the Book in Japan

The reprinting of this book is made possible through a cooperative arrangement between the University of Hawai'i Press and Brill (Leiden, The Netherlands), the purpose of which is to make available in affordable paperback editions some of the most important scholarship on Asia of recent years.

the Book in Japan

A Cultural History from the Beginnings to the Nineteenth Century

PETER KORNICKI

 University of Hawai'i Press • HONOLULU

First published by Brill (Leiden, The Netherlands), 1998
© Koninklijke Brill NV, Leiden, The Netherlands

Paperback edition
© 2001 University of Hawai'i Press

All rights reserved

Printed in the United States of America
06 05 04 03 02 01   5 4 3 2 1

Library of Congress Cataloging-in-Publication Data

Kornicki, Peter F. (Peter Francis)
  The book in Japan : a cultural history from the beginnings to the nineteenth century / Peter Kornicki.
    p. cm.
  Originally published: Leiden ; Boston : Brill, 1998. (Handbuch der Orientalistik. Fünfte Abteilung, Japan ; 7. Bd.)
  Includes bibliographical references and index.
  ISBN 0–8248–2337–0 (pbk. : alk. paper)
  1. Books—Japan—History. 2. Printing—Japan—History. I. Title.
Z8.J3 K67 2001
002'.0952—dc21   00–064896

University of Hawai'i Press books are printed on acid-free paper and meet the guidelines for permanence and durability of the Council on Library Resources.

Cover designed by Santos B. Barbasa
Printed by Versa Press

CONTENTS

	Preface	ix
	Conventions	xiii
	Chronologies	xvi
	List of illustrations	xvii
	INTRODUCTION	1
1	THE HISTORY OF THE BOOK AND JAPAN	8
1.1	*Books and the state*	11
1.2	*Books and the colonial experience*	17
1.3	*The advent and consequences of print*	20
1.4	*Calligraphy and the block-printed book*	26
1.5	*Literacy and reading*	30
2	BOOKS AS MATERIAL OBJECTS	39
2.1	*Paper and the roll*	40
2.2	*Forms of the book*	43
2.3	*Printing and the book*	47
2.4	*Illustration and the arts of the book*	56
2.5	*Printed maps, serial publications and ephemera*	60
2.6	*Conservation*	74
3	MANUSCRIPT CULTURE	78
3.1	*Manuscripts in the Nara period*	78
3.2	*Manuscripts up to 1600*	87
3.3	*Manuscripts in the Tokugawa period*	99

4		PRINTED BOOKS	112
4.1		*Printing before 1600*	114
4.1.1		The Hyakumantō darani	114
4.1.2		The Heian, Kamakura and Muromachi periods	117
4.2		*Movable type: the early phase*	125
4.2.1		The Jesuit mission press	125
4.2.2		Korean movable type	128
4.2.3		Japanese movable type	129
4.3		*Blockprinting in the Tokugawa and early Meiji periods*	136
4.3.1		Commercial publishing	136
4.3.2		Official publishing	143
4.3.3		Private publishing	149
4.3.4		Reprints of non-Japanese works	153
4.4		*Later movable type and copperplate*	158
4.4.1		Wooden movable type	158
4.4.2		Western-style movable type	163
4.4.3		Copperplate	166
5		THE BOOK TRADE IN THE TOKUGAWA PERIOD	169
5.1		*Publishing and bookselling*	170
5.1.1		Bookshops and publishers	170
5.1.2		Production and the guilds	179
5.1.3		Sales and prices1	184
5.1.4		Marketing and advertising	187
5.2		*The growth of the publishing trade*	192
5.2.1		Publishing in Kyoto	194
5.2.2		Publishing in Osaka	197
5.2.3		Publishing in Edo	199
5.2.4		Publishing in the provinces	205
5.3		*The publishers*	207
5.3.1		Murakami Kanbee	208
5.3.2		Suwaraya Mohee	210
5.3.3		Eirakuya Tōshirō	213
5.3.4		Obiya Ihee	215
5.3.5		Tsutaya Jūzaburō	218
5.3.6		Kawachiya Mohee	221

6	AUTHORS AND READERS	223
6.1	*Authorship*	223
6.1.1	The evolution of the author	225
6.1.2	Royalties	239
6.1.3	Copyright	242
6.2	*Readership*	251
6.2.1	Readers and reading before 1600	251
6.2.2	Readers and reading after 1600	258
6.2.3	Literacy	269
7	TRANSMISSION	277
7.1	*Transmission to Japan*	277
7.1.1	Pre-Tokugawa imports from China	278
7.1.2	Pre-Tokugawa imports from Korea and Parhae	293
7.1.3	Later imports of Chinese and Korean books	296
7.1.4	Imports of European and American books	300
7.2	*Transmission from Japan*	306
7.2.1	Exports of Japanese books to China and Korea	306
7.2.2	Exports of Japanese books to the West	313
8	CENSORSHIP	320
8.1	*Censorship before the Tokugawa period*	321
8.2	*Censorship in the Tokugawa period*	324
8.2.1	The exclusion of Christianity	325
8.2.2	Secular censorship and the book trade	331
8.2.3	Calendars	353
8.3	*Censorship in the early Meiji period*	358
9	LIBRARIES AND COLLECTORS	363
9.1	*Libraries and book collecting before 1600*	364
9.1.1	Nara and Heian periods	364
9.1.2	Kamakura and Muromachi periods	371
9.2	*Libraries and book collecting after 1600*	376
9.2.1	Ieyasu, Yoshimune and the Bakufu Library	376
9.2.2	Institutional libraries	384
9.2.3	Other libraries and collections	388
9.2.4	Commercial lending libraries	391
9.3	*Ownership*	398
9.4	*The Meiji transition and modern collections*	406

10	CATALOGUES AND BIBLIOGRAPHY	413
10.1	*Catalogues and categories*	414
10.1.1	Pre-Tokugawa	416
10.1.2	Tokugawa period	427
10.2	*Bibliography in the Tokugawa period*	437

Afterword	446
Appendix	450
Glossary	455
Abbreviations	457
Bibliography	461
Index	478

PREFACE

The author of any such work as this must be guilty of hubris. Books have a very long history in Japan and there are already an intimidating number of specialised monographs and articles on most aspects of bibliography as traditionally conceived, of the sociology of texts, and of the history of the book. In consequence, most of the topics covered herein have already been treated in Japanese with greater expertise and insight than I can muster. The subjects covered in each chapter, therefore, deserve book-length treatment, many of the sections should be substantial chapters, and some of the footnotes should be sections. Although this could not be described as a short book, it is undoubtedly far too short to do its subjects full justice. Why undertake it at all, then?

Firstly, although authorial intentions may count for nothing, one objective I had lay in the desire to globalize the study of the book in Japan, that is to take it out of the purview of Japanese specialists and make it accessible for a global study of the book. Certain assumptions that are suggested by the experience of the book in Europe are at least questionable in the context of the Japanese book or the Arabic book, and for this reason this book may offer something of heuristic value to those studying the phenomenology of the book in other cultures. To this end no knowledge of Japanese is assumed, although readers will have to put up with a sprinkling of Chinese characters on every page.

Secondly, students of Japanese history, ideas and literature have long lacked any guide to bibliographical questions bearing on the production and consumption of texts and few have paid such issues any attention, with occasionally unfortunate results. What is needed first of all is a work such as *Scribes and scholars: a guide to the transmission of Greek and Latin literature* by L. D. Reynolds and N. G. Wilson (third edition; Oxford: Clarendon Press, 1991). As Reynolds and Wilson elegantly demonstrate, the transmission of classical literature is of great importance when considering the extent of the extant corpus and the nature of the texts that have come down to us, as well as casting light on the intellectual world of those who shaped the tradition in later generations. Similar questions confront all who approach pre-modern Japanese texts, and I hope that this book may begin to show the way to some answers.

Thirdly, in spite of what I have said above, there are some sections of this book, particularly in chapters six, seven and ten, in which I have had to sail in relatively uncharted waters. This is partly because my agenda has been to some extent determined by studies of the history of the book in countries other than Japan, for the interests of Japanese scholars have not necessarily coincided with those of their Western counterparts. Thus they have written much on the history of libraries but little on collecting or readership. I have also, rashly I admit, attempted an initial coverage of some new areas of interest that have not hitherto featured in histories of the book in Japan, principally the history of reading. I have not been able to give these more than anecdotal treatment at this stage, but I hope that they may stimulate further efforts.

Any small merits that this book may have, then, are covered by the three considerations above. It is embarrassing to express it in such terms, though, for this book has been long in gestation and so my institutional and personal debts are correspondingly large. While I was teaching at the University of Tasmania in 1979–82 the Australian Research Grants Committee generously funded three trips to Japan and Europe to familiarise myself with various collections of early Japanese books in libraries from Stockholm to Kyoto. Subsequent research visits to libraries in Japan and elsewhere have been funded by the Research Institute for the Humanities at Kyoto University, by the British Academy, by the Leverhulme Trust, by the University of Cambridge, and by Robinson College, Cambridge. Most recently the Humanities Research Board of the British Academy enabled me to take an extra term's leave, which got me within sight of the end. My humble thanks are due to all these bodies, which have shown great patience.

I hesitate to name the many scholars and friends who have generously offered their assistance and saved me from many egregious errors, for fear that they may be associated with the mistakes and deficiencies that undoubtedly remain. My interest in the history of the book was first aroused by Nigel Wilson when I was a raw freshman at Oxford reading classics, and his superb guide to the transmission of classical literature, mentioned above, has served as a standard, albeit one far out of reach. My first explorations in this area with respect to Japan were tentatively presented at the 1978 conference of the Asian Studies Association of Australia in Sydney, and it was Hal Bolitho's comments on that occasion that encouraged me to pursue the topic further. On subsequent visits to the British Library the late Ken Gardner kindly gave a young and inexperienced academic the fruit of years of bibliographical experience and knowledge: he would surely have had many improvements to suggest and corrections to make if he had had a chance to see my drafts, but it is to my loss that he died before I had anything worth showing him.

While I was on the staff of Kyoto University from 1982 to 1984, Professor Asukai Masamichi, the late Professor Yoshida Mitsukuni, Professor Hamada Keisuke and Professor Yokoyama Toshio gave unstintingly of their advice and assistance. Later, following my move to Cambridge in 1985, I was fortunate to make the acquaintance of Professor Hayashi Nozomu, from whom I have learnt a lot and who has continued to assist and advise me after his return to Japan. My colleagues here, especially Richard Bowring, Mark Morris and Stephen Large, have been ever supportive and generous with their advice; David McMullen, Charles Aylmer and Roger Thompson have helped me locate numerous sinological texts and have sorted out my inane sinological queries; and in the University Library Noboru Koyama has helped me enormously by making it possible for me to consult all the items needed for this study, no matter where they might be located.

Outside Cambridge I am deeply indebted to Tim Barrett, Robert Borgen, Fujimoto Yukio, Christoph Harbsmeier, Alexandr Kabanov, James McMullen, Margaret Mehl, Mark Setton, Ivo Smits and Yokoyama Toshio who have all guided me to useful material way outside any claims I may have to an area of expertise. Tim Barrett, Richard Bowring, Tim Clark, Joseph McDermott, James McMullen, Francesca Orsini and Ivo Smits have read sections and have not only saved me from numerous errors but have also suggested new lines of thought. Their encouragement, interest and gentle corrections have been deeply appreciated. My editor at Brill, Patricia Radder, has been patient and sympathetic during the unduly long gestation of this book, and I am grateful to her for her forbearance.

Finally, I make no apologies for concluding with some personal remarks. My children, Martin and Alice, have been puzzled by my preoccupation with the subject of this book, but they have taken my inattention with good humour. Since the death of my wife and their mother in 1995 we have all been sustained by Francine Adams, Fiona Blackburn, Rosemary Boyle, Iris Hunter and Eleanor Smith and their families: their generosity and kindness in spite of other pressing demands on their time and attention have made all the difference to our lives. Francesca has been a wonderful critic and companion during the final stages of this book, and to her I owe more than I can say here.

Cambridge, 28 February 1998

CONVENTIONS

1 *Dates*

Time in years is divided in Japan into eras of unpredictable length which begin and end suddenly in the middle of the calendar year. The Genroku era, for example, began on the 30th day of the ninth month of the year in Japan that corresponds to A.D.1688 and ended on the 13th day of the third month of the year that corresponds to 1704. Until 1872 various lunar calendrical systems were in use successively in Japan and in consequence dates do not correspond with those in use in the West at the time. Accordingly, the tenth year of the Genroku era corresponds roughly to the year 1697 in the West, but the first day of the first month of that year corresponds to 23 January 1697 in Europe, and the last day of the year corresponds to 10 February 1698. Nevertheless, I shall use 1697 to refer to that year in Japan, even though, for example, somebody born at the end of that year would, strictly speaking, have been born in 1698. When it has been necessary to refer to days and months as well, I have done so in the form 1697.5.17, meaning the 17th day of the fifth month of the tenth year of Genroku. The same is true of pre-modern dates applying to China and Korea.

Late in 1872 Japan adopted the Gregorian calendar and 1872.12.3 became 1 January 1873. Thereafter dates in Japan correspond exactly with those elsewhere and so they will be given here in the form '1 Jan. 1873'.

2 *Names*

As discussed in §6.1.1, many Japanese in the past have enjoyed a plethora of names and there is a sore need for an agreed standard. In this book I have consistently used the names in the form in which they appear in Nagasawa Kōzō 長沢孝三, *Kanbun gakusha sōran* 漢文学者総覧 (Kyūko Shoin, 1979), for sinologists, and in Kokugakuin

Daigaku Nihon bunka kenkyūsho 国学院大学日本文化研究所, ed., *Wagakusha sōran* 和学者総覧 (Kyūko Shoin, 1990), for scholars of Japanese studies. These two invaluable works, however, cover only the Tokugawa period and there are many individuals who do not fall under either of these rubrics. In the case of others I have turned to *Kotenseki sōgō mokuroku* or the new *Kokusho jinmei jiten* 国書人名辞典 (Iwanami Shoten, 1993–), or, in the case of the names of publishers, to the glossed list of publishers in *Genshoku ukiyoe daihyakka jiten* 原色浮世絵大百科事典, 11 vols (Taishūkan Shoten, 1980–82), 3: 135–44.

Kanji (Chinese characters) have been given on their first appearance for technical terms, and for personal names not easily accessible in standard works of reference, and for the titles of some books. The birth and death dates of people mentioned in the text have been given where I have thought it useful, but again only on the first appearance of a name in the text.

In the text, following the standard convention, persons with pennames are subsequently referred to by the penname, but those without pennames are referred to by their family name. Thus Kyokutei Bakin becomes Bakin, while Yashiro Hirokata becomes Yashiro.

3 Titles and terms

So as not to burden the text with more italics than there already are, I have where possible used English equivalents for titles. The English versions of Japanese officials and offices in the Tokugawa period are taken from Conrad Totman, *Politics in the Tokugawa Bakufu, 1600–1843* (Berkeley: University of California Press, 1967). A few, notably shōgun and daimyō, have been left in Japanese, for they are now included in English dictionaries. I have not followed Totman in his translation of *machi-bugyō* as 'city magistrate' and have used instead 'city commissioner': *bugyō* was the title of many senior officers in the Bakufu's administrative apparatus and in many of these no judicial functions were involved, so it is misleading to use the word 'magistrate'.

The use of certain Japanese terms and suffixes is unavoidable. The names of temples, which almost always end with the suffix *-ji*, are left as they are, so Kan'eiji means the 'Kan'ei temple'. The names of literary genres, printing terminology and so on are explained on their first occurrence and in the glossary. A table of the historical periods in Chinese, Japanese and Korean history follows these remarks.

4 *Footnotes and cross references*

The footnotes take the form of bare references. Items referred to in more than one section are given in abbreviated form (eg, Mori 1933) with the relevant page numbers, and full details are contained in the main bibliography at the end of the book. Items referred to once are not contained in the main bibliography. At the end of each section is a short bibliography of the most important relevant work: items also referred to elsewhere appear in the usual abbreviated form, while other items appear with full details; in the case of Japanese authors, characters are only given for those whose names do not appear in the main bibliography. The abbreviations used in the notes are listed at the end of the book before the bibliography, with details of the books, journals or series to which they refer. Cross references in the text to other parts of the book are given in the form '§9.1.2', which means 'see chapter 9, section 1, subsection 2'.

CHRONOLOGIES

CHINA
Qin	c. 221–206 B.C.
Former Han	206 B.C.–8 A.D.
Later Han	25–220
Three kingdoms	c. 220–c. 280
Northern and Southern dynasties	c. 317–c. 589
Sui	c. 581–618
Tang	618–c. 907
Northern Song	960–1126
Southern Song	c. 1127–1279
Yuan	c. 1280–1368
Ming	1368–1644
Qing	1644–1912

JAPAN
Nara	710–794
Heian	794–1185
Kamakura	1185–1333
Muromachi	1333–1600
— Tokugawa	1600–1868
— Meiji	1868–1912

KOREA
Three kingdoms	
Paekche	?–660
Koguryŏ	?–668
Silla	?–660
Unified Silla	660–935
Koryŏ	918–1392
Yi	1392–1910

LIST OF ILLUSTRATIONS

Except in the cases of Figs. 1, 3, 11, 16, 18, and 19, which are taken from books in my own collection, the material illustrated here is taken from items in the collections of Cambridge University Library and is reproduced by permission of the Syndics of Cambridge University Library.

1 The end of the preface to Shikitei Sanba's comic novel *Shirōto kyōgen monkirigata* (1814)   28

2 Pages from the 1729 and 1780 editions of Tachibana Morikuni's *Ehon tsūhōshi*.   50–1

3 The colophon of *Inkyō jishi* (1663): an instance of *umeki*.   53

4 A *kawaraban* showing a procession of officials from the kingdom of Ryūkyū, probably published in 1796   64

5 A calendar for 1850.   68

6 *Yūshi bukan* 有司武鑑, a directory of Bakufu officialdom published in a revised edition in 1868.   70

7 The beginning of *Keian taiheiki* 慶安太平気, a manuscript concerning a plot to overthrow the Bakufu.   107

8 The beginning of Kūkai's *Sangō shiiki* 三教指帰 in an edition printed on Mt Kōya in 1580.   120

9 A movable-type edition of the *Ōkagami* 大かがみ published in the early years of the seventeenth century.   133

10 The end of Motoori Norinaga's *Uiyamabumi* (1799).   151

xviii   LIST OF ILLUSTRATIONS

11 The colophon of *Settōken zenji shōko hyakusoku shōtei*, published by a provincial temple in 1842.   154

12 The beginning of *Nanbandera kōhaiki*, published in 1868 in movable-type edition.   161

13 A scene from *Tōkaidō meisho zue* (1797) showing the premises of the Edo publisher and bookseller Izumiya Ichibee.   172

14 A catalogue of the books written by Hirata Atsutane and his followers, which has been bound into a copy of his *Kishin shinron*   190

15 The beginning of the text of *Junshi* (Ch. *Xun zi*) in a Japanese edition published in 1825.   228

16 A scene from Shikitei Kosanba's *Gesaku hana no akahon sekai* showing an author reading out his work to a publisher   234

17 The frontispiece of *Shingaku michi no hanashi*   237

18 A label affixed to books by a haberdashery shop that also functioned as a commercial lending library.   392

19 Seal of a *kashihon'ya* called Kameya   395

20 The ownership seal of Naitō Masaaki   400

21 The seal of the Wagaku Kōdansho, the institution for the study of Japanese texts established by Hanawa Hokiichi.   401

22 Label attached to the front cover of a copy of *Hyakunin isshu Saga no yamafumi*   403

23 The seal of the Minakuchi domain school   404

INTRODUCTION

Books in one form or another, imported or domestically produced, have been a part of Japanese cultural life for around 1,500 years. Superficially the continuities are impressive, and so too are the use of printing in the eighth century, the vast resources of medieval temple libraries, and the relative weakness of systems of censorship and political control. The history of the book in Japan is thus not the history of a marginal form of cultural production and consumption but of a central one over at least a millenium.

The bookishness of Japan is partly a result of the essentially literate character of Buddhism and Confucianism: written texts were central and indispensible for their transmission. On the other hand, oral traditions have existed in Japan in abundance, and some are still alive today, so there is inevitably a danger, in an account which privileges the book as a means of cultural construction and dissemination, of distorting the relationship between literate and oral cultures in Japan. Some measure will be taken here of that relationship, but the focus will be overwhelmingly on books and written texts, which have themselves created the authority and orthodoxy of literate culture in Japan and continue to do so. Oral texts have been squeezed into a subordinate position, at least until textualized in the form of writing, and will only have any place here to the extent that they impinge on the production of written texts and books.

What, then, is the subject of this book? It is easier first to say what it is not, for it does not purport to be a history of the Japanese book. The very concept of 'Japanese book', or in Japanese *kokusho* 国書, is one of only limited historical and analytical value, for it represents only a portion, at times a small portion, of the encounter with the book in Japan, which until the late nineteenth century was as likely to be with Chinese books or Chinese texts as with Japanese. One of the most graphic illustrations of the limitations of the concept of *kokusho* is *Kokusho sōmokuroku*, a monumental bibliography of pre-modern Japanese books and manuscripts which is now supplemented by a sequel, *Kotenseki sōgō mokuroku*. These exceptionally useful, indeed indispensible, compilations have one major shortcoming, and that is that they concern themselves only with *kokusho*. They therefore casually omit all the Chinese texts copied by hand in Japan or printed in Japan whether or not they contain glosses, annotations, or additional material written by Japanese. This fundamental distortion of the history of texts and books in Japan is largely attributable to the genetically close relationship between the development of Japanese literary studies and scholarship and the Kokugaku or so-called Nativist tradition of the eighteenth and nineteenth centuries, with its inbuilt antipathy towards sinology and insistence on the value of Japanese texts. These two essential bibliographies have their roots in that tradition, and its pervasiveness is apparent from the major exhibition on 'The cultural history of books and publishing in Japan' held in Kyoto in 1996, which paid scant attention to books other than those written by Japanese and printed in Japan.[1]

But why is it that a preoccupation with Japanese books is such a distortion? In the case of Buddhism the answer is obvious, for the textual history of Buddhism in Japan is the history of the transmission to Japan of Chinese translations of Sanskrit sūtras and of exegetical works in Chinese, and the history of how they were copied, printed, circulated and interpreted in Japan. Not one, however, of the innumerable manuscripts and printed versions of these Chinese translations and original commentaries appears in the pages of *Kokusho sōmokuroku* or its sequel. The same is true, *mutatis mutandis*, of works of Chinese literature or Confucian texts, which at times enjoyed a huge circulation in Japan, to say nothing of Daoist or medical texts from China. Since most Chinese texts reproduced in Japan, with the exception of Buddhist texts, customarily came equipped with diacritics and glosses inserted by Japanese editors to make it easier for Japanese readers to construe them, in addition to prefaces and postfaces contributed by Japanese scholars, they were to a greater or lesser extent 'japanized', and to omit them is to exaggerate the importance in Japan of texts written wholly by Japanese in the Japanese language and ultimately, as I have suggested, to distort the history of books in Japan.

---

[1] On the relationship between Kokugaku and literary studies in the Meiji period, see Michael C. Brownstein, 'From *Kokugaku* to *Kokubungaku*: canon-formation in the Meiji period', *HJAS* 47 (1987): 435–60. The catalogue of the exhibition held in Kyoto in 1996 has been published: *Zuroku: Nihon shuppan bunkashi ten '96 Kyoto* (図録) 日本出版文化史展'96京都 (Nihon Shoseki Shuppan Kyōkai, 1996).

The two catalogues mentioned above have a second shortcoming, which is just as serious in its consequences. With but one or two exceptions, they do not list works preserved in libraries outside Japan. Many of the great collections of books from Japan now to be found in Europe and North America were originally put together in the second half of the nineteenth century by diplomats, missionaries, globetrotters and the first generation of enthusiastic japanophiles. Some critics have suggested that these collections are a testimony to the cultural plunder of Japan by the Great Powers, but it is essential to remember that the collections were built up at a time when old books were valued far less in Japan than contemporary books such as translations from or adaptations of works in European languages, which served more practical if mundane ends. In this connection we are fortunate that we have a full list of the prices paid by the Swedish explorer Adolf Nordenskiöld when he acquired his books in Japan in 1879, which shows that he paid more for a bundle of current newspapers or for recent works of fiction than for a Gozan edition printed in 1296.[2] As a result of the fact that books of previous centuries were undervalued by comparison with new publications, it was possible for a shrewd collector to make some good acquisitions, and now in many cases the copies preserved in libraries from Moscow to San Francisco are the only ones that have survived. Books printed or produced by hand in Japan have, therefore, to be sought outside Japan as well as within, for the literary patrimony of Japan is not confined to Japanese shores, however much that might now be regretted by those of nationalistic persuasion.
   There is yet another sense in which too much focus on Japan can lead to distortion. Throughout the entire history of books in Japan the transmission of texts across the seas has been of crucial importance. The history of the book in Japan must, therefore, include the importation of books from China, from Korea and, from the sixteenth century onwards, from Europe. Some, but not all, of these books were transformed in Japan into new texts, as mentioned above, while others circulated in manuscript or in the printed form in which they arrived. But for the transmission of texts in this way, the transplantation to Japanese soil of Chinese Buddhism, of Confucianism and the other intellectual traditions of China and Korea, and of Western

---

[2] Edgren 1980: 5 #10, 89 #263, 343 #1068.

medicine and astronomy, could not have taken place. Further, it would be mistaken to conceive of Japan as merely a passive receiver in this process. In the first place 'passive' is the wrong word, for a process of active selection was at work. In the second place, it is abundantly clear that Japan also acted as a transmitter, exporting texts overseas, and this is important irrespective of the reception accorded to those texts, for it is expressive of a desire to transmit and to participate in the learned culture of East Asia.

In several important respects, therefore, the history of the book in Japan has to take account of the international context of book production in Japan, which owed much to parallel developments in China and Korea, and of the multiculturalism of pre-modern Japan in which Japanese literary and cultural production was balanced by a leaning towards that of China, particularly the Confucian classics and the fiction of the Ming dynasty, and later towards that of Europe. As Gavan McCormack has recently argued, the prominence of the slogan '*kokusaika*' (internationalization) since the eighties has not engendered any significant internal transformations in Japanese society or shifts in the interpretation and presentation of Japan's past. Yet books, and the bookish culture they represent, cannot be adequately situated in Japan's past unless the conventional vision of Japan as a monocultural society and the ideology of Japanese homogeneity are recognised as the distortions that they are.[3]

As in other societies, it has been customary for discussions of the book in Japan to omit certain categories of publication, particularly those emanating from the commercial press in Tokugawa Japan. Examples include printed ephemera, which are revealing of the outreach of print and the penetration of literacy; commercial reprints of classical literature, which are ignored because they have nothing to contribute to the textual tradition, even though they have much to tell us about the circulation and marketing of the classics in the Tokugawa period; and commercial maps, because many have little to add to cartographic knowledge, though they are important for what they reveal of perceptions and demarcations of space. These all deserve fuller treatment than it is possible to give them here, but they

---

[3] Gavan McCormack, 'Kokusaika: impediments in Japan's deep structure', in Donald Denoon, Mark Hudson, Gavan McCormack and Tessa Morris-Suzuki, eds, *Multicultural Japan: palaeolithic to postmodern* (Cambridge: Cambridge University Press, 1996), 274ff.

are an important component of the thick texture of print culture in the Tokugawa period, which reached a level of penetration that was matched in few other societies in the nineteenth century.

It is obvious that there can be no precise starting point to a history of the book in Japan, since we are never likely to know when the first books were imported from the Korean kingdoms and China. The problem, then, is where to conclude this history. The book is very much alive in Japan today, in spite of the development of electronic media, and the publishing industry still produces a prodigious number of new titles every year. In that sense the history of the book is seamless and any break must be acknowledged to be an arbitrary one. How can we separate the contemporary publishing industry from that of the early nineteenth century, or from earlier periods, without distorting the picture?

A strong argument could be made for resorting to 1600 as a boundary marker. Before 1600 there was no publishing industry to speak of and quantities of books printed were small. After the imposition of the Pax Tokugawa and the sponsorship of printing by Tokugawa Ieyasu, however, a commercial publishing industry grew to maturity in Kyoto in a remarkably short space of time and transformed the production and consumption of books. The marriage of commerce and books, then, starts around the year 1600 and continues to the present day. Commerce, however, is not all there is to the history of the book in Tokugawa Japan, and there are also important continuities between the Tokugawa period and what came before it, such as the dissemination of Chinese books.

The dividing line that has been borrowed to mark off the 'modern' on so many occasions in many different fields is the year 1868, the year in which the Tokugawa Bakufu collapsed and the Meiji Restoration launched the Meiji period: the year in which Japan is supposed to have suddenly become 'modern'. It goes without saying that this is completely arbitrary in fields other than politics, as well as highly unsatisfactory for our purposes here. Nevertheless, it continues to be used in literary and historical studies; 1868 is the cut-off year for entries in *Kokusho sōmokuroku* and its sequel, and numerous studies of the book start or finish around that year. What is wrong with that is that it is difficult to determine what of importance changed in the Meiji period.

Western books, for one, were not new to Meiji Japan. As chapter seven shows, Western books had been making an impact on Japan since the early eighteenth century, and after the 'opening' of Japan in the 1850s had become more easily available and in a variety of languages. It is true that the supply increased and the market grew after 1868, but there is no dramatic shift to be identified here. What of printing, then? Woodblock printing continued to dominate the printing industry for more than ten years after the Restoration and only gave way to metallic movable type and steam presses around 1890. And in any case movable type was not new to Meiji Japan either, for it was extensively used in the early seventeenth century and was becoming more widely used again in the middle of the nineteenth century. The shift from manual printing to the steam press was a dramatic one, but that did not happen in 1868 or even early in the Meiji period. Furthermore, the tastes of readers, far from undergoing any sudden transformation, remained wedded to the recent literature of the late Tokugawa period: this is as true of intellectuals as it is of the 'common reader'. There are, then, strong continuities between the late Tokugawa and Meiji periods that need to be addressed.

This is not to say that the new technologies and intellectual orientations did not make a difference, simply that the changes in book production and the new intellectual climate of Meiji Japan were far slower to take effect than is commonly appreciated. By 1900 books, and the products of the newly emergent periodical press, were vastly different in technologies of production and in appearance from anything that had been available in 1800, and more closely involved with the state and the holders of political power; they also pose quite different sorts of bibliographic problems. There is some sense, then, in detaching the output of the capital-intensive publishing industry of the twentieth century from that of earlier centuries and less industrialized conditions of production, but in response to the powerful continuities that cannot be ignored I have resorted to a fuzzy boundary in this book. It will therefore overspill the Tokugawa period, but by an indeterminate amount which will vary from chapter to chapter. In the case of censorship there is a clear shift in the institutions responsible for supervising publications in the early Meiji period, but some of the principles do not change so quickly and furthermore the exercise of censorship in those years reveals by contrast how much more severe the censorship system in the Tokugawa period could have been. In similar ways, in each chapter something,

I feel, has been gained by crossing that tyrannical year 1868 and examining the developments of the early Meiji period. The modern publishing industry, however, in its capital-intensive, technologically-sophisticated and market-oriented variety is now far removed from its roots in the nineteenth century and must be the subject of a separate study.

CHAPTER ONE

THE HISTORY OF THE BOOK AND JAPAN

1   Books and the state
2   Books and the colonial experience
3   The advent and consequences of print
4   Calligraphy and the block-printed text
5   Literacy and reading

The encounter with the book in Japan raises issues that are best confronted with a degree of abstraction, for they are of course common to all societies in their accommodation to the cultures of the manuscript and printed book. This is a much easier task to undertake now than it would have been twenty years ago, for the history of the book has become an established, if still not fully mature, discipline, at least in Western scholarship. As a distinct field of study the 'history of the book' has acquired a very distinct articulation in order to differentiate it from the narrowly focussed studies of printers, libraries, textual bibliography and so on that constitute the essential foundations but are limited in their scope. It has developed a more ambitious agenda, a more essential understanding of the ways in which books in their plurality have selected, stored, mediated, ordered and transmitted knowledge and texts, and of the connections between books and texts on the one hand and the social, cultural and intellectual lives of men and women (much more rarely children) on the other. It is not yet a fully mature discipline in the sense that it is still largely eurocentric in its concerns and is informed mostly by the European experience; this has its drawbacks, as will be apparent below.

There is an irony in that the impact of the book in its widest senses is attracting serious attention at the very time when we are being told that the electronic revolution will make books redundant and that the days of the book are numbered. Or perhaps it is not so much an irony as something akin to the awakening process whereby oral historians such as Lyn Macdonald and Martin Middlebrook only turned to the survivors of the First World War when it was nearly too late. Has our awareness of the protean impact of the book on human society possibly been aroused by a sense, however inaccurate, of its imminent demise?

Be that as it may, the development of this field of study has been vigorous and, in addition to the usual tokens of activity such as conferences, new journals and academic associations, has nurtured stimulating visions of the ways forward, of the prospects for realising its potential. For example, David Hall has argued for a new emphasis on readers and the act of reading, in acknowledgement of the materiality of texts in the social and geographic worlds in which they are circulated; John Feather has presented an agenda for future study, which emphasizes the need to understand books as more than merely vehicles for conveying texts and to treat them as commodities, as commercial goods subject to market forces; Robert Darnton has advocated a holistic approach that focusses on the 'circuit for transmitting texts', on the mechanisms, constraints and mediators that affect the movement, reception and impact of texts; and in the work of Roger Chartier and others the history of books has become a tool for the analysis of societies and their cultural and political constructs, the foundations of a new cultural history.[1]

Needless to say, new interest in the history of the book has not been slow to emerge in Japan, as elsewhere, but for the most part it has taken the form of studies of what is known as *shuppan-bunka* 出版文化, perhaps best translated as 'print culture'. It is concerned, therefore, almost exclusively with the world of commercially published books in the seventeenth, eighteenth and nineteenth centuries. In a sense this has been a welcome development, for the products of the commercial press and their significant impact on Japanese culture

---

[1] David D. Hall, 'The history of the book: new questions? new answers?', *Journal of library history* 21 (1986): 27–38, and *On native ground: from the history of printing to the history of the book* (Worcester, Mass.: American Antiquarian Society, 1984); J. Feather, 'The book in history and the history of the book', *Journal of library history* 21 (1986): 12–26, and 'The commerce of letters: the study of the eighteenth-century book trade', *Eighteenth-century studies* 17 (1984): 405–24; Robert Darnton, *The kiss of Lamourette: reflections in cultural history* (London: Faber and Faber, 1990), 125; Chartier 1989, 1994. See also D. F. McKenzie, *Bibliography and the sociology of texts* (London: The British Library, 1986).

and society have for too long been treated with the scorn of élite culture. To take just one example, studies of the textual traditions of the literary classics of the Heian and Kamakura periods routinely exclude the block-printed editions of the Tokugawa period even though it was those editions that canonized and standardized the texts for a mass reading public and visualized the past for the contemporary reader through the medium of illustrations. Virtually all of the many seventeenth-century block-printed editions of *Tsurezuregusa* [Essays in idleness], written in the early fourteenth century by Yoshida Kenkō, contain illustrations of the same scenes and this combination of text and illustrations undoubtedly reached much larger numbers of readers than either the manuscripts or the movable-type editions. These commercial editions may not be important in the textual history of *Tsurezuregusa*, but they have much to tell us about the canonization and dissemination of Japanese literary classics in the seventeenth century.

Although the focus on print culture promises to shed much-needed light on the sociology of texts in Japan, it inevitably entails neglect of the continuing manuscript traditions of the Tokugawa period, that is of the diversity of the means of access to texts, and in practice has yet to tackle the problem of reading. Further, as mentioned in the Introduction above, the history of books in the Tokugawa period is not just the history of books written and produced in Japan but of an intertextuality with books from China, Korea and the West, but studies of print culture in Japan have yet to appreciate this adequately or to address the transcultural character of the book-market in Japan and the osmosis of other concepts of books and texts from outside Japan.

Future studies of the history of the book in Japan must address some of these issues. A study such as this, limited in scale by comparison, for example, with the four volumes of *Histoire de l'édition française*, and impossibly comprehensive in scope, must necessarily skim the surface and satisfy itself with creating agendas for future work.[2] However, at this stage it is still possible and worthwhile to demonstrate what is heuristically of value in the history of the book in Japan and to integrate that history into larger debates that concern questions of reading, censorship, print culture, and so on. In the

---

[2] Henri-Jean Martin, Roger Chartier and Jean-Pierre Vivet, *Histoire de l'édition française*, 4 vols (Paris: Promodis, 1983–86).

sections that follow, therefore, I shall take up some of the issues discussed in later chapters and consider them here in a more global context.

1.1 BOOKS AND THE STATE

A central issue in the history of the book in East Asia, one that is not often addressed in those terms except in connection with censorship and control, is the relation between books and the state, or between books and political power. In this connection a comparison with the history of the book in China is particularly instructive and highlights one of the characteristics of the ecology of the book in Japan. In China the state has long had an important, even central, role in the history of the book: in the case of censorship and the destruction of books this is obvious, but it is also true of book collecting, the search for rare books, and the preservation of the canon. 'A dynasty's stewardship of the canon', Kent Guy has argued, 'and its invocation of classical sanction were vital bases of its legitimacy. ... a government's ability to collect books, correct texts, and pass judgements on them had become a sign of its power', and this proposition has now been magisterially corroborated and articulated by Mark Lewis.[3]

From the Han dynasty onwards there had been initiatives emanating from and sponsored by the imperial court for the collection of lost texts, for the control of textual transmission, and for the manipulation of texts into hierarchies and ranks. This urge reached its most ambitious form in 1772 when the Qianlong emperor initiated the *Siku quanshu* 四庫全書 project in order to compile a collection of rare and valued texts from the whole of China. Provincial officials at all levels were instructed to search out rare texts and more than 10,000 were examined with a view to inclusion in the final, authoritative anthology. But the project was not altogether benign in its conception, for it was accompanied by a campaign of censorship and repression which

---

[3] R. Kent Guy, *The emperor's four treasuries: scholars and the state in the late Ch'ien-lung era* (Cambridge, Mass.: Harvard University Press, 1987), 2, 12; Mark Edward Lewis, *Writing and authority in early China* (New York: SUNY Press, forthcoming).

sought to eradicate undesirable books, especially those expressing opposition to the ruling Manchu dynasty: in 1781 it was reported, for example, that 52,480 wooden printing blocks used for the production of seditious books had been broken up for firewood. As Yu Yue (1821–1907) described it, *Siku quanshu* 'was written to control thought rather than contribute to scholarship.' Irrespective of the motives, however, the intervention of the state in the transmission of texts is pervasive in the long history of the book in China, and the *Siku quanshu* project is just one important instance of that.[4]

In Japan, by contrast, there are very few parallels to be found to this central role of the state in the transmission of texts. There are two aspects to this issue, the negative, which concerns censorship and bookburning, and the positive, which relates to the formation of canons. As regards the first, both censorship and the physical destruction of books by state authorities have of course a long history in many societies: there are numerous recorded instances in China, in the Qin dynasty and more recently in the Qing dynasty, and in the Islamic world this was the fate of books deemed unacceptable for religious reasons.[5] The Roman empire offers another example: bookburning began in the reigns of Augustus and Tiberius, as an *ad hoc* response to criticisms of the Augustan régime, and in AD 25, for example, the works of one such critic were burnt in Rome and wherever else they were found, and it was made a crime to read them or to own them.[6] In Japan, however, until the seventeenth century there is very little sign of the censorship or the destruction of books we find in China and Rome, and yet this is not for lack of dissent. It may be that dissent was rarely articulated in Japan in the form of texts or it may simply be that instances of censorship or bookburning went unrecorded, or that the pertinent records have failed to survive. But it is surely significant that before the Tokugawa period printed books and manuscripts for the most part lacked means of publication, in other words they lacked the means of becoming in any sense public property. In the cases of China and Rome publication is clearly at issue, not solely the articulation of dissent, and without publication

---

[4] Guy, *The emperor's four treasuries*, 10–13, 106–7, 157ff.

[5] Franz Rosenthal, '"Of making many books there is no end": the classical Muslim view', in Atiyeh 1995: 39.

[6] Frederick H. Cramer, 'Bookburning and censorship in ancient Rome', *Journal of the history of ideas* 6 (1945): 157–96, especially 167ff and 191–4.

organized mechanisms for censorship and the destruction of banned books make little sense.

What, then, of the Tokugawa period, when we can conceptualize books as public property, and what of the bleak reputation for severity and strictness of control enjoyed by the Bakufu, the government of the shōgun? In fact, notwithstanding its reputation, the Tokugawa Bakufu did not entertain any ambitions to intervene in the transmission of texts, except to the extent that it sponsored the publication of a small number of works (§4.3.2), nor was it particularly effective at controlling, let alone suppressing, works deemed undesirable (§8.2.2). It is only in modern times, particularly during the period from the Meiji Restoration to the end of the Second World War, that control has been bureaucratically organized and applied in a rigid and authoritarian manner (§8.3).

In practice, the censorship system in the Tokugawa period, such as it was, created a distance between commercial publishing and the state by forbidding even laudatory references to the present or past shōguns or to current political events; instead, therefore, of being politically bound to a posture of flattery and fawning, commercial publishers inhabited a world that was completely detached from secular power and politically independent in the sense that they were not dependent on the state for patronage or even for approval: apart from the desultory application of *ad hoc* censorship legislation which was left in the hands of the guilds, the Bakufu took surprisingly little notice of the transformation of Japan into a print society and did not impose any postures of deference or subordination on publishers. This is not to say that they were able or willing to take advantage of that distance to indulge in the publication of political criticism; it is rather to show that secular power in the Tokugawa period so far removed itself from commercial publishing as to be unable even to use it for its own ends. The régime signally failed to appreciate the power and potential of print for what had become a mass reading public, both in the sense of harnessing that power for the purpose of propaganda and in that of subjecting the commercial publishers to consistent and rigorous control.

As in France under the Ancien Régime, and more recently in the countries of the former East Bloc, legitimate publishers acted as their own police in the application of self-censorship to preserve their privileges, and it was through the underground that unpublishable material circulated. The 'chroniques scandaleuses' of pre-Revolutionary France had their Japanese equivalent in the *jitsuroku*, which similarly had the effect of undermining the reputation and stability of the régime, and booksellers in Japan too resorted to verbal disguises to mask the identity of illicit books, just as obscene, irreligious or seditious works were known in the French book trade as 'livres philosophiques' (§3.3).[7] The existence and survival of this underground market for books, in spite of legislative attempts to control it, is further evidence of the failings of the Tokugawa Bakufu as a police state by comparison with the much more rigorous control instituted in the Meiji period.

And what of the more positive possibilities open to the state? States have in the past attempted to determine the canon, to control production or preservation, or to use bibliography for the purpose of determining what should and what should not be read. The *Siku quanshu* project mentioned above is the most striking example from China; another case is the support given by the government in Milan in the early nineteenth century to the publication of a new canon of Italian classics by the Società dei Classici Italiani which sought to apply new linguistic and literary criteria to the selection of 'classic' texts for a modern Italy; and the Roman Catholic church's opposition to the publication in 1545 of Konrad Gesner's *Bibliotheca universalis* on the ground that bibliography without selection preserves the memory of heretical books falls under this head.[8]

Again, the Japanese case differs markedly, and few parallels can be found to the cultural politics represented by these examples. It is true that in the eighth century the reigning empress Shōtoku sponsored a major printing exercise, but the items printed were not circulated and had no influence on the dissemination of texts (§4.1.1). During the Heian and Kamakura periods the court sponsored the compilation of a number of anthologies of court poetry which laid down the literary values and recognized the valued works of successive generations, and it cannot be denied that in effect inclusion ensured survival and so shaped the poetic canon. To what extent this was a

---

[7] Robert Darnton, *The literary underground of the old regime* (Cambridge, Mass.: Harvard University Press, 1982), 21, 122, 143–7, 187–8.

[8] Marino Berengo, *Intellettuali e librai nella Milano della Restaurazione* (Torino: Einaudi, 1980), 8–19; Balsamo 1990: 46–7.

statist, a political act remains, however, to be determined.[9]

Much later, in the seventeenth century, Tokugawa Ieyasu used his secular power to amass a large collection of books which formed the core of the Bakufu Library (§9.2.1). There can be no doubt that he was the first in Japan to use political power for the purpose of collecting books, and even of enforcing the movement of books from one collection to another: in 1609–13 he transferred to the Zōjōji in Edo the Korean Buddhist canon held by the Enseiji 円成寺 in Yamato, the Yuan canon held by the Shūzenji 修禅寺 in Izu, and the Song canon held by the Kanzanji 管山寺. He was demonstrably proud of his ownership of books intimately associated with some of the most precious cultural traditions of Japan, such as items in the hands of Kūkai and Fujiwara no Teika, and it is evident that he had some notion of being responsible for the literary legacy of Japan. But there is no sense that his régime depended on its treatment of books, or that his ambitions came remotely close to those of the Qianlong emperor in China. Similarly, in the early eighteenth century Tokugawa Yoshimune actively sought out books from China and various parts of Japan for the Bakufu Library while simultaneously tightening up the censorship apparatus (§§7.1.3, 8.2.2, 10.2). But the Library was in no sense a national repository of Japanese books: indeed, its holdings were mostly in Chinese. And it was never the case in Japan, as it was in China, that the largest and most important library belonged to the state. The imperial and Bakufu collections were always inferior to private holdings, which were never seriously in danger of confiscation and came under no form of state control.[10]

The Bakufu in the Tokugawa period was only concerned with the definition of a canon in the limited context of Chinese Confucian philosophy, and only actively in the last eighty years of its existence. The Kansei Prohibition of Heterodoxy of 1790 did require the Bakufu Academy to foster the study only of orthodox Zhu Xi neo-confucianism, but it was not compulsory for the domain schools to

---

[9] On the anthologies see R. H. Brower and E. Miner, *Japanese court poetry* (Stanford: Stanford University Press, 1961); Konishi Jin'ichi, 'Association and progression: principles of integration', *HJAS* 21 (1958): 67–127; and Mark Morris, 'Waka and form: waka and history', *HJAS* 46 (1986): 551–610.

[10] Ōba & Wang 1996: 72-3; Udaka Yoshiaki 宇高良哲, *Tokugawa Ieyasu to Kantō bukkyō kyōdan* 徳川家康と関東仏教教壇 (Tōyō Bunka Shuppan, 1987), 165, 284–5.

follow suit and there is no sign that the Prohibition affected the expression or publication of views dissenting from Zhu Xi orthodoxy (§8.2.2). The Prohibition was therefore not normative, and in any case its potential effect was attenuated by the existence of alternative, competing canons, particularly that of the Japanese classics espoused by the Kokugaku school and that of Western scientific thought promoted by the so-called Rangaku school of 'Dutch studies'. At around the same time the Bakufu was also giving support to *Gunsho ruijū*, a project launched by Hanawa Hokiichi to publish and therefore preserve rare Japanese texts (§10.2). Although it is significant that the Bakufu was in this way lending its support to the publication of Japanese texts, its involvement was largely financial and the collection did not enjoy canonical status.

There is then, up to the end of the Tokugawa period, very little evidence of the impact of a monolithic state on canon formation or preservation. One is forced to conclude that the state in Japan has played a negligible role in this respect by comparison with other societies in which for reasons of religion, political control or a sense of national identity the state has been much more inclined to intervene. And even in the negative sense of censorship and the destruction of print it is only in the Meiji period, and particularly in the twentieth century, that the Japanese state has sufficiently appreciated the power of print to wish to introduce rigid systems of ideological control and to enforce them (§8.3).

The climatic conditions for the growth and development of the book in Japan have been unusually beneficent, and one of the causes of this was undoubtedly the élite preoccupation with sinology which gave Japanese books room to manoeuvre. In Europe, as Benedict Anderson has argued, 'the fall of Latin exemplified a larger process in which the sacred communities integrated by old sacred languages were gradually fragmented, pluralised and territorialised', but in Japan the fall of Chinese, which was the language of both Buddhism and Confucianism, and the disintegration of the communities it bound together, did not take place until the end of the nineteenth century.[11] It is surely no coincidence that it was at that point that the state in Japan began to give much more serious consideration to the control of books and other publications in Japanese. It is, I suggest, the

---

[11] Anderson 1991: 19.

disintegration of the old hierarchies of texts and reading, and the collapse of the privileged position in the conception of the Japanese state which sinology had for so long enjoyed, that made a revised perception of what books and texts meant to the state possible and then paved the way for the introduction of much more rigid mechanisms of control.

1.2 BOOKS AND THE COLONIAL EXPERIENCE

Irrespective of the degree of state control and intervention, books as commodities travel easily and render national histories of the book a degree artificial. I have already argued in the Introduction above that the history of the book in Japan must, in a literal sense, reach for broader horizons and encompass the manifold literary, intellectual and commercial connections with China and Korea, and later with the West, that brought Japan into communion with the book culture of the outside world. In chapter seven, which explores the transmission of books to and from Japan, it becomes obvious that the shifting dependence of Japanese cultural life on input from the East Asian mainland and Japanese endeavours to participate in the sinological culture of Korea and China require such broader horizons. But this is of course not only true of Japan, for the intertextuality of book cultures is universal, although sometimes obscured by scholarly nationalisms.

This intertextuality manifests itself in different modes, which need to be articulated more clearly, since they are expressive of unequal political or cultural relationships. One of these possible modes is best described as colonial and expressive of cultural subordination. The provision of books from England for expatriate readers in eighteenth-century Jamaica, nineteenth-century Tasmania and other British colonies falls indubitably under this head.[12] The movement of books in these and similar cases is largely one-way, from Britain out to the colonies, and the local reliance on imports is a token of disdain for local production, such as it existed, and of cultural identification

---

[12] Roderick Cave, 'Early circulating libraries in Jamaica', *Libri* 30 (1980): 53–65; Wallace Kirsop, 'Books and readers in colonial Tasmania', in Michael Roe, ed., *The flow of culture: Tasmanian studies* (Canberra: Australian Academy of the Humanities, 1987).

with the 'homeland'. It has been claimed, in the case of Australia, that imports 'helped to forge a more diversified and more intertextually and interculturally literate colonial audience' than would have been the case without imports. This revisionist perspective is, as yet, based on hypothesis rather than detailed study of colonial reading, although it is suggestive of a more subtle understanding of the nature of colonial readership and of the orientations of colonial audiences.[13] Nevertheless, the fact of dependence on imports remains, as does the fact that colonial books were only very rarely transmitted to Britain.

In the case of Japan, in spite of a few attempts to reverse the flow and to broadcast local cultural achievements, the vital flow of books from China from the fifth century up to the nineteenth is difficult to distinguish from this characteristic colonial imbalance. This is particularly true of the early centuries, but even in the eighteenth and nineteenth centuries imports from China were still highly valued and the Bakufu Library still consisted overwhelmingly of Chinese books, some admittedly in Japanese reprints. And it is a fact that as a transmitter of book culture Japan played a very minor role, even in the case of books written in Chinese by Japanese authors; to the small extent that there was a flow of Japanese books out of Japan, from the seventeenth century onwards, it was at the initiative of curious Europeans (§§7.2.1, 7.2.2). Japan was a cultural receiver, not a transmitter, whereas China was a transmitter rather than a receiver. There is a sense, then, in which reading in China was perforce a hermetic experience, while in Japan it potentially required constant accommodation with the Other. It is possible that in Japan too 'a more diversified and more intertextually and interculturally literate colonial audience' was the result, in the sense in that it was constantly engaged with both Japanese and Chinese texts, but further study is needed before such conclusions can be drawn.

Although politically Japan was never subject to colonial status, there are times and senses, then, in which the literate culture of Japan has partaken of a characteristically colonial orientation. This argument needs some modification, however, for unlike Jamaica and Tasmania Japan had a thriving publishing industry of its own which

---

[13] John O. Jordan and Robert L. Patten, *Literature in the marketplace: nineteenth-century British publishing and reading practices* (Cambridge: Cambridge University Press, 1995), 11.

by the nineteenth century was as vigorous, commercial and prolific as those of most Western countries. What I have called a colonial orientation, therefore, describes the dominance of sinology in Japanese intellectual life in the Tokugawa period, a dominance that demanded and was supplied with imports from China, Japanese reprints of Chinese works with notes and guidance for Japanese readers, sinological handbooks and curricula, and so on. Although to some extent akin to the revival of the Classics in nineteenth-century Europe, it had a more highly-charged political character, both because of its association with the educational policies of the régime and because of the sense of national negation which made it the cynosure of criticism from scholars belonging to the Kokugaku or Nativist movement.[14]

A corollary to this 'colonial orientation' may also be found in the later nineteenth century, when the flow of Chinese books to Japan was replaced by that of books in English, French and German, and to a lesser extent in other European languages. From the 1850s onwards they were on sale in Yokohama and later became available in other cities, and in the Meiji period they were extensively translated and published in condensed or adapted versions in Japanese, and they spawned a secondary literature of commentaries and guides (§7.1.4). Although Western texts gradually replaced Chinese texts in the course of the late nineteenth century, they were not, however, for the most part accorded the canonical status that Chinese texts had enjoyed, as is evident from the fact that they circulated in translation or even in truncated versions.

Conversely, very few Japanese works were being translated at all at this time into any foreign languages, and there were indeed very few Westerners with the ability to undertake that task. Consequently, it cannot be said that at this stage the book market in Japan was in communication with those of Western societies, for there was none of the two-way traffic that characterized, for example, the flow of books among the countries of western Europe; that two-way traffic contained its own political and cultural imbalances, but between Japan and the West it simply did not take place. On the contrary, the traffic was almost exclusively one-way, and it cannot be said even today

---

[14] Cf. Richard Jenkyns, *The Victorians and ancient Greece* (Oxford: Blackwell, 1980).

that Japanese books, even literary works in translation, are as available, say, in Europe as are European books in the original languages or in translation in Japan.

1.3 THE ADVENT AND CONSEQUENCES OF PRINT

It is now a commonplace that the development of printing technology had profound consequences for the nature and ecology of texts, as books with new characteristics, such as uniformity, replaced manuscripts. The results of that process are assumed to be universal, as may also be the current shift towards digitalized texts that are globally accessible and globally uniform, although the reading and reception of those same texts may of course not be. But that is not to say that the path followed by all manuscript cultures towards print was the same, and it is essential to be aware of the particularities of the Japanese case from the outset. Not that I wish to claim that the Japanese case is unique, for, as will become clear, the variety of paths is striking and the shift to print in Russia, in Arabic-speaking societies and in Korea also has peculiarities that expose the contingencies of the shift to print in western Europe in the fifteenth century.

The point can be put most succinctly in this way: although printing began in Japan in the middle of the eighth century, it would not have been possible for a Japanese Francis Bacon to claim that printing had changed 'the appearance and state of the whole world' until some time in the first half of the seventeenth century. As recounted in chapter four, printing was resorted to only sporadically between the eighth and the eleventh centuries, and then for ritual purposes rather than for producing texts for people to read. From then until the end of the sixteenth century, the printing of books for the purpose of reading did begin to take effect, but they were few in number (fewer than 500 titles printed in 500 years), they were produced by Buddhist monastic institutions rather than by commercial publishers, they were almost exclusively in Chinese and they were almost entirely Buddhist scriptures or doctrinal works. Very few of them, therefore, were published in the sense of being produced with the intention or possibility of making them public property and were rather for the use of the monastic community, often just that of one particular

Buddhist sect.

By 1700 the situation had been transformed out of recognition and urban, educated Japan had become dependent on print and the book had accomplished its transformation into a commercial entity. So printing was in Japan a dormant technology and its potential latent until the seventeenth century. This critical delay in the application of an available technology is strikingly different from the European experience, but it is by no means unique to Japan. In Russia, for example, the printing press reached Moscow around the middle of the sixteenth century, a hundred years after the printing of Gutenberg's Bible, and the oldest surviving products of the press date from the 1560s, but thereafter the press languished. In the early eighteenth century, Peter the Great attempted to kick-start a European-style publishing industry in St Petersburg, but his death in 1725 brought an end to the enthusiasm and it was not until the end of the eighteenth century that we find such unmistakable signs of a nascent print culture as the foundation of publishing houses for Moscow University and for the military academies, the emergence of commercial publishing houses and the activities of commercial circulating libraries. It may well have been the Enlightenment that succeeded where Peter had failed in creating a buoyant market for the printed book in Russia, for a landmark publication was the three-volume set of articles from Diderot's *Encyclopédie* put out by Moscow University Press in 1767.[15]

The issue in the case of Russia is unequivocally the lack of the infrastructure in the form of means for commercial production and distribution and the lack of a literate and reading public. Peter found, for example, that the demand for the products of his presses was so poor that some books had to be given away, while civil servants were compulsorily required to purchase others in order to reduce stocks. To some extent these points hold true for Japan before 1600 as well: the means for commercial production and distribution may have existed, but political disunity prevented the emergence of a

---

[15] On the emergence of print culture in Russia see Gary Marker, *Publishing, printing, and the origins of intellectual life in Russia, 1700–1800* (Princeton: Princeton University Press, 1985), Marker, 'Russian journals and their readers in the late eighteenth century', *Oxford slavonic papers* 19 (1986): 88–101, and A. A. Zaitseva, '"Kabinety dlya chteniya" v Sankt-Peterburge kontsa XVIII - nachala XIX veka', in *Russkie biblioteki i chastnye knizhnye sobraniya XVI–XIX bekov* (Leningrad: Biblioteka Akademii Nauk, 1979).

national market for goods that could be readily exploited. And to what extent can we speak of a 'public' in Japan before 1600, one that was not only functionally literate but was also a potential market for books? How such a literate public emerged and then developed into a market in the early seventeenth century has yet to be explored, but at this stage it appears likely that print culture reached the point of take-off in Japan simultaneously with the emergence of a literate public. In Europe, by contrast, so rapid was the development of print culture in the second half of the fifteenth century that it is clear some form of literate public was already in existence; indeed, if what needs explaining in the case of Japan is the delay in applying a technology, what needs explaining in the case of Europe is the delay in developing the technology to meet the need.

A further instance of the delay in taking to print is that of the Islamic world.[16] The process from scribal cultures to print cultures (based on lithography before typography) was a long and tortuous one in the Islamic world and lasted until the end of the nineteenth century, but it is clear that this was not because of ignorance of the art of printing or because of the supposed technological difficulty of printing in Arabic: the Quran had been printed in Arabic in Venice in 1530, but copies of religious texts printed in Europe in Arabic turned out to embody errors that achieved permanence and diffusion by virtue of being printed.[17] Print was slow to establish itself in Islamic cultures primarily because the *ulama*, the body of Muslim scholars, objected to the use of print for religious books; other books might be acceptable and in the Ottoman Empire permission was given in 1727 for the printing of non-religious books in Arabic.[18] Francis Robinson argues that the principle reason for the objection was the perception that printing undermined the oral transmission and the sources of scriptural authority for the Quran, and in addition

---

[16] On Islam and print see the essays contained in Atiyeh 1995; Johannes Pedersen, *The Arabic book*, trans. G. French (Princeton: Princeton University Press, 1984), ch. 10; Francis Robinson, 'Technology and religious change: Islam and the impact of print', *Modern Asian studies* 27 (1993): 229–51; Robinson, 'Islam and the impact of print in South Asia', in Nigel Crook, ed., *The transmission of knowledge in South Asia: essays on education, religion, history, and politics* (Delhi: Oxford University Press, 1996), 62–97.

[17] Muhsin Mahdi, 'From the manuscript age to the age of printed books', in Atiyeh 1995: 1–4.

[18] Atiyeh 1995: 235.

there is evidence for a perception of defilement through printing and of unease about sacred books falling into the hands of infidels by virtue of being printed and becoming easily available.[19] When the *ulama* in north India decided to embrace print in the early nineteenth century, ahead of other Islamic societies, it was primarily because they feared for the future of Islam in its confrontation with Christianity and Hinduism, and this step was initially not understood as an abandonment of the oral tradition, for readers were reminded that it was dangerous to read scriptural books without clerical supervision.[20]

Here the reluctance to commit Islamic scriptures to print is in stark contrast with the readiness in Europe to print the Bible and the importance of print for the Reformation. In Catholic Europe there were of course measures taken to control or restrict the printing of Bibles, especially in translation, but by comparison with the fate of the Quran it is striking that there was so little resistance in Europe to the printing of Christian scriptures, even though some Bibles contained, and therefore perpetuated and disseminated, shocking misprints.[21] In Japan, and in the East Asian Buddhist world dependent on Chinese translations of Buddhist sūtras, there was similarly no antipathy towards printing sacred texts. On the contrary, there is considerable evidence to suggest that in early India the physical reproduction of Buddhist texts was in itself a pious act and that the first efforts to reproduce Buddhist texts were not only scripturally sanctioned but were designed to produce texts that nobody would read: the texts in question, such as the so-called Buddhist creed, were reproduced by impressing a stamp in damp clay but the impressions were then permanently sealed inside a stūpa. Here the reproduction of texts starts out as a ritual, with a potential for the production of texts for readers yet to be realised. This practice was certainly known in China, Tibet, Korea and Japan and was responsible for the oldest surviving items of print hitherto found in Korea and Japan (§4.1.1), and possibly

---

[19] E. W. Lane, *An account of the manners and customs of the modern Egyptians*, 3rd edition (London: Charles Knight & Co., 1842), 1: 431.

[20] Francis Robinson, 'Technology and religious change: Islam and the impact of print', *Modern Asian studies* 27 (1993): 240–42.

[21] Eisenstein 1979: 346–9; Kenelm Foster, 'Italian versions', and M. H. Black, 'The printed Bible', both in *The Cambridge history of the Bible* vol.3: *The West from the Reformation to the present day*, ed. S. L. Greenslade (Cambridge: Cambridge University Press, 1963), 358–60, 408–75.

for the origins of printing in East Asia.[22]

So in East Asia print was used first for ritual purposes, for the meritorious reproduction of Buddhist texts, and only later for the production of texts, Buddhist or secular, for people to read. But even at that later stage, which began in Japan in the eleventh century, there is no sign of any of the objections and unease evident in the Islamic world. In the first place this is because Buddhist texts, although they partook of the sacred, were not 'the word of God'. Secondly, in East Asia Buddhist texts were transmitted in the form of Chinese translations of mostly Sanskrit sūtras which required, particularly in Japan, visual contact with the text and which, for linguistic reasons, virtually precluded oral transmission. Thirdly, there was no Buddhist equivalent of the Islamic *ulama* safeguarding the authority of the tradition. And fourthly, because of the ritual practice of reproducing texts, there was no distaste about the association of sacred texts with means of reproduction. Buddhism, in the form in which it reached Japan, was a profoundly textual religion and far from obstructing the use of print actually monopolized it for centuries. As a consequence of this, the *Tale of Genji*, the great poetry anthologies, the medieval war-tales and the entire secular literary production of early Japan circulated in manuscript and did not appear in print until the seventeenth century.

The origins of printing, the emergence of print culture and the engagement of print with religious traditions, in Japan and in other societies, brings into focus some of the contingencies which mark these developments and experiences in the case of Europe. Elizabeth Eisenstein's celebrated study, *The printing press as an agent of change*, and her more recent work on the 'printing revolution', come perilously close to technological determinism in associating social and intellectual changes with the spread of typography.[23] As Clanchy has put it, 'printing succeeded because a literate public already existed': he argues that in Europe a literate public came into being in the twelfth

---

[22] Jeremiah P. Losty, *The art of the book in India* (London: British Library, 1982), 10; Walter Liebenthal, 'Sanskrit inscriptons from Yunnan, I', *Monumenta Serica* 12 (1947): 1–40; F. D. Lessing and A. Wayman, *Introduction to the Buddhist Tantric systems, translated from Mkha Grub Rje's Rgyud spyiḥi rnam par gźag pa rgyas par brjod* (Delhi: Motilal Banarsidass, 1978), 107; Lawson 1972.

[23] Eisenstein 1979; Eisenstein, 'On revolution and the printed word', in R. Porter and M. Teich, eds, *Revolution in history* (Cambridge: Cambridge University Press, 1986), 186–205.

and thirteenth centuries and that it was formed by the phenomenal growth of record-keeping, in other words by bureaucracy, and by the rise of vernacular education. Simon Franklin has cast some doubt on the association of record-keeping with literacy, but the key point here is the pre-existence of a 'literate public' as a market for print, for outside Europe the emergence of a literate public for the most part followed rather than preceded the development of printing technologies.[24]

Eisenstein's emphasis is undoubtedly a consequence of her concentration on Europe, for the advent of print did not have results so far-reaching, so rapid or so revolutionary in many societies outside Europe for several centuries. Print, be it typography, xylography or lithography, does not contain within itself the seeds of its own success, and the reasons for its success in creating print cultures in sixteenth-century Europe, Song-dynasty China, seventeenth-century Japan and eighteenth-century Russia must be sought elsewhere, just as the consequences of literacy must be explained without reference to an untenable determinism that attributes given social changes simply to the spread of literacy.[25] In the next section I consider just what difference it makes that printing in Japan, as in China, was dominated until the nineteenth century by xylography, the art of printing with carved wooden blocks.

Finally, although Eisenstein has set important agendas for future research and has forced us to think about the social, cultural and intellectual consequences of print, the relationship between print and the consequences attributed to it is not easy to pin down, and the consequences themselves need not necessarily be seen in benign terms. For example, Eisenstein argued, plausibly enough, that 'typographical fixity' made a rationalized view of the past possible by providing it with a 'permanent temporal location' in print, but print also provided 'ways in which traditional resources of meaning are codified, fixed, and dramatized' and print materialized culture in ways that urgently need to be explored.[26] What is missing, in other

---

[24] M. T. Clanchy, *From memory to written record: England 1066–1307*, 2nd edition (Oxford: Blackwell, 1993), 1, 16, 19, etc.; Simon Franklin, 'Literacy and documentation in early medieval Russia', *Speculum* 60 (1985): 1–38.

[25] On this see Thomas 1990, esp. chs 1 and 2.

[26] Eric J. Leed, 'Elizabeth Eisenstein's *The printing press as an agent of change* and the structure of communications revolutions', *American journal of sociology* 88

words, is the plurality of audience responses to texts and of audience perceptions of authority in printed texts before we can draw confident conclusions about the effects of print.

1.4 CALLIGRAPHY AND THE BLOCK-PRINTED TEXT

As will be clear from chapters four and five, there is no room for doubting that by the end of the eighteenth century Japan had already become a highly-developed and diversified print culture. Nevertheless, it proved difficult for the Europeans and Americans who resided in or visited Japan from the 1850s onwards to recognise this and to see Japan as essentially 'Western' in its adaptation to and dependence on the printed word. Edward Morse, for example, who lived and worked in Japan as a scientist for several years in the 1870s and 1880s and who observed the lending libraries doing their rounds in Tokyo, had no idea of the hinterland of publishers and of the national market for printed books.[27] This failure of perception is perhaps eurocentric in part, and attributable to the very obvious physical differences between Japanese books and Western books: how could the flimsy, soft-covered Japanese book compare with the leather-bound volumes of the West, weighty literally and by inference metaphorically as well? More importantly, it is due to the fundamental difference between contemporary Japanese and Western books in the manner of their production as printed books: Japanese books were until the 1880s almost exclusively block-printed books. This was not because of technological backwardness, for movable-type printing was practised in Japan from the early seventeenth century, albeit on a modest scale. So block-printing represented a choice, and one that poses certain epistemological problems.

The problem is this: are we justified in treating block-printed books as equivalent to movable-type printed books, in discussing the advent of print without reference to the different technologies involved? The consequence of the domination of wood-block printing

---

(1982): 415–7.

[27] Morse 1:120. Some of the ideas in this section were originally contained in a short essay, 'The emergence of the printed book in Japan: a comparative approach', in Andrew Gerstle and Anthony Milner, eds, *Recovering the Orient: artists, scholars, appropriations* (Chur: Harwood Academic publishers, 1994), 229–43.

was that each book had a different personality, and one that was closely related to calligraphy, to the written hand. Typography is not, of course, a neutral or universalistic medium, and different typefaces convey messages and arouse generic expectations, and the proliferation of computer fonts is currently extending the visual diversity of print. Nevertheless, every typeface, every font, is designed to be a standard, at least within a given item of print, and usually over a large number of printed items: the letter 'g' in a given font will be identical in its every appearance in a book printed in that font, and identical to all occurences of that letter in other books printed in the same font. This is not the case with the block-printed book. Since the printing blocks are prepared by pasting a manuscript onto a block of wood and carving away all but the text, block-printing is in effect the reproduction of manuscripts and a block-printed text shares many of the characteristics of manuscripts. A given character or syllabic sign will not be identical throughout the text but is subject to the infinite variety of handwriting, and it will not be identical to occurrences of that character or sign in other printed texts, even if the manuscript was written out by the same scribe. Each block-printed text, by virtue of being a reproduced manuscript, is therefore unique and unrepeatable. And the distinction here is not simply between a block-printed Japanese text, using a large number of different characters and syllabic signs, and a Western text printed with movable-type and making repeated use of the limited number of letters in the alphabet; it is a distinction that holds between block-printed copies of a Japanese text and copies of the same text printed with movable type.

The consequences of this are profound, and can only be briefly explored here. Frederick Mote has noted that the relationship between calligraphy and the block-printed Chinese book evolved in a different and more intimate manner than the more distant relationship between calligraphy and typography in the West, and a similar point may be made of Islamic calligraphy and the Arabic book. He argues that 'the nature of the Chinese script succeeded in imposing its demands on the forms of printing technology in East Asia' and that 'this aspect of printing in East Asia gives it an important place in the history of art'.[28] To be sure, the calligraphic character of a block-printed book,

---

[28] Mote and Chu 1988: 10–15 (quotations from p. 12). Unfortunately, although this book is titled *Calligraphy and the East Asian book*, none of the contributors

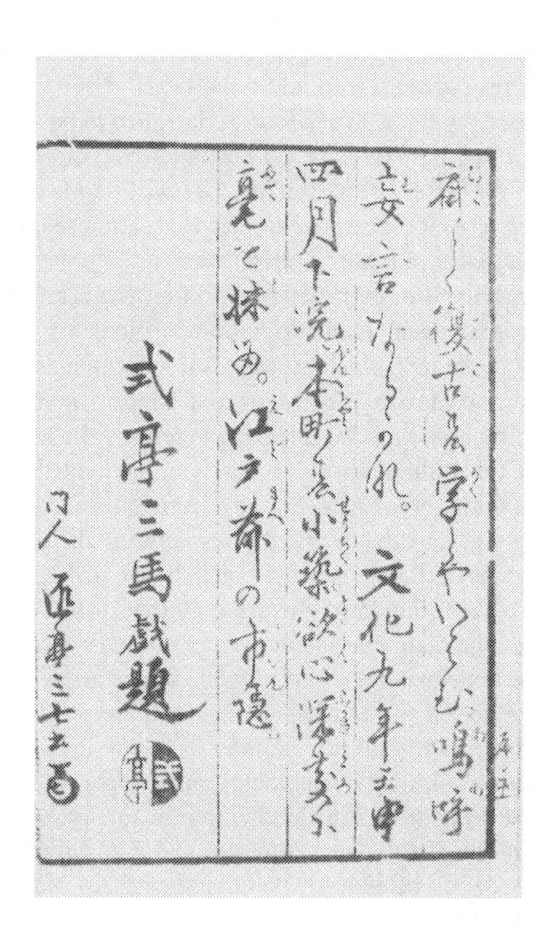

Fig. 1 The end of the preface to Shikitei Sanba's comic novel *Shirōto kyōgen monkirigata* 素人狂言紋切形 [A stereotype of amateur dramatics] (1814). The penultimate line informs the reader that Sanba himself composed it and concludes with a printed impression of his personal seal, and the last line, in reduced size, makes it clear that the text of the preface was actually written out by one of his followers.

---

address the questions raised below.

its claims to artistry, were significant considerations in Japan, and the calligraphic appeal of a text was often enhanced by appending a preface by the author and/or one or more commendatory prefaces by some well-known person or persons, all in their own reproduced hands. Prefaces and texts, they reproduce unique samples of unique calligraphic hands, and those hands can be judged in terms of their aesthetic appeal, or lack of it in the case of the cheapest forms of literary production, they can be understood in terms of the age and personality of the calligrapher, and appreciated as the product of a particular calligraphic tradition in a particular time and place.

All this is important, but what is at issue is not so much the artistry of the block-printed book as the consequences of that artistry, the fact that block-printed books enforce a more particularistic relationship between reader and text than was possible with movable type. The calligraphic personality of a book did more than just provide it with a genre-specific identity, it also created a relationship between the reader and the scribe or calligrapher which in turn affected the reading of texts in ways that need to be examined. For example, the flowing, sometimes archaic, Japanese calligraphy of most of the works produced by the scholars of the Kokugaku or Nativist movement in the eighteenth and nineteenth centuries gives their published works a nationalistically Japanese personality that is deliberately expressive of their resistance to the dominant sinological traditions and to the impact of China on Japan. And what does it do for the presence of an author in a text when it is preceded by a preface in his (very rarely 'her' in the Tokugawa period) own hand? The encounter of readers with block-printed texts is not merely with texts but calligraphic personalities as well.

I have suggested here the advantages, from the point of view of the reception of texts, of seeing block-printed books as reproduced manuscripts. It is important to remember too that the rapid spread of block printing in the seventeenth century did not lead to the end of manuscript traditions and that manuscripts continued to be produced and to coexist with printed books throughout the Tokugawa period (§3.3). The character of block-printed books and the persistence of hermetic scribal traditions relating to such individually transmitted artistic traditions as the tea ceremony are part of a larger set of phenomena in the Tokugawa Japan which emphasize the particularistic

30   CHAPTER ONE

rather than the universalistic, including the oral or colloquial component of popular literature, theatrical forms dominated by the actor rather than by the text, and a legal system that punished according to class, locality and occasion. Thus although the publication explosion in the seventeenth century worked important transformations on Japanese society, care needs to be taken to distinguish the impact of print in the West from that of block-printed books in East Asia. Typography clearly needs to be understood differently from block-printing or from lithography not only as a means of reproducing texts but in terms of the distance created between print and manuscript and of the development of scribal cultures into print cultures.

1.5   LITERACY AND READING

In chapter six I have made a brief exploration of the issues of literacy and reading in pre-modern Japan. It is undoubtedly the case that literacy rates in Japan in the mid nineteenth century were high by contemporary world standards, and that raises questions. What explanations can be put forward to explain this, and, more importantly, what were the functions and consequences of this high degree of literacy? Was it overwhelmingly urban and male? Unfortunately, too little research has yet been done on Japanese literacy, or rather literacies, to be able to shape answers these questions, but we do know enough to be able to address some related issues.

In their discussion of the consequences of literacy, Niezen and Parry have argued that Goody's earlier attempts to associate high rates of literacy with the generation and diffusion of knowledge and rationalism need some qualification. Referring to the circumstances of reformist Muslims in West Africa and the Brahmanical tradition in India, they suggest that literacy cannot bear the explanatory weight attached to it in connection with the growth of knowledge. They stress that the social structures and organizations within which literacy 'works' need to be given more attention, and this point has also been pressed by Rosalind Thomas and others.[29] If literacy does not

---

[29] R. W. Niezen, 'Hot literacy in cold societies: a comparative study of the sacred value of writing', *Comparative studies in society and history* 33 (1991): 225–54; J. P. Parry, 'The Brahmanical tradition and the technology of the intellect', in J. Overing, ed., *Reason and morality* (London: Tavistock, 1985), pp. 200–25. See

necessarily lead to the growth of knowledge, it is partly because the engagement of literate readers with texts cannot be assumed to be uniform and it is now clear that the study of literacy needs to be accompanied by the study of audiences, of modes of reading, and of what Jonathan Rose has called 'mass intellectual responses to reading'.[30]

Further, the modern enthusiasm for the spread of literacy to all corners of the globe has tended to associate literacy and access to books too closely with such desired goals as democracy and pluralism, but it is essential to retain a number of reservations. Literacy brings new readers into a world of books and print which is not immune from the politics of control or domination. Control in its overt form is of course familiar from censorship régimes around the world. But control in more subtle forms is equally worthy of our attention. Ann Douglas, for example, has shown how the reading market in nineteenth-century America, manipulated by the transformation of publishers into technology-dependent and capital-intensive commercial enterprises, came to be dominated by middle-class women consumers, and takes up the case of Margaret Fuller, a dissident who 'distrusted New England bookishness and its oppressive role in the process of feminine socialization' and for whom 'the revolt against books, against the role of reader ... was a symbolic protest against the derivative lives to which their society consigned them'.[31] In this connection we should remember that in Japan literary production for most of the nineteenth century was almost totally in the hands of men, and it was not until later that women writers began to articulate resistance, to recreate themselves as writers, to publish alternative views, and to find new readers. There is an urgent need for a study of the impact of gender on the shifting constructs of author and reader and the feminization of the reading public in late nineteenth-century Japan. At this stage it is possible to do little more than note the resistance to existing concepts of readership and authorship in the careers of women

---

also Thomas 1990. For Goody's arguments, see Jack Goody and Ian Watt, 'The consequences of literacy', *Comparative studies in society and history* 5 (1963): 304–45, and J. Goody, *The domestication of the savage mind* (Cambridge: Cambridge University Press, 1977).

[30] Rose 1992: 48.

[31] Ann Douglas, *The feminization of American culture* (New York: Knopf, 1977), 60–66, 82–6, 267–70. See also D. P. Pattanayak, 'Literacy: an instrument of oppression', in Olson and Torrance 1991: 105–8.

writers such as Yosano Akiko (1878–1942).[32]

But the question of literacy in Japan has also to confront the plurality of literacies made possible by the intellectual dominance of sinology, by the pervasive use of sino-japanese for bureaucratic purposes, and by the plurality of possibilities for writing Japanese, from script that is dense with Chinese characters to script that uses them sparingly and then glosses them with a phonetic pronunciation guide. Here too 'literacy' is replete with messages of control and far removed from supposed 'democratic' effects. Mark Lewis makes precisely this point when he 'situates writing not within the technologies of communication but in the forms of control', and in pre-modern Japan language and hence literacy are inextricably tied to systems of state control and determine access to élite culture. This is at its most obvious in the context of the court in the Nara and Heian periods, which operated by means of documents in Chinese, and of the sinological cast of élite male culture up until the nineteenth century.[33]

At the same time, the transformation of the spoken language into the language of a growing proportion of the output of the commercial publishers in the Tokugawa period, in other words into a print language, is not without its own significance. By the end of the seventeenth century we can see in the published works of Ihara Saikaku and other writers of fiction based in Osaka the breakdown of allegiance to the conventions of the formal written language and the incursion of colloquial vocabulary. At this stage, the print language of popular literature is a blend of formal written Japanese with the colloquial language of western Japan, particularly Osaka and Kyoto, where the publishing industry was at its most active. By the middle of the nineteenth century, Edo (=Tokyo) had become the centre of the publishing industry: the colloquial language of western Japan was replaced by that of Edo, and since the representation of colloquial speech itself became the focus of several popular genres of fiction,

---

[32] S. L. Sievers, *Flowers in salt: the beginnings of feminist consciousness in modern Japan* (Stanford: Stanford University Press, 1983). On Akiko see Phyllis Hyland Larson, 'Yosano Akiko and the re-creation of the female self: an autogynography', and G. G. Rowley, 'Making a living from *Genji*: Yosano Akiko and her work on *The Tale of Genji*', both in *Journal of the association of teachers of Japanese* 25 (1991): 11–26, 27–44.

[33] Mark Lewis, *Writing and authority in early China* (forthcoming), 1.

the colloquial speech of Edo gained a prominence in popular literature that no regional form of speech had had before.[34] Since, in addition, the market for books had already long since spread to cover almost all areas of Japan, it is evident that the language of Edo, as reproduced in books circulated throughout Japan, became one of those 'unified fields of exchange and communication' that Benedict Anderson has associated with print languages and 'laid the basis for national consciousness'. As Edo came in the late eighteenth century to dominate commercial publishing and to disseminate its products by means of networks of book distributors and lending libraries that covered all urban communities of Japan, so the language of Edo was carried to readers who had never been there and became for them the language of access to mass-market popular literature and culture, a language that was uniformly transmitted throughout Japan.[35]

But the Edo dialect as found in the colloquial fiction of the nineteenth century was by no means the only print language. There were in fact a plurality of print languages each with their own demands, conventions and social and cultural boundaries. There was the Chinese of works produced in China and reprinted in Japan, from the classics to Ming vernacular fiction; there was the Chinese written by Japanese authors, so-called *kanbun*, which was written to be decoded as Japanese and which might, as in the case of Ogyū Sorai, pass muster as Chinese in China, but which might equally well not; and there was the formal written Japanese of scholars in the Kokugaku tradition and of certain writers of fiction at the top end of the market. It is only in the late nineteenth century, with the development of a form of written Japanese that marries features of the spoken and formal written languages, that a unitary print language emerged.[36]

What is significant about this multiplicity of print languages in pre-modern Japan is that they did not form a simple hierarchy that

---

[34] On these colloquial genres see Robert Leutner, *Shikitei Sanba and the comic tradition in late Edo fiction* (Cambridge, Mass.: Harvard University Press, 1986), and Alan Woodhull, 'Romantic Edo fiction: a study of the *ninjōbon* and complete translation of *Shunshoku umegoyomi*', unpublished Ph.D. dissertation, Stanford University (1978).

[35] Anderson 1991: 44–5. On the shift in dialects see Honda Yasuo 本田康雄, 'Sharebon no hōgen byōsha' 洒落本の方言描写, *Kokugo to kokubungaku* 57.2 (1980): 39–47.

[36] Nanette Twine, 'The Genbunitchi movement: its origin, development and conclusion', *MN* 33 (1978): 333–56.

can be correlated with levels of educational or cultural attainment. The choice, for example, between *kanbun* and formal written Japanese was an ideological one as much as a linguistic one, representing a choice made between sinological and nationalistic orientations. Consequently literacy too in Japan has to be seen not so much as a ladder which you climbed to move from illiteracy to functional literacy and from there to higher rungs: there were choices to be made which were not simply a matter of levels and functions but which simultaneously carry ideological weight. This also applies, of course, to the acquisition of Dutch to gain access to Dutch scientific texts, the only ones available in the Tokugawa period: knowledge of Dutch was not only a badge of membership of the Rangaku school (Dutch studies) but also a token of rejection of Chinese science and its practitioners in Japan.

Furthermore, the binary division between illiteracy and literacy that mars many earlier discussions of these issues clearly needs to be blurred. In many ways a more useful division is that between those that have in some way access to the world of print and those that do not. In seventeenth-century England, as Margaret Spufford has argued, 'the presence of even one reader amongst a group of rural labourers could act as a significant bridge to the literate world'. In precisely this way in nineteenth-century Russia the widespread practice of reading aloud to illiterate peasants, the emergence of professional newspaper reciters, and the subsequent oral transmission of print-derived material, including, for example, news of the Russo-Japanese war in 1904–5, all brought illiterate peasants within the fold of print culture. In the Middle East, similarly, reading was often conducted as a group activity in coffee houses and by this means 'the illiterate and poorly educated also imbibed the printed word through the reading of extracts and passages out loud by their more literate companions'. In Japan too in the nineteenth century and earlier the practice of reading works of fiction aloud clearly functioned in the same way to afford aural access to printed books. But in these contexts what difference does it make that print rather than oral traditions are the source of the entertainment, enlightenment or information? If, as seems likely, print is here acquiring an authority that oral sources cannot contend with, then it is likely that aural access to print itself functions as a nudge in the direction of literacy, of direct access to the authority of print. Just as the servant in Gogol's *Dead souls* does not care what he is reading provided that he is engaged in the process of reading, the acquisition of a measure of literacy, before it even affords access to the world of books, offers a means of identifying oneself with the social standing of those who can read.[37]

How, then, did Japanese readers read? How did they position themselves before a text in the form of a book? The history of reading, as opposed to readership, in Japan is still at an inchoate stage, and the recovery of pre-modern reading practices has barely begun. The anthropology of reading demands something more subtle than the crude distinction between vulgar or passive readers and élite readers who create their own rereadings, and points to the significance, for example, of the choice of posture. The archetype of the scholar or litterateur reading at a low desk in a book-lined study bespeaks a fundamentally different textual orientation from that of a bath-house customer sprawled on the floor with a book or a courtesan reading in idle moments. And beyond questions of posture there are other important issues. How do authors conceptualise their readers and represent those conceptualizations in their works, for example in their prefaces? When the male authors of *ninjōbon*, a genre of nineteenth-century romantic fiction, apostrophise their readers as 'women and children' this conveys not simply their expectations about their likely readers but also, in the Tokugawa world of gender and age hierarchies, of their superior stance. Similarly, the various words used in Japan after the author's name at the head of the text to convey authorship are themselves replete with suggestiveness about the author's relation to the text and the relation readers were expected to have with the text (§§6.2.1, 6.2.2).[38]

Further, as Roger Chartier has emphasized, there is a significant space between text and book, and the formal presentation of a text in the form of a book can 'modify both its register of reference and its mode of interpretation'. In the case of Japanese printed books of the Tokugawa period, an obvious instance of that space being appropriated

---

[37] Margaret Spufford, *Small books and pleasant histories: popular fiction and its readership in seventeenth-century England* (London: Methuen, 1981), 32; Jeffrey Brooks, *When Russia learned to read: literacy and popular literature, 1861–1917* (Princeton: Princeton University Press, 1985), ch. 1, esp. 13, 27–29; Geoffrey Roper, 'Fāris al-Shidyāq and the transition from scribal to print culture in the Middle East', in Atiyeh 1995: 216; Maeda 1973: 132–8.

[38] Jesper Svenbro, *Phrasikleia: an anthropology of reading in ancient Greece*, trans. Janet Lloyd (Ithaca: Cornell University Press, 1993), 5–6.

for new presentations of texts is the provision of illustrations, for the simplicity of including line illustrations in the printing blocks made the visualization of pre-existing texts possible. The commercial appeal of illustrated versions is apparent both from advertising material and from the use of titles that highlight the presence of illustrations, for example adding to any title the prefix *ehon* 絵本, 'illustrated book'. Similarly, calligraphic styles used for the printing blocks, the use of bindings of different quality, and so on created indelible impressions of modernity, style and value that, we must hypothesize, interfered with the responses of individual readers.[39]

There is also a need to take the question of reading further, to develop a sociology of reading that can move from the atomized experiences of individual readers to the patterns of mass reading. Chartier, for example, has noted that for the literate élite of sixteenth- and seventeenth-century Europe reading 'became the act par excellence of intimate, private, and secret leisure', 'a withdrawal from the affairs of the city': 'the act of reading defines a new consciousness that is constructed outside the sphere of public authority and political power, and outside the network of interrelationships that make up social and domestic life.'[40] What needs to be problematized here is the 'outside': to what extent does reading *per se*, and do reading tastes, actually constitute a political act in themselves, a rejection or alternatively espousal of the values of the holders of political power? In Japan the reading habits of literati (*bunjin* 文人) is one such case. By definition they were intellectuals who had withdrawn from public life, and they turned away from orthodox sinology toward the colloquial fiction of the Ming and contemporary Qing dynasties: this new orientation in sinology can certainly be interpreted as a rejection or an escape. But also, the very profusion of popular vernacular literature and its extensive readership can be interpreted as a rejection of the sinophilic stance of the Tokugawa Bakufu and the sinological intelligentsia.

At the same time there is an obvious need to be wary of what Jonathan Rose has called the 'receptive fallacy', the assumptions that readers read the same messages into texts as those intended by

---

[39] Chartier 1994: 10–11.
[40] Roger Chartier, 'Leisure and sociability: reading aloud in early modern Europe', trans. Carol Mossman, in Susan Zimmerman and Ronald F. E. Weissman, eds, *Urban life in the Renaissance* (Newark: University of Delaware Press, 1989), 103–104.

their authors or read by other readers. An intriguing example in Japan is the claim, made in 1903, that the long historical novels of Kyokutei Bakin were and should be read as a political critique of the Tokugawa Bakufu and that 'the Revolution of 1868 [ie, the Meiji Restoration] may be ascribed more or less to the works of Bakin'. The suggestion here that a covert reading tradition has been lost is a valuable reminder of the instability of texts in the hands of their readers, an instability that becomes even more obvious when Japanese readers confronted Chinese or Western texts. With what spectacles did they read them? How can we understand what configurations Japanese readers in the nineteenth century fitted, say, Dickens into? The need to historicize reading practices and the repertoire of interpretive strategies is acute, for we cannot assume that Japanese read Dickens either as we do or as nineteenth-century British readers did. In cases such as this there is a huge gap between the 'audience' who actually read a book and the 'public' to which it is addressed. [41]

The profusion of popular literature mentioned above also raises the question of the shift from intensive to extensive reading, which has been discussed by Robert Darnton and others.[42] For intellectuals in Japan in the early seventeenth century, as for Chinese intellectuals in the Song dynasty, the startling leap in the availability of books contained the danger of 'over-reading', that is of the shallow reading of too many books (§6.2.2). The same point is made by Pope in his parody of the effects of print in the *Dunciad*, for as a result of the increasing accessibility of books 'truth becomes more obscure and understanding diminishes'. The 'reading revolution' in Europe, the shift to extensive reading, has been connected to the 'desacralization of the printed word', and to some extent this holds true of Japan too. As already mentioned, Buddhism monopolized the use of print from the eleventh century until the late sixteenth, but not in the sense in which Christianity was central to the output of the press in Europe,

---

[41] Rose 1992: 49; T. Asada, 'Life of Bakin', *The Sun trade journal* 9.13 (1903): 21–2. The distinction between 'audience' and 'public' is taken from Natalie Zemon Davis, *Society and culture in early modern France* (Stanford: Stanford University Press, 1975), 192–3.

[42] Robert Darnton, *The kiss of Lamourette: reflections in cultural history* (London: Faber and Faber, 1990), 133, 165–7. See also Rolf Engelsing, *Der Bürger als Leser: Lesergeschichte in Deutschland 1500–1900* (Stuttgart: J. B. Metzler, 1974) and Erich Schön, *Der Verlust der Sinnlichkeit oder die Verwandlungen des Lesers: Mentalitätswandel um 1800* (Stuttgart: Klett-Cotta, 1987).

for Buddhist texts at that time were for the most part not 'published', that is they did not become public property by becoming commodities and being made available to an interested public. The publishing activity of the early seventeenth century was by contrast overwhelmingly secular: even though Chinese Confucian texts did take on some of the mantle of sacredness, what is far more striking is the impact commercial publishing had on the range and availablity of printed books of all kinds. The sheer multiplicity of books of itself functioned to strip the sinological classics or Buddhist sūtras of their prominence and their aura and left them, in Alvin Kernan's words, 'epistemologically as well as ontologically only a few among many'. It is at this point in Japan that we can talk of a reading revolution, and we can trace it, for example, in the intertextuality of popular fiction, such as that of Ihara Saikaku, which requires of readers a range of literary experiences hitherto difficult to achieve.[43]

Although literacy and reading remain largely unexplored terrain in Japanese social history, it is clear that the stimulating work that has been done on European literacy and reading is replete with suggestiveness. But is also clear that literacy and reading in Japan and China present some variant perspectives. These are of interest in their own right, and offer insight into the modes of access to texts in pre-modern Japan, but at the same time they reveal some of the contingencies of Western practices and experience and expose the range of possibilities inherent in the encounter between human beings and books. In the chapters that follow the emphasis will be on the particularities of the book in Japan, particularities that have shaped the ontology of the book and its impact in Japan and that acquire a different layer of meaning when considered in apposition to the experience of the book in other societies.

---

[43] Kernan 1987: 12, 156.

CHAPTER TWO

BOOKS AS MATERIAL OBJECTS

1   Paper and the roll
2   Forms of the book
3   Printing and the book
4   Illustration and the arts of the book
5   Printed maps, serial publications and ephemera
6   Conservation

This chapter focusses on the incarnation of texts on paper as rolls and as books, and considers them as material objects which mediate between the text and readers and which also, as the most tangible and numerous surviving artifacts from earlier centuries, mediate between us and the mental worlds of the past. The physical forms of the book in Japan, their visual characteristics, the procedures that go into their making, and their artistic qualities are all quite different from those of European books, but they do of course have some features in common with Chinese and Korean books, and attention must be drawn to some of these features. What will be considered here, then, is the use of paper and the transition from rolls to books, block-printing and the conventions for the representation of texts on printed pages, the use of illustration and the arts of the book, and so on. The calligraphic nature of Japanese books is given less consideration here; it is undoubtedly of great importance as the medium through which texts reach their readers, but it has been given some consideration elsewhere (§§1.4, 4.2.3). The final two sections cover first the range of printed matter other than 'books' in the Tokugawa period, for books were part of a larger world of print that embraced other printed material objects such as maps and broadsheets, and then the traditions of conservation that have been partly responsible for the transmission and survival of texts.

2.1 PAPER AND THE ROLL

The paper roll is the earliest form of book known in Japan. It is in this form that texts first reached Japan from China, for papermaking was already several centuries old in China by the time the first rolls may be thought to have reached Japan. How and when the art of papermaking was transmitted is unknown, but the first documentary reference to papermaking in Japan dates from 610, when it is recorded that the king of Koguryŏ, the northernmost of the Korean kingdoms, sent two monks to Japan, one of whom knew the *Five Classics* and was skilled in making paper and ink. It is likely that papermaking was introduced to Japan before this, but in any case by the early Nara period the manufacture of paper had developed and spread to such an extent that many provinces were involved in production, and that domestic supplies were able to keep pace with the gargantuan appetites of the state bureaucratic system and with the extensive copying of sūtras that was being conducted both privately and by the state. Further, the papers preserved in the Shōsōin reveal that the producers experimented with a great variety of vegetable materials in their papermaking and could already by that time produce luxury decorated and coloured papers.[1]

In the early ninth century, if not before, the Zushoryō 図書寮, a state body responsible for the conservation of books (§9.1.1), established its own facilities for manufacturing the consumables it needed. Four men were employed to make paper, another four to make ink, and ten to make brushes, and the annual production of paper in the Zushoryō was, by some time later in the century, supposed to be 20,000 sheets. Later in the Heian period, when printing was beginning to be used for the reproduction of texts, the demand for paper must have risen further, but little is known about supplies of paper over the succeeding centuries until the beginning of the seventeenth.[2]

Coloured papers were in use in the Nara period for sūtra-copying and in the Heian period the use of coloured and decorated papers for

---

[1] On Chinese papermaking and inkmaking see Tsien 1985: 23–47, 233–47. *NKBT* 68:194–5; Shōsōin Jimusho 正倉院事務所, *Shōsōin no kami* 正倉院の紙 (Kunaichō, 1970).

[2] *NST* 3: 162; *KT* 26 *Engishiki* 387–8.

this purpose became more common. By the Muromachi period the production of decorated papers was well-established: in 1348 prince Son'en 尊円 (1298–1356) wrote out an ordination certificate, possibly to be used as a calligraphic model, on paper with a pine-branch design and flecks of gold and silver leaf. Later, decorated papers were used for some of the Sagabon printed in the seventeenth century, some with patterns drawn with mica. And at their most luxurious they could have patterns printed in colour and crests stamped in gold and silver, as did the paper used by the calligrapher and courtier Karasumaru Mitsuhiro 烏丸光広 (1579–1638) for some poems he copied out in the 1630s.[3]

The rapid growth of the publishing industry in the Tokugawa period and the proliferation of books led to an equally steep increase in the demand for paper, particularly in the cities that formed the core of the publishing industry. In 1798 a wholesale paper-dealer published an illustrated guide to papermaking which explained the process and made it accessible, but by that time the paper industry had already developed into an organised network of manufacturers, suppliers and retailers. By the early nineteenth century, if not before, there was a formally recognised guild of paper suppliers in Edo with a fixed quota of 47 members, while in a guide to Kyoto published in 1833 the names of 16 suppliers of paper are listed, some specialising in Chinese or provincial Japanese papers or in special decorative papers. In the closing years of the period the quality of Japanese papers and the range of decorated papers, some of which were used for manuscripts, luxury editions and book-covers, drew the attention of the British Minister in Japan, Sir Harry Parkes, who at the request of Gladstone made a collection of paper samples which represents the variety available at the end of the Tokugawa period.[4]

The invention of paper during the Han dynasty had made possible

---

[3] Rosenfield *et al.* 1973: 112–7 and plates VI–VII.

[4] Seki Yoshikuni 関義城, *(Edo Meiji) Kamiya to sono kōkokuzushū* （江戸明治）紙屋とその広告図集 (privately published, 1968), 33, 195, etc. Kunisaki Jihei, *Kamisuki chōhōki: a handy guide to papermaking*, translated by Charles E. Hamilton (Berkeley: The Book Arts Club, University of California, 1948). On the paper samples collected by Parkes see *Umi o watatta Edo no washi: Pākusu korekushonten* 海を渡った江戸の和紙ーパークス・コレクション展, catalogue of an exhibition held at the Tabako to shio Hakubutsukan and Gifu-shi Rekishi Hakubutsukan in 1994, (Kami no Hakubutsukan, 1994).

in China the production of paper rolls, at least by the second century A.D., but the roll form itself in China derived from the use of strips of bamboo or wood bound together, or later of sheets of silk. Throughout East Asia, paper rolls were made by pasting together sheets of paper and then attaching one end to a rod made of wood, or in some cases ivory or some other substance, around which the paper would be rolled. The loose end was commonly reinforced, usually with silk, and a tag attached to prevent it from unrolling; rolls were often kept in silk bags and either placed in book-chests or stored horizontally in wooden cases. The roll is known in Japan as *kansubon* 巻子本, and it is in this form that the book reached Japan and that books continued to be produced, exclusively so for several centuries, until new forms of book reached Japan from China. The roll had obvious disadvantages, as Martial pointed out when recommending the parchment codex as a superior form of book at the end of the first century A.D., for it took up more space in libraries and was difficult to consult. It remained the standard in China until the Tang dynasty when the introduction of printing and the compilation of reference books (*lei shu* 類書, J. *ruisho*) inspired the development of an alternative.[5]

However, in Japan, even after the introduction of texts in the form of books, such as Song printed editions imported from China (§7.1.1), the roll format remained in use for several centuries. It was used extensively for manuscripts of literary or religious texts, and notably for the illustrated scrolls known as *emakimono* 絵巻物 which were produced in the Heian period. It was also used for some of the printed books produced during the centuries before 1600, particularly the Buddhist texts printed in Nara and on Mt Kōya (§4.1.2). Finally, during the Tokugawa period, its use went into decline, as the printed book, bound and easy to use, became the dominant form in which texts were reproduced and consumed. It was still, however, occasionally used for printed books, such as *Kan'ei gyōkōki* 寛永行幸記 (1626), a roll depicting an imperial procession (§4.2.3), and for some other printed works depicting, for example, the processions of Korean diplomatic missions in Edo or scenic views, such as those of the Sumida river in *Sumidagawa ryōgan ichiran* 墨田川両岸一覧, published in 1781. Also, printed books were sometimes disassembled

---

[5] C. H. Roberts & T. C. Skeat, *The birth of the codex* (Oxford: Oxford University Press, 1987), 24–5; Tsien 1985: 227–30.

and mounted as scrolls by their owners, and scrapbooks containing printed ephemera often took the form of rolls too, as did other miscellaneous collections of written material, even in the nineteenth century.[6]

BIBLIOGRAPHY

On papermaking see Nishijima Tōshū 西島東洲, *Nihon kamigyō hattatsushi* 日本紙業発達史 (Osaka: Kamigyō Shuppansha, 1942); Seki Yoshikuni 関義城, *Wakan kami bunken ruijū* 和漢紙文献類聚, 2 vols, 'Kodai chūsei hen' and 'Edo jidai hen' (privately published, 1973–6). On calligraphy in East Asian books see Mote & Chu 1988; and on forms of the book in China, see Tsien 1985 and Chen 1984: 139–63.

2.2 FORMS OF THE BOOK

The development of alternatives to the roll in China is difficult to date, but it appears that at some time during the Tang period long rolls consisting of sheets of paper pasted together began to be folded alternately one way and the other to produce an effect like a concertina. It has been supposed that this form was suggested by the palm-leaf books which transmitted Buddhist texts from India to China. However that may be, it is in any case a fact that the concertina form was primarily used in China, and subsequently in Japan, for Buddhist texts. Books of this format are called *orihon* 折本 in Japan, and the format survived until the nineteenth century and beyond for printed Buddhist sūtras and occasionally for other books, such as reference lists, calendars, and folding maps.[7]

It was also during the Tang that the so-called 'butterfly binding', *kochōsō* 蝴蝶装, came into use, and was subsequently transmitted to Japan. This involved folding each sheet of paper in half and laying it on its predecessor and then gluing a cover to the folded edges: it derives its name from the fact that when opened each pair of pages tends to stand up with an effect resembling the wings of a butterfly. This technique was mostly used for printed books, unlike the *yamato-*

---

[6] Nakano 1995: 72–4; Hayashi and Kornicki 1991: #119–22.
[7] Tsien 1985: 230–31; Nakano 1995: 74–82; Hayashi & Kornicki 1991: #246, 1097, 1590, 1594, 1842, 1849, 2018–24, etc.

toji 大和綴 (also known as *techōsō* 綴葉装), a technique that appears to have no parallel in China and to have been developed independently in Japan. In this the folded pages were placed one inside the other until a fascicle or booklet had been formed, whereupon thread was used to sew them together along the fold, several of these fascicles being put together to form one volume. This technique was widely used from the late Heian period onwards, and particularly for manuscripts of Japanese literary works. By the Tokugawa period it was seldom used for printed books, except for the Nō texts published in Saga in the first half of the seventeenth century (§4.2.3) and some Buddhist texts pertaining to the Jōdo sect. It continued, however, to be used for manuscripts, mostly for luxury productions intended as bridal gifts (*yomeiribon* 嫁入り本) or for the collections of daimyō and members of the court aristocracy in Kyoto.[8]

In the Tokugawa period, however, it was a different technique that rapidly came to dominate and to determine the shape of at least 90% of all printed books and manuscripts, the *fukuro-toji* 袋綴. Here each page, carrying printed or handwrittten text on one side only, is folded with the text on the outside, and placed on top of its predecessor; the assembled pages were then sewn together, with the stitches passing through the blank margins next to the loose edges, so that the sewn edges form the spine and the folds form the edges of the pages. This method of binding seems to have been practised in China as early as the Tang but only became widespread in the Ming; it was transmitted to Japan and used for some of the Gozan editions in the Muromachi period, by the end of which it had become the standard form of binding for printed books.

Japanese books, particularly in the Tokugawa period, customarily consisted of a number of separately bound volumes (*satsu* 冊), but books had their own internal divisions that might or might not correspond with the physical divisions. Books were commonly divided into a number of *maki* 巻, a term which connotes 'roll' and derives from the time in China when the roll was the standard form of the book. Towards the end of the Tokugawa period, however, the internal architecture of books became more complex, particularly in the case of the longer forms of fiction such as the *yomihon* 読本 and *ninjōbon* 人情本, which were divided into a number of *hen* 編 or *shū* 輯, each

---

[8] Nakano 1995: 87; Hayashi and Kornicki 1991: #367, 937.

of which was again subdivided into five or ten *maki*. This was partly a consequence of the fact that works in these genres were often published in instalments, but it is also a reflection of the increasingly complex fictional structures represented in the texts. There was also a tendency for books to consist of much more than simply the text. While prefaces were by no means unknown before the Tokugawa period, they came to assume greater prominence and it is far from unusual for a book to contain four or five prefaces and, at the end, postfaces, in addition to a table of contents and possibly other preliminary material as well as advertisements. The prefaces often played a significant role in a market that was becoming increasingly sensitive to authorship, for it was common to attach a preface by a well-known name to the work of a lesser-known or unknown writer (§6.1.1).

At the end of a book it was usual to find a colophon. In the case of manuscripts, two kinds must be distinguished. Firstly, there is the *hon-okugaki* 本奧書, which is a text written by the author relating to the composition of the work to which it is attached, and which is often copied together with the text when later copies were made. And then there is the *shosha-okugaki* 書写奧書, which is a further note added by the person responsible for making a copy of a pre-existing manuscript, which often consists of little more than a name and a date, but which sometimes provides important information about the provenance of the original manuscript from which the copy has been made. With printed books, two forms of colophon are common, though they are not always carefully distinguished. One is the *kanki* 刊記, which is to be found at the end of the text on the (usually) last printed sheet, and the other is the *okuzuke* 奧附, which is a separate sheet attached to the inside of the back cover, and which is often lost when works are rebound. Since printing blocks often changed hands in the Tokugawa period, it is common for printed colophons to be altered or to be replaced altogether, but in many cases too the new publisher simply left the old *kanki* in place and added a new *okuzuke* of his own. In the second half of the Tokugawa period, it became common practice also to use the inside front cover, hitherto a blank sheet, for publicity purposes, and the printed sheet thus attached, called *mikaeshi* 見返し or *hōmen* 封面, often carried information about the publisher and date of publication in addition to the title and the name of the author (Fig. 17).

Covers will be treated below (§2.4), but in addition to their artistic qualities and their value as information distinguishing one genre from another, they also carried from the early seventeenth century onwards a title slip, or *daisen* 題簽. Mostly these simply gave a version of the title, but occasionally they also gave a summary of the contents (*mokuroku-daisen* 目録題簽) or were illustrated (*edaisen* 絵題簽). By virtue of their position on the cover they were fragile; often they became detached from the cover, and when covers were replaced the *daisen* was rarely transferred. Further, it is often the case that the external title on the *daisen*, which is known as the *gedai* 外題, differs from the internal title at the start of the text, which is known as the *naidai* 内題: the differences may be small, but sometimes, when the printing blocks had passed to another publisher, new *daisen* were prepared which differed from the old, sometimes in order to trick incautious purchasers into supposing that it was a new and different work.

Because of the softness of their covers, books were generally stacked on their sides and this is how they were kept in bookshops in the Tokugawa period, as contemporary illustrations show (Fig. 13). Sometimes wrap-around boxes were made of stiff cardboard with a cloth covering, and these are known as *chitsu* 帙, but for the most part books had a fragile quality, until in the early Meiji period stiffer cardboard covers came into fashion for books printed with modern metallic movable type in order to give them a 'Western' appearance. This fragile quality, however, lay principally in the eyes of Western beholders: as collectors and librarians they tended in the nineteenth century to discard the original covers, often losing the *daisen* and the *okuzuke* in the process, and even in the twentieth century to furnish Japanese books with Western-style hard covers. It is perhaps because of the visual unfamiliarity of Japanese books that so few of the European and American travellers, missionaries and others who visited Japan in the 1850s and 1860s recognised how bookish a society it was, but books in the form described here had by then long since established themselves as the principle vehicle for texts and as commercial products available alongside other commercial goods of everyday use.

BIBLIOGRAPHY

On the techniques of various styles of binding, see Kōjirō Ikegami, *Japanese bookbinding: instructions from a master craftsman*, adapted by Barbara B. Stephan (New York: Weatherhill, 1986). On *detchō* and *yamato-toji*, see Tanaka Kei 田中敬, *Detchō kō* 粘葉考, Tanaka Kei chosakushū 2 (Hayakawa Tosho, 1979; facsimile of 1932 edition) and Kushige Setsuo 櫛笥節男, 'Yamato-toji ni tsuite' 大和綴について, *Shoryōbu kiyō* 48 (1996): 64–84. On the forms of the book in the Tokugawa period, Nakano 1995 is a superb guide. The forms taken by *kanki* and *okuzuke* is a neglected field, but for examples from the Kan'ei era (1624–44), see Oka & Wada 1996. On *okugaki* in manuscripts see Hashimoto 1974: 184–241.

2.3 PRINTING AND THE BOOK

Until the late nineteenth century the dominant printing technology was that of woodblock printing. Very little is as yet known about the techniques and procedures used for block-printing before 1600, but the commercialization of printing and publishing in the Tokugawa period has ensured that some details concerning later practices have come down to us, although we still know surprisingly little about the processes whereby a manuscript was turned into a printed book. Furthermore, although some work has been done on the process as it applied to illustrated books or works of fiction, non-fictional works have for the most part been ignored, even though they constituted the bulk of the output throughout the period.

How did the block-printing process turn a manuscript text into a printed book in the Tokugawa period? Firstly, the manuscript was passed to a copyist, called *hanshitagaki* 板下書き or *hikkō* 筆耕, who wrote out a clean copy or *hanshita*; in cases where the publisher set store by the calligraphic quality of the finished product, an able calligrapher might be asked to do this, but in other cases, particularly the cheaper genres of fiction in the nineteenth century, it is clear that calligraphic quality was not a consideration and the task might be carried out in-house. In some cases authors prepared their own *hanshita*, or had one of their pupils do this. It is only in very rare instances that the *hanshita* survives, for it was normally used at once to prepare the printing blocks, but in some cases the author's own mansucript does survive, such as Bakin's manuscript of his *Keisei suikoden*, showing red corections to the text and his outline sketches of the illustrations he wanted the artists to provide.[9]

The *hanshita* was then passed to the block-carver, or *horishi* 彫師, who pasted the *hanshita* face-down on the wooden block and carved away the white parts, thus leaving the text, borders, and illustrations in relief. By the nineteenth century some authors and publishers had come to appreciate the importance of the work of the copyists and carvers in the production of calligraphically attractive books, and it became increasingly common to give them the recognition of naming them in the colophons of, for example, Kyokutei Bakin's longer novels. The carved blocks were then passed to a printer, or *surishi* 刷師, who inked the block, laid a sheet of paper on it, and rubbed the paper with a device known as a *baren* in order to make a good impression. In some cases (see below) a proof was printed for correction before any further printing was undertaken, but this appears to have been a rarity. Once sufficient copies had been printed they were passed to another worker for page alignment, *chōai* 丁合; meanwhile, a maker of covers, *hyōshiya* 表紙屋, had prepared front and back covers and these were passed with the printed pages to a binder, who sewed them together. Finally, at least in the second half of the Tokugawa period, the finished book was placed in a protective wrapper that gave the title and often further details, and it was then ready to be placed on sale. In the larger publishing establishments it was common for all or most of these stages to be carried out in-house, but smaller-scale publishers contracted some parts of the process out to sub-contracting specialists like block-carvers and binders, and cover-makers ran their own separate firms from the early seventeenth century onwards.[10]

---

[9] For the relationship between the author's manuscript and the eventual printed text in the context of nineteenth-century *gōkan*, and for authors' own perceptions of the processes whereby books were produced, see Hayashi Yoshikazu 1987 and *NKBT* 59: 87–105. *GUDJ* 3: 83.

[10] For accounts of block-printing techniques see 'Tokuno's description of Japanese printmaking', in M. Forrer, ed., *Essays on Japanese art: presented to Jack Hillier* (London: Sawers, 1982), 125–34, and T. Volker, *Ukiyoe quartet: publisher, designer, engraver and printer* (Leiden: E. J. Brill, 1949); for the printing process in the nineteenth century, see the illustrations to a work of fiction by Jippensha Ikku in Suzuki Toshio 1980: 1.32–3. On copyists and carvers, see Mori 1979: 1.70–88, and Kimura Yoshitsugu 木村嘉次, *(Jihori hangishi) Kimura Kahei to sono kokuhon* (字彫り版木師) 木村嘉平とその刻本, *NSGT* 13 (1980). For illustrations of carving tools, *baren*, etc, and lists of known *horishi* and *surishi*, see *GUDJ* 3: 84,

The use of wooden blocks for printing in the way briefly described above might seem to imply a certain fixity in the reproduction of texts, but it is important to note that in fact it was replete with instability. In two important ways texts printed from woodblocks might not be what they seem. The first is the use of a technique called *kabusebori* 覆せ掘り to produce a facsimile of a given text: in this process printed pages from an earlier edition are used as the *hanshita* and are pasted onto the blocks for carving. This results in blocks that produce a text very similar to, but never, owing to the vagaries of the carvers, identical, to the original. This technique was certainly in use before the Tokugawa period, for some books printed in Japan in the Muromachi period were in fact reproductions of Song or Ming editions imported from China, or occasionally Korean editions, and in some cases even reproduce the original colophon. In the Tokugawa period *kabusebori* editions of Ming and then Qing works were common. Let us take as an example a Japanese edition of *Zhuzi yulei* 朱子語類 (J. *Shushi gorui*), a record of Zhu Xi's discussions with his followers that was compiled seventy years after his death in 1270. In 1668 a full Japanese edition was published in Kyoto in 60 volumes: for the carving of the blocks a copy of a Chinese edition printed in 1604 was used but reading marks were added by Ukai Sekisai and another scholar before the blocks were carved. The same process was used also for Qing editions as they became available in Japan (§7.1.3), such as the collected works of the major Tang poet Du Fu 杜甫 (712–70) published in Japan in 1812, for which a copy of the Chinese edition of 1784 was used.[11]

Kabusebori was also used for the preparation of a new set of blocks when a book had already sold so well that the original blocks were worn out or when the blocks had been lost in a fire: it was for that purpose that publishers got into the habit of lodging one copy of every work they published with a shrine, so that in case of loss at least one copy would be available with which to make a new set of

---

87–8, 105–8.
[11] *Kabusebori* facsimiles are known as *fukkokubon* 覆刻本, while reprints using blocks carved from a text written out in Japan are known as *honkokubon* 翻刻本. *ARI* 3: 73; Okada Takehiko 岡田武彦, 'Shushi gorui no seiritsu to sono hanpon' 朱子語類の成立とその版本, in *Wakokubon Shushi gorui taizen* 和刻本朱子語類大全, 8 vols (Kyoto: Chūbun Shuppan, 1973), 1: 1–20; Nagasawa 1976–80: 1.24; Hayashi & Kornicki 1991: #2390.

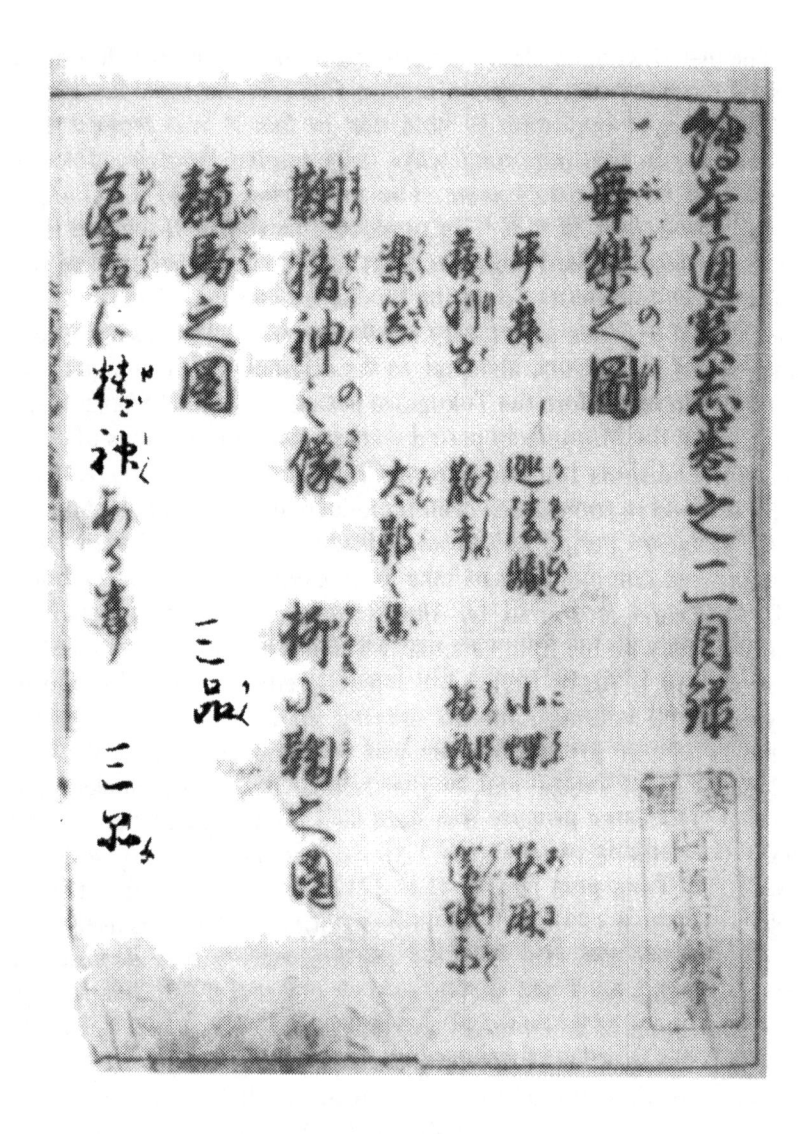

Fig. 2 This and the figure opposite furnish an example of *kabusebori*. An books of illustrations by Tachibana Morikuni 橘守国 was published in 1729 under the title *Ehon tsūhōshi* 絵本通宝志 by Kashiwaraya Seiemon 柏原屋清右衛門 of Osaka. In 1780 the same publisher reissued this work in a *kabusebori* edition based on the 1729 edition. On this page there is the list of contents of volume two of the 1729 edition, and on the opposite page of the 1780 edition, which is very similar but not, on close inspection, identical: Hayashi & Kornicki 1991: #2160 & 2161:

BOOKS AS MATERIAL OBJECTS

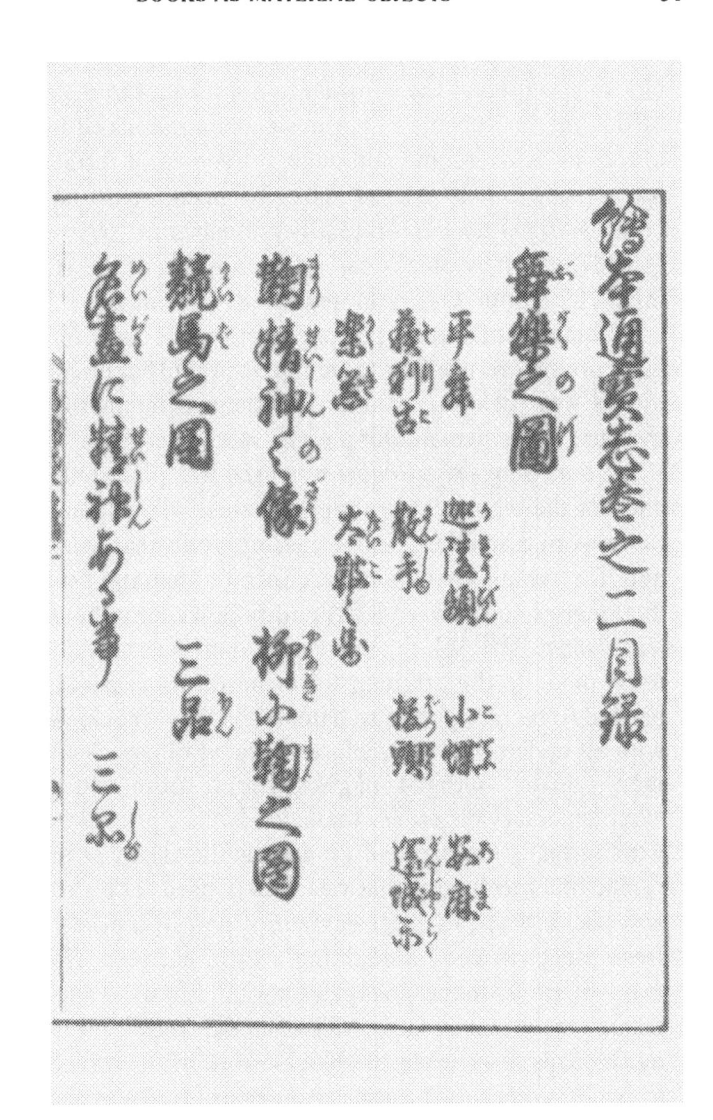

絵本通宝志巻之二目録

舞樂之圖
　平舞
　切りこ
　義刑古　観者
　衆怨　　太郎くわ
鵜情神之像
　　　　　柳ふ鞠之圖
競馬之圖
　　　　　三品
鷄盆に精神ある事
　　　　三品

blocks (§§5.1.2, 5.1.3). In such cases a copy printed from the old blocks was used as the *hanshita* to produce a *kabusebori* edition. Use of this method enabled the physical limitations of wooden printing blocks to be overcome, although at the cost of further investment in having new blocks carved. Thus Miyazaki Yasusada's agricultural manual *Nōgyō zensho*, originally published in 1697, was republished in 1787 with new blocks carved from pages of the 1697 edition, and this 1787 edition was reprinted in 1815: from this it is clear that the 1697 blocks sufficed to produce sufficient copies for the market for 90 years before needing to be replaced. Different editions produced in this way look very similar, but their differentiation provides one measure of the demand for a given work over time.[12]

In some books *kabusebori* was used to replace only selected pages and not the whole. This often happened when some blocks became more worn than others, in the case of works that were reprinted often and for which there was a constant demand, such as Chinese dictionaries (*gyokuhen* 玉編) and popular household encyclopedias (*setsuyōshū* 節用集). In other cases when extensive alterations needed to be made to the original, for example when personnel directories needed to be brought up to date (§2.5), new blocks would be carved with an updated text to replace outdated blocks. Such a book would then consist both of pages printed from old blocks and of 'supplementary pages' (*hokokuchō* 補刻丁) printed from new blocks, with an easily detectable difference in the clarity of the impression.

The other technique that was widely used for a variety of purposes was *umeki* 埋木, the replacement of part of a printing block with a fresh piece of wood containing a different text. This was used for many purposes in the Tokugawa period. Firstly, it was used to correct textual errors that had occurred when the *hanshita* was being prepared by the copyist or when the blocks were being carved: it is not clear to what extent proofreading of printed texts was carried out before publication in the Tokugawa period, but the survival of some corrected proofs from the late eighteenth century shows that it was at least carried out for some of the more substantial genres of fiction from that time, both to correct errors and to make emendations for avoidance of censorship problems. *Umeki* was also used to replace worn or broken parts of the blocks, and very frequently to alter the colophon

---

[12] Yayoshi 1988–93: 1.17; Hayashi & Kornicki 1991: #2066.

Fig. 3 The colophon of *Inkyō jishi* 韻鏡字子, a study of Chinese phonetics by Ōta Shiki 太田子規: the date given is Kanbun 3 (=1663) and the publisher named is Nagao Heibee, who is known to have been active in Kyoto from 1663 until 1700. However, it is clear from the broken lines of the border at the bottom that this colophon has been inserted by *umeki* to replace an earlier one: this was done in order to change the date, for an earlier edition, under the title *Inkyō shachūshō* 韻鏡遮中鈔, was published in 1660.[13]

for a later reprint by changing the date and/or the name of the publisher or publishers. It was also used to change the names of actors in publications related to the theatre, or the names of prominent officials named on maps or in directories (§2.5). More alarmingly, it was also used by somewhat unscrupulous publishers to alter the title of a work that would then be presented as if a new and entirely different work. And finally, it was used to make minor alterations to illustrations for reasons that are often obscure. For all these reasons it is rarely safe to assume that apparently identical books do indeed carry an identical text, although few reprints pay any attention to these textual variations and facsimile editions are rarely sufficient to make detection of *umeki* alterations easy.[14]

It is not only *umeki* and *kabusebori* that create difference, for copies of books printed from the same set of printing blocks in the Tokugawa period encompass an almost infinite variety. Publishers in the Tokugawa period tended to use their printing blocks not to produce a large number of copies in one operation but to print from them at intervals in response to the perceived demands of the market. When a publisher, then, got out a set of blocks and printed from them, the results were inevitably different from those of the previous and subsequent printings. The text might be identical, with no alterations perhaps even to the details in the colophon, but the quality and size of the paper, the decoration of the cover, the title slip, the booksellers advertisements and other end matter were all subject to variation, and as a result it is rare indeed for any two surviving block-printed books to match each other in all respects. This is, as Nakano Mitsutoshi has reminded us, largely because block-printed books were hand-made, but also because the blocks tended to be used over long periods of time with consequent changes in materials, decoration and sometimes too the publishers.[15]

---

[13] *KSM* 1.331.1; *Kotenseki sōgō mokuroku* 1.58.3; Inoue 1981: 438.

[14] On proofreading see Takagi 1995: 370–88. Hasegawa Tsuyoshi 長谷川強, *Ukiyozōshi shinkō* 浮世草子新考 (Kyūko Shoin, 1991), 194–213 and illustrations at the front of the book. For books with changed titles, cf Hayashi & Kornicki 1991: #648, 658, 664. Comparison of the two copies of *Ehon imayō sugata* in the Fitzwilliam Museum, Cambridge, reveals minor but deliberate alterations to the illustrations: Hillier 1989: 671–2. For other examples of alterations to illustrations see Suzuki Jūzō 1979: 230–31 and *passim*.

[15] Nakano 1995: 8–10; the most thorough demonstrations of the nature and value of these differences have been provided by Matthi Forrer in 'The publication history

Although methods of block-printing underwent very little change in the Tokugawa period, there were changes in the ways in which the text was presented on the page. Books in the seventeenth century, and sinological texts for a longer period, tended to exhibit some of the decorative features of Chinese books, including a double line marking the margins of the text, rules separating each line of text, and elaborate 'fish-tail' (*gyobi* 魚尾) devices decorating the central fold, or *hanshin* 版心, which also carried a version of the title and the pagination. Books in the Kokugaku tradition of nationalist learning rejected all these signs of Chineseness, presenting the text without margins or *hanshin* decoration and placing the pagination elsewhere. This is clearly done for ideological reasons, but it is nevertheless true that as the Tokugawa period progressed there was a tendency for these features of page ornamentation to be simplified and for the printed page to become sparer in appearance.[16]

Finally, some mention must be made here of the argument that in the Tokugawa period books, as a product of a society that was rigidly hierarchical, visibly and symbolically reflected that hierarchy. It is certainly true that certain genres of writing became associated with certain sizes and certain styles of cover decoration, and that as a result a sinological text, a 'serious' novel and a piece of light fiction could be told apart from a distance. It is also true that publishers were organizationally divided along lines that discriminated between what were considered serious and light books (§5.1.1). However, the suggestion that books thus also partook of the status system, as, for example, did the various forms of theatrical entertainment, should not obscure the fact that they were, unlike the theatre, commercially available to all without discrimination. Books did carry physical signs of their status but that did not restrict access to them.[17]

BIBLIOGRAPHY

Nakano 1995 is an excellent guide to the forms of the printed book in the Tokugawa period. For Chinese books see Chen 1984. For illustrations and discussion see Nagasawa Kikuya, (*Zukai*) *Shoshigaku nyūmon* (図解) 書

---

of a Japanese illustrated book as told by one block', in Yu-Ying Brown 1990: 211–18, and Forrer 1985.
[16] Tsien 1985: 222–3; Chen 1984: 101–6.
[17] Nakano 1995: 16, 60–69.

誌学入門 (Kyūko Shoin, 1976). See also *NKC* 4: 205–28.

2.4 ILLUSTRATION AND THE ARTS OF THE BOOK

The arts of the Japanese book are to be found in their covers, their paper, their calligraphy and their illustrations, but the subject is too large to be given more than a cursory treatment here. Calligraphy and paper have been touched upon elsewhere (§§1.4, 2.2), and the brief discussion of covers and illustration that follows will be confined to the printed books of the Tokugawa period, which have already been extensively treated by Jack Hillier, Suzuki Jūzō and others. Some aspects of manuscript illustration are considered elsewhere (§§3.1, 3.2).

Although the covers of many early manuscripts are themselves works of art, it was only in the Tokugawa period that attention began to be paid to the covers of printed books. The covers used for *fukuro-toji* bindings consist of paper with a thick backing, but the Gozan editions of the Muromachi period and most early seventeenth-century printed books commonly had undecorated covers in a single colour. An early exception was the Sagabon, books printed with movable type in Saga and consisting of Nō texts and Japanese prose literary texts (§4.2.3). In many cases these books used, for both the printed text and the covers, paper that was decorated with mica in designs that were either abstract patterns or representations of natural phenomena like bamboo and cranes. Other movable-type books of the same period had mostly plain covers, but the binders made use of scraps of paper to back the covers, and some of these have turned out to be bills and parts of other printed books, which have revealed much about the early organization of printing workshops.[18]

From the seventeeenth century onwards cover design began to have artistic pretensions, and this was connected with the growing commercialization and marketing of books. Covers became increasingly elaborate, as embossed designs and colour printing were

---

[18] Omote Akira 表章, *Kōzan Bunkobon no kenkyū - yōhon no bu* 鴻山文庫本の研究―謡本の部 (Wan'ya Shoten, 1970), 158–9, 206–29; Watanabe Morikuni 渡辺守邦, *Kokatsujiban densetsu* 古活字版伝説, *NSGT* 54 (1987), 1–85; Hayashi Nozomu 林望, 'Edo jidai seihon kakitome' 江戸時代初期製本書留(仮題)―ケンブリッジ大学所蔵古活字版『狭衣』表紙裏貼, *Tōyoko kokubungaku* 21 (1989).

used to give each book a more distinctive appearance and character, and in addition to the changing fashions and tastes that can be identified, there are also styles that became associated with particular kinds of book. This is most obviously the case with some of the lighter genres of fiction, which even for contemporaries came to take on genre names derived from the usual colour of the covers, such as *akahon* 赤本, 'red books', and *kibyōshi* 黄表紙, 'yellow covers'. This practice began in Kyoto in the seventeenth century but is most characteristic of Edo publications in the eighteenth century, and it was succeeded by the use of lavish block-printed illustrated covers in the nineteenth century for the genre known as *gōkan* 合巻. Later the range of designs was extended further with the use of roman letters for their visual effect, such as the cover of Kanagaki Robun's satire on superficial westernization, *Aguranabe* 安愚楽鍋 (1871), which carries the legend 'SEI Shi do oo', a rather odd representation of the name of the publisher, Seishidō 誠之堂.[19]

Although many early manuscripts of Japanese literature were illustrated, it was only rarely in the centuries before the Tokugawa period that printed books included illustrations. From the early years of the seventeenth century, however, when works of Japanese literature were printed for the first time, illustrations began to be a regular accompaniment of Japanese texts. It was probably the Sagabon that established the role of illustration in Japanese printed books, particularly in the case of literary texts. Certainly, most of the versions of the Japanese classics which were printed in the early years of the seventeenth century contained monochrome illustrations. By the end of that century it had became the norm for almost all books in Japanese to include some form of illustration, including not only literary works but also, for example, mathematical and botanical studies, encyclopedias, cooking manuals and guide books. With but a few exceptions these were line illustrations, and in the first half of the seventeenth century some literary works in Japanese were published with line illustrations that were coloured by hand (*tanrokubon* 丹緑本). There were a few isolated instances of colour printing, but even after the development of the techniques of polychrome illustration later in the eighteenth century most book illustration remained monochrome, with the exception of frontispieces

---

[19] Nakano 1995: 147–8; Suzuki Jūzō 1979: 13–37.

in later works of fiction and of picture books such as Utamaro's famous book of insects, *Ehon mushierami* 画本虫撰 (1788).[20]

The inclusion of illustrations was of course facilitated by the fact that they were produced by the same block-printing process as the text, and this made it possible for illustrations to fill a whole spread by occupying the verso of one page and the recto of the next, to occupy a fraction of a page, to dominate the page with the text fitting into the empty spaces, to take the form of small visual interruptions to the text, and so on. In this way Japanese books, but very rarely Chinese books printed in Japan, became profoundly visual in the Tokugawa period so that, for example, a reader's encounter with a work of fiction encompassed not only an engagement with a text and the conventions and expectations aroused by that, but also with a calligraphic style reproduced in the printed text and with a visual style in the illustrations. In many fictional works the illustrations helped to locate the text in a particular place or time through the depiction of costume and hairdressing styles, of recognisable places, or of figures identified by crests on their clothing or other visual clues. In the case of works with a transparent historical disguise adopted as a defence against censorship, the illustrations commonly subvert the disguise by means of contemporary visual references such as hair-styles.

Illustrations also fulfilled a marketing role, as is clear from the use of subtitles and title suffixes such as *eiri* 絵入 (with illustrations), *ehon* 絵本 (illustrated book), and the like. Even in the seventeenth century artists responsible for illustrations were being identified in colophons, and thereafter it became common for the names of illustrators to be prominently displayed. This was undoubtedly due to the selling power attached to the names of the many prominent ukiyoe artists who also engaged in book illustration, and it was this feature of the printed book in the Tokugawa period that led Jack

---

[20] M. Collcutt, 'An illustrated edition of the *Tale of the Heike* (*Heike Monogatari*) in the Gest Library', *GLJ* 4 (1991): 9-26; Harley Harris Bartlett & Hide Shohara, *Japanese botany during the period of wood-block printing* (Los Angeles: Dawson's Book Shop, 1961). For cooking manuals see *Daitōkyū Kinen Bunko zenpon sōkan* 大東急記念文庫善本叢刊 vol. 10 (Daitōkyū Kinen Bunko, 1977). On colour illustration see Kogorō Yoshida, *Tanrokubon: rare books of seventeenth-century Japan* (Tokyo: Kodansha International, 1984) and D. B. Waterhouse, *Harunobu and his age: the development of colour printing in Japan* (London: British Museum, 1964).

BOOKS AS MATERIAL OBJECTS 59

Hillier to argue that 'in no other country do prints in book and album form attain so high a degree of significance relative to the national art as a whole'. What remains to be explored, however, is the ways in which illustrations were read, particularly in conjunction with texts but also, in the case of *ehon* consisting solely or almost entirely of illustrations, on their own. Timon Screech has recently shown how the 'Western scientific gaze' made an impact on the visual cultures of eighteenth and nineteenth century Japan which can be detected in book illustration, but what effects did this alternative mode of vision have on those who consumed it in the form of illustrations? The vogue for *manga* 漫画 books of disconnected cartoons, initiated by the first volume of *Hokusai manga* 北斎漫画 in 1814, and later for *musha-ehon* 武者絵本, illustrated books devoted to warriors, pose different problems. Our impressions of the deconstruction of art amid the social and political malaise of the closing decades of the Tokugawa period in the one case and of a patriotic and belligerent tone in response to the growing threat from the West in the other seem plausible enough, but must remain conjectural in terms of readership in the absence of a clear understanding of how readers confronted the visual.[21]

The sheer flexibility and simplicity of the means of providing illustrations was responsible for the publication not only of *ehon* but also of other kinds of illustrated book, non-literary and often without artistic pretensions, such as kimono pattern books, stylistic guides for carpenters and other craftsmen, ikebana manuals and studies of the game of *go*. In such cases as these, publication had the effect of making public, and available throughout Japan, certain visual languages that would otherwise have been transmitted only in the limited contexts of workshops and private schools devoted to artistic pursuits.[22] Given that most books were produced in the three cities of Edo, Kyoto and Osaka in the Tokugawa period, it is evident that it was the visual languages of artists and illustrators from those cities that were disseminated throughout Japan, but to what extent they had

---

[21] Hillier 1988: 32; Jack Hillier, *The art of Hokusai in book illustration* (London: Sotheby Parke Bernet, 1980); Screech 1996. On *manga* and *musha-ehon* see Hillier 1988: 813–26, 884–93.
[22] On kimono pattern books see Hillier 1988: 112–6; the other genres mentioned have yet to be studied, but for design books for carpenters see Hayashi & Kornicki 1991: #2081–86 and Asakura 1983: 3.214–5.

a normative role or conditioned modes of envisioning the present and the past throughout Japan remains to be seen. Finally, it is important to note that these visual languages were overwhelmingly Japanese and that illustration was itself a token of a Japanese book, for very few of the large number of sinological texts printed in Japan carried any illustrations at all.

BIBLIOGRAPHY

Covers have been much neglected hitherto, but see Hillier 1988: 1048–55, Nakano 1995: 128–51, Nakamura Yukihiko, 'Hyōshi - shoshigaku no uchi to soto' 表紙ー書誌学の内と外, *Biburia* 95 (1990): 38–47, and the series of illustrated articles on covers in *Chōsa kenkyū hōkoku* 調査研究報告 from no. 1 (1980) onwards; for colour reproductions see the volumes in the *Nihon koten bungaku zenshū* 日本古典文学全集, *Tenri Toshokan Zenpon sōsho* 天理図書館善本叢書, *Daitōkyū Kinen Bunko zenpon sōkan* 大東急記念文庫善本叢刊 and *Waseda Daigaku zō shiryō eiin sōsho* 早稲田大学蔵資料影印叢書 series. Urushiyama Matashirō 漆山又四郎, *Ehon nenpyō* 絵本年表, 6 vols, *NSGT* 34 (1983–87), C. H. Mitchell, *The illustrated books of the Nanga, Maruyama, Shijo and other related schools of Japan: a biobibliography* (Los Angeles: Dawson's Book Shop, 1972), Hillier 1988, Suzuki Jūzō 1979 and Brown 1924 are invaluable guides to the illustrated books of the Tokugawa period, and Laurance P. Roberts, *A dictionary of Japanese artists: painting, sculpture, ceramics, print, lacquer* (New York: Weatherhill, 1976) is a convenient guide to artists' names and pseudonyms. See also Ekkehard May, 'Buch und Buchillustration im vorindustriellen Japan', in Formanek & Linhart 1995: 45–73.

2.5 PRINTED MAPS, SERIAL PUBLICATIONS AND EPHEMERA

Printed maps in the Tokugawa period closely resembled books: they were folded to one or other of the standard book sizes and equipped with two protective covers. For the most part these maps had little to contribute to the development of cartographic knowledge in Japan, although it is true that they did increasingly reflect the results of Bakufu-sponsored land surveys. As the market for commercially published maps grew rapidly towards the end of the seventeenth-century they became for the Japanese reading public the primary means of envisioning their spaces, from the city to the province, to the whole of Japan and even the world. These published maps thus testify to the spread of the spatial literacy maps call for and to the increasing functional significance of maps in Tokugawa society.

This market was dominated by urban maps, at first those treating Edo, Kyoto and Osaka, but later other large towns and also, in the closing years of the Tokugawa period, those towns made newly significant by the presence of foreign traders, such as Kōbe, Yokohama and Niigata. In the case of Edo the regular publication of maps began after the disastrous Meireki fire of 1657 destroyed most of the city and prompted a restructuring with the aim of fire prevention. In 1676, for example, four different maps of Edo were published, three advertising their claim to be up to date by including the word *shinpan* 新板, 'new edition', in the title, and in 1859 alone more than a dozen different maps of Edo were printed.[23]

Two features of these urban maps are of particular importance here. Firstly, they consist to a greater or lesser extent of pictorial maps, and many advertise the fact in their titles (*ezu* 絵図, picture map). They therefore include non-cartographic features, and other features are out of scale for the sake of prominence: thus the mountains around Kyoto are usually pictorially represented, temples and other historic sites are highlighted, and the residences of officials, such as that of the *shoshidai* (shōgunal representative in Kyoto), contain the name and title of the current office-holder. The growth of tourism and leisure travel undoubtedly created a steady market for these maps as also for the schematic itinerary maps which gave details of routes and post stations in a non-cartographic linear format, but they also provided residents with a political and visual representation of the space they inhabited and the practical knowledge needed to navigate the growing city. Secondly, these were rarely 'new' maps, that is to say they were reissued constantly until the blocks were worn out and new ones had to be prepared; the leading publisher of Edo maps, Suwaraya Mohee, customarily published two maps of Edo every year, one large and one small. In some cases it was simply the year in the colophon that was changed, to maintain the impression that the map was up to date, but in others changes were made to the blocks to take account of changes such as new areas of reclaimed land, new housing districts, and the names of newly-appointed officials. In this way a set of printing blocks could be used over many years: Iida Ryūichi, for example, has found that the blocks of

---

[23] Iwata Toyoki 1980: 12, 188–92, 225, etc.

an edition of *(Shinpan) Edo ōezu* first printed in 1676 were used up to 1714 with many alterations and some changes of publisher along the way.[24]

One of the most interesting developments in map publishing at the end of the period is that of *kiriezu* 切絵図, collections of pocket-sized small-scale maps covering the whole of Edo in 30 or so separate maps. There were two rival series of these, published between the 1840s and 1860s, and each map covered a district of Edo in great detail and with full colour. They retained some pictorial features, such as temples and other places of tourist interest, but their most obvious characteristic is the plethora of names: most of these are of samurai residents, together in some cases with an indication of the domain to which they belong, but others are of commoners, of restaurants, and so on. Accordingly, they were in need of frequent revision in order to keep them up to date with changes in the residences of samurai officials, and surviving copies bear the evidence of multiple alterations to the printing blocks by *umeki* to accomplish this. These series of maps have no parallel elsewhere in Japan, and although they doubtless were of use to tourists it was surely not tourists who needed up to date information on the residences of samurai: the functions these maps may have had for residents of Edo needs further exploration, but it is probable that the highly charged political atmosphere of the 1850s and 1860s in Edo created a new demand for access to information about who lived where, in addition to the utility of such information for mercantile purposes.[25]

Maps were not the only forms of publication to be issued regularly, but as information they were less politically sensitive than news. As a direct result of the censorship régime of the Tokugawa Bakufu, which placed current events strictly off limits (§8.2.2), newspapers

---

[24] On maps of Kyoto and Nagasaki see Ōtsuka Takashi 大塚隆, ed., *Kyōtozu sōmokuroku* 京都図総目録, *NSGT* 18 (1981), and N. H. N. Mody, *A collection of Nagasaki colour prints and paintings showing the influence of Chinese and European art on that of Japan* (London: Kegan Paul, Trench, Trubner & Co., 1939) respectively. Iida Ryūichi 飯田竜一, 'Hangi no inochi' 板木のいのち, in *Kochizu kenkyū: gekkan Kochizu kenkyū nihyakugō kinen ronshū* 古地図研究―月刊古地図研究二百号記念論集 (Nihon Chizu Shiryō Kyōkai, 1988), 235–7.

[25] Saitō Naoshige 斎藤直成, *Edo kiriezu shūsei* 江戸切絵図集成, 6 vols (Chūō Kōronsha, 1981–84), 5: 118, etc. Saitō identifies many of the subsequent changes to these maps in later editions, but his lists are not exhaustive and editions not noted by him exist: Kornicki 1993a: 283–8 #200a, b, g & z.

and magazines did not come into existence in Japan until the closing years of the Tokugawa period. News relating to political events and scandals was therefore passed around by word of mouth, publicized in graffiti, or circulated in the form of illicit manuscripts, and it is clear that there was a lively market for manuscripts purporting to offer scandalous news (§3.3). Further, news-gathering was a function of many diarists and keepers of miscellaneous records known as *zuihitsu*, and in the first half of the nineteenth century the proprietor of a second-hand bookshop in Edo employed information gatherers to compile a record of current events and made manuscript copies of this available for purchase.[26]

This is not to say, however, that no news was printed at all, for broadsheets were printed and distributed for most of the Tokugawa period. They are known today as *kawaraban* かわら版, although the etymology of this word is uncertain, and were sold on the streets by pedlars known as *yomiuri* 読売, who customarily wore sedge hats which hid their faces and were presumably worn to conceal their identity, for there can be no doubt that their wares were at best semi-legal. This was certainly happening by the end of the seventeenth century, for a record from 1682 refers to the practice, noting that 'some fool collected contemporary gossip and printed it', and there is an illustration of *yomiuri* peddling their sheets in one of Saikaku's fictional works. And an edict was issued in 1684 making it forbidden to print or make available for purchase on the streets printed sheets and the reference is unmistakably to *kawaraban*: this was repeated several times and evidently was not being heeded (§8.2.2).[27]

Ono Hideo cites as the first *kawaraban* one that deals with the battle at Osaka castle in 1615, but there is no indication that this was actually produced in that year, and given the existence of other *kawaraban* marking anniversaries and the lack of any other surviving *kawaraban* from the following fifty years there are grounds for doubting this dating. Although *kawaraban* for the most part avoided

---

[26] Asakura Haruhiko 1990: 179–80; Yoshihara Ken'ichirō 吉原健一郎, *Edo no jōhōya: Bakumatsu shominshi no sokumen* 江戸の情報屋－幕末庶民史の側面 (Nihon Hōsō Shuppan Kyōkai, 1978); Suzuki Tōzō 鈴木棠三 and Koike Shōtarō 小池章太郎, eds, *(Kinsei shomin seikatsu shiryō) Fujiokaya nikki* (近世庶民生活史料) 藤岡屋日記, 15 vols (San'ichi Shobō, 1987–95); Konta Yōzō 1978.

[27] Groemer 1994: 236–8; *OKS* 990–91, 1234, #2014–5, 2668.

Fig. 4   A *kawaraban* showing the procession of officials from the kingdom of Ryūkyū (now Okinawa, and one of the prefectures of Japan, but independent of Japan before the nineteenth century), probably published in 1796, the year in which the mission came to Edo. It was published by Hayashiya Mohee of Edo, and is the first item in a scrapbook in roll form containing, amongst other things, some other *kawaraban*: Hayashi & Kornicki 1991: #120.

dealing with explicitly political events, they did feature news and current events of a non-political nature, such as love suicides in the early eighteenth century, vendettas, natural disasters such as fires and floods, and the appearance of supposed freak animals. As such they were in fact in contravention of the censorship edicts banning the mention of current events in publications and as a result rarely carry any indication of the author or publisher: in 1793 they were singled out for condemnation both on the grounds of subject matter and of avoidance of the guild censorship system, but for this very reason producers were difficult to detect and there is no sign that they were cowed or otherwise affected by these edicts.[28]

Kawaraban were condemned by the authorities as 'false' or 'baseless' but in fact they purveyed information that potentially functioned at several different levels. For example, natural disasters resulting in damage to the rice harvest could affect the price of rice and such news therefore had an economic value; and much information about disasters and freaks also took on the character of portents reflecting a supposed heavenly displeasure with those in power. Further, as the period neared its end *kawaraban* producers became more daring and encroached more and more on the political preserves of the Bakufu, reporting, for example, on the arrival of Commodore Perry in 1853–54, the marriage of princess Kazunomiya to the shōgun in 1861, the shōgun's visit to Kyoto in 1863, and the Bakufu's operations against the Satsuma and Chōshū domains in 1864–65. So by the end of the Tokugawa period *kawaraban* were taking on some of the functions of newspapers even though they were still produced for the occasion, they were on the margins of legality and they were aimed at a popular market for purchase on the streets. They did not, therefore, have the potential to develop into regularly-issued newspapers with critical content, and when newspapers were published in Japan their inspiration clearly came from European newspapers.[29]

The first newspaper published in Japan was the *Nagasaki shipping list and advertiser* of 1861 and there were other Western-language newspapers produced in the treaty ports in the years leading up to the Meiji Restoration, but these were all produced by and for the foreign communities. The first Japanese newspaper was the *Kanpan*

---

[28] Ono Hideo 1960: 13–18; *TKKZ* 5: 253 #2948.
[29] Ono Hideo 250–54, 258–9; Nakayama 1974: 63–77; Konta Yōzō 1978.

Batabiya shinbun 官板バタビヤ新聞, produced in 1862 at the direction of the Bakufu by the Institute for the investigation of Western books (Yōsho shirabesho, the successor to the Institute for the investigation of barbarian books). It consisted of translations from *Javasche Courant*, a Dutch newspaper published in Batavia (=Jakarta), for Dutch remained the only accessible European language for all but a handful of Japanese, and it was commercially distributed by the Edo bookseller Yorozuya Heishirō 万屋兵四郎, but it only lasted for 23 issues in the first two months of that year and an attempt to revive it later that year under a different title was similarly unsuccessful. The first private newspaper was *Kaigai shinbun* 海外新聞, which consisted of translated extracts from English-language newspapers, was produced in 1865–66 by Joseph Heco [Hamada Hikozō], a Japanese castaway who had spent some years in the United States, but it did not prove to be a success. Similar was the *Bankoku shinbunshi* 万国新聞紙, which was produced by an English clergyman in 1867–69 and was widely distributed from Hakodate to Nagasaki.[30]

It was not, therefore, until the turbulent year 1868, when the Bakufu was on the point of collapse, that the first serial publications giving domestic news were published, the news magazines known as *shinbunshi*. More than a dozen such 'newspapers' appeared in that year, some block-printed, others printed with wooden movable type. They were all preoccupied by the political events of the day and were closed down by the new régime by the end of the year. They took the form of booklets and none were published on a daily basis. However, in the early years of the Meiji period government newspapers began to appear, such as the *Dajōkan nisshi* 太政官日誌, which had actually begun publication in the second month of 1868, and these were in competition with private ventures, such as the *Tōkyō nichinichi shinbun* 東京日々新聞, the ancestor of the modern *Mainichi shinbun*, which began to appear in 1872. Most newspapers and magazines at this stage were still being printed with woodblocks, but from its second issue the *Tōkyō nichinichi* shifted to movable type, which naturally proved easier to manage than carving new blocks for each issue once it became standard for newspapers to appear on a daily basis. All, however, were subject to the strict control of the Meiji government, which enacted its first laws restricting the freedom of

---

[30] Asakura 1990: 180; Hayashi & Kornicki 1991: 197, #138.

speech in 1868 and in subsequent legislation developed mechanisms for the effective control of the press (§8.3).[31]

Japanese-language newspapers and magazines were also published overseas, for the most part in the Japanese immigrant communities, almost exclusively in the nineteenth century in San Francisco and Honolulu. The first two such ventures, however, were different, and were initiated by Europeans with a strong interest in Japan. In 1868 the pioneer French japanologist Léon de Rosny (1837–1914) started publishing *Yo-no ouvasa* [*yo no uwasa*, 'rumours of the world']: it was short-lived and copies are now extremely rare, but de Rosny, who never visited Japan, was very enthusiastic in his promotion of the study of Japanese in France and in the same year became the first professor of Japanese in France. A few years later, in 1873, the *Taisei shinbun* 大西新聞 was launched in London by James Summers (1828–91), who was professor of Chinese at King's College, London, and who had already been studying Japanese for some time. The *Taisei shinbun* only lasted for one issue and Summers left in the same year for Japan. Although there were small numbers of Japanese residents in both Paris and London at this time, it is significant that the initiative at this stage came from non-Japanese, although subsequent publications aimed at the growing Japanese overseas communities owed their existence to the initiative of Japanese expatriates.[32]

Although there were no newspapers or magazines in Tokugawa Japan, there were a number of other publications which were issued regularly and correspond with serial publications. The most obvious of these, and probably the most widespread, were printed calendars, which were subject to strict publishing controls (§8.2.3). However, since they provided the only means of knowing the shape of each year, given the need for intercalary months and other *ad hoc* adjustments in the lunar calendrical system, they were a source of essential information for urban and rural life alike, in order to determine market days, monthly accounts and so on. In addition they also provided information of an astrological nature, informing readers of auspicious and inauspicious days which also acted as determinants

---

[31] Asakura 1990; Altman 1975; Séguy 1993: 62–72.
[32] Ebihara Hachirō 蛯原八郎, *Kaigai hōji shinbun zasshi shi* 海外邦字新聞雑誌 (facsimile of 1936 edition; Meicho Fukyūkai, 1980), 27–52.

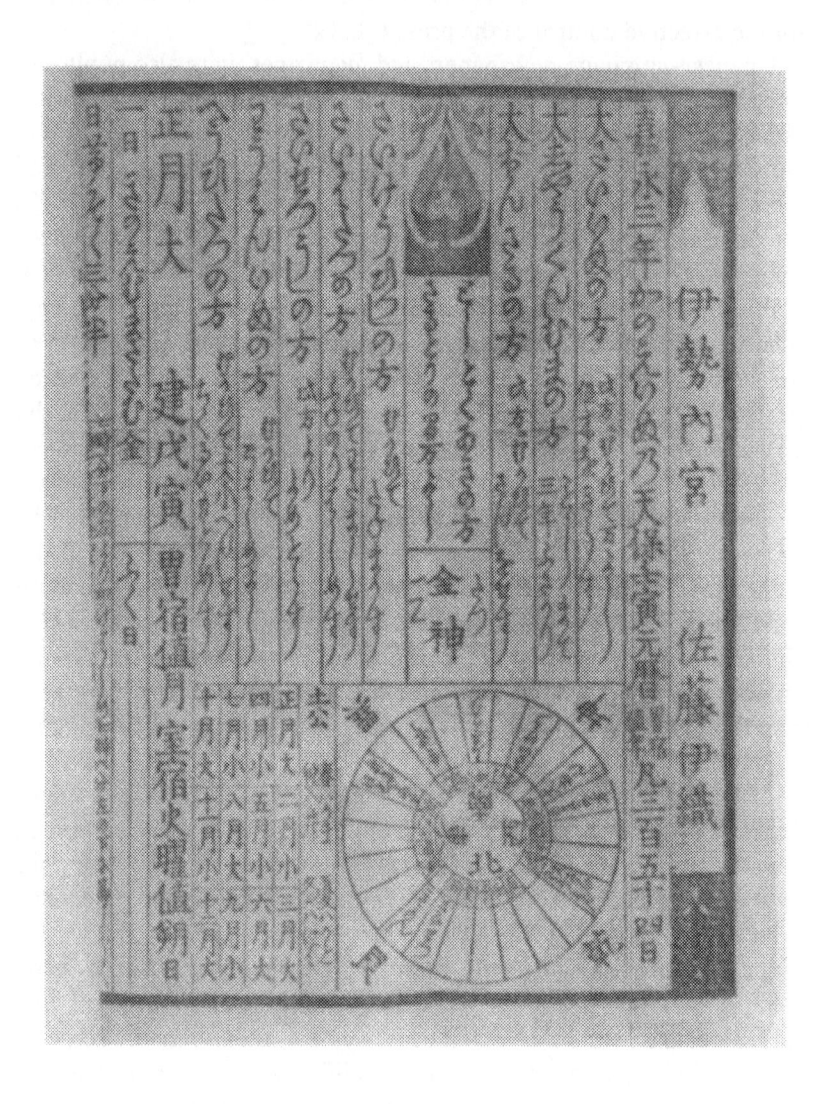

Fig. 5 The opening page of the calendar for 1850 published by the Ise Inner Shrine in 1849. Here geomantic and other astrological information for the year is given. Hayashi & Kornicki 1991: #2019.

on commercial and agricultural life. Consequently, for most of the Tokugawa period, and certainly for the eighteenth and nineteenth centuries, calendars were published on a regular basis at the end of each year for the year to come.

The directories of Bakufu officialdom known as *bukan* 武鑑 were another form of serial publication, for they were always available and constantly updated. Indeed, most surviving examples show signs of alterations to the printing blocks as publishers attempted to keep pace with personnel changes in the Bakufu, even making changes on a monthly basis by the end of the Tokugawa period. Directories of this sort were in existence in the early seventeenth century, but it was in 1687 that a bookseller affiliated to the Bakufu as an official publisher issued one with the word *bukan* in the title and from then onwards it was the standard term. At the end of the seventeenth century various publishers, all based in Edo, were producing *bukan* but by the early eighteenth century the market had been cornered by Suwaraya Mohee and Izumoji Izuminojō 出雲寺和泉掾.

What is surprising is that it was two commercial publishers who dominated this market: the *bukan* they published were not in any sense official publications, they did not carry the imprimatur of the Bakufu and were by no means free from error. On the other hand they were not illicit publications and evidently enjoyed the tacit approval of the Bakufu. This fact, together with the evident importance of keeping them up to date, is some indication of their functional value in the complex bureaucratic world of Edo and it must be supposed that they were an important source of information, although as yet we have little knowledge of how they were used and by whom. The British diplomat Ernest Satow noted in his memoirs that foreigners in Japan in the 1860s were prohibited from purchasing either maps or 'the official list of *daimios* and government officials', by which he was clearly referring to *bukan*. It remains remarkable, in the light of this and of the insistence of censorship edicts on avoiding reference in print to contemporary officials, that the Bakufu tolerated the exposure of its personnel to the public gaze in this way.[33]

---

[33] *KD* 12: 35–9; *YMC* 3: 155–83; Ernest Satow, *A diplomat in Japan* (Tokyo: Oxford University Press, 1968), 67. For the texts of *bukan* see Watanabe Ichirō 渡辺一郎, ed., *Tokugawa bakufu daimyō hatamoto yakushoku bukan* 徳川幕府大名旗本役職武鑑, 4 vols (Kashiwa Shobō, 1967); Ishii Ryōsuke 石井良助, ed., *Bunka*

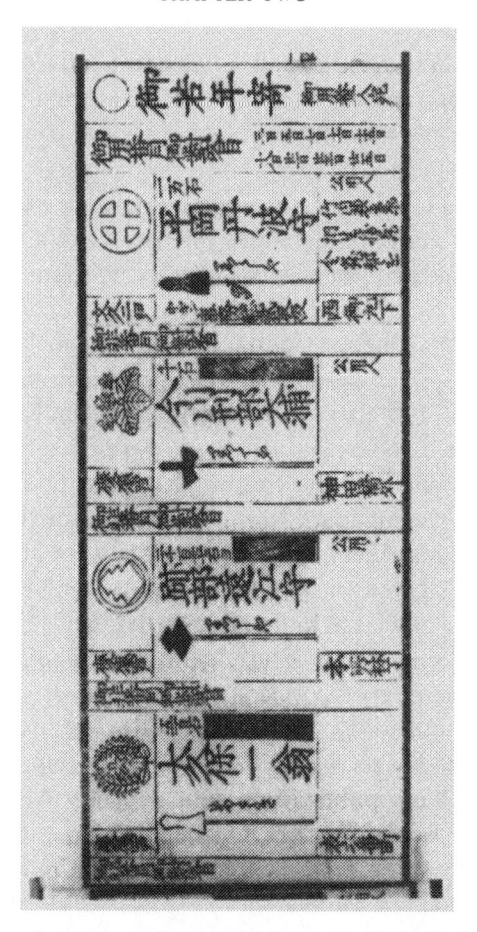

Fig. 6 *Yūshi bukan* 有司武鑑, a directory of Bakufu officials, published in 1867 and revised in 1868. This page gives details of the junior councillors (*wakadoshiyori*) in office at the time, but on the preceding page the places for the names of the senior councillors (*rōjū*) are blank in a dramatic indication of the political chaos in the last few months of the Bakufu's power. Each entry here gives crest, year of appointment, annual income in *koku*, surname and title, residence, and other information. Hayashi & Kornicki 1991: #1837.

---

bukan 文化武鑑, 7 vols (Kashiwa Shobō, 1961–82); Ishii Ryōsuke, ed., *Bunsei bukan* 文政武鑑, 5 vols (Kashiwa Shobō, 1982–92) and Hashimoto Hiroshi 橋本博, ed, *Daibukan* 大武鑑, 13 vols (Daikōsha, 1935–6; revised edition, Meicho Kankōkai, 1965).

Similar to *bukan* was another group of directories which focussed on the imperial court in Kyoto and which are generically known as *kuge-kagami* 公家鑑. The oldest example known dates from 1667 and is clearly modelled on the samurai directories which were already in existence, but *kuge-kagami* did not become regular publications that were frequently updated until the final decades of the Tokugawa period. By that time there were two rival formats, that of *Unjō meikan* 雲上名鑑, first published in 1758, and that of *Unjō meiran* 雲上名覧, first published in 1837, both giving a detailed view 'above the clouds', of the imperial family and its offshoots, of the court aristocracy and their roles, and of the religious institutions connected to the throne. While these directories may have been functionally useful for Kyoto residents with extensive dealings with the court, including members of the aristocracy themselves, the frequency of their publication in the middle of the nineteenth century with up-to-date information about personnel changes can only be taken as a sign of the growing consciousness of the emperor and imperial court as political entities and of their increased political visibility as a potential alternative to the Bakufu.[34]

Another regular publication that needed constant updating was the guidebook to the Yoshiwara pleasure quarters in Edo, which was known as *Yoshiwara saiken* 吉原細見. The oldest extant copy with a date was published in 1689 and claims to be subject to monthly revisions, but for the most part they seem to have been issued twice a year. Unlike the courtesan critiques (*yūjo hyōbanki* 遊女評判記), which were also frequently reissued but highly subjective in their judgments of the courtesans, the *saiken* offered a factual street by street guide to the establishments in the Yoshiwara and listed the courtesans by rank rather than by supposed charm or accomplishments. *Saiken* were, like *bukan*, a competitive and evidently profitable market for commercial publishers and in the 1770s the innovative Edo publisher Tsutaya Jūzaburō 蔦屋重三郎 successfully competed with the two established firms in this sector by introducing a new format and inducing novelists and poets to write prefaces for him. Although most surviving *saiken* deal with the Yoshiwara, some were published

---

[34] *KD* 2: 205–6, 4: 733–4; Hamish Todd, 'A glimpse above the clouds: the Japanese court in 1859', *British Library journal* 17 (1991): 197–220, is an examination of the contents of the 1859 edition of *Unjō meiran taizen*.

in other cities as guidebooks to the local pleasure quarters, clearly modelled on those for the Yoshiwara, but there are none extant for the Shimabara in Kyoto or Maruyama in Nagasaki, and it appears that only the large Edo market of potential customers for the Yoshiwara was sufficient to support a regular publication of this kind.[35]

As yet very little work has been done to reveal the extent or nature of printed ephemera during the Tokugawa period. The survival rate has inevitably been low, but examples have been preserved in scrapbooks kept by contemporaries with an interest in the profusion of print and they reveal a variety of subjects and styles from the celebratory to the magical. They include advertising material and handbills, which are known to have been in use from the early eighteenth century at least, for the blocks survive for an elaborate one issued by a cake shop in Edo in 1723; broadsheets, dealing with such subjects as the passage to Edo of missions from the Korean court or the king of the Ryūkyū islands (=Okinawa); theatre programmes; ranking lists (*banzuke* 番付) for sumō wrestling and, derived from that pattern, ranking lists of actors, hotspring resorts, places to visit in Edo, producers of soy sauce, and, in the early Meiji period, prominent bureaucrats and their salaries; talismanic prints for keeping smallpox at bay; and so on. By the early nineteenth century printed ephemera of these sorts were all commonplace and they testify to the commercial value and marketability of print.[36]

The profusion of all the forms of blockprinted text and image described in this section demonstrate that print had become an accessible, familiar, and increasingly essential part of daily life. In urban households it might take the form of the household encyclopedias and almanacs known as *setsuyōshū*, and in rural households of farming

---

[35] Yagi Keiichi 八木敬一 and Tanba Kenji 丹羽謙治, *Yoshiwara saiken nenpyō* 吉原細見年表, *NSGT* 72 (1995); Satō Yōjin 佐藤要人, 'Yoshiwara saiken shuppan jijō' 吉原細見出版事情, *Bungaku* 49.11 (1981): 114–24; Mukai Shinobu 1995: 331–9; Nakano Mitsutoshi 中野三敏, 'Yoshiwara igai no saiken' 吉原以外の細見, *Sharebon taisei furoku* 11 (1981): 6–8, & 12 (1981): 6–8; Niwa Kenji 丹羽謙治, 'Tenri Toshokan zō yūjo hyōbanki saiken mokuroku kō' 天理図書館蔵遊女評判記細見目録稿, *Biburia* 106 (1996): 45–88.

[36] There are many such scrapbooks in Ōsaka Furitsu Nakanoshima Toshokan; see also Hayashi & Kornicki 1991: #119–22. For the handbill of 1723 see Tani Minezō 谷峯蔵, *Edo no kopiiraitā* 江戸のコピーライター (Iwasaki Bijutsusha, 1986), 19–21.

manuals such as *Nōgyō zensho*, which was first published in 1697 and remained in print until the late nineteenth century, and of famine herbals which provided information about alternative foods at times of crop failure. But there can be no doubt that by the early nineteenth century, well before the advent of Commodore Perry and Admiral Putyatin in 1853 brought the pressures of the West from the United States and Russia respectively to bear upon Japan, print had completed its transformation from a Buddhist-dominated and élite medium into a secular medium that had overcome social or geographical boundaries to reach into the consciousness of the greater part of the Japanese population.[37]

BIBLIOGRAPHY

On printed maps, see Kazutaka Unno 1994; George H. Beans, *A list of Japanese maps of the Tokugawa era* (Jenkintown: Tall Tree Library, 1951; Supplement A 1955; Supplement B 1958); Kurita Mototsugu 栗田元次, *Nihon kohan chizu shūsei* 日本古板地図集成 (Osaka: Hakata Seishōdō, 1932); F. M. Woodward, '300 years of Japanese tourism: a look at the collection of Edo maps in the University of British Columbia Library', *World Association of Map Libraries information bulletin* 24 (1993): 161-174. On *kawaraban* see Ono Hideo 1960; Groemer 1994; M. William Steele, 'Goemon's world view: popular representations of the opening of Japan', *Ajia bunka kenkyū* 17 (1989): 69–83; Sepp Linhart, '*Kawaraban* - Die ersten japanischen Zeitungen', in Formanek & Linhart 1995: 139–66; and for reproductions and texts see *Kawaraban shinbun Edo Meiji sanbyaku jiken* かわら版新聞江戸明治三百事件, Taiyō Korekushon, 4 vols (Heibonsha, 1978). Leon M. Zolbrod, 'Mass media of the Tokugawa period: background of Japanese popular literature and journalism', in Harry J. Lamley, ed., *East Asian occasional papers II*, Asian studies at Hawaii 4 (Honolulu: Asian Studies Program, University of Hawaii, 1970), 123–43; and the special issue of *Rekishi kōron* 歴史公論 (113, 1985.4) devoted to 'Edo jidai no masumedia' 江戸時代のマスメディア. On advertising see Yamamoto

---

[37] On *setsuyōshū* see Toshio Yokoyama, '*Setsuyōshū* and Japanese civilization', in S. Henny & J-P. Lehmann, eds, *Themes and theories in modern Japanese history: essays in memory of Richard Storry* (London: Athlone Press, 1988), 78–98, and 'Some notes on the history of Japanese traditional household encyclopedias', *Japan forum* 1 (1989): 243–55; on farming manuals and famine herbals see Kornicki, 'Agriculture, food and famine in Japan', forthcoming in P. K. Fox, ed., *Cambridge University Library: the great collections* (Cambridge: Cambridge University Press, 1998).

Taketoshi 山本武利 and Tsuganezawa Toshihiro 津金沢聡広, *Nihon no kōkoku* 日本の広告 (Nihon Keizai Shinbunsha, 1986), 2–11; also Masuda Taijirō 増田太次郎, *Hikifuda ebira nishikie kōkoku* 引札絵びら錦絵広告 (Seibundō Shinkōsha, 1976), which I have not been able to consult. On sheets relating to missions from the Ryūkyūs, see Yokoyama Manabu 横山学, *Ryūkyūkoku shisetsu torai no kenkyū* 琉球国使節渡来の研究 (Yoshikawa Kōbunkan, 1987), 185–247. On *banzuke* see Hayashi Hideo 林英夫 and Haga Noboru 芳賀登, eds, *Banzuke shūsei* 番付集成, 2 vols (Kashiwa Shobō, 1973), and the pages following *KD* 11: 796; on smallpox prints see Hartmut O. Rotermund, *Hōsōgami, ou la petite vérole aisément* (Paris: Maisonneuve et Larose, 1991), 135–61; Hartmut O. Rotermund, Krankheitsbilder in Krankheits-Bildern', in Formanek & Linhart 1995; 107–37; and Sōda Hajime 宗田一, *(Zusetsu) Nihon iryō bunkashi* （図説）日本医療文化史 (Kyoto: Shibunkaku, 1989), 306–10. On early newspapers see Altman 1975; Asakura Haruhiko 1990; Ebihara Hachirō 1980; Hoare 1975; Christiane Séguy 1993; James L. Huffman, *Creating a public: people and press in Meiji Japan* (Honolulu: University of Hawai'i Press, 1997); and for the texts of the earliest Japanese newspapers see *Bakumatsu Meiji shinbun zenshū* 幕末明治新聞全集, 5 vols (Taiseidō, 1934–35). On calendars see the works cited in the bibliography to §8.2.3, and for illustrations see *Nihon no koyomi* 日本の暦, catalogue of an exhibition at the National Diet Library (Kokuritsu Kokkai Toshokan, 1984).

2.6 CONSERVATION

The humidity that characterizes the Japanese summer has always made life difficult for books, and so have a variety of insects which have an appetite for them and which flourish in the moisture that soon permeates them in the summer months. Also, the papers used in Japanese and Chinese books before modern times may have been tough and resistant to the depradations of time but they were also more absorbent of moisture and more hospitable to insect life than modern papers. For these reasons the protection of books, from the climate as well as from the dangers of fire and theft, has characterized the maintenance of collections at least from the eighth century, when sūtras and other roll books were stored in boxes.

The remedy, certainly in use in China by Han times, was to expose books to sunshine and the air to get rid of the moisture, the mould and the silverfish (*shimi* 紙魚). The formal name for this process is *bakusho* 曝書 or *bakuryō* 曝涼, although it is also known as *mushiboshi* 虫干し and *mushibarai* 虫払い. It was evidently known, and presumably practised, in Japan by 751, for the word *bakusho* occurs in a poem in *Kaifūsō*, an anthology of Chinese poems written by Japanese which was completed in that year. What is certainly true is that in the eighth century the contents of the Shōsōin repository in Nara were subject to general airings: precisely what items were aired is not made clear, but books and documents may safely be supposed to have been among them. By the tenth century rules had been laid down in the *Engishiki* for regular airings every six years of the book collection at the palace library, the Zushoryō, and every three years at the University, and the Heian poet Ōe no Masafusa 大江匡房 (1041–1111) later picked the seventh day of the seventh month as the day on which to carry this out, probably, as Kutsukake has shown, under the influence of Chinese texts which also stipulated this day. At any rate, this became the standard day for *bakusho* for several centuries, as shown in the twelfth- and thirteenth-century diaries of the statesman Kujō Kanezane 九条兼実 (1149–1207) and the celebrated poet Fujiwara no Teika. By the fifteenth century, however, the date was no longer observed and airings were rather carried out whenever the weather was most suitable.[38]

In the Tokugawa period *bakusho* was taken very seriously at the Momijiyama Bunko, the Bakufu Library in Edo which owed its origins to Ieyasu's collections. Ieyasu and his librarians appreciated its importance, and there are records of books being aired at his library in Sunpu on 1612.7.4 and at his other library in Edo castle on 1631.7.6. At the Momijiyama Bunko airing was an annual exercise which took place over several weeks, and the preparations, the equipment and the progress of the exercise were always recorded in the library diary. The librarians also undertook to air the books of other Bakufu officials. At the Hayashi school, which was the semi-official Bakufu Academy, airing was also taken seriously and sometimes, as in 1668, the exercise was combined with the task of taking an inventory and producing a catalogue of the holdings.[39]

---

[38] Kutsukake 1983: 44, 60–83, 87–8; *Zōtei kojitsu sōsho* 17: 243; *KT* 26: 384, 387, 525; *GY* 3: 719; *Meigetsuki* 名月記, 3 vols (Kokusho Kankōkai, 1911–12), 2.521, 3.109, 224, 302, 372, etc.

[39] *Sunpuki* in Ono Shinji 小野信二, ed., *Ieyasu shiryōshū* 家康史料集, Sengoku shiryō sōsho 6 (Jinbutsu Ōraisha, 1965), 56; *KT* 39: 519; *DNKS Bakufu shomotsukata nikki* 1: 27,155, etc.; Ono Noriaki 1978: 208; Kutsukake 1983: 98–110.

At a less exalted level, Kaibara Ekken, whose advice on reading is discussed elsewhere (§6.2.2), explained in simple language how to make sure ones books got a proper airing, adding that he had been doing this for years and as a result his books were unharmed. The more punctilious diarists, such as Kyokutei Bakin in the early nineteenth century, mentioned airing their books, but for the most part it became such an ordinary chore that it goes unmentioned. For foreigners arriving in Japan later in the century, however, it was a curiosity and so worth recording. Francis Hall reports what he saw at the Bukenji temple, Kanagawa (=Yokohama), on 20 July 1862: 'In one cottage ... were three young monks taking care of the library by opening the books to give them light and air, and so free them of the mold which attacks everything at this season. Not less than three hundred volumes thus lay open on the mats.'[40]

There was more to conservation than airing, as the Bakufu librarians were well aware. The library records furnish details of a process that most collectors undertook if they valued their books but that they did not think to record. Camphor, for example, was widely used to deter silverfish: at the Momijiyama Bunko it was wrapped in paper and put in the large, wooden boxes in which the books were kept, while others simply put folded pieces of paper containing some camphor between the leaves of their books. This practice was also recommended by Kaibara Ekken in his writings on airing and the care of books cited above, and it explains why scraps of folded paper, which once held camphor, are sometimes encountered in block-printed books. Shiraishi Chōkō 白石澄江, who acted as Ernest Satow's librarian in the 1860s, adopted this practice with Satow's extensive collection of early Japanese books, and in many of Satow's books the scraps of paper he used survive: they were torn from a notebook in which Satow practiced his calligraphy and recorded Japanese conversations he had heard.[41]

Books in Japan have had a high mortality rate, partly because of the disorder that accompanied political change but principally because of the prevalence of fires. Libraries carefully sited or surrounded by ditches might survive better than others, but conflagrations such as the fire that destroyed Edo in 1657 reduced many fine collections to

---

[40] *EZ* 1: 350, 498; *BN* 1: 365–6; Notehelfer 1992: 445.
[41] Hayashi and Kornicki 1991: #29.

ashes, not to mention the terrible human cost. Conservation could do nothing about such enemies of the book as these, but it could alleviate the dangers of climatic stresses and insect damage, and the consequence of failure to take such precautions was books so badly wormeaten that they fall apart in the hands. The early development of conservation techniques in Japan was therefore a rational response to an enemy of the book not encountered in so virulent a form in the West. It also expressed an awareness of the fragility of books as material artifacts: books could only be the temporary guardians of texts, and their transience was emphasized by the doleful frequency of fires and by the insect damage which affected even the most carefully preserved collections. For us at the end of the twentieth century the sense of that fragility is reinforced by the long list of texts that have not survived the ravages of time and climate: of the 493 works listed in *Honchō shojaku mokuroku*, a bibliography of Japanese books which was compiled in the Kamakura period, only 299 are still extant (§10.1.1). And there are not a few published works printed in the Tokugawa period that have not survived. Consequently, the precautions taken to protext books should not blind us to their essential materiality and vulnerability, or to the fact that the corpus of texts we have available to us can never be more than an incomplete one, and one that may not be as representative as we may like to suppose it is.[42]

BIBLIOGRAPHY

Kutsukake Isakichi 沓掛伊佐吉, 'Bakusho shikō' 曝書史稿, in Kutsukake 1983: 38–132; Fukui 1980: 97–117. On conservation in China, see Tsien 1985: 84.

---

[42] Wada Hidematsu 1936.

CHAPTER THREE

MANUSCRIPT CULTURE

1 Manuscripts in the Nara period
2 Manuscripts up to 1600
3 Manuscripts in the Tokugawa period

Manuscript production in Japan has a surprisingly long history in view of the early development of woodblock printing. In the first place this is because, until the end of the sixteenth century, printing was almost exclusively used for Buddhist texts and a few Chinese secular texts, while Japanese literary traditions were maintained in manuscript. Secondly, even after the advent of commercial printing and publishing in the seventeenth century, manuscripts continued to serve a function, both as a medium for texts that were too politically sensitive to be published in the form of print, and as a mechanism for restricting access to texts intended for initiates in such traditions as the tea ceremony and flower arrangement. It is only, therefore, in the late nineteenth century that manuscript culture begins to disappear, and this is at the same time as the scribal or calligraphic quality of block-printing described above (§1.4) is replaced by the more neutral medium of movable type. It is important to remember, therefore, that the production of manuscripts described in this chapter overlaps extensively with the production of printed books, chronologically, calligraphically and in terms of subject matter.

3.1 MANUSCRIPTS IN THE NARA PERIOD

We are never likely to know anything certain about the first manuscripts produced in Japan, but it is possible to say something about the circumstances that led to the origins of scribal culture in Japan. In the first place, there are the linguistic preconditions. Since systems for representing the Japanese language in writing only developed well after the introduction of the Chinese script, the first explorations in writing in Japan must necessarily have taken the form of Chinese script and Chinese texts. Further, at the stage when knowledge of Chinese was superficial and fragile in Japan and was confined to a few, we may suppose that at first any scribal activity consisted of producing copies of texts that had originated in China and then been transmitted to Japan. Indeed, it is likely that the first manuscript copies of Chinese texts made in Japan were written not by Japanese but by immigrants from the Korean kingdoms, whose knowledge of Chinese and experience of sinified monastic or bureaucratic culture placed them in influential positions in a barely literate Japan. It is doubtless from immigrants that Japanese learnt not only the written Chinese language but also the terminology of Chinese Buddhism and the calligraphic skills needed to write Chinese characters.

Secondly, there is the question of the motives for producing copies of texts transmitted from China or from the Korean kingdoms to Japan. In the case of secular Chinese texts, the uncertain supply of copies from China must, it may be supposed, have required the production in Japan of further copies for educational and other purposes, particularly as literacy in Chinese became an increasingly necessary skill for those in official positions. As discussed elsewhere (§7.1.1), we have some knowledge of what secular texts were transmitted to Japan by the Nara period and of the educational needs they served, but as yet we have little knowledge of the production of manuscript copies of these texts, of who copied them and how. We know much more, on the other hand, about the copying of Buddhist texts in their Chinese translations. There must also have been a need for more copies of these too for teaching needs, but a further motive for making copies of Buddhist texts was an appreciation of the notion that the copying of sūtras was in itself a meritorious act, a notion that is articulated in several sūtras that had been transmitted to Japan before the Nara period.[1]

The oldest extant manuscript, as opposed to inscription, executed in Japan is the copy in the Imperial Household Ministry of *Hokekyō gisho* 法華経義疏, a commentary on the *Lotus sūtra* allegedly

---

[1] Tanaka 1974: 4; Komatsu 1976: 46–51.

composed and written out by Shōtoku Taishi 聖徳太子 (d. 622) who acted as regent during the reign of empress Suiko. Whether or not it is in his hand is uncertain, but it is widely accepted that it dates from the early seventh century. It is written in Chinese and, assuming that it was not in fact composed and written by an immigrant, it indicates that by this time it had become possible for some Japanese at least to acquire sufficient understanding of Chinese and knowledge of Buddhism to be able to compose a commentary on a Buddhist text and in addition to have gained a familiarity with the practice of Chinese calligraphy. These levels of linguistic, doctrinal and calligraphic skills made it possible for this work and another attributed to Shōtoku Taishi to be transmitted to China and the Korean kingdoms in the seventh and eighth centuries, possibly the first works written in Japan to travel (§7.2.1). However, there can be little doubt that the greater part of the efforts devoted in the seventh and eighth centuries to the production of manuscripts was given over to the copying of Buddhist texts transmitted from China rather than the copying of secular Chinese works or of texts composed in Japan, of which there were still very few.[2]

The practice of sūtra-copying (*shakyō* 写経) reached a peak during the Nara period, but it had earlier origins and has continued, albeit at reduced levels of activity, up to the present day. The oldest extant sūtra copied in Japan is a privately-owned copy of the *Kongōjō daranikyō* 金剛場陀羅尼経, (Skr. *Vajramaṇḍādhāraṇisūtra*) which bears a date that corresponds to 686 and carries a colophon stating that it was copied as an act of devotion on behalf of the sponsor's ancestors and of all living things. However, it is certain that by this time sūtra-copying had been practised already for several decades, for there is a record of a complete copy of the Buddhist canon, presumably meaning all the Buddhist texts that had by that time been transmitted to Japan, being made at the Kawaradera in 673. Although there are few records of the activity of copying sūtras in the seventh century and few copied texts from that time have survived, there can be no doubt that the large number of temples that had been established by 700, and the quantities of monks and nuns residing in them, required the production of multiple copies of sūtras, for Buddhism

---

[2] Ishida Mosaku 1977–8: 3.9–25.

was a highly textual religion and temples needed texts as well as images. Tanaka Kaidō has suggested that sūtra-copying by Japanese began in earnest in the middle of the seventh century, and this is probably right, although it remains difficult, in the absence of references or surviving copies, to estimate the continuing contributions made by immigrant specialists rather than by Japanese.[3]

The centre of sūtra-copying activity in the Nara period was the Shakyōjo 写経所, or sūtra scriptorium, established as a government enterprise and financed by the state. The years of its foundation and demise are unknown, but it was definitely in existence by 727. The colophon of a copy of the *Daihannyakyō* 大般若経 (Skr. *Mahāprajñāpāramitā-sūtra*) made at the request of prince Nagaya the following year names the various copyists and proofreaders involved in its production and was clearly undertaken at the Shakyōjo. For some years the scriptorium seems to have been under the control of Kōmyō, emperor Shōmu's consort, but it underwent subsequent shifts in bureaucratic affiliation. By the end of the Nara period it appears to have been defunct and there is no sign that it survived the transfer of the capital from Nara to Heian-kyō (Kyoto) in 794.[4]

The work of copying sūtras at the scriptorium was undertaken by *kyōsei* 経生, who were either bureaucrats selected on a temporary basis on account of their calligraphic skills or others who passed an examination in which they were required to write several lines as a sample of their calligraphic ability. But the scriptorium also employed others such as *daishi* 題師, who supervised the work of the *kyōsei* and wrote the titles on the covers of the finished copies, and *kōsei* 校生, who proofread the finished copies to check for errors and omissions. The entire operation was subject to bureaucratic controls and a number of documents testifying to the operations have survived in the Shōsōin, including reports on the errors and omissions detected by the *kōsei*, and from these it is apparent that experienced copyists managed around 7 sheets, or 3000 Chinese characters, a day.[5]

---

[3] Tanaka 1973: 3, 25; Nara Kokuritsu Hakubutsukan 1983: 19; *NKBT* 68: 411. On the large number of temples in pre-Nara Japan see Tanaka Shigehisa たなかしげひさ, *Narachō jiinshi no kenkyū* 奈良朝寺院址の研究 (Kyoto: Shirakawa Shoin, 1978).

[4] Ishida Mosaku 1930: 187–254; Nara Kokuritsu Hakubutsukan 1983: 21–2.

[5] Tanaka 1974: 7–11.

In addition to this central sūtra-copying scriptorium there were others established to fulfil particular short-term needs at temples and other places. Mostly these were located in and around Nara. Sūtra-copying was not, however, the prerogative of these institutions nor was it confined to Nara and its environs. It is amply evident from documents preserved in the Shōsōin that sūtra-copying was also going on in the provinces far removed from these centres of sūtra production: in 757, for example, two women in Echizen province had 100 copies of the *Lotus sūtra* (*Myōhō rengekyō* 妙法蓮華経, often known in Japan as *Hokekyō* 法華経; Skr. *Saddharmapuṇḍarīka-sūtra*) made as an offering for the health and safety of the empress Kōken and her father, the abdicated emperor Shōmu.[6]

What is not clear in almost all cases of sūtra-copying is the nature of the exemplars being copied. In the early years many must have been Sui and Tang manuscripts imported from China, and this must have continued to be the case as long as new Buddhist texts or texts in new Chinese translations were being transmitted to Japan, in other words well beyond the end of the Nara period. For the most part, however, it must be supposed that copies were being made of copies that had themselves been made in Japan, and this must particularly have been the case after official contacts between Japan and China came to an end in the Heian period, which inevitably reduced the flow of manuscripts to Japan.

The reasons for undertaking the copying of sūtras in particular cases ranged from the severely practical, that is the production of a copy for use in a given temple, to the strictly devotional, but they often encompassed both practical and devotional ends. Many extant copies carry a special colophon (*ganmon* 願文) indicating the name of the person who had sponsored or requested the undertaking and the reasons for doing so, but in practice, at least in the Nara period, it was uncommon for the instigator to make the copies himself or herself. The particular devotional intentions underlying the copying of sūtras are usually made apparent in the colophons. The most common are those relating to the health or salvation of the instigator's parents, but sūtras were also copied for the sake of ones Buddhist teacher, of the state, or of ones own salvation. Kōmyō's dedicatory

---

[6] Tanaka 1974: 7–8.

colophon to the copy of the complete canon she had made in 740 reveals the range of intentions:

> Through her [ie, Kōmyō's] humble vow, she has placed her trust in the source of victory, to offer [her parents] a means to escape the darkness of hell, to spend eternity in the shelter of the Tree of Enlightenment and take the long journey to the harbour of wisdom. Moreover, she offers her vow for the sake of the rule of the Emperor Shōmu, that his good fortune and blessings shall expand continuously and extend down to all his subjects, and that they be loyal and honourable to the utmost. Moreover, [she] vows in her own right to extend relief to those in great peril, and with all zeal to eradicate spiritual vexation and hindrance.[7]

These colophons also reveal much about the context in which sūtra-copying took place. Firstly, those who initiated sūtra-copying projects, particularly the larger ones, tended to come from the ruling family, the higher aristocracy or the highest echelons of the Buddhist clergy. Thus particularly prominent were the emperor Shōmu, his consort Kōmyō, and their daughter, who reigned twice, first as Kōken and later as Shōtoku, and such monks as Genbō, who brought a huge quantity of Buddhist texts back from China in 734 (§7.1.1), Rōben, who was the founding abbot of the Tōdaiji, the Chinese monk Jianzhen 鑑真 (J. Ganjin), who reached Japan in 756, and Dōkyō, who became politically powerful during the reign of Shōtoku. Humbler names can also be found, such as those of nuns, lesser monks and lay Buddhists, but the surviving copies reveal that sūtra-copying was very closely connected to the court and associated Buddhist institutions.[8]

It is apparent both from surviving copies and the quantity of references in the documents preserved in the Shōsōin that the *Lotus sūtra* and the *Daihannyakyō* were much the most frequently copied texts in the Nara period. The precise reasons for this are not clear, although it is known that the latter was often the subject of recitations or copying exercises for devotional reasons connected with the protection of the state. But what is particularly striking about sūtra-

---

[7] Ishida Mosaku 1977–78: 3.50. Rosenfield *et al.* 1973: 33; for the Japanese text see Tanaka 1974: 127 and Ariga 1984: 16–17.
[8] Ishida Mosaku 1977–78: 3.44–9.

copying in the Nara period is the huge scale of some of the projects undertaken. There were at least 21 instances of copies being prepared of the complete Buddhist canon (*issaikyō* 一切経), which in the form in which it had reached Japan by that time consisted of more than 5000 volumes and was growing in size as newly-translated texts were being transmitted to Japan: in ten of these cases we have surviving parts to testify to the project and in the other 11 only documentary evidence. If it is indeed the case that in each of these 21 cases the whole canon was copied, then, as Rosenfield has pointed out, they must have consumed 'several million man-hours of labour' and in consequence the Nara period 'must rank as an epic moment in man's reverence for the written word'. But in addition to these *issaikyō* projects there were also a large number of cases in which multiple copies of the same sūtra were made: Genbō, for example, had 1000 copies of the *Senshu sengankyō* 千手千眼経 made in 741, and as many as 4000 copies of another sūtra were made in 750.[9]

Most sūtras in the Nara period were copied in black ink on paper that had been dyed pale yellow in what was the traditional way in China of preventing insect damage, but some were copied using gold or silver ink on papers dyed indigo or, less commonly, purple or other colours. This practice seems to have been transmitted to Japan from China or the Korean peninsula, although few Chinese examples survive, and one of the earliest references to it in Japan dates from 741, when Shōmu instructed that copies of a sūtra written in 'gold letters' were to be distributed to each of the provincial temples (*kokubunji* 国分寺) he had established. Apart from the 'conspicuous consumption' suggested by these luxury copies of sūtras and by the construction of the Tōdaiji, various doctrinal explanations have been offered for their production, which in the Heian period were decorated even more lavishly: Ishida Mosaku considers the primary purpose to have been to awaken in the reader a sense of respect for a text so magnificently presented and thus sees the practice as one of enhancement of the dignity of the Buddhist text, while Tanaka Kaidō connects it with the rise of belief in Amida and the association of light with Amida.[10]

---

[9] Ishida Mosaku 1977–8: 3.28–34; Kimoto 1989: 296–8, 422–4; Tanaka 1974: 122–49; Rosenfield *et al.* 1973: 26–8.

[10] *SNKBT* 13: 388–9; for the earliest reference to decorated sūtras in Japan (739)

Although we have far less information concerning the copying of secular Chinese works in and before the Nara period, we know that by the end of the period a considerable quantity of such works had been transmitted to Japan and, given the existence of educational institutions and a bureaucratic need for familiarity with Chinese writings, it must be assumed that many copies at least of standard texts were made in Japan (§7.1.1). Very few, however, have survived, except for a few texts copied in the early Nara period, including part of the account by the Tang monk Yijing 義浄 (635–713) of his travels to India and several literary works which do not appear to have survived in China. Some copying of secular texts was undertaken by the Zushoryō 図書寮, a state library established by the lawcodes of 702. This had a staff of 20 copyists who were supposed to make copies of both secular and Buddhist texts, but it is not possible now to identify any of their productions (§9.1.1).[11]

Although most of the bureaucratic, religious and literary manuscripts produced in the Nara period have long since been lost, the corpus of Nara manuscripts has recently been growing as a result of the discovery of the so-called *urushigami* 漆紙 fragments. These are torn scraps of paper used to cover and preserve supplies of lacquer, which have themselves been preserved by the lacquer, and they were first discovered at the Taga castle site in 1978. Since then many have been found at sites all over Japan, and they have included sections of calendars for the years 803 and 804, presumably disposed of at the end of the year, as well as parts of bureaucratic documents. And at the Izawa castle site in northern Japan have been found some fragments of the *Xiao jing* from an eighth century scroll produced in Japan; since the castle was founded in 802, it appears likely that the scroll was taken there, possibly for educational purposes and disposed of after about 100 years of use.[12]

Further texts have also come to the light in the form of *mokkan* 木簡, wooden tablets used for bureaucratic and other purposes, including writing practice. These have been found in great numbers,

---

see *DNK* 2: 168, 183. Ishida Mosaku 1977–8: 38; Tanaka 1974: 19–20.

[11] Sorimachi 1997: 1.75, 108–9, 154–5; *NST* 3: 262–8. On sūtra copying in the Zushoryō see Ogawa Tōru 小川徹, 'Zushoryō to shakyō jigyō' 図書寮と写経事業, *Toshokanshi kenkyū* 1 (1984): 11–36.

[12] Hirakawa Minami 平川南, *Urushigami monjo no kenkyū* 漆紙文書の研究 (Yoshikawa Kōbunkan, 1989), 225–60.

predominantly from the area around Nara, and the texts written on them in ink have added much to our knowledge of the Nara period, but they were not used for longer texts and are only peripherally related to the scribal culture of early Japan.[13]

The scribal culture of pre-Heian Japan follows an unsurprising trajectory, starting with the copying of Chinese works, Buddhist and secular, and then moving on to the composition of new works in Chinese and finally the composition of new works in Japanese, written out in Chinese script. The calligraphic styles follow a similar path, as far as can be told from surviving examples, which represent just a fraction of all that was copied in the Nara period. Immigrant scribes, and Japanese scribes who had been trained by them, naturally tended to use Sui or Tang styles, but in the late Nara period there was growing divergence from Chinese practice and by the tenth century Japanese calligraphic styles had taken over.[14] Unfortunately, however, we have at present only a very partial picture of scribal activity and the circulation and consumption of manuscripts in the centuries before the move to Heian-kyō (Kyoto) in 794, and although a number of works written in Japan in Chinese and Japanese survive from this period we still know very little about the manuscript traditions that underlie these surviving texts.

BIBLIOGRAPHY

On the Shakyōjo and sūtra-copying see Ishida Mosaku 1930 (contains English summary), Tanaka 1974, Komatsu 1986 and the works cited in *KD* 7: 205. Nara Kokuritsu Hakubutsukan 1983 contains photographs and discussions of most surviving Buddhist manuscripts of the Nara period. On surviving copies of sūtras from the Nara period see Tanaka 1973, and on sūtras mentioned in Nara period sources see Kimoto 1989. On copies of the *Lotus sūtra* see Kabutogi 1983. For the annotated texts of a number of sūtra dedications see Ariga 1984: this work and others such as Shinkawa Seifū 新川晴風, *Shakyō no mikata kakikata* 写経の見方・書方 (Tōkyōdō Shuppan, 1980) are intended both as studies and as guides for those wishing to undertake

---

[13] On *mokkan* see Tōno 1977; *KD* 13, plates following p. 828; Joan R. Piggott, '*Mokkan*: wooden documents from the Nara period', *MN* 45 (1990): 449–70; and Kiyotari Tsuboi and Tanaka Migaku, *The historic city of Nara: an archaeological approach*, trans. David W. Hughes & Gina L. Barnes (Paris: UNESCO; Tokyo: Centre for East Asian Cultural Studies, 1991).

[14] Tanaka 1974: 41–3.

sūtra-copying for themselves. For illustrations see Nara Kokuritsu Hakubutsukan 1983, Ishida Mosaku 1952, Ōya 1926, Christie's 1988: 10–13, and Rosenfield *et al.* 1973.

3.2 MANUSCRIPT PRODUCTION UP TO 1600

It was in the Heian period that printing began to be used to produce texts for people to read, but until the end of the sixteenth century almost all those texts were in Chinese and were Buddhist in content (§4.1.2). Consequently, most secular Chinese texts and all Japanese texts circulated only in manuscript during these centuries, and scribal culture continued to dominate book production until the seventeenth century.

The practice of sūtra-copying, discussed in the previous section, continued in the Heian and following periods in spite of the increasing availability of Buddhist texts printed in Japan or Song editions imported from the late Heian period onwards, but not on the scale as had been seen in the Nara period. The rise of new sects of Buddhism, particularly Shingon and Tendai, and the decline of the six Nara sects, led to changes in emphasis and a reduction in the demand for copied sūtras. Although there was a new need for the texts of esoteric Buddhism, these were more likely to be copied within temples for their own use rather than to be copied by other institutions or as devotional exercises. And devotional sūtra-copying tended to be undertaken by the initiator himself or herself and for his or her own salvation, rather than by others as public exercises: the great poet and scholar Fujiwara no Teika (1162–1241), for example, himself made many copies of the *Lotus sūtra* and other scriptural texts in his lifetime. Further, the enhanced belief in the powers of the *Lotus sūtra* is reflected in the fact that more copies of this sūtra have survived in devotional copies from the Heian period than of all other sūtras put together.[15]

Sūtra-copying in the Heian period also took some new forms. One

---

[15] Tanaka 1974: 15–7; Komatsu 1976: 46–51. On the *Lotus sūtra* in Heian culture see George J. Tanabe, Jr. & Willa Jane Tanabe, eds, *The Lotus sutra in Japanese culture* (Honolulu: University of Hawaii Press, 1989). On Teika's sūtra copying see Ishida Yoshisada 石田吉貞, *Fujiwara Teika no kenkyū* 藤原定家の研究, revised edition (Bungadō Ginkō Kenkyūsha, 1969), 684–92.

of these is the 'letter sūtra' (*shōsokukyō* 消息経), which denotes a sūtra copied on letters written by somebody who had died as a devotional exercise for the benefit of the deceased. Sometimes the text of the sūtra was written on the back of the letters and sometimes mica was sprinkled on the text of the letters enabling the sūtra to be written over the original. The earliest known instance of this is when, after the death of emperor Seiwa in 886, his widow used some of his letters for this purpose, but the practice continued at least until the sixteenth century. Sometimes also books owned by a person who had died were used in the same way after washing off the original texts.[16]

It was in the Heian period too that the use of sūtras for devotional purposes reached the extreme measure of burying them, usually in metal containers, in what have come to be known as sūtra mounds (*kyōzuka* 経塚). The earliest known instance of this is the celebrated case of the politician and arbiter of taste Fujiwara no Michinaga, who in 1007 took the *Lotus sūtra* and five other sūtras he had written in 998 and buried them on Mt Kinbusen: they were excavated in 1671 and parts survive in several collections. The practice of burying sūtras along with Buddhist images and ritual implements continued into the Kamakura period and is commonly associated with the millenial notion of *mappō* 末法, the 'Latter days of [Buddhist] law', which connoted decline and turned attention from the present to a distant future in Buddhist cosmology in which Maitreya would bring salvation. In many cases, including that of Michinaga, the sūtras and other objects were buried explicitly to await the coming of Maitreya.[17]

In certain textual senses too the practice of sūtra-copying in the Heian and Kamakura periods began to differ from that of the Nara period. In addition to the shift from Chinese to Japanese styles of calligraphy, we also find, from the middle of the Heian period onwards, increasing use of diacritical marks (*kunten* 訓点) to facilitate reading Chinese texts in Japanese; these differed, however, from the later, standardized forms of *kunten*, for a number of different techniques were used by different temples and sects. In the Kamakura period

---

[16] Tanaka 1974: 27–28. Komatsu 1976: 93–101 (pp. 96–7 contain a list of extant *shōsokukyō* from 886 to 1510). For an illustration see Ishida Mosaku 1952: 1.52 and 2, plates 152–4.
[17] Tanaka 1974: 27; Rosenfield *et al.* 1973: 50–51; Ariga 1984: 58–61.

there are also occasional versions of the *Lotus sūtra* written out in Japanese rather than Chinese, such as one that was written in a mixture of the *hiragana* syllabary and characters in the mid Kamakura period.[18]

The use of paper dyed indigo and of gold and silver inks for copying sūtras had begun in the Nara period, as mentioned in the previous section; from the eleventh century onwards it became increasingly common to furnish these sūtras with a frontispiece. This practice originated in China, but the earliest Chinese example surviving is in fact the printed frontispiece to the celebrated copy of the *Diamond sūtra* in the British Library, which was printed in 868. However, some fragments of a frontispiece recently been found in Korea are thought to date from the eighth century: these consist of line drawings in gold ink on dark-blue paper and appear to reflect Tang styles of illustration. The earliest Japanese example is attached to a copy of the *Lotus sūtra* written in silver ink in the ninth century and is probably copied directly from a Tang exemplar. This frontispiece consists simply of stylized ornamentation, but later Japanese examples commonly illustrate variations on the theme of Śākyamuni Buddha preaching to disciples, albeit with increasing elaboration.[19]

In the Heian period sūtra decoration assumed new forms. Sometimes each character was written in gold inside the outline of a stūpa (pagoda) drawn in silver, but much more elaborate and artistic styles of decoration were also employed. There is, for example, a contemporary description in the *Eiga monogatari*, compiled in the eleventh century, of the preparation of a decorated version of the *Lotus sūtra* in 1021, in the midst of an epidemic, by a number of court ladies-in-waiting, each of whom contributed a chapter:

---

[18] On *kunten* sūtras and varieties of *kunten* see Tanaka 1974: 91–2 and Tsukishima Hiroshi 築島裕, *Heian jidai kuntenbon ronkō* 平安時代訓点本論考, 2 vols (Kyūko Shoin, 1996). On *kana* sūtras see Sorimachi 1997: 1.233; Ishida Mosaku 1952: 1.59 and 2, plate 188.

[19] Sudō Hirotoshi 須藤弘敏, 'Kodai Ajia no kyōe' 古代アジアの経絵, *Bukkyō geijutsu* 172 (1987): 50; Hang Suyŏng 黄寿永, 'Shiragi hakushi bokusho Kegonkyō ni tsuite' 新羅白紙墨書華厳経について, *Bukkyō geijutsu* 127 (1979): 11–20; Sudō Hirotoshi, 'Heian jidai no teikei kyōkan mikaeshie ni tsuite' 平安時代の定型経巻見返絵について, *Bukkyō geijutsu* 136 (1981): 86–7. For illustrations of Japanese examples see Murase 1986: 5-1, Egami 1989, and Rosenfield *et al.* 1973: 76–82.

> The sūtra was indescribably magnificent. Some chapters were true chrysographed texts, inscribed in gold on lustrous cobalt-blue paper. Others were written over pictures superimposed on damask, or contained pictures above and below the text, or provided textual illustrations - the "Gushing Forth" chapter, for instance, depicted the emergence of multitudes of bodhisattvas from the earth, and the "Eternal Life" chapter showed the Buddha's eternal abode on Vulture Peak. ... But it would be impossible to describe them all. Their splendour and sumptuousness made them resemble collections of elegant verse rather than sūtras.

Although the copies described here have not survived, the decorative procedures are thought to have been in use by the early eleventh century, and they are exemplified in the twelfth-century *Heike nōkyō* 平家納経, which have survived in the Itsukushima shrine at Miyajima. The *Heike nōkyō* is a copy of the *Lotus sūtra* and some other texts in which the chapters were each written by a member of the Taira (Heike) family alliance, including the leader Taira no Kiyomori himself, and they were deposited in the Itsukushima shrine in 1164.[20]

In the cases mentioned so far the illustrations have been Buddhist in their inspiration, but some sūtras were also decorated with secular scenes, including figures and what appear to be scenes from *monogatari*. How these are to be interpreted is a matter of some controversy: it might be thought that the texts are intended to sacralize secular life in some way, or to provide some benefit to the owner. What is undeniable is that the secular world is brought in closer touch with the religious and that that secular world is depicted within the conventions of contemporary Japanese art; in this way the japanization of sūtra-copying has gone as far as it could go without actually translating the texts from Buddhist Chinese into Japanese.[21]

After the Heian period sūtra-copying continued to be practised as before, but rarely to such artistic effect. This-worldly concerns remained of importance, as when in the 1340s, during a period of drought, sūtras were copied with dedications indicating the hope that

---

[20] Sorimachi 1997: 1.231. William H. & Helen Craig McCullough, *A tale of flowering fortunes: annals of Japanese aristocratic life in the Heian period*, 2 vols (Stanford: Stanford University Press, 1980), 2: 531–2; *NKBT* 76: 43–4. On the *Heike nōkyō* see Komatsu 1986, which includes a volume of colour plates.

[21] Egami 1989: 45–9; cf Richard Bowring. 'The *Ise monogatari*: a short cultural history', *HJAS* 52 (1992): 446–7.

they might bring rain. And in 1354 Ashikaga Takauji, the founder of the Muromachi Bakufu, had a number of monks at different temples copy out the whole Buddhist canon for the sake of peace in his realm and even for the sake of his foe, emperor Go-Daigo, who is named in the dedication. By this time a number of copies of Song printed versions of the Buddhist canon had been imported and there were no longer compelling practical reasons to undertake copying exercises of this kind (§7.1.1), but sūtra-copying retained its devotional appeal.[22]

In many respects we know far more about the copying of sūtras in early Japan than about the copying of secular Chinese works and of works of Japanese authorship whether in Chinese or Japanese. And far more copies of sūtras copied in the Nara and Heian periods have survived than of secular works. In part this must be due to the sheer quantity of Buddhist texts that were copied in those centuries, but it is also to be attributed to the public nature of sūtra-copying projects. While organs of the state supported these projects, and major temples intimately associated with the state housed the copied texts, secular texts were more private in their generation and transmission and this undoubtedly affected their chances of survival. The Zushoryō, which was the institution responsible for the custody and transmission of texts in the Nara and Heian periods, certainly had the staff and facilities for copying texts (§9.1.1): guidelines were laid down in the Heian period for the layout of manuscripts copied there, the fines to be levied for errors made by scribes or proofreaders, the amounts of text to be copied and proofread daily, varying according to seniority, types of paper used, the size of the script required and so on. But what texts were being copied? It is probable that they were mostly either Buddhist texts or sinological texts for educational use, but it may be that Japanese historical documents and texts, and possibly even the imperially commissioned anthologies of *waka* poetry (*chokusenshū* 勅撰集), were also copied there.[23]

If so, however, this did not have the effect of facilitating the survival of Japanese literary manuscripts: the haemorrhage of texts was unremitting, as we know from the many titles listed in the thirteenth-century in *Honchō shojaku mokuroku* which have not survived (§10.1.1). Furthermore, an alarming number of works from

---

[22] Ariga 1984: 176–7, 184–8.
[23] Hashimoto 1974: 66–9; *KT* 26: 383–92.

these periods have survived in just one copy, and those that have survived in multiple copies tend to exhibit much greater textual variation than copies of sūtras or secular Chinese works. Since none of these literary texts were printed in Japanese until the early seventeenth century they must of necessity have circulated in manuscript for several hundred years. In the early Tokugawa period the texts of many of them were stabilized in print but in forms which rarely took account of the various manuscript traditions: as a consequence, although it was through these printed editions that Japanese literary texts broke out of the narrow confines they had inhabited and became established in a public sense as 'classics', they are still largely disdained as *rufubon* 流布本, or 'popular versions', and are mostly ignored in studies devoted to textual traditions.

There were, as we have seen, identifiable religious motives for copying, circulating and preserving copies of texts taken from the Chinese Buddhist canon, and there were educational motives, dictated by the sinological requirements of the bureaucracy, for the copying and use of the central texts of the Chinese tradition.[24] Political and bureaucratic motives may have underpinned the transmission of certain Japanese texts, especially the six official histories starting with *Nihon shoki*, which were all written in Chinese, but literary texts written in Japanese, such as the prose narratives known as *monogatari*, the poetic diaries and anthologies of court poetry, seem to have been rooted less securely in the systems for transmission, circulation and preservation. To what extent this was because they were written in Japanese and were closely associated with the women's quarters of the palaces is unclear, but it is a fact that for most texts we have to rely on copies made many centuries later and that very few copies from the Nara or Heian periods have survived. The oldest surviving literary examples are a *waka* poem written *c*749 on a bureaucratic document preserved in the Shōsoin by one of the copyists working in the Shakyōjo, and part of another poem which appears as a graffito on an inside part of the pagoda of the Hōryūji and which is probably somewhat older. Surviving items from the Heian period include an important fragment containing extracts from the writings of Ono no

---

[24] On sinological texts and Heian education see Robert Borgen, *Sugawara no Michizane and the early Heian court* (Cambridge, Mass.: Council on East Asian Studies, Harvard University, 1986), 96–7, etc.

Takamura (802–52), Sugawara no Michizane (845–903) and Ki no Haseo (845–912), which is attributed to the hand of Fujiwara no Kōzei (972–1072), and two copies of the early eighth-century poetry collection *Man'yōshū*, in addition to a number of illustrated rolls to be mentioned below. But overall the quantity is unimpressive when compared with the numbers of Buddhist texts surviving from this period.[25]

To a remarkable extent it is the activities of Fujiwara no Teika that seem to have rescued many earlier texts from obscurity and almost certain oblivion, such as the *Sarashina nikki*, for which we have only a copy in Teika's own hand and a number of secondary copies derived from Teika's copy and made centuries later in the Tokugawa period. The recently-opened rich store of texts in the Reizeike Bunko (§9.4) is adding to our understanding of Teika's role in the transmission of Heian and early Kamakura literature, but it is clear that even by his time the instability of Japanese literary texts was obvious and that copying texts was less of a mechanical than a scholarly exercise.

For example, there is the case of the *Tosa nikki*, the poetic diary compiled by Ki no Tsurayuki in the early tenth century. The original, in the hand of Ki no Tsurayuki himself, was somehow preserved in the Rengeōin 蓮華王院, the palace library (§9.1.1), until the Kamakura period but it later passed into the hands of Ashikaga Yoshimasa, the eighth Ashikaga shōgun, and its subsequent fate is unknown. Teika made a copy of this manuscript in 1235, writing as follows in the colophon:

> The thirteenth day of the fifth month, second year of Bunreki, in the sickness of old age, with my sight failing, unexpectedly I saw Ki [no Tsurayuki]'s copy in his own hand (the copy in the treasure house of the Rengeōin). ... Unable to control my emotions I copied it out myself, finishing the task in two days, yesterday and today.

Since the Rengeōin original has not survived, it is not clear on what basis Teika was able to state that it was in Ki no Tsurayuki's own hand, but it is evident that even he, after a lifetime of scholarship,

---

[25] Hashimoto 1974: 7–9; *Ōcho bijutsu meihinten* 王朝美術名品展 (catalogue of exhibition held at Tōkyō Kokuritsu Hakubutsukan in 1976): #16, 18 & 20.

had not known of its existence, or at least had not recognised its importance, before encountering it in 1235. That he had great respect for the text in front of him is certain, for he is careful to describe the state of the manuscript, noting that it was written on 26 sheets of unruled white paper and providing other information about its size and presentation. Furthermore, he undertook not simply to copy the text (*shasho* 写書, in contemporary terminology) but to copy the layout, orthographical usages and even calligraphy (*mosho* 摸書) so as to create as far as possible a handwritten facsimile of the original. This important copy made by Teika has survived to the present day, as also have a number of secondary copies of it, and it was this text that was used as the basis of study and of published texts up until the 1920s. However, a number of other copies of the Rengeōin text were made, and it appears that for all his care and reverence Teika did not manage to produce the best copy. His son Tameie made one the year after he did, in 1236, and, although this only survives in a secondary copy of it made in 1600, it is clear that Tameie made fewer orthographic mistakes, copying errors, omissions or involuntary additions than Teika. The original colophon, which is reproduced in the 1600 copy, is revealing:

> Twenty-ninth day of the eighth month, second year of Katei. I made this copy from Ki [no Tsurayuki]'s original (Rengeōin book), not departing from it even in one letter. There were some passages I was unable to make out.

Although Tameie makes the ritual claim of accuracy (*ichiji tagaezu* 一字不違), he did in fact make some errors and in a number of places corrected himself; it is evident that even he, like his father before him, found it not an easy task to read the original from which he was copying. In 1490 and 1492 further copies were made of the Rengeōin original, the former at imperial command and the latter by the important textual and literary scholar Sanjōnishi Sanetaka 三条西実隆; again these copies only survive in secondary copies made much later. Thus all the surviving manuscripts of the *Tosa nikki* originate from one source, the copy alleged to be in Ki no Tsurayuki's own hand. This has certainly facilitated the recovery of the text in the form in which Teika and the others found it, but it also raises serious questions about the circulation of the *Tosa nikki* in the Heian period.[26]

The case of the *Tosa nikki* demonstrates the familiar fragility of manuscript traditions and textual survival, and reminds us that Japanese literary works were particularly at risk because of the lack of an institutional place for them. Like both Chinese secular and Buddhist works, the value of copies was dependent on the personal qualities of the scribes, their educational levels, commitment to accuracy, appreciation of the work they were copying, palaeographic expertise, motives for making the copy, and so on. But whereas almost all the works in Chinese transmitted to Japan survived on the mainland and were in addition preserved in temple libraries in Japan, Japanese works had for the most part nowhere to survive but in the private collections of interested scholars. The example of the *Sarashina nikki*, another poetic diary, has already been mentioned, and Teika's colophon to the copy he made shows how fortunate we are to have the text at all:

> I obtained a copy of this book some years ago; I lent it to somebody and lost it. Then I made a copy of a copy that somebody had made of that book. As a result of its transmission [from copy to copy], there were many mistakes in the writing and I have marked with red ink the places that seem doubtful to me.

We know nothing of the book that Teika originally had, and although there were clearly other copies in circulation at the time none of these have survived even in secondary copies.[27]

The diary of Murasaki Shikibu, as the author of the *Tale of Genji* is known to us, reveals something of the presence of manuscripts and bound books in the women's quarters of the palace in Heian-kyō (Kyoto) in the early eleventh century. She notes a distinction between the special copies of imperial anthologies of *waka* poetry (*chokusenshū*) presented as gifts to the emperor's consort and personal poetry collections which, 'since they were for more everyday reading, had been written by someone quite unknown and looked very up-to-date and unusual'. She also records spending days with the emperor's consort binding copies of the *Tale of Genji* preparatory to sending them out, and complains that Michinaga had taken her fair copy of it

---

[26] Hashimoto 1974: 12–23, 52, ; Ikeda 1941 vol. 2.
[27] Hashimoto 1974: 52–4.

for his daughter. It appears from this and other diaries that books were a not uncommon commodity at court at this time, although most of the references to the circulation of works of Japanese literature are to be found in women's diaries and therefore concern their circulation among women of the palaces.[28]

The *waka* poetry of early Japan was both an oral and a written tradition, as the two poems written in the Nara period and mentioned in the previous section testify. When the first of the imperial anthologies, the *Kokin wakashū* (*Kokinshū*) was being compiled in the early years of the tenth century, it is recorded that the monarch ordered poets to submit 'family collections and old poems handed down from the past', and this implies the existence of written collections of poetry in the early Heian period. The *Kokinshū* went through a complex period of gestation, in which there was a first version and then a second version which went through five drafts before the submission to the throne of the dedication copy. The first version is only partially extant, but among the many surviving manuscripts there are copies of all the drafts of the second version, particularly of the fifth draft; Teika himself made at least 16 copies of the fifth draft between 1209 and 1237. It is evident that the successive drafts, far from being destroyed, circulated and created textual traditions of their own, and this is indicative of the plurality of manuscript traditions which has affected the transmission of many works of Japanese classical literature.[29]

The most important tradition of illustrated manuscripts in these centuries is that of the *emaki* 絵巻 or *emakimono*, which were in roll form. This probably has its origins in the Nara period in copies taken from imported Chinese rolls. The oldest surviving example in Japan is the *E ingakyō* 絵因果経, a copy of a Chinese original executed some time in the late Nara period; it consists of a roll in which the text of the *Kako genzai ingakyō* 過去現在因果経 (translated into Chinese in the fifth century from a Sanskrit original now lost), occupies the bottom half and scenes illustrating the text fill the top half. There

---

[28] Bowring 1982: 93, 95, 101, 143; Hagitani 1971–3: 1.493–4, 2.34, 387.
[29] *SNKBT* 1: 348–9. On the manuscript traditions see the 'Kaisetsu' by Kyūsojin Hitaku 久曽神昇 in *Kokin wakashū*, Yōmei sōsho kokushohen (Kyoto: Shibunkaku, 1977), 1–20; this contains a facsimile of a copy, made in 1305 by Reizei Tamesuke, of a copy of the fifth draft made by his grandfather Teika in 1226, described by Tamesuke as a 'family treasure' (*sōden hihon* 相伝秘本).

are records of several copies of this circulating in the Nara period, and in 1528 Sanjōnishi Sanetaka recorded seeing a copy dated 735 in the hand of emperor Shōmu, which is thought to have been based on a text imported from China. In the Heian period *emaki* became japanized and concerned themselves with *monogatari* prose literature, popular tales, legends concerning the origins of temples and shrines, the lives of famous monks, festivals, and other secular events, either in the divided format of *E ingakyō* or with illustrations alternating with passages of text. Multiple copies survive of some of these, such as the *Genji monogatari emaki*, the *Murasaki Shikibu nikki emaki* and the *Kitano Tenjin engi*, but the artists are known in only a few cases, and they usually lack a colophon giving even the barest details of their preparation. In the case of some of those dealing with temples, shrines and famous monks, they do survive with colophons which suggest that they were used in connection with the performance of oral narratives and sermons. One example is the *Yugyō shōnin engi e* 遊行上人縁起絵, which consists of a number of passages concerning the life and teachings of Ippen, the founder of the Jishū sect; this survives in a copy made in the fifteenth or sixteenth century of an original evidently dated 1307 and bearing a colophon which explicitly refers to its function as an aid to salvation for those who see and hear it. For the most part, however, the *emaki* remain an elusive presence as a manuscript tradition in Heian Japan and the centuries that follow, and it is difficult to ascertain how they might have been copied, read and circulated.[30]

The manuscript culture of the later Kamakura and the Muromachi periods has yet to be elucidated, but there is much material contained in diaries, and the manuscript traditions underlying the survival of some individual works have already been extensively explored, particularly in the case of the imperial anthologies of court poetry. A commanding presence in the Muromachi period, parallel in some ways to that of Teika in the thirteenth century, is that of Sanjōnishi

---

[30] For details of surviving *emaki* and of reproductions of each see *KD* 2: 365–72. On *E ingakyō* and *Yugyō shōnin engi e* see *Nihon emakimono zenshū* 日本絵巻物全集, 24 vols (Kadokawa Shoten, 1958–68), 16: 52–4 and *passim*, 23: 19, 21–6. *Sanetaka kōki* 実隆公記, 13 vols (Zoku Gunsho Ruiju Kanseikai, 1931–63), 7: 208. On questions of patronage in the production of *emaki* and of their transmission, including some on more vulgar subjects, in the fifteenth century, see Karen L. Brock, 'The Shogun's "Painting match"', *MN* 50 (1995): 433–84.

Sanetaka (1455–1537), whose voluminous diary attests to his active and scholarly involvement in the manuscript culture of Japanese and Chinese literature. By his early forties his reputation had spread so far that he was asked by litterateurs living in the provinces to make copies of poetry collections. During his lifetime he made copies of more than 20 different manuscripts of the *Tale of Genji*, but for reasons of poverty he was forced to sell some of the best items from his own collection, and he was constantly borrowing texts of Japanese historical and literary works and of the Chinese classics in order to make copies of them for his own use.[31]

Secular Chinese texts answered educational, intellectual and literary needs in the Kamakura and Muromachi periods as in the Heian, but until the beginning of the seventeenth century only a handful of texts were printed and for the most part they circulated in manuscript. This was true even of new Chinese texts imported in Song printed editions, for the supply of imports was insufficient to meet the demand in Japan. The neo-Confucianism of Zhu Xi and his followers was transmitted to Japan in this way, but once in Japan manuscript copies were made to facilitate their study and circulation. In some cases manuscript copies are furnished with colophons giving the date of copying and perhaps the name of the copyist, but for the most part our knowledge of the circumstances in which copies of secular Chinese texts were made is thin.[32]

Towards the end of the Muromachi period a new tradition of illustrated manuscripts emerged, which now bears the confusing name of *Nara ehon* 奈良絵本, although they have nothing to do with Nara. These mostly consist of the texts of the late Muromachi stories known as *otogizōshi* 御伽草紙 interspersed with richly coloured illustrations, but in some cases the texts were extracted from earlier works of prose literature, such as *Taiheiki*, *Ise monogatari* and the *Tale of Genji*. In the Muromachi period they were often in roll form, but in the first century of the Tokugawa period, when they seem to have been produced in quantity and with some standardization of the illustrations, they were more likely to take the form of bound books.

---

[31] Haga Kōshirō 芳賀幸四郎, *Sanjōnishi Sanetaka*, Jinbutsu sōsho series (Yoshikawa Kōbunkan, 1960), 97, 142, 153, 160, 179, 226–7; Haga 1981:1.106–110.

[32] Ashikaga Enjutsu 1932, separately paginated supplement giving details of manuscript copies made in Japan of neo-Confucian texts.

For the most part, however, they are anonymous and lack colophons, and we consequently have very little information on their circulation and the manuscript culture that supported their production.

BIBLIOGRAPHY

On sūtra copying see the works cited in the bibliography to the previous section. On sūtra mounds and buried sūtras see Hosaka Saburō 保坂三郎, *Kyōzuka ronkō* 経塚論考 (Chūō Kōron Bijutsusha, 1971) and *BKK* 1: 143–326. For illustrations of sūtras and secular manuscripts see Murase 1986. On the manuscript traditions of early historical and legal texts see Yoshioka Masayuki 吉岡真之, *Kodai bunken no kisoteki kenkyū* 古代文献の基礎的研究 (Yoshikawa Kōbunkan, 1994). Ikeda 1941 is a pioneering bibliographic study, which offers a detailed study of the manuscript traditions of the *Tosa nikki* and an exposition of the bibliography of Japanese manuscripts; Hashimoto 1974 gives an expert guide to the bibliographical problems presented by early manuscripts of Japanese literary texts. On the terminology of manuscript bibliography see Sugiura Katsumi 杉浦克巳, *Shoshigaku komonjogaku: moji to hyōki no rekishi nyūmon* 書誌学・古文書学ー文字と表記の歴史入門 (Hōsō Daigaku Kyōiku Shinkōkai, 1994). For facsimiles and studies of *Nara ehon*, see *Zaigai Nara ehon* 在外奈良絵本 (Kadokawa Shoten, 1981) and *Nara ehon emaki shū* 奈良絵本絵巻集, 12 vols, *bekkan* 3 vols (Waseda Daigaku Shuppanbu, 1987–9); in English James T. Araki, '*Otogi-zōshi* and *Nara-ehon*: a field of study in flux', *MN* 36 (1981): 1–20.

3.3 MANUSCRIPTS IN THE TOKUGAWA PERIOD

Although print came into its own in the Tokugawa period, it did not completely supplant the manuscript, and manuscripts continued to be produced for a variety of reasons. The survival of manuscript culture right up to the nineteenth century is not, however, simply a matter of old traditions being maintained with little regard for the spread of print. On the contrary, manuscript culture survived because it still had functions to perform in the midst of print culture and in certain important respects these complemented the functions of printed books, particularly in the case of books that could not be printed because of possible contravention of the censorship laws.

Of course, a number of older manuscript traditions also survived the efflorescence of print culture, but with new significance. Sūtra-copying was certainly practised throughout the Tokugawa period, but this no longer had anything to do with the production of copies of texts for the use of others, for commercial publishers printed a large range of sūtras and other Buddhist texts in the seventeenth century and beyond (§4.3.4). Sūtra-copying now had only a devotional role and was generally undertaken by the initiator or initiators rather than being entrusted to professional copyists. In 1678, for example, following the death of Tōfukumon'in (1607–78), emperor Go-Mizunoo's consort, 28 people connected with her, including members of the imperial family, senior members of the aristocracy, and high-ranking Buddhist monks, each copied out one of the sections of the *Lotus sūtra* for the sake of her happiness in the afterlife, and in 1785 emperor Kōkaku himself copied out part of another sūtra for similar intentions on the seventh anniversary of the death of emperor Go-Momozono. Similarly, in 1702 the court official and litterateur Konoe Iehiro 近衛家熙 (1667–1736), who later took the tonsure, wrote out a sūtra in gold ink on blue paper two days after the death of his mother, stating in the colophon that it had been 'reverently copied to ensure the spiritual enlightenment of his departed mother'; he then donated it to a subtemple of the Daitokuji in Kyoto. These sūtra copies have been preserved in all likelihood because of the hands that wrote them, but now that the texts were widely available in printed form there was little reason to preserve the sūtras copied for devotional reasons by those of humbler status and with less distinguished calligraphic hands to boast of.[33]

The increasing availability of printed secular texts from the seventeenth century onwards does not seem to have materially reduced the demand for manuscripts with calligraphic or artistic qualities to commend them, particularly in the first century of the Tokugawa period, when there were still many earlier texts that were yet to be printed for the first time. In the 1630s, for example, Karasumaru Mitsuhiro, who was a distinguished calligrapher and also wrote a number of works for publication in printed versions, copied out a set of poems that had been composed by Ashikaga Takauji, the founder of the Ashikaga shogunate in the Muromachi period, and by some of his companions in the fourteenth century. It is for similar reasons too that manuscript texts of works which had been printed already

---

[33] Tanaka 1973: 359–60, 366; Rosenfield *et al.* 1973: 38–9.

continued to be produced: this is particularly the case with works of classical Japanese literature of which illustrated manuscript copies continued to be produced by Kyoto court calligraphers as bridal gifts (*yomeiribon*) or for private collections. One example of the many that could be given is that of the numerous manuscript copies of Fujiwara no Teika's *Hyakunin isshu*: even after 11 blockprinted and movable-type editions had appeared in the early decades of the seventeenth century, copies were still being produced in Kyoto by distinguished calligraphers, members of the court aristocracy and even by emperor Gosai (1637–85).[34]

Another reason for producing a work in manuscript without seeking to have it published was the desire to keep the contents known only to a selected circle of people. This is the case with many of the *hiden* 秘伝, or secret traditions, such as the various schools of flower arrangement, of the tea ceremony, of swordsmanship and even of medical practice. For example, the Majimaryū school of ophthalmology, founded in the fourteenth century by Majima Seigan, was only transmitted to accepted practitioners orally and by manuscript, and copies of texts explaining the school's techniques survive only in manuscript. Similar cases are the Chūjō school of midwifery and perinatal medicine, and the works of Hanaoka Seishū (1760–1835), the pioneer anaesthetist and surgeon, which also remained unpublished and circulated only amongst his pupils and followers.[35]

For similar reasons, or for lack of an anticipated market, many earlier works remained unpublished until the end of the Tokugawa period, when they were printed for the first time by Hanawa Hokiichi in the *Gunsho ruiju* series which ensured the survival of countless texts that had for long circulated only in manuscript (§10.2). Another case is that of *Ishinpō* 医心方, the oldest extant medical treatise of Japanese authorship, which was compiled in the late tenth century by Tanba Yasuyori 丹波康頼 on the basis of a large number of Chinese medical and pharmaceutical texts. Several Heian period manuscripts

---

[34] Rosenfield *et al.* 1973: 114–7 (also plate VII). Yoshikai Naoto 吉海直人, *Hyakunin isshu nenpyō* 百人一首年表, *NSGT* 75 (1997), #59, 69, 74, 76, 83, 89, etc.

[35] For some examples of medical manuscript traditions see Kornicki 1997: #28–9. Kure Shūzō 呉秀三, *Hanaoka Seishū sensei oyobi sono geka* 華岡青洲先生及其外科 (Kyoto: Shibunkaku, 1971; facsimile of 1923 edition), 381–7.

of this text survive, but there are also many extant manuscripts from the Tokugawa period, for it was not until 1860, when the Bakufu's Medical Academy sponsored the publication of the first edition, that printed copies became available, and until then it was in the form of manuscript copies that *Ishinpō* was circulated and studied. If this was true of works written before the Tokugawa period, it was also true of many written since 1600 as well which could well have been published but which, for a variety of reasons, were never published. This applies, for example, to the many manuscripts prepared by Kōriki Enkōan 高力猿猴庵 (1756–1831), a Nagoya samurai who wrote many accounts of Nagoya life in the format of printed books with coloured illustrations from his own hand; almost all of these remained unpublished, but some circulated in the hands of lending libraries.[36]

Some at least of these works were available for sale and were in effect published in the form of manuscripts. For example, some time in the eighteenth century the Kyoto publisher and bookseller Hayashi Gonbee 林権兵衛 (also known as Yoshinoya 吉野屋 Gonbee) put out an advertisement for books by the Confucian scholar Itō Jinsai and his son Tōgai in which several works were identified as manuscripts and were presumably included because they were available to be purchased. Similarly, the Edo bookseller Masuya Chūbee 舛屋忠兵衛 put out an advertising catalogue listing a number of manuscript books on the games of Go and Shōgi, or Japanese chess; in it he described them as suitable for beginners and implied, probably falsely but with an eye to publicity, that they were books from a secret tradition (*hisho* 秘書).[37]

Given the growth of the market for fiction in the Tokugawa period it might appear unlikely that there would be any room for manuscript traditions to survive there. However, as will be mentioned below, there was a popular genre of fictionalized scandals which for reasons

---

[36] Sugitatsu Yoshikazu 杉立義一, *Ishinpō no denrai* 医心方の伝来 (Kyoto: Shibunkaku Shuppan, 1991), 26–33; Hayashi & Kornicki 1991: #2051. On Enkōan's manuscripts, see *Enkōan to sono jidai: Owari hanshi no egaita Nagoya* 猿猴庵とその時代―尾張藩士の描いた名古屋 (Nagoya: Nagoya-shi Hakubutsukan, 1986), 14–45.

[37] On the concept of publishing manuscripts, see Harold Love, 'Scribal publication in seventeenth-century England', *Transactions of the Cambridge bibliographical society* 9 (1987): 130–54. For the advertisements see Asakura 1983: 4.226–31, 328–9.

of censorship could only circulate in manuscript, and in addition it is clear that in certain cases works circulated initially in manuscript before being published. This is certainly the case with the genre of romantic fiction known as *ninjōbon*, for there is evidence that some of these works were written by 'amateurs' and circulated as manuscripts, and that some published *ninjōbon* were actually based on 'amateur' originals that have now been lost.[38]

In addition to the manuscript traditions described above, it was surprisingly common in the Tokugawa period for manuscript copies to be made of printed books. Individual readers wishing to own a copy of a rare or unobtainable book might borrow it from an acquaintance and make a handwritten copy for themselves or have one made for them. This was partly a consequence of the lack of public libraries, for access to old or rare books depended on private networks. But another reason for making a copy of a printed book is recorded by the Meiji critic and writer Uchida Roan (1868–1929), namely the high cost of some of the more substantial genres of fiction, particularly *yomihon*, in the second half of the Tokugawa period. He recounts that rather than attempting to purchase a copy interested readers wishing to own one used to borrow them from the commercial lending libraries known as *kashihon'ya* 貸本屋 (§9.2.4) and make whole or partial copies. Making such copies was, according to Roan, the work of retired men in the family, and in his youth in the early Meiji period it was still customary for elderly males to be engaged in making copies for the use of the family circle; this was, he claims, a hobby for them as well as a way of saving on the cost of books.[39]

A third reason for making a manuscript copy of a printed book was the desire to obtain a copy of a banned book. Since the censorship system that operated in the Tokugawa period was based on self-censorship exercised by the publishing guilds, and since the guilds

---

[38] Maeda Ai 前田愛, 'Edo murasaki – ninjōbon ni okeru amachua no yakuwari' 江戸紫－人情本におけるアマチュアの役割, *Kokugo to kokubungaku* 411 (1958): 57–67.

[39] Uchida Roan 'Hakkenden dan'yo' 八犬伝談余, in *Nansō Satomi Hakkenden* vol 3, Nihon meicho zenshū, Edo bungei no bu 18 (Nihon Meicho Zenshū Kankōkai, 1928), 2 (separately paginated). It is also reported that *kashihon'ya* employed their own copyists to make multiple copies of expensive printed books for which there was a good demand: Tsukahara 1910: 9.

could not always anticipate Bakufu reactions, it happened from time to time that published books met with disfavour and were banned and that the printing blocks were destroyed (§8.2.2). By the time that this had happened some copies of the offending work had inevitably been sold but further copies could not be printed, and it was common practice in such cases for manuscript copies to be made and these ensured the continued circulation of censored works. One example is *Sangoku tsūran zusetsu* 三国通覧図説, a description of Korea, the Ryūkyū islands (= Okinawa) and Ezo (= Hokkaidō and the various islands to the north of it) which was published in 1786. The author, Hayashi Shihei 林子平 (1738–93), is more famous for a later work, *Kaikoku heidan* 海国兵談, in which he exposed what he saw as Japan's inadequate defensive capabilities and which led to his imprisonment, and it may be that this drew attention to his earlier work. Whatever the truth, it was not until 1793 that *Sangoku tsūran zusetsu* was banned, on the grounds that it contained false information: the printing blocks were destroyed, Hayashi was sentenced to further imprisonment, the publisher was fined, and the four guild representatives responsible for monitoring works about to be published were also fined. This was seven years after publication, and many copies must have been sold by this time, but evidently demand outstripped the supply, for numerous manuscript copies of the printed version survive, many of which betray their origin by reproducing the original printed colophon as well. Similarly, it appears that in the eighteenth century some of the Chinese works by European Jesuits in China, which had long been banned, circulated extensively in manuscript but were kept well hidden from the authorities; Ogyū Sorai, for example, was shown a copy of one of Ricci's banned works in the 1720s and made a copy for himself (§8.2.1).[40]

What particularly distinguishes the manuscript culture of the Tokugawa period from that of previous centuries is the development of subversive genres of writing that could not be published in printed

---

[40] Yayoshi 1988–93: 3.502. On Hayashi's problems, see Donald Keene, *The Japanese discovery of Europe*, revised edition (Stanford: Stanford University Press, 1969), 39–45. For examples of manuscript copies see Hayashi & Kornicki 1991: #1550, 2510; in Europe other manuscript copies of the printed version of *Sangoku tsūran zusetsu* can be found in the Società Geografica Italiana in Rome, in the Staatsbibliothek in Berlin, in the Musées Royaux d'Art et d'Histoire in Brussels, and elsewhere.

form on account of the censorship edicts but that were increasingly published, that is, made publicly available, in the form of manuscripts. The origins of this practice are obscure, but the extent it had reached by 1771 can be ascertained from a list of forbidden books published by the Kyoto booksellers' guild in that year, *Kinsho mokuroku* 禁書目録, 'Catalogue of banned books'. This was published to assist members of the guild in their efforts to comply with the law and to avoid handling such books, but the largest section consists of a list of 122 illicit manuscripts, and a note at the end reveals the scale of the problem:

> Apart from those listed above there may be many other manuscript books including accounts of things heard (*kikigaki* 聞書) and miscellaneous records (*zatsuroku* 雑録), but there is not time to refer to them all. Even though they may not be included in the list above, it is strictly forbidden to handle any book that records recent events or deals with matters concerning the court aristocracy or samurai households, let alone matters concerning the court or the shōgun's household.[41]

In drawing up these restrictions the guild appears to be doing more than dutifully following Bakufu edicts: although various edicts in the 1720s had banned the printing of books containing this sort of subject matter, no edicts seem to have survived which take up the issue of illicit manuscripts before the publication of *Kinsho mokuroku* in 1771. In 1790, however, a new edict explicitly banned the practice of making manuscript versions of 'baseless rumours' and charging people a fee for reading them, a belated acknowledgement of the fact that the commercial lending libraries known as *kashihon'ya* were doing just that. And in 1853, when the Kyoto booksellers' guild drew up a new set of guidelines for its members, the provisions made it clear that books of the kinds described above were banned whether they were circulating in print or in manuscript and added that this also applied to printed books or manuscripts conveying 'rumours' about foreign countries.[42]

Just what, then, was so offensive about the illicit manuscripts listed in *Kinsho mokuroku*, and about those that were produced after

---

[41] Munemasa and Wakabayashi 1965: 84.
[42] *OTS* 2: 809–10, #6417; Munemasa and Wakabayashi 1965: 198–9.

1771, and when did such manuscripts begin to appear? The earliest recorded instance known to me occurred in 1681 when a monk named Ichion 一音 was banished to Hachijō island for having written a manuscript account of a daimyō succession dispute in the Takada domain. However, the subject matter of many of the listed manuscripts suggests that many of them are the product of manuscript traditions that go back much earlier than this. A considerable number, for example, deal with the controversial history of the relations between Toyotomi Hideyoshi, and later his son Hideyori, with Tokugawa Ieyasu, who went back on the promises he had made to Hideyoshi and established his own régime in 1603, and who in 1615 extirpated the remainder of the Toyotomi family. There were never any edicts in the seventeenth century forbidding books on this subject, but it was in practice avoided in printed books, and publications which attempted to deal with the subject were suppressed by the Bakufu (§8.2.2). The same goes for books concerning the history of the Christian missions in Japan in the sixteenth and seventeenth centuries, and consequently the list includes several works which treat the Shimabara uprising of 1638, in which Christian symbolism and Japanese Christians had a prominent part (§8.2.1). Several others take up the story of Yui Shōsetsu 由井正雪, who led a number of discontented *rōnin* (masterless samurai) in a plot to overthrow the Bakufu which was discovered in 1651. These and other works discussing the genesis of the Tokugawa régime and the public events of Ieyasu and his successors were not publishable, as the earliest edicts from the late seventeenth century make clear (§8.2.2), and it is likely that they were already circulating in manuscript in the seventeenth century.[43]

In the eighteenth century there were many scandals and public events which were written up for circulation as manuscripts, most notably the act of revenge carried out by 47 (actually 46) *rōnin* for the disgrace and forced suicide of their lord, which had occurred on 1702.12.14, and their subsequent mass suicide on 1703.2.4. Several of these are included in the *Kinsho mokuroku* list, but there were in reality far more in circulation. Further, not only did many of these illicit manuscripts bear seemingly innocuous titles by way of disguise, but also they often circulated under a range of different titles, and for

---

[43] *KT* 42: 416; Munemasa and Wakabayashi 1965: 177–83.

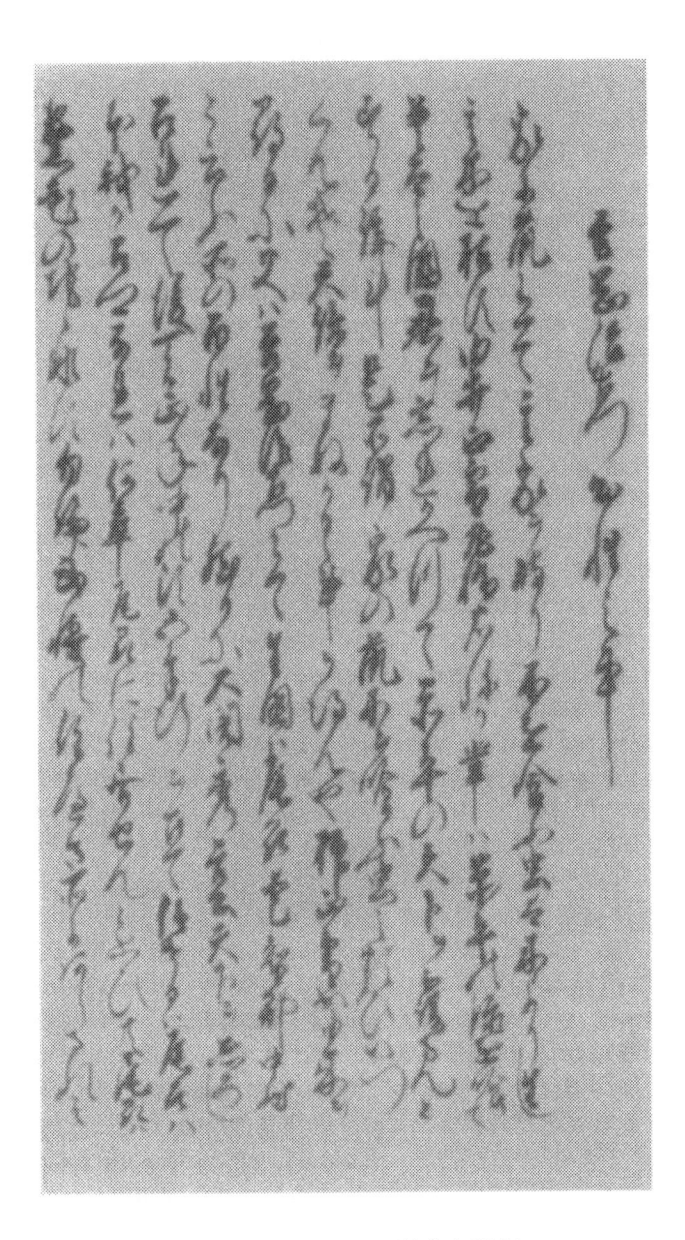

Fig. 7 The beginning of *Keian taiheiki* 慶安太平気, an anonymous account of a plot to overthrow the Bakufu which was led by Yui Shōsetsu and discovered in 1651. This manuscript copy was made in the second half of the Tokugawa period, judging by the style of calligraphy: Hayashi & Kornicki 1991: #1297.

these reasons it was not easy, as the compilers of the list were evidently aware, to judge by the title alone and booksellers could find themselves handling such manuscripts inadvertently.[44]

Many of these illicit manuscripts in the eighteenth and nineteenth centuries concern troubles in the daimyō domains (*oie-sōdō* 御家騒動), which appear to have attracted increasing interest and to have generated a covert literature of their own. These works usually contain an admixture of fictional elements not only for the purpose of disguise but also to increase their appeal to a readership expecting to find familiar styles of narration, and they are commonly referred to as *jitsuroku* 実録 or *jitsurokutai shōsetsu* 実録体小説. Although these owe varying amounts to fictional imagination, especially in the dialogue and incursions into the minds of the characters, some of whom are clearly invented, they retain a factual basis and often end with reproductions of legal documents, such as those passing down sentences on the miscreants. The *Kinsho mokuroku* list includes many of these, and specifically notes that a number of copies (perhaps versions?) of one entitled *Atan yume monogatari* 阿淡夢物語 were in circulation. This tells the story of Matsudaira Shigeyoshi 松平重喜, who was the daimyō of Awa (阿波: the title hints at this by adopting the first character and adding to it the character 淡, which can also be read 'awa'), and who conducted mock naval battles with real deaths for his own amusement: he was eventually dismissed from office in 1768.[45]

The most notorious producer of illicit manuscripts of this sort was undoubtedly Baba Bunkō 馬場文耕 (1718–58). He was a popular performer of oral narratives, in which he appears to have dealt with political topics under transparent disguises, but he also turned these narratives into manuscript books which were published by having multiple copies made either for sale or for circulation in the hands of lending libraries. One of them, for example, *Morioka mitsugi monogatari* 森岡貢物語, deals with a dispute in the shōgun's castle in Edo between the senior councillors of the Bakufu and the daimyō and domain officials of the Nanbu domain, and the copy in Kyoto

---

[44] For the titles of many manuscripts with various titles on the revenge of the 47 *rōnin* see Yukio Fujino, *Catalogo dei libri Giapponesi dei periodi Edo e Meiji* (Rome: Biblioteca Nazionale Centrale Vittorio Emanuele II, 1995), 129–32.
[45] On *jitsuroku* see *Mitamura Engyo zenshū* 三田村鳶魚全集, 28 vols (Chūō Kōronsha, 1975–83), 22: 299–342, and Kornicki 1982.

University Library contains a label indicating that it was circulated by a commercial lending library in Kanazawa, evidence that his works travelled well beyond Edo. It was another of his works, *Hiragana mori no shizuku* 平仮名森の雫, that brought about his death. This concerns the daimyō of the Gujō 郡上 domain in the province of Mino, whose name, Kanamori Yorikane 金森頼錦, is concealed in the title. As a result of the corrupt and harsh administration of his domain there was an appeal by the peasant cultivators to the Bakufu, which eventually responded by depriving him of his domain in 1758. Before the year was out Baba Bunkō had put together a version of these events which he made the subject of oral narratives and which he also distributed as a manuscript text to commercial lending libraries for circulation. When this came to the attention of the Bakufu he was executed, and six lending libraries were also punished.[46]

It should be noted here that Baba Bunkō was by no means the only oral performer who drew his material from current events and other topics that were too sensitive to publish in print. Other examples are noted by Kodera Gyokuchō 小寺玉晁 (1800–78), a litterateur and observer of contemporary life who lived in Nagoya. He records in his diary frequently attending performances of oral narratives in the 1820s and 1830s, including narratives on such topics as Hideyoshi, the revenge of the 47 *rōnin* and other vendettas, and political scandals involving the daimyō. This subversive oral culture was by no means undermined by the pervasive spread of print, for print could not touch these subjects, or even by the circulation of manuscript versions of the narratives, which in all probability did not reach such large audiences.[47]

Even more sensational than the scandals involving various daimyō was the sex scandal at the Enmeiin 延命院 in Edo in 1803. Although some details remain obscure, it appears that the abbot of the Enmeiin became the lover of several ladies from the women's quarters of the shōgun's palace, who visited the temple under the guise of attending

---

[46] Konta Yōzō 今田洋三, 'Baba Bunkō to sono chosaku ni tsuite' 馬場文耕とその著作について, in *(Haga Kōshirō sensei koki kinen) Nihon bunkashi kenkyū* (芳賀幸四郎先生古希記念）日本文化史研究 (Kasama Shoin, 1980), 357–81. Okada 1987: 309–13.

[47] *NS* 17: 330, 345, 362, 422, 438, 494, etc. See also Maria Teresa Orsi, 'Recitativi e narrativa nel Giappone degli anni Tokugawa-Meiji', *Il Giappone* 17 (1977): 53–70.

all-night vigils. The abbot was executed in the same year, and several versions of these events carry the same date, and were probably in circulation by the following year at the latest. However, it was not until 1805 that a samurai who had apparently been responsible for one of the written accounts was apprehended: he was exiled from Edo and 15 lending libraries who had furnished copies to their customers were sentenced to spells in handcuffs.[48]

Towards the end of the Tokugawa period, several bookshops were advertising *jitsuroku* manuscripts for sale quite openly.[49] It is abundantly clear that these manuscripts, including many of those listed in *Kinsho mokuroku*, circulated widely, and copies of many of them survive. Nevertheless, in only the few cases mentioned above does it seem that they came to the attention of the authorities, and in general it seems that the Bakufu's attempts to control the circulation of illicit manuscripts was not successful. Another category of illicit manuscript which similarly evaded the Bakufu's control, but which is missing from *Kinsho mokuroku* and appears to have been even more deeply hidden, is the narratives of peasant uprisings, which 'tell the tale of underground heroes, men whom the ruling authorities tried to erase from popular memory'.[50]

It is evident that the survival of manuscript culture in the Tokugawa period functioned among other things as an efficient and safe means of circulating books that could not be published. These books served partly to disseminate news and information and in doing so undermined the authority of the Bakufu by revealing matters that were not supposed to be publicized. They also led to the development of a new form of writing, which combined familiar narrative techniques with contemporary subject matter and characters drawn from the forbidden world of politics. But these were just part of an extensive scribal

---

[48] The advertisements are discussed in Kornicki 1982: 508-9; Sekine 1903-4: 1422-4; Okada Tetsu 1987: 308-13; for a full account of the Enmeiin affair see Kornicki 1982. Konta 1981: 129-35.

[49] For advertisements mentioning *jitsuroku* see Nogami 1975: 221; Kornicki 1982: 509-10.

[50] Anne Walthall, *Peasant uprisings in Japan: a critical anthology of peasant histories* (Chicago: The University of Chicago Press, 1991), 16. See also Yokoyama Toshio 横山十四男, *Hyakushō ikki to gimin denshō* 百姓一揆と義民伝承 (Kyōikusha, 1977).

culture that survived the commercial development of blockprinting in the seventeenth century. In the Tokugawa period manuscripts existed alongside printed books and were read by the same readers, for they continued to meet needs that printed books could not, needs for subversive or calligraphically artistic books, or for books that were intended for restricted circulation only.

BIBLIOGRAPHY

Konta 1981. Kornicki 1982. Some of the best-known *jitsuroku* are reprinted in *Kinsei jitsuroku zensho* 近世実録全書, 20 vols (Waseda Daigaku Shuppanbu, 1928–9). Reprints of several of Baba Bunkō's works are contained in Okada Tetsu 1987. On the evolution of *jitsuroku* versions of the Shimabara rebellion see Kikuchi Tsunesuke 菊池庸介, '*Amakusa gunkimono* jitsuroku no seiritsu' 「天草軍記物」実録の成立, *Kinsei bungei* 66 (1997): 41–53.

CHAPTER FOUR

PRINTED BOOKS

1   Printing before 1600
      1   The Hyakumantō darani
      2   The Heian, Kamakura and Muromachi periods
2   Movable type: the early phase
      1   The Jesuit mission press
      2   Korean movable type
      3   Japanese movable type
3   Block-printing in the Tokugawa and early Meiji periods
      1   Commercial publishing
      2   Official publishing
      3   Private publishing
      4   Reprints of non-Japanese works
4   Later movable type and copperplate
      1   Wooden movable type
      2   Western-style movable type
      3   Copperplate

Printing in Japan has, by global standards, an extraordinarily long history, but it is equally extraordinary that, after the introduction of printing technology in the eighth century, nearly a thousand years elapsed before printing established itself as the principle means for the production of books. That shift occurred when printing became a commercial operation in the early seventeenth century, and it is from that point onwards that we can begin to talk of a print culture in Japan, and not before. As we have already seen, that delay in the application of printing technology is by no means unique to Japan and has close parallels in Russia and the Middle East (§1.3), and as a result of it print culture, in those cases as well as in that of Japan, overlapped much more extensively with manuscript culture than was the case in Europe (§3.3).

The origins of printing in East Asia remain something of a mystery and I do not propose to consider the matter in depth here. Although there have been claims for the autonomous development of printing in Japan, these can be discounted and it is accepted now that printing in East Asia had its origins in China. The techniques of printing have often been associated with the use of blocks for dyeing fabrics and the use of carved seals, but there is also an important connection with the ritual duplication of texts in both Buddhism and Daoism. Indeed, in terms of the multiplication of texts for ritual purposes, the antecedents of printing can be found in India, in the practice of stamping Buddhist texts onto soft clay tablets, which was observed and described by Chinese monks.[1]

The oldest surviving examples of printing in East Asia, which were produced in Japan and Korea in the eighth century, are of ritual Buddhist printing, and in Japan it is not until the eleventh century that we have any examples of the printing of texts for people to read, although in China, in the case of both calendars and Buddhist texts, printing for the purpose of reading was already well established by then. The assumption underlying this chapter, then, is that printing reached Japan from China in the form of a ritual practice in the eighth century and that it was some centuries before it was put to more pragmatic use.[2]

Successive sections deal with the centuries of domination by woodblock printing and then with the use of metallic and wooden typography, and finally with Western-style typography, which only finally came to dominate at the end of the nineteenth century. There is not space here to deal with the infinite variety of the output of the press, particularly that of the world of commercial publishing which developed so rapidly in the seventeenth century. However, reprints of non-Japanese works are given separate attention, for they are

---

[1] Tokushi 1951: 16–17; Lawson 1982: 6–28, 54, etc.
[2] On this subject see Kanda Kiichirō 神田喜一郎, 'Chūgoku ni okeru insatsujutsu no kigen ni tsuite' 中国における印刷術の起源について, *Nihon gakushiin kiyō* 日本学士院紀要 34 (1976): 89–102; Tsien 1985; Twitchett 1983; Drège 1986; Michel Strickmann, 'The seal of the law: a ritual implement and the origins of printing', *Asia major*, third series, 6.2 (1993): 1-83; and T. H. Barrett, 'The *Feng-tao k'o* and printing on paper in seventh-century China', *BSOAS* 60 (1997): 538–40.

outside the mainstream of 'Japanese books' and have hitherto been inadequately studied, apparently on the ground that they are not in Japanese. Serial publications and printed ephemera, which have similarly been neglected because they are not 'books', have been discused elsewhere (§2.5).

4.1 Printing before 1600

4.1.1 *The Hyakumantō darani*

The oldest extant printed texts in Japan are the large numbers of invocations or dhāraṇī which were, according to the early chronicle *Shoku nihongi*, printed between 764 and 770 and placed inside miniature wooden pagodas. Since a number of the surviving pagodas bear dates that correspond with these years, there is little room for doubting that the invocations were in fact printed at that time. Whether these were the first items printed in Japan is, however, more difficult to say. Given the quantity of them evidently printed in those years it is unlikely that the *Hyakumantō darani*, as they are collectively known, were completely without precedent in Japan, for the very scale of the project suggests some familiarity with the process, and it has been suggested that a likely carrier of the art of printing to Japan was the Chinese monk Jianzhen (J. Ganjin), who reached Japan in 753.[3] As yet, however, no documentary or archaeological evidence has come to light to give substance to this supposition.

These dhāraṇī used to be, and sometimes still are, said to be the world's oldest printed artifacts, but in 1966 a similar printed dhāraṇī was found in a stone pagoda at the Pulguksa 仏国寺 temple in Kyŏngju, Korea. Although it is not dated and there is no documentary record of the printing, it is thought to date to some time before 751 on several grounds. Firstly, the text from which the dhāraṇī were taken is known to have reached Silla by no later than 706, for an inscription on the inside of a reliquary box states that a copy was placed inside a pagoda at a different temple in Kyŏngju in that year. Secondly, the Pulguksa records state that all work on the pagoda was

---

[3] Tokushi 1991: 182; Kimiya 1932: 1–17; *SNKBT* 15: 280–81.

completed in 751, and there is no mention of any further work. And thirdly, the other objects found in the pagoda are recognisably of Silla provenance. The likelihood is that the Korean example is older than the Japanese dhāraṇī, and indeed it is to be expected that the art of printing would have travelled from China to Korea before it reached Japan. The notion once held by some scholars that printing was an autochthonous development in Japan is not tenable.[4]

Both the Korean and the Japanese dhāraṇī were printed not for distribution, nor even for reading, but for the ritual reproduction of texts. The texts in question were taken from a sūtra known in Japanese as *Muku jōkō dai daranikyō* 無垢浄光大陀羅尼経, which was translated into Chinese by Mitraśanta, a Tokharian monk, in 704. This sūtra expounds the benefits to be derived from reproducing the texts of dhāraṇī and inserting them inside pagodas, and this practice is known from archaeological finds in India and elsewhere, where texts were stamped in clay and the 'printed' texts then placed inside stūpas. Knowledge of it is also known to have been transmitted to China by monks who had observed this practice in India, and it must be supposed that it subsequently reached Korea and Japan: the text of *Muku jōkō dai darani kyō* must obviously have reached Japan some time between 704 and 764. It was in the context of Buddhist ritual, then, that printing was first undertaken in Japan, and it was removed from practical considerations relating to the multiplication of texts for readers.[5]

The Japanese dhāraṇī printed in the eighth century are known collectively as the Hyakumantō darani, the 'dhāraṇī of the one million

---

[4] On the find in Korea see Li Hungjik 李弘稙, 'Keishū Bukkokuji shakatō hakken no Muku jōkō dai daranikyō' 慶州仏国寺釈迦塔発見の無垢浄光大陀羅尼経, *Chōsen gakuhō* 朝鮮学報 49 (1968): 457–82 [this is a Japanese translation of an article that appeared in *Paeksan hakbo* 白山学報 49 (1968): 457–82] and Kawase Kazuma, 'Shiragi Bukkokuji Shakatō-shutsu no Muku jōkō dai daranikyō ni tsuite' 新羅仏国寺釈迦塔出の無垢浄光大陀羅尼経について *Shoshigaku* 書誌学, 2nd series, 33/34 (1984): 1-9. For an example of the autochthonous view, see Asakura Kamezō 朝倉亀三, 'Nihon kokokusho shi' p. 3, in *Kokusho Kankōkai shuppan mokuroku/ Nihon kokokusho shi* 国書刊行会出版目録／日本古刻書史 (Kokusho Kankōkai, 1909).

[5] *T*, 55: 369c, 867a; Lewis R. Lancaster with Sung-bae Park, *The Korean Buddhist Canon: a descriptive catalogue* (Berkeley: University of California Press, 1979), 126–7; Hirako 1908: 1; *T* 54: 226, 51: 920; J. Takakusu, *A record of the Buddhist religion as practised in India and the Malay Archipelago (A.D. 671–695)* (Oxford: Clarendon Press, 1896), 150.

pagodas', and the implication of the passage in the *Shoku nihongi* and other sources is that one million of these dhāraṇī were printed and placed inside the miniature pagodas, of which thousands in fact survive in Nara along with their contents. Extraordinary though this is, there is good evidence to suggest that certainly a very large number were printed and that pagodas containing them were distributed to a number of temples: records survive, in a number of contemporary sources, of buildings constructed to house the pagodas. In spite, however, of the numbers of surviving exemplars, there is no consensus about the method used to undertake the printing. For long the dominant view has been that metallic plates must have been used, since surviving printed dhāraṇī did not appear to show the wear and tear that would be expected of wooden blocks. More recently, microscopic evidence of woodgrain in the printed characters in some of the dhāraṇī has lent support to the alternative view, that wooden blocks were used as indeed became customary for printing throughout East Asia. The issue is yet to be resolved satisfactorily.[6]

Another issue, which has attracted far less attention, is the question of motivation. There is a tradition, preserved in the records of the Tōdaiji temple in Nara, that this whole exercise was undertaken to atone for the loss of life that ensued when a rebellion led by Fujiwara no Nakamaro (also known as Emi no Oshikatsu) was put down in 764, and this has been widely accepted. However, the precise connection between the printing and the atonement is unclear. Further, this explanation takes no account of the sheer quantity involved, both of pagodas and of printed dhāraṇī, for the *Muku jōkō dai darani kyō* stipulates only that 99 be produced. Other sūtras, however, which were similarly translated into Chinese and transmitted to Japan by the middle of the eighth century, stipulate as many as 100,000. What seems clear is that any explanation must take account of the following issues. Firstly, the injunctions of this and related sūtras, which attach merit to the multiplication of texts, were most easily answered by means of printing. Secondly, the sūtras were translated into Chinese during the reign of empress Wu, and are closely associated with her,

---

[6] Tsutsui Eishun 筒井英俊 ed., *Tōdaiji yōroku* 東大寺要録 (Kokusho Kankōkai, 1971; facsimile of 1944 edition published by Zenkoku Shobō, Osaka), 105; Hirako 1908: 2–3, 10–12; Nakane 1987: 21–9, 56–8, etc.; 'Hyakumantō darani no insatsu saikō' 百万塔陀羅尼の印刷再攷, *Biburia* ビブリア 31 (1965): 13–51.

and it appears probable that in several respects Shōtoku modelled herself on Wu. Thirdly, the Hyakumantō darani project was undertaken during the reign of empress Shōtoku, whose leaning towards elements in the Buddhist establishment rather than towards the court bureaucracy is a matter of record and whose reign in this respect bears comparison with that of Wu. And fourthly, there was clearly a close association between Shōtoku and the ambitious monk Dōkyō, who is known to have been familiar with dhāraṇī and esoteric Buddhism and who may have provided her with access to the sūtras in question. The Hyakumantō darani, which not only utilized a novel technology but did so on a grand scale that must have consumed considerable human and material resources, have without doubt other layers of meaning.[7]

BIBLIOGRAPHY

Hirako 1908; Nakada Sukeo, 中田祐夫, 'Hōryūji hyakumantō darani no insatsu' 法隆寺百万塔陀羅尼の印刷, *Bungaku* 49 (1981): 72–85; Nakane 1987; Drège 1986; Mitchiko Ishigami-Iagolnitzer, 'Les Hyakumantô-dhârani et les débuts de la xylographie au Japon (VIIIe – XIIe siècle),' in Drège, Ishigami-Iagolnitzer and Cohen 1986: 163–85; Brian Hickman, 'A note on the Hyakumantō Dhāraṇī,' *MN* 30 (1975): 87–93; Mimi Hall Yiengpruksawan, 'One millionth of a Buddha: the Hyakumantō Darani in the Scheide Library', *Princeton University Library chronicle* 48 (1986–7): 225–38. The Hyakumantō dhāraṇī and their background will be dealt with more fully in a longer study I am preparing on the subject.

4.1.2 *The Heian, Kamakura and Muromachi periods*

Other than the *Hyakumantō darani*, no other samples of printing from the Nara period survive. There is slight evidence to suggest that the Chinese monk known in Japan as Ganjin may have engaged in printing while resident in Nara, but this is widely discounted because there is no mention of this in contemporary accounts of his activities. It is certain, at any rate, that *inbutsu* 印仏, the stamping of images of

---

[7] Kimoto 1989: 377; *T* 9: 161, 21: 885; Nabatake Takashi 名畑崇, 'Nara jidai mikkyō juyō no sokumen' 奈良時代密教受容の側面, in Bukkyōshi gakkai 仏教史学会, ed., *Bukkyō no rekishi to bunka* 仏教の歴史と文化 (Kyoto: Dōhōsha, 1980), 464–6.

the Buddha on paper, was practised in the Nara period, and it is quite conceivable that some texts were printed too, albeit for similar devotional rather than practical purposes.[8]

It is in the Heian period, however, that we encounter more persuasive evidence of printing in Japan. *Inbutsu* continued to be practised, and some examples from the Heian period have survived. But by this time printed books were reaching Japan from China (§7.1.1), and some of the Tendai and Shingon monks who travelled to China in the ninth century explicitly record them amongst the books they brought back. This is not surprising because the *Diamond sūtra*, the oldest dated Chinese book extant, was printed in 868 and was doubtless one of many Buddhist texts available in printed form by then.[9]

The first unequivocal record of textual printing in the Heian period comes from 1009, when Fujiwara no Michinaga recorded in his diary that 1,000 copies of the *Lotus sūtra* had been printed, although no copies of this seem to survive. However, this was not for the production of copies of reading; rather, it was an alternative to hand-copying for devotional purposes. In other cases of this kind both the dedications appended to surviving copies and the term commonly used at the time for printing, *shūsha-kuyō* 摺写供養, indicate that the motivation did not lie in the dissemination of texts. Diaries and other records from the late Heian period indicate that the reproduction of sūtras was resorted to at times of sickness or on the occasion of a death, and it is clear that the point lay in the meritorious act of producing multiple texts, and that their subsequent fate was of no concern to the sponsor. It is for this reason, as Tokushi Yūshō argues, that there was no need to use good-quality paper or to preserve the printed copies, although some do survive from this period.[10]

Printing for practical rather than devotional purposes can also be dated to the eleventh century, when Song-dynasty printed texts were

---

[8] Kimiya 1932: 16; Tokushi 1951: 41–42; on the oldest surviving *inbutsu*, which date from the Heian period, see Kaneko Kazumasa 金子和正, '(Tenri Toshokan zō) Heian Kamakura jidai no inbutsu suributsu yonshu' （天理図書館蔵）平安鎌倉時代の印仏摺仏四種, *Biburia* 91 (1988): 37–43.

[9] *T* 55: 1084, 1091, 1110, 1111; on the *Diamond sūtra* and other early printing in China, see Tsien 1985: 151–6.

[10] Tokushi 1951: 68–72, 81–8; *Midō kanpakuki* 御堂関白記, in *DNKK* 2: 34; Kawase 1945: 1503–50; Kimiya 1932: 34–7; *NKC* 2: 90–92.

becoming sought after in Japan, and it is associated with sūtra commentaries and doctrinal works: in such cases textual reproduction did not serve the devotional purposes of sūtras. The oldest extant example bearing a date is the *Jōyuishikiron* 成唯識論, which was printed in Nara by monks of the Kōfukuji temple in 1088. Whereas devotional printing appears to have been undertaken mostly in Kyoto, where the aristocratic sponsors resided, practical printing in the Heian period was undertaken mostly if not exclusively in Nara, and only at the wealthy Kōfukuji, which was the family temple of the Fujiwara family. These editions are known as Kasuga-ban 春日版, on account of the close association between the Kōfukuji and the nearby Kasuga shrine, and a small number survive from the last century of the Heian period. All of them are of course Buddhist texts in Chinese.[11]

In the Kamakura period printing became more firmly established and spread to other parts of Japan. *Inbutsu* were still being produced for devotional reasons, and amongst them images of Amida and Jizō were becoming more common, but printing was in general increasingly concerned with the practical business of producing texts for reading. The Kōfukuji continued to be active in this respect, and was joined by other temples in and around Nara, such as the Saidaiji 西大寺, Tōdaiji and Daianji 大安寺. The monasteries of Mt Kōya also began to use printing for the reproduction of Shingon texts, including works by the Japanese monk Kūkai 空海, such as his *Sangō shiiki* 三教指帰, which was printed in 1253 and is the oldest extant 'Kōya edition', or Kōya-ban 高野版. Unlike most other temples, which only concerned themselves with printing sporadically, Mt Kōya remained active in the publication of Shingon works right up to the nineteenth century.

In the Kamakura period, if not before, the temples of Kyoto began to take up printing, and this marked the beginning of a period of some five hundred years during which Kyoto established itself as the centre of printing. Prominent amongst them in the thirteenth century was the Sen'yūji 泉涌寺: its founder, Shunjō, had visited China and had brought back with him some printed books, and under his influence the temple was particularly active in printing works relating to monastic

---

[11] Tokushi 91–98; Kimiya 1932: 42–3; Ōya 1923: 33–119; Gardner 1993: 791. For an example of devotional printing in 1165 on Mt Kōya, one of the few instances known outside Kyoto, see Fukakusa Nobuto 深草陳人, 'Kōyaban no kigen ni kansuru isshiryō' 高野版の起源に関する一史料, *Ryūkoku shidan* 龍谷史壇 2.2 (1930): 29–30.

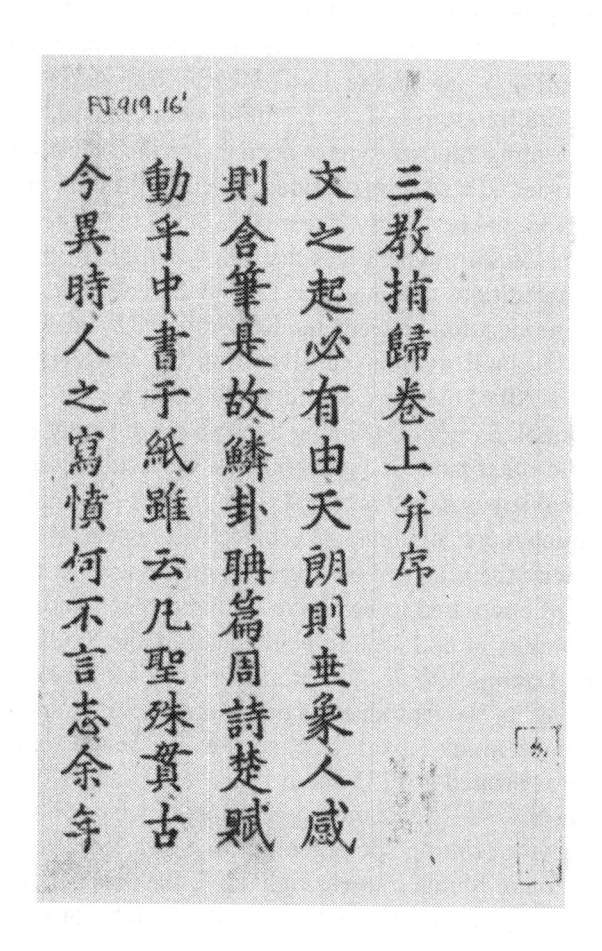

Fig. 8 The beginning of Kūkai's *Sangō shiiki* 三教指帰, a study of Buddhism, Daoism and Confucianism, in an edition printed on Mt Kōya in 1580. Three rectangular ownership seals are impressed in this copy: immediately underneath the first line of text is that of the doctor and sinologist Shibue Chūsai 渋江抽斎 (1805–58); underneath it is that of the sinologist and wide-ranging intellectual Tōjō Kindai 東条琴台 (1795–1878), and to the right is one reading Tamonritsuin 多聞律院, and probably belonging to a temple called Tamon'in in what is now Nara prefecture. Hayashi & Kornicki 1991: #260.

discipline, often producing them by making *kabusebori* facsimiles of imported Song editions. Other Kyoto temples which were associated with the Pure Land sect seem to have been responsible for the many editions of texts related to the doctrines of this sect, although most extant editions carry no indication of where they were printed. One of the earliest was the 1168 edition of *Ōjō yōshū* 往生要集, a treatise on the 'essentials for salvation' by the Japanese monk Genshin (942–1017), which is not extant but appears to have been the only work written by a Japanese author to be printed in the Heian period. Further, it is undoubtedly due to the populist nature of Pure Land Buddhism in Japan that the first book to be printed in Japanese was a book emanating from this sect, *Kurodani shōnin gotōroku* 黒谷上人語灯録 (1321). This was a collection of the sayings of Hōnen (1133–1212), who established the Pure Land sect in Japan, and it was printed in Japanese with *hiragana* and characters glossed with *furigana*, explicitly to make the tenets of the sect accessible to those unable to read Chinese. Later in the fourteenth century other works by Hōnen were also printed in Japanese, and also a single sheet containing a portrait of Hōnen together with a short text. Largely because of its proselytizing stance, the Pure Land sect was the most active in the Kamakura period in trying to reach a larger audience through the medium of print.[12]

The sect that probably had the most impact on printing in the late Kamakura and the Muromachi periods was Zen, and the editions produced by Zen temples are known as Gozan-ban 五山版. They were printed in the five Zen monasteries of Kyoto and the five of Kamakura, which had become the locus of political power with the foundation of the Kamakura shōgunate, and later they were also printed at certain other Zen temples. The earliest Gozan-ban known was printed at the Kenchōji 建長寺 in Kamakura in 1287, but other temples in Kamakura, such as the Gokurakuji 極楽寺, were also involved in printing at this time, and all five of the Kyoto Zen temples were active by the early fourteenth century. Given the distance between Zen and the more textual varieties of Buddhism, it may appear surprising that Zen temples had much use for printing, but

---

[12] Kawase Kazuma, 'Sen'yūjiban ni tsuite' 泉涌寺版について, *Shoshigaku* 書誌学 15 (1969): 1–12; Tōdō 1976: 26–7, 58–9, 63–5; *NKC* 2: 93, 101–2; Ono 1944: 438–442; Chibbett 1977: 55–6.

many of the texts printed, such as the recorded sayings of former Zen masters (*goroku* 語録), were intended for the training of novices or for the enlightenment of lay contemporaries and so had an educational role. And when they did print sūtras it appears that in many cases the printing was undertaken for devotional purposes at the behest of sponsors, rather than at the initiative of the monasteries themselves.[13]

The Gozan-ban consisted exclusively of texts in Chinese, mostly of Chinese authorship although a few were written by Japanese monks. They were also Chinese in appearance, for many were *kabusebori* facsimiles of Chinese editions. A further factor was the participation of Chinese immigrants in the production of Gozan-ban in Kyoto in the fourteenth century. In 1367 eight Chinese monks experienced in printing came to Japan at the request of a senior Japanese monk and settled in Saga, to the west of Kyoto, and by the end of the year they had already been involved in the printing of a Zen text. For the most part they seem to have worked as block-carvers and printers on behalf of Japanese monks and temples who were financing the production of books, and in many cases they left their names in the colophon, in the central fold, or in the margin. Some of them, particularly Yu Liangfu 俞良甫, who was involved in the printing of at least 13 works, undertook some printing at their own initiative and expense.[14]

Although most of the Gozan-ban are either Zen texts or other Buddhist texts, roughly a quarter are secular Chinese texts, and this reflects the role of Zen monks as the custodians of Chinese culture in Japan. It seems to have been in the fourteenth century that the first non-Buddhist works were printed in Japan, but by the end of the sixteenth a considerable number of secular Chinese texts had been printed, mostly by Zen temples. The first was *Hanshan shi* 寒山詩 (J. *Kanzan shi*), a collection of the poems of the Tang-dynasty monk Hanshan, which was printed in 1325 in a *kabusebori* facsimile of a Southern Song edition. Later in that century Shun'oku Myōha 春屋妙葩, who was a monk at the Tenryūji 天龍寺 in Kyoto and was

---

[13] Seki Yasushi 関靖 and Kumahara Masao 熊原政男, *Kanazawa Bunkobon no kenkyū* 金沢文庫本之研究, *NSGT* 19 (1981): 399–405; Gardner 1993: 733–5; Kawase 1970: 5–8, etc.; Kawase 1945: 1582–9.

[14] Kawase 1970: 1.142–60; *NKC* 1: 65–75.

responsible for the printing of at least 18 works, produced three collections of Yuan dynasty literature, all again *kabusebori* versions of Yuan editions. The first canonical Chinese work to be printed was the Confucian *Analects*, which was first printed in Sakai in 1364 with the commentary of the third-century Chinese scholar He Yan 何晏. It appears that the printing blocks for this edition were destroyed in the Sakai fire of 1399, for new blocks were later prepared and these were used to continue producing copies until the end of the sixteenth century.[15]

Over the succeeding two centuries the output of secular Chinese works was dominated by three categories: there were the canonical texts, although there were surprisingly few editions of the *Four Books* of Confucianism; there were dictionaries and other sinological reference works; and there were poetical works. The last included recent poetry composed by monks and the works of some of the major poets of the Tang and Song dynasties as well as practical guides to poetry composition, such as *Shi xue da cheng* 詩学大成 (J. *Shigaku taisei*), a Yuan dynasty work which was published in Japan in the fourteenth century, again a *kabusebori* version of a Yuan edition. In addition to these were some Chinese medical texts, of which the first was the Ming *Yi shu da quan* 医書大全 (J. *Isho taizen*), which was printed in 1528. Not all the secular works were published by Zen monasteries, but a quarter of all the Gozan-ban were secular works, and were being printed in Japan for the first time. Without the interest of the Japanese Zen monastic community in secular Chinese culture, especially Confucianism and poetry, it is doubtful if they would have been printed at all.[16]

Unlike the sinological texts published in the succeeding Tokugawa period, almost all these secular Chinese texts were published in editions consisting of the 'raw' Chinese without any of the reading marks (*kunten*) making it possible for Japanese readers to construe Chinese as if it were Japanese. Many surviving copies, however, have reading marks added by hand, sometimes by contemporaries and sometimes by later scholars in the Tokugawa period. It is also evident from these surviving copies that in many cases the blocks were used to

---

[15] *NKC* 1: 60, 63–5; Kawase 1970:1.91–3, 2.35-6; Gardner 1993: 17–20; Christie's 1988: 104–5.

[16] *NKC* 1: 89–90; Ōe 1935: 123ff.

print copies over a long period of time; in some cases wear and tear on the blocks has necessitated the preparation of *kabusebori* blocks to replace the defective ones. This indicates a buoyant demand for printed copies of these texts in the Muromachi period, even though only a few copies of each work have survived to the present day.[17]

A few works of Japanese authorship were printed during the Kamakura and Muromachi periods, almost all of them written in Chinese. Some have been mentioned above, but the most widely circulated of these printed Japanese texts was probably *Ōjō yōshū* (see above): at least nine editions of this are known to have been produced before 1600, of which the edition printed in 1253 survives in many copies.[18]

Printing in the centuries before 1600 was dominated by Buddhist institutions and it was used to print mostly Buddhist texts in Chinese. It was not centralized, however, and one characteristic of this period is the geographical diffusion, for in addition to the temples of Kyoto, Nara, Mt Kōya and Kamakura, some other provincial temples also engaged in printing, such as the Negoroji 根来寺 in the province of Kii, which printed many titles from the fourteenth to the sixteenth centuries. It was also in a provincial temple, the Chōrakuji 長楽寺 in Kōzuke, that the oldest extant printed illustration in Japan was produced in 1239 as the frontispiece to a sūtra. In addition to temples, some daimyō and other provincial figures also undertook printing: one example is the Satsuma edition of *Da xue zhang ju* 大学章句, Zhu Xi's commentary on the *Da xue*, which was printed at Kagoshima in 1481 and was the first edition of this work to be printed in Japan.[19]

It is evident that by the beginning of the sixteenth century printing was well established in Japan for the production of books to read, and that it was not yet subject to any external controls. But it was not yet commercial, and although some at least of the texts printed may have been made available for purchase, we know as yet very little

---

[17] For examples of reading marks added by hand in the Muromachi period and of later printings with replaced pages (*hokokuchō* 補刻丁), see 'Iwasaki Bunko kichōsho shoshi kaidai 4' 岩崎文庫貴重書書志解題 (四), *Tōyō Bunko shohō* 東洋文庫書報 19 (1987): 6, 8, 12–13.

[18] Nishimura Keishō 1987: 42–4.

[19] Mizuhara Gyōei 水原堯栄, 'Negoroban' 根来版, *Shoshigaku* 1.6 (1933): 1–10; Gardner 1990; on illustrations see Kawase 1970: 12–27, Ishida Mosaku, *Kodai hanga* 古代版画 (Kōdansha, 1961), and Chibbett 1977: 97–108. Ono 1944: 456–61.

about the contemporary book trade or about the mechanisms whereby these books circulated in pre-Tokugawa Japan.

BIBLIOGRAPHY

For surveys of printing in this period see Chibbett 1977: 39–60, Gardner 1990, and *NKC* 2: 89–121; for descriptions and illustrations of the fine collection in the British Library see Gardner 1993. For good collections of illustrations, see Kawase Kazuma, *Ishii Sekisuiken bunko zenpon shomoku* 石井積翠軒文庫善本書目, 2 vols (Ishii Mituso, 1942); Wada Tsunashirō 1918; Ishida Mosaku 1952; Ōya 1926. On the printing of non-Buddhist works, see *NKC* 1: 55–97. On Kasuga-ban see Ōya Tokujō, 'Kasugaban chōzōkō' 春日板雕造攷, originally published in 1940 and now contained in *Bukkyō kohangyō no kenkyū* 仏教古板経の研究, Ōya Tokujō chosaku senshū 9 (Kokusho Kankōkai, 1988), 212–72, and Ōya 1923; on Kōya-ban, Mizuhara 1932 and Mizuhara Gyōei, *Kōyaban eisui* 高野版英萃 (Kyoto: Dōmeisha, 1981; reprint of 1932 edition); on Gozan-ban, Kawase 1970, of which the second volume includes many illustrations; on the printing of the *Analects*, Nagata Tomisaku 長田富作, *Shōheiban Rongo no kenkyū* 正平版論語之研究 (Osaka: Dōjinkai, 1934); on editions of the *Lotus sūtra*, Kabutogi Shōkō 兜木正亨, *Hokke hangyō no kenkyū* 法華版経の研究 (Daitō Shuppansha, 1982).

4.2 MOVABLE TYPE: THE EARLY PHASE

4.2.1 *The Jesuit mission press*

In the 1540s and 1550s Francis Xavier had had some of his works translated into Japanese and had evidently intended to have them printed, but it was not until 1590, when Alessandro Valignano brought a printing press to Japan for the use of his fellow Jesuit missionaries, that the Jesuits were actually able to undertake printing in Japan. This press was first installed in the Jesuit college at Kazusa before being moved to Amakusa and later Nagasaki, but it appears that there were other presses used by the Jesuits in Japan too, such as the one in Kyoto which was used to print a Japanese translation of *Contemptus mundi* in 1610. In addition to the European printing press, Valignano also brought back a Japanese known only as Constantino Dourado, who had studied printing in Lisbon and had undertaken some printing at Goa, and it was probably this Dourado who undertook some of the initial printing work of the mission.[20]

Fewer than 40 works printed by the Jesuits in Japan have survived, and some of them in only a single copy. How many copies were printed is unknown, but many must have been destroyed when the persecutions in the seventeenth century made it dangerous to be a Christian, and we know that in 1626 'a mountain of books' belonging to the mission was burnt by the Japanese authorities in Nagasaki. However, the letters and records of the Jesuits refer to many other works and it is likely that as many as 100 titles were printed before the persecutions silenced the press.[21]

The first work printed at Kazusa may have been a church calendar in Japanese: one was certainly in existence by 1590 or early 1591, and it appears that they were produced annually at least until 1618, although not one copy has survived. From this it is clear that soon after the arrival of the press a Japanese font was cast, probably consisting of the *katakana* syllabary; to that was added later a *hiragana* syllabary and some characters. The press operated in the usual European fashion, with the type being impressed onto the paper, and it was used to print a variety of works for the use both of the missionaries and their students. For the students, for example, there were texts in Latin, such as some of Cicero's speeches and some Virgil as well as some devotional works. Devotional works were also printed in Japanese script and in romanized Japanese transcription, but the secular works are of particular interest. These included part of the *Heike monogatari* in an adapted and romanized version, which was produced at Amakusa in 1592 and was the first work of Japanese literature ever to be printed in Japan, and Aesop's *Fables*, translated into romanized Japanese; these were probably intended to assist the Jesuits in their language study, as were also an edition of the *Rakuyōshū*, a

---

[20] Laures 1940: 2, 5–6; Tenri Toshokan 1973: 39–40.
[21] Laures 1940: 60. For references to books which have not survived see Laures 1940: 55–63, and Ohara Satoru 尾原悟, 'Kirishitanban ni tsuite - Iezusukai Nihon nenpō o chūshin ni' キリシタン版についてーイエズス会日本年報を中心に, *Jōchi shigaku* 28 (1983): 50–86, 29 (1984): 68–71, 31 (1986): 1–15, 32 (1987): 1–15. On recent discoveries see Yagi Sōichi 八木壯一, 'Shinhakken no kirishitanban Nabarusu no zange' 新発見のきりしたん版「ナバルスのざんげ」, *Nihon kosho tsūshin* 682 (1986): 2–4, and Angela Dillon Bussi, 'Due nuovi esemplari di edizioni cinquecentine della missione gesuitica in Estremo Oriente', *La bibliofilia* 82 (1980): 23–31.

Chinese-Japanese dictionary, and a dictionary and grammar of Japanese by the scholar Rodrigues (1561–1633).[22]

In spite of the intense activity over a small span of years, the influence of the Jesuit publications on printing in Japan seems to have been slight. This is partly because of the association with Christianity and partly because the press operated for the most part in Kyushu, far from the centres of power and patronage. Shinmura Izuru argues that the use of the *hiragana* syllabary in some of the Jesuit publications may have stimulated the development of printing Japanese with *hiragana* in the early decades of the seventeenth century, but there is no evidence to support this view, and it is dependent certain assumptions about the likely circulation of Jesuit publications beyond Kyushu.[23] It seems therefore that it was the Korean tradition of movable type that proved far more influential on printing in Japan, for the techniques imported from Korea were taken up first by successive emperors and political leaders and then by private and commercial publishers in the seventeenth century.

BIBLIOGRAPHY

Laures 1940; Tenri Toshokan 1973; Adriana Boscaro, 'I Gesuiti e gli inizi della stampa Cristiana in Asia Orientale', L. Lanciotti, ed., *Orientalia Venetiana I* (Firenze: Olschki, 1984), 43–67; Ernest Mason Satow; *The Jesuit Mission Press in Japan 1591–1610* (privately printed, 1888); *Tenri Toshokanzō kirishitanban shūsei kaisetsu* 天理図書館蔵きりしたん版集成解説 (Tenri: Tenri Daigaku Shuppanbu, 1976); Diego Pacheco 1971, 'Diego de Mesquita, SJ, and the Jesuit Mission Press', *MN* 26 (1971): 431-43; Ebisawa Arimichi 海老沢有道, 'Amakusa kirishitanban shoshi' 天草キリシタン版書誌, *Ajia bunka kenkyū* 10 (1978): 13–45. For a convenient list of extant copies and a guide to facsimiles see the table in *KD* 4: 438–9.

---

[22] Laures 1940: 55–6.
[23] 'Katsuji insatsujutsu no denrai' 活字印刷術の伝来, in *Shinmura Izuru zenshū* 新村出全集, 15 vols (Chikuma Shobō, 1972–3), 5: 111–25.

4.2.2 *Korean movable type*

Although it appears that movable type was first developed in China in the tenth century in the form of ceramic type and subsequently used on a very limited scale in the form of wooden type, this had no discernible influence on printing in Japan.[24] The independent Korean tradition of printing with movable type, however, which reached Japan in the late sixteenth century, had a decisive impact, and it had the additional effect of secularizing the use of print in Japan.

The use of metallic movable type in Korea can be safely traced back to the early thirteenth century, and in 1392 the court established a Printing Office (書籍院 *sŏjŏkwŏn*) for type-casting and the publication of books. The titles of some books printed in the thirteenth century are known but no printed copies are extant and the earliest surviving books printed with movable type date from the late fourteenth century. As is well known, these antedate the products of Gutenberg's press by several decades, and mark the beginning of typography as a means of publishing books in East Asia. What is not so clear is the reason for turning to typography: it has been suggested that a shortage of wood suitable for blockprinting was a factor, but in fact block printing continued to be practised alongside typography. In any event, the particular Korean contribution to typography was undoubtedly the invention of a means of casting metallic type: thanks to a contemporary description by Sŏng Hyŏn (1436–1509) we know some of the details of this process in the form in which it reached Japan. At the same time, from around the late fourteenth century Korean printers were also making use of wooden movable type, and this too was a technique that was adopted and extensively used in Japan during the seventeenth century.[25]

The year in which the Printing Office was established, 1392, was the year in which the Yi dynasty came to power and it is particularly significant that the new régime privileged Confucianism over Buddhism, for the preponderance of titles printed by the Office were secular works in Chinese, mostly Confucian texts. Consequently, when the Korean typographic tradition was transmitted to Japan it was predominantly secular in nature, and as such contrasted with the

---

[24] Tsien 1985: 201–3.
[25] Son 1971: 37–9; Son 1987: 128–9, 148–9; Ch'ŏn 1976: 79–112, 123–7.

Buddhist domination of blockprinting in Japan. This 'transmission' to Japan was effected forcibly, during the invasion of the Korean peninsula undertaken by Toyotomi Hideyoshi in the closing years of the sixteenth century; in the course of it large numbers of printed books were looted, and printing type was removed from the Printing Office and taken to Japan. No contemporary accounts of the looting are extant, but the survival in Japan of large numbers of books taken from Korea at this time is some indication of its extent (§7.1.2). Further, it appears that Korean type was immediately put to use to print the text of the supposed 'old' version of the *Xiao jing* or *Classic of Filial Piety* (*Kobun kōkyō* 古文孝経), in 1593, although no copies of this appear to have survived. In 1597, in the postface to another work printed in Japan with movable type, a monk who was present at Hideyoshi's headquarters acknowledged that typography in Japan had come from Korea. It is not clear whether any Korean printing artisans came to Japan as well as a result of the invasion, but in any event the impact on Japan of Korean typography, both technologically and intellectually, was far greater than that of the Jesuit Mission Press, principally because the imported Korean typography was much closer to the centres of power in Japan than the increasingly precarious Jesuit missions.[26]

BIBLIOGRAPHY

On typography in Korea see Ch'ŏn 1976; Son 1987; Peter H. Lee, ed., *Sourcebook of Korean civilization*, vol 1 'From early times to the sixteenth century' (New York: Columbia University Press, 1993), 536–9; and Kim Tujong 金斗鍾, *Hanguk koinswae kisulsa* 韓国古印刷技術史 (Seoul: T'amgudang, 1974). On the looting of Korean books by Hideyoshi's armies see Yi Hongjik 1954: 147–65 and Yi Chun'gil 1986: 207–22. On the impact of Korean typography on Japan see Kawase 1967: 1.151–2, 178.

4.2.3 *Japanese movable type*

The printing equipment and type looted from Korea by Hideyoshi's troops was presented to emperor Go-Yōzei and used, as mentioned above, to print the *Xiao jing* in 1593. This inaugurated a period of

---

[26] Son 1987: 165; Kawase 1967: 151–2, 178.

some 50 years in which movable type was used extensively for the production of books, and these are known collectively as *kokatsujiban* 古活字版 (old movable-type editions). It should be remembered, however, that blockprinting was by no means completely eclipsed during those 50 years and that blockprinted books continued to be produced, especially if they were extensively illustrated or were *kabusebori* facsimiles of Chinese editions, such as the 36-volume set of the Ming herbal *Ben cao gang mu* 本草綱目 (J. *Honzō kōmoku*), which had a profound impact on the development of botanical and pharmaceutical knowledge in Japan and was published in 1637 in a facsimile of a late sixteenth-century Chinese edition.[27]

Soon after 1593 Go-Yōzei had a font of wooden type cut and this was used by him and by his successor, Go-Mizunoo, to print a number of works that are now known as *chokuhan* 勅版, 'imperial editions'. What is significant about these works, all printed between 1595 and 1621 is that they are all secular. Most of them are Chinese, and include a set of the *Four Books* of the Confucian tradition, which were printed together for the first time in 1599, but in the same year the beginning sections of the *Nihon shoki*, a chronicle of Japan compiled in the eighth century, were also printed, again for the first time.[28]

During these same years, Tokugawa Ieyasu, who was to become the *de facto* ruler of Japan in 1600 and inaugurated what became the Tokugawa Bakufu in 1603, was also taking an interest in printing. His interest in books was of long standing (§9.2.1), but even before the decisive battle of Sekigahara in 1600 he had 100,000 pieces of wooden type cut. Between 1599 and 1606 these were used to print a number of works at Fushimi, south of Kyoto. Except for the *Azuma kagami* 吾妻鏡 (see below), these were all secular Chinese texts and they were produced under the direction of San'yō (1548–1612), the head of the academy known as the Ashikaga Gakkō. Some years later, after his retirement to Suruga, Ieyasu instructed his adviser Hayashi Razan, later the founder of what turned into the Bakufu Academy, to undertake some printing using bronze type. This was probably the type prepared for emperor Go-Yōzei earlier, but some extra type was cast by Korean immigrants, and it was used to print

---

[27] On blockprinted books in the early seventeenth century see Okuno 1982.
[28] Gardner 1993: #19; Kawase 1967: 177–97.

two Chinese texts in Suruga in 1615–6.[29]

Although many secular works were now being printed, it should not be supposed that movable type ended the close association between Buddhist texts and printing, for throughout the seventeenth century they constituted an important sector of the market (§4.3.4). Indeed, a number of temples, some of which already had a history of blockprinting, experimented with movable type to print mostly Buddhist works in the late sixteenth and early seventeenth centuries, and the oldest dated book printed with movable type is in fact *Tiantai si jiao yi ji jie* 天台四教儀集解 (J. *Tendai shikyōgi shūge*), a Song commentary on a Tendai Buddhist text, which was printed at the Honkokuji in Kyoto in 1595. Several other temples in Kyoto engaged in printing, especially the Yōhōji 要法寺, and further afield the temples on Mt Hiei and Mt Kōya and two temples in the province of Shimōsa all had facilities for printing with movable type at their disposal. The Mt Hiei temples were particularly active, and one book published in 1626 contains a list of 38 other titles, which are presumed to have been published on Mt Hiei. In some cases, such as the publications produced by the Honnōji in Kyoto, there is evidence that temples were collaborating with local printing establishments run by laymen, presumably on a commercial basis, and this is the first sign of a transition from printing under patronage to commercial printing by city residents.[30]

An important question about the movable-type editions printed by emperors, political leaders and temples is what happened to the copies that were printed. In some cases we know from references in the colophon that only a hundred copies were printed, but we do not know how and to whom they were distributed, nor do we know if any found their way onto the market, such as it was. However, it is known that a number of private individuals also took to printing at this time, including several doctors, such as Oze Hoan (1564–1640), who printed four Chinese medical works in 1596–97, and in these cases it is probable that while some copies may have been privately distributed others became available from booksellers.[31]

The most significant private printing with movable type was that

---

[29] Kawase 1967: 208–31; Gardner 1993: #21–2, 26, 57–8, 96–7; Christie's 1988: 133–5.
[30] Kawase 1967: 255–328 (especially 281, 305–7); Tōdō 1976: 153–67.
[31] Kawase 1967: 329–36.

of the so-called Sagabon 嵯峨本, the books printed between 1599 and c1610 in Saga, Kyoto. These were a product of the collaboration between Hon'ami Kōetsu, a man of protean talents who was the outstanding calligrapher of his day as well as a renowned maker of pottery for the tea ceremony and lacquerware maker, and Suminokura Soan (1571–1632), a merchant intellectual. It is not clear what roles each played, but Kōetsu undoubtedly provided the calligraphy from which the wooden type was cut, and presumably the artistic direction as well, while Soan probably provided the finance and organized the printing. The extensive use of ligatures, enabling the print to represent the flow of calligraphy, together with the inclusion of illustrations and the use in some cases of fine papers, coloured, patterned and decorated with mica, resulted in books of great beauty. The Sagabon consist almost entirely of Japanese texts, particularly *Ise monogatari*, which was the first secular Japanese book to be illustrated and which survives in many variant editions, indicating that a considerable number of copies were printed. Although they may never have been put on sale and may not have been 'published' in the commercial sense, the Sagabon are significant for having established the importance of including illustrations in printed Japanese texts, which became the norm for the rest of the Tokugawa period, and for the use of *kana*. Soon after the introduction of movable type, wooden fonts of type had been cut not only for characters but also for both *katakana* and *hiragana* and were being put to ever greater use as the attention of printers turned to Japanese texts.[32]

Although it had been mostly Chinese secular works that were printed in the initial phase of movable type, by the 1620s large numbers of Japanese texts had been or were being printed, some in the form of Sagabon. These included the *Man'yōshū*, a poetic anthology compiled in the eighth-century; the prose literature of the Heian period, such as the *Tale of Genji*, *Makura no sōshi* and many other works; and the war tales, such as *Heike monogatari* and *Taiheiki*. These editions were important in that they fixed in print and established the forms in which these texts were to circulate for the rest of the

---

[32] For colour illustrations of some Sagabon, see Christie's 1988: 122–27, Kawase 1967: 410–76, and *OATD* 191. On Soan, see Hayashiya Tatsusaburō 林屋辰三郎, *Suminokura Soan* (Asahi Shinbunsha, 1978). A hitherto unrecorded variant of *Ise monogatari* is in Cambridge University Library: Hayashi & Kornicki 1991: #543.

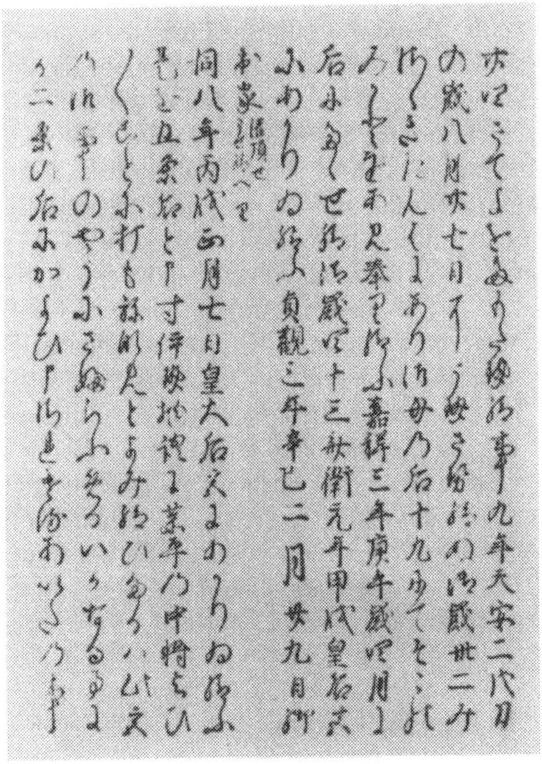

Fig. 9 A movable-type edition of the *Ōkagami* 大かがみ [Great mirror] published in the early years of the seventeenth century without a colophon: Hayashi & Kornicki 1991: #578.

Tokugawa period. But it was not only the classics that were printed, for the gap between composition and printing was narrowing and a number of works written in the 1620s were soon published, including prose fiction like *Urami no suke* 恨の介, and as many as six editions of *Isoho monogatari* 伊曽保物語 (based on Aesop's *Fables*). The growing immediacy is also evident from *Kan'ei gyōkōki*, which is an illustrated account of emperor Go-Mizunoo's procession to Nijō castle in Kyoto on 1626.9.6 and was published later the same year. Most of these Japanese works carry neither date nor publisher, but those that do have colophons carry what are evidently the names of merchant publishers. Apart from the Sagabon, they were mostly, it seems, put out by commercial publishers and it is with these Japanese works, then, that printing for the market appears to have begun (§5.1.1).[33]

Movable-type printing had effectively come to an end by the 1650s, although it was later to be revived at the end of the eighteenth century (§4.4.1). While the technologies imported from Korea and Europe were both based on metallic type, wooden type was much more widely used in Japan, probably because of the cost involved in preparing a huge font of characters in bronze and the technological difficulty of casting the type. The abandonment of this technology and the reversion to blockprinting raises difficult questions. Is this a case of 'technological lock-in', whereby an 'established but inferior technology continues to dominate because of secondary advantages, that derive from the consequences of its prior establishment?' Blockprinting was certainly well-established before the introduction of typography, but it is by no means obvious that it was inferior in all respects.[34]

Although the Sagabon had shown that movable type was capable of producing aesthetically satisfying books, the calligraphic variety that was simple to achieve with wood-blocks was only possible if new fonts of type were to be cut in different calligraphic styles, and of course each font had to consist of a large number of pieces to

---

[33] Kawase 1967: 507–626; on *Kan'ei gyōkōki* see Kawase 1967: 623–5, 945, and Kokuritsu Kokkai Toshokan 1989: 188–91.

[34] Mark Elvin and Su Ninghu, 'Engineering the sea: hydraulic systems and pre-modern technological lock-in in the Harngzhou Bay area, circa 1000–1800', in Itō Shuntarō and Yasuda Hoshinori, eds, *Nature and humankind in the age of environmental crisis* (Kyoto: International Research Center for Japanese Studies, 1992), 79–137 (quote on p. 134).

accommodate all the Chinese characters that would be needed. Inserting reading marks (*kunten*) in Chinese texts was again much easier in the case of blockprinted books, and, even more importantly, blockprinting proved better able to handle the growing market for books in the seventeenth century: reprinting movable-type books required resetting the type, while blockprinting simply required taking the blocks out of storage. Consider, for example, the seventeenth-century editions of *Azuma kagami*, a thirteenth-century account of the foundation of the Kamakura Bakufu. In 1605 Tokugawa Ieyasu had this text printed for the first time at Fushimi and there were two further movable-type editions in the early seventeenth century: thus type was set up to print *Azuma kagami* three times in about 20 years. In 1626 a blockprinted edition was published with reading marks, and these blocks were used to print up to and beyond 1661, and in 1668 a separate *hiragana* version was also published. It is evident that there was a continuing and growing market for *Azuma kagami* which the same set of blocks was able to satisfy for more than forty years. Similarly, in the case of *Kan'ei gyōkōki* and many other works mentioned above, blockprinted editions replaced the movable-type ones, in some cases simply by preparing *kabusebori* facsimiles of the latter, and the printing blocks for the new editions remained in use for decades.[35]

The use of movable type by two emperors and especially Ieyasu to print secular Chinese and Japanese works served to liberate print from the Buddhist context which had dominated it for centuries, and the subsequent use by merchant publishers gave texts in Japanese a place in the print culture of Japan that they had not enjoyed before. However, as commercial publishers took over from the patronage arrangements of the early part of the century, they reverted to blockprinting in order the better to respond to the demands of the market, and it is this familiar technology which governed the production of books for the remainder of the Tokugawa period.

BIBLIOGRAPHY

For illustrations see Kokuritsu Kokkai Toshokan 1989, Tenri Toshokan 1961, Gardner 1993, and Kawase Kazuma, *Sagabon zukō* 嵯峨本図考

---

[35] *ARI* 3: 361–75; Kawase 1967: 627–30.

(Isseidō, 1932). Kawase 1967 is the authority on early movable-type books. In English see Chibbett 1977: 61–78, and the English summary at the back of vol. 2 of Kawase 1967.

4.3 BLOCKPRINTING IN THE TOKUGAWA AND EARLY MEIJI PERIODS

4.3.1 *Commercial publishing*

As described in the previous section, commercial publishers in Kyoto in the early seventeenth century made extensive use of movable type before reverting around the middle of the century to blockprinting. The structure and organization of the book trade will be covered in the next chapter; here the focus will be on the potential and limitations of blockprinting and on what was published.

The blockprinting process itself changed little in the Tokugawa period and essentially built on what was already a well-established tradition. The use of illustration became much more widespread, and indeed an expected feature of works of fiction, and by the end of the seventeenth century books consisting almost entirely of visual matter were being published. The one major development was that of colour printing using multiple blocks, which evolved in the seventeenth century on a modest scale, and from the middle of the eighteenth was employed more and more extensively in published books for illustrations using a multiplicity of colours (§2.4). In the nineteenth century colour illustrations increasingly began to appear even in the cheaper genres of fiction, and colour printing was also used for the production of picture cover titles (*edaisen* 絵題簽) for pasting on the covers of some of those cheaper genres.[36]

Two other techniques were developed for printing books of calligraphic samples. One was *hidarihan* 左り版 or *inkokubon* 陰刻本, in which the relationship between the text and the surround was reversed so that it was the text that was carved away from the blocks with the result that the text appeared as white against a black background, like a rubbing of an incised inscription. This was in use

---

[36] On illustrations and picture books see Nakada 1950, Hillier 1988, and D. B. Waterhouse, *Harunobu and his age: the development of colour printing in Japan* (London: British Museum, 1964).

from the early seventeenth century onwards, but around 1700 a new technique came into use, *shōmenzuri* 正面摺り, which involved in effect taking a rubbing from the blocks rather than applying ink to them in the usual way, and which was apparently thought to produce a superior impression of the flow of the calligraphy.[37]

What was particularly different about blockprinting in the Tokugawa period, then, was not so much the techniques as the fact of its transformation into a series of commercial operations. These were undertaken with increasing specialization as block-carvers, printers, and binders developed their skills to the point that in some cases their names were given in the colophons of books they had produced. Further, once publishing became a commercial operation and fostered a market which it sought to supply with books, the number of copies printed ceased to be arbitrary and began to be influenced by perceptions and evidence of demand. This had already happened in the case of some of the movable-type books, which had appeared in several successive editions as their publishers tried to make more copies available to a market that was ready to take them.

This raises the question of print runs and the printing capacity of wooden printing blocks. Here it is important to note first of all that the kind of wood used is crucial, for softer woods were easier to carve but quicker to wear down, and the wood most commonly used in the Tokugawa period was the wild cherry, which was difficult to carve but which could be used to print many more copies. However, there is unfortunately no hard evidence concerning the numbers of copies of a text that could be printed from wood blocks, although Hamada Keisuke's estimate of 8,000 as a maximum is probably near the mark. In the seventeenth century, however, it seems likely that even popular works were not achieving print-runs of that magnitude. It is recorded in a contemporary work, for example, that *Kiyomizu monogatari* 清水物語 (1638), a best-seller in its day, sold between two and three thousand copies, and the fact that the blocks of many seventeenth-century books were still being used in the eighteenth or even the nineteenth centuries without needing to be renewed is further evidence of this. By the nineteenth century, however, the situation was different. Kyokutei Bakin, who was unusually interested in the process of publishing and is generally reliable, wrote in 1823 that a

---

[37] Nakano 1995: 29–30, 37–8.

work of light fiction published that year, *Moroshigure momiji no aigasa* 諸時雨紅葉合傘, had sold 18,000 copies in three months, and if this is true then it must be supposed that two if not three sets of blocks were used, presumably relying on the *kabusebori* technique to prepare the second and third sets. Another best-seller by the standards of the day was Ryūtei Tanehiko's *Inaka Genji*, which is said by a contemporary to have sold more than 10,000 copies. In the nineteenth century it seems that sales of the lighter and cheaper genres of fiction were in the order of 6,000 over several months, but the more expensive genres, particularly the historical novels for which Bakin himself was famous, sold much more slowly, perhaps a couple of hundred a year.[38]

The flexibility of blockprinting was exploited in a variety of ways in the Tokugawa period. Illustrations were manipulated on the page with or without accompanying text; characters were glossed with *furigana*, and Chinese texts customarily had reading marks added throughout; commentary and notes were added either in the form of doubled columns of smaller characters or they made use of the space outside the margins of the text; and the techniques of *kabusebori* and *umeki* (§2.3) were extensively used to extend the lives of books which were suffering from worn printing blocks in the one case and in the other either to make alterations to a text or to bring it up to date. Further, the possibility for calligraphic variation was exploited with the result that the calligraphic quality of the printed text became a token of the publisher's, and to a lesser extent the author's, estimate of the demands, and the capacity for aesthetic appreciation, of particular audiences.

The fragmentation of the market for books had indeed already begun in the early seventeenth century with the publication of Japanese and secular Chinese books, as mentioned in the previous section. The narrowing of the gap between writing and printing, which resulted in the publication of works in the year in which they were written from as early as 1626, created a new market for current rather than classical works in Japanese, and the remainder of the Tokugawa period saw an increasing diversity of publications and the development

---

[38] *Gion monogatari* 祇園物語, in *(Kinsei bungaku mikanbon sōsho) Kanazōshi-hen* (近世文学未刊本叢書) 仮名草子篇 (Tanba: Yōtokusha, 1947), 51; Hamada 1953: 23–7.

of niche markets. The market for prose literature came to maturity in the late seventeenth century, particularly with Ihara Saikaku's fictions based on the sexual possibilities and economic realities of the lives of the merchant classes in Osaka. Prose dominated literary publishing for the remainder of the Tokugawa period, although the continuing demand for, and publication of, playbooks and poetry collections should not be underestimated. Until the end of the eighteenth century it was the publishers of Kyoto and Osaka that controlled this market and were the source of fiction consumed in Edo and elsewhere, but the emergence of entrepreneurial publishers like Tsutaya Jūzaburō and the development of new genres of fiction in Edo in the 1780s and 1790s, which daringly satirized official life or treated the world of the Yoshiwara pleasure quarter of Edo with only transparent disguises, signalled a shift to Edo. In the nineteenth century it was in Edo that fiction was written and produced and new Edo genres, such as the *ninjōbon* pioneered by Tamenaga Shunsui and the *yomihon* of Kyokutei Bakin and Santō Kyōden, exported the tastes, fashions, language and outlook of Edo to the rest of Japan. But this is only to consider the literary market, which has been relatively well explored, and it is important to keep in mind that prose literature lived in a context in which there were buoyant markets for illustrated books (*ehon*), for dictionaries and household encyclopedias (*setsuyōshū*), for sinological texts of varying degrees of difficulty, for Buddhist texts, and for a multitude of other kinds of books. The place of prose literature in all this has undoubtedly been exaggerated: the writers, illustrators, publishers and readers of the Edo genres of fiction were all involved in the public world of print in several different ways and capacities, and it is a distortion to detach them from that world with an exclusive focus on the fictional literature.[39]

By the early nineteenth century, and in many cases well before that, niche markets existed in cookbooks, books on flower arrangement, medical books, mathematical treatises, *senryū* poetry, popular educational works, and so on, and some publishers began to describe themselves as specialists in one or another niche market (§5.1.1) or to issue specialist catalogues.[40] Another very substantial market,

---

[39] *Hanpon* (1990) is a useful visual exploration of the varieties of blockprinted books, but with a bias in favour of Japanese prose literature and illustrated books.

[40] For examples of specialist catalogues see Asakura 1983: 1.40–41, 98–100, 104–5, 216–21, 3.214–5, etc.

which catered to the growing need and demand for literacy, was that for the popular educational works known as *ōraimono* 往来物. These have had a poor survival rate and have hitherto been treated in a bibliographically cavalier manner, but it is clear that they were produced in many parts of Japan for local use and that by the early nineteenth century they were a substantial part of the market for print.[41]

Print culture in the Tokugawa period matured rapidly into a phenomenon with all the complexity and variety that is customarily associated with only the most advanced Western countries before modern times. Nunn has attempted to quantify the output using samples of data taken from *Kokusho sōmokuroku* and concluded that in both the first and second halves of the period more than 3,000 titles were published on average each year. There are problems here with the word 'published', for, as explained in the Appendix below, the criteria used in *Kokusho sōmokuroku* are far from ideal. However, it is, if anything, likely that his estimate is too low, for *Kokusho sōmokuroku* does not include reprints of Chinese or Buddhist works, of which there were huge quantities as well (§4.3.4).[42]

Well in excess of 90% of the publications of the Tokugawa period were commercially produced, and the combined output of official and private publishing, which will be considered in the subsequent sections, was by comparison small both in terms of numbers of titles and in terms of numbers of copies. Further, while the range of subject matter covered by commercial publishing was extensive, this was not true of other forms of publishing. The books published by the Bakufu and the domains were mostly sinological, although some scientific works were also published in the middle of the nineteenth century, and private publishing was limited to certain very specific categories of book. Literary works were almost entirely within the

---

[41] On *ōraimono* see Okamura Kintarō 岡村金太郎, *Ōraimono bunrui mokuroku* 往来物分類目録 (Keimeikai Jimusho, 1925), Ishikawa Ken 石川謙, *Joshiyō ōraimono bunrui mokuroku - Edo jidai ni okeru joshiyō shotō kyōkasho no hattatsu* 女子用往来物分類目録－江戸時代に於ける女子用初等教科書の発達 (Dainihon Yūbenkai Kōdansha, 1946), and L. I. Okazaki-Ward, 'Women and their education in the Tokugawa period of Japan', unpublished M.Phil thesis (Centre for Japanese Studies, University of Sheffield, 1993). For texts see Ishikawa Matsutarō 石川松太郎, *Ōraimono taikei* 往来物大系, 100 vols (Ōzorasha 1992-1994).

[42] Nunn: 1969: 118.

domain of commercial publishing, with the exception of the collections produced by some poetry groups specialising in *haikai* or *waka* poetry, and works produced by alternative intellectual traditions such as Kokugaku may have initially been privately published but often passed into the public domain and were then commercially distributed (§4.3.3). Thus the print society of the Tokugawa period was one in which the commercial setting was dominant. Given the context of guilds and self-regulation in which commercial publishing operated, it may well be that this dominance exerted its own influence on the political complexion of what was printed, particularly in view of the fact that some politically doubtful books were privately printed with wooden movable type, which took them right out of the world of commercial blockprinting, which tended to avoid politically sensitive matters (§4.4.1).

In the Meiji period, in spite of the introduction of Western-style movable-type technology, blockprinting continued to dominate the market until the 1880s, except in the case of newspapers, which rapidly turned to movable type (§2.5, 4.4.2). This is evident from the published catalogues of the Meiji holdings of the National Diet Library, which reveal that many new works were first published in the Meiji period in blockprinted form. These catalogues do not take account, however, of the innumerable books printed in the Meiji period with pre-Meiji blocks; many of these reprints are undated but can be assigned to the Meiji period when the addresses of the publishers in the colophon betray their Meiji origins through the use of new geographical and administrative terminology. Many publishers continued to be active well into the Meiji period, some turning to new fields of publishing such as textbooks for school use and translations of Western books; they now used their surnames rather than their old tradenames (*yagō*) and many are included in a list of Tokyo publishers produced in 1873, although few survived into the 1890s. Many of those who published with movable type were newly established firms and many of the older ones who were accustomed to blockprinting failed to adapt. The last important literary works to be published in block-printed editions were the series *Shinsaku jūniban no uchi* 新作十二番之内, which was launched by Wada Tokutarō 和田

篤太郎 in Tokyo and included new novels by Aeba Kōson and other contemporary writers.[43]

The last innovative use of block-printing for books was the series of illustrated crepe-paper books produced by Hasegawa Takejirō (1853–1938). These were mostly printed in English, French or German, and consisted for the most part of translations of Japanese folk-tales by Basil Hall Chamberlain, James Curtis Hepburn, and other missionaries and scholars of Japanese; the first was *Momotaro; or, Little Peachling*, published in 1885. They were obviously aimed at the foreign communities resident in Japan, and were in effect curios intended to appeal to those with a love for 'old' Japan. They were quite at variance with the trend in book-publishing, which was in the 1880s moving over to movable type. By this time blockprinting had had its day and the growth of the market was such that the balance of the economic argument had shifted in favour of movable type.[44]

BIBLIOGRAPHY

On some of the niche markets, see R. Imazeki & R. G. Wasson, '*Kinpu*: mushroom books of the Tokugawa period,', *TASJ* (3rd series) 11 (1973): 81–92; Kawakami Kōzō 川上行蔵, *Ryōri bunken kaidai* 料理文献解題 (Shibata Shoin, 1978); Okada Kōzō 岡田幸三, *Kanpon kadōsho nenpyō* 刊本花道書年表 (Kyoto: Shibunkaku, 1973); Ikenobō Gakuen Tanki Daigaku Toshokan 池坊学園短期大学図書館 (ed.), *Kadō bunken mokuroku* 華道文献目録 (Kyoto: Kadō Bunka Kenkyūsho, 1957); Ogawa Teizō 小川鼎三, *Igaku kosho mokuroku* 医学古書目録 (Nihon Igaku Bunka Hozonkai, 1976); Okamoto Sokuroku 岡本則録, *Wasan tosho mokuroku* 和算図書目録 (Teikoku Gakushiin, 1932); Takasaka Tarō 高阪たらう, 'Senryū shomoku kaidai' 川柳書目解題, *Shoshigaku* 4 (1935): 2.37–48, 4.23–6; and P. F.

---

[43] Kokuritsu Kokkai Toshokan 1971–6; for examples of Meiji reprints using pre-Meiji blcoks, see Hayashi & Kornicki 1991: #2056, 2067, 2107, etc.; for Tokyo publishers in 1873 see Asakura & Sakuma 1971: 187–201. Contemporary newspapers abound with advertisments for translated books either for sale or available for borrowing from commercial lending libraries: see *Tōkyō nichinichi shinbun*, 1873.4.4: 2, 1874.2.24: 2, etc. It should be noted here that use of the name 'Tokyo' for Edo was not uncommon well before the official adoption of the new name: it appears, for example, in the copy of *Ehon kōkyō* which was published in 1864 and is in the Museo d'Arte Orientale Edoardo Chiossone in Genoa.

[44] Frederic A. Sharf, *Takejiro Hasegawa: Meiji Japan's preeminent publisher of wood-block illustrated crepe-paper books*, Peabody Essex Museum Collections vol. 130, no. 4 (Salem: Peabody Essex Museum, 1994).

Kornicki, 'Agriculture, food and famine in Japan', in P. K. Fox, ed., *Cambridge University Library: the great collections* (Cambridge: Cambridge University Press, 1998). For early Meiji booksellers' catalogues see Asakura & Sakuma 1971.

4.3.2 *Official publishing*

In China it was during the Song dynasty, at the latest, that the state made use of printing technology for the purpose of producing official publications, and in Korea similar developments took place in the Koryŏ dynasty. In Japan, by contrast, the state's appropriation of print came very much later, around the turn of the seventeenth century, when emperor Go-Yōzei, and Tokugawa Ieyasu first sponsored the use of movable type, as discussed above (§4.2.3). Ieyasu's motives for doing so are said to have lain in the act of publication, of making texts more readily available, and what was significant about his involvement was the fact that, after centuries of Buddhist domination of print, the works published were all secular. With the exception of the *Azuma kagami*, a historical account of the foundation of the Kamakura shōgunate, they were all sinological texts, it is true, but it is undeniable that they launched the secularization of the press which was to be such a marked feature of the publishing world of the Tokugawa period.[45]

The usual term for 'official publication' in the Tokugawa period is *kanpan* 官版, probably a borrowing from Ming government usage, although sometimes other words such as *kankoku* 官刻 were used instead. But all these terms refer strictly to the involvement of the Bakufu or its attendant institutions; they were not used for publications sponsored by the domains or their academies. Furthermore, it is not the case that, following Ieyasu's example, the Bakufu consistently made use of the technology of print for its own purposes; on the contrary, an appreciation of the utility of print was reached only in the eighteenth century, when the Bakufu was simultaneously becoming aware of the dangers of print in the hands of commercial publishers, and it has to be said that until the nineteenth century the Bakufu's commitment to print was at best half-hearted.

---

[45] *KT* 38: 339.

Ieyasu's publications were more a matter of personal sponsorship than institutional publication on the part of the infant Bakufu, and the same is true of the next set of official publications following his death, those sponsored by the fifth Tokugawa shōgun, Tsunayoshi, at the end of the seventeenth century. These are most likely associated with the lectures on sinological texts which Tsunayoshi gave to selected audiences of daimyō and other notables in the years 1690–1700; they may have been distributed at the time and in any case do not appear to have been put on sale, although some of them displayed the word *kanpan* to indicate their official status.[46]

In the early eighteenth century it was similarly the personal interest of the eighth shōgun, Yoshimune, whose role in the codification of censorship legislation, in the import of books for the shōgunal library and in the encouragement of learning are discussed elsewhere, that led to the appearance of six, and possibly more, official publications in the 1720s and 1730s. The nature of the texts printed at Yoshimune's request bespeaks a desire to disseminate knowledge. The first was the *Liu yu yan yi* 六諭衍義 (J. *Rikuyu engi*), a Chinese guide to practical morality, which was published in 1721 with punctuation added by the celebrated sinologist Ogyū Sorai to facilitate reading by Japanese, and this was followed the next year by a translation of the same work into Japanese by Muro Kyūso, which was later widely used as a primary education text. Later publications included a medical encyclopedia and a handbook on Japanese medicinal herbs compiled to order, and edicts were issued by the Bakufu requiring them to be sold at fixed prices.[47]

As these edicts suggest, Yoshimune's *kanpan* were distributed through the commercial networks: the carved blocks were made available to commercial publishers in return for a fee and they printed and distributed copies as much as the market could absorb them, appending colophons giving the names of the responsible publishers and distributors. This was an arrangement that Ogyū Sorai objected to, observing that 'since there is no place in which the blocks might be stored, the printing is carried out by the *chōnin* [townsmen] who make great profit from the business, and the name [*kanpan*] is thus inappropriate'. With reference to Chinese precedents, he argued that

---

[46] Fukui 1985: 59–68.
[47] Fukui 1985: 71–96, *OKS* 994–5, #2023–4.

the whole operation should be removed from commercial control and carried out entirely in Bakufu schools. As in other areas of public policy his advice was not followed and until the end of the Tokugawa period it remained the case that the Bakufu relied upon the networks of commercial publishers to distribute and sell copies of official publications.[48]

After Yoshimune's time there was again a hiatus until 1799, when the Bakufu Academy, the Shōheizaka Gakumonjo, began a publishing career that lasted until 1867 and produced in all 197 works. Wooden movable type was used for four of them but the remainder were blockprinted, and all but two of them were sinological texts, either *kabusebori* facsimiles of Chinese and Korean books or new reprints. The Academy had its own printing workshop where books were printed for internal use, and the costs involved were covered by the Academy's own budget. Although the Academy's publications were thus divorced from commercial realities, the commercial publishers of Edo were permitted to borrow the blocks for a fee and to market the books they printed from them. According to an edict issued in 1798 commercial publishers were supposed to remove the word *kanpan* from the cover and/or title pages of books, but many surviving copies equipped with commercial colophons also carry the *kanpan* designation, so the ruling was evidently ignored, possibly because a commercial cachet was attached to publications of the Academy. In 1842 the head of the Academy noted that the Academy's publications were not being well circulated and approved an application from Izumoji Bungorō, a well-established Edo publisher, to handle the printing and distribution henceforth, thus evincing a concern that the books reach a wide audience.[49]

In addition to the Academy, several other Bakufu institutions also engaged in publishing in the nineteenth century. The Observatory officials (Tenmonkata 天文方) published several copperplate maps of the world based on European sources; the Medical Academy (Igakkan 医学館) published two Song-dynasty medical texts and in 1860 the *Ishinpō*, a compendium of information derived from Chinese

---

[48] *NST* 36: 440; J. R. McEwan, *The political writings of Ogyū Sorai* (Cambridge: Cambridge University Press, 1969), 137–8. *Rikuyu engi* was later printed and distributed by the Edo publisher Suwaraya Mohee: Hayashi & Kornicki 1991: #2326.

[49] *OTS* 2:811, #6420; *DNKS* Shichū torishimari ruishū 18: 38–41; Ono Noriaki 1978: 233–8.

texts and compiled in Japan in 982–4; the Institute for the investigation of barbarian books (Bansho shirabesho 蕃書調所, later Yōsho shirabesho 洋書調所, and later still Kaiseisho 開成所) published language textbooks, translations and newspapers in the 1850s and 1860s; and the Military Academy (Rikugunsho 陸軍所) published 17 texts between 1864 and 1867, mostly translations of Dutch and English works on military science. Finally, the office of the Nagasaki city commissioner (Nagasaki bugyōsho 長崎奉行所) published five books in Dutch with the Bakufu's permission in 1856–9, including an English primer and an infantry manual as well as books on the Dutch language.[50]

The switch from sinology to so-called Western studies is striking, and it was maintained in the early Meiji period by the Council of State (Dajōkan 太政館), Ministry of Education (Monbushō 文部省) and University (Daigaku Nankō 大学南校), which published translations and guides to Western studies under the *kanpan* heading. By the 1850s at least, then, there seems to have been a clear appreciation in Bakufu circles of the possibility of providing intellectual leadership through the medium of print. Before that time the accommodation with the commercial world of publishing seems to have been at best a reluctant one.

Although their publications were not eligible to be designated *kanpan*, the daimyō domains and their academies also engaged in publishing. The various domain academies (*hankō* 藩校) owed their existence to the growing interest of daimyō in education, but this was slow to develop and more than half of the total 278 academies were founded in the nineteenth century, as many as 48 of them in the few years between the Meiji Restoration and the abolition of the domains in 1871. They were predominantly sinological in their curricula and their concerns, but in the late eighteenth century some large domains established their own medical academies and in the nineteenth some established academies of Western learning, military science and Kokugaku. For all this, however, fewer than half took any interest in publishing, and this was eventually noticed by the Bakufu, which in 1842 set about encouraging the domains to follow the lead of the Bakufu Academy in this respect. The number of publications produced by each domain was in rough correlation with

---

[50] Fukui 1985: 153–297.

its assessed income, and the three domains most active in publishing were the collateral Tokugawa houses of Mito, Owari and Kii. For smaller domains the financial burden may have been too great, but the economics of domain publishing remains to be explored.[51]

From 1630 onwards domains were beginning to use blockprinting technology to produce paper currency, known as *hansatsu* 藩札, but few in the seventeenth century showed any interest in the publication of books. Rather, in parallel with the trend in the foundation of the academies themselves, it was not until the second half of the eighteenth century that domain publications began to reach significant numbers. More than half of all the domain publications appeared between 1751 and 1844, but since the total was only 786 for all domains throughout the period, it is obvious that the output was puny compared with that of the commercial publishing industry. Furthermore, it is pertinent to enquire in what sense the domains were actually engaged in 'publishing'. In some domains the emphasis was on producing essential sinological texts for use in their own academies and these texts were distributed locally, sometimes at artificially low prices or even for no charge. In such cases it is clear that the education of the domain samurai, together with the exercise of control over the texts they came into contact with, were of more concern than a desire to publish. Nevertheless, in some domains there was an identifiable interest in making works widely available beyond the domain's borders. This is particularly true of Mito domain, the most active of all, which through its academy, the Kōdōkan 弘道館, and its special historiographical institute in Edo, the Shōkōkan 彰考館, published more than 60 items including the *Dainihonshi* 大日本史, a massive history of Japan, and numerous other japanological rather than sinological works. Furthermore, although most domains retained the printing blocks and the rights in them, some surviving copies carry colophons with lists of commercial publishers. The precise nature of the relationship between the domain academies and commercial publishing in such cases is unclear, and it may be that the printing and physical preparation of the books was entrusted by some domains to commercial publishers, but at the very least they were clearly

---

[51] *KT* 49: 465; Kasai 1962: 60–61, 65. On the domain academies see Kasai Sukeharu 1960, *Kinsei hankō no sōgōteki kenkyū* 近世藩校の総合的研究 (Yoshikawa Kōbunkan, 1960).

entrusted with the commercial sale and distribution throughout Japan of copies of some works.[52]

It should come as no surprise that domain publications were predominantly sinological, for so too were the curricula of most of the domain academies. Many were simply editions of the *Four Books* and *Five Classics*, like those produced in the 1830s by the Morioka domain academy explicitly for the purposes of recitative reading (*sodoku* 素読). These were prepared for publication by one of the academy teachers, and this was a common characteristic of domain publications, which often served to provide local scholars with a public, even a national public in some cases. An example is the edition of *Qun shu zhi yao* 群書治要 (J. *Gunsho chiyō*) prepared by Yamamoto Gentan, director of the Wakayama domain academy, and published by the academy in 1847 explicitly to make a good text widely available. This edition is remarkable in that it was printed using the font of bronze movable type used for some of Ieyasu's printing projects early in the seventeenth century: a few domains, such as Fukuyama and Morioka, did make use of wooden movable type, but for the most part they followed the lead of the commercial publishers and relied on blockprinting.[53]

In the closing decades of the Tokugawa period the profile of domain publications changed. Some domains, especially Mito, focussed on Japanese studies, particularly historical works, while the new academies devoted to Western studies published language primers, medical works and most commonly works on Western military science. The first of these was a translation, via a Dutch version, of a German work on the formation and strategic use of infantry, artillery and cavalry units, which appeared in 1846, but most were published in the years following the arrival of American and Russian naval units in 1853, when the need for defensive preparations had become very obvious. For example, in 1867, the year in which a French team of military instructors came to Japan to build up a Western-style army for the Bakufu, the Satsuma domain academy published a translation of an English infantry training manual, *Jūtei eikoku hohei renpō* 重

---

[52] On *hansatsu*, see Kokuritsu Shiryōkan 国立史料館, ed., *Edo jidai no shihei* 江戸時代の紙幣, Shiryōkan sōsho 史料館叢書 bekkan 2 (Tōkyō Daigaku Shuppankai, 1993). Kasai 1962: 58–60, 68–83.
[53] Kasai 1962: 92, 102, 104–5, 394–5, 549–93; Gardner 1993: #57.

訂英国歩兵練法. This is a revised edition of a translation that had first appeared in 1865: it was translated by Akamatsu Kozaburō 赤松小三郎, who was one of the domain teachers and was assassinated in 1867. During these dangerous and tense years before the Restoration, it is clear that sinology was declining in appeal and that the detachment of the domain academies from market considerations was an advantage as they sought to produce works with a limited audience but a severely practical value.[54]

BIBLIOGRAPHY

On official publications associated with the Bakufu see Fukui 1985, and Fukui Tamotsu, *Edo Bakufu hensanbutsu* 江戸幕府編纂物, 2 vols (Yūshōdō, 1983), and on domain publications Kasai 1962: all are exhaustive. On domain publications see also the contemporary study by Tōjō Kindai 東条琴台, 'Shohan zōhan shomoku hikki' 諸藩蔵版書目筆記, in *Kaidai sōsho* 1916: 234–74.

4.3.3 *Private publishing*

Publishing in the Tokugawa period that was not undertaken by commercial publishers or by official institutions such as the Bakufu and the domains is here termed private publishing. It was undertaken both by individuals and by bodies such as temples and academic or literary associations, either because the works in questions could not be published commercially or because the publishers desired to control the processes of publishing and distribution. Here the focus will be on private publications that were blockprinted, while others that were printed with wooden movable type will be considered separately (§4.4.1).

Private publications are distinguished by the word *zōhan* 蔵版, retention of the printing blocks, which denotes ownership of the blocks and hence printing rights; it was sometimes used by commercial

---

[54] Kasai 1962: 313, 541–3, 641–7; on the circumstances behind the transmission of Western military science and its growth in Japan see Satō Shōsuke 佐藤昌介, 'Kokusaiteki kankyō to yōgaku no gunjikagakka' 国際的環境と洋学の軍事科学化, in Nakayama Shigeru 中山茂, *Bakumatsu no yōgaku* 幕末の洋学 (Kyoto: Minerva, 1994), 15–50.

publishers to assert their ownership of the blocks, but was widely used by private publishers. Books that were privately published often indicated the ownership of the blocks in a special colophon with a space in which a vermilion seal was impressed in each copy to indicate authenticity, but sometimes the impression of the seal was a part of the printed text. In other cases there is an indication of the ownership of the blocks on the inside front cover (*mikaeshi* 見返し or *hōmen* 封面) or on the central fold of the page (*hashira* 柱 or *hanshin* 版心). During the early years of the seventeenth century many movable type publications were in fact private, such as those of Suminokura Soan which have been mentioned above (§4.2.3), but the concept and practice of *zōhan* dates from the end of the seventeenth century and becomes increasingly common in the eighteenth.

Although in some cases use of the word *zōhan* may have literally meant that the private publisher actually retained the blocks in a storehouse, it appears that the concept gradually took over from the reality and that it became increasingly likely for all or most of the blocks to rest in the hands of commercial publishers. Private publishing was theoretically detached from the market and therefore required the investment of a capital sum, known as *nyūgin* 入銀, to cover the costs: although few details are available, it seems likely that the carving of the blocks, the printing and the binding were entrusted to commercial enterprises for a fee, while the distribution was at first handled by the private publisher.[55]

Numerous surviving copies of private publications carry not only a *zōhan* colophon but also a colophon attached by commercial publishers acting merely as distributors. In some of these cases it is clear that the private publisher has subsequently sought to use commercial channels to distribute the work more widely, and presumably received some payment from booksellers who saw a market for it. In other cases, copies were being commercially distributed long after the publisher's death and commercial publishers had evidently taken over possession of the blocks, possibly in return for a payment to the heirs: it is clear that here the work has effectively entered the public realm. It may still carry a statement that it is 'so-and-so *zōhan*', but if there is a place in the colophon for the

---

[55] On the finances of *zōhan* publication, the contractual arrangements, and the speed with which private publication could be carried out, see Okamoto 1980.

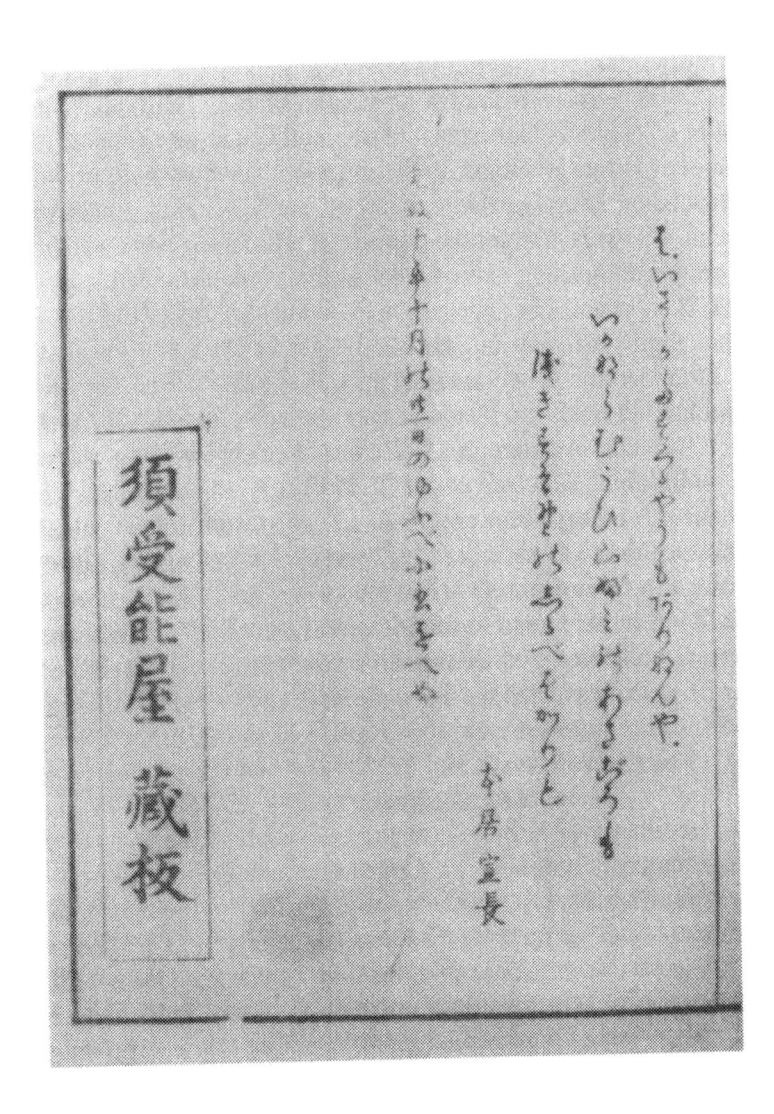

Fig. 10 The end of Motoori Norinaga's *Uiyamabumi* うひ山ふみ [First steps into the mountains], published in 1799. The cartouche reads 'Suzunoya *zōhan*', indicating that ownership of the blocks remained with the Suzunoya, Norinaga's school in Matsuzaka: Hayashi & Kornicki 1991: #253.

impression of a *zōhan* seal it is usually empty and the *zōhan* status is essentially dead.[56]

The most active private publishers were undoubtedly the schools of some of the most well-known Kokugaku scholars, particularly the Suzunoya of Motoori Norinaga and his intellectual descendants and the school of Hirata Atsutane. In the nineteenth century both of these were producing many works by Motoori and Atsutane respectively or by their followers, and for the purpose of advertising were attaching to their publications long lists of other works available or forthcoming (Fig. 14). This practice became common in other fields too. In medicine the Taki family of doctors who had long been in service to the Bakufu founded their own medical school in Edo in 1765 known as the Seijukan 躋寿館. Until it was taken over by the Bakufu as the Bakufu's Medical Academy in 1791, the Seijukan published several books, including *Kōkeisai kyūhō* 広恵済急方, a manual for the treatment of emergency conditions. Like some other private publications, this was distributed by commercial publishers, but the reasons for this arrangement are not always clear: it may be that the work had too limited a market for commercial publication and hence that private publication with commercial distribution offered the only means of ensuring it reached an audience, or it may be that the publisher wished to maintain some degree of control. In the case of books relating to traditional arts like ikebana and the tea ceremony or produced by circles of *haikai* poets, which are commonly found without indications of commercial distribution, it appears that the desire for control, or at least for a limited circulation, is foremost.[57]

Some temples also engaged in publishing during the Tokugawa period, including the temples of Mt Kōya and temples of the Nichiren sect. It was also in this period that the first Japanese editions of the Buddhist canon were published in private ventures undertaken by temples, rather than by commercial publishers. The first was produced by the Kan'eiji in Edo and was produced in 1637–48, mostly with movable type, and the second by the Ōbaku sect in Kyoto in 1669–81. In general it appears that Buddhist works that were not commercially marketable, especially scholarly texts or huge compilations like the

---

[56] Hayashi & Kornicki 1991: #154–5, 2039, etc.

[57] Eg., Hayashi & Kornicki 1991: #993, 2234; Kornicki 1997: 500, #25. On publishing by the Taki family, see Mori 1979: 2.250–91.

full canon, were privately published by temples, but hitherto there has been little study of the temple imprints of the Tokugawa period.[58]

BIBLIOGRAPHY

Nakano 1995: 196–201; *NKC* 2: 132–6. On Kōya and Nichiren-sect editions see respectively Mizuhara 1932 and Kanmuri 1983.

4.3.4 REPRINTS OF NON-JAPANESE WORKS

Given the place that Confucianism and sinology in general had in the educational ethos of Tokugawa Japan it is only to be expected that the Chinese classics in particular would always be available in Japanese reprints, at least for educational purposes. Indeed it was Chinese works that were printed with movable type in the late sixteenth and early seventeenth centuries by Tokugawa Ieyasu and successive emperors, thus initiating the secularization of print, and many of the domain schools published sinological texts for classroom use (§§4.2.3, 4.3.2). If, in addition, we include the large number of Buddhist works in Chinese reprinted in the Tokugawa period, it is obvious that printing in Chinese produced at the very least a significant proportion of the printed books available.

The texts of the Chinese works printed in Japan during the Tokugawa period were for the most part derived either from late Ming editions or, later in the period, from Qing editions. As a result there was a major shift in Japan in the textual authority for secular Chinese books, which had in the past been represented in Japan by the manuscript traditions of the Song dynasty or earlier. The relationship between seventeenth-century Japanese imprints and Ming editions is often physically obvious: in many cases Chinese originals were sacrificed by being pasted directly onto the blocks to form a *kabusebori* facsimile of the original (§2.3). But in most cases the Chinese texts printed in Japan were to some extent japanized. It was rare for them not to have reading marks (*kunten*) added to enable

---

[58] On the Ōbaku edition of the canon, a reproduction of a Ming edition and produced by the monk Tetsugan 鉄眼, see *KD* 2: 469–70, and Takemura Shin'ichi 竹村真一, *Minchōtai no rekishi* 明朝体の歴史 (Kyoto: Shibunkaku, 1986), 120–63.

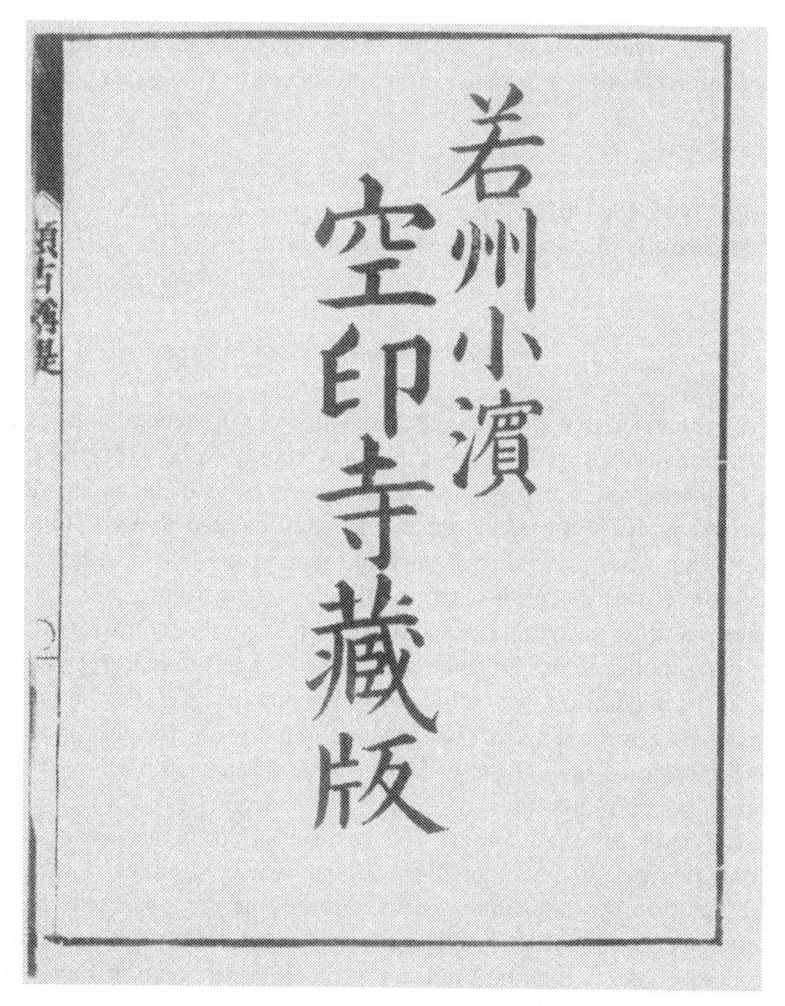

Fig. 11 Part of the colophon of *Setchōken zenji juko hyakusoku shōdai* 雪竇顕禅師頌古百則称提, a work in the Sōtō Zen tradition by the Chinese monk Xuedou 雪竇 (980–1052) edited and supplied with diacritics to facilitate the reading of the Chinese text as Japanese by Mensan Zuihō 面山瑞方 (1683–1769). This copy was published in 1842 by the Kūinji in Obama, in the province of Wakasa, and distributed by Ogawa Tazaemon 小川多左衛門 of Kyoto; the other side of the colophon includes the word *saikoku* 再刻 (recut), indicating that it is a reissue of the 1788 edition with new blocks.[59]

---

[59] *BKD* 6: 310.

Japanese readers to construe the text, and in many cases marginal notes, extracts from Chinese or Japanese commentaries, prefaces by the Japanese editors, and so on, are present too. It is for this reason that the hard-line distinction between 'Japanese' and 'Chinese' books in catalogues and studies seems unsatisfactory, for it fails to take account of the scholarship and interpretive strategies of Japanese thinkers in their encounter with Chinese texts.[60]

It is impossible to quantify or to characterize the reprinting of Chinese works in the Tokugawa period: they were a fundamental part of the output of most commercial and official publishers, although for the most part they have yet to receive much attention. Perhaps the most extensively reprinted work of them all was the *Classic of filial piety* (Ch. *Xiao jing* 孝経, J. *Kōkyō*), which was first printed in Japan in 1599 as one of emperor Go-Yōzei's movable-type editions. From the 1650s until the 1860s a dated edition was published almost every year, and when account is taken of undated reprints it is evident that copies were permanently available. The demand can further be seen from the various published versions of an edition of this work compiled by Dazai Shundai, which was first published in 1744 by the Edo publisher Suwaraya Shinhee 須原屋新兵衛. This same publisher had to prepare completely new sets of blocks for Shundai's edition eight times between 1783 and 1866: given that this was an expense which a publisher would normally only undertake when the blocks were too worn or damaged to print any more viable copies, it is evident that there was a huge demand for Dazai Shundai's edition alone.[61]

The Confucian *Analects* and the other central texts of the canon were also produced in innumerable editions and reprints, both by commercial publishers and by the domain academies (§4.3.2). Chinese medical texts were also extensively published in Japan, since it was only in the second half of the Tokugawa period that Chinese medicine came under any threat from Western medicine. Take, for example, the *Shisi jing fa hui* 十四経発揮: this is an account of the theory and

---

[60] *NKC* 2: 277–85.
[61] Nagasawa 1976–80: 1.19–26 (for the Suwaraya Shinhee editions see p. 19); Hayashi Hideichi 林秀一, 'Nihon *Kōkyō* kankō mokuroku' 日本孝経刊行目録, *Shoshigaku* 3.1 (1934): 37–54, 3.2: 41–48; Morikawa Akira 森川彰, '*Kōkyō* no wakoku' 孝経の和刻, in *Chūgoku bunka sosho* 中国文化叢書, 10 vols (Taishūkan Shoten, 1967–8), 9: 285–96.

practice of acupuncture which was written in 1341 by Hua Shou 滑寿 and first printed in 1364. It reached Japan in a Ming edition, was printed using movable type in 1596 and on three further occasions in the early seventeenth century, and also appeared in numerous blockprinted editions up to 1805, not to mention the Japanese commentaries on, and translations of, this work. Much later, in the 1850s, some of the medical writings of Benjamin Hobson (1816–73), a missionary doctor working in China whose introductory works on Western medicine were published in Chinese, were reprinted in Japan making recent advances in Western medicine accessible to Japanese doctors, who could generally read Chinese but not English.[62]

The reprinting of Buddhist texts in the Tokugawa period has yet to be extensively studied. There can be no doubt, however, that they represented a substantial proportion of the output of the commercial publishers in the seventeenth century particularly, and this is not to mention the role of temples as private publishers from the seventeenth century onwards, which were responsible, for example, for the first two Japanese printings of the Buddhist canon (§4.3.3). Towards the end of his life Suzuki Shōsan 鈴木正三 (1579–1655), a Zen teacher and writer of popular literature, noted that 'Buddhist books sell exceptionally well, and for that reason they are gradually seeking out even old sermons and publishing them'. Hard evidence of the prominence of Buddhist books in the market can be found in the booksellers' catalogues of the seventeenth century. In the first place, it is Buddhist books that have pride of place at the head of all the seventeenth century catalogues that are organized into categories. And secondly, they constitute a very substantial proportion of all the books listed: for example, in the undated catalogue of the 1660s, which is the oldest to survive, the entries, which start with sūtras and continue with the doctrinal works associated with each of the sects, occupy 117 of the 266 pages. Buddhist books are rather less prominent in the booksellers' catalogues of 1755 and 1772, and were by the nineteenth century a less significant part of the market and hence of the output of commercial publishers. This trend is probably attributable to the revival of Shintō at the expense of Buddhism and the growth of anti-Buddhist sentiment.[63]

---

[62] Nagasawa 1976–80: 1.33–6; Kornicki 1997: 491–5.
[63] *Suzuki Shōsan dōjin zenshū* 鈴木正三道人全集 (Sankibō Busshorin, 1975),

PRINTED BOOKS 157

Although in the early Tokugawa period a number of Korean editions of Chinese Confucian works were reprinted in Japan, works by Korean authors were not so extensively reprinted as those by Chinese authors. Such Korean writings as were reprinted in Japan were exclusively Confucian, naturally in Chinese, and most of the reprinting took place in the first half of the Tokugawa period, with a little coming in the second half. Yamaguchi has identified some 35 works, including *Iphak tosŏl* 入学図説, a work by Kwŏn Kŭn 権近 (1352–1409) which was printed in Japan in 1634, but the neo-Confucian writings of Yi T'oegye 李退渓 (1501–70) dominate and his most important works were reprinted several times. His influential *Ch'ŏnmyŏng tosŏl* 天命図説, when reprinted in Japan in 1646 and 1651, carried a preface by Hayashi Razan testifying to the high esteem in which both he and Fujiwara Seika held this work, and Yamazaki Ansai (1618–82) and his followers were deeply influenced by Yi's various writings on the neo-Confucianism of Zhu Xi (§7.1.2). Abe Yoshio goes so far as to say that Yi T'oegye was more widely read in Japan than in Korea, and it is certainly true that he was a major intellectual presence in Japanese neo-Confucianism, and this was the main consequence of the reprinting of Korean works in the Tokugawa period.[64]

Although Western works were reaching Japan via the Dutch East India Company's settlement at Nagasaki (§7.1.4), none of them were reprinted in Japan in their original languages. Rather, they were published in Japanese translation or in Japanese versions loosely based on the Dutch originals. Some printing of words and phrases in European languages was undertaken in blockprinted Dutch dictionaries and primers, which were often presented so as to look like Western books, but only in the last few years of the period was there any publication of books in Western languages, and that was mostly undertaken using movable type (§4.4.2).[65]

---

312. For the booksellers' catalogues see Shidō Bunko 1962–4, especially in this connection 1: 19–34. Nunn 1969: 114; for the diminished but not insignificant output of Buddhist books in early nineteenth-century Kyoto, see Munemasa & Wakabayashi 1965: 1–111. On opposition to Buddhism in early nineteenth-century Japan see James Edward Ketelaar, *Of heretics and martyrs in Meiji Japan: Buddhism and its persecution* (Princeton: Princeton University Press, 1990), 15–42.

[64] Abe 1965: 423, 426, etc.
[65] See the illustrations in Sugimoto Tsutomu 杉本つとむ, *Edo jidai rangogaku*

BIBLIOGRAPHY

Nagasawa 1976-80 is the most detailed catalogue available of Japanese reprints of Chinese works, but it is not exhaustive and it excludes Japanese reprints of Buddhist works in Chinese, for which the only source of information is *BKD*. Nagasawa has also edited several series of facsimiles of Tokugawa-period reprints of Chinese works which were published by Kyūko Shoin in the 1970s, for example *Wakokubon kanseki zuihitsu shū* 和刻本漢籍随筆集, 20 vols (Kyūko Shoin, 1972-8). See also Nakamura Yukihiko 中村幸彦, 'Wakokubon' 和刻本 and 'Hon'yaku chūshaku hon'an' 翻訳注釈本案, in *Chūgoku bunka sosho* 中国文化叢書, 10 vols (Taishūkan Shoten, 1967-8), 9: 260-71, 272-84. On medical reprints, see Kosoto Hiroshi 小曽戸洋, Seki Nobuyuki 関信之 & Kurihara Mariko 栗原萬理子, 'Wakokubon kanseki isho sōgō nenpyō' 和刻本漢籍医書総合年表, *Nihon ishigaku zasshi* 日本医史学雑誌 36 (1990): 459-94. De-min Tao, 'Traditional Chinese social ethics in Japan, 1721-1943', *GLJ* 4 (1991): 68-84. On Korean reprints, see Abe 1965: 423-51, Yi Chun'gil 1986: 263-72, and Yamaguchi Masayuki 山口正之, 'Tokugawa jidai ni okeru chōsen shoseki no honkoku' 徳川時代に於ける朝鮮書籍の翻刻, *Bunkyō no chōsen* 文教の朝鮮 48 (1929): 52-70. Since Chinese books are not included in *KSM*, locating copies of Japanese reprints is difficult: recourse has to be made to the published catalogues of individual libraries and to the series published by Tōkyō Daigaku Tōyō bunka kenkyūsho fuzoku Tōyōgaku Bunken Sentā 東京大学東洋文化研究所付属東洋学文献センター, *Kanseki shozai chōsa hōkoku* 漢籍所在調査報告 (1980-85), which covers various provincial libraries.

4.4 LATER MOVABLE TYPE AND COPPERPLATE

4.4.1 *Wooden movable type*

Although the movable type technology of the early seventeenth century fell into disuse, it did not completely disappear. In the second half of the seventeenth century there were a few works printed with movable

---

no seiritsu to sono tenkai 江戸時代蘭語学の成立とその展開, 5 vols (Waseda Daigaku shuppanbu, 1976), 3: 110, 581, 595, 596, 654-5, 690, 714, 927; on translations see Goodman 1986 and S. Miyashita, 'A bibliography of the Dutch medical books translated into Japanese', *Archives internationales d'histoire des sciences* 25 (1975): 8-72.

type, such as some calendars printed in Aizu and some Zen texts, and between 1727 and 1743 the Zōjōji temple in Edo printed a number of texts relating to the Pure Land (Jōdo) sect of Buddhism. Otherwise there was very little until the revival of the use of wooden movable type towards the end of the eighteenth century. Books printed in this way in the second half of the Tokugawa period are known as *kinsei mokkatsujiban* 近世木活字版 ('movable-type editions of the early modern period') to distinguish them from the earlier movable-type editions. This is a valuable distinction, for while typography became for a time the dominant printing technology in the early seventeenth century, these later movable-type editions posed no threat to woodblock printing. However, the accepted boundary of 1653 as the first year of *kinsei mokkatsujiban* is somewhat artificial: the few works printed with movable type between 1653 and the 1770s occupy a twilight zone and owe more to a lingering tradition than to a renewal of interest.[66]

So why was typography revived at all, and why did it pose no threat? There can be no doubt that the revival was at least partly due to the importation from China in 1779 of the *Imperial Printing Office Manual for Movable Type,* and in 1783 and 1786 of some of the movable type editions produced by the Office. The revival of movable type in China in 1773 was at the initiative of the superintendant of the Office, Jin Jian 金簡, and the *Manual* is an illustrated guide to the process. Another sign of the connection between Japan and China in this respect is the use of the term *shūchinban* 聚珍版 to refer to movable-type books in Japan, for this clearly derives from the term given by the Chinese emperor to the type used in the Office, *juzhen* 聚珍. How widely the *Manual* circulated, why the earlier Japanese tradition of movable-type printing appears to have been forgotten, and why some printers were inspired by the *Manual* to revive the practice are questions that cannot yet be answered.[67]

---

[66] Kishimoto 1986: 75–7; Tōdō Sukenori 藤堂祐範, *Jōdokyō kokatsujiban zuroku* 浄土教古活字版図録 (Kyoto: Kichō Tosho Eihon Kankōkai, 1934), 40–49; Kawase 1967: 132–3; Nagasawa 1976: 38.

[67] Ōba 1967: 419, 421, 703, 718. Ōuchida 1981: 61, 64. On the Office and the *Manual* see Kaneko Kazumasa 金子和正, *Chūgoku katsujiban insatsuhō* 中国活字版印刷法 (Kyūko Shoin, 1981), and R. C. Rudolph, 'Chinese moveable type printing in the eighteenth century', *Silver Jubilee Volume of the Zinbun-Kagaku-Kenkyusyo* (= *Tōhō gakuhō* 25.1, 1954), 317–35.

Movable-type printing was taken up by Bakufu institutions of learning on a limited scale, by some domain academies, by private schools of learning, or by private individuals. Commercial publishers kept their distance, with the exception of one each in Sunpu and Wakayama, and there were good reasons for them to do so. Owing to the fact that the type was wooden and carved by hand there were inevitably minute variations in the depth of each piece of type and few were completely true. As a result, when a page was printed by placing a sheet of paper on the composing tray with its pre-inked type and brushing the paper to ensure that the ink adhered to the paper, there was never an even impression. Consequently, it is easy to distinguish a book printed with wooden movable type from a block printed book, for in the former some of the characters make a good impression and others a poor one, and in any case the alignment of the pieces of type is rarely perfect, while in the latter these problems do not arise since the whole page is carved as one block. Aesthetically, therefore, wooden typography could rarely compete with block-printing, although it had done so in the early seventeenth century.[68]

But that is not all. While it was simple with blockprinting to include textual glosses or the reading marks used to punctuate Chinese texts for the convenience of Japanese readers, it was not so easy with wooden movable type. It was not impossible, however, and some of the Buddhist texts printed on Mt Hiei, such as *Kachū Myōhō rengekyō shō* 科註妙法蓮華経鈔 (1625), an annotated edition of the *Lotus sūtra*, included reading marks and even *furigana* glosses. However, this required the use of a separate font of smaller *kana* and *kunten* symbols, and it was undoubtedly easier to achieve with blockprinting. Consequently, a few movable-type books containing quotations in Chinese actually used woodblocks for those pages so as to include the reading marks, in an eloquent testimony to the greater flexibility of block-printing. Nevertheless, although few commercial publishers showed any interest in printing with movable type, it is clear from a dispute that arose in 1792 between the booksellers' guild in Osaka

---

[68] For a clear statement by a contemporary of the poor aesthetic quality of movable type books, see Makita 1968: 2.164. On the Wakayama publisher who also produced movable type books, see Tajihi Ikuo 多治比郁夫, 'Kishū shoshi Shūseidō no katsujibon' 紀州書肆聚星堂の活字本, *Biburia* 81 (1983): 130-36; Kishimoto 1986: 84.

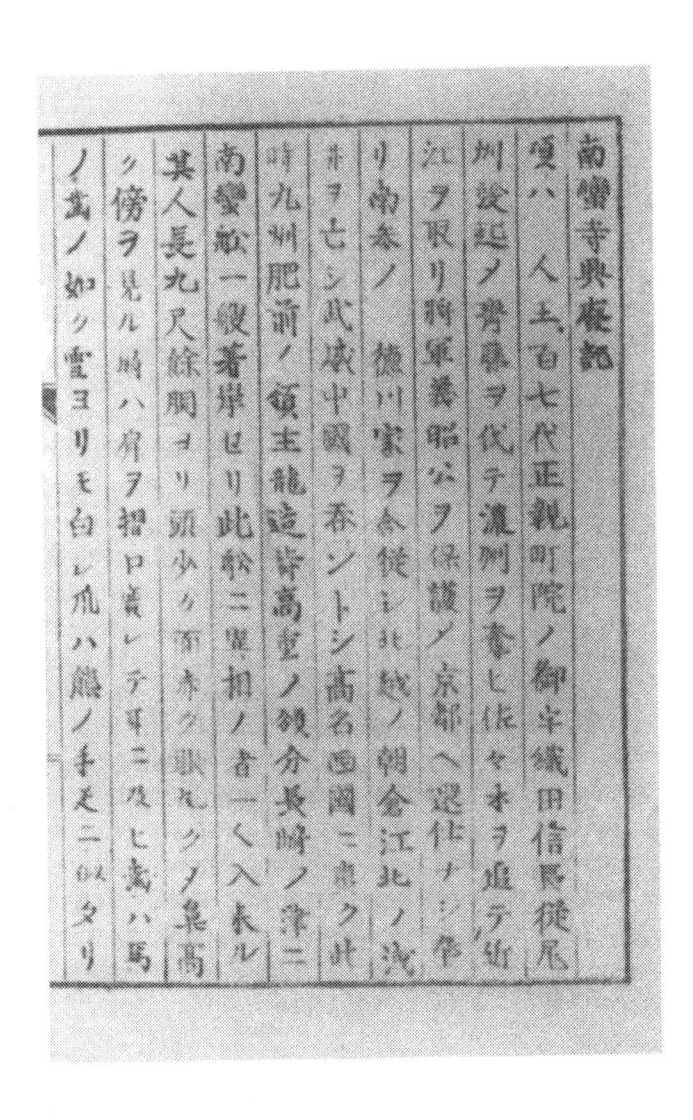

Fig. 12　The beginning of *Nanbandera kōhaiki* 南蛮寺興廃記 [The rise and fall of the temples of the Southern Barbarians], an account of the Christian churches in Japan which was published in 1868 in a movable-type edition. As can clearly be seen, the characters are not fully aligned and their impression on the paper is uneven: Hayashi & Kornicki 1991: #409.

and a Confucian scholar that the booksellers saw movable type as a potential threat to their livelihood, for their monopoly was confined to blockprinting. The scholar sought permission to publish some rare or elusive texts in movable-type editions for the benefit of scholars who were poor or far removed from good collections of books and the guild raised objections.[69]

The greater fragility of wooden type precluded running off large numbers of copies, and in fact far from being used to achieve economies of scale, movable type was utilized for relatively small editions by the standards of the second half of the Tokugawa period. Many indicate the size of the print run, and the maximum given is 300 copies, but 100 or less is much more common: Kumazawa Banzan's *Daigaku wakumon* was published in an edition of 100 copies under the title *Keizaiben*, and a work on naval defence was published in just 35 copies for circulation to 'fellow enthusiasts in this branch of study' (同学の志士). These two works, like many others which touched upon political matters or were works that had earlier led to difficulties, were clearly intended for restricted circulation because of the danger of censorship: until 1842.9.26, when an edict was issued requiring the manuscripts of books which were to be printed with movable type to be submitted for inspection like other books, there seem to have been no provisions for the censorship of books that were not blockprinted. This was probably both because books printed with movable type tended not to be offered for commercial sale and because they left behind no printing blocks from which almost unlimited copies could be printed. As a result most books printed with wooden type do not carry a colophon, which was required for other books, and consequently it is sometimes difficult to determine the date of publication, and the identity of the publisher can sometimes only be determined from the inside front cover (*mikaeshi*) or from the central fold of the page (*hanshin*).[70]

---

[69] Kawase 1967: 651–2; for an illustration of *Kachū Myōhō rengekyō shō*, see Kawase Kazuma, *Nihon shoshigaku yōgo jiten* 日本書誌学用語辞典 (Yūshōdō Shoten, 1982), 244. Ōuchida 1981: 65–9; Makita 1968: 2.158–66. Ōuchida Sadao 大内田貞郎, 'Shutsujō shōgo no ihan ni tsuite' 出定笑語の異版について, *Biburia* 36 (1967): 20–28.

[70] Sōda Ichirō 早田一郎, 'Kinsei mokkatsujiban kenkyū shiryōshū' 近世木活字版研究資料集, *Biburia* 81 (1983): 149, 151; Kishimoto 1986: 88–90; *BOS* 5: 301 #4714.

In many respects, then, as Ōuchida Sadao has suggested, the *kinsei mokkatsujiban* were more akin to manuscripts than printed books, for they were produced in small numbers of copies, sometimes *sub rosa*, and were mostly not for commercial distribution. Altogether more than 1,000 of these later movable-type editions have been identified, and although this is a small number compared with the numbers of blockprinted editions produced during the same period, the use of this alternative method of production either for scholarly or for political works is interesting. Kishimoto argues that it was an attractive alternative not only because it was free of censorship but also because on a small scale it proved possible for amateurs to undertake and was preferable to manuscripts as a means of producing a small number of copies. It is possible that a further attraction was the greater control that the publisher could exercise over the publication and distribution, as in the case of private publishing (§4.3.3), but without having to leave blocks in the hands of commercial publishers. Finally, what is not clear is whether those who turned to movable type were also interested in it as an alternative technology, and one that was used to print the Dutch books that were being imported into Japan (§7.1.4).[71]

BIBLIOGRAPHY

Kishimoto 1986; Ōuchida 1981; Tajihi Ikuo 多治比郁夫 and Nakano Mitsutoshi 中野三敏, *Kinsei katsujiban mokuroku* 近世活字版目録, *NSGT* 50 (1990), which contains a full bibliography. For the fullest set of illustrations, see Gotō Kenji 後藤憲二, ed., *Kinsei katsujiban zuroku* 近世活字版図録, *NSGT* 61 (1990).

4.4.2 *Western-style movable type*

For reasons that have been mentioned above, the introduction of typography from Korea only had any impact on Japan in the seventeenth century. Metallic movable type went rapidly out of use, although wooden movable type continued to be used, albeit on a small scale after 1650 and for non-commercial purposes. When metallic movable type came back into use in the middle of the

---

[71] Ōuchida 1981; Kishimoto 1986: 74.

nineteenth century, however, it was not as a revival of the earlier typographic traditions but as a technology imported from the West, and in this the Dutch East India Company at its base on Deshima in Nagasaki had a decisive role to play.

In 1848 a printing press and fonts of Dutch type arrived in Nagasaki on a ship of the Dutch East India Company. They were purchased in the same year by Motoki Shōzō 本木昌造 (1824–1875) and three other Dutch interpreters in the employ of the Bakufu in Nagasaki, and in 1851–2 Motoki managed to print *Ranwa tsūben* 蘭和通弁, a simple Dutch-Japanese dictionary. He used the Dutch type he had purchased and some crude Japanese *katakana* type he had cast for the purpose, but it is not clear what stimulated his interest in typography or how he managed the casting and printing processes. In 1855 the Nagasaki city commissioner purchased his press and applied to the Bakufu for permission to use it for the publication of books. Permission was granted not only to publish but also to seek more equipment from Holland, and between 1856 and 1859 several Dutch books were printed on this press in Nagasaki under Motoki's direction, including an introduction to natural science, and these have been described as the first 'modern' books produced in Japan, for they were bound in Western style. This press was joined in 1857 by another brought to Deshima by the Dutch East India Company, which was used there by the Company's representatives to print at least eight items between 1857 and 1862, including an edition of the treaty between Japan and the Netherlands, an infantry training manual, an almanac for 1861, and various works by Philipp Franz von Siebold and J. L. C. Pompe van Meerdervoort.[72]

The only other Western-style press active in Japan in those years was one given by the Dutch government in 1850 to Keiki, the last Tokugawa shōgun. This was entrusted to the Institute for the investigation of barbarian books (Bansho shirabesho), and was used to print a number of works in Dutch and English, mostly language primers, which were bound in Western style. There were some other attempts made to experiment with movable type in the 1850s and 1860s, notably by the Satsuma domain, which used the services of Kimura Kahei 木村嘉平, a well-known block carver from Edo, and

---

[72] Kawada 1981: 49–74; Fukui 1985: 177–255; Reinier H. Hesselink, '333 years of Dutch publications on Japan: 1566–1899', in *NYK* 9: 1–41, especially 20–21.

by Ōtori Keisuke 大鳥圭介, who printed two Japanese translations of Dutch works in Edo using his own *katakana* and *kanji* type in 1860–61. Later his type was taken over by the Rikugunsho, the Military Academy recently established by the Bakufu, and used in the 1860s to publish translations of English works on military science.[73]

By this time Europeans and Americans resident in Edo were beginning to publish newspapers and books in European languages. The *Nagasaki shipping list and advertiser* was the first newspaper to appear in Japan, on 22 June 1861, and within a few years there were several being published regularly in Yokohama and elsewhere. These were, however, published for the expatriate communities and had little discernible influence outside them.[74]

In the early Meiji period Motoki resumed his typographic activities and his pupils carried the skills of type-founding and typography to the main centres of population in Japan. In 1869 he appears to have invited William Gamble, head of the US presbyterian mission press in Shanghai, to Japan and this led to the popularization of Ming-style type (*minchōtai* 明朝体), which had been introduced in the Ōbaku edition of the Buddhist canon in the seventeenth century and which remains the standard style of typeface to this day. In that sense the growth of typography in Japan for printing in Japanese rather than in Western languages owes a considerable amount to the use of typography for printing in Chinese. In the 1870s typography was used to print growing numbers of newspapers and magazines in Japanese, initially using wooden type but rapidly adopting metal type, with the result that by the end of the Meiji period typography was the dominant means of printing while blockprinting was all but extinct for the production of books. However, it is important to recognise, as the catalogues of Meiji publications in the National Diet Library in Tokyo show very clearly, that blockprinting still had the upper hand until the 1880s. The substantial capital investment required for Japanese typography, with the need for huge fonts of characters, could only be justified by the expansion of the market for books and newspapers, and it was not until the end of the nineteenth century that this point was reached in all categories of publication.

---

[73] Kawada 1981: 60–74.
[74] Altman 1975: 52–3; Ebihara 1980: 15–78.

The limits on the number of copies that could be produced using wooden blocks ensured that once the market had grown beyond those limits blockprinting would cease to have any commercial advantages over typography, particularly when mechanical and then steam-powered presses made it possible to produce copies more quickly. Even then, blockprinting continued to be used for Buddhist sūtras and for colour illustrations, to preserve the customary format of sūtras published in Japan in the one case and in the other because no mechanical means yet existed of surpassing what could be achieved by blockprinting in the realm of colour illustration.[75]

BIBLIOGRAPHY

Albert Avraham Altman, 'Modernization of printing in mid-nineteenth century Japan', *Asian and African studies* (Jerusalem) 4 (1968): 85–105; Kawada 1981; Tsuda Isaburō 津田伊三郎, *(Honpō kappan) Kaitakusha no kushin* (本邦活版)開拓者の苦心 (Nagoya: Tsuda Sanseidō, 1934). On the books published by the Nagasaki city comissioner's office and the Institute for Western studies, see Fukui 1985: 177–255. On the Deshima editions see Itazawa 504–14, Fukui 1985: 179–80, and Kanzaki Jun'ichi 神崎順一, 'Tenri Toshokan shozō no Nagasakiban narabi ni Deshimaban ni tsuite' 天理図書館所蔵の長崎版並びに出島版について, *Biburia* 103 (1995): 158–124 (in reverse pagination). On the subsequent development of a modern publishing industry in Japan see Junko Bauermeister, *Entwicklung des modernen japanischen Verlagswesens*, Berliner Beiträge zur social- und wirtschaftswissenschaftlichen Japan-Forschung 6 (Bochum: Studienverlag Dr. N. Brockmeyer, 1980) and the works cited therein.

4.4.3 *Copperplate*

Copperplate printing was first introduced to Japan by Jesuit missionaries in the late sixteenth century, and it was under their direction that Japanese artisans learnt the art of engraving and applied it to the production of religious images. The earliest surviving

---

[75] Kawada 1981: 87–138; Kokuritsu Kokkai Toshokan 1971–6; on the connections between Motoki and Gamble and the *minchōtai* question see Yahagi Katsumi 矢作勝美, 'Meiji kappan insatsu no seiritsu to Bikashokan no eikyō' 明治活版印刷の成立と美華書館の影響, *Bungaku* 49.11 (1981): 149–60.

copperplate print evidently produced by a Japanese is an image of St Peter dated 1590, and during the years in which the Jesuit Mission in Japan flourished, copperplate printing was used for the production of a number of prints for devotional purposes: some of the books printed by the Mission Press contain copperplate illustrations and in addition various single-sheet prints have also survived. However, the suppression of Christianity and the expulsion of the missionaries in the seventeenth century inevitably brought about the decline of copperplate printing, which had been inextricably associated with the Europeans and the Catholic missionaries.

The revival of the art of copperplate printing in Japan, and the introduction of the use of the etching technique, are both due to the interest of Shiba Kōkan 司馬江漢 (1738–1818). Dutch books containing copperplate illustrations were certainly imported to Japan from the seventeenth century onwards, and in the eighteenth century single-sheet copperplate 'views' were also being imported via Deshima. These attracted the interest of Shiba and others, and in 1783 he succeeded in learning enough from Dutch sources to master the technique of etching and to produce copperplate prints. In the following years he applied his skills to the production of views of Japan, maps and pictures of animals, and the technique he and his pupil, Aōdō Denzen 亜欧堂田善, developed became more and more widely used. In the early nineteenth century it was particularly used for maps, medical illustrations and for 'views', and as such was predominantly associated with the Rangaku school and its empirical vision. An emblem of this was the frequent inclusion of legends not in Japanese script but either in romanized Japanese or in Dutch.[76]

In the 1830s there were two centres for the production of copperplate prints, Edo and Kyoto. In Edo, however, copperplate printing went into a decline, probably in connection with the negative intellectual and political climate which confronted Rangaku supporters in Edo and which made publishing Rangaku works more difficult (§8.2.2). In Kyoto, on the other hand, there was already a specialist shop dealing with copperplate prints, and Matsumoto Yasuoki 松本保居

---

[76] An early example of an imported book with copperplate illustrations is Dodonaeus's *Kruid boek*, presented to the shogun in 1659 (Kornicki 1997: 509). On Shiba's sources, see Sugano Yō 菅野陽, 'Shiba Kōkan no dōbanga no gihō no genten ni tsuite' 司馬江漢の銅版画の技法の原典について, in Asakura Haruhiko et al., eds, *Shiba Kōkan no kenkyū* 司馬江漢の研究 (Yasaka Shobō, 1994), 288–94

(1786–1867), a former student of oil painting, founded the Gengendō 玄々堂 firm which became the dominant producer of copperplate prints for a growing market up to the Meiji Restoration. In the Meiji period copperplate printing continued to flourish, partly because the fine detail that could be achieved was inextricably associated with the 'West', which by then of course enjoyed great cultural prestige. The techniques were also of practical value for the production of banknotes, postage stamps and share certificates, but in such areas the adoption of contemporary Western techniques was principally due to the contributions of the Italian artist and engraver Edoardo Chiossone, who was invited to Japan in 1875 to head the new government Mint.[77]

The history of copperplate printing in pre-modern Japan is thus one that mirrors the shifting image of the West. The fineness of line was understood to be a part of the Western way of 'seeing' things and it was applied to Japanese subjects, particularly urban views, in a demonstration of new ways of representing Japan using a European vision.

BIBLIOGRAPHY

Nishimura Tei 1941; Sugano 1974. Masanobu Hosono, *Nagasaki prints and early copperplates*, translated and adapted by Lloyd R. Craighill (Tokyo: Kodansha International, 1978). On Shiba Kōkan, see Calvin L. French, *Shiba Kōkan: artist, innovator, and pioneer in the westernization of Japan* (New York: Weatherhill, 1974), 41–52; Screech 1996: 95–103, deals with Shiba and with Japan's encounter with Western vision.

---

[77] Nishimura Tei 1941: 342–9, 347–65, 386–8. On Chiossone see Donatella Failla, *Edoardo Chiossone: un collezionista erudito nel Giappone Meiji* (Genoa: Comune di Genova, 1996) and Lia Beretta, 'Edoardo Chiossone', *TASJ*, 4th series, 10 (1995): 69–84.

CHAPTER FIVE

THE BOOK TRADE IN THE TOKUGAWA PERIOD

1   Publishing and bookselling
      1   Bookshops and publishers
      2   Production and the guilds
      3   Sales and prices
      4   Marketing and advertising
2   The growth of the publishing trade
      1   Publishing in Kyoto
      2   Publishing in Osaka
      3   Publishing in Edo
      4   Publishing in the provinces
3   The publishers
      1   Murakami Kanbee
      2   Suwaraya Mohee
      3   Eirakuya Tōshirō
      4   Obiya Ihee
      5   Tsutaya Jūzaburō
      6   Kawachiya Mohee

Although booksellers are known to have existed before 1600, it is in the Tokugawa period that the book became primarily a commercial artifact. Every facet of book production became the subject of commercial considerations, from the carving of the printing blocks and the printing itself to the sale of new copies and the operations of commercial lending libraries. Even privately published books, or books published by the Bakufu and the domains, were subject to the same conditions of production and of circulation, for the book trade in its various manifestations became the primary mechanism for the dissemination of books, including in some cases manuscripts.

170

CHAPTER FIVE

This chapter, then, focuses on the commercial environment in which books were produced, on the conditions it imposed and on the ways in which it shaped cultural production in the Tokugawa period. Although that environment undoubtedly had its negative consequences, not least in the matter of censorship, it also had the effect of expanding the market for books. The productive capacity of a set of printing blocks was, in the seventeenth century at least, far in excess of the numbers of potential purchasers in the town in which the publisher operated. Even in the seventeenth century, therefore, publishers were beginning to devise partnerships with booksellers in other towns so as to increase sales, and to develop means of advertising their wares. By the early nineteenth century at the latest, and most likely much earlier, we can speak of there being in Japan a national market for books, and this is one of the most important consequences of the development of commercial publishing in Japan.

5.1 PUBLISHING AND BOOKSELLING

5.1.1 *Bookshops and publishers*

To what extent books were a commercial commodity before the Tokugawa period is difficult to say, for the evidence is sparse. There is a record of the wife of a maker of sūtras going around Kyoto selling books in 1140, and there appear to have been bookshops on Mt Kōya in the fourteenth century, presumably selling books connected with the Shingon sect. However, although Japanese collectors and scholars had by then already been sending money to China for the purchase of Song printed editions, it is not clear if there was a book trade to speak of before the seventeenth century.[1]

In the course of the seventeenth century books became one of the visible commodities available in shops on the streets of Kyoto. In *Kyō suzume* 京雀 (1665), an early guide to Kyoto, an illustration shows a Buddhist monk examining books at the front of a shop on Teramachi street, and the sequel to this work, published a few years later, refers to two areas where there were dealers in second-hand

---

[1] Yayoshi 1988–93: 1.1–5.

books. Other seventeenth-century illustrations show shops displaying advertisements for books they had for sale, book-pedlars on the streets of Osaka, and customers examining books at the shop-front. By 1692, when a guide to shopping and goods around Japan was published, bookshops were evidently an attraction in the largest cities: the guide lists sellers of serious books and Chinese books in Kyoto (3), Edo (2) and Osaka (1), and lists separately sellers of books for the puppet theatre (3, 5 & 10, respectively). Eighteenth- and nineteenth-century illustrations show larger and busier establishments, with a big display of books, several clerks and an accounting desk, advertising signboards in the street, and customers, who are both male and female, adults and children, and from different social classes (Fig. 13). But it is clear that there were also much smaller businesses, for a guide to the sights of Osaka published in 1798 shows a tiny stall, next to a fishmonger, with the proprietor sitting, with a small display of books, under a sign declaring that picture books and playbooks were for sale. Books had become an everyday commodity well before the end of the period, and the market was sufficiently large and varied to be able to support substantial enterprises as well as neighbourhood stalls. By the time Francis Hall visited Edo in 1860 and noticed 'bookstores gaudy with high colored pictures arranged to attract notice', techniques for attracting the attention of customers were far from new.[2]

In addition to these specialist bookshops, there were other means of purchasing books, even in the seventeenth century. A story written no later than 1640 mentions book-pedlars on the streets of Kyoto, and by 1671 books were available at the regular markets held at the Kitano shrine, also in Kyoto. Pedlars also seem to have been operating in the Yoshiwara pleasure quarter of Edo in the late seventeenth century, providing books for the courtesans, who were expected to be able to read and are often depicted in prints doing so, and also providing guidebooks (§2.5) for the customers. Also, in 1773 Tsutaya

---

[2] Hanasaki Kazuo 花咲一男, ed., *Shokoku kaimono chōhōki* 諸国買物調方記 (Watanabe Shoten, 1972), 40. For contemporary illustrations showing bookshops in Kyoto and Osaka see Tajihi Ikuo 多治比郁夫, 'Keihan hon'ya zuroku 1 - hon'ya tentōzu' 京阪本屋図録 1 － 本屋店頭図, *OHNK* supplement to vol. 2 (1976), and idem, 'Keihan hon'ya tentōzu (hoi)' 京阪本屋店頭図（補遺）, *Ōsaka furitsu toshokan kiyō* 29 (1993): 1–16. For illustrations of shops in Edo, see Hayashi Yoshikazu 林美一, *Edo tenpo zufu* 江戸店舗図譜 (Miki Shobō, 1978), 47–49, and of shops in Nagoya, Ōta 1995. Notehelfer 1992: 268.

Fig. 13 The premises of the Edo publisher and bookseller Izumiya Ichibee 和泉屋市兵衛 (here written 泉屋市兵衛), who was active over several generations from the end of the seventeenth century to the late nineteenth century and published popular books and *ukiyoe* prints as well. The illustration is taken from vol. six of *Tōkaidō meisho zue* 東海道名所図会, a guide to the sights along the route from Osaka to Edo published in 1797: Hayashi & Kornicki 1991: #1475.[3]

---

[3] Inoue Takaaki 1981: 68.

Jūzaburō opened a shop just outside the Yoshiwara quarter and sold courtesan critiques and guidebooks right on the spot. Books were also commonly sold along with other goods, such as stationery, haberdashery and medicines.[4]

To what extent books were available in the provinces is still far from clear, particularly in the seventeenth century. One of the few explicit records we have is the diary of Ishibashi Seian 石橋生庵 covering the years 1642–97 in Wakayama, which was one of the larger provincial castle towns. As is evident from many other such records, an important source of books for intellectuals was frequently the libraries of their friends and acquaintances, and, as mentioned before, they often made it a practice to make partial or complete copies of books they borrowed in this way (§3.3). However, it is also clear that there were several booksellers in Wakayama, at least by the 1660s: Seian took books home on approval, paying later for those he wanted and returning those he did not. Further, he records the visits to Wakayama of booksellers from Osaka and Kyoto, from whom he also made purchases. Since at this stage there was no significant publishing activity in Wakayama or in any other provincial castle town, the books he purchased must of necessity have been published in Osaka or Kyoto, or possibly in some cases Edo. It is impossible to generalize from this one case, but given the presence in the larger castle towns of intellectuals whose milieu included domain academies and libraries (§§4.3.2, 9.2.2), it is probable that this pattern was replicated elsewhere, with local retail booksellers furnishing books from the centres of cultural production. Most were probably selling other goods as well. How they acquired their supplies of books is as yet unknown, but in most cases they would probably have come by ship.[5]

In the first half of the seventeenth century the books that were being made available for sale were for the most part produced in

---

[4] Nagatomo Chiyoji 長友千代治, 'Kinsei - gyōshōhon'ya, kashihon'ya, dokusha' 近世-行商本屋、貸本屋、読者, *Kokubungaku kaishaku to kanshō* 45.10 (1980): 94–6; Hanasaki Kazuo 花咲一男, *Edo Yoshiwara zue* 江戸吉原図絵 (Miki Shobō, 1976), 232; Hayashi Yoshikazu 林美一, *Edo kanban zufu* 江戸看板図譜 (Miki Shobō, 1977), 163, 280.

[5] Nagatomo 1987: 59–122; there is a complete facsimile of the diary in *(Kishūhan Ishibashi-ke) Kejō* （紀州藩石橋家）家乗, 5 vols (Osaka: Seibundō, 1984).

Kyoto. Commercial publishing developed there in the early decades of the century, but it is apparent that the financial capital for the establishment of printing shops and the commercialization of culture in Kyoto at this time came not from bodies that were already sponsoring the production of books, such as the court or Buddhist temples, but from established members of the mercantile elite. The first identifiable mercantile publisher was Nakamura Chōbee-no-jō 中村長兵ヱ尉, whose name appears in the colophon of a Zen text, *Goke shōjūsan* 五家正宗贊, published in Kyoto in 1608. Even more explicit is the name Hon'ya Shinshichi 本屋新七, which appears in a book published the following year and which indicates (*hon'ya* means 'book dealer') that the owner had something to do with the book trade, probably as a retailer of new and antiquarian books. Both of these books were printed with wooden movable type, and over the next 50 years many commercial publishers made use of the new technology, following the lead set by Tokugawa Ieyasu and other patrons of printing around the turn of the century. During this period it became common for book colophons to carry the names of what were unmistakably people of the merchant class living in the mercantile quarters of Kyoto. For example, an edition of a book of *haikai* poetry, *Hanabigusa taizen* はなひ草大全, was published in 1628 with the name of Sakaiya Magobee 堺屋孫兵衛, of Teramachi street in Kyoto, in the colophon: his address and use of a trade-name ending in *-ya* (*yagō* 屋号), instead of a surname, identify him as a townsman. It should be mentioned here that a trade-name such as Sakaiya Magobee was both the name of the firm and that of the successive heads of the firm; thus established firms would carry the same names over several generations.[6]

By the 1640s there were more than a hundred shops functioning in Kyoto as publishers of books, but some produced just one book, presumably as a side-line from their main business of retail operations. Doubtless in some cases commercial failure was the simple reason for their disappearance. While movable type was dominant at first, it did not completely replace blockprinting, which gradually assumed greater importance for the commercial production of books. The reasons for this shift have been discussed already (§4.2.3), but mention should be made here of Nakano's argument that commercialization

---

[6] Konta *et al.* 1981: 5; Kawase 1967: 338, 349–52, 359; Oka & Wada 1996: 326.

itself was partly responsible for this: he suggests that, in commercial terms, sets of carved printing blocks represented in the seventeenth century a more durable investment than a font of movable type: in addition to lending themselves to easy reprinting operations, they also had a marketable value and, as will be seen below, were often sold to other publishers. But whatever the case, and irrespective of the technology used, the net result of the printing boom of the period from 1597 to the middle of the seventeenth century was the appearance of at least 500 newly-printed titles, a total which is greater than that of all the books printed during the previous two centuries. It is at this point, then, that commercial printing and publishing come into their own, and the pace quickens over the succeeding decades.[7]

Most publishers were also engaged in other aspects of the book trade, including retail selling, book-lending and the use of pedlars to sell books further afield, and the names and terms they used reveal something of their activities. By 1609 the word *hon'ya* was already in use to indicate somebody active in some part of the book trade. It usually connoted, as it does today, retailing rather than publishing, but throughout the Tokugawa period many publishers used this word as their trade name, indicating a current or past close involvement with the retail trade. There were a number of other terms that were also in use in the seventeenth century as trade-names: *sōshiya* 草子屋, implying at this stage a dealer in bound books, although later the word *sōshi* acquired connotations of lack of seriousness; *shomotsuya* 書物屋, which increasingly was used by dealers of more serious books, such as sinological texts; *shōhonya* 正本屋, indicating a dealer in playbooks for the *jōruri* theatre; *tōhonya* 唐本屋, indicating a dealer in books imported from China; *ezōshiya* 絵草子屋, the name for dealers in illustrated books; and *monohon'ya* 物之本屋, which was a generic term for bookseller and publisher in the first half of the seventeenth century. In colophons and advertisements a variety of terms are used to denote 'publisher', including *shorin* 書林, *shobō* 書房 and *shoshi* 書肆, all of which were used by booksellers whether or not they were engaged in publishing. In some cases they chose to indicate a specialism, referring to themselves as *haikai shorin* (seller of books of *haikai* poetry), or even *Shōmon haikai shorin* (seller of books of *haikai* poetry in the tradition of Bashō). *Haikai* books became

---

[7] Okuno 1982: 102–4; Nakano 1995: 31, 34–5.

in the late seventeenth century an increasingly profitable part of the market, and a number of firms established themselves as specialist *haikai* publishers, mostly in Kyoto.[8]

Even in the seventeenth century booksellers required specialist knowledge about books, and later some became bibliographers and scholars in their own right (§10.2). Most, however, developed a specialist form of knowledge. An example is provided by an Osaka bookseller, who included the following story in a lengthy advertisement. When travelling by boat from Kyoto to Osaka he was talking about books with two doctors and a priest, and impressed them with his knowledge of the authorship, dates of publication, number of volumes and authenticity of the works discussed. Then he revealed his trade, whereupon they laughed at his superficial knowledge.[9]

A work published in 1702 suggests that there were very few publishers or booksellers who could be called scholars or intellectuals, but then gives four names for Kyoto and two for Osaka with details of their intellectual interests. Just a few years later a Kyoto publisher and bookseller named Nakamura Magobee compiled a bibliographical guide for fellow members of the book trade, *Bengisho mokuroku* 弁疑書目録, which gives details of forthcoming books and of books with similar titles that could easily be confused (§10.2). By the nineteenth century some publishers were becoming involved in bibliography and scholarship, such as the third head of the firm Kariganeya Seikichi 雁金屋清吉, who in 1811 held a gathering for the appreciation of old books and works of art. This was attended by well-known writers such as Santō Kyōden and Ōta Nanpo, with whom Kariganeya was in the habit of exchanging rare books, and it became a monthly event.[10]

By the middle of the seventeenth century the flood of publications was so great that there was a perceived need for information and guidance, and it was provided by the booksellers' catalogues known

---

[8] The advertisements contained in Nogami 1975, mostly from the early nineteenth century, reveal the wide variety of activities booksellers customarily engaged in. Inoue Takaaki 1981: 111, 298–302, 337–8, 407–9, 542–58, 611; Asakura 1983: 1.98–100, 270. Kira Sueo 雲英末雄, 'Haikai shoshi no tanjō' 俳諧書肆の誕生, *Bungaku* 49.11 (1981): 95–111.

[9] Nogami 1975: 73.

[10] Miyako no Nishiki 1937: 397–8; *Ichiwa ichigon*, *NZT bekkan*, 2: 393–412; *ONZ* 19: 235–7.

as *shojaku mokuroku* 書籍目録. The earliest of these is a manuscript which can be dated to 1659, and it is either a copy of a printed version no longer extant or a manuscript intended for publication but never actually printed. It includes some of the commercially published movable-type books, but it also includes works which were yet to be published and in some cases never were. However, the information given was sparse, titles and numbers of volumes only: authors were not yet deemed significant, for the concept of authorship was still immature (§6.1.1). The oldest printed booksellers' catalogue, *(Wakan) Shojaku mokuroku* 和漢書籍目録, was published c1666, and it established standard categories for Japanese books which were followed by the trade thereafter.

Shojaku mokuroku were sold to scholars and bibliographers as reference works, but they were primarily intended for the book trade and this determined their character. It was reported in 1702 that many booksellers carried around copies with them. These catalogues therefore excluded private publications and the publications of the domain academies, except in cases where the blocks had been sold to commercial publishers. They also left out many ephemeral works, such as actor critiques (*yakusha hyōbanki* 役者評判記) and *jōruri* playbooks, and the catalogues published in Osaka and Kyoto tended to be patchy in their coverage of Edo publications. On the other hand, they did include forthcoming works, such as an edition of the Ming work *San cai tu hui* 三才図絵, which appeared in catalogues from the 1660s to the end of the century but was never published. The last new catalogue was issued in 1772, and the one that was issued in 12 volumes in 1801, *Gōrui shojaku mokuroku taizen*, was in fact a composite work that used the blocks of four earlier editions, with some alterations to the blocks in an attempt to bring it up to date. It is significant that there were no further attempts to produce a catalogue of books in print, even though it would have been relatively easy for the guilds, with their records of permissions to publish, to produce one. Possibly the quantities of books published had become too great to contemplate producing such a catalogue, but more likely the detailed catalogues put out by individual publishers, which often focussed on a particular writer or genre, fulfilled the same function.[11]

There is little precise information available about the second-hand

---

[11] Miyako no Nishiki 1937: 397; Nogami 1975: 72–3; Shidō Bunko 1962–64.

book market, although it is evident from booksellers' advertisements that many shops from the seventeenth century onwards sold both new and old books. These also reveal that there were specialists in antiquarian books willing to accept orders, and that booksellers produced leaflets offering to buy books that were no longer needed for good prices. In his final years Bakin sold off some of his books, giving them to an antiquarian book-market at Nihonbashi in the heart of Edo. According to a letter he wrote to a friend, they attracted a lot of interest because of their association with him, and 'booksellers were milling around like ants'. He apparently sold 700 titles, including many manuscripts, and noted that he made a loss on his Chinese books, as most went for half the prices he had paid for them. Iit seems likely that he is here referring to books imported from China rather than Japanese reprints, but it is not clear if the price had fallen because there was a small market for sinological texts without the reading marks most Japanese readers relied upon, or because such books were now easier to get and hence cheaper. The market was thrown into confusion by the enthusiasm for new and Western books in the first ten years of the Meiji period, when many Europeans and Americans built up good collections of books (§9.4). According to Mizutani Futō, however, it was the value of works of Japanese literature that was particularly hit, while Chinese books suffered less on account of the continuing importance of sinological education. And it was only in 1890 that the first catalogue of antiquarian books was issued, in Osaka.[12]

Finally, although the whole process of the production and distribution of books is commonly presented as if it were exclusively male, this picture needs some correction. In the first place, it seems that bookbinding was often undertaken, at least in the nineteenth century, by women in the publisher's household, and there is a record in a book published in 1716 to the effect that the copyist responsible for the *hanshita*, or clean copy, was a woman. More importantly, however, Sakamoto has demonstrated that a few women were active as publishers and booksellers, having inherited the family firms when there were no male heirs available. Thus a list of Kyoto publishers compiled in 1853 includes the names of three women. Given the strict rules which made female inheritance difficult, this opens up the question, as yet

---

[12] Nogami 1975: 50, 56–7, etc.; *MFC* 6: 198, 200–202, 206.

unanswerable, of the roles that may have been played by women in cases where the male heir of the business was either uninterested or incompetent.[13]

BIBLIOGRAPHY

Konta et al. 1981; Nakano 1995; Nogami 1975. Setsuko Kuwabara, 'Verleger und Künstler – zur zentralen Rolle des Verlagswesens in der Edo-Zeit', in F. Ehmcke und M. Shōno-Sládek, eds, *Lifestyle in der Edo-Zeit. Facetten der städtischen Bürgerkultur Japans vom 17.–19. Jahrhundert* (München: Iudicium, 1994). Robert W. Leutner, 'The Japanese book publishing industry before and after the Meiji Restoration of 1868', unpublished MA thesis (University of Michigan, 1970). For the booksellers' catalogues see the facsimiles and commentary in Shidō Bunko 1962–64.

5.1.2 *Production and the guilds*

It was in Kyoto that many of the patterns and practices that became standard features of publishing in the Tokugawa period were developed, but it should be emphasized here that there are many aspects, particularly relating to the capitalization of publishing projects, that remain obscure. For example, one of the ways in which publishers spread the risks or raised the capital for new publications was to cooperate with fellow publishers, sharing the costs and, to ensure good faith, sharing the printing blocks out amongst themselves, so that any reprints would have to be undertaken by all the participants acting together. Such publications are known as *aiaiban* 相合版, and the earliest known examples are two books printed with movable type in Kyoto in 1628 and 1630. In many later cases it is common for publishers cooperating with each other in this way to signal the fact in the colophon by placing the word *hakkō* 発行, or one of the synonyms for 'publish', under their names in such a way that it clearly refers to them all. While it is easy to understand how it might have been possible to make the necessary arrangements when both

---

[13] Suzuki Toshio 1980: 1.33; *Shin usuyuki monogatari* 新薄雪物語, colophon; Sakamoto 1982: 2–3; Makita 1968: 1.15–32. There are also some scenes in a series of prints by Utamaro show printing operations in which all the workers are women: *GUDJ* 3: 80–81.

publishers were in Kyoto, even though we know little about how the finances were actually managed, it is quite a different matter when publishers from two or more cities were cooperating with each other. How were the financial and contractual arrangements made in such cases? And since it was impractical to share out the printing blocks when the publishers operated in different cities, it is likely that the *tomehan* 留板 system was used. Under this system each participating publisher in a jointly capitalized publishing project retained one block, with one of their number storing the rest, but again little is known about the arrangements made between publishers in such cases.[14]

As explained elsewhere (§2.3), the printing of books in the Tokugawa period incorporated a number of procedures dependent on craft skills. Before, however, a book could even get to that stage it had to pass through bureaucratic procedures which could be even more time consuming, and it could take as long as several years in some cases before a work reached the stage of being put on sale in another city. By way of example let us first consider the case of the 'Kizai' section of Itō Tōgai's *Meibutsu rikujō* 名物六帖, which combines some of the functions of a dictionary and an encyclopedia. The inside front cover proclaims that it was printed in 1725 (Kyōhō kinotomi shinsen 享保乙巳新鐫) but the postface is dated 1726; this is the date under which it began going through the process of being examined in the Edo booksellers' guild, subsequent to its apparent publication in that year in Kyoto by Tōhon'ya Kichizaemon 唐本屋吉左衛門. But the final entry in the guild's records, which confirms the right to put the work on sale in Edo and identifies the authorized distributor as the Edo bookseller Tōhon'ya Seibee 唐本屋清兵衛, is dated the eighth month of 1727. It is evident that it took over a year to pass from the state of being ready to be published in Kyoto to that of being put on sale in Edo.[15]

The guilds of booksellers engaged in publishing played a crucial role in determining what could be published and which books could be put on sale. Informal arrangements seem to have existed in the seventeenth century whereby booksellers and publishers sought to protect their trade, but the guilds, or *hon'ya nakama* 本屋仲間, were

---

[14] Yayoshi 1988–93: 1.13–4; Okamoto 1980: 50. On the costs of producing directories in 1865 and of producing Motoori Norinaga's works see Minami 1975: 35–6 and Okamoto 1980: 48–9.

[15] *EHSK* 1.12.

formally recognised by the Bakufu authorities only in the early eighteenth century: in 1716 in Kyoto, 1721 in Edo and 1723 in Osaka. For the booksellers and for the Bakufu alike control was the central issue (§8.2.2). The bookseller-publishers in Osaka and Kyoto had for some years been having difficulties with alleged infringements of copyright and had been successful in persuading the Bakufu in 1698 to ban the publication of *jūhan* and *ruihan*, but copyright was still a problem in 1702, when publishers in both cities were evidently bemoaning the damage caused to their trade. Furthermore, since the guilds were the only avenue to legal publication, these arrangements gave publishers a legally recognised monopoly of publishing. For this, unlike many other guilds formed at around the same time, they do not seem to have been required to pay regular and substantial fees to the Bakufu. On the other hand, internal Bakufu documents dating from 1721 make it abundantly clear that the Bakufu's motive for recognising the guilds and making their members responsible was to exercise control over the production of 'novel' (*shinki* 新規) goods, which were considered inherently likely to be undesirable. But it should be noted that this did not apply to books alone, for a memorandum in which this policy was advocated addresses itself to the cases of haberdashers, cake shops, tailors and suppliers of small goods. Books were not singled out for control, and the association of them with other consumables of daily life, while perhaps partly expressive of Bakufu disdain for popular publishing, is also a token of the extent to which books had become everyday goods in Edo.[16]

The guilds were divided into sections (*kumi* 組) run by their own members, who took it in monthly turns to serve as the managers, or *gyōji* (written 行司 in Osaka and 行事 in Edo and Kyoto). The *gyōji*, who had no offices and carried out thier official business at their own premises, were primarily responsible for ensuring that published books did not contravene the censorship regulations and did not infringe the copyright of other publishers, and it was their task to represent the guilds in their dealings with the city commissioners and other authorities. If a work that they had approved was found subsequently to be undesirable by the Bakufu authorities then the *gyōji* were held to be responsible, along with the author and the

---

[16] *Kyōto machibure shūsei* 京都町触集成, 15 vols (Iwanami Shoten, 1983–89), 1: 62, #193; Makita 1968: 2.6–7; Miyako no Nishiki 1937: 321; *SR* 3: 53.

publisher, and were subject to punishment (§8.2.2).[17]

The actual publishing procedures employed in Kyoto, Osaka and Edo differed slightly on account of their different administrative structures, and they also underwent some changes over time, but in outline they were as follows. A publisher submitted to the *gyōji* in office in his section of the guild the manuscript of a work he wished to publish together with a request for permission to publish. The manuscript was then checked by the *gyōji* to ensure that it did not contravene censorship regulations and that it was not a *jūhan* or *ruihan* of a work that had already been published. In some cases the manuscript was also forwarded to the guilds in the other two cities to ensure that it was not a *jūhan* or *ruihan* of a work that had been published elsewhere. Once the manuscript had passed this scrutiny, it usually went, via other officials and with a certificate signed and sealed by the *gyōji*, to the office of the city commissioner, although some of the lighter works of fiction seem to have been exempt from this requirement. On receiving the approved manuscript back, the *gyōji* applied his seal simultaneously to the letter of request and to the guild's registers, and sent it back to the publisher, who was then able to begin the process of having the blocks carved. In some cases the publisher had finally to submit a printed copy together with the manuscript for another inspection, but in all cases a fee was payable to the guild in order to obtain permission finally to put copies on sale.[18]

This process, and the records kept by the guilds, ensured that publishers had their rights to their printing blocks, which represented each firm's capital investment, officially recognised. The blocks had a capital value, and a publisher's right to this, and sole right to print from them, was recognised by the guilds as their *hankabu* 板株. If the investment had been shared by several publishers, then the *hankabu* were also shared. The blocks could be sold, if another publisher or publishers saw a potential market for further printed copies, and the sales of blocks were usually reported to the guilds. Little of this documentation has survived, but, for example, in 1858 Fūgetsu Shōzaemon 風月庄左衛門 of Kyoto reported to the Kyoto

---

[17] On the duties of *gyōji* see Makita 1968: 1.55–8.
[18] On the procedures and the terms used by the guilds see Makita 1968: 1.65–7, Suzuki Toshio 1980: 2.30–31, 35–6.

booksellers' guild that he had sold the blocks of nine books to Kawachiya Wasuke 河内屋和助 of Osaka for a stated sum: in one case Fūgetsu only had the rights to a quarter of the blocks and in other just one sixteenth, and so he shared the proceeds with his fellow publishers.[19]

This example points to an important feature of the commercial publication of books in the Tokugawa period, namely that there was an alternative to the technical and bureaucratic procedures that had normally to be gone through. That alternative consisted simply of buying existing blocks. This was, for example, the strategy used by Kawachiya Mohee in Osaka (§5.3.6), and it depended on the ability to maintain sales for a title that had already been published. We do not know much about the circumstances in which publishers were prepared to sell their blocks and their *hankabu*; some must have been forced by financial circumstances to do so, while others may simply have wanted to raise money for other projects or may have seen limited future possibilities for sales. But it is a fact that the blocks and associated *hankabu* were frequently sold, and it is often possible, through surviving copies, to trace the passage of a particular set of blocks through the hands of three or more publishers over several decades. In some cases the colophons acknowledge this with the word *kyūhan* 求板 (also read *guhan*), meaning 'acquired blocks'. The purchase of used blocks did not, however, necessarily represent a sound financial investment, for the sales of copies depended on the continuing existence of a market for the work in question. In some cases we can see that blocks carved in the seventeenth century were still being used in the nineteenth to produce copies, which tells us something about the longevity of the market for that work and, simultaneously, since there had evidently been no need to carve new blocks, indicates that the total number of copies sold must have been less than 10,000 over a period of 200 years. On the other hand, the blocks of the books published by Hachimonjiya Jishō did not bring their later purchaser much financial success even though he tried to pass them off as new works by changing the titles.[20]

---

[19] Makita 1968: 1.86–90; Kishi 1981: 22–4.
[20] Nakamura 1961: 127–47.

BIBLIOGRAPHY

Suzuki Toshio 1980; on the guilds in Kyoto, Osaka and Edo see Makita 1968; Kōzato 1970.

5.1.3 *Sales and prices*

As indicated earlier (§4.3.1), we have very little data to go on with regard to print-runs and in consequence we know very little about sales. It may have been the case, as was reported by a contemporary, that *Kiyomizu monogatari* quickly sold between two and three thousand copies in the middle of the seventeenth century, but what exactly does this tell us? Presumably the figures were thought worth mentioning because they were high, but whether they were high when compared to books of all kinds or just to others of a similar kind is not possible to say. Further, since the contemporary observer reporting these figures did so in a work which set out to refute the claims made in *Kiyomizu monogatari*, it is conceivable that he may have been exaggerating, or even understating, its success. On the other hand, the blocks for another work, *Kashōki*, were recarved three times between 1642 and 1659: it seems unlikely that this capital expenditure would have been made unnecessarily and therefore it is probable that over those 17 years at least 10,000 copies were sold.[21]

In the first half of the nineteenth century it is evident that sales were closely related to the prices of different genres, and that sales of the bulky *yomihon* in particular, which were expensive and mostly bought by lending libraries, were dependent on the perceived state of their financial health. When the lending libraries were suffering from a poor cash-flow then there was little point trying to sell as many copies as normal. One publisher is reported to have sold only 60 copies of Santō Kyōden's *Ukibotan zenden* (1809) and to have been left with more than 800 copies on his hands owing to his misreading of the market. On the other hand, Bakin's publisher was overly pessimistic when putting out the ninth part of his monumental novel

---

[21] *Gion monogatari* 祇園物語, in *(Kinsei bungaku mikanbon sōsho) Kanazōshi-hen* (近世文学未刊本叢書) 仮名草子篇 (Tanba: Yōtokusha, 1947), 51; Nakamura Yukihiko, 'Kinsei no dokusha', *Ōsaka furitsu toshokan kiyō* 9 (1973): 87.

Hakkenden on 1837.1.2 and printed only 200 copies, all of which were sold by the afternoon of the same day: by the end of the month he had printed and sold 400 more in Edo, and an unknown quantity in Osaka and Kyoto. And it is evident from surviving copies of *Hakkenden* that the blocks continued to be used for many years, in some cases well into the Meiji period, as was also the case with other *yomihon* too. In the case of the lighter genres of fiction in the early nineteenth century, Hamada states that most sales were made in the first few days after publication, which usually came at the beginning of the year, and that the market would only last for several months.[22]

Most of the information we have concerning sales relates to literary works, and the sales patterns of other kinds of publication remain largely unknown. However, two publishers of samurai directories submitted in 1865 a detailed statement of the costs they incurred. From this it appears that they expected to be able to print up to 15,000 copies from each new set of blocks, to sell most of them within the year, and in subsequent years to sell several thousand copies brought up to date by applying *umeki* alterations. In the case of privately-published works, there appears to have been some delay in distributing copies, if the example of Motoori Norinaga's *Kotoba no kayoiji* (1829) is typical: in the first year only 103 copies were printed, of which 28 were distributed by the author and 75 were for retail sale. Only in later years would the distributor be permitted to produce more copies in accordance with the demands of the market, passing some of the proceeds from each sale back to the Motoori family, which had provided the capital for publishing in the first place.[23]

Books published in the Tokugawa period do not contain any indication of their retail price, nor is any indicated in advertisements. Some of the booksellers' catalogues, starting with *Shojaku mokuroku taizen* in 1681, do give prices, but there is no evidence that these were binding on retailers. Further, this catalogue notes that the prices given were for *gehon* 下本, that is for books printed on ordinary paper, and the preface to another issued in 1696, *Zōeki shojaku mokuroku*, states that the retail price varied according to the paper quality and, in distant places, to the transportation costs. Various

---

[22] Aeba 1900: 2–3; Hamada 1953.
[23] Minami 1975: 36; Okamoto 1980: 46–7.

attempts have been made to relate contemporary prices to modern monetary values but they have generally foundered on unsupported assumptions or the complexities of the monetary system of the Tokugaw period. However, there seems to be little doubt that the prices of books in the seventeenth century and most of the eighteenth were high by comparison with the prices of other commodities, but at least by the late eighteenth century the lighter genres of fiction had become cheap and readily available, and were perceived to be so.[24]

Although the prices of commercially published books were in general not subject to any controls, this does not seem to have been consistently so. For example, the prices of the samurai directories appear to have been subject to some forms of control, presumably because they must have been published with the Bakufu's permission and possibly even encouragement. In 1842 Izumoji Manjirō 出雲寺万次郎 requested permission from the city commissioner to reduce the wholesale and retail prices of the three types of *bukan* he published, partly to cooperate with current Bakufu policy aimed at reducing inflation. In the 1860s he and Suwaraya Mohee requested several price rises on account of the rising costs of paper and labour and the rising number of pages needed to accommodate all the information. Nevertheless, *bukan* were not cheap, and the high production costs left publishers with only 10% of the retail price by way of profit. A similar case was that of the books published commercially on behalf of the Bakufu. The books sponsored by Yoshimune in the early eighteenth century were to be sold at fixed prices, and a memorandum relating to the commercial publication in 1812 of *Doryōkō* 度量考, a study of weights and measures, contained a careful calculation of the profits to be permitted the publishers after the costs had been taken into account and determined the retail price.[25]

Several writers have noted that some books listed in both the 1681 and 1709 booksellers' catalogues show falls in price even though consumer prices were mostly going up at this time. Mizutani Futō's view was that this was due to the works in question going out of date and hence being subject to price reductions. However, it is hard to

---

[24] Shidō Bunko 1962-4: 3.18, etc; Utano Hiroshi 歌野博, 'Edo jidai no hon no nedankō' 江戸時代の本の値段考, *Nihon kosho tsūshin* 772 (1993): 11–14; Nakamura 1961: 321.
[25] Minami 1975; *OKS* 994–5 #2023; *SR* 3: 88–9.

see how this argument can apply to the Confucian works and texts of the *Tale of Genji* amongst them. Kurita Mototsugu argues instead that the fall represents the effects of larger print runs and that when blocks were used over a number of years it became possible, once the capital investment had been recouped, to lower the prices. It is also likely that the expansion of the reading public and the book market made it possible to increase profits by marking down prices to a point where sales would dramatically increase.[26] The economics of publishing and of reading have hitherto been given only scanty attention, however, and it is not yet possible to say much about the economic accessibility of books in the Tokugawa period other than to reflect the impression of contemporaries that they were for the most part becoming less costly.

BIBLIOGRAPHY

For the booksellers' catalogues with prices see Shidō Bunko 1962–4. Minami 1975. Okamoto 1980.

5.1.4 *Marketing and advertising*

The marketing of books was taken seriously in the Tokugawa period, and some of the mechanisms used have already been mentioned, such as the visual displays and advertising signs used by booksellers at their premises and their use of pedlars to hawk their wares further afield. The advertising signs, and in the later Tokugawa period even some of their publications, also carried their trademarks, and in some cases these are the only means of identifying a publisher, particularly in the case of *ukiyoe* prints and some of the flimsier genres of fiction.[27]

From the late seventeenth century, in a book market that was growing in complexity, publishers began to give their publications subtitles such as *shinpan* 新板, literally 'new blocks', to draw attention to their novelty, or, in the case of directories, *shinpan kaisei* 新板改正, 'new blocks, revised', to suggest that they had been brought up to date. Similarly, when the blocks of a work were worn and books

---

[26] Kurita 1979: 62–5; *MFC* 6: 191–200.
[27] For a table identifying publishers with their trademarks, see *GUDJ* 3: 146–8 or Inoue Takaaki 1981.

printed from them difficult to read, publishers would sometimes put the word *saihan* 再板, 'recut blocks', on the title slip or in the colophon, to appeal to readers who were looking for cleaner copies. However, in both cases these words were subject to abuse and cannot always be taken literally: 'new' books sometimes turned out not to be new but to be presented as such to encourage sales, and books claiming to be printed from recut blocks are often printed in fact from old blocks to which some alterations have been made. Similarly, the claim, which was made in the colophon of some of the directories and maps (§2.5), that they were revised every month cannot be taken as anything more than the publisher's awareness of the market value of presenting them as up to date.[28]

Other techniques used by publishers included the use in titles of particular catch-words that were associated with bestsellers or had other connotations, such as *kōshoku* 好色, which suggested eroticism and was also used in the titles of several of Saikaku's works, *katagi* 気質, which appeared in the successful character books of Ejima Kiseki in the early eighteenth century, and *keisei* 傾城, which meant 'courtesan' and hinted at connections with the pleasure quarters. Successful works often led to sequels riding explicitly on the backs of their predecessors, particularly in the nineteenth century when a popular formula could be turned into a long-running market line, as with the *ninjōbon* of Tamenaga Shunsui. Similarly, in what is a sign of the growing marketability of authors' names, the works of unknown authors would sometimes carry an endorsement by a more well-known figure, or some other connection would be claimed: thus a work published in 1851, *Shunshō yumiharizuki* 春宵弓張月, proclaimed on the inside front cover *Kyokutei-ō genkō* 曲亭翁原稿, 'original manuscript by the venerable Kyokutei', thus claiming that the work was inspired by Kyokutei Bakin's famous historical novel, *Yumiharizuki.* Sometimes publishers would contribute a preface or, more commonly, a laudatory passage known as a *kango* 刊語 which appeared on the inside front cover. It is also clear, from references in numerous prefaces, that publishers often solicited works from authors and in some cases even determined their contents, but their role in the genesis of literary and other works is yet to be explicated.[29]

---

[28] *NKC* 4: 216.
[29] On sequels see May 1983: 150–81; for examples of a *kango* and a publisher's

In the early eighteenth century, if not before, publishers also began to insert at the ends of their books catalogues of the other books they had published or had available for sale. These reveal the range of their publications, their consciousness of niche markets and how they positioned themselves in the market for books. In some cases, like the catalogue produced by the Osaka publisher Kashiwaraya Seiemon 柏原屋清右衛門 around the 1720s, the publisher aims at comprehensive coverage and lists everything from medicine and pharmacology to *ehon*, works of fiction, and collections of Japanese and Chinese poetry. This particular example, like many others, bears the title 'Zōhan ryakumokuroku' 蔵板略目録 (summary catalogue of publications) and indicates that it is a list of works for which the publisher had the blocks and hence the printing rights. Some of the works, therefore, would not have been new but could be reprinted from the old blocks in response to demand.[30]

Although there were many generalist booksellers like this, which sought to establish themselves as shops to which purchasers would go for all kinds of book, many others either specialized, or presented themselves as specialists, in particular kinds of book. Uemura Fujiemon 植村藤右衛門 of Kyoto, for example, published a wide range of books but put out separate catalogues for his books on Chinese poetry and poetic composition and for his medical publications. The same is true of Okadaya Kashichi 岡田屋嘉七 of Edo, who put out a separate catalogue of his mathematical books. In these cases the specialist catalogues were normally attached to books in that field and hence would be aimed at the restricted readership for such books. Booksellers also became aware of the increasing pull of authorship and began to put out catalogues of the works of particular authors. The earliest example known to me is one of the writings of Kaibara Ekken issued in 1721, but there are others for the works of Motoori Norinaga, of Ogyū Sorai, and of Izawa Banryū 井沢蟠龍 (1668–1730), a Shintō scholar and encyclopedist, and it was particularly common for private publications to carry a list of the other works of the author (Fig. 14). Some of the catalogues mentioned here are little more than lists, but publishers sometimes included further information about each book,

---

preface see *Bunshō kanazukai* 文章仮字用格 and *Ehon hitorigeiko* 絵本独稽古 respectively. Hamada 1953.
[30] Asakura 1983: 1.333–52.

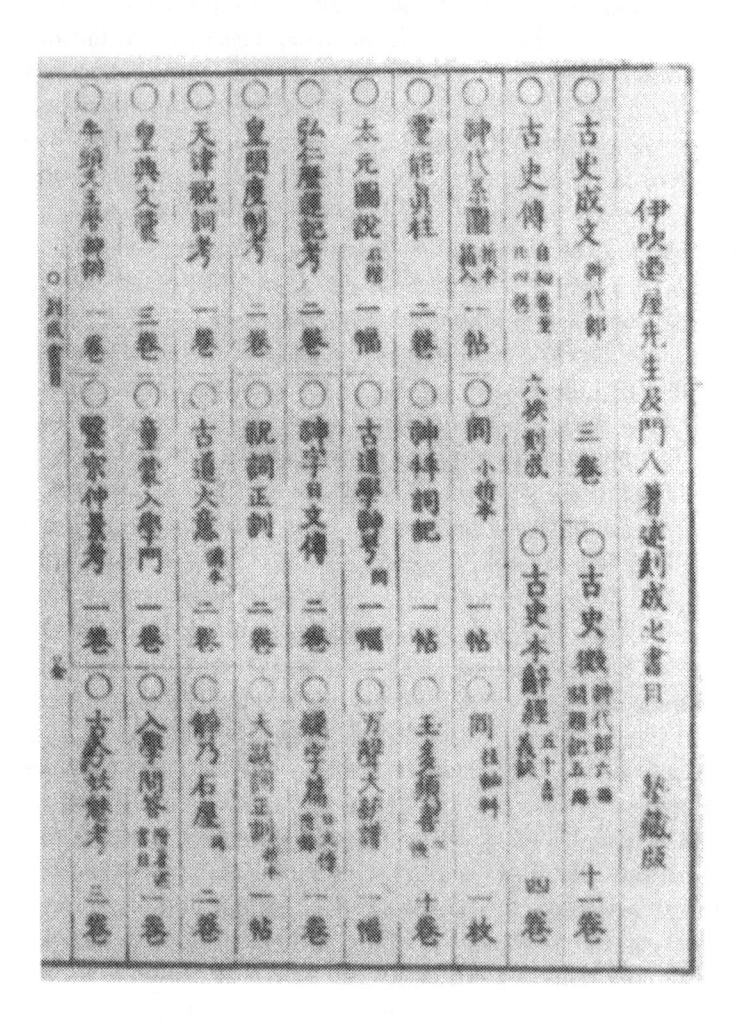

Fig. 14 A catalogue of the books written by Hirata Atsutane 平田篤胤 (1776–1843) and his followers at his school, known as the Ibukinoya, which was bound into a copy of his *Kishin shinron* 鬼神新論 (1820): Hayashi & Kornicki 1991: #204.

outlining the contents and explaining its merits.[31]

Publishers also produced handbills and more detailed advertisements dedicated to newly-published books, like the four-page advertisement for *Man'yōshū ryakuge*, a commentary on the *Man'yōshū*, which was put out by Eirakuya Tōshirō of Nagoya. Few of these have survived apart from some preserved in scrapbooks and others included at the ends of books. In some cases these handbills advise customers to purchase the book from their local bookshop, which displays a telling confidence in the systems for the distribution of books. And in rare cases booksellers even advertised their willingness to handle manuscripts on vendettas, daimyō disputes and other proscribed subjects. In the last years of the Tokugawa period and the early Meiji period, some of them began to use new language to advertise books, such as the nationalist language used to advertise an account of the products of Japan, *Kōkoku sanbutsu ōrai* 皇国産物往来. A handbill for *Kinmō kyūri taizen* 訓蒙究利大全, a translated introductory book on science, drew attention to the fact that its author was an American woman and described it as 'the best translation in these days of civilization and enlightenment'.[32]

By the end of the Tokugawa period some publishers, mostly in Edo, had acquired such substantial stocks of printing blocks ready to be used to produce books for sale that they took advertsiing a stage further. In effect they published separate catalogues of the books they had ready or could print for sale, and although most surviving examples date from the 1860s this practice dates probably from the early years of the nineteenth century. Kawachiya Kihee 河内屋喜兵衛 of Osaka, for example, issued such a catalogue in 1863 which consisted of more than 160 pages. A catalogue issued at about the same time by Suwaraya Shinhee 須原屋新兵衛 of Edo included more than 40 different editions of *Tōshisen* 唐詩選, an anthology of Tang poetry, varying in size and the nature or quantity of illustrations, notes and linguistic glosses.[33]

Finally, it should be noted that although all the publishers mentioned above operated in Edo, Kyoto or Osaka, this does not mean that

---

[31] Asakura 1983: 1.104–5, 110–11, 124–39, 149–52, 216–21, 360, 6.139–46.
[32] Asakura 1983: 1.49–52; Nogami 1975: 50, 75–6, 81.
[33] *(Kinsei kōki) Shorin zōhan shomokushū* （近世後期）書林蔵版書目集, 2 vols (1984), *SSS* 12, 1.77–244, 277–81.

these marketing techniques were limited to those cities, simply that the collections of published facsimiles consist almost exclusively of examples from them. Provincial booksellers also produced catalogues which they attached to the end of their publications. One example is a catalogue produced by Iseya Han'emon 伊勢屋半右衛門, the most prolific publisher in Sendai, who was active from the 1760s to the end of the Tokugawa period: it lists 23 titles including sinological works as well as maps and other items of local interest, and for each there is a short description referring to the author's achievements and the benefits or pleasures that the book will confer on the reader. Similarly, a handbill issued in 1854 for a map of the province of Bitchū by a local publisher in Kurashiki drew attention to its usefulness for tourists and for people travelling on business as a source of information concerning places of interest, local specialities, mileages, and so on.[34]

BIBLIOGRAPHY

For reproductions of advertisements see Asakura 1983, and of publishers' catalogues see *(Kinsei kōki) Shorin zōhan shomokushū* （近世後期）書林蔵版書目集, 2 vols (1984), *SSS* 12. For advertising techniques used by Kyoto booksellers see Makita 1978: 1.41. Forrer 1985: 44–6, and ch. 4.

5.2 THE GROWTH OF THE PUBLISHING TRADE

What does it mean to say that a work was 'published' in the Tokugawa period? Publishing of course implies a public, and that public expanded and changed in the course of the period. Many commercial publications from the seventeenth century carry in their colophons just the name of one publisher, in most cases a publisher from Kyoto. The implied public of these works is that of Kyoto, both its resident population and its visitors, although Kyoto books were available in Osaka and vice versa. To what extent they may have been available in Edo or in

---

[34] The Iseya catalogue is contained in a copy of *Gogyō ekishinan* 五行易指南 (1815) in my possession; on Iseya see Koikawa Yuriko 小井川百合子, 'Sendai no shoshi ni tsuite' 仙台の書肆について, *Sendai-shi hakubutsukan chōsa kenkyū hōkoku* 2 (1981): 15–19. Nogami 1975: 91–2. For a similar catalogue issued in Wakayama see Kornicki 1990: 196.

provincial towns is unclear, for little is yet known about the sales networks for books in the seventeenth century.

In the eighteenth century it became increasingly common for colophons to carry the names of several publishers, often one in each of the so-called 'three capitals' (*santo* 三都) of Kyoto, Osaka and Edo.[35] This raises difficult questions about the financing of publications and the identity of the 'real' or primary publisher, but at any rate by this time it is clear that sales networks encompassed all three cities and at least some of the larger castle towns as well. At the end of the eighteenth century and in the nineteenth there is a tendency for colophons to become more complex and to list a dozen or more publishers, mostly from Kyoto, Osaka and Edo but also sometimes from castle towns such as Nagoya, Hiroshima, Wakayama and Okayama. Take, for example the colophon found in some copies of *Ehon toyotomi kunkōki* 絵本豊臣勲功記: it lists 19 publishers and booksellers from Edo, 3 from Aizu Wakamatsu, 2 each from Yonezawa, Kanazawa, and Nagoya, and one each from Osaka, Kyoto, Fukushima, Takasaki, Utsunomiya, Tochigi, Sano, Sanjō, Nishiuraga, Zenkōji, Mito, Sahara, Kōfu and Sendai. This phenomenon not only bespeaks a greater density of circulation within the 'three capitals' but also the extension of circulation to major provincial towns, where these works were presumably available. Rural areas were for the most part dependent on their local castle towns, but even there supplies may well have been limited: in 1867 the headman of a village in what is now Niigata Prefecture travelled to Edo with orders from his fellow villagers for a number of books, including *Nihon shoki* and *Ehon taikōki*: it is interesting not only that they knew of their existence and could read them, but also that these books were evidently not available more close at hand. Well before this time books were already circulating widely through the network of commercial lending libraries (§9.2.4), but the point here is that publishers were consciously aiming their works at a national public.[36]

---

[35] Alternative names were used for each of the 'three capitals' during the Tokugawa period; while Kōto 皇都 for Kyoto and Tōto 東都 for Edo are common, Setto 摂都 for Osaka is much rarer, although it is occasionally encountered, for example in the colophon of Ōishi Matora's *Soga hyakubutsu* (1832).

[36] The example is taken from vol. 1 of the copy in Ōsaka Furitsu Nakanoshima Toshokan, which was first published in 1857, but the same colophon is found in the copies in the Chester Beatty Library in Dublin and Maidstone Museum of Art; all

If we define the actual publisher of a blockprinted work as the owner of the blocks, then all the other publishers listed in the colophon are present as distributors, and possibly also in some cases as financial collaborators, although this point is much less certain. It is generally understood that the last publisher named in a list in a colophon is the 'main' publisher, and it many cases this is clearly correct, especially when the last name alone is followed by the word *han* 板 or something similar to indicate ownership of the blocks. But in many cases this is not correct and then the publisher can only be identified by a publisher's catalogue or advertisements appended to the book, by an indication on the inside front cover, or by examination of the publishing records of the guilds. What these lists of publishers do indicate, however, is that publishing and distribution for sale were perceived as closely connected operations and that publishers made sure that the books they published were already locked into a distributing network on publication.[37]

5.2.1 *Publishing in Kyoto*

The origins of publishing in Kyoto have already been discussed, and it is likely that for most of the seventeenth century the population of Kyoto formed the bulk of the reading public for printed books in Japan, and that it was books produced in Kyoto that served the needs of readers elsewhere. The success of the Kyoto publishers can be traced statistically through the early editions of the booksellers' catalogues, which reveal very substantial growth in the numbers of publications as the century neared its end, and which explicitly began to exclude certain categories of publication, such as the erotic *kōshokubon*, on the ground that there were too many to include. But trade was not easy, for there were growing numbers of publishers and some of them were putting out imitations of successful works, thus diminishing the profits of the original publisher. By 1694, and

---

are later reprints from the original blocks, probably issued in the 1860s. Fuse Tatsuji 布施辰治, 'Tokugawa makki nengu shūnō no kunan o egaita Edo kikō' 徳川末期年貢収納の苦難を描いた江戸紀行, *Shakai keizai shigaku* 7.4 (1937): 106–16.

[37] Hasegawa Tsuyoshi 長谷川強, 'Kanki shoshi renmeikō' 刊記書肆連名考, *(Nagasawa sensei koki kinen) Toshokangaku ronshū* （長沢先生古希記念）図書館学論集 (Sanseidō, 1973), 511–40.

probably earlier, the publishers of Kyoto had therefore banded together to form an unofficial guild with its own *gyōji* system for their mutual protection, and it was this embryo guild which was recognised by the Bakufu in 1716.[38]

Before the guild had been officially recognised there were also private associations of publishers and booksellers, as there were of other trades as well, known as *kō* 講, which were often religious in their ostensible purpose. In Kyoto one was launched in 1685 which required members to make a monthly subscription. The capital sums accumulated in this way by the *kō* are said to have been available to members to borrow from, so that they could finance publication with a loan and repay it from the proceeds, but details are wanting. Further, one of these *kō* in Kyoto was associated with the Kitano shrine, and in 1702 this *kō* constructed a storage house for books in the shrine precincts in which publishers lodged one copy of any new book they printed. Apart from any religious meaning this act might have had, it also had the severely practical purpose of ensuring that if, through some mishap or as a result of fire, the printing blocks were destroyed, the copy lodged in the shrine could be used to prepare a facsimile edition by *kabusebori*. Although eminently practical, it is not clear if this was the purpose or merely a consequence of the formation of this *kō*.[39]

The numbers of booksellers engaged in publishing in Kyoto at the turn of the seventeenth century is difficult to establish. The contemporary writer Miyako no Nishiki stated in 1702 that there were 72, and he singled out the ten most important of these as the 'ten philosophers' (*jittetsu* 十哲) after the term used for the legendary ten disciples of Confucius, and these were in fact responsible for a very substantial proportion of the books published in the seventeenth century. The formation of the guild in 1716 did not lead to a fixed number of publishers operating in Kyoto, for the size of the membership was not fixed: unlike other guilds, where the point was to limit the numbers active in the trade, the booksellers' guilds in Kyoto and elsewhere were concerned with the control of the product, not of the numbers of publishers. Anybody could join if they could prove that they had the requisite skills and trade connections, and the *gyōji* of

---

[38] Shidō Bunko 1962–4; Makita 1968: 1.5–12.
[39] Yayoshi 1988–93: 1.14–7.

the three (later two) sections of the guild considered applications at their monthly meetings. Members could be expelled from the guild, and were indeed expelled on occasions: in such cases the facts were reported to the guilds in Osaka and Edo and all booksellers were forbidden, on pain of expulsion, to deal with the expelled member. On 1841.12.13, as a part of the Tenpō reforms which had far-reaching effects on the censorship system (§8.2.2), the Bakufu ordered the dissolution of all guilds, considering them to be one of the causes of the current financial crisis. Accordingly, the Kyoto booksellers had no choice but to dissolve the guild in 1842, which led to a predictable increase in the number of disputes between publishers. In 1851 the Bakufu reversed its decision and permitted guilds to re-form: the Kyoto booksellers' guild was revived in 1853 with 200 members.[40]

While it was in Kyoto that commercial printing and publication emerged and developed into a means of cultural production that reached most corners of Japan by the end of the seventeenth century, the subsequent development of publishing in Osaka and Edo has obscured the continuing role of Kyoto. Makita, for example, writes that by the nineteenth century Kyoto publishing erred on the conservative side and had been overtaken by Osaka and Edo except for the production of artistic and Buddhist books. It is certainly true that Kyoto had long since ceased to produce works of popular literature by then. However, given the buoyant market for the Buddhist texts and medical, philosophical and other academic texts published and constantly reprinted in Kyoto, it is probable that Kyoto publishers continued to supply books in quantities as significant as those produced by Edo publishers. It is largely the focus on current prose literature, which was overwhelmingly a product of Edo by the nineteenth century, that has skewed perceptions, and studies of non-literary publishing are needed to correct the balance.[41]

BIBLIOGRAPHY

The standard studies of the book trade in Kyoto are Makita 1968 and Munemasa 1982; see also Yayoshi 1988-93 vols 1 & 5 and Munemasa &

---

[40] Miyako no Nishiki 1937: 397; Makita 1968: 1.15-32, 51-4, 106-7; Kōzato 1970: 110-11.
[41] Makita 1968: 1.32; Konta et al. 1981: 7. Suzuki Toshio 1980, although a good guide to publishing in Edo, deals exclusively with literary publishing.

Wakabayashi 1965. The records of the Kyoto booksellers' guild are reproduced in facsimile in Munemasa Isoo & Asakura Haruhiko, eds, *Kyōto shorin nakama kiroku* 京都書林仲間記録, 6 vols, *SSS* 5 (1977–80). There is an index of Kyoto publishers in *(Shuppan bunka no genryū) Kyōto shoshi hensenshi* （出版文化の源流）京都書肆変遷史 (Kyoto: Kyōto-fu Shoten Shōgyō Kumiai, 1994).

5.2.2 Publishing in Osaka

The origins of publishing in Osaka are obscure, and it seems that at first the growing mercantile city's needs in the way of maps and books were most likely served by Kyoto publishers for the greater part of the seventeenth century. Hamada Keisuke has shown that extant books seemingly published in Osaka in the first half of the century have in fact got faulty colophons showing the wrong dates. And the oldest extant maps of Osaka, which were published in the late 1650s, carry no place of publication and were likely published in Kyoto.[42]

It has long been assumed that the first publisher operating there, in the 1660s, was Nishizawa Tahee 西沢太兵衛, and it is indeed true that in the eighteenth century this was an active Osaka publishing house, but it now appears probable that it was operating at first from Kyoto and that his publications in the 1660s and 1670s, which give his name and the date but do not give his address, were published there. The first work definitely published by Nishizawa in Osaka appeared in 1683, and even as late as 1698 the firm appears to have been active in both Osaka and Kyoto. At present, therefore, the earliest work that can definitely be shown to have been published in Osaka is *Aseishū* 蛙井集 (1671), a collection of *haikai* verse published by Ōmiya Jirōemon 近江屋次郎右衛門: his address does not appear in the colophon, but he is known from contemporary sources to have been operating in Osaka.[43]

---

[42] Sako Keizō, 'Meirekiban Ōsakazu no chōmei chōki ni tsuite' 明暦板大阪図の町名丁記について, in *Kochizu kenkyū: gekkan Kochizu kenkyū hyakugō kinen ronshū* 古地図研究－月刊古地図研究百号記念論集 (Nihon Chizu Shiryō Kyōkai, 1978), 289–97. On early maps of Osaka see Sakichi Keiga 佐吉慶賀, *Kohan Ōsaka chizu shūsei* 古板大阪地図集成 (Osaka: Seibundō, 1970).

[43] Hamada Keisuke 浜田啓介, '*Ikutama manku izen no Ōsaka kanpon o utagau*'

Publishing in Osaka, a predominantly mercantile town lacking the samurai and Bakufu presence of Edo and the scholarly and religious presence of Kyoto, became established by producing books for the local market. Chief among these were maps, books of *haikai* poetry, and the prose fiction of Ihara Saikaku, whose origins were in the Osaka mercantile community, and of other Osaka writers of similar background. By 1698 copyright infringements were proving so troublesome that 24 Osaka booksellers petitioned the city commissioner for a ban on publications that infringed the rights of other publishers, and the commissioner obliged by issuing such an edict. Following the recognition of the Osaka booksellers' guild in 1723, the guild frequently found itself having to adjudicate in disputes which arose between Osaka publishers and those in other cities, especially Edo. It is evident that by the early eighteenth century Osaka booksellers perceived the whole of Japan as a potential market which could be damaged by the production of pirated or copy-cat editions elsewhere. Between the 1720s and 1815 some 370 publishers were active in Osaka, of whom more than 150 were linked with Edo publishers. Together they published about 1,200 books in Edo: this constituted roughly 15% of the Edo total but 33% of the Osaka total, and is an indication of the dependence of the Osaka book trade on the Edo market. On the other hand, Osaka was simultaneously perceived as part of the market for Edo publishers, with the consequence that when Osaka firms infringed the rights of Edo booksellers, the latter protested. In 1751, for example, an Osaka publisher rashly put out an edition of *Tōshisen*, which was the monopoly of Suwaraya Shinhee of Edo: the offence was detected and the offender lost both the blocks and his supply of printed copies.[44]

In 1730 some Osaka publishers founded the Tenmangū gobunko kō 天満宮御文庫講, a voluntary association, or *kō*, based at the Tenmangū shrine in Osaka similar to that functioning in Kyoto. Publishers offered the shrine an early impression of each book they published, sometimes printed on high-quality paper or specially bound, both as an act of devotion and as a practical measure to ensure the

---

『生玉万句』以前の大阪刊本を疑う, *Ōsaka Furitsu Toshokan kiyō* 10 (1974): 21–36; Tajihi Ikuo 多治比郁夫, 'Kinsei Ōsaka insatsu shi' 近世大阪印刷史, in *Ōsaka insatsu hyakunenshi* 大阪印刷百年史, 2 vols (Osaka: Ōsaka-fu Insatsu Kōgyō Kumiai, 1984). On Nishizawa see Nagatomo 1994: 1–18.

[44] Makita 1968: 2.6–7, 93–6; Sakamoto 1982: 1.

survival of at least one copy that could be used to produce a facsimile edition by *kabusebori*. For even when the blocks of a book were burnt or lost, their owner retained his *hankabu* in the work. There was a similar *kō* attached to the Sumiyoshi shrine in Osaka, and at some stage the two combined to form one organisation, but most of the books were burnt in 1837 in the fire that followed the riot led by Ōshio Heichachirō.[45]

The publishing procedures that were in force in Osaka were similar to those in Kyoto and need not be rehearsed here. By comparison with Kyoto and Edo, the publishing world of Osaka has yet to be extensively studied. Although a number of powerful and active publishers can be identified such as Akitaya Taemon 秋田屋太右衛門, who was operating from the seventeenth century to the twentieth, their history and commercial strategies are mostly unexplored. The one exception is the Kawachiya group of booksellers, whose purchases of printing blocks in the nineteenth century made Osaka important as the centre of *yomihon* reprinting (§5.3.6). This strategy was, however, predicated on the use of capital not for the publication of new titles but for investment in existing ones. Nevertheless, Osaka remained throughout the eighteenth and nineteenth centuries an important segment of the market for books, and most published books were furnished with lists of distributors that include at least one from Osaka.[46]

BIBLIOGRAPHY

The standard study of the book trade in Kyoto is Makita 1968, which cites many documents that are not accessible. See also Yayoshi 1988–93 vol 2. The vast records of the Osaka booksellers' guild have been reprinted in *OHNK*, but the extracts contained and indexed in *OSSM* are still useful.

5.2.3 *Publishing in Edo*

By the end of the Tokugawa period Edo was at least on a par with Kyoto for the production of books, and dominated the market for

---

[45] *Ōsaka Tenmangū gobunko kokusho bunrui mokuroku* 大阪天満宮御文庫国書分類目録 (Osaka: Tenmangū, 1977), 1.

[46] For details of the Osaka publishing procedures see Makita 1968: 2.54–65.

prose literature, but it had taken some time to reach that position. For well over a century it was subordinate to Kyoto and Osaka, which led the publishing world and provided the books that the rest of Japan read. Edo had the highest population, with an estimated one million inhabitants by 1700, and therefore was the largest potential market. The history of publishing in Edo, therefore, is the history of its resistance to the domination of Kyoto and Osaka, and of the entrepreneurial development of new fields of publishing.

It has become something of a commonplace that in the second half of the eighteenth century Edo gradually took over from Kyoto as the centre of cultural production. In terms of the publication of literature there can be no doubt that this was true and that, in the nineteenth century, most fictional literature was published in Edo. However, so far there have been few studies of the publication of literature other than prose fiction, let alone of non-fiction, and it is far from clear that Edo's dominance extended to all fields of publication. On the contrary, as Munemasa Isoo has argued, it is perfectly possible that Kyoto may have remained the pre-eminent cultural producer right up to the 1860s once the publication of reprints as well as new titles is taken into account.[47]

The first books printed in Edo were produced with movable type by some Tendai monks in the 1620s, but the origins of commercial publishing are unclear. By the 1660s several publishers were active there, as is evident from their publications. These included Shōkai Ichirōbee 松会一郎兵衛; Izumoji Izumi-no-jō 出雲寺和泉掾, which was a branch of a Kyoto firm that started publishing in Edo c1655 and was, like Shōkai, an official supplier of books to the Bakufu; and Urokogataya Magobee 鱗形屋孫兵衛, who in 1660 published a guide to the Yoshiwara pleasure quarter and later published *jōruri* playbooks, illustrated books and works of light fiction. By 1687 it is recorded that there were 25 firms involved in the Edo book trade, comprising 16 bookseller-publishers (*shomotsuya*), five dealers in *jōruri* playbooks, three dealers in manuscripts of unspecified kinds, and one specialist in imported Chinese books. In the seventeenth century it appears that the strongest booksellers were those which had close ties with Kyoto or Osaka publishers, for they could draw on ready-made printing blocks rather than having to find the capital

---

[47] Konta Yōzō *et al.* 1981: 7.

to invest in new books.[48]

By 1675 publishing and the market for books in Edo had risen to the level that booksellers felt the need for a catalogue to bring some order to the trade. This was reissued in 1683, with a number of additions and with the pages rearranged so that Confucian books were given precedence, which is probably a reflection of the interests of the large samurai population of Edo. By this time there was already an embryo guild in existence, but it was not recognised and had no privileges. In 1657 the Bakufu attempted to restrict the formation of trade organizations of this kind and explicitly included publishers in the edict, but it is unclear how effective this was. In any case when in 1721 Bakufu officials summoned the 47 publishing booksellers of Edo to a meeting and explained the procedures to be followed in the future to prevent the publication of undesirable books and to reduce the number of copyright disputes, the effect of the new arrangements was simply to legitimize what was already established practice in Edo. The guild consisted from 1725 of three sections covering different areas of the city, and in 1730 they reached an agreement to control the sale in Edo of books imported from Kyoto and Osaka. The records of the guild survive for the years 1727–1815, but they are patchy compared to those that have survived for Osaka. The publication records for each book, in Edo as elsewhere, indicate the publisher, termed *hanmoto* 板元, and the distributor, termed *uridashi* 売出し. In addition they name the author, in what is clearly a recognition of authorship that has as much to do with censorship regulations as the growing public visibility of authors. Their value lies, however, in the fact that they clearly identify the publisher, as distinct from the distributors, in ways that extant books rarely do.[49]

In addition to the booksellers' guild, Edo also had its own guild of block-carvers, the *Hangiya-nakama* 板木屋仲間, which was only officially recognised in 1791. The members of this body were at first mainly involved in carving blocks for officially authorized calendars, which were then printed by artisans who acted as their employees. Later they began printing other works too, and in the 1660s they were compulsorily organised into a guild by the city authorities

---

[48] Inoue Takaaki 1981: 81, 105. On early Edo publishing see also Konta 1974: 113–8.
[49] Shidō Bunko 1962–4: 2.8–9, 53–160, *OKS* Meireki 3.9; Kōzato 1970: 103–10; *EHSK*.

expressly to exercise control over illicit publications. In the eighteenth century some of them continued to function effectively as publishers while others became contractual block-carvers and printers for Edo publishers. By 1790 there were 62 members of this guild, but the number had risen to 223 by 1852. This must be taken as an indication of the rising demand for print, not only for books but also for notices, advertisements and other ephemera. For reasons of censorship the members were required to obtain permission before undertaking to carve any blocks, and for similar reasons publishers were required to use members of the guild for their carving needs. However, it is clear that by 1802 some samurai were undertaking block-carving as a side employment, getting their work directly from publishers, and this may in some cases have been undertaken to escape censorship. Similarly, members of the block-carvers guild were also undertaking some illegal printing and, for example, contravening the requirement that even handbills should be subject to pre-printing censorship.[50]

The main Edo booksellers' guild was known as the *Shomotsuya nakama* 書物屋仲間, and its members handled both the publication in Edo of books initially published elsewhere and the publication of books produced in Edo, which were known as *jihon* 地本, 'local books'. The publishers of these 'local books', at first mostly illustrated *jōruri* playbooks but later the lighter genres of Edo fiction and prints as well, subsequently formed their own association, the *Jihon toiya nakama* 地本問屋仲間, the records of which have not survived. In 1790, Tsutaya Jūzaburō applied his entrepreneurial skills to the enhancement of the *Jihon toiya nakama* by attempting to incorporate within it the block-carvers' guild, but the move was resisted. Nevertheless, with the development of new genres of fiction, such as the *sharebon* that were set in the pleasure quarters, and the extensive range of illustrated light fiction known collectively as *kusazōshi*, the muscle of the *jihon* booksellers grew and there is evidence that they

---

[50] Yoshihara Ken'ichirō 1980: 254; Kitakōji Ken 北小路健, *Hangiya kumiai monjo* 板木屋組合文書 (Nihon Editā Sukūru shuppanbu, 1993), iv–ix; Yoshihara Ken'ichirō 吉原健一郎, 'Bakumatsu no Edo hangiya nakama' 幕末の江戸板木屋仲間, in Nishiyama Matsunosuke sensei koki kinenkai 西山松之助先生古希記念会, ed., *Edo no minshū to shakai* 江戸の民衆と社会 (Yoshikawa Kōbunkan, 1985), 505–521; and Yoshihara Ken'ichirō, 'Edo hangiya nakama to ihō insatsu' 江戸板木屋仲間と違法印刷, *Bungaku* 49.11 (1981): 138–48.

were finding markets for their wares even in distant parts of Japan.[51]

In the early nineteenth century, when Edo dominated the production of the historical fiction known as *yomihon*, a new publishing force began to challenge the role of the members of the booksellers' guild. Since *yomihon* tended to be bulky and expensive to purchase, most of their readers gained access to them through the commercial lending libraries, or *kashihon'ya* (§9.2.4): both the authors and the publishers were well aware of the crucial role these institutions played in the finely balanced economics of producing these works, and the leading writer, Bakin, was himself acutely sensitive to this nexus. But the *kashihon'ya* did not simply provide a distributing service, for in the early years of the nineteenth century it is clear that they also began to be active as publishers. Formally, of course, they did not have the right to publish and requests for permission to publish were made by members of the *shomotsuya* guild, but it has recently become clear that in many cases the owners of the blocks, who made the financial investment for publishing, were actually *kashihon'ya*. It is not clear how they came by the capital to finance the publication of *yomihon*, but it is apparent that the *shomotsuya* guild began to see them as a threat to their livelihood as publishers. That the *shomotsuya* booksellers were losing their financial muscle seems to be clear from the fact that they gradually sold so many of their *yomihon* printing blocks to Kawachiya Mohee of Osaka (§5.3.6). The circumstances that necessitated these sales and shifted the centre of *yomihon* reprinting to Osaka are as yet unclear. They may well be closely related to the shock occasioned the Edo publishing world by the consequences of the Tenpō reforms, which led, directly or indirectly, to the deaths of many of its leading authors (§8.2.2).[52]

Although Edo is most famous in publishing terms for the prose literature it produced in the second half of the Tokugawa period, it is important to remember that this was just part of the commercial publishing operations undertaken there. The large samurai population were not only a market for *yomihon* but also for the *bukan*, or directories of Bakufu officialdom, of which Suwaraya Mohee acquired a virtual monopoly and which, as we have already seen, were updated at least

---

[51] Konta 1974: 139–143, 163–4; Suzuki Toshio 1980: 1.58–61; Yoshihara Ken'ichirō 1980: 250–52.

[52] Hamada 1953; Takagi 1995: 20–48.

annually and possibly sometimes monthly (§2.5). Another product that was evidently much in need, at least for the constant flow of visitors to Edo, was maps. The buoyancy of this market is indicated by the profusion of different kinds of maps of Edo and the frequency of copyright disputes. In an effort to reduce their occurrence, the *gyōji* of the *shomotsuya* and *jihon toiya* guilds drew up in 1817 a register of the *hankabu* (rights in printing blocks) of all the maps in print so as to be able to monitor infringements more easily.[53]

As the Tokugawa period drew to a close, Edo was bereft of the prose authors whose names had sold books since 1790 and their epigones could not match their selling power. In this climate what sustained the livelihood of the booksellers was more likely to be the sorts of publication for which there was a steady demand, such as maps and *bukan*, and those for which there seems to have been a growing demand, such as textbooks for school use. Although most of the major booksellers of Edo survived the political changes of 1868, by the 1880s many were in difficulties or closing down and their places were being taken by new firms. It seems likely that the older firms experienced difficulties in coming to terms with the end of the *hankabu* system, the introduction of new technologies, a more punitive and rigorous censorship system, and a market driven by new political and cultural energies, but the circumstances that caused the closures and determined the strategies of the new firms are yet to be fully explored.[54]

BIBLIOGRAPHY

The standard studies of the Edo book trade are Kōzato 1970 and Konta 1974, but see also Konta 1977, Suzuki Toshio 1980, Yayoshi 1988–93 vols 3–4, and May 1983. *EHSK* provides a facsimile of the guild records for the years 1727–1815, which are all that survive; see also Higuchi Hideo 樋口秀雄 and Asakura Haruhiko 朝倉治彦, eds, *(Kyōhō igo) Edo shuppan shomoku* （享保以後）江戸出版書目 (Toyohashi: Mikan Kokubun Shiryō Kankōkai, 1962), and Kaneko Kōji 金子宏二, '(Honkoku) *Sankumi shomotsu*

---

[53] Iwata Toyoki 1980: 255–322.
[54] Konta 1974: 190. The profiles of the publishing companies contained in *(Tōkyō) Shosekishō denki shūran* （東京）書籍商伝記集覧, *NSGT* 2 (1978; facsimile of edition of 1912), reveal how few pre-Meiji firms were still in business in 1912; see also the dates given in Inoue Takaaki 1981, although these need to be treated with some caution.

ton'ya shokitei' (翻刻)『三組書物問屋諸規定』, *Waseda Daigaku Toshokan kiyō* 18 (1977): 55–92. For a good illustrated collection of studies on Edo publishing at the end of the eighteenth century see the exhibition catalogue *Kansei no shuppankai to Santō Kyōden* 寛政の出版界と山東京伝 (Tabako to Shio no Hakubutsukan, 1995), in which much attention is paid to the impact of the celebrated censorship case in which Santō Kyōden and his publisher, Tsutaya Jūzaburō, were involved.

5.2.4 *Publishing in the provinces*

Publishing in the provinces, i.e. towns apart from Osaka, Kyoto and Edo, was more extensive than is generally recognised. Inoue Takaaki has compiled a statistical table which purports to show that over the whole of the Tokugawa period there were altogether 1,733 publishers active in Kyoto, 1,253 in Osaka, 1,652 in Edo and 585 in the rest of Japan. However, it is already evident that a significant number of provincial firms do not appear in his index of publishers and that the figure must be revised upwards. Further, since many provincial publications are not represented in major university and national libraries but only in provincial collections, their existence has often passed unnoticed. Many do not, for example, appear in the pages of *Kokusho sōmokuroku* and other bibliographic compilations.[55]

The presence in most castle towns of domain academies, intellectual circles and poetry groups was one of the consequences of the decentralized state in the Tokugawa period. Although they mostly came to an end with the collapse of the Tokugawa Bakufu and the establishment of the Meiji government in 1868, they nevertheless made these towns not just recipients of the urban culture of the 'three capitals' but also transmitters of their own cultural production. This is most obviously the case with Nagoya, which, partly because of its position on the busy Tōkaidō route between Edo and Osaka and partly on account of the support given by the powerful Owari daimyō, developed the most active publishing industry in the period. It was Eirakuya Tōshirō of Nagoya who was responsible for the

---

[55] Inoue Takaaki 1981: 5; Kornicki 1985; Ōwa 1991. On the concept of 'provincial' in the Tokugawa period, see Tsukamoto Manabu 塚本学, 'Edo ni okeru chūō to chihō' 江戸における中央と地方, *Shisō* 726 (1984): 45–59, and Kornicki 1985.

publication of such significant works as Motoori Norinaga's *Kojiki den* and of the *Hokusai manga* (§5.3.3). However, this was also true of other towns, and in the case of a number of them it can clearly be demonstrated that their publications, often the work of local intellectuals, poets or writers, were aimed at and reached a national market.

In some provinces publishing activity can be traced back to the late seventeenth century. In Kanazawa, Sangeya Gorōbee 三ケ屋五郎兵衛 published a number of *haikai* books from 1681, and in Mito the first publication appeared in 1691. This early activity was not followed up, however, and in Kanazawa there was no further publishing until the 1780s. It is at the end of the eighteenth century that in many castle towns booksellers began to add publishing to their retail and booklending operations, and began publishing careers that spanned several decades leading up to the Meiji Restoration. In Mito, Suwaraya Yasujirō 須原屋安次郎 began publishing in 1799 and the firm continued operating into the twentieth century; the same is true of Obiya Ihee of Wakayama (§5.3.4), and of many others.[56]

In order to reach a national market it was usually necessary for provincial publishers to form ties with publishers from the 'three capitals'. This did not mean that the books were really published there, for, even if some of the capital came from outside, the printing blocks were retained by the provincial publishers. Thus Obiya Ihee in Wakayama formed links with various publishers in Osaka, which was the nearest of the 'three capitals', while Kanazawa publishers worked with booksellers in Edo and Kyoto.

In the second half of the Tokugawa period provincial publishers were operating in at least 50 castle towns, and in ten of them the names of more than ten bookseller-publishers are known. The full picture is still hard to grasp, but the striking point is the ease with which booksellers could establish themselves as publishers in the Tokugawa period. They were free of the legal constraints which in England restricted publishing to London, Oxford and Cambridge between 1586 and 1695, and free too of the need for the major

---

[56] Yanagawa Shōji 柳川昇爾, 'Hansei jidai no Kanazawa no shorin' 藩政時代の金沢の書林, *Shoshigaku geppō* 8 (1983): 7–9; Ehara Tadaaki 江原忠昭, 'Mito no shoshi Suwaraya' 水戸の書肆須原屋, *Kyōdo bunka* (Ibaragi-ken Kyōdo Bunka Kenkyūkai) 10 (1969): 55–7.

capital investment required by movable-type printing. They afforded a means of communicating with the rest of Japan for poets, scholars and others residing in provincial castle towns and, in addition to their role as sellers of books published in the 'three capitals', they printed books for the local market which had a predominantly local appeal, such as guidebooks, the output of local *haikai* and *waka* poetry circles, and so on. The Tokyo-centric conception of Japan which became widespread from the Meiji period onwards has largely obscured the energy of local cultures in the Tokugawa period and has led to consistent underestimation of the vigour of the provincial book trade.[57]

BIBLIOGRAPHY

On Nagoya see Ōta 1995, on Sendai see *Kyū Sendai-ryō kankei shuppan shomoku kō* 旧仙台領関係出板書目考 (Sendai: Miyagi Kyōiku Daigaku Kokugo Purojekuto Chīmu, 1987), on Wakayama see Kornicki 1985. Asakura & Ōwa 1993 contains reprinted essays on Akita, Sendai, Aizu, Hitachi, Mie and Wakayama. For statistics see Ōwa 1991, which also contains a bibliography of writings on provincial publishing. See also Nakamura Yukihiko 中村幸彦, 'Kinsei chihōban kenkyū no teishō' 近世地方版研究の提唱, in *(Nagasawa sensei koki kinen) Toshogaku ronbunshū* (長沢先生古希記念) 図書学論集 (Sanseidō, 1973), 487–509, and Kornicki 1985 & 1990.

5.3 THE PUBLISHERS

To date there have been few studies of individual publishers. Although hardly any individual publisher's archives have survived, there is much material in the form of advertisements and catalogues, in addition to the evidence offered by their surviving books, which would make such studies possible, as Forrer has shown with his analysis of Eirakuya Toshirō's catalogues. There is a need for more studies of this kind to expose the strategies, ranges of publications and conceptions of the

---

[57] Ōwa 1991: 113. Cf J. Feather, *The provincial book trade in eighteenth-century England* (Cambridge: Cambridge University Press, 1985). For an instance of the influence of the Tokyo-centric perspective see 'Edo to chihō bunka' 江戸と地方文化, in *Kinsei bunka no kenkyū* 近世文化の研究, Nishiyama Matsunosuke chosakushū 4 (Yoshikawa Kōbunkan, 1983), 147–86.

market that publishers had in the Tokugawa period in different places and at different times, and to explore their relationship to the official ideology and cultural systems of their times. Here it is not possible to offer more than thumbnail sketches of six publishers whose cases reveal different approaches to the commercial exploitation of the market for books.[58]

5.3.1 *Murakami Kanbee*

The firm of Murakami Kanbee 村上勘兵衛, which also went under the name of Heirakuji 平楽寺, is not only one of the earliest Kyoto commercial publishers that can be identified, but it is also one of the few publishing enterprises of the Tokugawa period that is still in business, now publishing under the name Heirakuji Shoten. The firm was founded in the early years of the seventeenth century and, according to its records, initially printed sinology, Buddhist books and works of Japanese history with movable type. The oldest surviving book bearing the Murakami imprint is a medical text dated 1622. By the time the second head of the firm died in 1653 it had published more than 60 items, which already made it one of the most productive publishing houses in Kyoto.[59]

The third head of the firm changed the family allegiance from the Jōdo to the Nichiren sect of Buddhism and took the tonsure, leaving the business in the hands of his son, who put this connection to commercial use. In 1669 the firm, as *primus inter pares*, joined with three other Kyoto booksellers to publish 103 Buddhist texts, of which 43 were associated with the Nichiren sect and most of the remainder with Tendai Buddhism. The four, who called themselves *Hokke shūmon shodō* 法華宗門書堂, thus identifying themselves as publishers of books connected with these two sects, went on to publish other works together up to 1687. For the most part the titles they published in those years were not ones for which they had initiated publication, but were the result of substantial investment in the

---

[58] Forrer 1985. For case studies of other publishers see Munemasa 1982, Hattori Kiyomichi 服部清道, 'Edo no shoshi Izumiya Kin'emon' 江戸の書肆和泉屋金右衛門, *Fūzoku* 6.3 (1963): 16–21, and the bibliographic guides in the entries for some of the publishers listed in Inoue Takaaki 1981.

[59] Inoue Takaaki 1981: 602; Kanmuri 1983: 79.

purchase of existing printing blocks from other publishers. This move, then, demonstrates the substantial working capital that Murakami in particular had built up by this time. At the same time it shows that Buddhist texts, which hitherto had mostly been the preserve of temple publishing, now enjoyed a substantial commercial market.[60]

By the end of the century Murakami Kanbee was a major force in the publishing industry. The booksellers' catalogue of 1698 credited the firm with 371 publications, which means that he had the *hankabu* or rights to print them; while some of them were new, others had been published earlier and were still in print. This compares with 127 for his nearest rival, Takemura Ichibee 武村市兵衛. While both Takemura and Murakami both published a considerable amount of sinology, Murakami's greatest strength was in Buddhist books, which amounted to 68% of his total. In these circumstances it was quite natural for the contemporary writer Miyako no Nishiki to describe Murakami as one of the ten most important publishers in Kyoto, where there were already 72 of them in business.[61]

Throughout the Tokugawa period the Murakami firm continued to publish books connected with the Nichiren sect, particularly the *Lotus sūtra* in a range of different formats and editions, and these were the mainstay of its longevity as a bookseller and publisher. But in addition the firm acted as the publisher or distributor of many other works too, including for example pattern-books for carpenters, historical works, Kitamura Kigin's commentary on the *Tale of Genji*, and the popular household encyclopedias known as *setsuyōshū*.[62]

In the Meiji period the firm survived the transition while many of its erstwhile competitors fell by the wayside. In 1868 the new government, the Dajōkan, launched an official publication called *Dajōkan nisshi* 太政館日誌, which carried government decrees. This was a clear departure from the practice of the Bakufu, which had circulated all its legislation in manuscript and had mostly disdained the use of print for official purposes. The task of publishing *Dajōkan nisshi* was entrusted to Murakami Kanbee and a fellow Kyoto publisher, but later, when the new government moved to Tokyo, it

---

[60] Kanmuri 1983: 21–9, 81, 87–90.
[61] Kanmuri 87–9; Miyako no Nishiki 1937: 397.
[62] Muneamasa 1982: 94–5; Hayashi & Kornicki 1991: #507, 559, 1106, 2086, 2351, 2353; Munemasa 1982: 94–5.

was Suwaraya Mohee's firm that took over publication. Murakami was also involved in other government publishing ventures in the early Meiji period, including in 1872 directories of government personnel in the various ministries and in 1873 the law codes, but the strength of the firm still lay with its publication of sūtras and other texts associated with the Nichiren sect. A catalogue of the publications it had available for purchase in this field in 1880 contains 268 items: 150 of these were commercial publications, either produced by Murakami himself or books to which he had acquired the rights, and 118 were temple publications, including 27 items published by the major new Nichiren temple founded in Tokyo in the Meiji period, the Nichirenshū Daikyōin. The list includes many different editions of the *Lotus sūtra*, some with just the raw Chinese text and others with reading marks and other aids to comprehension, and these were all available in various versions with different kinds of paper and different prices accordingly. In spite of the government-led assault on Buddhism in the early Meiji period and in spite of new publishing trends, such as translations, which were inspired by the new orientation towards the West, it is clear that there was still a viable market for Buddhist books and texts, and the Murakami firm survived by catering to that continuing market rather than by moving into new areas of publication.[63]

BIBLIOGRAPHY

Kanmuri 1983: 79–126; Munemasa 1982: 94–5, 299–310. For some of the advertisements put out by Murakami see Asakura 1983: 4.348–60. For an incomplete list of Murakami's publications see Yajima 1976: 1.236–8, 2.88–9.

5.3.2 *Suwaraya Mohee*

The firm of Suwaraya Mohee 須原屋茂兵衛 was the leading publisher in Edo in the late eighteenth and early nineteenth centuries, and it was celebrated in numerous poems. Further, judging from the partial records of the Osaka and Edo publishers' guilds, this firm was clearly the most active of all in Japan in the second half of the Tokugawa

---

[63] Hayashi & Kornicki 1991: #1376–7, 1790, 1839; Munemasa 1982: 299–310.

period. Between 1727 and 1815, by Sakamoto's count, he was associated with 1,147 different works, some 350 as solitary or joint publisher and the remainder as distributor. Since, however, these records are far from complete, it is likely that these figures considerably understate the case. For example, the collection of 2,000 block-printed books in Cambridge University Library includes 332 items in which Suwaraya Mohee is mentioned in the colophon; doubtless in most cases the firm was acting as a distributor, but the ubiquity is striking. Furthermore, the firm spawned a number of offshoots, mostly original employees who had been given their independence, such as the firm of Suwaraya Ihachi 須原屋伊八, which produced its first book in 1744. By 1817 twelve of the 63 members of the *Shomotsuya nakama* bore the Suwaraya name and together they were associated with one third of all the books published or distributed in Edo.[64]

The founder of the Suwaraya Mohee firm moved from the province of Kii to Edo in the 1650s and set himself up as a bookseller in Nihonbashi, in the heart of the mercantile quarter. The earliest extant book bearing the firm's imprint is a sinological work dated 1674. Although it may have been publishing more ephemeral items such as *jōruri* playbooks before that, most likely the bulk of its business at first consisted of bookselling.[65]

By the 1720s Suwaraya Mohee had accumulated sufficient capital to acquire the *hankabu*, or rights, to some of the many versions of the directories of samurai officials (*bukan*) that were regularly published with Bakufu cognizance (§2.5). By the middle of the century he had seen off most of his rivals and enjoyed a near monopolistic position in what was a steady market. The annual sales of directories in Edo were evidently in the tens of thousands, and 'Suwaraya *bukan*' featured in a later guidebook for shoppers that listed the famous products of Edo. Other signs of the firm's economic strength were its establishment by the 1780s of a branch in Kyoto, which was a reversal of the earlier tendency of Kyoto booksellers to set up branches in Edo, and the publication of maps of Edo, for which too there was a constant demand and a constant need for updated editions.[66]

---

[64] Konta 1974: 171–2; Sakamoto 1982: 1–2; Inoue Takaaki 1981: 309, 315; Hayashi & Kornicki 1991: 463; *KD* 8: 183.
[65] Konta 1974: 175–7; Inoue Takaaki 1981: 315.
[66] *YMC* 3: 162–6, 177, 191 n. 5; Hayashi & Kornicki 1991: #1819–34; Minami 1975; *Edo meibutsushi* 江戸名物詩 (1836), 4a; Iwata Toyoki 1980.

By the end of the eighteenth century Suwaraya Mohee owned the blocks to at least 273 works in a bewildering variety of fields. His earliest dated list of publications was produced in 1752, but he was consistent in including such lists in his publications, and even drew up catalogues of books in certain niche markets he had effectively cornered, such as the catalogue he put out in 1764 featuring books of plans and designs for carpenters (*Daiku hinagatasho mokuroku* 大工雛形書目録). He also perceived a growing market in Edo for the Kokugaku works of Motoori Norinaga and in 1797 wrote to Norinaga requesting permission to distribute his works in Edo in return for the very substantial fee of 25 *ryō* a year.[67]

In the early nineteenth century the firm was in decline, partly because of the early death of the sixth head of the firm in 1803 and a fire in 1806 that damaged the premises, and partly because of rising costs that affected the economics of publishing. In addition there was the rise of new entrepreneurial publishers in Edo like Tsutaya Jūzaburō and increasing publishing activity in the provinces. The firm later recovered, published books on famine relief during the Tenpō famine in the 1830s and, while continuing to run a subsidiary pharmaceutical business, resumed its activities as a publisher and distributor on a national scale. In the last decades of the Tokugawa period Suwaraya Mohee's name appears almost invariably in the lists of distributors for new and reprinted books, and the same is true of reprints in the Meiji period. Like other publishers, he had by then abandoned his trade-name and used his surname, thus appearing as Kitabatake Mohee. The firm survived the transition to the Meiji period partly by continuing to reprint from blocks in the firm's possession and partly by acting as the printer and distributor of numerous government publications, but it was unable to adapt effectively to the new publishing world of movable type and closed its doors in 1904.[68]

BIBLIOGRAPHY

Konta 1974: 170–87; *YMC* 3: 155–83. For some of the advertisements put out by Suwaraya Mohee see Asakura 1983: 3.212–316. For an incomplete list of Suwaraya Mohee's publications see Yajima 1976: 1.121–6, 2.48–9.

---

[67] Asakura 1983: 3.214–5; Konta 1974: 177; Okamoto 1980: 50.
[68] *YMC* 3: 178–9; Konta 1974: 182; Hayashi & Kornicki 1991: #1377, 1788, 1835–6, 1838–9; Inoue Takaaki 1981: 315.

5.3.3 *Eirakuya Tōshirō*

Publishing in Nagoya dates from the 1680s when some booksellers collaborated with Kyoto firms to produce joint publications. By the middle of the eighteenth century there were around 30 publishers active there and it became the most important provincial publishing centre. Until 1794 they obtained permission to publish by going through the established routes in Edo, Kyoto or Osaka, but in that year they began applying instead to the Owari domain authorities for permission. This move evidently caused consternation. The booksellers guilds in the three cities protested that independent publishing in the provinces would put their livelihoods at risk, but the Owari domain authorities noted the convenience of having works written by Owari samurai published locally and gave its permission. Certainly by 1798, and possibly as early as 1794, there was a local booksellers' guild in existence and it came into frequent dispute with publishers in other cities over possible infringements of their copyright. One startling case involved the first parts of Motoori Norinaga's extensive commentary on the *Kojiki*, *Kojiki den*, which was initially banned in the three cities in 1794 on the ground that it included the text of the *Kojiki*, the rights to which, it was claimed, lay with other publishers. Although some Nagoya publishing was provincial, in the sense that it concerned the works of local authors, this did not mean that it had a purely local market. Motoori's works, which were produced at his school in Matsuzaka, had a large potential market in Edo, as the leading Edo publisher Suwaraya Mohee was well aware (§5.3.2).[69]

There can be no doubt that Nagoya was the largest of the provincial publishing centres. There were around 100 booksellers active as publishers at different times in the Tokugawa period from 1688 onwards, and the fact that several Kyoto booksellers set up branch operations there in the eighteenth century is some testimony to the size of the market. To sustain this publishing activity there must have been local block-carvers, printers and the other artisans whose skills were necessary for the manufacture of books, but it is only in a botanical work published in 1828 that we have the first clear indication

---

[69] Kishi Masahiro 岸雅裕, 'Bishū shorin nakama no seiritsu to santo' 尾州書林仲間の成立と三都, *Bungaku* 49.11 (1981): 125–36; Ōta 1995: 135–41.

of a carver and printer based in Nagoya.[70]

The Eirakuya Tōshirō firm was the largest in Nagoya and was one of two mentioned by Bakin following his visit there. The other was Fūgetsudō Magosuke 風月堂孫助, which had started publishing in 1714, and it was here that the founder of the Eirakuya firm was apprenticed until he set up business on his own in 1776. The initial publications of the firm were mostly sinological, but after the death of the first Eirakuya Tōshirō in 1795 his successor, a former apprentice whom he had adopted, extended the range of publications to include *ehon* and books of poetry. He also established branch operations in Ōgaki, in the province of Mino, and, uniquely for a Nagoya publisher, in Edo. It was in the time of the second head of the firm that it established itself as the publisher of Motoori Norinaga's *Kojiki den*, which was completed in 1822 and was kept in print by the firm until at least 1875. The firm also published *ehon*, and other kinds of picture books and illustrated books by Hokusai and other well-known artists. In some cases Eirakuya acquired the blocks from other publishers, presumably by purchase, but in others he initiated the publication or acted as the distributor for a private publisher. Amongst his lasting successes was the *Hokusai manga*: the first volume was published in 1814, consisting of sketches done by Hokusai during his visit to Nagoya in 1812, and 14 more volumes were published up to 1878, mostly in collaboration with Kadomaruya Jinsuke 角丸屋甚助 of Edo. By the 1830s he owned the blocks of a considerable number of picture books, as indicated by advertisements attached to his publications, and had established a strong presence in that niche market. However, in the Meiji period the firm went into a decline and the blocks for many of its books were sold to Yoshikawa Hanshichi of Edo, who then put out his own impressions.[71]

The firm only finally closed in 1951, but its significance lies in the role it played as a provincial publisher in the nineteenth century. Eirakuya Tōshirō was, as the most active and prolific publisher operating outside the three cities, the most visible sign of the diffusion of cultural production in the Tokugawa period. The firm was not

---

[70] Ōta Masahiro 太田正弘, 'Nagoya no shoshi' 名古屋の書肆, *Bungaku* 49.12 (1981): 95–104; Ōta 1995: 116.

[71] Forrer 1985: 84–8, 155–6, 170–77, 196–221, 237–41, etc; Hayashi & Kornicki 1991: #1138–9, 2132–5, 2140–42.

merely publishing for Nagoya but identifying talent that could appeal to a national market, and it was consequently able to market its books in Edo, Osaka and Kyoto, as the lists of distributors attached to its books show.

BIBLIOGRAPHY

Forrer 1985 offers a detailed study of Eirakuya's publishing activies in addition to a good general account of books and publishing in the Tokugawa period. For some of the advertisements put out by Eirakuya see Asakura 1983: 1.141–97. For lists of Eirakuya's publications see Kishi Masahiro 岸雅裕, 'Edo jidai Bishū shorin shoshibetsu shuppan shomoku shūran' 江戸時代尾州書林書肆別出版書目集覧, *Nagoya-shi Hakubutsukan kenkyū kiyō* 5 & 6 (1981 & 1982), and Yajima 1976: 1.36–8, 2.12–3. On publishing in Nagoya see Ōta 1995 and the illustrated exhibition catalogue *Nagoya no shuppan* 名古屋の出版 (Nagoya: Nagoya-shi Hakubutsukan, 1981).

5.3.4 *Obiya Ihee*

As in most major provincial towns, publishing in Wakayama only began to take off at the end of the eighteenth century. By 1800 there were at least six publishers producing books there; the most prolific were Kasedaya Heiemon 綛田屋平右衛門, who was active at least from 1787 to 1857 and produced more than 70 titles, and Obiya Ihee 帯屋伊兵衛, which started business c1790 and still exists as a bookshop in Wakayama today. The founder of the Obiya Ihee firm was Takechi Shiyū 高市志友 (1751–1823), who was born in Wakayama but spent some years apprenticed to a pharmacist in Edo; he was back in Wakayama by 1778, evidently practising as a pharmacist at the same time as being engaged in the numismatic trade. During his lifetime he established the first theatre in Wakayama and appears to have enjoyed the trust of the daimyō. He also enjoyed some fame as a *haikai* poet.[72]

Exactly when and why Obiya turned to publishing is unknown. The earliest evidence of his activities in this area is a travelogue published in 1790, *Kumano sensei nanzan kikō* 熊野先生南山紀行.

---

[72] Tanaka Keichū 田中敬忠, *Kishū konjaku* 紀州今昔 (Wakayama: privately published, 1927), 121–30.

This is a private publication for which four 'Wakayama booksellers' (和歌山書肆), including Obiya and Kasedaya Heiemon, and two others from Osaka acted as distributors. Obiya was clearly operating as a bookseller by this time, and the involvement of four booksellers from Wakayama is probably to be explained by the fact that the author, who is otherwise unknown, is identified in the colophon as a Wakayama man.[73]

During the 1790s Obiya Ihee published on average just one new title each year. It follows that he must have had some other business interests, and it seems that he was engaged in the book trade at the same time as being a member of the guild of pharmacists. Most of the works he had a hand in publishing then were books of *haikai* or *kyōka* poetry, all with some Wakayama connection. *Kyōka kaiawase* 興歌かひあわせ(1796), for example, is a collection edited by a Wakayama man and published by Obiya, Tsutaya Jūzaburō and one bookseller each from Kyoto and Osaka.[74] A few years earlier, in 1793, he had joined with two Osaka publishers to produce *Mikusazashi* 三種尺, a collection of *haikai* poetry; the identity of the pseudonymous author is unknown, but he refers to Obiya as his friend in the preface.[75] The most interesting indication of his involvement in publishing in the 1790s is, however, *Shintei sanraizu* 新定三礼図, which was a Japanese edition of a Song-dynasty work. The blocks for this particular edition were prepared in 1761, but they were later acquired by Obiya Ihee and used by him in 1792 to reprint it in collaboration with several publishers from Osaka, Kyoto and Edo. In 1793, however, it became apparent that a Kyoto publisher Kitamura Shirōbee 北村四郎兵衛 had plagiarized part of this work and Obiya took the dispute

---

[73] The only copy I have seen is in the possession of Mr Takechi Isao 高市績 of Wakayama, the proprietor of Obii Shoten 帯伊書店, the descendant of Obiya Ihee's firm. The bibliographic details are as follows: 崖弘毅著、崖弘美校、2巻、大2冊、寛政2序刊 (鎰惟園蔵版)、(奥附書肆)和歌山書肆／新通三丁目 加勢田屋平右衛門／寄合町 亀屋六兵衛／西ノ店 山崎屋嘉兵衛／中細工町 帯屋伊兵衛／大阪書林、池田屋長十郎・平野屋九兵衛.

[74] Again, the only copy I have seen is in the possession of Mr Takechi Isao (see previous note). The bibliographic details are as follows: 巴水亭貞三編、1巻、半1冊、寛政8刊 (奥附書肆)書林／京 菱屋孫兵衛／江戸 蔦屋重三郎／大坂 河内屋太助／紀州若山 帯屋伊兵衛. For the identity of the author see *OSSM* 152.

[75] *Mikusazashi* was later reissued by the same three publishers with the date at the end of the preface removed; copies of both versions are in the Wataya Bunko in Tenri Library (ざ183-4).

to Edo, where it was agreed that Kitamura would pay Obiya the substantial sum of 70 *ryō* for the blocks of *Shintei sanraizu*. It is clear from this episode that Obiya had by this time accumulated sufficient capital to be able to purchase printing blocks and with them the right to print works originally published elsewhere.[76]

For the most part Obiya's publications, like those of other publishers in Wakayama, Hiroshima, Sendai and other major castle towns, consist of works which have some connection with Wakayama, either in terms of subject matter or more commonly of authorship. This does not mean, however, that they were of purely parochial interest, as the collaboration with publishers in other cities shows, for, like other castle towns, Wakayama had intellectual and poetic talents for whose works there was conceivably a larger market. The best indication of this in the case of Obiya Ihee is his most important publication, *Kii no kuni meisho zue* 紀伊国名所図会. This is a well-illustrated topographical study devoted to the sites of the province of Kii, of which Wakayama was the main town, and it was published by the Obiya firm in four parts between 1811 and 1851. It was inspired by the series of illustrated local topographies known as *meisho zue* which was launched by Akisato Ritō 秋里離島 in 1780 with a set of volumes on the sites of Kyoto, *Miyako meisho zue* 都名所図会. The first Obiya Ihee, Takechi Shiyū, himself began the research in 1796 for the first three parts, with the explicit support of the daimyō and the domain authorities, and he wrote the text of the first two parts, which were published before his death. The firm retained the rights to all four parts, but an Osaka publisher made haste to acquire the rights to distribute them in Osaka and they were put on sale there, in Edo and Kyoto.[77]

The Obiya Ihee firm also published some medical texts written by staff at the Wakayama domain medical academy, and some Kokugaku works written by the intellectual descendants of Motoori Norinaga, including Motoori Ōhira (1756–1833), who composed an obituary poem on the death of the founder of the firm in 1823. In later years the firm published an increasing number of collections of *waka* poetry

---

[76] The only copy of Obiya's edition of *Shintei sanraizu* I know of is in Tenri Library (122.4-221); it has attached to it a four-page catalogue of books Obiya was handling at this time. The legal document is reprinted in Tanaka Keichū, *Kishū konjaku*, 125-6 (see note 72 above).

[77] *OHNK* 9: 263, 274, 284.

and some pharmacological works and educational books for women. After the Meiji Restoration its role as a transmitter of Wakayama cultural output to other parts of Japan came to an end, as intellectuals and writers moved to Tokyo, and, like other provincial publishers, it became dependent on the publication of textbooks distributed by the Ministry of Education in Tokyo.

Like the case of Eirakuya Tōshirō, Obiya Ihee's publications demonstrate the vigour of local culture. However, whereas that of Nagoya is now recognised, the local cultures of Wakayama and other castle towns like Kanazawa and Hiroshima remain to be fully explored in the context of their contributions to the national market for books.

BIBLIOGRAPHY

For one of the advertisements put out by Obiya Ihee see Asakura 1983: 1.270; a much larger one is to be found in the British Library copy of *Kii no kuni meisho zue* (BL 16113.c.29) and is partially illustrated in Kornicki 1990: 196. For an incomplete list of Obiya's publications see Yajima 1976: 1.51–2. Kornicki, 'Obiya Ihei, a Japanese provincial publisher', *British Library Journal* 11 (1985): 131–142. On publishing in Wakayama see Kornicki 1985 and Ōwa Hiroyuki 大和博幸, 'Wakayama no shuppan to shoshi' 和歌山の出版と書肆, in Asakura and Ōwa 1993: 192–223.

5.3.5 *Tsutaya Jūzaburō*

Tsutaya Jūzaburō is notable for having quickly established a commanding and innovative presence in the Edo publishing world. He enjoyed some fame as a *kyōka* poet, was acquainted with a number of leading writers and intellectuals, and is credited with 'the gift of discovering genius', particularly that of Utamaro. At various times he offered lodgings to Kyokutei Bakin, Santō Kyōden and Utamaro himself, who stayed with Tsutaya until the latter's death in 1797.[78]

Tsutaya Jūzaburō, or Tsutajū as he was commonly known, was born in the Yoshiwara pleasure quarter in 1750. In 1773 opened a bookshop at the entrance to the quarter selling the guidebooks, or *Yoshiwara saiken* (§2.5), published by the firm of Urokogataya

---

[78] J. Hillier, *Utamaro: colour prints and paintings* (London: Phaidon Press, 1961), 12.

Magobee, which had been in business since 1660. The following year he launched his career as a publisher with a courtesan critique, and in 1775 he produced his own guide to the Yoshiwara. In doing so he was probably taking advantage of the fact that Urokogataya was at the time beset with problems connected with a copyright-infringement case, but at the same time he was clearly, by devising a new format, giving some attention to the development of a new kind of product. For a while the Tsutajū and Urokogataya versions appeared side by side but by 1783 Tsutajū had overwhelmed his erstwhile patron, who ceased publishing around 1803, and had monopolized the right to publish *Yoshiwara saiken*. Well before this, however, he had begun to branch out, employing artists such as Katsukawa Shunshō to illustrate his guidebooks and, from 1776, publishing illustrated books of *haikai* poetry, *ehon* and *sharebon*. In 1783 he moved from the Yoshiwara to a new permanent home for his growing business.[79]

In the 1780s Tsutajū was publishing the works of the leading *kyōka* poets and writers of light fiction in Edo. These included a number of the satirical *kibyōshi* that appeared in the tolerant years before the advent of the Kansei reform and the imposition of harsher censorship laws in 1791. In that year, he published three of Santō Kyōden's *sharebon*. These were subsequently made an example of by the new régime in power in the Bakufu, with the result that not only was Kyōden punished but also Tsutajū, who had gone through the correct procedures to gain permission to publish, had half his wealth confiscated, and the *gyōji*, or guild officials, were banished from Edo (§8.2.3).[80]

After the troubles of 1791, Tsutajū, who had hitherto been a member of the *jihon* booksellers' guild, sought admission to the *shomotsuya nakama*, the guild of publishers of 'serious' books. From this time onwards he published more of the sort of books appropriate to members of that guild, but it is not the case that he was seeking to change the character and emphasis of his bookselling operations, for, as Ōwa Hiroyuki has argued, his main purpose was to re-establish the financial basis of his publishing business and to raise capital. Thus the main focus of his activity in the early 1790s was actually not 'serious' publishing but single-sheet *ukiyoe* prints of beauties

---

[79] Inoue Takaaki 1981: 105; Matsuki 1988: 15, 18–22, 47.
[80] Matsuki 1988: 79–82, 100–104; Kornicki 1977.

and actors by Utamaro, Sharaku and others. One example is the series of eight prints by Utamaro depicting leading courtesans of the Yoshiwara pleasure quarter, each with a *kyōka* poem in a cartouche, that was probably published in 1793. After 1794 he concentrated his efforts on illustrated books of *haikai* poetry: he began buying up the blocks of such books from other publishers and reissuing them under his own imprint, and in 1796 he published his first new work in this area.[81]

Tsutajū died in 1797. Although the firm survived for some years under his chief clerk, it lacked the entrepreneurial energy that had propelled it from obscurity to the point where it was celebrated in verse as the equal of Suwaraya Mohee.[82] His case contrasts strongly with the careers of many other publishers in Edo, whose activities by this time were built upon years of more conservative business practice: precisely because they were less dependent on entrepreneurial talent they were able to survive as publishers for several generations, holding on to their valuable positions as members of the guilds.

BIBLIOGRAPHY

Matsuki 1988; Mukai 1995: 54–65; Suwa Haruo 諏訪春雄, 'Tsutaya Jūzaburō no kisetsu - kinsei shuppan no senkakusha' 蔦屋重三郎の季節—近世出版の先覚者, *Bungaku* 49.11, 12 (1981), 50.1 (1982). Suzuki Toshiyuki 鈴木俊幸 has compiled a bibliography year by year of Tsutaya's publications, 'Tsutaya Jūzaburō shuppan shomoku nenpyō kō' 蔦屋重三郎出板書目年表稿, which appeared in *Kinsei bungei* 35 (1981): 71–90, 36 (1982): 53–73 and 39 (1983): 67–74, and is due to be published in the *NSGT* series as *Tsutajū shuppan shomoku* 蔦重出版書目. For some of the advertisements put out by Tsutaya see Asakura 1983: 3.352–61.

---

[81] Ōwa Hiroyuki 大和博幸, 'Jihon toiya Tsutaya Jūzaburō no shomotsu ton'ya kanyū no ito' 地本問屋蔦屋重三郎の書物問屋加入の意図, *Nihon rekishi* 594 (1997): 53–70; Asano & Clark 1995, Text volume, pp. 105–7, #69–74; Matsuki 1988: 106–24.

[82] Inoue Takaaki 1981: 391.

5.3.6 *Kawachiya Mohee*

Kawachiya Mohee 河内屋茂兵衛 was a latecomer on the publishing world in Osaka, and only made an impression in the nineteenth century. But the firm developed rapidly, and by the end of the Tokugawa period had acquired the blocks, and of course the rights to print from them, of a substantial number of *yomihon* and other genres of fiction, including many works that had originally been published in Edo or Kyoto. Records of the Osaka publishers' guild show that in 1818 a total of 110 Osaka publishers had the rights to 5,160 books; at the head of the list was Kichimonjiya Ichiemon 吉文字屋市右衛門, one of the founder members of the guild, who had the rights to 600. But in 1870, when there are records of the rights to 8,270 titles in Osaka shared between 224 publishers, Kichimonjiya's total had slipped to only 130, while Kawachiya Mohee, who had not been active in 1818, had as many as 1,140. He was clearly the tough businessman Bakin's letters reveal him to be. Furthermore, the Kawachiya stable of publishers had grown as had that of Suwaraya in Edo, and 35 of the 224 publishers recorded in 1870 were Kawachiyas. As a result, the Kawachiya share of Osaka publishing rights had risen from 32% in 1818 to 54% by 1870. They are reported to have treated each other as brothers, and hence they enjoyed an unrivalled domination of the Osaka publishing world: in 1866 they all signed a cooperative agreement that enabled them to work together more effectively.[83]

Few *yomihon* were published in Osaka after 1818, but between 1818 and 1870 the various Kawachiya firms increased their hold of *yomihon* publishing rights from 217 to 436 works, with 109 going into the hands of Kawachiya Mohee alone, largely in the 1850s. It is clear that that most of these works must have originally been published in Kyoto and Edo, and that the rights to them were acquired by Osaka publishers. It is for this reason that many surviving reprints of works published in Edo carry the Kawachiya Mohee imprint. But this also raises the question of why Edo publishers were disposing of their blocks in such quantities. It also points to the domination of Osaka publishers in a market that still valued *yomihon* up to the

---

[83] Hamada 1956.

1880s.[84] What is significant about the Kawachiya Mohee firm is that it was built on the purchase of used blocks: it was only very rarely involved in the publication of new books which would require the preparation of new printing blocks and the long process of acquiring guild permission. The founder, the first Kawachiya Mohee, died in 1863, and by the time his successor died in 1886 the business was in trouble, so his successor turned to the clothing trade. It is no coincidence that it was at this time that blockprinting, too, went into a decline: the Kawachiya Mohee business was built on the *hankabu* system that was peculiar to the guilds of the Tokugawa period and that had no corollary in the Meiji period.

BIBLIOGRAPHY

Hamada 1956. For some of the advertisements put out by Kawachiya Mohee see Asakura 1983: 2.143–84. For an incomplete list of Kawachiya Mohee's publications see Yajima 1976: 1.73–4, 2.29–30. Inoue 1981: 213.

---

[84] Hamada 1956: 15–28.

CHAPTER SIX

AUTHORS AND READERS

1   Authorship
      1   The evolution of the author
      2   Royalties
      3   Copyright
2   Readership
      1   Readers and reading before 1600
      2   Readers and reading after 1600
      3   Literacy

6.1 AUTHORSHIP

In 1968 Roland Barthes announced the death of the author: in a polemic that undermined author-based criticism and sought to recover the experiences of readers he declared that 'the birth of the reader must be at the cost of the death of the Author.' Although the point of this is clear, the history of the book cannot be written without an understanding of the concept of authorship, of the rhetoric with which authors proclaim themselves in their texts, and of the social constructs of authorship. It is the category and career of the author, and the changing legal, commercial, social and intellectual functions of the presence or absence of authors in the books of which they are the purported authors, that Foucault sought to recover in 1969, though of course he was equally scathing about '"man-and-his-work" criticism'. In consequence, there has in recent years been a revival of interest in 'authors' and authorship, one generated by these new perspectives.[1]

---

[1] Barthes 1977: 148; Chartier 1994: 25–59; Michel Foucault, 'What is an author?", in Josué V. Harari, ed., *Textual strategies: perspectives in post-structural criticism* (Ithaca, NY: Cornell University Press, 1979), 141–60.

Much of this new interest has focussed on the legal and economic determinants of the emerging category of 'author', but it is also clear that a writer's relationship to the products of his or her intellect has undergone some fundamental changes. In eighteenth-century Europe, as Martha Woodmansee describes it, 'writing was considered a mere vehicle of received ideas which were already in the public domain', but the growth of the book trade and of book piracy, tolerated or even defended by trade interests, led to an affirmation of the rights of ownership of authors in their work and ultimately to Herder's 'radically new conception of the book as an imprint or record of the intellection of a unique individual' which in turn required new reading strategies. At the same time, Carla Hesse's study of the laws of authorship in revolutionary France shows that Foucault's equation of the emergence of the Author with the privatization of knowledge needs some revision because of the existence of other possible conceptualizations of authorship. The efforts of the revolutionary government in the 1790s to afford authors some recognition of their rights in their texts were tied first to an emphasis on their 'accountability and responsibility' rather than creativity, and ultimately to a perception of the author 'as a hero of public enlightenment rather than as a private individual creator': they 'explicitly intended to dethrone the absolute author ... and recast him, not as a *private* individual ... but rather as a *public* servant'.[2]

In the following sections I consider the evolution of the author in Japan, the payment of royalties and the development of a copyright system, but much more work needs to be done in these areas, particularly the first, for the preponderance of author-based criticism in Japan has yet to give way to an appreciation of the social fact of authorship. Nevertheless, it is evident that the articulation of the author has followed a different trajectory in Japan from those found in Europe, particularly in the realm of printed books in the Tokugawa period. On the one hand authors were not in legal terms public figures. Legal protection, such as it was, focussed on the rights of commercial publishers in their investments rather than on the

---

[2] Martha Woodmansee, 'The genius and the copyright: economic and legal conditions for the emergence of the "Author"', *Eighteenth-century studies* 17 (1984): 425–48 (quotes from 434, 447); Carla Hesse, 'Enlightenment epistemology and the laws of authorship in revolutionary France, 1777–1793', *Representations* 30 (1990): 109–37 (quotes from 120, 128, 130).

intellectual rights of authors in their works: authors were protected, but for the wrong reasons, so to speak. Similarly their economic rights were legally and contractually unrecognised and their economic returns at best unstable, although, as argued below, authorship as a career and as a presence in texts began in the seventeenth century and by the nineteenth had developed into professional authorship. We look in vain, then, for a legal context in the hierarchical world of Tokugawa Japan, a world in which authorship was not an acknowledged category of being. On the other hand, authors were not fully private either. While not dependent on patrons, most were of course, dependent on commercial publishers at least for publication if not for their living, but that commercial nexus generated an enhanced visibility for the author as the selling power of successful or popular authors coincided with the logic of commerce. Further, the presence of Japanese writers in their published texts, especially in popular literature, represented an important shift. Publicly acknowledged authorship had in the early seventeenth century been largely confined to the long-dead authors or putative authors of the Chinese classics, and was in effect a sacralized relationship, but that relationship was appropriated by Japanese authors in the Tokugawa period, and authorship became a category borrowed from the sages and scholars of the Chinese past.

6.1.1 *The evolution of the author*

As many users of Japanese libraries and catalogues have noticed, even today the 'author' is paid less respect in library systems in Japan than in the West. Author indices and author catalogues are still a rarity, although they are becoming less uncommon, and the principal means of access to library catalogues remains the title rather than the author, whereas, until the age of the computer catalogue, title catalogues were a rarity in the West and readers were expected to know the author's name. The ascendancy of the title over the author is not, however, either a recent, or an exclusively Japanese, phenomenon. The earliest catalogues of collections of books in Japan, whether Chinese or Japanese, customarily gave no indication of authorship and this commonly remained the case until the publication of the 1670 edition of the booksellers' catalogue *(Zōho) Shojaku mokuroku* (see §10.1.2). It is in fact at this point, when the book trade had been through a period of phenomenal growth and had reached a certain maturity and an appreciation of the commercial value of authorship, that authors began to be a presence in their texts as they were made commercially available as printed books and that authors began to write with publication in mind, or even at the suggestion of publishers.

The evolution of the author in Japan can and should, of course, be considered in the context of the history of texts from the earliest times. In the case of the court anthologies of *waka* poetry in the Heian and Kamakura periods the names of the poets, both men and women, have been preserved as an integral part of the text, and the compilers of those anthologies enjoyed public identification in the process of commissioning. By contrast, the names of the authors of most Japanese prose works written by women in the Heian period are quite detached from the text and indeed are not known, so that we have only a court title or a family identity to go on. These texts had authors, but their identity is not attached to the texts they wrote. The reason for this lies in the essentially 'private' rather than 'public' circumstances of female existence in Heian Japan, and since it was mostly women who wrote prose in Japanese, their prose had a private character that men's writing in Chinese did not have.[3] In fields such as medicine and mathematics in the Heian period the very concept of authorship, that is of authoring a complete text, was much slower to develop and most writing consisted of patchworks of quotations from earlier works, often Chinese works. In the case of Buddhism the development of rival schools in Japan encouraged followers to lay claim to authority by attributing texts to the founder of their school, thus equating putative authorship with authority.

Further, in the Tokugawa period many works in the genre of popular historical fiction known as *yomihon* show signs of extensive reliance on works of Ming fiction for ideas and even for language: *yomihon* authors invariably claimed authorship of their works at the beginning of their texts, but that claim did not, even at this stage, necessarily constitute a statement of creative originality and could still encompass dense intertextuality. In the Meiji period this continued

---

[3] Cf. Richard Bowring, *Murasaki Shikibu: the Tale of Genji* (Cambridge: Cambridge University Press, 1988), 10–11.

to be the case. Indeed, it could be argued that under the impact of the acceptance of Western science and social organization the notion of authorship came under increased strain, for many Japanese writings were perforce heavily reliant on foreign texts and there was a gap between the claims and facts of authorship. This even applies to classics such as Shiga Shigetaka's *Nihon fūkeiron* 日本風景論 (1894), a study of the Japanese landscape and of mountaineering which borrows extensively and without acknowledgement from Francis Galton's *The art of travel* (1855). In other cases translations appear without the name of the original author but with the name of the translator alone making a claim for authorship. This is not so much a problem of plagiarism as an indication of a loose sense of authorship: to present onself as an author still does not at this stage constitute a claim to be the intellectual creator, simply a claim to be the compiler of a text published as a book.

The question of authors and authority in pre-modern Japan, then, is a complex issue and one that deserves a study in its own right, but since it has less to do with books as physical objects I shall not pursue it any further here. What is important to keep in mind, however, is the fact that the word 'author' as used below, and its Japanese equivalents, embrace a variety of possible relationships to a text, that the claims to creativity and authority they suggest to us often need to be examined with care.

What then is an author in the Tokugawa period? In the first place it is necessary to distinguish between different kinds of authorship for they were terminologically differentiated and so in visible language made different kinds of claims. At the élite end of the spectrum there was *sen* 撰 which customarily followed the name of the authors or putative authors of Chinese texts. This increasingly gave way to *cho* 著, which was predominately associated with scholarly writing but not necessarily sinology, for Kokugaku writers used it too, and it was also applied to Chinese authors. At the bottom end of the spectrum there was *saku* 作, which was associated with authorship of the more popular genres of fiction; the implications were sometimes amplified in the form *gesaku* 戯作, which connoted frivolity and lack of seriousness of purpose but came to be the standard form of reference to self and others by writers of popular fiction. It commonly followed the names of writers of popular fiction at the head of the text, and Kyokutei Bakin, for example, referred to his contemporaries Tamenaga

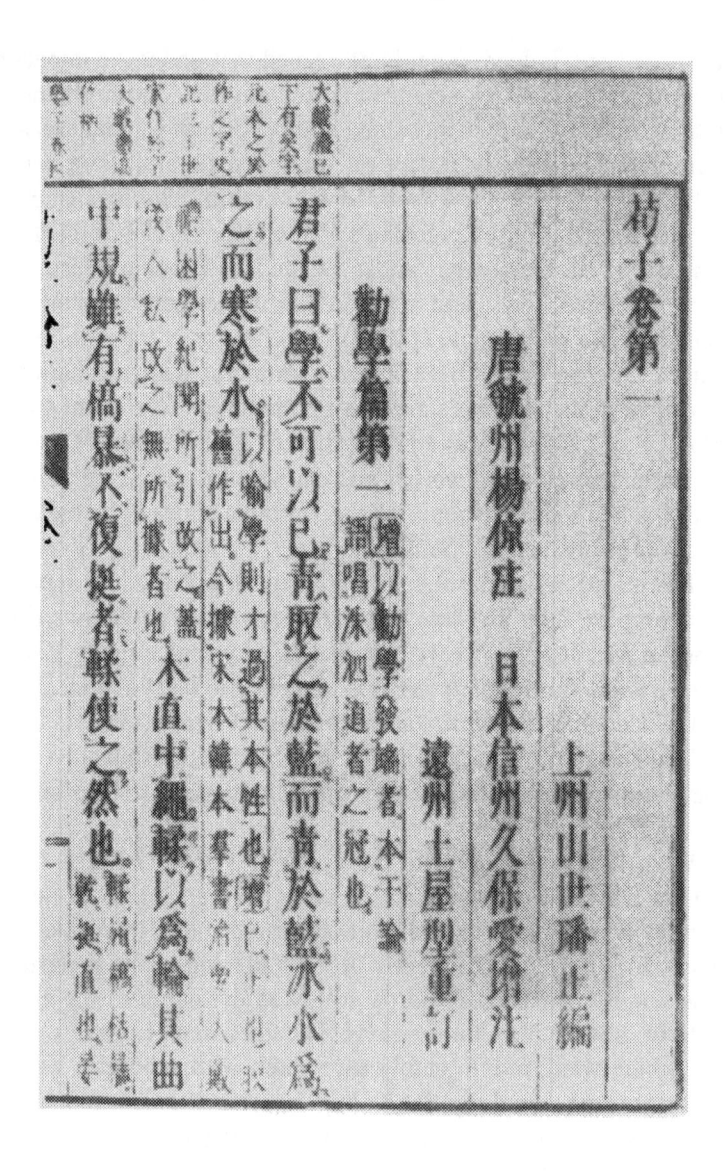

Fig. 15 The beginning of the text of *Junshi* (Ch. *Xun zi*) in a Japanese edition published in 1825. Identified here are the Chinese annotator, Yang Liang of the Tang dynasty, and three Japanese annotators and editors. Attached to the name of each man is his place of origin and a term indicating the part he had played in the preparation of the text. See Hayashi & Kornicki 1991: #2435.

Shunsui and Shōtei Kinsui as *gesakusha*, '*gesaku* writers'. In his historical novels, however, Bakin appended to his name the character *shū* 輯 or some other term such as *henji* 編次 carefully avoiding the connotations of *saku* and *gesaku* while at the same time forbearing to claim the status that went with *cho*. He was only prepared to lay claim to *cho* in his more scholarly works, such as *Gendō hōgen* 玄同放言, where he also uses a different form of his name from that found in his fiction. There is a clear sense here of a hierarchy of conceptions of authorship.[4]

It is in the Tokugawa period that authors, compilers, editors and the like begin to assert themselves in public in their publications, when commercial publication came to dominate the means of book production. Before that it is extremely rare for either manuscripts or printed books to carry any indication of authorship, except in the case of poetry collections. Even in the seventeenth century it is highly unusual for those associated with the intellectual preparation of published works to be mentioned at all, whether it be a matter of authorship, of illustration, or of punctuation of a Chinese text for the convenience of Japanese readers.

This contrasts with the practice in China, where in works published in the Ming it had already been common for the main title at the commencement of the work to be followed by explicit identification of the author and any others involved in editing or proofreading, and this practice is also sometimes found even in Song editions.[5] It was, of course, in the Song that commercial publishers came into their own in China, and it is tempting to see this development both as a device to sell books on the part of the publishers and at the same time as a statement of intellectual property and of the author's place within the Confucian tradition: thus commentaries are careful to indicate not only the names of the original author and the editor but also to make clear their respective roles in the creation of the new text. Japanese reprints of sinological works, and not only those which are simply *kabusebori* facsimiles of Chinese editions, followed this practice. Thus, for example, the 1648 edition of *Jia li yi jie* 家礼儀節 (J. *Karei gisetsu*) carried at the head of the text the name of the

---

[4] Nakamura Yukihiko 1966; *Kyokutei ikō* (Kokusho Kankōkai, 1911), 511, 521.
[5] See for example the illustration of the 1589 edition of *Nanqishu* 南斉書 in Chen Guoqing 1984: illus. 7b.

putative author, Zhu Xi 朱熹, and the name of the Ming editor, Qiu Jun 丘濬, but not the name of the Japanese editor who added reading marks for Japanese readers.[6]

It was a long time before Japanese authors asserted themselves as boldly as did Chinese authors. Japanese sinological works published in the seventeenth century usually carried no direct indication of authorship, although often the followers of a well-known scholar would append a preface or postface identifying the author and, by referring to him as *sensei* 先生, 'teacher', simultaneously positioning themselves as his disciples and inviting readers to join them in their allegiance. Similarly, it was possible for the disciples of Hayashi Razan to publish a collection of his works as *Razan sensei bunshū* 羅山先生文集 but unthinkable yet for him to append his own name to works published in his lifetime. In Tokugawa Japan authors first positioned themselves in their texts, if they did so at all, not in the explicit manner used in Chinese texts but via the medium of a preface. Itō Jinsai, for example, in 1684 signed the preface to his *Gomō jigi* 語孟字義 with his real rather than his scholarly name and concluded with the words *tsutsushinde shirusu* (謹識 in the *kanbun* original), 'I write this respectfully': this is expressive of a deferential stance towards the reader, however conventional it may later have become.[7]

By the eighteenth century, this shyness, or rather sense of hubris about asserting authorship in the same manner as Chinese scholars, had disappeared and both Confucian scholars and Kokugaku scholars customarily placed their names solidly at the head of their texts. Ogyū Sorai placed his name at the head of *Bendō* 弁道 (published in 1737) as follows: 日本 物茂卿著 (Nihon Butsu Mokei *cho*): by 'Nihon' he identifies himself as Japanese and distinguishes himself from Chinese Confucian scholars, 'Butsu' is the Sino-Japanese pronunciation of the first character of the surname Mononobe from whom the Ogyū traced their descent and which Sorai contracted to form a Chinese-style surname, 'Mokei' is one of his personal names in Sino-Japanese pronunciation, and the final *cho* claims authorship of a serious work.[8]

Sorai and other writers were now following Chinese practice in

---

[6] Based on the copy in Cambridge University Library: FB.349.1–2.
[7] *NST* 33: 115.
[8] *NST* 36: 10.

positioning their names prominently on the first page of the text immediately after the title, and this remained the standard procedure until the Meiji period. But what kind of presence do they establish? Sinologists created a Chinese-style persona for themselves, not commonly going as far as Sorai in the example referred to above, but customarily identifying their geographical ties, sometimes the domain which they served, and giving both their 'real' names and one or more of their pen-names. They also frequently added the names of one or more followers supposedly or actually responsible for some of the editorial work in preparing the text for publication: their names are usually smaller and prefixed with the word *monjin* 門人, a word that connotes an intellectual or literary pupil and of course indicates in such contexts the status of the author as some kind of 'teacher'.

In the second half of the Tokugawa period texts sometimes assume baroque forms at the outset, identifying not only the author but also a whole host of editors, helpers, illustrators, block carvers and the like, often members of his family or his followers. This was common in Kokugaku books and finely produced books such as the topographical *meisho zue*, but it is also found in other works where the hierarchy of 'authors' bespeaks a desire to make a public statement of affiliation to a particular scholar or school of learning. Behind this practice is evident a growing acknowledgement of book-production as a team effort involving an author and assorted editors and copy-editors to produce a text and a skilled block carver to translate that text into a calligraphically acceptable book.

In the case of popular literature, few seventeenth-century works identify their author, and even in the case of the celebrated Ihara Saikaku our knowledge of the extent of his oeuvre is based mainly on textual evidence and indications by his contemporaries, although in his later years he did sign his prefaces with one of his many pseudonyms. Clear indications of authorship commence with his successors, and probably arise from the tension between Ejima Kiseki 江島其磧 and Hachimonjiya Jishō 八文字屋自笑, who both combined publishing with the writing of popular works of fiction known now as *ukiyozōshi* 浮世草子. The prefaces of their works customarily end with some such formula as 作者八文字自笑 (*sakusha* [author] Hachimonji[ya] Jishō), suggesting that Jishō was the author when it is now thought that Kiseki had actually written the text; in some cases both of their names appear at the end of the preface as 'authors', and in the colophon as joint publishers, but in most of these Kiseki is again thought to have written the text.[9]

The association here with commercial publishing is crucial, for the economics of publishing had already made it obvious that recognised writers sold books and thus shown that it was commercial good sense to exploit their names. The commercial value of artists' names, on the other hand, seems to have been recognised somewhat earlier: Yamamoto Shunshō 山本春正 introduced himself to the readers of *Eiri genji monogatari*, an illustrated version of the *Tale of Genji* published in 1650, by signing the postface as the responsible artist, while the colophon on the same page gives the date and the name of the publisher rather more prominence. Hishikawa Moronobu's earliest illustrated books, published from 1672 onwards, carry his name in the colophon, and some of Ejima Kiseki's works, even when they do not identify the author, at least identify the illustrator. In 1710 a bibliographic guide for booksellers was published called *Bengisho mokuroku* which contained a section on authors and their works, revealing a perception of books as the products of authors; and in the 1780s a leading publisher of Edo, Tsuruya Kiemon 鶴屋喜右衛門, produced something more elaborate. Publishers were taking authorship more seriously, and this was taken much further at the end of the Tokugawa period when many books carried publicity material on the inside front cover making much of the supposed fame of the author or illustrator and sometimes carrying a list of his (almost exclusively 'his' in the Tokugawa period) other works (§5.1.4).[10]

In 1722 a censorship edict required that the colophons of published books carry the real name of the author as well as the publisher, and from this time onwards it therefore became a legal requirement as

---

[9] Richard Lane, 'Saikaku's prose works: a bibliographical study', *MN* 14 (1958–59): 1–26.; *Hachimonjiyabon zenshū* 八文字屋本全集, ed. Hasegawa Tsuyoshi 長谷川強 *et al.* (Kyūko Shoin, 1992–), 1: 460, 2: 269, 3: 322, 7: 449, etc.

[10] See Matsudaira 1988; *Hachimonjiyabon zenshū*, 3. 322. My comments on *Eiri genji monogatari* are based on a copy of the 1654 reprint in the possession of Dr James McMullen. For *Bengisho mokuroku* and Tsuruya's catalogue, see *NSMT* 3: 77, 121–32, and Kunii Kuniko 国井邦子, 'Shojaku mokuroku sakushayose' 書籍目録作者寄, in *Toshokangaku to sono shūhen (Amano Keitarō sensei koki kinen ronbunshū)* 図書館学とその周辺（天野敬太郎先生古希記念論文集）(Gannandō, 1971), 474–533. For examples of author-related publicity material, see Hayashi & Kornicki 1991: #2006, 2011, 2045, etc.

well as good commercial sense.[11] In practice, however, the letter of the law was not always followed, for the author's name is usually to be found at the head of the text rather than in the colophon. Furthermore, it is rarely the case that the author's 'real name' is used wherever it may appear, for common practice was to use a pen-name which carried greater public recognition and hence commercial potential. This becomes apparent in papers relating to censorship problems, where official documents customarily use the legal name of the offender rather than the pen-name appearing in the works. An obvious exception to compliance with the law was illegal publications: erotic books naturally eschew colophons and all other means of identifying responsible authors, illustrators and publishers, but some carry parodies of the legal format in lewd pseudonyms (*ingō* 淫号) coined for the nonce, such as Henkadō Injin 辺佳堂淫人.[12]

The identification of authors with their work is carried further in the nineteenth century with a growing tendency for authors to apostrophize their putative readers. The first consistent practitioner of this was probably Tamenaga Shunsui, who regularly inserted asides labelled 'Sakusha iwaku' (the author speaks) in which he sought to legitimize his genre of romantic fiction and in so doing imposed himself much more visibly on his readers than had previous generations of writers. It is interesting in this connection to note that his creation of a public persona for himself contributed to his downfall in 1841 when officials in the city magistrate's office in Edo urged their superiors to take action against him by name because of the moral damage they claimed his works wreaked on the population.[13]

The growing perception of the author as creator is also found in literary critiques. An early example, using what is now the standard word for author, is the passage in Miyako no Nishiki's *Genroku taiheiki* 元禄大平記 (1702) entitled 'kindai sakusha no yoshiashi' 近代作者のよしあし, 'an appraisal of contemporary authors'. He uses the opportunity, however, to attack his rival, Ihara Saikaku,

---

[11] *OKS* 993–4, #2020.

[12] The author of *Shunjō awase kagami* 春情啊和世鏡, of which the only copy known is in the library of the Wellcome Institute for the History of Medicine in London.

[13] The only thorough treatment of authors' apostrophes known to me is May1983: 181–92; cf. also Kornicki 1982b: 30. On Shunsui's downfall see *DKS* Shichū torishimari ruishū 18: 7–15.

Fig. 16   A scene from Shikitei Kosanba's *Gesaku hana no akahon sekai* 戯作花赤本世界 [The frivolous world of the *akahon* chapbooks] (1846). The upper half purports to show the public image of an author of light fiction, as a bookish man with some scholarly dignity, and the lower half to depict the reality as he reads out his work to his publisher, who is unimpressed.

whom he famously described as 'illiterate and ignorant of grammar'. The attachment of criticism to authors rather than their works subsequently became standard and is followed, for example, in Kyokutei Bakin's extensive survey of popular literature in his time, *Kinsei mono no hon Edo sakusha burui* 近世物之本江戸作者部類, which, as the title indicates, is explicitly concerned with the categorization of authors. Bakin himself exemplifies Barthes' formula of 'the very consciousness of men of letters anxious to unite their person and their work through diaries and memoirs', for he was the first popular writer to leave a diary, and it touches frequently on his literary production and negotiations with publishers. In the Meiji period these trends accelerated and up to the present day author-based criticism remains the staple of *kokubungaku* (Japanese literature) studies both within and outside Japan.[14]

What did it mean to be an author in the Tokugawa period, and what can we say about the construct of 'author'? As already shown, authors positioned themselves on a hierarchy of different kinds of writing: there was no one word which could be used to apply both to Ogyū Sorai as a sinologist writer and to Ihara Saikaku as a writer of fiction. Consequently, 'author' covered a plurality of constructs, at least in the eyes of writers themselves. To some extent this plurality was melting down by the end of the period as the dividing lines between 'scholar' and 'novelist', for example, began to break down and some novelists, especially Kyokutei Bakin and Ryūtei Tanehiko, began to engage in and to publish their scholarly work (§10.2). But for the reader, irrespective of the terminological differences between categories of author, the positioning of the names at the head of the text was the same and it is possible that the distinctions made by authors were not appreciated by readers.

Nevertheless, the different categories of author did differ in other respects as well, such as their social and economic circumstances. Sinologists for the most part had paid employment as teachers, commonly in service to daimyō or in the employ of the Bakufu or domain academies. They were therefore not dependent financially on their writing, and many of their works were in fact published by the institutions for which they worked, at least in the first instance. So their writing was a step removed from commercial publishing, even

---

[14] Miyako no Nishiki 1937: 324; Barthes 1977: 143.

if it did eventually circulate on the commercial market. Scholars in other disciplines, such as medicine, mathematics, Kokugaku or Rangaku, either enjoyed daimyō patronage or derived an income from their teaching activities; for the most part their works were commercially published or published by themselves, and it is likely that they derived additional income from their writing (§6.1.2). Much *haikai* and *waka* poetry was published privately by circles of poets, while virtually all fiction was commercially published in Edo, Kyoto and Osaka.

It is clear, then, that different categories of author enjoyed quite different relationships with the commercial world of publishing. In a physical sense, writers of fiction gravitated towards Kyoto and Osaka in the first half of the Tokugawa period and Edo in the second, because that was where the publishers and markets they increasingly came to depend upon were to be found. On the other hand, writers of scholarly books, for example, had less need of such direct and dependent contact with publishers and were able to remain in the provinces without losing the ability to see their works printed and disseminated, as was the case, for example, with the works of the great Kokugaku thinker and writer, Motoori Norinaga, who remained in Matsuzaka. In more existential terms, for writers of fiction without other sources of income, it was commercial publishing that made the career of author possible, at least by the early nineteenth century but probably earlier, and that relationship of dependence is apparent from innumerable prefaces in which the role of the publisher in soliciting work and managing the careers of authors is clearly expressed. In other kinds of writing, from poetry to sinology, such references to, and acknowledgement of, the world of commercial publishing are rare or non-existent.[15]

In various ways authors also came to be more public figures as the Tokugawa period drew towards its end. Publishers gave their names greater prominence on the book wrappers and the inside front covers, giving star-like status to some by appending ō 翁 [venerable old man] or *sensei* [teacher] to their names. Simultaneously visual representations of authors became more common, portraying them as writers seated on the floor at their desks or as men about town. And

---

[15] On some of these issues with regard to Bakin see Hamada 1953: 242-3; on Santō Kyōden's relationship with his publishers, see Kornicki 1977.

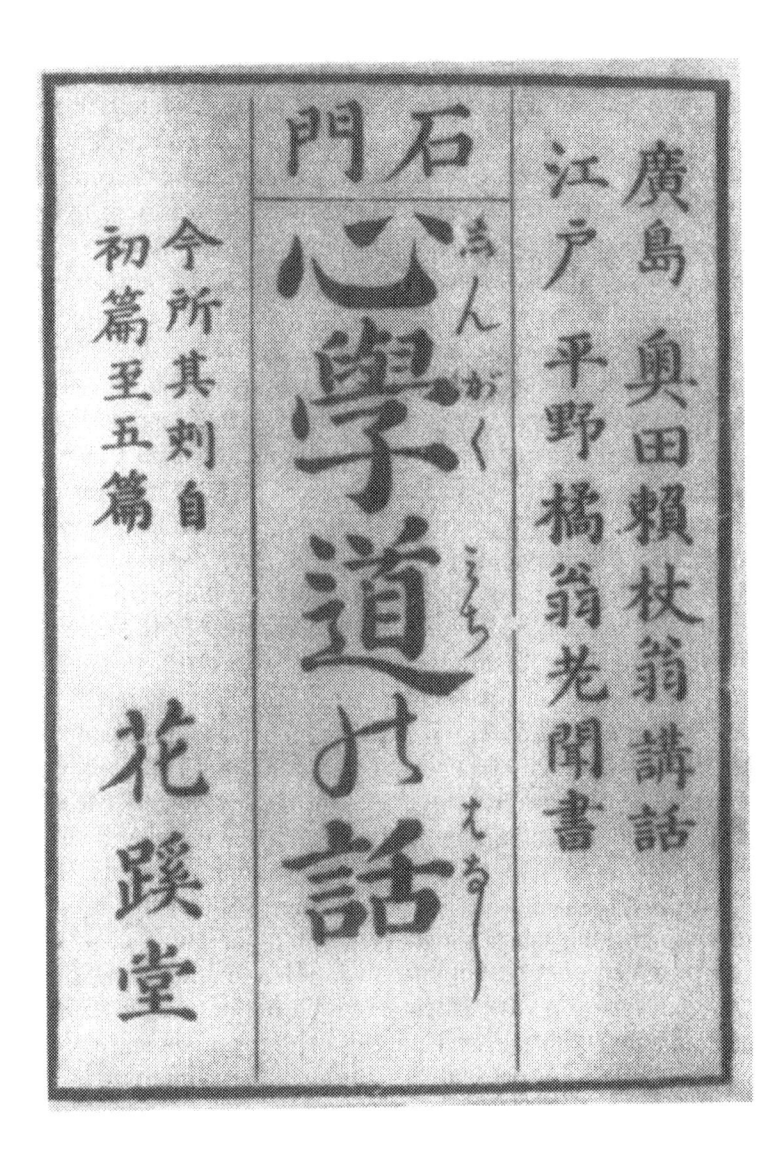

Fig. 17 The frontispiece of *Shingaku michi no hanashi*, a work in the tradition of popular moralism known as Shingaku; the first part was published in 1843 but sequels were published over a number of years. At the extreme right the 'venerable' (ō) Okuda Raijō of Hiroshima is identified as the lecturer whose discourses are contained in the book, and the next lines identifies the copyist who took down his words. See Hayashi & Kornicki 1991: #1982.

some writers of popular fiction in Edo published books which reflexively dealt with the act of authorship and in which the author himself was the hero.[16] Although there is a need for much more work on the figures of the author in the Tokugawa period, it is evident that by the early nineteenth century the author was a much more visible and significant presence, and that this had more to do with publishing than with rights of ownership in their work.

Finally, a word about names, for they were a significant but protean symbol of the writer's identity in the Tokugawa period. pen-names are in abundance in the writings of the Tokugawa period and bedevil the identification of the oeuvre of many a writer. As already indicated some writers made use of a number of different pen-names, either changing their usage over time or using different pen-names for different kinds of writing, for there were no legal restrictions on the generation or usage of alternative names.[17] Some of the pen-names are designed to conceal identity altogether, such as those found in erotic books. Others, used by Confucian scholars, mirror Chinese practices and styles and become the public identity of the owner, such as 'Sorai sensei'; in some cases authors sinify their family names by reducing a binary surname to a single character, thus rendering Fujiwara 藤原 as Tō 藤. Kokugaku scholars customarily eschewed the use of a pseudonym altogether in their published works, which must be read as a statement of resistance to the practice of the sinologists. In the case of popular literature practice is more diverse and less easy to summarize. Certain writers, notably Kyokutei Bakin, used different pen-names for different kinds of writing with the evident intention of creating a distance between their more serious or scholarly writing and their popular fiction. Most, however, simply hid behind a barrage of pseudonyms which created a public persona different from their non-authorial identity. Shikitei Sanba, whose real name was Kikuchi Taisuke and who ran a perfumery, is an obvious case.

---

[16] Hayashi Yoshikazu 1987; *NKBT* 59: 87-105.

[17] There are now, fortunately, two useful indices of the names used by sinologists and by scholars in the Japanese tradition in the Tokugawa period which include all variants and suggest a standard name in each case: Nagasawa Kikuya and Nagasawa Kōzō 1979, and Kokugakuin Daigaku Nihon bunka kenkyūsho 1990. Also, the index to *Kotenseki sōgō mokuroku* includes a considerable amount of cross-referencing and proposes readings for all names. There is still a real need for an agreed standard: Bakin, for example, appears in some sources and catalogues as Kyokutei Bakin and in others as Takizawa Bakin, and this is just one example among many.

To what extent this practice of semi-concealment is related to the ambivalence felt by many popular writers towards the business of fictional writing, as discussed by Nakamura Yukihiko, is yet to be closely examined.[18]

BIBLIOGRAPHY

May 1983: 81-107 is one of the few to deal with the problem of the author in Tokugawa fiction. On Bakin, see Hamada 1953. Nakamura Yukihiko 1966 is a classic exploration of the intellectual context in which popular literature flourished and of writers' reflexivity. Very little has been written on female authorship, but see *Joryū chosaku kaidai* 女流著作解題 (n.p.: Joshi Gakushūin, 1939). On the development of the concept of the author in China, see M. E. Lewis, *Writing and authority in early China* (New York: SUNY Press, forthcoming).

6.1.2 *Royalties*

It is received wisdom that Kyokutei Bakin was the first professional writer in Japan in the sense that he was the first to be able to make a living from his profession alone, although certain playwrights are thought to have been in the same position. In spite of the fact that he was of samurai status, Bakin was unwilling to serve as a samurai; he learned to write whilst living under the roof of the most entrepreneurial publisher of the 1790s, Tsutaya Jūzaburō, and attempted to restore the reputation and fortunes of his family through writing.[19]

However, Aeba Kōson, an early Meiji writer who took an informed interest in the literary world of Edo, claimed that the first to receive a payment for his work was Santō Kyōden in respect of one of the three works of fiction in the genre known as *sharebon* which brought him into trouble in 1791. It is certainly true that the official record of enquiry (*ginmisho* 吟味書) into the publication of these *sharebon* makes it clear that Kyōden received a substantial payment from his

---

[18] Nakamura Yukihiko 1966. Pseudonymous writing and the textual functions of the use of different types of pseudonym in Japan need close examination: see Maurice Laugaa, *La pensée du pseudonyme* (Paris: Presses Universitaires de France, 1986).

[19] Hamada 1953; Leon M. Zolbrod, *Takizawa Bakin* (New York: Twayne, 1967), 26-8, 60.

publisher upon handing over the manuscripts. But it also states that Kyōden had come to an arrangement 'five or six' years earlier whereby his publisher would buy his manuscripts from him, and that for these three *sharebon* he had received a down payment and had also been due to receive a further payment related to sales figures. There is nothing to indicate that there was anything novel about these arrangements. Kōson's assertion, then, that prior to 1791 writers had had to make do with presents or, in the case of best-selling authors of the booklets known as *kibyōshi*, with a night on the town at the theatre or in the pleasure quarters in the company of his illustrator and at his publisher's expense, would seem to be false.[20]

Kōson also argues that it was the length of the historical novels known as *yomihon* that led to a payment system, presumably because of the commitment of time on the part of the author; he had access to the early parts of Bakin's diaries which are now lost, and on the basis of those states that one of Bakin's early *yomihon*, *Chinsetsu yumiharizuki*, was so popular that his publisher gave him an exceptional payment of 10 *ryō* and a specially commissioned portrait of Minamoto no Tametomo, the hero of the novel, painted by Hokusai. Further evidence of Bakin's receipt of payments has been collected by Hamada Keisuke, who also demonstrates that Jippensha Ikku, a writer of popular comic works, unashamedly claimed to be writing for money as early as 1802, and Hattori Hitoshi has worked out from Bakin's diaries the limits of his income in the 1830s to show that he was indeed a professional writer by then at least.[21]

However, there is some evidence to suggest that payments were not uncommon even in the late seventeenth century. In his *Genroku taiheiki*, the popular writer Miyako no Nishiki included a section purporting to show Ihara Saikaku in a bad light. Saikaku is alleged to have received 300 *momme* in silver in advance fees from a publisher for a work entitled *Kōshoku ukiyo odori* 好色浮世躍 and to have spent the money in five days on a binge in the pleasure quarters; he is supposed to have kept promising delivery of the non-existent manuscript until his death six months later. Miyako no Nishiki had

---

[20] Aeba 1910; *ZEJ* 2: 176–8.
[21] Aeba 1910; Hamada 1953; Hattori Hitoshi 服部仁, 'Tenpō shonen ni okeru Bakin no shūnyū' 天保初年に於ける馬琴の収入, *Kokugo kokubungakkai shi* 国語国文学会誌 18 (1974): 21–30

no love for Saikaku (see above, §6.1.1) and this story of Saikaku's supposed bad faith may have no basis in fact whatsoever. However, the assumption behind this story is that such payments were credible, and, furthermore, the title of this section uses the word *shahonryō* 写本料 to indicate a payment to an author for a manuscript, and the inescapable conclusion is that some popular authors at least could expect payment upon submission of a manuscript to a publisher.[22] To date little has come to light concerning payments to authors in the eighteenth century. A passage in *Iwademo no ki* 伊波伝毛之記 states that the publishers Tsutaya Jūzaburō and Tsuruya Kiemon conspired in the 1790s to fix payments for Bakin and Santō Kyōden so as to keep them from the clutches of other publishers and that before this time writers, such as Hiraga Gennai, Hōseidō Kisanji and Koikawa Harumachi, had merely enjoyed the presents and junketings mentioned by Aeba Kōson. However, this does not allow us to conclude, although many have done so, that payments were unknown before this, for two reasons. Firstly, the three writers mentioned all enjoyed samurai status and indeed adopted pseudonyms that partially concealed their identities, and they therefore had alternative sources of income. Secondly, the passage cited here is exclusively concerned with popular literature in Edo: it has nothing to say about circumstances in Kyoto or Osaka, or about payments to authors of other works, such as illustrated maps, gazetteers or popular educational works, all of which enjoyed substantial markets at the time.[22]

What little attention has been paid to royalties and the professionalization of authors so far has concerned literary works. Many non-literary works were of course not commercial and had to be sponsored in some way but others offered good commercial prospects, amongst them the writings of Kokugaku scholars such as Motoori Norinaga and his successors. His correspondence with the doyen of Edo publishers, Suwaraya Mohee, has survived and in a letter of 1797 Suwaraya offered him 25 *ryō* a year for permission to publish his works in Edo.[23] Information on the royalties paid to other non-fictional writers is scarce, but it is unlikely that Motoori was unique or the first to receive payment. Until much more work

---

[22] Miyako no Nishiki 1937: 348–50; *Shin enseki jisshu* 新燕石十種, 5 vols (Kokusho Kankōkai, 1912–13), 4: 199.

[23] Okamoto 1980: 50.

has been done on this subject it will be difficult to reach substantive conclusions, but the evidence that has so far come to light suggests that received wisdom is wrong and that the professionalization of authors has its roots in the seventeenth century.

BIBLIOGRAPHY

Aeba 1910 was the first to consider the history of royalties. See also Kōzato 1970: 171–7; May 1983: 81–5. On Bakin see Hamada 1953.

6.1.3 *Copyright*

'Copyright', argues Mark Rose, 'is founded on the concept of the unique individual who creates something original and is entitled to reap a profit from those labours', but there can be no gainsaying that the concept, and the ancillary concepts of 'individual' and 'original', have been long in gestation, in Japan as elsewhere. For the most part copyright has in various parts of the world long been intimately associated with the commercial business of book publishing rather than with authorship. There were exceptions, such as the acceptance in France in 1586 of the argument that 'the author of a book is wholly its master, and as such he can freely do with it what he wills'. John Feather, writing on the historical development of copyright in England, has described it as 'a device developed within the London book trade in the sixteenth century to protect the investments of those involved in printing and publishing' without any statutory framework. Further, since the rights of authors were only fully embodied in legislation in England in the 1842 Copyright Act, then it behoves us to think of copyright in evolutionary rather than binary terms.[24]

The development of copyright in Japan, both as a commercial measure and as a recognition of intellectual property rights, has to be considered in connection with publishing in the Tokugawa period and not before, for the lack of legislation or even copyright disputes before the seventeenth century precludes any attempt to move the

---

[24] Mark Rose 1993: 2, 20; John Feather, *Publishing, piracy and politics: an historical study of copyright in Britain* (London: Mansell, 1994), 4, 125–48.

argument to earlier periods. There is no evidence that manuscripts have ever been considered to be anything other than 'public property', with the exception of those explaining secret traditions in such fields as *ikebana*, *Nō* and *waka* theory, which were jealously preserved by the owners. Thus manuscripts could be and were freely copied by those who owned or borrowed them. Similarly, even in the Tokugawa period when printed books were available in abundance, rare printed books were frequently borrowed and copied in their entirety by hand, and to date no evidence has come to light suggesting that this practice was anything but widely accepted (§3.3). In pre-Tokugawa Japan there is not even any counterpart to the controls practised in China, first recorded in a decree issued in 835 and reinforced in 1009, which were intended to prevent the unauthorised reproduction of texts deemed to be the exclusive preserve of the state, such as calendars, almanacs, maps and the classics.[25]

The question of whether in any meaningful sense copyright existed in pre-modern Japan has been raised by Suwa Haruo, but his understanding of the concept is based on an unhelpful extrapolation of modern concepts and practice. Suwa's argument is that the *hankabu* system (see §5.1.2), which was operated by the guilds from the seventeenth century onwards and functioned to protect publishers' investments in their publications, determined who owned the rights to the printing blocks but did not protect either the financial interests or the intellectual property rights of the author. To support this claim he cites the constant reworkings and rewritings of earlier works in the theatrical world and the adaptation of *jōruri* plays for the *kabuki* theatre and vice versa, the free adaptation of Chinese originals by a host of prose writers from Ihara Saikaku to Ueda Akinari, the use by poets of Matsuo Bashō's school of parts of earlier poems, and even the practice of *honkadori* 本歌取り, whereby *waka* poets drew on earlier poems. Most of this activity he describes, improbably, as plagiarism and concludes, unhelpfully, that it would be legally problematic today. He also draws attention to the lack of professional writers until Bakin's time and argues that writers did not in the Tokugawa period receive a royalty but sold their rights in their work

---

[25] Mark Rose 1993: 9. On books as 'public property' in Roman libraries see T. Keith Dix, 'Public libraries in ancient Rome: ideology and reality', *Libraries and culture* 29 (1994): 281–96.

for a single payment. Even if this were true, it would not necessarily mean that authors' financial interests in their work were non-existent, but, as suggested above (§6.1.2), we are in any case right to question this particular piece of received wisdom.[26]

There are two parallel issues here to keep in mind: on the one hand the development of measures to provide publishers with some commercial protection, and on the other the evolution of a concept of intellectual property. Munemasa Isoo rightly rejects Suwa's argument that there was no concept of the property rights of individual authors, pointing out that he restricted his view to lower-status literary genres and that in the case of 'serious books', *mononohon* in the booksellers' jargon, authors maintained rights in their work at least until death. Further, the censorship edict of 1722 required that the colophons of published books carry the name of the author as well as the publisher (see §8.2.2). Although this was to ensure that the authors of banned books could be identified, it simultaneously amounted to a public recognition of the concept of authorship. Some support has been added to Munemasa's arguments by Okamoto Katsu, who has examined the circumstances surrounding the publication of some of the works of Motoori Norinaga and his correspondence with his publishers in Edo in the late eighteenth century and who can demonstrate that Norinaga did indeed enjoy financial and intellectual rights in his work.[27]

Although it is evident that authors could retain some rights in their work, this was most likely to be the case where the capital investment for publishing came from the author or from an institution responsible for the author in some sense. Thus the simplest way to retain absolute rights in a work was to make the necessary capital investment and to retain the printing blocks. Many books were privately published in the Edo period in this way and they characteristically carry in the colophon or some other place an indication of who owns the blocks in the form 'XX *zōhan* 蔵版' (§4.3.3). These *zōhan* publications were produced by private individuals with substantial means but more commonly by circles of *haikai* poets, by private academies, especially those attached to Kokugaku scholars such as Hirata Atsutane, by domain schools, or by Bakufu institutions such as the

---

[26] Suwa 1978.
[27] Munemasa 1979; Okamoto 1980: 51–52.

Medical Academy, Igakkan 医学館. It was usually the case that *zōhan* publications were distributed commercially by booksellers in the major cities, and often the printing blocks eventually passed into the public domain as the property of a bookseller: again, we know little of the financial side to the transfer of ownership in the blocks, but it is difficult to suppose that the owners were not compensated for the capital investment represented by the blocks.

If, on the other hand, an author was dependent on his, or much more rarely her, publisher for the necessary capital investment, then the question of copyright became, as it was in England, an issue closely tied to the commercial interests of that publisher. In 1698 Osaka booksellers petitioned the city authorities to issue a ban on copyright infringements and this was indeed done later that year in an attempt, vain as it turned out, to reduce the frequency of disputes between publishers.[28] It was repeated in 1723, 1819 and 1857. The third repetition followed the abortive dissolution of the *hon'ya nakama* or booksellers' guilds during the Tenpō era (1830–44) when, according to a plaintive letter from the Osaka guild, all sorts of amateur publishers had taken advantage of the lack of control to flout the regulations and make money out of plagiarism. To the extent, then, that the city commissioners in Edo and elsewhere issued edicts relating to copyright and were prepared to adjudicate in disputes which the booksellers' guilds were unable to resolve, copyright as an issue clearly was officially recognised. But it was not embodied in formal legislation, being instead, like most matters relating to the non-samurai population, the subject of *ad hoc* decrees and edicts. Further, that recognition was not due to any commitment to the notion of copyright on the part of the Bakufu, but rather to the desire to eliminate disputes between publishers. In this, as we shall see, it was unsuccessful.

Two different terms, and on occasion a third, were used to describe different kinds of copyright infringements. *Jūhan* 重板 (also pronounced *chōhan*) was the most serious and it referred to pirate editions with the original text unchanged or with no more than minor changes, for example to the title. A *jūhan* edition might, at the most

---

[28] A similar edict was issued in Kyōto in the same year, and doubtless also in Edo, although that does not appear to have survived: *Kyōto machibure shūsei* 京都町触集成, 15 vols (Iwanami Shoten, 1983–89), 1: 62, #193. The text of the Ōsaka edict is in Makita 1968: 2.87.

blatant, be simply produced by cannabalizing a copy of the original text to create a *kabusebori* facsimile text or it might, in more subtle hands, be created by having a calligrapher rewrite the text, perhaps with some minor cosmetic changes, for the preparation of new blocks under a new title. Although it seems improbable, a *jūhan* edition could be the result of an innocent misunderstanding, for example if a publisher bought or inherited a set of blocks not knowing them to belong to a *jūhan* edition. In such cases the dispute was often resolved by having the innocent offender buy the blocks of the original edition or join with the original publisher to produce a joint edition. For the most part, however, they were not produced in good faith and when discovered resulted at least in the confiscation of the illegal blocks and of all remaining printed copies of the offending work, and sometimes also in the offending publisher's exclusion from the book trade.[29]

Ruihan 類板, on the other hand, referred to works that were partially or conceptually similar to another. This could, of course, be interpreted in many ways and the inherent vagueness led to large numbers of cases. In some it was the plot or the contents that had supposedly been copied, in others extracts from the original had been lifted and included in the new work, or the original had been condensed into an abbreviated version, and so on. In many cases similar titles were adopted as publishers hoped to benefit from the success of a popular work put out by a rival. Resolution of *ruihan* disputes was often difficult, and if they could not be settled within the guild they ended up in the offices of the *bugyō*, or city commissioner. But the usual result was some form of compromise: if the blocks and printed copies of the offending work were confiscated then often the original publisher was required to make some form of payment to the *ruihan* publisher to compensate him for his capital investment. Makita Inashiro has extracted from the guild records sufficient case material to show that many different measures were available to guild officials seeking to resolve disputes and concluded that the most common was to ban the *ruihan* edition but simultaneously require the original publisher to cede one or more blocks of the original work to the offender. This had the result of requiring him to

---

[29] On *jūhan* and the other kinds of copyright infringement see especially Makita 1968: 1.95–105, 2.87–115.

pay a *hanchin* 板賃, or block fee, every time he wished to reprint the work and so of diminishing his profits; thus the victims lost money even when the disputes were resolved, hence the eagerness of the guilds to prevent as far as possible *ruihan* books getting to the stage of being published.

The third category was known as *sashikamai* 差構, a term that also referred to a complaint made against any perceived infringement. Cases of *sashikamai* occurred when a publisher copied only the title or covers or some other external feature of another work without copying the contents or infringing the original publisher's *hankabu* rights.

In spite of the prohibitions, contemporary testimony and surviving legal documents show that the publication of *jūhan* and *ruihan* editions was almost routine, especially if they involved, for example, pirating or imitating a Kyoto publication in Edo. Such cases presumably had their origins in the assumption that the original publishers would not discover the infringement, but the assumption was false and the details of many intercity disputes survive, particularly in the records of the Osaka booksellers' guild, even though the plaintiffs were required to shoulder the burden and expense of travel to the jurisdiction of the accused to state their case. In 1751, for example, Suwaraya Shinhee, one of the leading publishers of Edo, discovered that a pair of publishers from Osaka and Kyoto had produced a *jūhan* version of his edition of *Tōshisen*, a popular anthology of Tang poetry: they forfeited 20 printing blocks and 220 copies, but ten years later three Osaka publishers tried the same trick, with the result that all three were expelled from the guild and lost their livelihood. Few such cases would have come to light but for the vigilance of the booksellers' guilds in each city, and in 1818 the Osaka guild made a present to its counterpart in Edo in thanks for the care taken to detect the many aspiring *jūhan* and *ruihan* offenders in Edo.[30]

At present very little is known about publishing organization and control outside the 'three capitals' of Kyoto, Edo and Osaka, although most of the large castle towns had their own printing and publishing industries, substantial ones in the cases of Nagoya, Wakayama, Sendai and Hiroshima at least. No domain edicts relating to *jūhan* and *ruihan* have yet come to light, but it is clear from a case involving one of

---

[30] Makita 1968: 2.93–7, 102–3.

the household almanacs known as *setsuyōshū* that provincial publishers were bound by the same rules. *Setsuyōshū* were one of the mainstays of the publishing industry and were probably the most likely book to be found in a house of few books. In 1752 two Osaka publishers put out a new kind of product with a rapid-finder index system called *Hayabiki setsuyōshū* 早引節用集 and this was a commercial success, to the extent that it spawned numerous imitations. The publishers' claim that any other *setsuyōshū* with a similar index system would constitute a *ruihan* was upheld by the guild but imitations continued to appear: in 1865 the guild reminded booksellers that the sale of nine named *ruihan* versions was prohibited, but in 1869 yet another *ruihan* edition was published, in Kyoto, only to be banned on the application of the current holder of the copyright. Well before this, three provincial publishers had taken the risk: in 1771 one in Matsumoto had to give up his blocks and all printed copies of his *ruihan* edition; the same happened to one in Sendai, who had foolishly put copies on sale in Edo, and one in Kōshū in the early nineteenth century had his edition banned. In some way, evidently, the tentacles of the copyright protection system, such as it was, spread over much of Japan: it could do nothing to bring an end to the disputes, but it could provide for their resolution so as to protect the rights of publishers.[31]

Disputes within one jurisdiction were also legion. In 1782, for example, Tsuruguya Kyūhee discovered that an employee of a fellow Osaka publisher had been distributing copies of a *jūhan* edition of his *Banreki ryōmen kagami* 万暦両面鑑: the offender's employer was held to be responsible and lost not only the blocks but also an astonishing 996 copies. While this was an extreme case, as indicated by the substantial loss suffered by the offender, many *ruihan* cases reveal a high degree of sensitivity to what we might call intellectual property, albeit intellectual property owned by a publisher. In 1734 a publisher complained about an edition of *Monzen jibiki* 文選字引, a concordance to the Chinese text *Wen xuan*, on the ground that it included indications of the tones of the characters just as his quite different dictionary did.[32]

As will already be clear, when disputes arose it was the publishers

---

[31] Makita 1968: 3.99–105.
[32] Makita 1968: 2.101, 112.

rather than the authors that made the official complaints; and when settlement was reached it was made between publishers, not between authors. Nevertheless, this does not mean that the concept of copyright was alien to the book trade in the Tokugawa period; on the contrary, it was a matter of articulation and dispute from the seventeenth century onwards, and was officially recognised to the extent that the city magistrates were required to resolve cases hinging on alleged infringements. What is more, it does not mean either that authors could not enjoy rights, whether legally enunciated or not, and it is clear from the case of Motoori Norinaga that publishers sought the permission of authors at the respectable end of the market before reprinting their works and offered substantial sums in lieu of royalty. The eagerness of publishers to protect their financial investment in the works they published thus generated at least by the eighteenth century a system, organised by the guilds and recognised by the authorities, that did provide authors with some protection too. Before this system came properly into being it was much easier to get away with plagiarism and the false attribution of works to well-known authors, as one of the victims of this practice, Kumazawa Banzan, testified.[33]

At the end of the Tokugawa period, in the 1840s, there are some signs that the authorities were enlarging upon their recognition of publishers' copyright and edging nearer to an understanding in which the author's intellectual interests assume as much importance as the publisher's commercial interests. The first sign of this appears in 1842 in a report on a *jūhan* case involving almanacs submitted by the *shichū torishimarigakari* 市中取締掛. This was a new post which had been established in the city magistrates' offices in 1841 under the Tenpō reforms and the incumbent was responsible for control of the urban population in various respects, including the publication of books. In his report on this case he stated that the offender had 'stolen the accomplishments (*kō* 功) of the original author', and he banned publication of the proposed *jūhan* edition. Where one would have hitherto expected to find a reference to the inconvenience caused to the original publisher there is here an unequivocal expression of concern for the author's interests. Similarly, in 1843 Bakufu officials

---

[33] *Banzan zenshū* 蕃山全集, 6 vols (Banzan Zenshū Kankōkai, 1941–43), 2: 66–67.

responsible for censorship were instructed to forbid publication in cases where the author had not given permission for his work to be published. A further sign is to be found in a still unpublished edict issued early in 1844, most of which consists of the usual rehearsals of old prohibitions but which also contains the following: 'it is forbidden to take a work written by another person and to submit the manuscript for publication without that person's permission.' It is likely that this phrase was a response to a particular problem that had recently arisen; at any rate it is neither repeated nor developed further during the remainder of the Tokugawa period. Nevertheless, underlying it is acceptance of the concept of author's copyright, poorly articulated though it is at this stage.[34]

After the Meiji Restoration the government gave immediate attention to the control of publishing in an edict issued in 1868, and in the Publication Ordinance, *Shuppan jōrei* 出版条例, of 1869, which recognised the rights of publishers to sell the works of an author during the author's lifetime but did nothing for authors themselves. It was Fukuzawa Yukichi 福沢諭吉 who first campaigned for the legal embodiment of the concept of copyright as he had encountered it on his journeys to the West before the Restoration. His enthusiasm for copyright had not a little to do with the fact that he was a victim of disreputable publishers in Osaka and Kyoto who pirated his best-selling works *Seiyō jijō* 西洋事情 and *Gakumon no susume* 学問のすすめ. In 1872-73 he complained vigorously to the newly-established city authorities in Kyoto and Tokyo and argued in the press that without the institution of copyright, which he translated as *hanken* 版権, authors would not write, and if authors did not write then there could be no progress.[35] In 1875 the *Shuppan jōrei* was revised and a new article, employing Fukuzawa's term, stated that exclusive rights in books lasted for thirty years. It did not, however, explicitly attach these rights to the author. In 1887 the laws relating to *hanken* were detached from the *Shuppan jōrei* and were separately promulgated as *Hanken jōrei*, but it was not until 1899, when Japan became a signatory to the Berne Convention, that a copyright law,

---

[34] Minami 1976: 8-9; *Kaihan shishin* 開版指針, unpublished manuscript in the National Diet Library, 2:15a; Nakamura 1972: 156-8.

[35] Kurata Yoshihiro 倉田喜弘, *Chosakken shiwa* 著作権史話 (Senninsha, 1980), 9-12; *Fukuzawa Yukichi zenshū* 福沢諭吉全集, vol. 19 (Iwanami Shoten, 1962), 441-78.

Chosakken hō 著作権法, was introduced. This established the concept of copyright in the international context of authors' rights and fixed as the modern term for copyright a word that unequivocally asserted the rights of authors rather than those of publishers. The modern word for 'copyright', *chosakken* 著作権, was in use certainly by the 1880s, although it did not have any legal force until 1899. It should be noted finally that the Japanese term, which may be translated as 'rights of authorship', is actually more explicit in protecting the rights of authors than the term 'copyright'.

BIBLIOGRAPHY

Suwa 1978; Munemasa 1982: 164–67, and *idem* 1979. On *jūhan* and *ruihan*, see Makita 1968: 1.95–105, 2.87–115, and May 1983: 62–67; Mitchell 1983: 26–8, deals with the *Shuppan jōrei*. For copyright in pre-modern China, see Alford 1995: 9–29.

6.2 READERSHIP

6.2.1 *Readers and reading before 1600*

So far very little work has been done on reading in pre-modern Japan. In particular, our knowledge of habits and patterns of reading before the Tokugawa period is extremely sparse and hitherto little attention had been paid to the fate of books in the hands of their readers. This is a complex issue, for the forms texts took in the Nara, Heian and Kamakura periods confronted readers with meanings that are now difficult to reconstruct. In the Tokugawa period the market for books expanded out of all recognition and commercialization intervened in the reader's approach to texts, although, as discussed elsewhere (§1.4), they retained certain features of manuscript culture. The question of readership in the Tokugawa period has been discussed by several writers, but mostly in connection with literary works and mostly with an eye to the reading public, its access to books, and requisite levels of literacy. There is, therefore, much work to be done on reading in Japan, and this section will therefore perforce have to be an almost anecdotal introduction to the subject.

The earliest references to reading in Japan relate to Buddhist texts, but it is extremely difficult to determine what is meant by 'read' (*doku* 読) in many contexts in which the word is used. Indeed, it should be remembered at the outset that in many cases what was of crucial importance was the actual production of Buddhist texts either in manuscript or in print, and that 'reading' them was a secondary consideration, if they were even intended to be read at all. This is not, of course, to deny that sūtras were read and carefully studied, for they were, of course; rather it is to recognise that 'reading' was one of a range of possible engagements with Buddhist texts, some of which were more akin to ritual than to what we think of as 'reading'.

Early historical records such as the *Nihon shoki*, *Shoku nihongi* and *Genkō shakusho* contain many references to the 'reading' of sūtras, without identifying the kind of reading involved: silent or chanted, individual or mass. Some of these do, however, explicitly concern mass acts of 'reading', involving as many as 2,100 nuns and monks on 651.12.30 when those assembled read through the entire Buddhist canon. This is often cited as the first known performance in Japan of *tendoku* 転読, a term that confusingly embraces both the act of reading through a text and the act of skipping through a long text. According to a much later text, *Zenrin shōkisen* 禅林象器箋 by Mujaku Dōchū 無着道忠 (1653–1744), *tendoku* in this second sense ('flipping', perhaps) meant 'reading' seven lines from the beginning of a volume, five lines from the middle and three from the end. There are, unfortunately, no earlier references closer in time to the seventh century which make it unequivocally clear what is going on, and so it is possible, for example, that the 2,100 nuns and monks in 651 each read a different portion of the canon simultaneously. The apparent ambiguity of the term is extremely unhelpful.[36]

The variety of techniques of 'reading' Buddhist texts in Japan has yet to be studied, but whatever conclusions might emerge, it is clear that in the Nara and Heian periods public performances at which large numbers of clerics in some abbreviated sense 'read' prodigious quantities of text, often the entire *Daihannya kyō*, took place on a number of occasions in order to derive some form of worldly protection or benefit. This practice, it must be supposed, came from China, and there are several references to it in the diary Ennin kept during his

---

[36] *NKBT* 68:317, *SNKBT* 13:158, etc.; Shibata Otomatsu 柴田乙松, ed., *Zenrin shōkisen* (Seishin Shobō, 1963), 532–3, sections on 'tenzō' and 'ten daihannyakyō'.

stay in China. On 838.10.19, for example, he states that following the appearance of a comet monks at several temples were ordered to 'read' two sūtras, using the word *tennen* 転念 (Ch. *zhuan nian*), which together with *tengyō* 転経 (Ch. *zhuan jing*) was, it seems, used in China in the same sense as *tendoku*. The clearest indication he gives of this practice is shortly after his safe arrival back in Japan: over five days he records having 'read' 5,000 scrolls, noting, for example, on 847.12.1 that '[b]efore noon I read through five hundred scrolls [of scriptures] on behalf of the Famous God of Chikuzen'. Even if, as Edwin Reischauer suggests, he paid monks to do 'this pious chore' for him, it is hard to see how they could have read through so much in such a short time unless they were doing *tendoku* in the 'flipping' sense. Elsewhere in his diary Ennin gives numerous examples of the instrumental recital of scriptures to get a favourable wind on the voyage or some other desired benefit, and it is evident that the engagement with Buddhist texts in China and Japan at this time encompassed a variety of modes of 'reading', which have yet to be examined in full.[37] It may be that public reading rituals were more common than private reading of texts, but as yet we know too little about how the literate engaged Buddhist texts in this period to be able to put *tendoku* in a context.

Secular Chinese texts were also put to certain ritual uses in the Heian court. In the Dokusho no gi 読書儀 ceremony, which is described in Murasaki Shikibu's diary, twice a day for the first seven days after the birth of a male child to a member of the imperial or any noble family, set passages were read out from the *Shi ji* 史記, *Han shu* 漢書 or other texts. Similarly the Dokusho hajime 読書始 was performed when a male child reached the age of being able to read Chinese, usually somewhere between the ages of 7 and 10, and parts of *Xiao jing* 孝経 or *Shi ji* were read aloud first by a teacher and then by a pupil. The difficult problem here, as also with Buddhist reading, is to know just how the text was read aloud: was it in increasingly unrecognisable attempts to pronounce Chinese by Japanese who had never been there, was it in the Japanese derivatives of different Chinese pronunciations we now know as *on'yomi*, or was it in unashamed

---

[37] *Ennin's diary: the record of a pilgrimage to China in search of the law*, trans. Edwin O. Reischauer (New York: Ronald Press, 1955), 46, 114, 123–4, 287, 348, 407, and notes 203 & 1543.

yomikudashi, that is to say a conventional instant rendering of Chinese into Japanese? It appears likely that by the ninth century, as ties with China were becoming attenuated, even scholars were finding it difficult to read texts with Chinese articulation, but too little is yet known on this subject.[38]

Japan's first encounter with writing was with Chinese texts and the transmission of those texts was carried out by Chinese immigrants, by the sinologically literate élite of the Korean kingdom of Paekche or by Japanese educated in China. It must therefore be assumed that reading practices at least at first were close to those practised by literate élites in China, but here too we have little to go on apart from exhortations to study and emphasis on repetitive reading and memorization. As is clear from ninth- and tenth-century pupils' copies that have survived at Dunhuang, memorization was to be achieved by reading aloud and by repetitive copying out of the text. Jean-Pierre Drège has noted that reading Chinese texts at this time meant for scholars a continual process of collation, textual criticism and punctuation rather than engagement with a ready text, and this process must have been more daunting for Japanese aspiring to literacy in Chinese, if only for reason of the paucity of texts and the difficulty of establishing an accurate text.[39]

Of all the readers of the Heian period we have best knowledge of Fujiwara no Yorinaga, whose voluminous diary *Taiki* 台記 contains frequent references to the books he read. In 1143 he recorded the books he had read over the years 1136–41, amounting to 60 different works in 578 volumes, and thereafter regularly noted down his reading up to 1155. All the works mentioned are Chinese, mostly from the Confucian canon but also poetry collections and other works, and many he reread on several occasions. The sheer quantity of his reading is impressive, and he records using time travelling in carts and boats to read, but in addition to reading texts he was also constantly engaged in the ancillary activities of editing, punctuating and finally lecturing on the texts he was reading. It is difficult to suppose that he never read works written in Japanese but if he did he did not record it: for

---

[38] Bowring 1982: 61, 186–9; Hagitani 1971–3: 2: 583–4; Tsunoda Bun'ei 角田文衛, ed., *Heian jidaishi jiten* 平安時代史事典, 3 vols (Kadokawa Shoten, 1994), 1752–3; Hayashi Hideichi 林秀一, *Kōkyōgaku ronshū* 孝経学論集 (Meiji Shoin, 1976), 358–83. Ōe Fumiki 1935: 47–52.

[39] Drège 1991a.

Yorinaga 'reading' meant sinological scholarship and study. Further, he appears to have undertaken his reading in something akin to a ritualistic context. On 1143.12.8 he set down in his diary the circumstances in which he read the *Book of Changes* that day.

> At noon began reading *Zhouyi*; got to the nine-five hexagram and stopped, because that is an auspicious hexagram. I began reading it because today is an auspicious day for the commencement of studies. First I placed the book on my desk; after bowing to it twice I began reading. I washed my hands and rinsed my mouth out, and put on my *eboshi* hat and my *nōshi* apparel before reading. This is how it will be in the future too, for this book is particularly worthy of respect.

Although of great interest, this passage raises more questions than it answers. Where did he derive these practices from, assuming they were not of his own invention? What books did he consider suitable for this treatment? How did he approach other books? The formality of Yorinaga's respect for books is similar to that advocated by Zhu Xi (1130–1200) in China a little later, and the probability is that they came from the same source, with allowances made for Japanese tastes in clothing.[40]

We know a little more of secular Japanese reading in the Heian period, although here too there are huge gaps in our knowledge. Richard Okada has declared that in the Heian period, 'the act of "reading" was a far cry from the passive and individual act it has become today; it was a communally oriented, integrative process that not only required linguistic and poeticohistorical competence but also summoned calligraphic, vocal, and even painterly talent and freely allowed a degree of rewriting, or re-creation.' This is of course no more than a hypothesis, and the issue is controversial and unresolved. In 1950 Tamagami Takuya put forward his thesis that *monogatari*, or 'tales' in the unsatisfactory but conventional rendering, were read aloud in intimate company and that their genesis lay in this process of a shift from oral to written text. At the centre of his argument is a scene in the picture scroll of the *Tale of Genji* showing

---

[40] Kojima Shōgorō 小島小五郎, *Kuge bunka no kenkyū* 公家文化の研究, (Kokusho Kankōkai, 1981; facsimile of 1942 edition), 66–101; *(Zōho) Shiryō taisei-* (増補) 史料大成, 45 vols (Rinsen Shoten, 1965), 23: 107. On Yorinaga's reading see also *YMC* 2: 207–30.

Ukifune and Nakanokimi looking at pictures while the maid Ukon reads a text out aloud. But what text? Pointing out that the text is more likely to be an *ekotoba*, that is a condensed version supplementing the pictures, than the *monogatari* itself, Nakano Kōichi has rejected Tamagami's thesis, and has argued for a more subtle understanding of the variety of modes of reading. In his view what we see in the scroll is a 'lower level' of reading, as opposed to that of the author of the *Sarashina nikki* (c1008), who clearly did enjoy reading as a 'passive and individual act' and may not have been exceptional, particularly in the provinces where books and fellow readers were evidently hard to come by. Nakano's argument is marred by the implication that reading aloud is for children and illiterates, but he has shown that the readership of *monogatari* was broader and reading habits more varied than Tamagami allowed. Certainly, while the author of *Sarashina nikki* naively hoped to meet in the real world people like the heroes of the tales she read, Sei Shōnagon's list of *monogatari*, all now lost, bespeaks a more detached and critical reading and implies an individual engagement with the texts.[41]

For the centuries that follow we have virtually no clues as to reading practices, except for the diaries of learned monks and courtiers, which rarely record anything but titles of books read. For example, *Shaken nichiroku* 蔗軒日録, the diary of the monk Kikō Daishuku 季弘大叔 (1421–87), which gives details of his reading in the 1480s, betrays his reading of Ming vernacular literature, as do also the diaries of other Zen monks. But was this 'leisure reading', as Ōba suggests, or was it seen as something else, such as familiarization with contemporary forms of Chinese?[42]

The diaries of court scholars in Kyoto in the Muromachi period reveal something of the practice of *kōdoku* 講読, a form of public or private instruction involving both the recitation and exposition of canonical Chinese texts. *Kōdoku*, at least of Buddhist texts, is certainly a practice that goes back to the Nara period, but it later came to

---

[41] Okada 1991: 23; Tamagami Takuya, *Genji monogatari kenkyū* 源氏物語研究, Genji monogatari hyōshaku bekkan (Kadokawa Shoten, 1966) 143–55; Nakano Kōichi 中野幸一, 'Kodai monogatari no dokusha no mondai - monogatari ondokuron hihan' 古代物語の読者の問題－物語音読論批判, in *Genji monogatari I*, Nihon bungaku kenkyū shiryō sōsho (Yūseidō, 1969), 194–202; Morris 1971: 41, 55, 87; *NKBT* 19:249.

[42] Ōba & Wang 1996: 66–67.

include secular texts, even in Japanese in the case of the *Tale of Genji*, once it had achieved the status of a canonical work. It seems often to have been a long and painstaking process: an extreme example is the five years it took Nakahara Yasutomi 中原康富 (c1400–57) to go through the text of *Mencius* with Wakamatsu Sadatsugu 若松定嗣 (1437–54) from 1444 to 1449, starting when he was under ten years of age. Sanjōnishi Sanetaka had the *renga* poets Sōgi 宗祇 and Shōhaku 肖柏 come to his house on 1485.3.28 and start a *kōdoku* of the *Tale of Genji*, which took 14 months to complete, and he himself undertook a *kōdoku* of part of the *Genji* before the emperor and crown prince in 1490–91. Various other texts were the subject of *kōdoku* reading, including sinological works and the early Japanese histories such as *Nihon shoki*, which was the subject of several *kōdoku* given by Ichijō Kanera 一条兼良 (1402–1481) in the mid fifteenth century.[43]

Sanjōnishi Sanetaka records in his diary what appears to be recreational reading aloud of the *Heike monogatari* 平家物語 after parties or poetry competitions, and there is other fifteenth-century evidence to suggest that oral recital of texts already existing in written form was a common practice. Nakahara Yasutomi reported the existence of an aged nun who gave *Genji* readings, and Sanetaka records that in 1474 a reading of the *Taiheiki* was given before the emperor over two months. And the Japanese tales of this period often end with an address to 'the reader' or 'the listener', suggesting that they were read both aloud and in silence, but in what circumstances is unclear.[44]

We know even less concerning women's reading, although the Kanazawa Bunko preserves some undated letters showing that in the Kamakura period the library was used not only by men but also by women, who sought to borrow, or perhaps just read at the library, some of the classic works of Heian literature, such as the *Tale of Genji*, the *Tales of Ise*, and the *Pillow book* of Sei Shōnagon. One letter from Kyoto complains that there are no longer any good copies of the *Pillow book* to be had there and that books were moving to the

---

[43] Inoue Masamiochi 1972: 450–512; Haga 1981: 1.111, 119, 131–2. For a Nara-period reference to the practice of *kōdoku*, see *SNKBT* 15: 172–3.

[44] Haga 1981:1.147, 104–5, 148; Furuhashi Nobuyoshi 古橋信孝, 'Kodai kara chūsei made' 古代から中世まで *Kokubungaku kaishaku to kanshō* 国文学解釈と鑑賞 45.10 (1980): 89.

east, presumably following the movement of political power. This reference apart, women are invisible readers over the centuries of the Kamakura and Muromachi periods.[45]

It is too early to draw any conclusions about reading in the Muromachi period, other than that there were many modes of reading being practised. Reading could be either a public or a private activity, it could be either ritualistic or recreational, and it could be carried out aloud or in silence. To some extent the nature of the text seems to have dictated the mode of reading, but it is clear that all texts were still to varying degrees tied to oral modes of dissemination.

BIBLIOGRAPHY

On *tendoku*, see *Bukkyō daijiten* 仏教大辞典, ed. Ryūkoku Daigaku 龍谷大学 (Fuzanbō, 1922), 3413-4, and M. W. de Visser, *Ancient Buddhism in Japan: sūtras and ceremonies in use in the seventh and eight centuries A.D. and their history in later times*, 2 vols (Leiden: E. J. Brill, 1935), 9, 22, 494-519. On reading in the Heian and Tamagami's thesis on the *Genji*, see Okada 1991: 23, 175-80. On the reading of monks in the Muromachi period, see Ōba & Wang 1996: 62-6, and on reading in China see Drège 1991a.

6.2.2   *Readers and reading after 1600*

In the Tokugawa period readership underwent some fundamental shifts as book production and distribution became commercialized and the book became a commodity like any other. Before the end of the seventeenth century some books, such as *Kiyomizu monogatari*, were being sold in thousands; they were being sold on the streets by pedlars; they were stocked with other goods such as medicines and haberdashery; and they were available either for purchase or for rent. By 1808, as Nakamura Yukihiko has noted, there were as many commercial lending libraries in Edo as barbershops and public bathhouses. Access was no longer a problem, even for the illiterate, who could take advantage of others reading aloud, or for the impecunious, who could borrow for small sums. By the early nineteenth century, it

---

[45] Seki Yasushi 関靖, 'Kanazawa Bunko no saiginmi (7)' 金沢文庫の再吟味, *Rekishi chiri* 62.5 (1933): 23-26.

is clear that something akin to a nationwide network of booksellers and circulating libraries existed, which created a national readership for books. Again, reading had as a habit spread socially as well as geographically well before the onset of the nineteenth century. For many readers access to books came through the commercial lending libraries known as *kashihon'ya* rather than purchase: the historical novelist Tsukahara Jūshien (1848–1917), recalling his youth in Edo before the Restoration of 1868, noted that *kashihon'ya* went the rounds of daimyō residences, those of their retainers and of the shōgun's vassals, retired merchants, brothels, and so on.[46] And in response to the commercialized culture of print that had established itself by the seventeenth century, perceptions of books and modes of engagement with them were also beginning to change. (§5.1.1, 9.2.4)

The rapid pace at which books had become ubiquitous and easily accessible had consequences that did not have to be perceived as necessarily benign. This particular problem had been faced already in China some centuries earlier when Zhu Xi, one of the most influential figures in the Confucian tradition in Japan and Korea as well as in China, developed a critical theory of reading, *Dushu fa* 読書法. Printing was decidedly a mixed blessing in his perception: '[b]ecause nowadays the number of printed texts is large, people don't put their minds to reading them'; '[t]he reason people today read sloppily is that there are a great many printed texts.' Zhu Xi's prescriptions for reading are predicated on a sense of crisis in the Confucian educational tradition. Reading was supposed to be practised in order 'to observe the intentions of the sages and worthies': he understood it instrumentally, as a tool for moral education, and as such it had to be a demanding discipline: '[o]rdinarily, in reading a book we must read and reread it, appreciating each and every paragraph, each and every sentence, each and every word. Furthermore, we must consult the various annotations, commentaries, and explanations so that our understanding is complete. In this way moral principle and our own minds will be in perfect accord.' To this end he urged students to read less: the pressures put upon them to read more by the examination system and by the ever growing weight of a long tradition were inimical to proper reading and understanding. The ideal reader should be able to know the core texts so well that he is free of the written

---

[46] Nakakura Yukihiko 1973: 95; Tsukahara 1910.

word. It goes without saying that the reading of which Zhu Xi is speaking is that dedicated to the Confucian canon: reading popular fiction and reading as a form of leisure cannot be considered to be real reading at all under this head.[47]

What impact did Zhu Xi's theory of reading have in Japan? We know that it reached Japan, for it was contained in the large collection of his sayings, *Zhuji yulei* 朱子語類, which was published in a Japanese edition in 1668 and subsequently reprinted in 1791 and again in the nineteenth century. There is also an epitome of his views of reading, *Shushi dokusho no yō* 朱子読書之要, which was published some time in the seventeenth century in an edition prepared by Yamazaki Ansai (1618–82).

The earliest echo of Zhu Xi's theory of reading I have seen is in *Shogaku dokushohan* 初学読書範 (1699), a guide to reading practice by Amano Shinkei 天野信景. Amano is concerned to guide students to the right texts so as to fulfil the moral purpose of reading, which was to rectify the mind so that in turn the family, the nation and ultimately the world would enjoy order and harmony. He quotes from Zhu Xi's *Dushu fa*, urging students to read less and absorb more, and enjoins them to adopt a reverent attitude and respectful posture when reading. Of course, he is only talking about serious books, beginning with the *Four Books* of the Confucian canon. He concludes with an appendix listing Japanese books that may be read, which is dominated by the early histories of Japan composed in Chinese, such as the *Nihon shoki*, but also includes the *Man'yōshū* and the official anthologies of court poetry. The perceived danger of excessive reading taking the place of thorough reading, which Amano takes up here from Zhu Xi, was also a concern of some of the domain schools established later in the period: at the Sakura domain school, for example, the school rules warned students against reading too much.[48]

---

[47] Chu Hsi, *Learning to be a sage: selections from the Conversations of Master Chu, arranged topically*, translated with commentary by Daniel K. Gardner (Berkeley: University of California Press, 1990), 129, 139–40; see also Daniel K. Gardner, 'Transmitting the Way: Chu Hsi and his program of learning', *HJAS* 49 (1989): 141–172, and Steven Van Zoeren, *Poetry and personality: reading, exegesis, and hermeneutics in traditional China* (Stanford: Stanford University Press, 1991), 230–46.

[48] Nagatomo 1987: 380–407 contains a facsimile of *Shogaku dokushohan*; *NKSS* 1: 257.

Kaibara Ekken (1630–1714), a writer in the Confucian tradition who concerned himself with popular education, also picked up some of the themes articulated by Zhu Xi, although without developing them into a sustained argument. In doing so, he reflects some of the concerns the changes brought about by print were arousing, but at the same time he takes it as given that books are freely available, a situation that was new to the seventeenth century in Japan and directly attributable to the marriage of commerce and book production. In *Rakkun* 楽訓 (1710), his book of instruction in the pleasures of life, Ekken assigns high importance to reading and describes it as the best of pleasures available to man, and one to be savoured alone. But he was not speaking of reading in general, rather, as he goes on to explain and like Zhu Xi, of reading the Chinese classics, which he saw as the best reading matter of all, and after them works on Chinese and Japanese history, without a knowledge of which one would live as if in a dream.

In *Wazoku dōjikun* 和俗童子訓 (1710), his instructions on the upbringing of children, he gave far more detailed prescriptions for reading. Readers should wash their hands beforehand, adopt a reverent attitude, kneel formally before their desk with good posture and place the book properly on the desk in front of them. Books should not be thrown about, stepped over, used as pillows, have their pages folded back or turned with fingers moistened with spittle. Pages from discarded books with the words of the sages upon them should be disposed of with respect and not put to humiliating uses. Naturally, one does not laugh, move about or leave the room while engaged in reading. How, then, actually to read? His prescriptions here are predicated on his understanding of the objectives of reading. One reads so as to remember, and so not in a hurry but carefully and slowly, with ones eyes, ones mind and ones mouth: he is not necessarily talking here of reading aloud, but he is at least talking of mouthing the syllables. Care should be taken to make sure that the characters are given their correct pronunciation and that the Chinese is correctly read as Japanese. So he is principally concerned with Chinese texts, glossed, to be sure, with reading marks (*kunten*) to enable Japanese to construe the text as if it were written in Japanese. He does not exclude the notion of reading Japanese texts, for when addressing the question of texts for children to read he makes a point of deprecating *jōruri* and *kouta* texts, all *waka* poetry suggestive of sexual relationships and, for the same reason, Japanese classics such as the *Tale of Genji* and the *Tales of Ise*, by implication allowing other Japanese texts.[49]

Ekken was undoubtedly reacting to contemporary practices that were of recent origin and bespoke the everyday familiarity of books and printed texts. The printed page was not any longer so precious that one refrained from using it as toilet paper. Nagatomo Chiyoji, who refers to Ekken's prescriptions as ideals which differed greatly from the realities of reading as practised by the urban population at large, has suggested that reading for pleasure, that is as a leisure activity, first emerged in the Genroku era (1688–1704), but that is surely too late, as prints showing courtesans reading date from much earlier. Nevertheless, he is right to argue that the need for a basic sinological education of the sort prescribed by Ekken was widely accepted, and that the pill of a morally didactic system of education was gradually sweetened as moral justification was found for reading an ever wider range of texts. In 1672 Samukawa Masachika 寒河正親 saw the message of Japanese warrior tales as appropriately Confucian and in 1719 Nishikawa Joken 西川如見 extended the range, with caution, to include old *jōruri* texts. Later still, at the end of the Tokugawa period, the Meirindō domain school of the Owari domain in Nagoya issued a syllabus that included, in addition to the standard sinological texts, new and radical histories of Japan written in Chinese, such as Rai San'yō's *Nihon gaishi* 日本外史, and even the early Japanese war-tale *Heike monogatari*. What the students actually read in their spare time is, of course, entirely another matter: the Daisō lending library in Nagoya, which counted many samurai among its customers, certainly had much less demanding reading matter to offer the students (§9.2.4).[50]

In the Meiji period this tradition of sinological reading and education by no means came to a dramatic end. On the contrary, since the new state schooling system introduced in 1872 turned away from the traditional sinological orientation of education, scholars well trained in sinology at domain schools or the Bakufu Academy opened private schools (*kangakujuku* 漢学塾) which taught pupils

---

[49] *EZ* 3: 197–205, 632–4.
[50] *NST* 59: 43, 117, 129–30; Nagatomo 1987: 408–19 contains a reprint of the Meirindō syllabus.

how to read and construe Chinese texts in order to cater to the large market that that still valued these skills. There were also private schools specializing in English, Frnnch or German, but they were few in number at first because of the shortage of teachers; reading foreign texts demanded skills enjoyed by only a tiny minority, and for most access to such texts was at second hand, through the medium of translations. There were guides to reading translated books, such as Yano Fumio's *Yakusho dokuhō* 訳書読法 (1883), which sought to guide readers through the unfamiliar terrain of translations of books on subjects they did not understand, by European and American writers they had never heard of, but there were also guides, such as *Dokusho shidai* 読書次第 (1893) by Nishimura Shigeki, which retained a place for sinology in a demanding programme of reading that also included works of classical Japanese literature, recent Japanese translations of Western writings and even books in English such as Herbert Spencer's *Principles of sociology*.[51]

Let us now return to Kaibara Ekken. It will be clear already that his precepts were addressed not to intellectuals but to ordinary town-dwellers, hence their easy, accessible style in Japanese, rather than the difficult sino-japanese that was the normal language of Confucian scholarship. Although, as indicated below, we know that many urban readers did not take his advice, what is at this stage much less clear is the nature of reading as practised by his fellow intellectuals. Zhu Xi was widely read in Japan in the Tokugawa period but there are few echoes in Japanese Confucian writings of his theory of reading and it is not evident why this should be so. While more work is needed on this area, there is one important aspect of reading common among intellectuals that Ekken does not mention at all. It is the felt need to copy passages from books you do not own. Many diaries testify to this widespread practice, as also do the many surviving manuscript copies of books that had already been printed. In the case of rare books this practice is understandable, but equally common was selective copying. Hosono Yōsai 細野要斎 (1811–79), for example, a Confucian scholar of Nagoya and teacher at the Meirindō domain school, kept a detailed diary of his reading from 1836 until

---

[51] Kutsukake 1983: 164–77; Kannabe Yasumitsu 神辺靖光, 'Tōkyō ni okeru kangakujuku no jittai' 東京における漢学塾の実態, *Shigaku kyōiku kenkyūsho kiyō* 史学教育研究所紀要 7 (1963): 99–125.

the year of his death, and in it he records both borrowing books in order to make a complete copy and 'copying down some passages that moved me'.[52]

In the eighteenth and nineteenth centuries numerous introductions to sinology were published which propounded views of canonical reading. One example is *Keishishi yōran* 経子史要覧, which was first published in 1804 but purports to be a text composed orally by Ogyū Sorai and written down by his follower Miura Chikkei 三浦竹渓 (d. 1756). This cites some of the more mundane of Zhu Xi's prescriptions and then tells the student how to read the Chinese texts and what meanings to read into them. There is a suspicion that this is not so much an introduction as a bluffer's guide to sinological discourse. This suspicion becomes a certainty in the case of *Gedai gakumon* 外題学問, 'title scholarship', which explicitly offers a handy guide to the basic texts. Both of these works were of course written in Japanese, and at the same time as attesting to the prestige of sinological discourse in Japan they show the market for short-cuts which bypassed Zhu Xi's notions of reading altogether.

As Kaibara Ekken well knew, there were already in his time many books available to the contemporary reader of sorts that he was unlikely to approve of, and we know that they were being read, and read in ways that Ekken had warned against. The upper floors of bath-houses were places of entertainment and relaxation, and sometimes sexual activity as well, but books were also commonly available. An illustration published in 1798 shows a group of men relaxing after a bath with books scattered on the floor, some open, though they are paying more attention to the bath-house girls or to their food than to the books. An account of the hotsprings at Arima similarly refers to ghost stories and other light reading matter being made available by commercial lending libraries for customers to 'while away their time after taking the waters'. Other indications of the familiarization of readers with books are legion: a poem from the 1730s referring to medicine spilled on books; and others about using books to cover the face for a nap (1723), using them as a temporary pillow (1789), turning pages with ones mouth (1800), sprawling on the floor to read (1804), and so on.[53]

---

[52] *NS* 19: 273, 285.
[53] *Settsu meisho zue* (1798) 10:10b–11a; *Hyakka zuihitsu* 百家随筆, vol 3

As Nagatomo has argued, one of the most common means of access to books for the bulk of the urban populations of the large towns and cities was the *kashihon'ya*, commercial lending libraries (see §9.2.4). This was certainly true in the eighteenth century, and in Osaka and Kyoto in the seventeenth too. In the 1830s Tamenaga Shunsui included in his *ninjōbon* numerous scenes in which young rakes or courtesans borrow his books from *kashihon'ya*, which not only testify to the familiarity of the practice but also show readers how they can gain access to his works. He also frequently refers to his readers as 'ojōsama and ojochūsama', young women and maids, but this was a pose, for there is much evidence to suggest that his works were just as popular with men. A similar pose encountered in some genres of fiction is that they were for children: but this cannot be taken as literally as Koike Masatane takes it, for this was a ploy to evade close censorship examination.[54]

It is possible to gain some measure of the extent of readership for individual works in the Tokugawa period by means of their printing history. In a few rare cases we have a good idea of how many copies of a given work may have been printed, but these crude figures do no more than convey a minimal extent of readership, for the habits of patronizing commercial lending libraries or borrowing from acquaintances enabled each copy to reach a plurality of readers that is unquantifiable today. However, the comparative demand for given works is reflected in the existence of multiple editions of the same work, such as the many editions of *Taiheiki* and *Heike monogatari* printed in the seventeenth century, and in the need to renew the blocks of works that had been printed until the blocks had worn out.[55] Further, the sustained demand for a given work over time can be determined from the frequency with which the blocks were brought out from storage and reprinted. For example, the works of Ihara

---

(Kokusho Kankōkai, 1918), 244-5; *MZS* 13-ki, section 7, p.11a. See Nagatomo 1982: 176-8 for the examples cited, and *idem* 1987: 185-7 on reading in hotspring resorts.

[54] Tsukahara 1910; *NKBT* 64: 68, 383; Koike 1980: 44-5.

[55] On the *Taiheiki*, for example, see Takahashi Sadaichi 高橋貞一, *Taiheiki shohon no kenkyū* 太平記諸本の研究 (Kyoto: Shibunkaku, 1980): this focuses on the manuscripts and only considers the printed editions of the early seventeenth century, although it is clear from *KSM* 5: 475 and Hayashi & Kornicki 1991: #594-5 that there were many commercial editions later in the seventeenth century.

Saikaku, popular though they were in the late seventeenth and early eighteenth century, clearly excited little interest later in the period, for they were very little reprinted, whereas various other seventeenth-century works were reprinted at intervals throughout the period.

Although we have some good evidence showing us how readers gained access to books in the Tokugawa period, we have little that gives us any insight into how they read, and in particular how popular fiction was read. In this connection Nagaidō Kiyū's *Fūzoku haijin katagi* (1763) contains a scene of interest. A money-lender's mistress is ill, and although she likes reading stories and has tried to do so, the doctor has told her not to, as it could damage her health, and instead to have somebody read to her. The money-lender's wife is jealous so he cannot do this himself and sends his employee, Sasuke, along to read to her: she gives him some works of fiction which had been published 40 or more years earlier and which she has borrowed from a circulating library. The implication of this passage, if we can extrapolate from the fictional setting, is that intimate reading alone, and probably in silence, was a common practice by this time.[56]

Nevertheless, popular fiction retained oral elements, particularly in the exact representation of speech. Of all the popular writers of the Tokugawa period Shikitei Sanba was the most attentive to his readers in seeking to direct their reading with a particular view to vocalisation. The orality latent in his published works has often been noticed: he devised his own diacritics and transcription conventions to represent dialectal differences of pronunciation, idiosyncrasies of speech or even speech defects, all with parallel explanatory glosses. In the preface to his *Namaei katagi* 酩酊気質 (c1806), a virtuoso series of drunken monologues, he provided readers with close instructions for reading alone or reading aloud in company to get the full feel of the personalities and moods of the speakers. The romantic genre of *ninjōbon* also has ties with orality, as Maeda Ai has noted, drawing attention to the use of punctuation to facilitate reading aloud. The main exponent of this genre, Tamenaga Shunsui, is reported to have given public readings of some of his works, and there are several passages in his writings where reading *ninjōbon* aloud is taken for granted, as when a young man proposed to read one aloud

---

[56] *Chinpon zenshū* 珍本全集, 3 vols, Teikoku Bunko (Hakubunkan, 1895), 1: 737.

to two courtesans clearly able to read for themselves.[57]

Just as manuscripts coexisted with a sophisticated print society in the Tokugawa period, so too did silent reading coexist with reading practices that were encouraged by the persistence of texts with marked oral and aural features. The fundamental shift was the transformation of means of access to texts: printed texts and their ready availability from the second half of the seventeenth century onwards brought books within the physical reach of new readers hitherto cut off by geography or social class or economic circumstances from contact with books. They had access to books from bookshops, from *kashihon'ya* and from acquaintances, for many diaries testify to the widespread practice of lending books to fellow readers (§9.2.3). How they read and understood the texts they had access to is yet to be discovered, but the Tokugawa world that encountered the global world in the middle of the nineteenth century was already a nation of readers.

Maeda Ai has drawn attention to the survival of reading aloud in the Meiji period, citing several diaries and autobiographies that note reading aloud in childhood of works of fiction like Bakin's *Hakkenden* and of other reading matter such as newspapers and Fukuzawa Yukichi's *Gakumon no susume*. He argues that reading aloud in the Meiji period took two forms. The first provided a means of communication for those who were poorly educated, as instanced by a father reading *Hakkenden* aloud to the whole family, maids included. The second derived from the *sodoku* recitation practices of private schools of Chinese learning: *sodoku* was the traditional technique by which most beginning students learnt how to 'read' Chinese without any understanding of the text.[58] In the Meiji period, when Chinese studies were deemphasized in the curriculum of the national elementary schools, private schools of Chinese flourished and continued to rely on the *sodoku* method of basic training; and the pupils applied this

---

[57] *NKBZ* 47: 207. See also Robert W. Leutner, *Shikitei Sanba and the comic tradition in Edo fiction* (Cambridge, Mass.: Harvard University Press, 1985), 104–6, and Honda Yasuo 本田康雄, 'Sharebon no hōgen byōsha' 洒落本の方言描写, *Kokugo to kokubungaku* 国語と国文学 57.2 (1980): 39–47. Maeda 1973: 136–7; Tamenaga Shunsui 為永春水, *Umegoyomi* 梅暦, 2 vols, Iwanami Bunko (Iwanami Shoten, 1951), 2: 65.

[58] Maeda 1973: 132–67. On *sodoku*, see Richard Rubinger, *Private academies of Tokugawa Japan* (Princeton: Princeton University Press, 1982), 52–3.

required habit of reading aloud to the novels of Bakin or to the new political novels of the 1880s.

Maeda's argument needs some refinement now. Firstly, while it is undoubtedly true that in some cases reading aloud did provide the illiterate with access to the literate world, it is also clear that reading aloud to the whole family was also an expression of family solidarity and of paternal authority. Secondly, it is not clear, in the case of students who read aloud even to themselves, how much this practice had to do with the appreciation of rhythm and how much with the custom of reading in groups either in class or for sociability. Further, one practice not mentioned by Maeda is that of reading newspapers aloud: newspapers report men called *shinbun-yomi* 新聞読み (newspaper-readers) going around villages and reading passages out, including the advertisements, for a set sum per newspaper as late as 1884.[59]

Finally, it is important to note that there were no dramatic changes in the reading allegiances even of intellectuals in the first twenty years of the Meiji period. In spite of the emphases on the 'new' and the 'useful', sinological literature and the fiction of the recent Tokugawa period continued to enjoy considerable esteem and continued to be available at commercial lending libraries, and they were extensively reprinted on the new movable-type presses in the 1880s. And when, in 1889, 69 leading writers, scholars and journalists were asked to list their ten favourite books, only three chose any Japanese works published since 1868 while 27 chose works of Tokugawa literature. Even a cursory examination of readership in the Meiji period thus suggests that the cultural revolution that accompanied the Meiji Restoration was, after all, far more insecure than is often supposed.[60]

BIBLIOGRAPHY

Nakamura Yukihiko 1973, and 'Yomihon no dokusha' 読本の読者, in Nakamura Yukihiko 1961; Noma Kōshin 1958; Koike 1980: 44–7; Nagatomo Chiyoji 長友千代治, 'Edo shomin no dokusho' 江戸庶民の読書, *Bungaku* 文学 45 (1977): 99–109; and Nagatomo 1987: 31–37, 59–122, etc.; Yokota

---

[59] *Yomiuri shinbun*, 17 February 1884, p. 3.
[60] Kornicki, 'The survival of Tokugawa fiction in the Meiji period', *HJAS* 41 (1981): 461–82.

1995. On reading aloud in the 19th century see Maeda 1973: 132–67, and on guides to reading in the Meiji period see Kutsukake, 'Meiji jidai ni okeru dokushoron no keifu' 明治時代における読書論の系譜, in Kutsukake 1983: 162–93.

6.2.3 *Literacy*

The study of literacy in pre-modern Japan is of recent origin and most writers have concentrated on levels of commoner literacy in the nineteenth century with the stated or unstated agenda of elucidating the contribution of a literate population to the 'modernization' of Japan. A full-scale study is not possible within the compass of this book, but some pertinent observations can be made by way of introduction to the subject.

It was claimed by a Shintō scholar in the thirteenth century that Japan had had its own system of writing before the introduction of Chinese characters, and this idea was taken up by several scholars of nationalist persuasion in the Tokugawa period who produced samples of the script to support their claims. These were forgeries, and we can only agree with Christopher Seeley that this mythical scipt, known as *jindai-moji* 神代文字, 'letters from the age of the gods', was 'a fabrication dreamed up by Shintoist scholars who were unwilling to acknowledge that writing was one of the many cultural appurtenances for which Japan was at first dependent on China and Korea.'[61]

The representation of the Japanese language in writing came some considerable time after the introduction of the Chinese writing system. The first stage is what Seeley calls the 'hybrid style', in which the exigencies of the Japanese language began to transform the Chinese word order, and the earliest example of this dates from 596. At least by the end of the seventh century characters were being used as phonograms to represent the sounds of Japanese nouns and in the eighth century this practice was extended much further, especially in the case of poetry in Japanese, which is represented entirely by phonograms and so constitutes the first corpus of written Japanese. In the *Man'yōshū* (*c*759), an anthology consisting largely of Japanese poems with Chinese notes, we find extensive use of characters as

---

[61] Seeley 1991: 4.

logograms, that is to say being used not for their sound value like phonograms but for their sense-value from which the Japanese equivalent is to be derived, and we also find a variety of other orthographic conventions in order to represent the Japanese language. In the ninth century the use of phonograms gave rise to the evolution of the *kana* syllabic writing systems, *katakana* and *hiragana*. The word *katakana* is attested in the tenth century but *hiragana* does not appear until 1603 in a Portuguese source. The word often used in texts of the Heian period for the cursive *hiragana* was *onna-de* 女手, 'women's hand', while *otoko-de* 男手, 'men's hand', denoted Chinese characters. The implications of this will be considered below.

It was in the Nara and Heian periods that literacy first came to be functional, for Buddhism was a scriptural religion and required familiarity with written texts. These texts were of course mainly Chinese translations of Sanskrit or Prākrit sūtras and this continued to be the case until the Tokugawa period when some sūtras were translated into Japanese: it is only in modern times that Buddhist texts have been widely available in Japanese translation. Buddhism therefore required literacy in Chinese, and adherents in Japan, Korea and other countries on the periphery of China simply had to be able to read Chinese. This requirement was reinforced by the bureaucratic nature of the state in these early periods. As the wooden documents known as *mokkan*, which have been found in such profusion in recent years, have clearly shown, reports from the provinces, official communications, and even missing-person notices were all written in Chinese and depended upon a population with Chinese literacy manning (only men were employed as officials) the central organs of the state and its provincial outposts. The education system for the University (*Daigakuryō* 大学寮), therefore, laid down a syllabus of texts that closely followed the Tang educational system and sought in the same way to prepare privileged young men for careers in the bureaucracy (§7.1.1).

It is customarily supposed that women in the Nara period were generally illiterate, that women in the Heian period were *kana*-literate if they were literate at all, and that women who were literate in Chinese were rare. This may not, however, have been the case. The *Tale of Genji* contains an often-cited passage in which a young man tells Genji and his friend of a woman he once knew: 'Her letters were lucidity itself, in the purest Chinese. None of this Japanese nonsense for her.' Genji and his friend comment that, 'she seems a most unusual woman', and this has been taken to refer to her Chinese ability and to imply that such ability was seldom found, but the young man, we are told, is 'aware that the great gentlemen were amusing themselves at his expense': Genji's remarks might even have an ironical cast here, but in any case this fictional exchange cannot be taken to prove that women's literacy in Chinese was 'unusual'. What is a fact is the survival of a number of poems by women in Chinese in the *Keikokushū* 経国集, the third and last court anthology of poetry and prose in Chinese, compiled in 827: they include empress Shōtoku, who reigned in the middle of the eighth century, princess Uchiko (807-847), and others. It is clear from Sei Shōnagon's *Pillow book* that she too was familiar with Chinese historical and other works, and Murasaki Shikibu herself reveals in her diary that she could read Chinese books and that 'I read with [her majesty] the two books of Po Chü-i's *New Ballads* in secret', because she did not want a court gossip to find out. It is quite possible to conclude from this, as Robert Borgen has recently done, that there was 'diversity among Heian court ladies, with the more intellectual ones having learned some Chinese and the less intellectual ones making fun of them'.[62]

After the end of the Heian period we have even less to go on for the next four centuries. Buddhism, of course, remained a textually based religion and Zen monks in particular concerned themselves increasingly with secular Chinese texts. The bureaucratic pretensions of the Nara and Heian periods, however, had given way to a more modest apparatus under the Kamakura and Muromachi shōgunates and in the struggle for territory and power literacy was less functional than it had been. Those playing by the book and trying to legalize their claims naturally had to be literate in order to do so. The literacy required was not so much in Chinese as in the sino-japanese written language known as *kanbun* 漢文. It is perhaps fair to claim that for much of this period the literate were mostly to be found in the Zen monasteries, but of literacy in Japanese and women's literacy there are but few traces.

---

[62] Murasaki Shikibu, *The Tale of Genji*, trans. Edward G. Seidensticker (London: Secker & Warburg, 1976), 35; *NKBT* 24: 265-6, etc.; *NKBT* 19: 249; Bowring 1982: 133, 139; Hagitani 1971-3: 2.253, 294-5; Borgen's comment was made on the H-Japan network on the Internet on 22.10.1996.

There can be no doubt that it was in the Tokugawa period that literacy rates made their most dramatic rise, but this has yet to be demonstrated satisfactorily. The most powerful factor working in favour of this shift towards a literate society was the enhanced functionality of literacy. The Tokugawa Bakufu was to an unprecedented extent in Japan a paperwork régime and it used the formalized written style, known as *sōrōbun* from the ubiquitous use of the auxiliary verb *sōrō*, as a system of subordination: respondents and writers of reports and petitions in towns and villages were required to use this language in their dealings with officialdom, that is in their written dealings with officialdom. Edicts and public prohibitions posted on the *kōsatsu* notice-boards were all written in this style and required a knowledge not only of a number of characters but also of the somewhat bizarre conventions of *sōrōbun*. Further, commercial development, and particularly the development of a national market for goods, produced a parallel dependence on paperwork for the purpose of account-keeping and maintenance of credit records.

To meet these needs there was an increasingly extensive network of educational institutions. On the one hand the domain schools (*hankō*) offered an orthodox sinological education, while for those who were not samurai there were the commoners' schools, *terakoya* 寺子屋, in increasing numbers throughout Japan offering basic instruction in reading, writing and arithmetic, and for allcomers a variety of private academies offering advanced study of various unorthodox disciplines. The latter included Rangaku, or 'Dutch studies', which comprised mostly the study of Western science through the medium of texts in Dutch. Itazawa Takeo has estimated that by the nineteenth century there were at any one time several hundred who were literate in Dutch; other European languages were largely unknown until the 1850s, although on 1808.10.9 the Bakufu did instruct the Nagasaki interpreters to apply themselves to Manchu, Russian and English.[63]

Umehara Tōru has demonstrated that there were huge increases in the numbers of *terakoya* and private academies in the first half of the nineteenth century. There are problems here with the data for the earlier periods, which may be seriously underreporting the numbers before the nineteenth century, but that there was a surge in the

---

[63] Itazawa 1959: 465; Katagiri 1985: 82-4.

foundation of new educational institutions in the cities is hard to controvert. His attempts to derive percentages of children attending school from the data are less successful because they are tied to a modern definition of what constitutes 'attending school' and hence lead to an underestimation. An important point, however, is that for urban women in families involved in retail trades acquisition of the basis skills of reading, writing and arithmetic was a significant means of preparing for marriage given the importance of women's labour in retail businesses.[64]

The extent of peasant literacy is difficult to measure. However, it is clear from the publication of Miyazaki Antei's guide to farming practice *Nōgyō zensho*, which was written for peasant cultivators and first published in 1697, from a host of later works in the same vein, and from early nineteenth-century famine herbals that suggested alternative sources of food for the starving, that literacy among cultivators of the earth was becoming less uncommon and indeed more functional. There are several cases too of altruistic individuals making their collections of books open to the public and explicitly indicating that members of both the farming and mercantile classes were welcome. One such public library opened in Fukuoka in the 1750s was closed down later by the domain authorities on the ground that encouraging farmers to study would disturb the social order.[65]

It is of course a mistake to see the cultivators as a monolithic mass in the Tokugawa period, for we know that economic and social stratification became marked by the eighteenth century, but at the top end literacy was probably essential, for communications with domain authorities were conducted in writing, as also were appeals for reduced taxation in years of crop failure and calls to fellow cultivators for collective protest. Diaries kept by village headmen testify to their literacy and in some cases provide some insight into their reading habits. And in villages in the vicinity of Osaka it was not unusual for village headmen to possess their own personal libraries, sometimes amounting to several hundred volumes, even in the early eighteenth century. The diary of the Mori family of Kusakamura

---

[64] Umehara Tōru 梅原徹, *Kinsei no gakkō to kyōiku* 近世の学校と教育 (Kyoto: Shibunkaku, 1988), ch. 8.
[65] Thomas C. Smith, *The agrarian origins of modern Japan* (Stanford: Stanford University Press, 1959), 88–9, 178; Ono 1952: 186, 188–89.

shows that they had constant contact with the colporteurs of Osaka booksellers and sometimes placed orders for books they wished to purchase or rent, and they were involved in a network of fellow readers in the neighbourhood with whom they were constantly exchanging books, from current fiction to works of classical literature such as the *Taiheiki* and even to commentaries on Chinese medical texts. Their library, like that of the Sanda family also in the vicinity of Osaka, contained ample evidence of literacy in Chinese in the form of Confucian texts and collections of Chinese poetry. Literacy of this order was not widespread, but it is unlikely that the colporteurs would have travelled in the countryside for just one or two customers, and we are justified in concluding from their regular visits that there was enough of a population that was literate and interested in reading at least current fiction to make such visits worthwhile.[66]

As Aoki Michio has shown, many foreigners who visited Japan in the years before the Restoration were surprised at the levels of literacy and education they found. To take just two examples, Golovnin, who spent three years in captivity in 1811–13, declared that there were no Japanese who could not read or write, and Heinrich Schliemann, who visited Japan in 1867 well before he became famous as the discoverer of Troy, wrote that there was no Japanese man or woman unable to read. How well they were able to judge this is of course a problem, but Golovnin explicitly compared the high overall educational level of Japan with that of Russia, where, he said, there were more men of scientific genius than in Japan but far more who could not read at all.[67]

In the face of the evidence showing the spread of literacy among the ordinary population of towns and even in rural areas, literacy sufficient at least to read current works written mostly in *kana* and a small number of characters, Lawrence Stone has drawn attention to the absence of any association between literacy and social and political radicalism as found in England. This issue needs further consideration, however, for it has now become clear that literacy was an indispensible tool used to gather support for protests and to commemorate the deeds of martyred protesters, and as such had a part to play in the

---

[66] Noma 1958: 66; Nagatomo 1982: 87–105 and 1987: 420ff.

[67] V. Golownin, *Memoirs of a captivity in Japan*, 3 vols (London: Oxford University Press, 1973; facsimile of 2nd edition of 1824), 3: 27ff, etc. H. Schliemann, *La Chine et le Japon* (1867).

millenarian cries for *yonaoshi* 世直し or 'world renewal' in the mid-nineteenth century. Similarly, when preparing his uprising in Osaka in 1837, Ōshio Heihachirō wrote an appeal urging the rural population to rise up with him against injustice and had it secretly printed for distribution on a large scale. In the event he was betrayed and was forced to bring the uprising forward, with disastrous consequences, but surviving copies of the appeal are addressed to the village headmen, elders, farmers and peasants in four provinces near to Osaka. Literacy could indeed have radical consequences.[68]

The figures commonly cited for literacy rates in the early 1870s are 40% for males and 15% for females, but as Rubinger among others has shown, the methods of arriving at these figures pose many problems. The figures were derived from *terakoya* attendance statistics collected later in the Meiji period, but these unquestionably understate the numbers of *terakoya* throughout Japan. They also exclude altogether other, more informal systems of education, such as those accompanying the apprenticeship system. More important is the fact that these are national averages and that they certainly conceal great urban-rural variation. Since literacy was at its most functional in the major cities, for reasons of employment, leisure and dealings with the authorities, the strong likelihood is that male literacy in, for example, Edo was much higher than this and that female literacy did not lag far behind. In rural areas, where there were fewer uses for literacy, the rates were, it must be supposed, much lower. Here a literacy test given to 882 males in Tokiwa village in Nagano prefecture in 1881 and distinguishing carefully between different levels of literacy is revealing, even though the lack of similar material from other villages makes wholesale extrapolation dangerous. Nevertheless, the fact that 312 could not read or write anything and that a further 363 could only write their name and address, leaving just 207, or 23% of the sample, with some degree of literacy, supports the suggestion that literacy in rural areas lagged far behind the cities. Women were not tested in Tokiwa, but probably would have enjoyed even lower literacy rates. Further, this was already 13 years after the Meiji

---

[68] Marius B. Jansen and Lawrence Stone, 'Education and modernization in Japan and England', *Comparative studies in society and history* 9 (1966–7): 227; Walthall 1991: 26–30; the text of Ōshio's appeal is contained in Kōda Shigetomo 幸田成友, *Ōshio Heihachirō* 大塩平八郎 (Sōgensha, 1942), 261–7.

Restoration and nine after the introduction of an embryo national education system: literacy rates in Tokiwa, if not in other rural communities, must have been lower in the Tokugawa period.[69]

BIBLIOGRAPHY

On the history of writing see Seeley 1991 and Richard Bowring, 'The female hand in Heian Japan: a first reading', in Domna C. Stanton, ed., *The female autograph: theory and practice of autobiography from the tenth to the twentieth century* (Chicago: University of Chicago Press, 1987). On education in the Nara and Heian periods and the Chinese texts used, see Momo Hiroyuki 桃裕行, *Jōdai gakusei kenkyū* 上代学制研究 (Meguro Shoten, 1947). On literacy see Rubinger 1988; Aoki Michio 青木美智男, 'Bakumatsuki minshū no kyōiku yōkyū to shikiji nōryoku' 幕末期民衆の教育要求と識字能力, in Aoki and Kawachi Hachirō 河内八郎, eds, *Kaikoku* 開国, Kōza Nihon kinseishi 7 (Yūhikaku, 1985), 219-69, and the works cited in Yokota 1995 note 3. See also R. P. Dore, *Education in Tokugawa Japan* (London: Routledge & Kegan Paul, 1965), Herbert Passin, *Society and education in Japan* (New York: Teachers College Press, 1965), and Richard Rubinger, *Private academies of Tokugawa Japan* (Princeton: Princeton University Press, 1982).

---

[69] Rubinger 1988: 15.

CHAPTER SEVEN

TRANSMISSION

1 Transmission to Japan
    1 Pre-Tokugawa imports from China
    2 Pre-Tokugawa imports from Korea and Parhae
    3 Later imports of Chinese and Korean books
    4 Imports of European and American books
2 Transmission from Japan
    1 Exports of Japanese books to China and Korea
    2 Exports of Japanese books to the West

7.1 TRANSMISSION TO JAPAN

As mentioned in chapter one, the transmission of Chinese books to Japan has played a fundamental role in the formation of Japanese book culture and intellectual enquiry from the earliest times right up to the nineteenth century. Indeed, so extensive were these imports from China that a number of works eventually lost in China, mostly but not exclusively Buddhist works destroyed during the persecutions of Buddhism, turned out to have survived in Japan and were subsequently re-exported back to China. In this chapter, therefore, the focus will be on the movement of books from China to Japan, although it is clear that some Chinese books also reached Japan from the Korean kingdoms and from the state of Parhae (Bohai). Korean books have had a limited impact in Japan, except for some neo-Confucian studies in Chinese which were influential in the early seventeenth century; of books in Korean rather than Chinese there is no trace in Japan. The only other imports that must be mentioned are the Dutch books that began reaching Japan in the seventeenth century: they had a profound influence on scientific and intellectual enquiry in Japan and undoubtedly prepared the way for the 'turn to the

West', the shift in intellectual orientation from China to Europe and America that took place from the middle of the nineteenth century onwards.

On the other hand, Japanese books seem to have had only a limited impact on the outside world. There are but few traces of Japanese books in China and Korea, and they are in any case almost all books written in Chinese rather than in Japanese. While there is some evidence that certain Japanese writers were eager for their writings in Chinese to be circulated in China, there appears to have been no interest in sending books to Europe even when it became possible. Nevertheless, Japanese books, both in Japanese and Chinese, did begin reaching Europe in the seventeenth century via several routes and eventually provided material for the first stirrings of European intellectual interest in Japan. The influence these books had on Europe pales into insignificance, however, when compared with that of the Dutch works imported into Japan, let alone with that of the flow of Chinese books. Japan's role in the transmission of books is in pre-modern times that of a receiver rather than that of a transmitter, and that imbalance is reflected in this chapter.

7.1.1 *Pre-Tokugawa imports from China*

In spite of attempts by nineteenth-century nationalists to prove otherwise, there was of course no indigenous script in Japan until after contact with Chinese civilization, and so Japan's initial experience of books was with books in Chinese, most probably brought over from the Korean peninsula. It is clear from the scattered references in the first of the Japanese chronicles, *Nihon shoki* (720), that books and those who could read them were held in high esteem and both were deemed suitable presents for the purpose of cementing political relationships. The first mention comes in the account of the fifteenth year of Ōjin's reign, traditionally but unreliably equated with A.D. 284 (perhaps really c405). In that year, we are told, the king of Paekche on the Korean mainland sent to Japan a man who 'could read the [Chinese] classics well' and he became tutor to the heir apparent. The following year, it is reported, a man called in Japanese Wani is said to have come to Japan and to have lectured on various books to Ōjin's heir apparent, and the *Kojiki* (712) adds that he brought with him copies of the Confucian *Analects* (*Lun yu* 論語) and *Qian zi wen* 千字文. It is not possible to assign a reliable date to this episode, and Wani, if indeed there ever was such a person, must have been preceded by literate immigrants or the gifts he brought would have been of no use in Japan.[1] Over the next couple of hundred years, in the reckoning of *Nihon shoki*, there were a number of other occasions when gifts of books or teachers reached Japan, but we have no means of ascertaining their reliability, to say nothing of the dates. The safest guess is that Chinese books had reached Japan via the Korean kingdoms at least by the fifth century and probably by the end of the fourth.

When we come to the early seventh century, we can begin to identify some of the books that must have reached Japan, for, as Kawase Kazuma has shown, quotations in Shōtoku Taishi's so-called Seventeen-Article Constitution reveal knowledge of 18 identifiable books, although of course some of these quotations may be at second-hand. Similarly, quotations and references in *Nihon shoki* and the eighth-century poetry collections *Kaifūsō* 懷風藻 (751) and *Man'yōshū* reveal familiarity with many more texts, although again some of these may have been derived from compendia or other secondary sources.[2]

Most of these texts, it must be supposed, reached Japan in the hands of the numerous people of continental or peninsular origin who settled in Japan in the seventh and eighth centuries and many of whom were proficient in bureaucratic procedures and other professions requiring not only literacy but also familiarity with books. Others must surely have been brought back by members of the official missions to the Sui and then the Tang courts in China, the court in Silla on the Korean peninsula, and the court in Parhae (Bohai) in what is now Heilongjiang and neighbouring provinces in north-eastern China and the Russian Maritime Province up to Khabarovsk. There is, for example, a report in a later source that the Japanese ambassador sent to the Sui court in 608 was instructed to buy books in China: the likelihood is that this was usual rather than exceptional. And it is

---

[1] *NKBT* 1: 248–9; 67: 370–1, 373–4; 68: 28–9, 34–5, 100–101, 108–109, 140–41, 194–5. See Inoue 1972: 15–28. Wang, in Ōba & Wang 1996: 353, cites the Korean text *Haedong yŏksa* 海東繹史 in support of the *Nihon shoki* account, but this is a Yi dynasty text and this passage is probably based on *Nihon shoki* itself.

[2] Kawase 1934.

difficult to imagine that the scholar monk Minabuchi no Jōan, who also took part in the mission of 608 and did not return to Japan until 640, failed to bring any books back with him, but there is no hard evidence. In the case of Yamanoe no Okura's participation in an official mission to China in 702, his long poems contained in the *Man'yōshū* reveal his familiarity with some ephemeral popular works which he had doubtless acquired during his stay and some of which, otherwise no longer extant, have subsequently been found in the caves at Dunhuang. Participation in the missions gave those interested a precious opportunity to extend their knowledge of Chinese texts beyond those that happened to be available in Japan, and it is likely that most followed Yamanoe no Okura's example and acquired what they could.[3]

The wooden tablets or shavings often used as tallies and now known as *mokkan* provide some further evidence of books in Japan in the Nara period, for some carry the titles of books, and others contain quotations or extracts, apparently for writing practice or memorization. Most *mokkan* offering evidence of this sort come from Nara and its environs, but some have also been found in Dazaifu in Kyushu; together they testify to the presence of the Confucian *Analects*, *Wen xuan* 文選 and other texts. Hardly any of the many manuscripts that reached Japan in these early centuries have survived, but in Tokyo National Museum there is a manuscript of the works of the Tang poet Wang Bo, *Wang Bo ji* 王勃集, copied before 690 and bearing an ownership seal of the Kōfukuji temple dating from the Nara period. A few others are also known, including an early Tang manuscript of *Han shu* 漢書 bearing the seal of the Shikibushō 式部省, one of the departments of state in the Nara and Heian periods.[4]

The accumulation of books in Japan remained passive and subject to the vagaries of chance probably until the early eighth century, when scholars and monks began actively to seek out books in China, and probably in the Korean kingdoms as well. This was only to be expected, for other states in the cultural orbit of China were already making official requests for books: in 686 the king of Silla sent a request for *Li ji* 礼記, and in 738 the government of Parhae asked for

---

[3] Ōba (1996), 290. For tables showing details of the Japanese overseas missions, see *KD* 5: 173, 176, 205–6, 224.

[4] For the *mokkan*, see Tōno 1977.

San guo zhi 三国志 and other works.[5] The earliest Japanese bookbuyer of whom we have record is the head of the mission that reached the Tang court in 717, who is reported to have spent all the allowances he received on books.[6] Accompanying the ambassador was the scholar and politician Kibi no Makibi 吉備真備 (693–775), who spent the years 717–35 in China as a government-sponsored student and later made a second trip, a rare privilege, as vice-ambassador on a mission in 752–3. The official chronicle mentions four books by name that he brought back in 735, and another mentioned in *Nihonkoku genzaisho mokuroku* (see below) is said to have been brought to Japan in a copy made by him after extensive but fruitless searches for a complete version of the text.[7] Kibi is almost certainly the man mentioned in the *Tang shu* 唐書 as a Japanese envoy keen on acquiring books, and it is evident that his appetite for them made an impression on the Chinese court. It is *a priori* likely that he brought back far more than the five books of which we have knowledge.

There is some evidence that there was resistance in the Tang court in the early eighth century to the practice of allowing 'barbarians' access to any Chinese books they wanted. It was suggested, for example, that there was a strategic danger in letting certain military, geographical and historical works fall into the hands of potential enemies and these questions were discussed when the Tang court was considering in 730 how to respond to requests for books made by a Tibetan envoy. Wang Zhen-ping's view is that the court was indeed cautious about making such texts available to foreign envoys, but at present these circumstances do not seem to have affected the supply of Chinese books to Japan, and there do not appear to have been any restrictions placed on the purchases made by students and monks.[8]

The texts imported from China had an impact in Japan not only in Nara but also in the provinces. In 769 local officials in Dazaifu in northern Kyushu complained that they only possessed copies of the *Five Classics* and requested copies of some historical works as well. In response the government in Nara sent a number of works including

---

[5] *Tang hui yao* 唐會要, (Shanghai: Guji Chubanshe, 1991), 1:777–8.
[6] *Jiu tang shu* 旧唐書 199上「日本」.
[7] *SNKBT* 13: 288–9; see also Ōta 1959.
[8] Wang Zhen-ping 1991: 45–6.

Han shu 漢書 and *San guo zhi*. As Mori Katsumi has argued, this reveals two things: firstly, that imports were firmly in the hands of the central government even though Dazaifu was much closer to the mainland, and secondly that there was a demand for Chinese texts in the provinces, which was undoubtedly stimulated if not created by the establishment of provincial academies (*kokugaku* 国学). Nevertheless, some books did reach Dazaifu directly: *c*838 Fujiwara no Takemori 藤原岳守 found a copy there of the collected poetic works of Yuan Zhen and Bo Juyi in a merchant ship that had arrived from China.[9]

The demand for Chinese texts can also be gauged from the syllabuses laid down for the University and the provincial academies, which are prescribed in the earliest surviving law codes and which for the most part closely followed Tang practice in selecting a core group of nine Confucian texts. What we know of educational practices in the Nara period suggests that *Shi ji* and other historical texts were also used, and the texts used for the private education of children of the aristocracy included some Daoist works and literary works as well.[10]

Two catalogues and a compendium of texts from the Heian period give a much more complete picture of the secular Chinese works that had reached Japan by this time. The compendium is *Hifuryaku* 秘府略, compiled by Shigeno no Sadanushi 滋野貞主 in 831 in 1,000 volumes, of which only two survive. Even the two volumes extant reveal familiarity with a large number of Chinese works, although some of the quotations were probably made at second hand from Chinese compendia.[11] The first of the two catalogues, *Nihonkoku genzaisho mokuroku*, was probably compiled before 898 by Fujiwara no Sukeyo at his sovereign's command (on both the catalogues see

---

[9] *SNKBT* 15: 264–5; Mori 1975: 207 ff; *KT* 3, *Nihon Montoku tennō jitsuroku*, 31; *NST* 3:262–8.

[10] On textbooks, see Momo Hiroyuki 桃裕行, 'Jōdai ni okeru kyōkasho no henkan' 上代に於ける教科書の変換, *Rekishi chiri* 歴史地理 66.2 (1935): 1–18.

[11] Kawaguchi 1964: 137; for an index of the books cited by Shigeno, see Yoshida Kōichi 吉田幸一, '*Hifuryaku* in'yō shomei sakuin' 秘府略引用書名索引, *Shoshigaku* 13.3 (1939): 28–32. On the sources used for *Hifuryaku*, see Katsumura Tetsuya 勝村哲也, 'Shūbunden goran tenbu no fukugen' 修文殿御覧天部の復元, in Yamada Keiji 山田慶兒, ed., *Chūgoku no kagaku to kagakusha* 中国の科学と科学者 (Kyōto: Dōhōsha, 1978), 659–68.

also §10.1.1). It may be a catalogue of books that survived the fire at the palace library in 875, as has been suggested, but is more likely to be a catalogue of books circulating in Japan, although how far and wide the compiler may have searched is unknown: it certainly omits some books known to have reached Japan by this time and a few that are known to have survived. It also contains a number of items not recorded in Sui or Tang catalogues, others that have not survived in China and a few that have only turned up this century at Dunhuang. The other catalogue is *Tsūken nyūdō zōsho mokuroku*, which purports to be the catalogue of the library of Fujiwara no Michinori (1106–59) and which lists Chinese works by both Chinese and Japanese authors. As Ivo Smits has demonstrated, both of these catalogues have been somewhat neglected and serve to show, for example, that the texts of all the major Tang poets were available in Heian Japan. Bo Juyi was the most influential of the Tang poets in Japan: a copy of his collected works was imported *c*838, as mentioned above, and it appears he was aware that his works were available in Japan and Korea. It is apparent, however, that there was still a considerable time lag between secular manuscript production in China and transmission of copies to Japan, and so there is very little evidence of any of the Northern Song poets being available even in Fujiwara no Michinori's time.[12]

As mentioned above, citations alone are not sufficient to prove the transmission of a particular work to Japan, for some citations came at second-hand from the Chinese compendia or encyclopedias known as *lei shu*. Kojima Noriyuki has explored this question with respect to Japanese texts of the Nara and Heian periods and has identified certain Chinese compendia known to have been available to Japanese writers by this time. However, it is clear from citations in Japanese legal commentaries, such as *Ryō no shūge* 令集解, which was compiled in the second half of the ninth century, that a number of contemporary Chinese commentaries on the Tang Code (*Tang lü* 唐律) had actually reached Japan, for these works were not featured in compendia.[13]

---

[12] Smits 1995: 35–44. Bo Juyi refers to the circulation of his works in Japan and Korea in a postscript dated 845: *Bo Juyi ji* 白居易集, *waiji* 外集 2 (Beijing: Zhonghua Shuju, 1979), 1553.

[13] Kojima Noriyuki 小島憲之, *Jōdai nihon bungaku to chūgoku bungaku - shuttenron o chūshin to suru hikaku bungakuteki kōsatsu* 上代日本文学と中国文学－出典論を中心とする比較文学的考察 (Hanawa Shobō, 1962); Rikō Mitsuo 利光三津夫, 'Wagakuni ni hakusai sareta *Tōritsu* no chūshakusho to sono itsubun' 我が

So far I have only mentioned secular texts, but well before this time the first Buddhist texts had been introduced to Japan: the lack of records make it impossible to state with certainty what texts had reached Japan by 700, but the writings attributed to Shōtoku Taishi enable us to make some deductions. In the Nara period the records of the court sūtra scriptorium (*shakyōjo*) include a number of catalogues of texts copied or of the contents of book chests dating from 733 onwards. From these and other records it is clear that a very large number of texts had reached Japan by this time and it is also possible to determine what specific texts were available in Nara. Further, a catalogue produced in 741 purports to give the numbers and types of texts in 9 chests constituting the Buddhist canon, which shows that by this time at least a large part of the canon had already reached Japan (§10.1.1).[14]

Kibi no Makibi, whose journeys to China have already been mentioned, was accompanied to and from China on his first visit by the monk Genbō (d. 746). Genbō is reported to have brought back more than five thousand volumes of Buddhist texts, probably both sūtras and exegetical works, all of course in Chinese. This may well have been the entire so-called Kaiyuan 開元 canon, which was catalogued as such in 5048 volumes just four years before Genbō returned home in 734 and which is known to have been available in Japan by 739. Some of the Chinese monks who came and settled in Japan in the eighth century are also known to have brought texts with them and this was probably true of them all. In the case of the most celebrated of them all, Jian Zhe (J. Ganjin), who arrived in 756, the titles of the works he carried with him are recorded in a contemporary biography.[15]

Textually, then, Nara Buddhism was well equipped. It must not be

---

国に舶載された唐律の註釈書とその逸文, *Shigaku zasshi* 67.11 (1958): 63–83; Endō Mitsumasa 遠藤光正, *Ruisho no denrai to Meibunshō no kenkyū* 類書の伝来と明文抄の研究 (Saku: Asama Shobō, 1984), 58–68.

[14] *DNK* 3: 84–91; 7: 495–500; 24: 17–22, 185–6, 197. Kimoto 1989 provides an exceptionally useful index to references to Buddhist texts in the Nara period.

[15] *SNKBT* 14: 30–31; Kimiya 1955: 198; *DNBZ Yūhōden sōsho* 1: 119. On the fate of the books Ganjin brought with him, see Sakachara Towao 栄原永遠男, 'Ganjin shōraikyō no yukue' 鑑真将来経の行方, in Ueda Masaaki 上田正昭, ed., *Kodai no Nihon to torai no bunka* 古代の日本と渡来の文化 (Gakuseisha, 1997), 95–116.

forgotten, however, that the collection and copying of texts also had something of a political character. This is both in the sense of an expression of Japanese cultural progress vis-à-vis China and the Korean kingdoms, and in the narrower sense of seeking ritual protection of the state through Buddhism. Furthermore, the copying of texts was also a meritorious activity and not necessarily related to the desire to propagate them (§3.3).[16]

We have far more detailed knowledge of the arrival of Buddhist texts from China in the Heian period, owing to the survival of the catalogues (*shōrai mokuroku* 請来目録) compiled by the monks responsible for bringing them back (§10.1.1). These catalogues constituted in effect official reports on their text-collecting missions, which were all sponsored by the Heian court, and which were intended to bring to Japan new texts and new translations. The first was that of Saichō, the founder of Japanese Tendai Buddhism, whose catalogue of 222 texts is dated 805. This is closely followed by that of Kūkai, the founder of Japanese Shingon Buddhism, which is dated 806. Kūkai's collection was rather more significant and includes 142 newly translated works and 42 Sanskrit texts. Subsequently, Jōgyō 常暁 in 839, Engyō 円行 in 839, Ennin 円仁 in 839, 840 and 847, Eun 恵運 in 847, Enchin 円珍 in 859 and Sōei 宗叡 in 865 submitted catalogues of the texts they brought or sent back from their travels in China: these demonstrate their transmission of Buddhist texts and exegetical works hitherto unknown in Japan, mostly in Chinese but some in Sanskrit, and of some secular Chinese works. However, the collection brought back by Genbō in 734 far outstrips those brought back by these eight: this is partly because of the length of his stay in China and partly because his eight successors were concentrating on bringing back new works or new translations. What is significant about their imports is the predominance of the texts of esoteric Buddhism, including Sanskrit texts, which prefigures the growing importance of esoteric Buddhism in Japan. Finally, it is probable that they also brought back secular texts as well, but because these were unrelated to their missions they are not included in their catalogues, except for that of Ennin.[17]

---

[16] M. W. de Visser, *Ancient Buddhism in Japan*, 2 vols (Leiden: Brill, 1935), 182–7, 436–7, 446–54.

[17] *T*, vol. 55, nos 2159–68, 2173–4. Kimiya 1955: 200 conveniently tabulates the data.

During the early Heian period, it is evident that Japanese Buddhism kept very much up to date with Chinese translation work and exegesis, but following the cessation of the missions to Tang China in the ninth century there was a *de facto* ban on Japanese travelling to China until the end of the Heian period. Monks could, exceptionally, secure permission to travel, on Chinese trading ships, but these ships were restricted to biennial visits from 911. A further difficulty was a Song prohibition on the export of certain books, but this could be circumvented. For example, the ambitious monk Chōnen (938–1016) petitioned the Song court in 984 for a free copy of the Kaibao 開宝 canon in 5048 volumes, which had been printed for the first time the previous year under imperial patronage, and for some other texts which had been translated by the revived court translation bureau. In an audience with the emperor he was granted all this and he brought them back in triumph in 986, although he was never able to make use of this success to achieve a position of influence in the Buddhist establishment in Japan. This copy of the Kaibao canon was placed in Fujiwara no Michinaga's temple, Hōjōji 法成寺; there, according to Wang, it 'served as the master copy for all Buddhist sūtras', it was consulted by monks from all over Japan in search of better texts, and it possibly rekindled interest in printing (§4.1.2).[18]

Unlike Chōnen, Jōjin 成尋 (1011–81) was unable to get permission to go to China but he left secretly anyway in 1072 along with five other monks, who returned to Japan the following year. He acquired a number of books in China, at Tiantai and Wutaishan; his attempt to buy some new sūtra translations from a temple was rebuffed on the ground that they could not be sold to foreigners, so, like Chōnen, he petitioned emperor Shenzong 神宗 and received 413 volumes of new translations. In addition, it is evident from his diary that he managed to obtain books of poetry, maps, and works on calendrical science and materia medica: all this, together with some printed Buddhist works that he acquired from the official Buddhist printing house, the Yin jing yuan 印経院, he sent back with his disciples and it was deposited in various temples.[19]

By the early tenth century printed editions of secular works were beginning to appear in China, and some printing was sponsored by

---

[18] Wang Zhenping 1994b.
[19] Fujiyoshi Masumi 1981 and Charlotte von Verschuer 1991.

the Song government. There is a vague reference in a Japanese source to Chinese printed books reaching Japan early in the tenth century, but the first Song edition known to have been brought to Japan was the Buddhist canon acquired by Chōnen in 986. In spite of the restrictions, Chinese merchants and Japanese monks seem to have had little difficulty getting hold, for example, of *Tai ping yu lan* 太平御覽, a highly-prized compendium in 1,000 volumes completed in 983. The government of Koryŏ on the Korean peninsula had requested a set many times before finally being granted one in 1100, but Taira no Kiyomori obtained a copy in 1178 and a diarist recorded later that Chinese merchants had brought over dozens of copies to Japan. Song printed editions were highly regarded in Japan, so much so that collectors would part with valuable manuscripts in exchange for them and that Chinese merchants in breach of Japanese law could evade punishment by 'donating' printed books to powerful collectors such as Fujiwara no Michinaga. Fujiwara no Yorinaga (1120–56), whose reading has been described in the previous chapter, was an avid collector of Song printed editions brought to Japan by Chinese merchants and he drew up a list of desiderata he hoped they could acquire for him. It is not clear how he knew of the availability of these works unless he had already seen copies in Japan, but in any case this list reveals expert familiarity with the contemporary book trade in China.[20]

During the Northern Song and Yuan dynasties there was a steady flow of Japanese monks travelling to China. Most of them were Zen monks in search of a Chinese master and, although they were less concerned with texts *per se* than previous generations had been, they did in fact bring back considerable quantities of books, amongst them many secular books. Chōnen was the only monk to bring a copy of the Kaibao canon, but a surprising number of copies of the various later Song printed editions of the Buddhist canon, such as the Dong chan si 東禅寺 (1080–1112) and Kai yuan si 開元寺 (1115–c1148) editions, were brought back in the Kamakura period, and at least 14 sets have survived to the present day. Several editions were printed in the Yuan dynasty, but the only one acquired by Japanese monks was the Da pu ning si 大普寧寺 edition, part of which survives in the Nanzenji (§7.1.2). The arrival of these various

---

[20] *GR* 1:904; Mori 1975: 224, 227–9; *ST* 20: 225, 28:292.

printed editions of the Buddhist canon from China, and later from Korea, stimulated interest in printing an edition of the canon in Japan. We know of two projects from the thirteenth and fourteenth centuries, but neither came to anything and it was only in the Tokugawa period that the Buddhist canon was finally printed in Japan.[21]

In addition to the Buddhist canon, monks also brought other Buddhist texts and various secular books. In 1211 Shunjō brought 2,013 volumes of Tendai and Ritsu texts and in addition 256 volumes of Confucian texts and 463 volumes of other secular texts. In 1241 the founder of the Tōfukuji, Ben'en 弁円, brought back a large collection of Chan (Zen) texts and literary, medical and Confucian works, and a catalogue of this collection survives. All the monks who travelled to China during the Yuan dynasty were Zen monks, and the Chan texts they brought to Japan consisted mostly of *yu lu* 語録, collections of the sayings of Chan masters. By this time most of the imported books were likely to be printed copies, and they stimulated Zen temples to undertake printing, usually at first simply *kabusebori* reproductions of Chinese printed editions of *yu lu* and the like.[22]

In the Muromachi period the Ashikaga shōguns established official relations with the Ming dynasty on terms that placed Japan in a subordinate relationship to China and allowed the resumption of trade. Ashikaga Yoshimasa used the opportunity to request a number of rare books from the Ming government and it is supposed by Kimiya Yasuhiko that there was a trade in books in addition to the books being imported by monks, but there is very little documentary evidence for this period. For example, Sakugen Shūryō 策彦周良 (1501–79), who visited Ming China twice in 1539–41 and 1547–50 as a member of tribute missions, noted only a total of 17 books he had bought or received as gifts while there. Yuan and Ming editions surviving in Japan provide some further indications, although these must be treated with caution unless there is reliable evidence of a *terminus ante quem* for their importation in the form of seals of ownership, for some may have been imported later. Finally, Japanese *kabusebori* reprints of Chinese works produced in the Kamakura and

---

[21] Kimiya 1955: 363–71, 477–80.

[22] *Fumon'in kyōronshōsho goroku jusho tō mokuroku* 普門院経論章疏語録儒書等目録, in *DNBZ*; Kimiya 1955: 371–8.

Muromachi periods, which sometimes even reproduce the original colophons of the Chinese editions, obviously demonstrate that these works had reached Japan and that they were considered important or useful enough to disseminate.[23]

From the twelfth century onwards monks and merchants had brought over the corpus of texts that lay the foundations for the transmission to Japan of the new Confucianism of the Song, or neo-Confucianism as it is now known, especially the commentaries and other works of Zhu Xi. For the most part we have no record of exactly when they were brought to Japan, but diary entries recording the use of these texts and dated inscriptions in surviving copies make it possible to arrive at a *terminus ante quem* for the transmission of many of the key texts.[24]

In sum, over the centuries up to 1600 a vast quantity of Chinese texts were imported into Japan. The significance this flow of books had for the development and maintenance of Chinese literacy in Japan, and for theological, philosophical, literary and medical study, does not need to be rehearsed here. What is important to notice is the privatization of this process after the middle of the Heian period, the growing secularization of the sinological interests supported by imported Chinese books, and the contribution to that made by Zen monks in the Kamakura and Muromachi periods. In this connection it is worth recalling that 78 of all the 273 works printed by the Gozan monasteries in the Muromachi period were secular Chinese works (§4.1.2). Well before the Tokugawa period, then, when the demand was definitely for secular rather than Buddhist works from China, there was already a substantial corpus of secular texts in Japanese being absorbed by the Zen monastic tradition.

The Ming writer Zheng Ruoceng 鄭若曾 (c. 1505–1580) included in his *Chou hai tu bian* 籌海図編 an extensive account of Japan, which includes a list of the things Japanese liked to acquire in China. The section dealing with books notes that they were keen on the *Five Classics* and the four basic Confucian texts, Buddhist books and old

---

[23] Kimiya 1955: 400, 480–85, 585, 594; Makita Tairyō 牧田諦亮, *Sakugen nyūminki no kenkyū* 策彦入明記の研究, 2 vols (Kyōto: Hōzōkan, 1959), 2:166–7.

[24] Ashikaga 1932: 17–35 and separately paginated supplement at the end reproducing many inscriptions on Confucian texts transmitted from China. Invaluable also is Shibunkai 斯文会, ed., *Nihon kangaku nenpyō* 日本漢学年表 (Taishūkan Shoten, 1977).

medical texts but had no time for Daoist books or for the works of Mencius.[25] This, in Ōba Osamu's view, accords well with what we know of Japanese imports from China up to this period, but we should not forget that both Daoism and *Mencius* had no small impact on Japan.

As Fukunaga Mitsuji and others have observed, there is much evidence to suggest that the impact of Daoism on early Japan was very considerable, even on the ceremonial of the court, quite apart from the links between the ascetic *shugendō* 修験道 tradition and Daoism. *Nihon shoki* contains a record of a Paekche monk travelling to Japan in 602 and bringing with him not only books on geography, astronomy and calendrical science but also *hōjutsu* 方術 books, that is, books on divinational and semi-magical practices associated with Daoism. By the eighth century it is certain that some Daoist practices and a number of Daoist texts, most perhaps related to medicine, were well known in Japan. Kūkai evidently had access to Daoist texts before he went to China, for in his *Sangō shiiki* (797) he makes a comparative evaluation of Buddhism, Daoism and Confucianism. Further evidence for the importation of Daoist texts can be found in *Nihonkoku genzaisho mokuroku*, which includes 63 Daoist books, all of which must have reached Japan by the late ninth century.[26]

It is difficult to ascertain what Daoist books may have reached Japan in the succeeding centuries. Kokan Shiren 虎関師錬 (1278–1346), the scholar-monk and author of a history of the Buddhist clergy in Japan (*Genkō shakusho* 元亨釈書), bemoaned the lack of Daoist books in Japan in his time and regretted that there was no copy of the vast Daoist canon (*Dōzō* 道蔵) to consult.[27] The Daoist canon, so far as is known at present, did not reach Japan until the Tokugawa period: according to the records of the Nagasaki censors, an incomplete copy in poor condition was imported in 1786. This

---

[25] *Zhongguo bingshu jichen* 中国兵書集成 (Beijing, 1990–), 15: 263; Ōba (in Ōba & Wang 1996: 81) mistakenly follows an erroneous attribution of this work to Hu Zongxian 胡宗憲; for a good discussion of this book and its authorship see L. Carrington Goodrich, ed., *Dictionary of Ming biography*, 2 vols (New York: Columbia University Press, 1976) 1: 205–7.

[26] Fukunaga Mitsuji 福永光司, *Dōkyō to kodai nihon* 道教と古代日本 (Jinbun Shoin, 1987); *NKBT* 68: 178; Nakamura Shōhachi 中村璋八, 'Nihon no dōkyō', in Fukui Kōjun 福井康順 et al., eds, *Dōkyō*, 3 vols (Hirakawa Shuppansha, 1983), 3: 3–47.

[27] *GBZ* 1:325.

may or may not be identical to the incomplete copy consisting of a substantial part of the edition printed in 5,305 volumes in 1445 which was acquired at about the same time by Mōri Takasue 毛利高標 (1755–1801), who was the daimyō of Saiki domain in Kyushu and the owner of a library of some 80,000 volumes. But by this time there was already available in Japan a substantial corpus of Daoist texts in imported Chinese editions, in Japanese reprints, and even in Japanese translations.[28]

As for *Mencius*, the first mention of the text by name is found in *Nihonkoku genzaisho mokuroku* (c898), but quotations of passages not found in compendia or encyclopedias enable us to push the date back much further to the early eighth century. The book of *Mencius*, it has often been said, was much criticized and barely read in Japan, and there was a story, repeated in several sources of the Tokugawa period, that ships carrying copies of *Mencius* to Japan invariably sank en route. These stories all have their origin in a text of the late Ming, *Wu za zu* 五雜俎, and it has not proved possible to trace them back any further. As the exhaustive study of Inoue Masamichi has conclusively demonstrated, however, they are quite without foundation. Up to the late sixteenth century there is no evidence whatsoever that *Mencius* was attacked or criticized in spite of its author's views on the replacement of incapable rulers, which have been thought to be unacceptable in Japan. In the Tokugawa period, it is true, certain unfavourable mentions can be found, and in lectures certain passages deemed ideologically offensive were omitted, but not in earlier times. And even in the Tokugawa period it is quite clear that *Mencius* was read and reprinted as commonly as other texts, and generated numerous commentaries and studies.[29]

---

[28] *Yoshioka Yoshitoyo chosakushū* 吉岡義豊著作集, 5 vols (Gogatsu Shobō, 1989–90), 2: 424–43; T. H. Barrett, 'The Taoist Canon in Japan: some implications of the research of Ho Peng Yoke', *Taoist resources* 5.2 (1994): 71–77; Ōba 1967: 412; Ozaki Masaharu 尾崎正治, 'Dōzō no seiritsu to sono shūhen' 道蔵の成立とその周辺, in Akizuki Kan'ei 秋月観暎, ed., *Dōkyō kenkyū no susume - sono genjō to mondaiten o kangaeru* 道教研究のすすめ―その現状と問題点を考える (Hirakawa Shuppansha, 1986), 79–109; F. G. Bock 1985, *Classical learning and Taoist practices in early Japan*, Center for Asian Studies Occasional Paper 17 (Arizona State University, 1985).

[29] Inoue Masamichi 1972: 3–4, 213–4, 512–7. For examples of reading *Mencius* in the Tokugawa period, see Inoue Masamichi 1972: 488–512, and Nagatomo 1987: 66; for reprints, see Nagasawa 1976–80: 36–47.

It seems, then, that Zheng Ruoceng's account of books that interested Japanese is wrong on two counts and not, after all, a reliable guide. On the other hand, it is more than likely that Japanese bibliophiles who travelled to China were selective in their purchases and that their tastes, viewed together, did not encompass all Chinese literary production. What needs to be examined in the future, therefore, is how that selectivity is reflected in the transmission of Chinese books to Japan. In the case of Bo Juyi, whose work enjoyed an esteem in Heian Japan far in excess of that enjoyed by any other Chinese poet in Japan, and higher than that he enjoyed in his own country, we can see that selectivity in action and discern the application of aesthetic sensibilities that were independent of Chinese sensibilities, but more work of this kind is needed before we can confidently evaluate the Japanese recreation of the Chinese tradition.[30]

BIBLIOGRAPHY

Books in Sino-Japanese relations are covered in Kimiya 1955: 197–213, 300–74, 477–485, 585, 594, etc.; Ōba 1996: 289–322; Ōba 1997; Ōba & Wang 1996; Inoue Masamichi 1972: 15–57, 109–39, 213–4; and Robert Borgen, 'State sponsorship of Chinese literature in early Japan', *Ajia bunka kenkyū* 16 (1987): 25–44. On Nara and Heian imports from China, see Kawase 1934; Ōta Shōjirō 1959; Ishida Hisatoyo 1982; Kawaguchi 1984: 135–55; Mori Katsumi 1975: 204–242; and Charlotte von Verschuer, *Le commerce extérieur du Japon. Des origines aux XVI*ͤ *siècle* (Paris: Maisonneuve et Larose, 1988), 59–62; and Smits 1995: 35–56, who gives serious and well-informed consideration to reconstructing the sinological libraries of Japanese poets. On Chōnen and Jōjin see Wang 1994b, Fujiyoshi Masumi 1981 and Charlotte von Verschuer 1991. Yan Shaodang 1992: 27–35 provides a convenient discussion and list of the 32 Tang manuscripts extant in Japan that were imported in the Heian period; also, on pp. 196–203, he examines the looting of public and private collections in China by the Japanese military between 1937 and 1945.

---

[30] On Bo Juyi in Japan see David Pollack, *The fracture of meaning: Japan's synthesis of China from the eighth through the eighteenth centuries* (Princeton: Princeton University Press, 1986), ch. 2; Jin'ichi Konishi, *A history of Japanese literature*, vol. 2 'The early middle ages' (Princeton: Princeton University Press, 1986), 150–55; and the various essays in *Haku Kyoi kenkyū kōza* 白居易研究講座, 7 vols (Benseisha, 1993–95).

7.1.2 *Pre-Tokugawa imports from Korea and Parhae*

Apart from what has been said in the previous section about the acquisition of Chinese books via Korea, little is known at present about the acquisition of books either from Korea before the fourteenth century or from Parhae (Bohai). It is, however, obvious from the references to and quotations from *Paekchegi* 百済記 (J. *Kudara ki*) and other works in *Nihon shoki* that at least three chronicles from the Korean kingdom of Paekche had reached Japan by the early eighth century, probably in the hands of immigrants. These quotations are in fact now all that survives of these three works.[31]

Much later, the two editions of the Chinese Buddhist canon printed in Korea attracted a great deal of interest in Japan. The first edition was prepared partly in response to the Song printed edition of 983: the Korean government officially requested a copy of this, which it received in 991. The blocks for the Korean edition were then carved from 1010 onwards and an important supplement was added at the end of the century, but the blocks were destroyed in 1232 during the Mongol invasion. No complete printed copies survive in Korea, or in Japan, but one part is known to have reached Japan in 1105 and some other surviving parts carry Japanese inscriptions dated 1400. The Nanzenji temple complex in Kyoto still possesses 1,715 volumes (*kan* 巻) of the first printing: they were acquired in 1613 when Ieyasu confiscated the Buddhist canon owned by the Zenshōji 禅昌寺 at Suma and deposited it in the Nanzenji. Almost half of this Buddhist canon consisted of part of the Yuan Da pu ning si edition, which had been imported to Hakata in Kyushu by 1394, when a monk in Hakata presented it to the Zenshōji. However, a substantial part of the remainder consists of a part of the first Korean edition, which was donated to the Zenshōji in or around 1400; when and how it reached Japan is unclear.[32]

---

[31] *KD* 4:805.
[32] Lewis R. Lancaster, with Sung-bae Park, *The Korean Buddhist Canon: a descriptive catalogue* (Berkeley: University of California Press, 1979), x-xiv; Egami Yasushi 江上綏 and Kobayashi Hiromitsu 小林宏光, *Nanzenji shozō "Bizangquan" no mokuhanga* 南禅寺所蔵『秘蔵詮』の木版画 (Yamakawa Shuppansha, 1994; contains English translation), 38 and *passim*; Ikeuchi Hiroshi 池内宏, 'Kōraichō no daizōkyō 1' 高麗朝の大蔵経, *Tōyō gakuhō* 13.3 (1923): 40-1; Yi Chun'gil 1986:

The blocks for a second edition, which was far more comprehensive a collection of sūtras and exegetical writings than anything previously produced in China or elsewhere, were cut from 1236 to 1251, more than eighty thousand of them in all. They were moved in 1399 to the Haeinsa 海印寺 temple, where they survive to this day almost in their entirety. The first recorded request from Japan for a printed copy of this second edition was made in 1389 by Imagawa Ryōshun, the Kyushu deputy of the Ashikaga shōgun. Owing to the chaos as the Koryŏ dynasty collapsed it seems to have been unsuccessful, although a second request from the same source to the new Yi dynasty was rewarded in 1395 with two sets. Over the following 150 years more than 80 requests for copies of the Korean edition of the Buddhist canon came from Japan, mostly either from the Ashikaga shōgunate or from the Ōuchi daimyō of south-western Japan, but also from the Sō daimyō of Tsushima and the king of Ryūkyū. Indeed, so frequent were these requests that the official missions sent by the Ashikaga were known in Korea as *ch'ŏnggyŏngsa* 請経使, or 'sūtra-seeking missions.'[33]

The most audacious request was made in 1423 when Ashikaga Yoshimochi sent a team of 135 men in the hope of actually acquiring the 81,258 blocks needed to print the entire canon; he was under the impression that there were two sets of blocks and considered that Korea could spare one set so that copies could be run off in Japan; even when informed that there was only one set, he still tried again in 1425, with, of course, no more success. In 1539 Ōuchi Yoshitaka (1507–51) sent the monk Sonkai 尊海 on a mission to Korea to acquire another copy of the canon for his temple at Itsukushima, but the request was turned down with the explanation that Korea did not respect Buddhism and there were no copies of the Buddhist canon to be had. Whatever the truth of the second half of this statement, it is certainly the case that the Yi dynasty had embarked on repressive measures aimed at weakening the Buddhist establishment, and no

---

19. On the Nanzenji Tripitaka see Suematsu Yasunori 末松保和, 'Nanzenji daizōkyō no bekken' 南禅寺大蔵経の瞥見, in *Seikyū shisō* 青丘史草 2 (privately published, 1966), 73–91 [this piece was originally published in *Chōsen* 191 (1931)].

[33] Eda Toshio 江田俊雄, 'Ashikaga Yoshimochi ni yoru Kōrai zōhan no kyōsei tenmatsu' 足利義持による高麗蔵板の強請顛末, in idem, *Chōsen bukkyōshi no kenkyū* 朝鮮仏教史の研究 (Kokusho Kankōkai, 1977), 269–7; Kanno Ginpachi n.d.: 14ff.

further attempts were made from Japan to obtain copies of the Korean Buddhist canon.[34]

In all 40 or so partial or complete copies were brought to Japan. What is not clear is what impact they had on Japanese Buddhism, or why so many copies were sought. Further, it is not known what secular works, such as the neo-Confucian writings of Kwŏn Kŭn or particularly Yi T'oegye, whose writings were so influential in Japan during the Tokugawa period, reached Japan during this period. Some books were certainly crossing the sea, for Ōuchi Yoshitaka had a collection of Korean books, some of which survive in the Tōyō Bunko. What we do know, however, is that the invasions of Korea carried out by Toyotomi Hideyoshi in 1592–8 resulted in the looting of large numbers of secular books in Chinese, especially works by Korean neo-Confucianists, as well as a printing press. One of Hideyoshi's generals, Ukita Hideie, is reported to have sent him 'several cartloads of books' from Korea, which Hideyoshi then gave to Manase Shōrin (1565–1611). These books were examined by Fujiwara Seika (1561–1619) and Hayashi Razan (1583–1657), who both abandoned monastic careers and became active proponents of neo-Confucianism in Japan. Their first acquaintance with the neo-Confucian tradition came through Korean editions of Chinese texts and the works of Korean neo-Confucianists, and Razan's library, which survives in the Naikaku Bunko in Tokyo, shows this very clearly. A record of Razan's reading in 1604 includes Chinese works in Korean printed editions and 17 books by Korean Confucianists such as Yi T'oegye, a number of which were later reprinted in Japan. Some Korean books from the same source also found their way into Tokugawa Ieyasu's library.[35]

The kingdom of Parhae sent some 34 missions to Japan in the eighth, ninth and early tenth centuries, and Japan sent at least 12 missions to Parhae, the last in 811. Via this route Parhae music reached Japan and also a copy of *Xuan ming li* 宣明曆 (J. Senmyōreki), the calendrical system drawn up in China in 822. This was brought

---

[34] Eda Toshio (see previous note); Nakamura Eikō 中村栄孝, *Nissen kankeishi no kenkyū* 日鮮関係史の研究, 3 vols (Yoshikawa Kōbunkan, 1965–69), 1: 742–4.

[35] On the import of Korean books in the 1590s and the impact of Korean neo-Confucianism on Japan, see Yi Chun'gil 1986: 144–67, 159–262; Abe Yoshio 1965 and in English his 'Development of Neo-Confucianism in Japan, Korea and China: a comparative study', *AA* 19 (1970): 16–39.

to Japan by a Parhae embassy in 859, and the system was adopted in 861 and remained in use until 1684. Of other Chinese books that reached Japan from Parhae we have unfortunately no knowledge.[36]

BIBLIOGRAPHY

On books from Korea see Yi Chun'gil 1986, Yi Honjik 1954: 147–65, and Kanno Ginpachi n.d.

7.1.3 *Later imports of Chinese and Korean books*

The main external source of books in the Tokugawa period was the tightly controlled trade with Qing merchants conducted at Nagasaki, and it is thanks to the tight controls operated by the Bakufu that we have detailed records of what books were imported and when. The trade was entirely at the initiative of the Chinese merchants, who provided the capital and the ships and who determined the cargoes, always, of course, with an eye to what would sell in Japan.

The number of Chinese ships arriving each year fluctuated unpredictably, with a peak of 193 recorded in 1688 and in some years in the eighteenth century fewer than twenty. In the first half of the Edo period most of the ships carried no books and the quantities carried by those that did were small, but from the middle of the eighteenth century onwards books became a more significant component of the cargoes, largely because the Chinese captains had become aware of the market for Chinese books in Japan. In Ōba Osamu's view, it is probable that only certain captains were interested in importing books and that they were supplied by bookshops which learnt to specialize in books for the Japanese market. In any case captains importing books were required to submit a *sairai mokuroku* 齎来目録 listing the books they had in their cargo: the earliest extant one dates from 1714 and it is not clear when this requirement came into force. The surviving *sairai mokuroku*, however, only provide us with raw information on the books imported by particular ships in

---

[36] Niizuma Toshihisa 新妻利久, *Bokkai kokushi oyobi nihon to no kokkōshi no kenkyū* 渤海国使及日本との国交史の研究 (Tōkyō Denki Daigaku Shuppankyoku, 1969), esp. 381–6, 400–402.

particular years for a total of fewer than twenty cargoes, so they offer at best a glimpse of what was being imported.[37]

The discovery in 1630 of some Christian books in a cargo of Chinese books brought into Nagasaki occasioned the establishment of a censorship bureau in Nagasaki operating under the jurisdiction of the city commissioner (see §8.2.1). This bureau was headed by the *shomotsu aratameyaku* 書物改役, a post hereditarily held by members of the Mukai 向井 family from 1685 onwards, and it consisted of a number of other officers, whose job it was to inspect all incoming cargoes of books. Inspection was a serious and laborious business and it had several objectives. They had to go through each book, page by page, in the first instance on the lookout for phrases concerning Christianity but also noting missing pages, handwritten annotations and other inscriptions, and so on. Then they had to compile a report, *taiisho* 大意書, which listed each book in the cargo by title, together with an indication of its authorship and the nature of its contents and any other pertinent matters; the report customarily concluded with a statement to the effect that the cargo contained no offensive books, if this was in fact the case. The *taiisho* was passed on to the city commissioner, who despatched it to Edo, where it served as a catalogue for the purpose of ordering books. There it was checked carefully by the *goshomotsukata* 御書物方, the librarian in charge of the Bakufu Library, who made any selections for the Library. The report seems also to have been made available to various other parties in Edo, including the Hayashi School and the Senior Councillors. Books chosen from these lists were usually paid for immediately and sent up from Nagasaki, sometimes on approval, and it was only when this process was complete that other books in the cargo could be offered for sale to the Nagasaki booksellers and through them to the general public. It should be noted that the quantities were not so great as to make it easy for anyone to acquire Chinese books: on the contrary, throughout the period they seem to have remained a rarity and to have become widely accessible only when reprinted in Japan.

The choice of what books to bring was the captain's, and it must be assumed that some of them did some market research, at least by enquiring of Nagasaki booksellers what books would sell. It was, however, possible for the shōgun, his librarian and certain other

---

[37] Ōba 1984: 49–51, 82-3. The following paragraphs rely heavily on Ōba 1984.

institutions and officials to channel requests via the Nagasaki city commissioner, whose task it was to brief the Chinese captains on books required in Edo. The whole process was slow and cumbersome: compiling the *taiisho* alone sometimes took up to two years. And in the mid eighteenth century efforts were made to simplify procedures by excluding from the inspection process all books ordered from Edo and all books that had previously been imported and found to be blameless.

If all the *taiisho* and *sairai mokuroku* were extant it would be possible to chart the progress of Chinese books to Japan in the Tokugawa period with ease, but that is unfortunately not the case. Nevertheless, the documents that have survived are sufficient to enable us to trace the movements of Chinese books and to discern some important trends. In the first place it is important to stress that many of the books imported were not new: the trade was not one in newly published books. The *taiisho* which was prepared for the Nagasaki commissioner on the books brought in 1782, for example, gives details of their condition and makes it quite clear that most were second-hand.[38] Secondly, we should note that shogunal demand for books from this source was subject to considerable fluctuation. Up to 1662 large numbers of books were despatched from Nagasaki each year, but the quantities fell off dramatically after that, and in some years no books were taken at all. Under the shōgun Yoshimune in the early eighteenth century, however, interest revived, and in 1726 a total of 307 Chinese books were sent to the Bakufu Library. This is directly related to Yoshimune's personal interest in books and to the relaxation in 1720 of the censorship rules to permit the importation of Chinese books mentioning but not advocating Christianity.[39] Thirdly, it is difficult to trace the movements of the books once they had reached Japan, except for those that entered the Bakufu Library and are now preserved either in the Naikaku Bunko or the Kunaichō Shoryōbu in Tokyo. From these we can see, for example, a particular concern in the early eighteenth century to collect commentaries on the Ming statutes and Chinese local histories, at least partly under

---

[38] Ōba Osamu 大庭脩, *An'ei kunen Awa Chikura hyōchaku Nankinsen Genjungō shiryō* 安永九年安房千倉漂着南京船元順号資料, Kansai Daigaku Tōzai Gakujutsu Kenkyūsho shiryō shūkan 13.5 (Suita: Kansai Daigaku Shuppanbu, 1991), 125–35.

[39] Ōba 1984: 190–200.

the direct inspiration of Yoshimune. These books apart, however, we have no knowledge of the fate of the books imported from China and it is impossible at present to determine what difference it may have made to Japanese intellectuals that such books were available.[40]

Although we do not have any clear idea of what imported books were made available to the book trade, probably the mostly widely disseminated of all recent Chinese texts in the Tokugawa period were some of the best-known examples of Ming fiction. The fictional literature of the Ming dynasty inspired and shaped a great deal of Japanese fiction in the late eighteenth and early nineteenth centuries, especially the genre of long and largely historical narratives known today as *yomihon*. Undoubtedly the most influential Ming work was *Shui hu chuan* 水滸伝, the 'Water Margin', which inspired a number of Japanese adaptations, such as *Honchō suikoden* 本朝水滸伝 (1773) and *Onna suikoden* 女水滸伝 (1850–53), and was also married to the story of the 47 rōnin in *Chūshin suikoden* 忠臣水滸伝 (1799–1801). Although there were some reprints in Japan of Chinese vernacular fiction, for the most part these Ming texts circulated in loose translations or adaptations (*hon'an* 翻案), and it is through these that the stories and their heroes became sufficiently well known to reappear in ever more unfamiliar guises.

The flow of books from China to Japan in the Tokugawa period differs markedly in character from the imports of earlier centuries. It is, of course, now overwhelmingly secular, but it is also largely passive, by virtue of the fact that Japanese were not permitted to travel to China to make their own selections of books and were perforce reliant on Chinese merchant captains. Furthermore, the imports were insignificant in quantity in the context of a mature publishing industry in Japan that was producing books for a mass home market. But the ties to China remained: they conditioned the literary imagination in the second half of the period, and in the closing years they brought a number of valuable Chinese accounts of the West to Japan at a time when the Bakufu was beginning to face up to the external threat.

Books from Korea only reached Japan in small quantities in the Tokugawa period. Following the resumption of friendly relations in the early seventeenth century a number of missions from the Yi

---

[40] Ōba 1984: 227–314; Henderson 1970–71.

dynasty travelled to Japan, and their political and cultural impact has recently attracted much attention. Relations with Korea were handled by the Sō family of daimyō on the island of Tsushima, and a catalogue of the daimyō's library prepared in 1683 shows that the collection contained a considerable number of seventeenth-century printed Korean books, all of course in Chinese. These may have been gifts presented by the Korean missions, or they may conceivably have been acquired by the Wakan 倭館, or residence, in Pusan maintained by the Sō. At any rate, from annotations in the catalogue we know that some of the books were sent on either to the Bakufu or to the Hayashi family, who were hereditary heads of the Bakufu Academy in Edo. Although intellectual interest in Korea was growing in the Tokugawa period, Korean books seems to have left few footprints in Japan, with the exception of the neo-Confucian texts mentioned in the previous section.

BIBLIOGRAPHY

Ōba Osamu is the authority on imports of Chinese books in the Tokugawa period: Ōba 1984 has superseded Ōba 1967, though the original material reprinted in the latter is not included in the former; see also his 'Imported Chinese books in late Edo period and their influences on Japan', *International Association of Orientalist Librarians Bulletin* 38 (1991): 55-60. See also Ōba 1997; Ōba & Wang 1996: 79-80. On Ming fiction and the fiction of the Tokugawa period see Asō Isoji 麻生磯次, *Edo bungaku to Chūgoku bungaku* 江戸文学と中国文学, 2nd edition (Sanseidō, 1955), and Ishizaki 1967, who also considers the study of spoken Chinese and the introduction and translation of colloquial texts. On Korean books, see Fujimoto 1981. On the reprinting of books by Chinese and Korean authors in the Tokugawa period, which in individual cases provides proof positive of the transmission of a given text, see §4.3.4 and the works cited therein.

7.1.4 *Imports of European and American books*

Western books were first imported to Japan by Portuguese missionaries, who printed copies for use in Japan in the late sixteenth century (see §4.2.1) Some of the books they printed have survived, but the subsequent suppression of Christianity has erased all trace of any other books they might have brought with them. The one exception is Aesop's *Fables*: a Japanese translation was published at Amakusa by the Jesuits in 1593 in the form of a transliteration into roman letters. Later a large number of movable type and woodblock editions of this work were published in the early seventeenth century under the title *Isoho monogatari* 伊曽保物語. If, as is commonly thought, there is no direct connection between the Jesuit edition and the various Japanese editions, then some European edition, no longer extant in Japan, must have been imported. The only other work of Western literature that may have been imported at this time was the *Odyssey*, which was recreated as the Japanese legend of Yuriwaka Daijin 百合若大臣, but James Araki's hypothesis is that it was transmitted orally rather than in the form of a book and the connection between the two still admits of some doubt.[41]

In the early years of the seventeenth century some members of the English Factory at Hirado brought books with them and lent each other, for example, copies of Suetonius and the works of Sir Walter Raleigh, but these were for private use and were probably taken back to England. The accounts of the factory refer to a 'Booke of Armes' in a list of items to be presented to the 'Emperor' (i.e., shōgun), but this is all, and books were not included in the list of English goods thought marketable in Japan.[42]

Dutch books, on the other hand, were imported via the Dutch East India Company's factory on Deshima in growing numbers from the second half of the seventeenth century onwards. According to entries made in the Company diary at Batavia (=Jakarta) in 1641 and 1642, books brought in to Deshima on the Company's ships were closely examined, and Bibles and other Christian books were placed in a sealed bag until departure, when they were returned to the ship. The Dutchmen were allowed to bring Bibles and hymn-books for their own use, but they were required to keep them from the eyes of Japanese. The head of the Factory prohibited them from giving or selling such books to Japanese, presumably for fear of jeopardizing the trading monopoly the Company enjoyed. The Company could, it seems, import books for sale, but the Nagasaki city commissioner permitted only the import of books on surgery, navigation and similar

---

[41] Kawase 1967: 604–5; James T. Araki, 'Yuriwaka and Ulysses: the Homeric epics at the court of Ōuchi Yoshitaka', *MN* 33 (1978): 1–36.
[42] Farrington 1991: 174, 209, 538, 1436.

subjects. However, as Itazawa Takeo has pointed out, Japanese knowledge of Dutch was at this stage hardly sufficient to make proper policing of imports possible, and when in 1643 some Christian books were imported, the Company evaded trouble simply by saying that they were books on history, astronomy and surgery. It seems, therefore, that, unlike translations of European works into Chinese, any restrictions on Dutch or other European books brought to Deshima by those employed by the Company were not effectively enforced (§8.2.1).[43]

What sort of a market for Dutch books there might have been in seventeenth century Japan is unclear, for knowledge of the language was at this stage confined to the official interpreters, the *oranda tsūji* 阿蘭陀通司. Some books were presented to the Bakufu by the successive heads of the Dutch Factory on their annual visits to Edo: in 1659 Zacharias Wagenaer presented a copy of Rembert Dodoens' herbal in the Dutch edition of 1618; in 1663 Hendrick Indijck presented a copy of the 1660 edition of a zoological treatise by Jan Jonston [=John Johnston]; and probably in 1672 Johannes Camphuijs presented a copy of Joan Blaeu's map of the world, which survives in Tokyo National Museum with annotations by Arai Hakuseki. Most of these books seem to have been little used, if at all, until Hakuseki brought them out in 1709 when questioning the Italian priest Sidotti who had smuggled himself into Japan the previous year. In 1717 the shōgun Yoshimune could not find anybody to explain Jonston's book to him, but by 1741 Noro Genjō 野呂元丈, who had entered the shōgun's service in 1720, had been able to make a Japanese version by using the interpreters to question members of the annual Dutch mission to Edo, and by 1750 he had done the same with the Dodoens herbal.[44]

Even as early as the middle of the seventeenth century orders for books were being placed with the Dutchmen. In 1650 the Bakufu itself ordered a book on dissection to be brought from Holland, and by 1814 at the latest Deshima received an annual order for Dutch books from the Bakufu. In the years 1838–42 Mizuno Tadakuni 水野忠邦, who in 1838 became chief councillor and *de facto* ruler of

---

[43] *Batabiyajō nisshi* バタビヤ城日誌, trans. Murakami Naojirō 村上直次郎, ed. Nakamura Takashi 中村孝志, 3 vols, Tōyō Bunko 170, 205 & 271 (Heibonsha, 1970–75), 2: 160–62, 200; this work consists of translated extracts from the *Dagh-Register gehouden int Casteel Batavia*. Itazawa 1959: 463–70, 664–83.
[44] Ueda 1982: 22–6.

Japan, ordered at least 30 Dutch books concerning military subjects. This, it must be supposed, was in connection with the rising anxiety about the supposed inadequacy of Japanese defences in the face of a growing Western presence in the waters around Japan.[45]

These various Dutch books consisted, it should be made clear at this point, not only of books written by Dutch authors but also of translations into Dutch of works originally written in English, French and German, for the Dutch language remained the only medium of access to Western books until the final years of the Tokugawa shōgunate. Although it was not easy to acquire Dutch books, the evidence is that some substantial collections were built up, the largest probably being that of the Nabeshima daimyō in Kyushu. In 1850 the Bakufu issued an edict noting the confusion caused by the popularity of 'Western studies'. All imported Dutch books were henceforward to be registered with the city commissioners and private translations, as opposed to those done by the Bakufu's own academies for the study of Western books and medicine, were banned. This was a feeble attempt to shut the stable door, and the horse had long since bolted.[46]

After the conclusion of the treaties with the Western powers in the mid-1850s, it became rather easier to get books, and the Bakufu, at least, had access to some catalogues sent by Amsterdam booksellers in 1857. In 1858 an office for the sale of Dutch books was opened in Edo by the agency permitted to sell imported goods from Nagasaki. Nevertheless, even the famous family of experts in Western studies, the Mitsukuri 箕作, appear to have possessed barely fifty Dutch books of their own, published between 1710 and 1866.[47] By 1860, as Itazawa has demonstrated, very large numbers of books were being brought to Deshima for sale in Japan. A list for that year that has survived, giving the prices being charged in Japan, and this reveals that 50 copies of an English grammar, 100 copies of a French grammar, and 300 copies of an infantry training manual were imported to cater to new demands, as well as numerous books on scientific

---

[45] Katagiri Kazuo 1985: 278–82.
[46] *BOS* 5: 307–8, #4725.
[47] Kanai Madoka 金井円, 'Tōkyō Daigaku Shiryō Hensanjo shozō Mitsukuri-ke kyūzō ransho kō' 東京大学史料編纂所所蔵箕作家旧蔵蘭書考, *Shigaku zasshi* 67.10 (1958): 95–106; for the sale of Dutch books see p. 106, but Kanai offers no source.

subjects, which were of course the staple of the Dutch book trade in Japan.[48]

The growing number of Dutch books circulating in Japan had led to the emergence in the eighteenth century of a distinct school of intellectual enquiry known as Rangaku or 'Dutch studies', which embraced medicine, calendrical astronomy, land measurement and a number of other fields. The importation and translation of Dutch books made possible, for example, the marriage of Western anatomical knowledge and Japanese pharmacology that Hanaoka Seishū (1760–1835) put to use in 1804 when he conducted the first successful operation under a general anaesthetic in the world. The intellectual impact of Dutch books was enormous, as Grant Goodman and others have amply shown, and no more need be said here.

English books only began to reach Japan in quantity after 1854, when Commodore Perry returned to Japan and concluded the Treaty of Kanagawa. On 13 March 1854 he handed over an impressive quantity of presents, including a number of books. For the 'Emperor' (ie, Shōgun) there was a rather bizarre assortment, consisting of copies of Audubon's *Birds of America*, the *Annals of Congress*, the *Natural history of the state of New York* and other items. For each of the senior councillors there was, in addition to ten gallons of whisky, a book: one received the *Geology of Minnesota*, another Downing's *Country houses*, and so on. These were not the first English books to reach Japan, for a small number were already recorded in the Bakufu Library (§9.2.1), but they were the first books of substance. Early the following year Commander Adams returned to Japan with a ratified copy of the Treaty of Kanagawa for presentation to the Bakufu, and the official record notes the interest in books: '[t]he Japanese were exceedingly desirous of obtaining English books, particularly on medical and scientific subjects; and many valuable works were given to them by our officers. But they coveted our books on any subject except religion.' What became of any of these books is unfortunately unknown.[49]

On his return to Japan in 1859, Philipp Franz von Siebold appears to have brought with him a large collection of European books in

---

[48] Itazawa 1959: 664–83.

[49] Roger Pineau, ed., *The Japan Expedition 1852–1854: the personal journal of Commodore Matthew C. Perry* (Washington DC: Smithsonian Institution Press, 1968), 233; Hawks 1857: 512.

English, French, Latin, German and Russian to facilitate research in Japan in various fields. Some additional books published in 1861 were evidently sent to him after his arrival. Many of these are the writings of European scholars on Japan and East Asia. His intentions in bringing these books are clear from the published catalogue, which lists 760 items and expresses his hope that they will be of use to Japanese scholars. However, the impact must have been small, given the tiny numbers in Japan at the time who knew any of these languages, and I know of no evidence to suggest that the collection was of any use to anybody. It subsequently ended up in the Ministry of Foreign Affairs and was finally dispersed. By this time English books were evidently available, albeit in limited quantities. Francis Hall, an American resident in Yokohama from 1859 to 1866, recorded in his diary in 1861 that, 'Japanese learning English frequently come to me with an English book they have procured but are puzzled to make some word or sentence [sic].'[50]

The history of the importation of Western books in modern times is yet to be told. In his autobiography, Fukuzawa Yukichi explains that his participation in an official mission to Europe in 1862 gave him the opportunity to purchase a large number of books in London, but unfortunately his list of his purchases has not survived. His claim, however, that 'This was the beginning of the importation of English books into Japan' is obviously belied by the items included among von Siebold's books, among others.[51] It may be supposed that other members of the various missions that left for the West in the last years of the Bakufu, or the men and women who travelled with the Iwakura Mission in 1872–73, purchased books to bring home with them, but the supply and availability of Western books at this time remains uncertain. This makes it difficult to reconstruct the libraries of early Meiji writers and so to solve some of the intertextuality problems that concern writers thought to have had access to Western books. The famous Maruzen establishment of Tokyo certainly had Western books to offer its customers by the late 1870s, and a number of the more progressive circulating libraries had foreign books to offer their customers by the 1880s, including works of fiction as well as legal studies and other books of a more practical nature, in English,

---

[50] Notehelfer 1992: 365.
[51] Fukuzawa 1966: 26.

French and German.[52] By this time, however, translations had already been made of many Western works from a variety of languages: these provide another index of the accessibility of European and American writings, although many of them placed readers at a considerable remove from the originals and freely omitted or added at will.

BIBLIOGRAPHY

Itazawa 1959: 463–70, 664–83; Ueda Yutaka 1982; J. MacLean, 'The introduction of books and scientific instruments into Japan, 1712–1854', *Japanese studies in the history of science* 13 (1974): 9–68; S. Miyashita, 'A bibliography of the Dutch medical books translated into Japanese', *Archives internationales d'histoire des sciences* 25 (1975): 8–72; and S. Yajima, 'Dutch books on science and technology brought to Japan in XVIII and XIX centuries', *Archives internationales d'histoire des sciences* 6 (1953): 76–79. The impact of these books is discussed extensively in Goodman 1986. The books brought to Japan by von Siebold are listed in *Catalogue de la bibliothèque, apporté au Japon par Mr. Ph. F. de Siebold pour servir à l'étude des sciences physiques, géographiques, ethnologiques et politiques et de guide dans les recherches et deecouvertes scientifiques dans cet Empire* (Dezima [Deshima]: Imprimerie Néerlandaise, 1862; a facsimile edition was published with introduction in Tokyo c1940, n.p., n.d.).

7.2 TRANSMISSION FROM JAPAN

7.2.1 *Exports of Japanese books to China and Korea*

The first two Japanese works known to have gone beyond Japanese shores are commentaries on two Chinese translations of Sanskrit sūtras, *Shōmangyō gisho* 勝鬘経義疏 (c611) and *Hokekyō gisho* (c611). Both are attributed to Shōtoku Taishi, and were, of course, written entirely in Chinese. Copies of them were apparently taken in 615 to the Korean kingdom of Koguryŏ by the Korean monk Hyeja 慧慈, and in 767 they were taken to China by a party of Japanese monks. Subsequently a Chinese monk, Mingkong 明空, produced a

---

[52] For details see Kornicki, 'The publisher's go-between: *Kashihonya* in the Meiji Period', *Modern Asian Studies* 14 (1980): 331–344.

commentary on the *Shōmangyō gisho*: Ennin came across a copy of this in China during his stay there and brought it back to Japan in 847. This is the only recorded case before modern times of a Chinese scholar writing a commentary on a work written by a Japanese, while the reverse, Japanese writing commentaries on Chinese works, pervades the history of Japanese scholarship.[53]

In the eighth and ninth centuries some of the envoys and monks sent to China took with them books from Japan, including *Hokekyō gisho* and other Buddhist writings in Chinese by Japanese monks and scholars. According to *Enryaku sōroku* 延暦僧録, which is a collection of biographies of monks compiled at the end of the eighth century but which survives only in quotations, two of the greatest sinologists of that century, Ōmi no Mifune 淡海三船 (722–85) and Isonokami no Yakatsugu 石上家嗣 (729–81), sent to China copies of Buddhist works they had written in Chinese. Their motives for doing so are not recorded, but what can be said is that even at this early date Japanese Buddhism had gone beyond the stage of passive acceptance of Chinese Buddhism and was beginning to play the part of a transmitter as well as that of a participant in the Chinese Buddhist tradition that extended over the whole of East Asia.[54]

Similarly, in 804 Saichō himself took Japanese copies of the three central texts of Tiantai/Tendai Buddhism, in Chinese translations that had earlier been imported to Japan from China, and presented them to the monastic complex at Mt Tiantai. They were written in gold by noted calligraphers at the behest of the crown prince, later emperor Heizei, and entrusted to Saichō for this purpose. It is difficult to see this as anything other than a grand statement of Japan's progress as a Buddhist state.[55] In 926 there is a clear example of the export of Japanese writings as a statement of Japan's cultural development vis-à-vis that of China when a monk from the Kōfukuji took to

---

[53] Hanayama Shinshō 花山信勝, *Shōmangyō gisho no Jōgūōsen ni kansuru kenkyū* 勝鬘経義疏の上宮王撰に関する研究 (Iwanami Shoten, 1944), 46–9; *DNBZ Shōtoku taishi den sōsho*, 44; *DNBZ Shōmangyō gisho*, 379; *DNBZ Bukkyō shoseki mokuroku*, 2: 72. The Chinese commentary is *Sheng man jing yi shu si chao* 勝鬘経義疏私鈔.

[54] On Isonokami, see *KT* 31: 90; on Ōmi, Wang (Ōba & Wang 1996: 209–10) cites a section of *Enryaku sōroku* apparently preserved in 金剛寺本龍論抄, but he provides no further details: I have not been able to trace this work and it is not included in *BKD*.

[55] *NST* 4: 168–9.

China books of Chinese poetry written by Sugawara no Michizane and others, together with examples of the work of the finest calligrapher of the day. These were perhaps the first secular works taken to China, but in any case, like all the previous exports of which we have knowledge, they were in Chinese. There is no record of any texts in Japanese, or even of Japanese historical records written in Chinese, reaching China at this time.[56]

In 983 Chōnen made what Wang Zhenping has described as 'a personal contribution to the Sung [Song] court's effort to enrich its war-damaged imperial book collection' when he took two works, *Shokuinryō* 職員令 and *Ōnendaiki* 王年代記, and presented them to emperor T'ai-tsung in 984. Neither of these works is extant in Japan but sections of the latter, interlaced with Chōnen's replies to the emperor's questions concerning Japan, have been preserved in *Song shi* 宋史: the compiler was the first official Chinese historian to have access to and use Japanese written records in order to compile an account of Japan. Wang further claims, on the strength of a citation from Ouyang Xiu, that 'the Japanese court had prohibited any Chinese works preserved in Japan to be [sic] exported to China', but the citation refers to a single work, the original hundred sections of *Shang shu* 尚書 which survived in Japan but not in China, and there is no evidence to suggest that there was any such general prohibition.[57]

Further attempts to export Japanese books to China can be traced in the following years. In 986 Genshin gave a copy of his *Ōjō yōshū* and other Buddhist works by Japanese monks to a Chinese monk he met in Hakata and asked him to send them to a temple on Mt Tiantai. And in 995 another Chinese monk, Yuanqing 源清, sent a copy of one of his own works to Japan in the hope of receiving in exchange some Chinese Buddhist texts no longer extant in China, which were duly copied and sent. By this time Chinese monks were well aware that some texts which had not survived the persecutions of Buddhism in China had been preserved in Japan and Korea. Earlier in the tenth century some merchants from the short-lived state of Wuyue discovered that the *Chishakyō* 智者経 in 500 volumes had survived in Japan and king Jian Hongchu 錢弘俶 sent money to Japan in

---

[56] Ōba 1997.
[57] Wang 1994b: 79, 94; Wang 1994a skilfully extricates what is left of *Ōnendaiki* from *Song shi*.

order to procure a copy.[58]

A more substantial contribution to the stock of books in China was made by Jōjin, who embarked on a Chinese ship in 1072 with more than 600 volumes of Buddhist books. The two catalogues of this collection are unfortunately lost, but some can be identified from his account of his trip, and it is clear that it included some works which had been lost in China as a result of the earlier persecutions of Buddhism, some works by Japanese Buddhists including Jōjin himself, and a donation of several sūtras in the hand of the retired emperor Go-Reizei. Some of these books he had not intended to donate but simply to collate with copies extant in China, but in the event they remained with him in China, where he died. It is in any case clear that he was aware of the efforts being made by the Song court to trace copies of lost Chinese Buddhist and secular works surviving in Japan and Korea. In the tenth and eleventh centuries the Korean court responded to Chinese requests for lost works possibly preserved in Korea with a number of texts that had indeed been preserved, and so, it is clear, did the Japanese court.[59]

There is little or no record of Japanese works reaching China over the centuries of the Kamakura and Muromachi periods, but during the Qing dynasty the flow of Japanese books to China picked up again. The only route by which they could leave was on the Chinese merchant ships trading at Nagasaki. *Azuma kagami*, a chronicle of the early history of the Kamakura Bakufu, was certainly circulating in China in manuscript by this time: in 1814 Weng Guangping 翁広平 published a critical edition of it in the course of which he named 36 other Japanese works he consulted. One of these was *Shichikei Mōshi kōbun hoi* 七経孟子考文補遺, a philological study of *Mencius* and seven canonical Chinese texts by Yamanoi Konron 山井崑崙 (1690–1728). On completing it in 1726 Yamanoi presented a copy to the shōgun Yoshimune who ordered Ogyū Sorai's son, Hokkei 北渓, to append some additional material and to repare it for publication. It was eventually published under the above title in 1731 and Yoshimune then ordered the Nagasaki city commissioner to export it to China by way of the Chinese merchants. It did indeed reach China, but its impact was delayed and the earliest Qing reference to it dates from

---

[58] Kimiya 1955: 300; *KT* 29 下: 304; Ōba and Wang 1996: 356–8.
[59] Son 1987: 124; Fujiyoshi Masumi 1981 and Charlotte von Verschuer 1991.

1761. It is referred to with praise, and a measure of surprise, by a number of Qing scholars in China and it was the only book written by a Japanese to be included in the *Siku quanshu* collection.[60]

This was by no means the only Japanese work of the Tokugawa period to reach China, but as yet details of the flow of Japanese books to China in the seventeenth, eighteenth and nineteenth centuries are wanting. Ogyū Sorai's two works *Bendō* and *Benmei* were published in China in 1838, although they were probably circulating there in Japanese editions well before this. Sorai's *Rongochō* also crossed the seas, in 1809 according to one account. The Qing Confucianist Yu Yue (1821–1906) found a copy in a bookshop in 1866 and this inspired him to build up a collection of Japanese sinology. In order to gain a much fuller picture of the transmission of Japanese Confucian literature to China what is needed is a close study of pre-modern Japanese editions surviving in Chinese libraries to determine if ownership seals can allow us to chart the arrival of texts more accurately.[61]

It is possible that some books on the sensational vendetta carried out by the 47 rōnin in 1703 reached China in the eighteenth century. A Chinese version was supposedly published in 1794 under the title *Hai wai qi tan* 海外奇談 and later imported to Japan. It was published there in 1815 under a new title, *Chūshingura* 忠臣庫, borrowing the title of the play that became synonymous with the whole story. It should be noted, however, that so far only copies of the later Japanese reprints have come to light and some have therefore doubted the existence of a Chinese original and have supposed that this work was in fact written by a Japanese.[62]

In 1793 two monks sought to reverse the flow of Buddhist texts from China to Japan. They collected copies of 76 Chinese texts they understood to be lost in China and despatched them with a message to the effect that they hoped the texts would be deposited at a temple where they could be consulted by learned monks. They sent at the same time a selection of Japanese writings on Buddhism in Chinese, including works by Kūkai, Saichō and Hōnen and Kokan Shiren's

---

[60] Wang in Ōba and Wang: 1996: 292–300.
[61] Ōba and Wang 1996: 311–31. On this question see also T. H. Barrett's review of Tai Chen on Mencius in *Orientalische Literaturzeitung* 88 (1993): 84–6.
[62] *Akō gishi jiten* 赤穂義士事典 (Kōbe: Sakamoto Katsu, 1972), 538.

Genkyō shakusho. The catalogue of what they sent is extant but the ultimate fate of the collection is unclear.[63]

It was not until 1880 that the full extent of the survival in Japan of texts that had been lost in China became apparent. In that year Yang Shoujing 陽守敬 (1839–1915) came to Japan at the invitation of the Minister at the Chinese embassy in Tokyo, and during his residence of four years he was surprised to discover a number of texts that had long been thought lost. Twenty-six of these were published in 1882–4 in *Gu yi cong shu* 古逸叢書. This was the last important case of the re-export of lost Chinese works, and by this time contemporary Japanese works were assuming much greater importance in China, especially the products of Japan's encounter with the Western world.

Roy Andrew Miller was mistaken to suggest that the export of Yamanoi's work was the first 'conscious attempt to reverse the flow of cultural influences from China to Japan', as we have seen, but his documented claim that it was 'at least one major factor in encouraging the pursuit of textual criticism and emendations among Chinese scholars' is justifiable.[64] It should be noted, however, that even this was a matter of 'encouragement' rather than inspiration, and the long history of the movement of Japanese works of sinological scholarship left but few ripples in Chinese scholarship. Overall, the export of these works meant far more to the exporter than the importer: it was a matter of pride that Japanese scholars were producing works that were deemed worthy of being exported, but in China they seem to have been treated as contributions to a China-centred world of scholarship in which japanology had no part. The commentary on Shōtoku Taishi's *Shōmangyō gisho* and the reception accorded to Yamanoi's philological investigations fall squarely under this head and the only exceptions in this long history are Weng Guangping's study of the *Azuma kagami* and the putative Chinese version of the affair of the 47 rōnin.

Little is yet known of the transmission of Japanese books to Korea in the Tokugawa period, but it has become clear that several Korean Confucian scholars of the so-called *sirhak* 実学 school had access to some of the writings of Japanese Confucian scholars. Yi Ik (1629–90) was the first to take an interest in Japanese scholarship, and was

---

[63] *NZT*, 1st series, 10: 389–93.
[64] Miller 1952.

familiar with the work of Yamazaki Ansai. The writings of Itō Jinsai were introduced by the Korean embassy to Japan in 1719 and were studied by An Chŏngbok (1712–91) and especially Chŏng Yagyong, who had in his possession copies of various works by Jinsai as well as by Dazai Shundai and Ogyū Sorai and who explicitly responded to their views in his exegetical works. These books had a discernible impact in Korea, but only on the school of Yi Ik, which was critically engaged with Confucian orthodoxy.[65]

The two obvious routes for the transmission of these books are the Korean diplomatic missions returning from Japan and the Japanese trading mission at Pusan. It is known that a volume of Arai Hakuseki's poetry in Chinese was taken back to Korea by a diplomat in 1711, and that although books were exported from Japan and formed part of the trade conducted at Pusan they were for the most part Chinese books which had earlier been imported and sold at Nagasaki. It is not clear what other books may have reached Korea during the later part of the Yi dynasty and there are no signs of any impact made on Korea, except in connection with the Confucian scholarship mentioned above.[66]

BIBLIOGRAPHY

Tsuji Zennosuke 辻善之助, 'Nihon bunka no gyaku yunyū' 日本文化の逆輸入 in *(Zōtei) Kaigai ryūtsū shiwa* 増訂海外流通史話 (Naigai Shoseki, 1930); Ōba and Wang 1996, chs 3–4; Wang Yong has also written on this subject in his *Zhong ri han zi jiao liu shi lun* 中日漢籍交流史論 (Hangzhou: Hangzhou daxue chubanshe, 1992), but I have been unable to consult a copy of this. For works relating to Chōnen and Jōjin, see the bibliography for §7.1.1. For Yang Shoujing's discoveries, see his *Riben fangshu zhi* 日本訪書志 (1901) and *KD* 14: 338. On the impact of Japan on Qing scholarship and Qing studies of Japan see Miller 1952; Kano Naoki 1973: 120–39; and Ishihara Michihiro 石原道博, 'Sakoku jidai shinjin no nihon kenkyū' 鎖国時代清人の日本研究, *Ibaragi daigaku bunrigakubu kiyō* 茨城大学文理学部紀要 16–17. On Japanese books exported to Korea see Yi Chun'gil 1986: 195–202.

---

[65] Mark Setton, *Chŏng Yagyong: Korea's challenge to orthodox Neo-Confucianism* (Stony Brook: State University of New York Press, 1997), ch. 4.
[66] George M. McCune, 'The Japanese trading post at Pusan', *Korean review* 1 (1948): 11–15; Yi Chun'gil 1986: 197; Tashiro Kazui 田代和生, *Kinsei nitchō tsūkō bōekishi no kenkyū* 近世日朝通行貿易史の研究 (Sōbunsha, 1981), 262–4.

7.2.2 Exports of Japanese books to the West

The first Japanese books to reach Europe probably did so in the hands of Jesuit missionaries, but no copies appear to have survived and no clear reference to their possession of Japanese books is known to me. On the other hand, in 1614 John Saris brought home from Japan certain 'lascivious books and pictures', which caused the East India Company considerable embarrassment. Richard Cocks, the manager of the English Factory in Hirado, sent back to the Company a Japanese almanac 'whereby yow may see their order of printinge figures & carectors': this was in 1619 shown to King James I but is unfortunately no longer extant. And in 1616 Cocks wrote in his diary, 'And I bought 54 Japon bookes printed, of their antiqueties & cronicles from their first begyning': this is possibly a reference to *Azuma kagami,* and the surviving odd volumes of this work in Trinity College, Dublin, and Cambridge University Library, which definitely reached Europe in the early seventeenth century, may be all that survives of his collection. The Bodleian Library acquired three Nō texts in 1629, presumably exported by a member of the English Factory, which closed down in 1623. Subsequent exports can only have left Japan via the Dutch Factory on Deshima in Nagasaki harbour. Nicholas Witsen (1641–1720), for long the mayor of Amsterdam, owned a small number of Japanese printed books, maps and other items supplied by his contacts in the Dutch East India Company. One of his protégés, Herbert de Jager, who was based in Batavia in the late seventeenth century, even drew up a list of desiderata which he sent to Deshima in the hope of acquiring books on subjects in which he and Witsen were interested. By this time it is clear that there was a small circle of men associated with the Dutch East India Company who were actively seeking books and information from Japan.[67]

---

[67] Tōkyō Daigaku Shiryō Hensanjo 東京大学史料編纂所 ed., *Igirisu shōkanchō nikki* イギリス商館長日記, Nihon kankei kaigai shiryō series (1978), 1: 343; Farrington 1991: 239, 265, 753; Izumi Tytler, 'The Japanese collection in the Bodleian Library', in Yu-Ying Brown, ed., *Japanese studies*, British Library Occasional Papers 11 (London: British Library, 1991), 114; Witsen's Japanese materials are listed in the auction catalogue of his possessions, *Catalogus Van een Heerlyk Kabinet Met Oost-Indische en andere Konstwerken en Rariteyten* ... (Amsterdam: 1728).

One of these men was Engelbert Kaempfer (1651–1716) who, during his residence on Deshima, acquired a collection of Japanese books with the bold assistance of his Japanese pupil; this is now in the British Library. Andreas Müller (1630–94) in Berlin, sinologist and librarian to the Great Elector of Brandenburg, also had a few Japanese books, either acquired via Witsen or via his own contacts in the Dutch East India Company. In the eighteenth century Karl Pieter Thunberg (1743–1828) and Isaac Titsingh both brought back books following their sojourns on Deshima, and it is clear from various auction catalogues in Paris and elsewhere in the early nineteenth century that it was possible to acquire Japanese books without going to Japan.[68]

A number of the Dutchmen who served spells of duty at Deshima in the employ of the Dutch East India Company in the nineteenth century built up personal collections of books. These included Jan Cock Blomhoff (1779–1853), who first went out to Deshima in 1809 and served as the head of the mission in 1817–23, Johan Frederik Overmeer Fisscher, who took part in the Hofreis, or Mission, to Edo in 1822, and Jan Hendrik Donker Curtius (1813–79). Curtius was appointed head of the Dutch factory on Deshima in 1853: in 1857 he wrote a grammar of Japanese, and in 1861 he sold his collection to the Dutch government.[69] But the most famous collector of Japanese books before collecting became easy in the mid nineteenth century was undoubtedly Philipp Franz von Siebold, who brought back a large number of books from his first spell on Deshima in 1830, after having got into considerable difficulties over his illegal possession of a map of Japan. The bulk of his books remained in Leiden, but some were sent to Austria and Denmark, and possibly other countries.[70]

Although the 'opening' of Japan is best understood in the context of pressures emanating not only from the United States but also from

---

[68] K. B. Gardner, 'Engelbert Kaempfer's Japanese library', *Asia Major*, n.s. 7 (1962): 74–9; Kornicki 1993a: 211–13 and 1993b.

[69] L. Serrurier, *Bibliothèque japonaise: catalogue raisonné des livres et des manuscrits japonais enrégistrés à la bibliothèque de l'université de Leyde* (Leiden: Brill, 1896), introduction.

[70] Eberhard Friese, *Philipp Franz von Siebold als früher Exponent der Ostasienwissenschaften: ein Beitrag zur Orientalismusdiskussion und zur Geschichte der europäisch-japanischen Begegnung* (Hamburg; C. Bell, 1986), 73–92.

Russia, France and Britain, Commodore Perry's mission to Japan in 1853–54 did result in the first direct transmission of Japanese books to the United States. Although Perry included a number of books in his presents for the shōgun and the senior councillors (§7.1.4), the presents he received on 24 March 1854 included no books. On the other hand, the official account of the expedition makes it clear that there were plenty of opportunities for the purchase of books. 'There were no printing establishments seen either at Simoda [Shimoda] or Hakodadi [Hakodate], but books were found in the shops. These were generally cheap works of elementary character, or popular story books or novels.' The compiler of the official account, Francis Hawks, included a discussion of Japanese pictorial art and book production on the strength of a number of 'illustrated books and pictures brought home by the officers of the expedition' and 'an unpretending child's book' purchased at Hakodate which he had at his disposal. One member of the party acquired at least a part of *Ehon ōshukubai* 画本鶯宿梅, an illustrated book by Tachibana Morikuni originally published in 1740. This was then published in Philadelphia in lithographic facsimile with translation and transliteration in 1855. In his preface he also refers to the purchase of some Japanese dictionaries at Shimoda, where Perry's expedition was accommodated.[71]

By the end of the 1850s the foreign population in Japan was steadily increasing and in 1859–61 the Bakufu made an attempt to prevent certain kinds of publication, hitherto freely available in bookshops, from falling into the hands of foreigners. On 1857.10.13 members of the booksellers' guild in Edo undertook to hide away any maps, geography books, directories of Bakufu and domain officialdom (*bukan*), military books, translations of foreign works or any 'unusual' books when any Americans were passing along the streets of Edo. In this context, 'unusual' probably meant manuscripts of doubtful legality (§8.2.2). On 1859.6.21 the Bakufu instructed Edo booksellers to hide away directories of the court aristocracy in Kyoto and 'manuscripts concerning the Tokugawa house' (*gotōke shahon* 御当家写本) when foreigners were passing. This is an

---

[71] Hawks 1857: 58, 369, 459, 462–3; *Japanese botany, being a facsimile of a Japanese book* (Philadelphia: J. B. Lippincott & Co., nd): the copy in the Oriental and India Office Collections in the British Museum is undated but an inscription indicates that it was purchased in London in October 1855. The Library of Congress has no knowledge of the present whereabouts of the books mentioned by Hawks.

astonishing acknowledgment of the fact that such illicit manuscripts were in fact circulating and bespeaks a much stronger concern that such material should not get into the hands of foreigners. Banning the display of books was not, however, the same as banning their sale, and to make good this deficiency an edict was issued in Edo on 1859.8.18, and repeated in Ōsaka on 1861.4.20, forbidding the sale to foreigners of books containing Bakufu laws, of court or Bakufu directories, of maps showing castles, of military texts and of unpublished manuscripts.[72]

It was possible, however, for the determined foreigner to get around this prohibition. Some time in 1862 a Prussian diplomat in Edo wishing to purchase a current *bukan* conducted a sit-in in a bookshop when the bookseller improbably claimed not to have a copy in stock, and he was eventually allowed to purchase one. As Ernest Satow (1843–1929) recalled, however, such extreme measures were unnecessary, 'as we could easily procure what we wanted in the way of maps and printed books through our Japanese teachers'. Satow, together with his compatriot and fellow consular official William George Aston (1841–1911), was undoubtedly the most active and discriminating of bookhunters in Japan in the years immediately before and after the Restoration. In 1868 he was the first European to enter Kyoto for decades if not centuries and he headed for the bookshops on Sanjōdōri as soon as he was free of ceremonial.[73]

So far I have only mentioned Japanese books collected by Europeans in Japan, but in a few cases we know of books taken overseas by Japanese. Travel overseas, except to Korea and the Ryūkyū islands by members of the Tsushima and Satsuma domains respectively, was forbidden for most of the Tokugawa period. On the other hand a number of ships were washed ashore on Kamchatka and the survivors found their way eventually to St Petersburg. All were provincial seafaring men but several are known to have possessed books, the most well known being Daikokuya Kōdayū 大黒屋幸太夫 (1751–1828), who was shipwrecked in 1783. He presented his collection to Catherine the Great, who in turn gave it to the Academy of Sciences in St Petersburg, where it remains. One of Kōdayū's

---

[72] *BOS* 5:582–3, #5092–3; Makita, 3.37; *Matsuzawa Rōsen shiryōshū*, 96–7.

[73] Ernest Satow, *A diplomat in Japan* (London: Oxford University Press, 1968), 67–68, 336.

companions, Shinzō, remained behind in Irkutsk and at least some of his books, by fair means or foul, entered the collection of Heinrich Klaproth, who met him there in 1805 and was the first European to learn Japanese from a native speaker outside Japan. In addition to these cases, it should be added that a number of the students sent to England in the years before the Meiji Restoration in 1868 appear to have taken with them large collections of blockprinted books which they then sought to sell to obtain funds when their remittances dried up in 1868.[74]

From the 1860s onwards Europeans and Americans with an interest in books began to visit Japan as diplomats, missionaries, teachers, globetrotters and so on, and it was during the next couple of decades that many of the great collections of Japanese books outside Japan were built up: in Stockholm by Adolf Nordenskiöld, in London and Cambridge by Aston and Satow, in Lille by Léon de Rosny, in Genoa by Edoardo Chiossone, in Kraków by Feliks Jasieński and in Moscow by Sergei Kitaev. One of the factors that facilitated collecting in the decades up to 1900 was the enthusiasm in Japan for Western learning and Western books, which greatly distorted the home market for antiquarian books. Mantei Ōga, a reactionary but popular writer, recorded soon after the Restoration that people were ready to sell quite blameless books for scrap paper. Mizutani Futō (1858–1943), recalled later that the first ten years of the Meiji period were a time of martyrdom for antiquarian books. Nordenskiöld, who visited Japan in 1879 carefully recorded the prices paid for the items in his collection and it is clear that some of the choice items, such as his copy of the 1296 edition of *Hannya haramitta rishushaku* 般若波羅密多理趣釈, cost only three times the price of a contemporary journal and considerably less than works of popular fiction or recent translations from Western literature and scholarship.[75] In this sense Western collectors were taking advantage not so much of the weakness of the Japanese currency as of the shift in contemporary tastes that brought many hitherto treasured items onto the market at absurdly low prices.

---

[74] Kornicki 1993a: 210–14; Kornicki 1993b.
[75] The prices are noted in Edgren 1980. For Ōga's comments, see *Meiji bungaku zenshū* 1.198; for Mizutani's recollections see *MFC* 6: 200–202.

Many of these collections have ended up in national libraries or museums or in university collections and have now been fully described in print. It is too early yet to write a history of 'collecting Japan' through the composition of these collections, but a few significant points may be mentioned. Firstly, Satow was unusual in focussing on works of bibliographical interest and seeking out rare editions, but he was one of the few collectors resident in Japan at the time with both the requisite linguistic knowledge and the bibliographical interest. Secondly, those who did have the linguistic knowledge acquired in the main books that were of use for their studies: two good examples are Léon de Rosny (1837-1914), who became in 1868 the first professor of Japanese in France, and Johann Joseph Hoffmann (1805-78), who became the first professor of Japanese at Leiden: neither of them ever visited Japan. Thirdly, the globetrotters and other visitors who knew little or nothing of the language unsurprisingly concentrated on illustrated books with little knowledge of what they were purchasing. There were obvious exceptions, such as Nordenskiöld, who knew nothing of Japanese but sought expert help to build up a representative collection of manuscripts and printed works of all kinds and from all periods.

The ultimate value of these many collections lies in the fact that they contain works which have either not survived in Japan or are extremely rare. It is true that the impact of Japanese books reaching Europe between 1600 and, say, 1900 was small, and much less significant than the flow of Dutch books to Japan in the Tokugawa period, to say nothing of the Western works of all kinds that were imported in the Meiji period. However, while the exports to China were almost exclusively of books written in Chinese, which in any case stimulated little interest in China, Klaproth and others relied upon the Japanese books they could consult in Europe to launch the study of Japan as a worthy subject in St Petersburg, in Vienna, in Paris and in Leiden.

BIBLIOGRAPHY

On early collecting in Europe see Kornicki 1993b; Kōdayū's collection is examined in O. P. Petrova, 'Kollektsiya knig Daikokuya Kodayu i eyo znachenie dlya Russko-Yaponskikh kul'turnykh svyazey', in *Istoriya, kul'tura, yazyki narodov Vostoka* (Moscow: Nauka, 1970), 51–58. On the students in England, see Utano Hiroshi 歌野博, 'Bakumatsu Eikoku ryūgakusei no shomotsu uribarai no hanashi' 幕末英国留学生の書物売り払いの話, *Nihon kosho tsūshin* 日本古書通信 806~8 (1996) and Kornicki 1993a: 214–6.

CHAPTER EIGHT

CENSORSHIP

1   Censorship before the Tokugawa period
2   Censorship in the Tokugawa period
    1   The exclusion of Christianity
    2   Secular censorship and the book trade
    3   Calendars
3   Censorship in the early Meiji period

This chapter is primarily concerned with the operation of censorship systems in the Tokugawa period and with their effects. This is not to say that censorship was unknown before 1600, as will become clear; rather, it is to emphasize that the emergence of mechanisms for the operation of censorship in Japan coincide with the development in the seventeenth century of a market for printed books, whether produced domestically or imported from China. The study of censorship in its fullest sense should encompass restrictions on the freedom of expression, publication and circulation of unorthodox views and their consequences, but the emphasis here is on books that can be identified and on attempts to prevent their dissemination. Since the control and suppression of books only became an organized part of the activities of the state in the Tokugawa period, that is where the focus will lie.

Although much has been made in the past of the supposed harshness of Tokugawa censorship, I suggest here that this has been unduly exaggerated. Both in terms of legislation and of enforcement, censorship was haphazard and unsystematic until after the Meiji Restoration. In comparison, then, with Meiji censorship or with censorship régimes in many other societies, Tokugawa Japan was more lenient and tolerant, in effect if not by intent. There were of course victims, and censorship undoubtedly had its effects on writing and book production, but, as mentioned in chapter one, the Bakufu created a distance between itself and commercial publishing that allowed the latter considerable freedom of movement. This freedom of movement did not lead to the publication of critiques of the Bakufu, but it did lead to the publication of alternative ideological systems, particularly those represented by the nationalist intellectual tradition of Kokugaku and by the empirical scientism of the Rangaku school. It also led to the efflorescence of a popular, urban printed culture that was quite at variance with the values of the Bakufu.

8.1 CENSORSHIP BEFORE THE TOKUGAWA PERIOD

Censorship in Japan is commonly treated as a phenomenon of the Tokugawa period and, of course, of modern times, but this view is in need of some modification. It is true that there was no parallel in pre-Tokugawa Japan to the burnings of books in China in the Qin dynasty, to the efforts made in the Tang dynasty to prevent the unauthorized reproduction and circulation of books pertaining to governance, such as calendars, almanacs laws and official histories, or to the measures taken in the Song dynasty to institute a form of pre-publication censorship.[1] Regulations designed to prevent the publication and dissemination of offensive books in Japan were not issued until the seventeenth century and so coincide with the emergence of commercial publication. It is at that point that printing passes onto the streets, and that commercial considerations rather than political or intellectual loyalties begin to affect the dissemination of printed texts and illustrations. This stage had been reached in China much earlier, for by the start of the Song dynasty printing had gone commercial, and well before that the control of writing and dissent had assumed an importance to the state that it did not have in Japan until the Tokugawa period.[2]

Nevertheless, there is certainly evidence of the suppression of particular books before the Tokugawa period and of what Brownlee has called 'ideological control' in the production of symbolic texts.

---

[1] Alford 1995: 13–15.
[2] On this issue see Mark Lewis, *Writing and authority in early China* (New York: SUNY Press, forthcoming).

In the law codes of the eighth century and in an edict issued in 729 there were prohibitions on the production or use of books concerning malevolent magical practices. These offences were punishable in Japan by exile, while in the Tang codes on which they were based the punishment was death. There is no evidence to show, however, that any such books were ever produced in Japan, let alone detected. The earliest references to actual cases of suppression are found in two chronicles of the ninth century. They involve the suppression of genealogical works which claimed that the Japanese monarchs were related to the ruling families in China or Korea, in contrast to the orthodox view, then and now, that the Japanese imperial family was entirely indigenous. Much later, in the early thirteenth century, there is reason to suppose that censorship was applied to the compilation of the ninth of the imperial anthologies of court poetry, the *Shinchokusenshū*. It appears likely that the exiled emperor Juntoku and others involved in the Jōkyū war of 1221, an abortive attempt by the court to reassert itself vis-à-vis the Bakufu in Kamakura, had contributed poems which were then excluded before the final version was presented to the throne in 1235.[3]

Further cases are cited by Miyatake Tobone (also known as Gaikotsu; 1867–1955), who was inspired to write an exhaustive account of instances of censorship as a result of a three-year prison sentence he served in 1889–92 for *lèse-majesté*.[4] However, most of these on further investigation turn out to be mistaken. There are just two exceptions which I have been able to verify. The first concerns the tempestuous monk Nichiren 日蓮. In the 1250s a series of fires, earthquakes, floods and other natural disasters struck Kamakura, the seat of the shōgunate, and in 1260 he wrote *Risshō ankokuron* 立正安国論, in which he laid the blame for these disasters on the Pure Land teachings of Hōnen. He submitted this work to Hōjō Tokiyori 北条時頼, who had in 1256 retired as regent but remained in *de facto* control of the Bakufu. The following year Nichiren was exiled

---

[3] *SNKBT* 13: 210–11; *NST* 3: 99; John S. Brownlee, 'Ideological control in ancient Japan', *Historical reflections* 14 (1987): 131–2; on the *Shinchokusenshū* I am indebted to Ivo Smits, 'The poet and the politicians', forthcoming.

[4] It was Miyatake who published the notorious lampoon by Adachi Ginkō of the promulgation of the Constitution in 1889 in which the emperor Meiji was represented by a skeleton; Miyatake himself contributed a parody of the Constitution: T. Fujitani, *Splendid monarchy: power and pageantry in modern Japan* (Berkeley: University of California Press, 1996), 198–9.

to Izu as a result of this work, but copies survived and were later printed without any further action being taken.[5]

The second case concerns the learned Zen monk Chūgan Engetsu 中巖円月 (1300–1375). It appears from the record of his life that in 1341 he wrote a history of Japan entitled *Nihonsho* 日本書, which is not extant, and that the following year he attempted to make a second trip to China. Miyatake misquotes and conflates the two entries, suggesting that they are connected. It may be that they are, but it does seem certain that he caused offence with this book, where he suggested that the Japanese ruling family originated in China, and that he suffered some temporary punishment.[6]

These are the only cases for which there is any reliable evidence of state censorship before the Tokugawa period, and none, it should be noticed, concerns a printed book. It appears, therefore, that print was untouched by censorship during the centuries when it was in the hands of Buddhist monastic institutions and that this lasted until publishing went commercial in the seventeenth century.

This is not, however, to say that there was no self-censorship or that there were no attempts to control the expression of doctrinal views in Buddhism. A notable example of the latter is the castigation of the Tachikawa school of tantric Buddhism from the thirteenth century onwards: it was increasingly termed a heresy, and in the 1470s Shingon monks burnt Tachikawa books in Kyoto, with the result that the school largely went underground.[7]

BIBLIOGRAPHY

John S. Brownlee, 'Ideological control in ancient Japan', *Historical reflections* 14 (1987): 113–33.

---

[5] Ishikawa Kyōchō 石川教張 & Kawamura Kōshō 河村孝照, eds, *Nichiren shōnin daijiten* 日蓮聖人大事典 (Kokusho Kankōkai, 1983), 273; Philip B. Yampolsky, ed., *Selected writings of Nichiren* (New York: Columbia University Press, 1990), 11–41; Laurel Rasplica Rodd, *Nichiren: a biography*, Occasional Paper 11 (Tempe: Arizona State University, 1978), 19–22.

[6] *GBZ* 2: 154; Tamamura Takeji 玉村武二, *Gozan zensō denki shūsei* 五山禅僧伝記集成 (Kōdansha, 1983), 449.

[7] James H. Sandford, 'The abominable Tachikawa skull ritual', *MN* 46 (1991): 2–4.

8.2 CENSORSHIP IN THE TOKUGAWA PERIOD

For Kondō Seisai 近藤正斎 (1771–1829), the historian of the book and a keeper of the shōgun's books, 'forbidden books' (*kinsho* 禁書) meant Christian books, specifically those by Matteo Ricci and other Jesuits which reached Japan in Chinese translations in the early eighteenth century, and censorship meant the treatment of such books. This is cautious if not disingenuous, for censorship meant far more than this in the Tokugawa period. Nevertheless, it is a line that has been followed by Itō Tasaburō and Shio Sakanishi, who had no need to share Seisai's caution.

Although we have the texts of many censorship edicts and the details of many cases of censorship in the Tokugawa period, some care is needed before we examine these, for five reasons. Firstly, matters relating to the non-samurai population were mostly dealt with by means of *ad hoc* decrees and edicts rather than codified law. As the texts of many of these edicts make abundantly clear, they were largely reactive, seeking to eliminate practices unacceptable to the Bakufu rather than to develop a body of law. As a result they were frequently repeated and often flouted, and it is not easy to trace changes of policy or even enforcement.

Secondly, the relationship between edicts and particular censorship cases in which offenders were punished for perceived transgressions is a tenuous one. The edicts were exhortatory rather than prescriptive, and action taken by the Bakufu in individual cases was not predicated upon the existence of these edicts. It is for this reason that a number of cases, some of which resulted in severe penalties, occurred well before any edicts on the subject had been issued, that in many cases it is not possible to connect an offending work with the provisions of any particular edict, and that enforcement of the edicts was capricious and unpredictable.

Thirdly, what I have referred to as edicts and decrees were not issued according to standardized procedures. As internal references in surviving texts make clear, there were many more edicts than have survived. The texts that we have consist mostly either of *tasshi* 達, which were instructions addressed to a specific official or office, or of *machibure* 町触, which in Edo were passed by the *machi-bugyō* (city commissioners) down to the *machidoshiyori* (city elders), thence to the *nanushi* (neighbourhood chiefs) and *tsuki-gyōji* (official of the month) and by them to the population at large. By no means were all of these edicts made public.[8]

Fourthly, although we have collections of edicts and some knowledge of the procedures followed in Edo, Kyoto and Osaka, we have nothing parallel from the other large towns where publishing was practised, such as Nagoya, Wakayama, Kanazawa and Hiroshima. It may be supposed that some of the Edo edicts made their way to the domain administrations in the provinces and were applied locally, but I know of no evidence to support such a supposition, and the published collections of domain legislation do not contain any edicts relating to these matters.[9]

And fifthly, as yet surprisingly little work has been done, since Miyatake Tobone's study appeared in 1926, to examine the documentary evidence for the various cases of censorship reported. Only in a few cases have legal documents survived to testify to the nature of the offence and the degree of punishment, and the reliability of the anecdotal evidence relating to other cases still needs to be carefully examined.

8.2.1 *The exclusion of Christianity*

It is appropriate to consider this aspect of censorship separately because it concerned books imported from China in the first instance rather than those produced in Japan. For this reason the controls were exercised at Nagasaki, the only port of entry for Chinese goods, and they were exercised under the direct supervision of the Bakufu's representatives there. Of course the ban on Christian books extended throughout Japan, but outside Nagasaki the controls were entrusted to the booksellers' guilds and were not directly administered by the city commissioners.

In Japan the suppression of Christianity began in the late sixteenth century and was applied with increasing severity in the seventeenth, with the effect of driving surviving Japanese believers underground.

---

[8] *KD* 9: 204, 13: 85.
[9] Some Kyoto edicts are referred to below. For Osaka edicts see *Ōsaka shishi* 大阪市史, 8 vols (Osaka: Seibundō, 1978–9; facsimile of 1927 edition), 3: 219, 221–2, 226–7, 4下:1359, 1552, 1562, 1620, 1869, 2197, 2215.

Nagasaki acted as the conduit for Chinese books reaching Japan throughout the entire Tokugawa period. It only became necessary to control the flow of books there early in the seventeenth century, when imports were found to include some of the Chinese works of Jesuit missionaries active in China and their followers, books on Christian doctrine as well as scientific works. A *caveat* is needed here: perhaps because the operation of censoring imported Chinese books was carried out with some secrecy, no contemporary documents have survived from the seventeenth or early eighteenth centuries. So for this crucial early period we are forced to turn to the writings of the shōgunal librarian Kondō Seisai, who, during a spell of duty in Nagasaki in the early nineteenth century, evidently had access to records belonging to the Mukai family of censors that appear now to be lost. Kondō quotes from a number of these documents *in extenso* and for the most part the contents agree with an official Nagasaki report on banned Christian books compiled in 1841, *Goseikin gomen shoseki yakusho* 御成禁御免書籍訳書.

According to Kondō, then, an edict was issued in 1630 banning 32 Chinese books by Li Madou 利瑪竇 (=Matteo Ricci) and other Europeans, but permitting trade in Chinese books containing only rumours about Christianity or concerning countries in which Christianity was practised.[10] Itō Tasaburō has raised doubts about which books were banned and when, doubts partly shared by Ōba Osamu, but it is accepted that some books at least were banned in 1630 and that others were added at least by 1676, when a catalogue of prohibited Christian books was drawn up by the office of the Nagasaki city commissioner.[11]

Li Madou was the Chinese name used by Ricci, and the other Jesuit missionaries, including Julius Aleni, were also designated by the Chinese names they had adopted. Among the titles listed by Kondō as having been banned in 1630 are Ricci's *Tian zhu shi yi* 天主実義, a refutation of Buddhism and exposition of Christian doctrine, Aleni's *Misa ji yi* 彌撒祭義, an account of the Mass, and *Tai xi shui fa* 泰西水法, a study of irrigation in the West by Sabbatinus de Ursis. The presence of this and a number of other works which have nothing to do with Christianity does not square with the provisions

---

[10] *KSZ* 3: 215–6.
[11] Itō 1972; Ōba 1984: 55–85.

of the edict as cited by Kondō. It may have been the case that all books by Europeans irrespective of the contents were banned, but that is not evident from the perhaps abbreviated text cited by Kondō.

It is not certain exactly when an apparatus was established to exercise some sort of control over books coming into Nagasaki, but it was probably before 1630. At any rate, by 1639 Mukai Genshō 向井元升, a local Confucian doctor and the author of several works on botany, had been appointed to participate in the censorship process. In 1685 his son Gensei 元成 (1653–1727) distinguished himself by discovering that a work that had passed through the censorship system and been auctioned off to booksellers actually contained passages advocating Christianity. The book was burnt and the captain of the Chinese boat was sent back with his cargo intact and banned from future trading voyages to Japan. As a consequence Gensei was appointed *shomotsu-aratameyaku* 書物改役, the term used henceforward for the chief censor at Nagasaki, and the post became hereditary in the Mukai family. It was probably at this point, if not before, that the censorship office was established with a staff of assistants and secretaries. It was at this point too, according to *Goseikin gomen shoseki yakusho*, that the regulations were made much stricter so as to prevent the importation of any book containing the slightest reference to Christianity.[12]

The procedure for dealing with imported books was as follows. Books ordered by the Bakufu were passed straight to the Nagasaki *daikan* 代官, the shōgun's representative, for transmission to Edo. The rest were passed to the censor's office at the Confucian Academy in Nagasaki and minutely examined by Mukai and his assistants. They wrote detailed descriptions of the contents of each book, noting titles, prefaces and contents, and presented them in the form of a report (*taiisho* 大意書) to the city commissioner. The commissioner had the power to order the destruction of any banned or other Christian books, to require the captain to take his cargo back and to ban him from future voyages. In the case of books with a passing mention of Christianity, the offending passage was customarily torn out or obliterated and the captain was ordered to take it back to China. The report was then sent to Edo where it functioned as a catalogue, and

---

[12] Ōba 1984: 85–99. Here and in much of what follows I am indebted to Ōba's comprehensive study.

books were selected from it for the Bakufu libraries and for individual senior members of the Bakufu's administrative apparatus. Itō has noted that in no case does it appear that the Bakufu sought to purchase any of the banned books for its own use.[13]

While the inspection of the cargoes of books on arrival was the principal means of control, the local booksellers, who bid for the imported books at an auction, were also required to assist with enforcement of the ban. In 1671 the five members of the local booksellers' guild signed a pledge in which they promised to bring to the attention of the authorities any books on military science, any Christian books or any 'rare' books they encountered, in Nagasaki or anywhere else. The word 'rare' in this context does not denote bibliographical rarity but books that were out of the ordinary and therefore subject to suspicion.[14]

Between 1685 and 1720, when the rules were relaxed, 16 books were either destroyed or returned with deletions. Most of them were of Chinese authorship and had only passing references to Christianity. For example, *Zeng ding guang yu ji* 増訂広輿記 (1696), a topographical work, was sent back in 1710 merely because it included a description of a Christian church in Beijing.

The relaxation of the rules in 1720 was directly the result of intervention by the shōgun Yoshimune (1684–1751), who took a keen interest in science and indulged his curiosity about Europe. According to the *Tokugawa jikki* 徳川実記, a chronological record of the entire Tokugawa period, Yoshimune put a number of questions concerning calendrical science to Nakane Genkei 中根元圭 (1662–1733). Nakane was unable to answer them and said that he would be able to do so if only he could have access to Western books, which were banned just for mentioning Christianity, and he begged Yoshimune to lift the ban.[15] By this time Dutch books were already being imported by the Dutch East India Company based at Deshima in Nagasaki (see §7.1.4), but knowledge of the language was still confined to the official interpreters, and Nakane was naturally unable to read it. Therefore, being unable to make use of Western books, he could only have recourse to the astronomical works by

---

[13] Itō 1936.
[14] *Tsūkō ichiran* 通航一覧, 8 vols (Kokusho Kankōkai, 1912–13), 4: 119.
[15] *KT* 46: 292.

Ricci and others which had been translated into Chinese and which had been banned.

Possibly as a result of this episode, in 1720 the Bakufu sent instructions to the Nagasaki city commissioner instructing him that works concerning Christianity would remain prohibited as before, but works just mentioning it in passing could even be publicly sold, although great care would have to be taken to ensure that undesirable books did not slip in.[16] As a result a number of works previously banned were now admissible, including, for example *Tai xi shui fa*, the study of irrigation in the West by Sabbatinus de Ursis mentioned above. Furthermore, a number of important Chinese works on mathematics and astronomy, which could not have been imported earlier because they mentioned Ricci by name, now reached Japan. Like the vast collectanea *Gu jin tu shu ji cheng* 古今図書集成 which arrived in 1736, they were purchased for the Bakufu Library.

After 1720 there are few recorded cases of books being sent back to China and the only one to be destroyed was a work on Islam in 1840, presumably through some misunderstanding. The last recorded cases involved *Hai guo tu zhi* 海国図志, a description of foreign countries which includes an account of Christian doctrines and was imported in 1851 and 1852. After some delay it was published in Japan with diacritics to aid Japanese readers. Works that might have caused problems and that would earlier have been sent back, after offending passages had been deleted, were now able to enter Japan once the passages had been removed. For example, *Wu za zu* contained a passage about Ricci but this was removed from imported copies in Nagasaki and when Japanese editions were published in 1661, 1795 and 1822, the passage in question was omitted. That is not to say that this passage was completely inaccessible, for Ogyū Sorai and others had access to copies of the unexpurgated Chinese text which they copied out. Again, a bibliographic work, *Hui ke shu mu* 彙刻書目, contained a table of the contents of a Christian book, so that was omitted when it was published in a Japanese edition by the Bakufu in 1827, but Yamazaki Yoshinari had access to a complete copy of the original text and copied it out.[17]

Although all the foregoing has concerned the censorship operation

---

[16] *KSZ* 3: 216–7.
[17] Itō 1936: 35–7.

in Nagasaki, the ban had consequences for booksellers elsewhere too. In 1698 the Osaka city commissioner prohibited local booksellers from dealing with any of the banned Christian books and had them hang up at the front of their shops a printed list of the titles under the heading *Gokokkin yaso shomoku* 御国禁耶蘇書目, 'list of Jesus books banned by the state'. The Osaka booksellers' guild remained extremely cautious so far as Christan books were concerned. In spite of the relaxation of the ban in 1720, it continued to forbid members to deal with any of the original banned books until at least 1794. There was some reason for this, since it appears that there were ways around the Nagasaki censorship system. According to Arai Hakuseki, the banned works by Ricci, Aleni and the others circulated extensively in manuscript form but were kept well hidden. Ogyū Sorai was shown a copy of one of Ricci's banned works in the 1720s and made a copy for himself, adding a note railing against the officials who tried to enforce ignorance. Other copies of various banned works are known to have circulated as well.[18]

Itō concludes that the ban obstructed the development of Japanese science and prevented Japanese scholars from obtaining an understanding of Christianity. That may be so, although the growth of Rangaku in the eighteenth century and the opportunity for direct access to Western scientific works gave a much greater stimulus than contemporary Chinese science was able to do. What is more striking than the rigidity with which the ban was implemented, long after there was any threat from Christianity, is the fact that it was relaxed at all when other regulations instituted in the early seventeenth century remained in force until the last years of the Bakufu. This seems to be entirely attributable to Yoshimune's initiative. Further, in spite of the seemingly impermeable system for controlling imports, banned books did find their way into Japan. Thanks to these Sorai and others were able to gain an understanding of Christian beliefs without subscribing to them, and in the nineteenth century thinkers such as Hirata Atsutane and Satō Shin'en were able to acquire copies and satisfy their curiosity about the religion of the West.[19]

BIBLIOGRAPHY

---

[18] Nakamura Kiyozō 中村喜代三, 'Edo Bakufu no kinsho seisaku' 江戸幕府の禁書政策, *Shirin* 11.3 (1926): 86. Arai's comments are in *Kottō zōdan*, a copy of which has not been available to me. See also Sorai's comments in *NST* 36: 434–5.

[19] Itō 1936: 39, 43–8.

For Kondō Seisai's records, partly based on material no longer extant, see *KSZ* 3: 215–41. Details of the books banned and the procedures are to be found in Itō Tasaburō 伊東多三郎, 'Kinsho no kenkyū 禁書の研究', in *Kinseishi no kenkyū* 近世史の研究, 5 vols (Yoshikawa Kōbunkan, 1981–4) 1: 183–249, Itō Tasaburō 1972 and Ōba Osamu, 'Sino-Japanese relations in the Edo period' part 3 'the discovery of banned books', *Sino-Japanese studies* 9.1 (1996): 56–74; see also Shio Sakanishi, 'Prohibition of import of certain Chinese books and the policy of the Edo government', *Journal of the Oriental Society of America* 57 (1937): 290–303. The larger issue of control of imported books is dealt with in Ōba 1984, which is a new edition of Ōba 1967. Makita 1968: 3.107–110.

8.2.2 *Secular censorship and the book trade*

The Bakufu, or at least its representatives in Kyoto, were alert to the dangers of the popular theatre from as early as 1629, when women were banned from appearing on the stage. Later they turned their attention to the contents of the plays performed, warning in 1644 that the real names of living people could not be used for rôles in plays, and in the 1650s they banned certain plays for dealing too overtly with the Shimabara pleasure quarter.[20]

The Bakufu was undoubtedly slower to wake up to the dangers posed by uncontrolled popular publishing, possibly because after Ieyasu's time it took no interest in printing and failed to monitor commercial publications. It was only in the 1720s that some system of control, albeit incomplete, was established. The oldest surviving edicts relating to the censorship of books date from the 1670s, but it is nevertheless clear that secular censorship has a longer history in the Tokugawa period than that date suggests. There are a few recorded instances in which books were banned before any edicts had been issued at all, so far as is known at present. This is important, for the Bakufu, as we shall see, was not beholden to any particular pieces of legislation in exercising control over publication, and the many edicts that have come down to us are for the most part addressed to the booksellers' guilds to guide their operation of the self-censorship

---

[20] Ihara Toshirō 井原敏郎, ed., *Kabuki nenpyō* 歌舞伎年表, 8 vols (Iwanami Shoten), 1: 57, 69, 75.

system.

The earliest known case of censorship in the Tokugawa period cited by Sekine Masanao and subsequently by Miyatake Tobone and other writers is that of the edition of *Kojōzoroe* 古状揃, published by Nishimura Denbee of Osaka in 1649. This consists of various letters including an exchange between Tokugawa Ieyasu and Toyotomi Hideyori, the son of Hideyoshi: in this Hideyori addresses Ieyasu in uncomplimentary terms and accuses him, with some justification, of treachery to Hideyoshi. Nishimura was supposedly beheaded for publishing this book. Konta Yōzō regards this as a mistake, and the same view is taken by other writers; Ishibashi Ken points out further that the exchange of letters between Ieyasu and Hideyori is also included in other editions of *Kojōzoroe* published in the seventeenth century without any unpleasant consequences. However, Sekine is unlikely to have fabricated this incident and the mistake, if such it is, is unexplained. It is difficult to come to any conclusion about this case: if it is true then it is indicative of a Bakufu that is at this stage much harsher in its dealing with publishers than it later was, but there must remain some doubt about it.[21]

Although there is no extant edict explicitly banning books dealing with Hideyoshi and Hideyori, in practice such books invariably got their authors and publishers into trouble. It was probably for this reason that *Chōsen seibatsuki* 朝鮮征伐記, a description of Hideyoshi's campaigns on the Korean peninsula in the 1590s, was banned after its publication in 1659. Similarly, although there was, as far as can be ascertained now, no specific ban on Japanese books mentioning Christianity, *Kirishitan taiji monogatari* 吉利支丹退治物語, an account published in 1665 of the transmission of Christianity to Japan and the methods used to suppress it, was banned, and so in 1672 was even a work by a renowned Confucian scholar, Utsunomiya Ton'an 宇都宮遯庵 (1633–1707), simply for referring in one sentence to Christianity. For the remainder of the Tokugawa period Hideyoshi and Christianity were taboo subjects for publishers and were carefully avoided in published works, although manuscripts dealing with such subjects circulated without occasioning any trouble (§3.3).[22]

---

[21] Ishikawa Ken 石川謙, 'Kojōzoroe no hattatsu' 古状揃の発達, *Kyōikugaku kenkyū* 20.1: 24.

[22] Miyatake 1974: 13–6, 19.

Another early case is that of Yamaga Sokō 山鹿素行. In 1666 he was banished and placed under house arrest for writing *Seikyō yōroku* 聖教要録, which had been published the preceding year. In this work he had been critical of the neo-Confucianism of Zhu Xi, but precisely what the Bakufu found offensive is not clear. There are two aspects to this case that are significant. Firstly, in this instance the author was punished and not, as was usually the case, the publisher. This indicates that the problem was one of the authorship of views rather than of publication *per se*. For similar reasons, Kumazawa Banzan 熊沢蕃山 (1619–1690) was in 1687 placed under house arrest for having written *Daigaku wakumon* 大学或問, in which, amongst other things, he had been sharply critical of Bakufu policies. He had submitted it to the Bakufu as a memorial and had not sought to publish it, so this is more a case of thought control than of censorship applied to a published book. Later, however, *Daigaku wakumon* was published in a watered-down version in 1788, when conditions were more favourable, and was subsequently reprinted. Secondly, *Seikyō yōroku* had not contravened any known edicts and this case consequently demonstrates that the edicts were for guidance, and the Bakufu took action on individual cases as it saw fit. Furthermore, both Yamaga Sokō and Kumazawa Banzan were samurai and as such they came under the jurisdiction of the samurai code of law, the Buke Shohatto 武家諸法度, while the edicts relating to censorship, when they were issued, were addressed to the publishing trade and were not concerned with the intellectual content of serious books.[23]

Cases such as these, in which the Bakufu became directly involved, were unusual and for most of the Tokugawa period the day-to-day supervision of commercial publication was left to the booksellers' guilds, whose responsibility it was to ensure that undesirable publications did not reach the bookshops. Self-policing systems of this type were for the Bakufu the normal means of exercising social control, and at stake for the guilds was the economic advantages conferred upon them by their trading monopolies.

What, then, constituted 'undesirable' publications? The oldest extant edict relating to publishing was issued in Kyoto by the Kyoto

---

[23] Shuzo Uenaka, 'Last testament in exile: Yamaga Sokō's *Haisho zampitsu*', *MN* 32 (1977): 128, 143ff; Miyatake 1974 24–8; Miyazaki Michio 宮崎道生, *Kumazawa Banzan no kenkyū* 熊沢蕃山の研究 (Kyoto: Shibunkaku, 1990), 119–26.

Deputy of the Bakufu in 1657. It touches on various matters unrelated to publishing but requires anybody wishing to publish *wahon no gunshorui* 和本之軍書類, 'Japanese military books', to apply first to the office of the city commissioner for instructions. What this is probably referring to is books concerning the conflicts from which Ieyasu emerged the victor.[24] It is possible that it was this edict that *Chōsen seibatsuki*, mentioned above, fell foul of when it was banned in 1659.

Much more detailed is an edict which was issued in Edo in 1673. In the opening sentence it refers to previous instructions, proving that there had already been edicts relating to publishing in Edo that have not survived. It advises booksellers that they have to seek guidance from the city commissioner's office if they intend to publish anything in any of the following coded categories:

i anything concerning *kōgi* 公義; this meant in practice anything concerning the shōgun and the Bakufu and their politics;

ii anything that might cause inconvenience to people; this does not, of course, mean 'any' people but in practice daimyō and other high-ranking samurai;

iii anything *mezurashii*, that is, rare or unusual; this refers to scandals and sensational events, such as revenge killings.

They were further advised that anybody who furtively engaged in publishing such works would be punished. It is clearly not intended that publishers bring all books before the city commissioner, so the system, such as it was at this stage, allowed publishers to test the waters and take risks, and it is perhaps for that reason that the regulations were tightened up in the early eighteenth century and a pre-publication self-censorship system introduced.[25]

There may have been other edicts issued in the Kanbun era (1661–73), for one purportedly issued then is repeated in an edict issued in 1823. This mentions the following additional categories of doubtful books:

i *gunsho* 軍書; these were military histories concerning

---

[24] This edict is preserved in a collection compiled in 1854, *Kamishimo Kyō machimachi kosho meisaiki* 上下京町々古書明細記: Harada Tomohiko 原田伴彦, ed., *Nihon toshi seikatsu shiryō shūsei* 日本都市生活史料集成, 10 vols (Gakushū Kenkyūsha, 1975–77), 1: 151.

[25] *OKS* 1071, #2220; Munemasa 1982: 158–9.

episodes in the history of China and Japan, and many were safely published in the Tokugawa period, so the reference is probably to those dealing with matters in which Tokugawa Ieyasu was engaged;

ii books of *waka* poetry; I know of no cases in which these caused offence and the point of this is unclear;

iii calendars; these were subject to a separate monopolistic arrangement under the control of the Bakufu, as will be mentioned below (§8.1.3), and no other calendars could be published;

iv rumours and criticisms of people; again, this concerns daimyō and other high-ranking samurai.[26]

v *kōshokubon* 好色本; this is the usual term for erotica, and although not intrinsically pejorative it connoted 'pornography' in edicts.

By 1682 at least, the Bakufu had become sufficiently aware of the potential power of publishing, and included on the public noticeboards (*kōsatsu* 高札) was a new prohibition on 'dealing in new books that are unsound'.[27]

These various edicts, explicit though they were for contemporaries in prohibiting certain categories of book, seem to have had little effect. In 1684 the edict of 1673 was reissued with a firmer tone and a notice to the effect that some publications had infringed the regulations and the offenders had been punished. Later the same year another edict banned the publication of popular ballads or items concerning 'strange events that have happened recently' and instructed that anybody selling such things on the streets would be arrested and taken to the city commissioner's office for questioning, which would result in punishment for the seller and for the publisher. This is undoubtedly a reference to the broadsheets known as *kawaraban*. These offered the only access to news other than word of mouth and private letters (see §2.5): already some had appeared on the streets after the fires of 1681 and 1682. This edict was repeated in 1698, 1703 and 1713, indicating that these practices were proving difficult to suppress. Indeed, the epidemic of love suicides (*shinjū* 心中) in the late seventeenth and early eighteenth centuries provided sensational

---

[26] *TKKZ* 5: 255–6, #2953.
[27] *KT* 42: 499.

copy for many such ephemeral publications, and an internal Bakufu memo of 1720 makes it abundantly clear that they were being recited and hawked on the streets of Edo.[28]

In the second month of 1703 a ban was placed on publishing books about, or mounting plays in the Edo kabuki theatres on the subject of, 'recent strange events'. This refers to the act of revenge carried out by the 46 *rōnin* (masterless warriors) for the disgrace and forced suicide of their lord, which had occurred on 1702.12.14. In view of the Bakufu's legislative practice with regard to the commoner population, it is much more likely that this ban was a response to the activities of enterprising publishers and theatre managers than a preventative measure. There is some evidence, although not completely reliable, that an Edo theatre put on a dramatized version of these events, ostensibly set in the distant past, just twelve days after the *rōnin* had been required to commit suicide on 1703.2.4, and it is certain that even before their suicides a Kyoto theatre had staged a play with obvious references to these happenings. In any case, the sensational nature of these events made them irresistible for dramatists, authors and publishers, and a number of prose versions published in the following years were banned, although the numerous dramatic versions escaped punishment, partly because of their sophisticated use of historical camouflage. One of the first of many books to tell the story using the real names of the participants was *Taihei gishinden* 太平義臣伝: surviving copies lack a colophon, presumably a precautionary measure on the part of the publisher, but one of the prefaces is dated 1719. According to a later commentator, the publisher told the author of this work that it was sure to be banned but that if they printed a large number of copies and sold them with all speed the profits would still be good. In the event the book was indeed banned in 1720, and the author and publisher had to endure spells of house arrest. Further, Osaka booksellers were required to hand in to the city commissioners any remaining copies they had in stock, but printed copies were reportedly in plentiful supply in the bookshops and manuscript copies were also in circulation.[29]

---

[28] *OKS* 990–991, 1234, #2013–5, 2668; *TKKZ* 5: 249, #2939; *SR* 3: 51; on *kawaraban* see Ono Hideo 1960: 20–24, and on their suppression Groemer 1994.

[29] *KT* 43: 502–3; Munemasa 1982: 160–64; Konta 1981: 139–46.; *NZT*, 3rd series 13: 452–3. The internal title of *Taihei gishinden* is *Sekijō gishinden* 赤城義臣伝.

In spite of all the edicts that had been issued so far, there are few signs of suppression and no evidence that any offenders were brought to book during this period, except in connection with the affair of the 47 rōnin. Miyatake reports a small number of cases, but the details and confirmation are mostly wanting; one that appears to be accurate is the banning in 1720 of *Iro denju* 色伝授 in Kyoto on moral grounds, but few details are available.[30]

It was not because publishers were erring on the side of caution that there were so few cases of censorship at this time. On the contrary, *kawaraban* were becoming more blatant than ever in dealing with love suicides, revenges and natural disasters, and *kōshokubon* were being published without any difficulty. Jinbō Kazuya has drawn attention to the publication in the 1690s and early eighteenth century of a number of *kōshokubon* containing descriptions of sexual activity or erotic illustrations. None of these were banned or subject to any suppression. Nakamura Kiyozō is therefore right to argue that the Bakufu had so far failed to appreciate fully the power of the popular commercial press and had signally failed to control it.[31]

In 1721 and 1722 the Bakufu under Tokugawa Yoshimune, who had the previous year relaxed the ban on the importation of Chinese books referring to Christianity, issued new and more thorough edicts which set the standard for the remainder of the Tokugawa period. The first, which was not for general circulation, began uncompromisingly by forbidding the production of new books, but stipulated that if publication was unavoidable, application had to be made to the city commissioner's office. It remained forbidden to produce broadsheets dealing with current events and to put them on sale, and luxury formats for books were deplored. The second, which took the form of a *machibure* for promulgation, laid the groundwork for the Bakufu's approach to the popular press for the remainder of the Tokugawa period. New books, the preamble made clear, were acceptable if they were ordinary Confucian, Buddhist, Shintō, medical or *waka* books, but any new books containing obscene matter or divergent views were strictly prohibited, and books dealing with the ancestors and family backgrounds of 'people' (i.e., daimyō and ranking

---

[30] Miyatake 1974: 46; *Kinsei fūzoku kenbunshū* 近世風俗見聞集, 4 vols (Kokusho Kankōkai, 1912–13), 2: 27.

[31] Jinbō Kazuya 1964: 202–6; Nakamura Kiyozō 1972: 52.

members of the Bakufu) with an admixture of falsehood would no longer be tolerated. Of more significance than these prohibitions was the fact that the edict, for the first time, provided for enforcement by requiring all books henceforward to display the real names of the author and the publisher in the colophon and by requiring them to be inspected before being put on sale.[32] These new requirements had a major impact on the publishing industry, driving certain kinds of book underground so that they were either printed illicitly without any indication of the publisher or circulated in multiple manuscript copies.

It was thus in the Kyōhō era (1716–36) that the system of internal pre-publication self-censorship by the booksellers' guilds began, for the burden of inspection and enforcement of the law fell squarely on the guilds. Members of the guilds wishing to publish a book were required to submit the manuscript for approval to the duty member acting as censor (§5.1.2). In the case of Osaka the complete record of applications has survived from the Kyōhō era to the Meiji period. For Edo the equivalent record, titled the Wariinchō 割印帳, was started in 1722 but has survived only for the period from 1727 to 1815. It opens with the text of the edict of 1722 mentioned above and with instructions from three members of the guild to the effect that the provisions of the edict were to be strictly obeyed and that careful treatment was needed of any new books lacking a date or the names of the author and publisher. Similar records for Kyoto and probably some provincial towns such as Nagoya and Wakayama must have existed but they have not survived. From those that have survived from Edo and Osaka it is clear that the process was taken seriously, presumably to protect the monopolistic privileges enjoyed by the guilds, and that changes were sometimes required before permission was given.[33]

Several further edicts were issued in the Kyōhō era, such as one noting that some books were appearing with incorrect dates or without the proper author's name in the colophon, and demanding vigilance to prevent such infringements. This testifies to the willingness of publishers to disguise their publications, but there is no record of any publisher being punished for such deception. Other edicts testified to

---

[32] *OKS* 1017, #2019; 993–4, #2020.
[33] *OHNK*; the Edo *Wariinchō* is reprinted in Higuchi & Asakura 1962.

the news value of the love suicides which were at a peak at this time. In spite of the bans people were still apparently turning such episodes into books and hawking them on the streets or making plays about them, so in future people selling them were to be arrested. Again, there is no evidence to suggest that any arrests actually ensued. The only significant change made in this period was to relax slightly the rule about the appearance in publications of the names of Ieyasu or his successor shōguns: this was to permit the appearance of the names only, but not of any associated stories or history, in serious publications; for 'light *kana* books', that is for popular publications, of course, the rule was unchanged.[34]

The Kyōhō edicts coincided with one of the three periods of political reform in the Tokugawa period, and it was not until the next period of reform, in the early part of the Kansei era (1789–1801), that there was on the part of the Bakufu any marked interest again in controlling publications. An important component of the Kansei reforms was the so-called 'prohibition of heterodoxy' (*igaku no kin* 異学禁). This originated in a letter written on 1790.5.24 by Matsudaira Sadanobu, the architect of the reforms, to Hayashi Jussai, the head of the Bakufu Academy, pointing out that 'a variety of novel doctrines have been preached abroad, and in some cases the prevalence of heterodoxy has ruined public morals'. Henceforward the Academy was only to concern itself with orthodox Zhu Xi neo-Confucianism and Hayashi was to endeavour to see that other schools followed suit. The prohibition, then, was only directly applied to the Academy, but in the event many domain schools found it prudent to follow the same line. However, this only applied to official schools and it had no discernible effect on the expression or publication of views dissenting from Zhu Xi orthodoxy, which may have entrenched itself in samurai education but did not enjoy a monopoly.[35]

In the Kansei era the Bakufu under Matsudaira Sadanobu issued several new edicts relating to censorship. These partly rehearse the provisions of the Kyōhō edicts, noting in doing so that observance of the law had become slack, but they also reveal awareness of some new developments in need of control. There were 'children's books'

---

[34] *OKS* 994, #2021–2; 1206–7, #2582; 995, #2026.

[35] Robert L. Backus, 'The Kansei prohibition of heterodoxy and its effects on education', *HJAS* 39 (1979): 55–106 (the quotation is from p. 56).

with fake historical settings but actually dealing with the contemporary world: this must be a reference to the satirical chapbooks known as *kibyōshi* which usually resorted to a transparent historical disguise to mask the satire. There were manuscripts containing baseless rumours which circulating libraries (*kashihon'ya*) were making available to their customers: these were mostly about scandals concerning daimyō or the shōgun and were usually handled as manuscripts by *kashihon'ya* (see §3.3 and 9.2.4). There were illicit publications lacking the name of the author or depicting current events like fires. And there were erotic works, which were damaging to public morality. The new edicts incorporated these practices within the compass of what was forbidden, but it is not clear that they had much effect on the book world. In the case of prints, however, censorship had a visible impact on the surface of legitimate prints in the form of the *aratamein* 改印, or censor's seal of approval, the use of which dates from 1790. Internal Bakufu documents of 1721 had suggested that some such seal of approval be impressed on single sheet prints, but the earliest instances known date from much later. Needless to say, illicit prints such as the erotic *shunga* failed to carry any such seal at any time.[36]

What did have an effect, however, was the treatment meted out in 1791, at the time of the Kansei reforms, to one of the most popular writers of the day, Santō Kyōden, and one of the leading publishers, Tsutaya Jūzaburō. The target was three works in the genre of *sharebon*, which were primarily concerned with the world of the pleasure quarters. It appears that after Kyōden had handed his manuscripts over to Tsutaya and received his fees he heard about the new edicts and became alarmed. However, Tsutaya took printed copies of the books, which had evidently not been inspected before, to the duty officers of the guild, who informed him that publication could go ahead, evidently unaware that the climate had changed. At the official investigation which followed he admitted that he had written 'depraved books', 'confessed that he made an unpardonable mistake', and was sentenced to 50 days in handcuffs. All three *sharebon* were banned, Kyōden's father was reprimanded, Tsutaya was fined half of his

---

[36] *OTS* 2: 809–10, #6417–8; *TKKZ* 5.252–3, #2947–8. On *aratamein* see Ishii Kendō 石井研堂, *Nishikie no aratamein no kōshō* 錦絵の改印の考証, revised edition (Isetatsu Shoten, 1932); *GUDJ* 3: 126–32; and Richard Lane, *Images from the floating world: the Japanese print* (New York: G. P. Putnam's sons, 1978), 213; *SR* 3: 55.

personal wealth, and the guild officials were banished from Edo.[37]

Kyōden's three *sharebon* were not pornographic and the illustrations were not erotic, nor did they have any political or satirical content whatsoever. Had such been the targets, it would indeed have been easy to find a more suitable victim. It may be, then, that Kyōden was singled out as a persistent offender, for it is reported that in 1789 he had already been fined for having illustrated *Kokubyaku mizukagami* 黒白水鏡, a fictionalised account of an assassination attempt on Tanuma Okitsugu, currently the most powerful of the senior councillors. At any rate, Kyōden wrote no more *sharebon*, and it has often been suggested that the punishment meted out to Kyōden spelled the end of *sharebon* and encouraged the development of the genre of romantic novels known as *ninjōbon*, which in turn became one of the targets of the Tenpō reforms in 1842.[38]

Kyōden was not the only victim of the Kansei reforms. In 1792 Hayashi Shihei was arraigned for having written of the poor state of Japan's military preparedness and other 'unorthodox views' in *Kaikoku heidan* (1791) and for having included misleading maps in *Sangoku tsūran zusetsu*, which had been published some years earlier in 1786. He was sentenced to an indeterminate period of house arrest, while his publisher, Suwaraya Ichibee 須原屋市兵衛, suffered confiscation of the blocks and of all remaining copies as well as a heavy fine. The four guild officials who had passed the manuscripts for publication were also fined.[39]

In the first years of the nineteenth century, when the heat of the Kansei reforms had died down, there was a revival of publishing interest in works concerning Hideyoshi. Owing to the connection with Ieyasu's rise to power, Hideyoshi remained a dangerous topic and for most of the Tokugawa period books on this subject had been circulated in manuscript. In the seventeenth century, however, before the Bakufu woke up to the extent of commercial publishing, one or two works were published without repercussions, notably Oze Hoan's classic biography, *Taikōki* 大閤記 (1661). In 1797 Okada Gyokusan produced an illustrated version, *Ehon taikōki*, which launched the fad for books and prints concerning Hideyoshi and the battles of the

---

[37] Kornicki 1977; *ZEJ*, 2: 176–8.
[38] Sekine 1903–4: 1424–5 (Sekine does not, however, cite any sources for his account of the fate of *Kokubyaku mizukagami*).
[39] Sekine 1903–4: 1426–9; Miyatake 1974: 87–8.

late sixteenth century. In 1804 an edict sought to put an end to the publication of these works by banning all references to warriors active from 1573 onwards and all pictorial representations, including crests, in prints. And it is reported that *Ehon taikōki* was banned and that Utagawa Toyokuni, Kitagawa Utamaro and other print artists spent 50 days in handcuffs as punishment for their productions during these years.[40]

After the Kansei era there were no edicts relating to the control of books until 1823, when stricter controls were applied to books on calendrical science and astronomy and to translations of Dutch works. All books in these categories had henceforward to be inspected by officials from the city commissioner's office. The intended point of this edict was presumably to restrict the spread of Rangaku, 'Dutch studies'. This was the first step in a process whereby the Bakufu sought to diminish the influence of Rangaku. As a note to the Bakufu astronomer made clear in 1840, translations of Dutch scientific works, including medical works, ought not to have unrestricted circulation. A new requirement, issued in 1842, that medical books had to be submitted in manuscript to the Bakufu Medical Academy, the Igakkan, for a pre-publication check was probably also aimed at Rangaku medicine, to which the Igakkan was not well disposed. In the following year one of the Edo city commissioners sought the advice of the head of the Igakkan on the possible publication of a volume of biographies of European doctors of medicine by Mitsukuri Genpo, a prominent Rangaku scholar. The response was that Chinese medicine had already been damaged enough by Rangaku and that publication was therefore undesirable. However, the city commissioner considered this reply to be biased and consulted the head of the Bakufu Academy. As a result the senior councillors themselves gave permission for publication and it appeared later the same year under the title *Taisei meii ikō* 泰西名医彙講. Finally, in 1850, when it was almost too late, an edict deplored the popularity of 'Western studies' and the confusion they were causing even in the case of medicine, applied new controls to the importation of Dutch books, and forbade private

---

[40] Sekine 1903–4: 1431–3; *Zoku zuihitsu bungaku senshū* 続随筆文学選集, 6 vols (1928), 6: 295–9; Minami Kazuo 南和男, 'Utamaro to Toyokuni no hikka ni tsuite' 歌麿と豊国の筆禍について, *Ukiyoe shūka* 浮世絵聚花, furoku 11 (1981), 1-8; Asano & Clark 1995, Text volume, pp. 243–4.

individuals to make their own translations.[41]

It was towards the end of the Tenpō era (1830–44) that commercial publishing came under the greatest legislative onslaught in the Tokugawa period as the Tenpō reforms sought to reimpose order and authority on urban society. Not only were the guilds themselves dissolved by order and the old edicts of earlier periods enforced with new vigour, but also new targets were identified and attempts made to channel popular publishing into new directions. Almost all of this legislation came in 1842 and it started with a ban on woodblock prints depicting kabuki actors or courtesans. These had been published for decades without causing offence but were now deemed undesirable, and in consequence neither could new prints be published nor old ones sold. The light fictional works known as *gōkan* were also banned, on the ground that the plots and illustrations were closely related to the kabuki theatre and indulged in luxury colour covers and wrappers. Authors were urged instead to write uplifting tales of filial piety and chastity, both of which were somewhat alien to the traditions of popular literature hitherto.[42]

Some of the Tenpō edicts rehearsed earlier provisions, but with renewed concerns for enforcement. Mizuno Tadakuni himself, the architect of the Tenpō reforms, wrote in 1842 to one of his officials reiterating bans articulated in previous edicts, but extending the controls to samurai engaged in private publishing. Since the guilds in Edo had been abolished the previous year, the guild-operated pre-publication censorship system had fallen into disarray, and the ultimate responsibility for censorship was now imposed upon the Bakufu Academy, the Gakumonjo. This continued to be the case even after the guilds were reconstituted in 1851, but it is unclear how much of the actual inspection was carried out at the Gakumonjo. Nevertheless, some pre-publication manuscripts of popular rather than scholarly books survive with impressions of the censorship seal (*aratamein*) of the Gakumonjo. It is clear that it did at least carry out some of the surveillance that had formerly been entrusted to the guilds. Even

---

[41] *OTS* 2: 812, #6426; *BOS* 297, #4706, 300, #4712, 307–8, #4725; *DNKS* Shichū torishimari ruishū 18: 79–86. On the impact of the Tenpō reforms on the publication of books on Western studies see Mori Mutsuhiko 森睦彦, 'Tenpō kaikaku to Yōgakusho no shuppan - toku ni Igakkan to no kankei ni tsuite' 天保改革と洋学書の出版－特に医学館との関係について, *Hōsei shigaku* 18: 71–80.

[42] *BOS* 298–305, #4708–20.

before the end of 1842 it had been noticed that the duty of inspection imposed a huge burden on the Gakumonjo and suggested that books on such subjects as cookery and flower arrangement could be dealt with by lower-level officials.[43]

It was certainly in the Tenpō period that commercial publishing came under the most severe pressure in the Tokugawa period, as already indicated by the number of edicts issued. In 1841, as a part of the Tenpō reforms, the new post of *shichū torishimarigakari* 市中取締掛 was established in Edo in the city commissioners' offices. The incumbent was responsible for control of the urban population in various respects, including the publication of books, and the extant records of the office just relating to books and publication for a handful of years, which fill four volumes, testify to the higher order of surveillance applied to books and commercial publication.

The principal literary victim of the new régime of enforcement was the genre of romantic novels known as *ninjōbon*. On 1841.10.21 the three subordinates of one of the Edo city commissioners submitted a document urging that *ninjōbon* be banned as they were morally offensive and putting the blame on the leading author of the genre, Tamenaga Shunsui 為永春水 (1790-1843). This was accepted by the commissioner and, following orders, they investigated all the published and forthcoming *ninjōbon* and *kōshokubon* in Edo, noting the names and addresses of the publishers who owned the blocks. Finally on 1842.7.7 a public edict was issued noting that *ninjōbon* were popular but offensive and stipulating that the printing blocks were to be confiscated and all sales prohibited. Even before this, in the last month of 1841, Shunsui had been summoned by the city commissioner, together with Chōjiya Heibee 丁字屋平兵衛 and seven other publishers, and questioned. By the second month of 1842 he was under house arrest in handcuffs. Five cartloads of *ninjōbon* printing blocks were confiscated and subsequently destroyed, representing a huge loss of capital investment; the publishers were sentenced to house arrest and heavily fined. This news changed the literary atmosphere and made Kyokutei Bakin, a popular writer of historical novels, decidedly nervous about the publication of his own works, even though they were safely and authentically set in the past.[44]

---

[43] Higuchi 1963: 180; *DNKS Shichū torishimari ruishū* 18: 124-32, 135-7.
[44] Higuchi Hideo 樋口秀雄, *Edo no hankachō* 江戸の犯科帳 (Jinbutsu Ōraisha,

Shunsui was not the only one to suffer. In the 1830s a Confucian scholar named Terakado Seiken 寺門静軒 had written in Chinese an account of Edo and its urban variety titled *Edo hanjōki* 江戸繁昌記 which was published serially in 1832-6. In 1841, however, he and his publisher, the same Chōjiya Heibee, were summoned to the city commissioner's office. It transpired that Chōjiya had been informed already that the work was unacceptable for unstated reasons but had surreptitiously continued to print copies and prepared printing blocks for two further sections. Seiken was sentenced to detention at the commissioner's pleasure and Chōjiya to a period of detention. In addition, the craftsman who had carved the printing blocks was fined and the fees he had received for his work on this book were confiscated. Of the numerous other cases at this time only a couple more need be mentioned. Ōno Hiroki 大野広城 published several works giving details of samurai regulations, residences and customs and although he took the precaution of stating that they were not for commercial sale he was sentenced to detention. And Ryūtei Tanehiko, another popular author, also found himself in trouble in connection with his successful *Nise murasaki inaka Genji* 偽紫田舎源氏, a contemporary version of the *Tale of Genji* set in the pleasure quarters. Shunsui, Seiken and Tanehiko all died within a year, some have suggested by suicide; whatever the case, the elimination of three popular writers gave the Tenpō reforms a particularly chilling air for writers and publishers.[45]

In one interesting area there was a relaxation of censorship practice in the Tenpō era. As mentioned above, in 1841 two books by Ōno Hiroki, *Tonoibukuro* 殿居嚢 and *Aobyōshi* 青標紙, were banned for having included the texts of Bakufu laws without authorisation. However, at the end of 1842, at the height of the campaign against popular publishing, a daring publisher sought the city commissioners' permission to publish a work entitled *Hōrei*

1963), 172-82; *DNKS Shichū torishimari ruishū* 18: 7-15; *BOS* 301, #4713; Miyatake 1974: 138-9; Sekine 1903-4: 1424; Minami 1976: 3-4; *Chosakudō zakki*, in *Kyokutei ikō* 曲亭遺稿 (Kokusho Kankōkai, 1911), 476; *Bakin nikki* 馬琴日記, 4 vols (Chūō Kōronsha, 1973), 4: 317.

[45] *Kyokutei ikō* (Kokusho Kankōkai, 1911), 476-7, 506; Miyatake 1974: 131-3, 136-7, 139-43. On the Tenpō reforms and Tanehiko see Andrew Lawrence Markus, *The willow in autumn: Ryūtei Tanehiko, 1783-1842* (Cambridge, Mass.: Harvard University Press, 1992), 182-7, 195.

burui 法令部類, which was a compendium of recent edicts. There was no precedent for permitting a publication of this sort, and it had been axiomatic that such official documents could not be published. However, the commissioners considered that it would be no bad thing to publish these texts, and that the laws might be better observed if people bought their own copies. They therefore brought the question before Mizuno Tadakuni himself, who gave permission for publication. This work was published in 1843 under the title *Ofuregaki shūran* 御触書集覧 with the subtitle *gomen* 御免 clearly indicating that official permission had been given. In that same year there was a similar request for permission to publish the texts of the notices displayed on the public noticeboards (*kōsatsu*): again, no objection was raised.[46]

Although the Tenpō reforms petered out following the dismissal of their instigator, Mizuno Tadakuni, in 1843, the Bakufu continued to keep a watchful eye not only on commercial publishing but on print in all its forms. In 1844 an edict issued in Edo noted that commercial and private publishers in Kyoto and Osaka had not been following the new policy of applying to the city commissioners for permission to publish, and stipulated that as a result books imported into Edo from other parts of Japan would henceforth have to be inspected by the Edo city commissioners before being put on sale. The following year the Tenmongata (Astronomical Bureau) was made responsible for approving the texts of all proposed publications in the fields of astronomy, mathematics and calendrical science, including translations of Dutch books. Further, publishers were required for the first time to deposit with the Tenmongata one copy of any book published after receiving permission in this way.[47]

In 1854–5 the Bakufu signed treaties with the USA, Britain, France, Russia and the Netherlands establishing minimal diplomatic relations and in the years that followed citizens of those countries, and others, began to settle in the permitted ports. This development also had consequences for the control of publication and information. Firstly, in 1856 the newly-established Bakufu Institute for the Investigation of Foreign Books, the Bansho shirabesho 蕃書調所, was made responsible for overseeing the publication of foreign books in Japan, whether in translation or in the original. People buying

---

[46] Minami 1976: 1–2; *DNKS* Shichū torishimari ruishū 18: 63–8, 110–112.
[47] *BOS* 305–6, #4721–2.

foreign books from the Western merchants at the open ports of Yokohama, Nagasaki and Hakodate were required to submit them to officials for inspection and the impression of a seal of approval, and they were advised that they would be punished if they had in their possession books concerning the banned religion, i.e. Christianity. Similarly, the Bakufu tried to restrict the books that could be sold to foreigners. It is open to doubt if any of these measures had any success. While it appears that none of them lead to any prosecutions, it is probable that this betokens not so much a new readiness to observe the law as a weakening of the Bakufu's means of enforcement in the last years before its collapse (§7.1.4).[48]

For most of the Tokugawa period, at least until the Tenpō reforms, the Bakufu left the supervision of pre-publication censorship in the hands of the various guilds. All the evidence suggests that from the outset the guilds took their responsibilities in the matter of censorship very seriously and acted as the Bakufu's willing agents. They were in effect complicit in the imposition of controls and made no attempt to protect their members when trouble arose. This was doubtless all in the interest of preserving their invaluable trading monopolies. When it came to the inspection of books, the duty members of the guild had internalized the Bakufu's concerns sufficiently to be able to object to passages in submitted manuscripts and require rewriting. Few examples of the process have survived, but a surviving pre-publication manuscript of a pictorial guide to northern Japan which was never actually published, *Ōshū meisho zue* 奥州名所図会, carries annotations on attached slips of paper outlining the objections to nine places in the manuscript.[49] The guilds were particularly alert when inspecting books to identify cases of copyright infringement (§5.1.2), but identifying offensive books involved fine judgement, except in the case of the more obvious infringements. The guilds, for example, must have passed all the satirical *kibyōshi* which appeared in the 1780s and the *sharebon* by Santō Kyōden, all of which, it turned out, were now unacceptable. Nevertheless, there is nothing to suggest that the guilds suffered for having failed to anticipate changes of policy, although the two officials concerned in Kyōden's case

---

[48] *BOS* 308–9, #4728, 4730; 582–3, #5092–3. See also *NKSS* 7: 660–1.
[49] Higuchi 1963: 175, 181; *Kōbunsō taika koshomoku* 弘文荘待賈古書目 34 (Kōbunsō, 1959), 118–20, #128.

were banished from Edo.

The guilds were much exercised, at least in public, about the possibility of members handling undesirable books in the retail sides of their businesses. In 1735 the Osaka guild issued a list of seven banned *kōshokubon* which members were supposed not to sell, and in 1740 introduced a system of fines for members found selling erotic pictures. In 1795 the guild was warned by a member of the urban administration that some bookshops had *kōshokubon* on display and that this could cause problems for the guild. Again, the Osaka guild does not appear to have suffered in any way from the willingness of its members to flout the law.[50]

The Kyoto publishers' guild was similarly concerned about the possibility of its members handling forbidden books, so much so that in 1771 it published a list of such books for circulation to the members, *Kinsho mokuroku*, 'Catalogue of banned books'. According to the preface, at regular publishers' meeting in the first, fifth and ninth months of every year the members were strictly enjoined to keep to the law and not to handle banned Chinese books (i.e., those relating to Christianity), banned Japanese books, erotica, or manuscripts touching on secret matters or baseless rumours. However, there were many such books and it was difficult to remember them all, and so it was decided to publish the list to help the members. In addition to the banned Christian works in Chinese, the list included many illicit manuscripts (§3.3), a number of banned books, including several works on the story of the 46 *rōnin*, and books that were not to be sold because of copyright infringements. Of course, the presence of a title in the list indicates that the compilers were actually familiar with the book in question and that such books were actually circulating in defiance of the law. *Kinsho mokuroku* could also be read, therefore, as a bibliographic guide to such works.[51]

Later, in 1853 when the Kyoto guild was reconstituted after its compulsory dissolution in 1841, the duty officials drew up a memo for the members to remind them of the various categories of books they were forbidden to handle. In addition to the categories already mentioned, these included printed books or manuscripts conveying

---

[50] Makita 1968: 3.110–12.
[51] The text of *Kinsho mokuroku* is contained in Munemasa & Wakabayashi 1965: 177–87.

rumours about foreign countries and imported Chinese pornography.[52] The implication of this is that in fact some members were actually handling forbidden material, knowingly or unknowingly. We know in addition that illicit publishing and the circulation of illicit manuscripts through the network of circulating libraries kept alive an underworld of books: the extent of this underworld we probably underestimate (§3.3).

It is perhaps significant that most of the cases mentioned in this section relate to publishers and booksellers operating in Edo, for several scholars have taken it for granted that censorship was prosecuted more vigorously in Edo than elsewhere owing to the watchful presence of the Bakufu in Edo castle. Internal Bakufu memoranda of 1721 written as part of the preparations for the edicts issued the following year stipulate that books brought to Edo from Kyoto, Osaka and other places should be checked. Those that were 'novel' (*shinki* 新規) and hence undesirable should henceforward be inspected at the city commissioner's office before being offered for sale, and books in playbook style imported from Kyoto should meet the same treatment. And, as mentioned above, an edict issued in Edo in 1844 noted that publishers in Kyoto and Osaka had not been following the new policy introduced in 1842 and ruled that as a result books imported into Edo from other parts of Japan would have to be inspected by the Edo city commissioners before being put on sale. This question needs further examination but the two documents cited here do suggest that, in the perception of the authorities in Edo, censorship was slack in other towns. However, Roger Keyes has noted that in Osaka there were no actor prints at all issued during the years 1842–7 following the Tenpō reforms, and this is at least an indication of stringent self-censorship by the publishing guilds, if not of strict supervision on the part of the city commissioners.[53]

Overall, the record of celebrated instances of censorship in the Tokugawa period is not impressive. A *caveat* is needed here, though. The cases cited by Miyatake cannot be taken at face value and need to be carefully reexamined, and since there has been no thorough study of this issue since 1926 it remains unclear what other cases

---

[52] Munemasa & Wakabayashi 1965: 177–87, 198–200.
[53] *SR* 3: 49–51; *BOS* 305, #4721; Roger S. Keyes & Keiko Mizushima, *The theatrical world of Osaka prints* (Philadelphia Museum of Art, 1973), 30.

might come to light. Nevertheless, it does seem apparent that punishment was rare and not severe by twentieth-century standards. In the period leading up to 1722 many items produced by the popular press seem to have escaped suppression altogether. Two ostensibly fictional works, which were published in 1688 and 1713, portray uprisings in Osaka and in a rural district respectively and were not banned. The same goes for a number of other fictionalized accounts of current events, such as adultery-related vendettas and the confiscation in 1705 of the untold wealth of the merchant Yodoya Tatsugorō. Numerous *kōshokubon* were published around that time, not to mention the erotic *shunga* produced by Hishikawa Moronobu, which were openly published from c1675 with the real names of the artist and the publisher in the colophon. After 1722 such works were for the most part no longer published, openly at any rate, and *shunga* went underground. The sections dealing with erotica were removed from the blocks used to print the booksellers' catalogues so that reprints lacked those pages. Some earlier works were reissued with more innocuous titles: thus *Kōshoku fumi denju* 好色文伝授 (1699), with the suggestive '*kōshoku*' in its title, was reprinted in 1753 as *Fūryū fumi hyōban* 風流文評判, and Saikaku's *Kōshoku gonin onna* 好色五人女 (1686) was reprinted later as *Tōsei onna katagi* 当世女気質. Also, as mentioned above, manuscripts dealing with scandals continued to be produced, were available for sale, and could be borrowed from *kashihon'ya* (§3.3).[54]

Disregard of regulations in the Tokugawa period was the norm. The constant repetition of the edicts is evidence enough of that, but so is the lack of means to enforce their prescriptions.[55] For example, in 1701 the commoner population of Edo were forbidden to drink *sake* except at weddings and special festive occasions, but there is no sign whatsoever that consumption was monitored.[56] Thus the requirement that the names of authors and publishers be given in the

---

[54] The two works, *ukiyozōshi*, are *Binjin taiheiki* 貧人太平記 and *Hyakushō seisuiki* 百姓盛衰記. See also Jinbō Kazuya 1964: 202–208; Shidō Bunko 1962–4: 3.8; Nakamura Kiyozō 1972: 85; and Richādo Rein [R. Lane], *Shinpen shoki hanga: makura-e* 新篇初期版画―枕絵 (Gakken, 1995), 100.

[55] On the futility and repetition of Bakufu edicts see Harold Bolitho, *Treasures among men: the Fudai daimyo in Tokugawa Japan* (New Haven: Yale University Press, 1974), 24.

[56] Donald H. Shively, 'Sumptuary regulations and status in early Tokugawa Japan', *HJAS* 25 (1964–5): 123–58.

colophon of printed books was routinely ignored, apparently without serious consequences. The erotic books now known as *enpon* 艶本 and the erotic prints known as *shunga* invariably failed to comply, although during the slack years of 1761–86 some artists' signatures did appear on *shunga*, often disguised as signatures on screens or hidden in the design. In 1842, in the midst of the Tenpō reforms, the Edo authorities noticed that prints were already being published with faked censorship seals suggesting that they had been approved in the hope of getting around the new restrictions, and surviving copies of a particularly flagrant example were confiscated. Later, in the late 1840s and early 1850s, some prints, such as a triptych by Utagawa Kunisada which contravened the recent ban on the representation of actors and courtesans in prints, carry the imprint of a seal advising retailers not to hang it up for display but to sell it 'under the counter' (*shitauri* シタ売). This is in a sense a form of self-censorship, but it also demonstrates the willingness of publishers to bend the rules.[57]

Censorship was not a joke in the Tokugawa period, but neither was it applied so harshly or consistently as to shackle authors and publishers and force them to publish works of the kind that were acceptable to the Bakufu. The publishing industry was nothing akin to the 'captive press' of Nazi Germany or the Soviet Union.[58] Indeed, the official system introduced by the Bakufu to control the flow of Chinese books into Japan, with a view to keeping Christian books out, was far more rigorous and thorough, and by comparison the censorship of domestically produced books was slack. After all, in spite of the disdain for popular publishing expressed in some of the edicts, and the officially expressed view that no more new works should be published, innumerable works of fiction were safely published and evidently tolerated by Bakufu officials. That was even true of works set in the pleasure quarters, of some satirical sketches and of some books dealing with current events.

To be sure, the shadow of censorship had its effect on the kinds of books published. It gave rise to systematic forms of deception, such as the transparent historical disguise adopted in the theatre and various

---

[57] Thompson 1991: 35, 53. The ban on the depiction of kabuki actors and courtesans in prints was issued on 1842.6.4: *BOS* 5: 298, #4708. *DNKS Shichū torishimari ruishū* 18: 138–42; *GUDJ* 3: 42.

[58] Cf Oron J. Hale, *The captive press of the Third Reich* (Princeton: Princeton University Press, 1964).

fictional works. Thus Chikamatsu Monzaemon's play *Keisei Shimabara kaeru gassen* (1719), which deals with the Shimabara uprising of 1638, is ostensibly set in the late twelfth century, and Santō Kyōden's *Nishiki no ura*, which is set in the contemporary pleasure quarters of Edo, pretends to be dealing with an eleventh-century brothel. Similarly, in the first half of the nineteenth century it was the fear of censorship that forced writers of the historical novels known as *yomihon* to turn to much earlier periods for their material rather than risk dealing with the controversial late sixteenth century and besmirching the memory of Tokugawa Ieyasu. Nevertheless, it remains true that the system was not an efficient one, as becomes only too clear when it is compared with the censorship systems of the police state that emerged in the early Meiji period. And whatever may be said of the censorship of printed books and prints, it is evident that the Bakufu did not have either the resources or the will to control the circulation of illicit or subversive manuscripts.

BIBLIOGRAPHY

Censorship legislation is contained in *TKKZ* 5: 248–57; *OKS* 990–6, 1017, 1071, 1206–7, 1234; *OHS* 466–7; *OTS* 2: 809–12; *BOS* 5: 297–310, 582–3; and also in Takagi Gen 高木元, '*Ruishū sen'yō* maki no yonjūroku - Edo shuppan shiryō no shōkai' 『類集撰要』巻之四十六―江戸出版史料の紹介, *Yomihon kenkyū* 2.2 (1988): 81–111; but these are not exhaustive. The legislation and its application is discussed in Sekine 1903–4, Nakamura Kiyozō 1972 and Higuchi 1963. Miyatake 1974, Jinbō Kazuya 神保五弥, 'Edo kinsho kaidai' 江戸禁書解題, *Kokubungaku kaishaku to kanshō* 29.12 (1964): 202–18, and Konta 1981 cover a number of case studies, although Miyatake is unreliable; and May 1983 and Kornicki 1977 and 1982 consider the literary consequences. For a thorough discussion of the impact on prints see Thompson 1991, and Fujikake Shizuya 藤懸静也, 'Tokugawamatsu no shuppankai ni okeru eshi to sakusha' 徳川末の出版界に於ける絵師と作者, *Shigaku zasshi* 29.6 (1918): 1–22 & 29.7: 36–66; for theatrical censorship see Donald H. Shively, 'Bakufu versus kabuki', *HJAS* 18 (1955): 326–56, and *idem*, 'Tokugawa plays on forbidden topics', in James R. Brandon, ed., *Chūshingura: studies in Kabuki and the Puppet Theatre* (Honolulu: University of Hawaii Press, 1982), 23–57. On *shunga*, see Richādo Rein [R. Lane], *Shinpen shoki hanga: makura-e* 新篇初期版画―枕絵 (Gakken, 1995) and Tom & Mary Anne Evans, *Shunga: the art of love in Japan* (New York: Paddington Press, 1975).

8.2.3 *Calendars*

The publication of calendars in the Tokugawa period was subject to special controls and it is evident from the repeated edicts forbidding the unofficial publication of calendars that the regulations were frequently flouted. The official calendrical system used in Japan from 862 until 1684 was imported from Parhae early in the ninth century and was known in Japan as the Senmyōreki (§7.1.2). Each year the calendar for the following year was calculated in accordance with this system and drawn up by the Onmyōryō 陰陽寮, or Institute of Divination, in Kyoto, and this formed the basis for calendars produced in Kyoto. By 1458 there was a guild of calendar printers in Kyoto with three members, who presumably enjoyed a local monopoly, but by the 1580s others were printing calendars without permission. The guild was under the control of an official of the Onmyōryō titled Daikyōshi 大経師, who was responsible for getting the calendar right: there are records of punishments being visited upon him when errors came to light. In the provinces calendars were sometimes independently calculated and compiled, and there were inevitably discrepancies both in the calendrical and in the astrological parts of printed calendars, but by 1657 the Daikyōshi had acquired the right to control the printing of calendars compiled in the provinces.[59]

As a result of advances in calendrical science and the increasingly obvious dissonance between the Senmyōreki calendar and observable astronomical phenomena, calls for a new system became pressing in the seventeenth century. In 1684 Shibukawa Harumi (1639–1715), one of the four masters of *go* in the shōgun's service, succeeded in persuading the court astronomical bureau in Kyoto to adopt a new calendrical system, which came into force the following year and was known as the Jōkyōreki 貞享暦. He himself was appointed to the headship of a new office in the Bakufu, the Tenmongata or Astronomical Bureau. This did not replace the old Court bureau of astronomy in the Onmyōryō in Kyoto; rather, the two worked in complement each year to fashion the following year's calendar. The Tenmongata took over the astronomical calculations to determine the long and short months and the occasional intercalary month, not

---

[59] Watanabe 1984: 74, 149–55.

to mention eclipses, while the Onmyōryō retained responsibility for the astrological elements.

The Tenmongata had the upper hand over the Court bureau when it came to revisions of the calendrical system. New systems were adopted in 1755 (Hōrekireki 宝暦暦) and 1798 (Kanseireki 寛政暦), and finally in 1843 the Tenpōreki 天保暦 was adopted, based on a Japanese translation of Joseph de Lalande's *Astronomie*, of which a Dutch version published in 1775 had reached Japan via Deshima. The Tenmongata, under the hereditary leadership of the Shibukawa family, cooperated with the Court bureau to maintain the formalities of presenting the calendar for the following year at the Grand Shrine at Ise, but the final proofreading was done by the Tenmongata, and it was through the Bakufu's network of city commissioners that approved copies were distributed to officially recognised publishers of calendars in Edo, Aizu, Mishima, Ise, Kyoto and Nara. After 1755 most of the controls were again exercised by the Tsuchimikado family in Kyoto, which dominated the Onmyōryō, but in 1798 they returned to the Tenmongata and remained there.[60]

The imposition of controls on the publication of calendars is usually considered to date from 1684, when the Jōkyōreki was adopted and privately-produced calendars were prohibited. Thereafter, all calendars were supposed to be calendrically and astrologically uniform. Any edicts that were issued on this subject do not, however, seem to have survived. It is clear, nevertheless, that in each town where the publication of calendars was permitted only recognised publishers could engage in this trade. They were generally known as calendar-makers (*rekishi* 暦師), and there was a fixed number in the towns where they were permitted. In Edo there was a different system, for there was an established guild of calendar publishers: originally there were 28 of them but, as a result of an internal dispute, in 1697 the number was reduced to 11 and all others were forbidden to publish calendars. Until the end of the Tokugawa period 11 remained the

---

[60] Watanabe 1984: 155–59, 162, 167; Masayoshi Sugimoto & David L. Swain, *Science and culture in traditional Japan: A.D. 600–1854* (Cambridge, Mass.: MIT Press, 1978), 252–8; Nakayama Shigeru, *A history of Japanese astronomy: Chinese background and Western impact* (Cambridge, Mass.: Harvard University Press, 1969), 118–122, 194–5, 200–202. Annick Horiuchi, 'La science calendérique de Takebe Katahiro (1664–1739)', *Historia scientiarum* 33(1987): 3–24. The Hōrekireki is sometimes mistakenly referred to as the Hōryakureki.

number of official calendar publishers in Edo, although the names of the members did change, as individual members dropped out to be replaced by other publishers. All guilds were abolished on 1841.12.14 in the course of the Tenpō reforms, but on 1842.4.18 it was made clear that the calendar publishers' and the Nihonbashi fishmongers' guilds alone were exempt and could continue to operate as before.[61]

In Edo numerous edicts were issued on the subject of calendars throughout the period. Following the edict of 1697 restricting publication to the 11 approved publishers, edicts with similar texts were issued in 1703, 1716, 1718, 1725, 1744, 1788, 1799, 1823, 1838, 1849, and 1851, and doubtless on other occasions as well. Several of these refer to the circulation of unauthorised calendars, presumably printed by those who were not members of the guild. On the one hand these edicts undoubtedly protected the guild's monopoly, to the extent that they were heeded at any rate, but they also testify to the constant supply of illicit calendars.

Just what were these illicit calendars? Two kinds explicitly mentioned in the edicts are 'abbreviated calendars' (*ryakureki* 略暦), which were simple calendars produced outside the guild before the Tenmongata had approved the final form of the calendar for the following year. They anticipated the approval of the official calendar and could, therefore, differ from it. These were banned, and so too were single-sheet calendars (*ichimaizuri* 一枚刷): they were sold in shops and even hawked on street corners, and offenders were to be severely punished, for, as the edicts put it, calendars were a 'serious matter' (*omoki gi* 重キ儀). It is difficult now to identify calendars falling under this rubric, but it almost certainly applies to the illustrated single-sheet calendars known as *egoyomi* 絵暦, and to some *surimono* prints which convey calendrical information. These were privately produced and for the most part for private rather than commercial distribution. Matthi Forrer notes that some of them carry publishers' trade marks, suggesting that they were not illegal, but he notes too that they were also issued in editions lacking the trade marks, and these may have been intended for furtive public sale. It may well be, as Forrer suggests, that they were tolerated so long as they were not commercially distributed to the public. At any rate, there are no

---

[61] Nakamura Kiyozō 1972: 51; Watanabe 1984: 75, 268, 299–303, 306–7.

records of punishments for those who flouted the law to publish or distribute illicit calendars.[62]

In 1799 two calendars were explicitly banned, and this is the only such case we know of as yet. They were the 1789 edition of *Koreki benran* 古暦便覧 and *Kaihō chōreki benran* 懐宝長暦便覧, which was published in separate editions in 1778, 1788 and 1794. The problem with both of these works, according to the edict banning them, was that they gave the calendars for ten years to come, in spite of the fact that they had not been officially calculated and approved yet. However, by the time these two books were banned they had both been on sale for several years, and unless there were earlier banning edicts which have not survived it is evident that the Bakufu took some time to catch up with illicit items.[63]

I have described above the system in operation for the control and publication of calendars in the Tokugawa period, but there was one exception to this system of control exercised from Edo. That exception was the domain of Satsuma at the southern end of Kyushu, which comprised the provinces of Satsuma, Ōsumi and Hyūga. Satsuma was uniquely permitted to devise and publish its own calendars but only for distribution within the domain. According to Watanabe, this was because of the distance from Edo, which made it difficult to obtain approved calendars in time, but it may also have something to do with the long tradition of calendar production in Satsuma, which went back to the Kamakura period. Satsuma accordingly had its own calendrical scientists, and when changes in the calendrical system were announced, they travelled either to Edo or to Kyoto to gain instruction in the new system. In 1779 the domain established its own school of astronomy and calendrical science, the Meijikan 明時館.[64]

The publication of calendars, which combined both calendrical and astrological information, was of course important for the conduct of official and commercial business as well as for agriculture and indeed many aspects of everyday life. Until they became available at the end of each year it was not possible to know in advance the exact

---

[62] Watanabe 1984: 301–2; *OKS* 991 #2016, *OHS* 466 #1356, *OTS* 2: 809 #6416, 811 #6421, 812 #6425, *BOS* 297 #4704, 307 #4724, 308 #4726; Forrer 1979: 12, 14, 26–27.
[63] *OTS* 2: 811 #6421; *KSM* 3: 590.3–4, 2: 46.4.
[64] Watanabe 1984: 339–43.

shape of the year to come. The Bakufu's control of publication, exercised through a recognised group of publishers, was partially designed to ensure uniformity and to prevent confusion, but, as was even more so the case in China, it was also a matter that went to the heart of the Bakufu's claims on legitimacy. The calendar was not simply a matter of computing the length of the year and dividing up time. It was also, in Confucian thought, a reflection of the harmony that was supposed to lie between the heavens and the governance of the state. Indeed, in the neo-Confucianism of Zhu Xi this belief that the movements of the celestial bodies 'maintained order and harmony according to perpetual principles and laws' lead him to make his own astronomical observations and to concern himself with calendrical science.[65] It is for these reasons that in China from 839 the state placed formal controls over the production and distribution of calendars. In Japan the Court and the Ise Shrine had long been at the centre of the process of devising the calendar for each year, although they had imposed no formal controls on the production of calendars elsewhere. In the Tokugawa period, however, the Bakufu came to see it as lying within its legitimate interests to exercise some supervisory control over the production and publication of calendars and to ensure that the calendrical and astrological information they contained were uniform.

In 1868, once the Meiji Restoration was under way, the Tsuchimikado family in Kyoto petitioned the new government for the restoration of its old rights. This request was granted, and henceforward the family had control of the whole process, including the right to give permission for publication. In 1870, however, responsibility for calendars was passed to the Bureau of Astronomy and Calendrical Science (Tenmon rekidōkyoku 天文暦道局), which had recently been established in Tokyo, and the Tsuchimikado were placed in charge of a branch office in Kyoto. On 1872.11.9 it was announced that the Gregorian calendar would be adopted on 1872.12.3, which would become 1 January 1873 and bring calendrical computation into line with the Western world. Frequent administrative rearrangements were made over the subsequent years but finally in 1883 responsibility for the

---

[65] Tomoeda Ryūtarō, 'The system of Chu Hsi's philosophy', in Wang-tsit Chan, ed., *Chu Hsi and neo-Confucianism* (Honolulu: University of Hawaii Press, 1986), 161–3; Alford 1995: 13.

distribution of calendars was entrusted to the Ise Shrine, and in 1888 the compilation of calendars was made the responsibility of the Tokyo Observatory (Tenmondai 天文台).[66]

BIBLIOGRAPHY

Watanabe 1984; Forrer 1979; *GUDJ* 3: 110–18; *Nihon no koyomi* 日本の暦, exhibition catalogue (Kokuritsu Kokkai Toshokan, 1984).

8.3 CENSORSHIP IN THE EARLY MEIJI PERIOD

There can be no doubt at all that censorship was more strictly enforced and more severely punished in the Meiji period than in the Tokugawa period. Saitō Shōzō lists more than 100 separate cases of censorship from the first ten years of the Meiji period (1868–1912) alone, many of them concerning the new media of newspapers and magazines. To some extent it seems that more rigorous censorship enjoyed the support of those who saw the reforms of the 1870s as an opportunity to enforce 'enlightenment' and moral cleansing. There were, for example, protests from newspaper readers about the continued popularity of romantic fiction and the continued availability of 'harmful literature' and 'harmful' theatrical performances. Erotica (*shunga*) and courtesans should be banned, argued one correspondent, and if people spent their time reading proper books, rather than ones that were useless or positively harmful, then popular morals would improve and Japanese civilization would move forward.[67] Although the control of the press and of publications never threatened to take such a utilitarian line, the Meiji government did not accept either the arguments for the freedom of the press put forward by Tsuda Mamichi and other intellectuals.[68]

The Meiji government established, immediately in 1868, an office for the publication of an official gazette, the *Dajōkan nisshi*, which was to carry the texts of government decrees. As mentioned above,

---

[66] Watanabe 1984: 357–99.

[67] *Tōkyō nichinichi shinbun*, 17 Nov. 1872, 23 Jan. 1873, 31 Jan. 1874, p.2.

[68] *Tōkyō nichinichi shinbun*, 10 May 1884, p. 2, and William R. Braisted, *Meiroku zasshi: journal of the Japanese enlightenment* (Cambridge, Mass.; Harvard University Press, 1976), 72–3.

the idea that publishing the texts of official ordinances was desirable had first been accepted in the Tenpō era (1830–44), but instead of being in the hands of commercial publishers the new gazette was to be firmly controlled by the government itself. In that same hectic first year of the new régime the government also found time to issue a number of decrees relating to publications. Books published without official permission were prohibited on 1868.4.28, in an edict which stipulated that only books given official permission could be put on sale. The word used for permission was a new one, *kankyo* 官許, which made it explicitly clear that the permission was to come from the government and not from the guilds, as had earlier been the practice.[69] On 1868.6.5 the first measure was taken to control the new phenomenon of news magazines, known as *shinbunshi* 新聞紙. The decree condemned the greed for profits that lay behind the appearance of such publications, deplored the confusion they caused amongst the populace, and stated that any publication which had not received permission would be punished. In the event none of the *shinbunshi* met with the new government's favour, largely because most of them were produced by Tokugawa loyalists, and they were either banned or just disappeared within a few months. Fukuchi Gen'ichirō, who was later to become one of the most well-known journalists and newspaper publishers of the Meiji period, was one of the first victims. His magazine, *Kōko shinbun* 江湖新聞, was banned for his vigorous opposition to the new government, he was required to hand over all the printing blocks and he also spent a short period in prison.[70]

The government had not as yet instituted a new system for the censorship of books or newspapers, but in Edo (not yet renamed Tokyo) the temporary military administration installed by the new government issued a decree on 1868.6.20 indicating that a new educational institution, the Gakkōkan 学校館, which was the Bakufu Academy under a new guise, would be responsible for inspection henceforward. In 1869 a system for the censorship of newspapers

---

[69] The word *kankyo* had been used occasionally in the Tokugawa period, but only in connection with books published by the Bakufu or by domains.
[70] Ishii Ryōsuke 石井良助, ed., *Dajōkan nisshi* 太政官日誌, 8 vols (Tōkyōdō Shuppan, 1980–2), 1: 81; *BOS* 310, #4732. James L. Huffman, *Politics of the Meiji press: the life of Fukuchi Gen'ichirō* (Honolulu: University of Hawaii Press, 1980), 53–60. On the emergence of *shinbunshi*, see Altman 1975.

was published as *Shinbunshi inkō jōrei* 新聞紙印行条例, but the provisions are reminiscent of earlier edicts of the Tokugawa period, requiring as they do indication of the real names of authors and publishers and avoidance of unorthodox views. However, the old system of pre-publication inspection was abandoned in favour of a system whereby proprietors submitted two copies of each issue upon publication: this applied also to newspapers in Japanese published by resident foreigners, which had not hitherto been subject to any control. A similar system of post-publication censorship was also instituted in the same year in an ordinance concerning the publication of books, *Shuppan jōrei* 出版条例.[71]

Over the following years the new government underwent a process of constant organizational change and in consequence responsibility for censorship passed from one body to another, ending up in the Ministry of Education, which was founded in 1871. At the same time the rapid growth of the press, the publication of leaks relating to internal differences of opinion within the government, and the hostility of many newspapers towards the government finally led the Ministry to prepare tougher regulations on the press, which were embodied in *Shinbunshi hakkō jōmoku* 新聞紙発行条目 on 19 October 1873. But even these did not prove sufficient to take the sting out of the press as the Freedom and Popular Rights Movement became stronger in its opposition to the government's authoritarian tendencies. Consequently, in 1875 responsibility for censorship was transferred to the Home Ministry, which promptly drafted new and more detailed laws to control the press and the publication of books and to prevent libel. These were partially reliant on French law, for the government had at its disposal a translation of the French penal code and a team of French legal advisers, and they were more thorough than all previous formulations.[72]

Under the new regulations newspapers now had to get permission to publish, their editors were criminally responsible for the contents and for any public order consequences arising from articles they

---

[71] Asakura Haruhiko 朝倉治彦, ed., *Dajōkan nisshi*, bekkan 4 vols (Tōkyōdō Shuppan, 1984–5), 1: 82; *Meiji bunka zenshū* 17: 369; Mitchell 1983: 21–7. The *Shinbunshi inkō jōrei* is translated in Séguy 1993: 64–5.

[72] Mitchell 1983: 28–46; Okudaira Yasuhiko 奥平康彦, 'Ken'etsu seido' 検閲制度, in *Kōza nihon kindaihō hattatsushi* 講座日本近代法発達史 (Keisō Shobō, 1967), 143-6.

published, and infringements were punishable by imprisonment for up to three years and suspension of publication. Newspapers also could only be published by Japanese subjects: this measure was aimed at John Black, whose Japanese newspaper, *Nisshin shinjishi* 日新新事紙, was the best-selling daily newspaper but who could not be punished for any transgressions because of the extraterritoriality rights he enjoyed under the treaties Japan had signed with the Western powers. Books were subject to equally stringent regulations, under which publications deemed by the Home Minister to be obscene or damaging to public peace or morals could be banned and their sale prohibited: this applied not only to new publications but also to existing books on sale, which were thus subject to re-censorship. And the Libel Law provided protection for government ministers and their officials from attacks in the press, for even matters that were true but reflected badly on them could not be reported.[73]

It is in effect at this point, in 1875, that censorship became an integral part of the Meiji government's policy of repression. Thereafter successive governments maintained an ever tighter control on the press and the publication of books until 1945. Further, it is at this point that censorship legislation ceases to be a loose collection of occasional edicts and ordinances and becomes a part of a fully articulated code of law with explicit punishments and appropriate means of enforcement. The contrast with the Bakufu, unfriendly towards popular publishing but inconsistent and indecisive in its attempts at control, is a stark one.

BIBLIOGRAPHY

Saitō Shōzō 斎藤昌三 provides a conspectus of instances of censorship in modern times in *Gendai hikka bunken dainenpyō* 現代筆禍文献大年表 (Suikodō Shoten, 1932). The best treatments of the development of censorship regulations in the early Meiji period are Okudaira Yasuhiko 奥平康彦, 'Nihon shuppan keisatsu hōsei no rekishiteki kenkyū josetsu' 日本出版警察法政の歴史的研究序説, parts 1 and 2, *Hōritsu jihō* 法律時報, April

---

[73] Mitchell, 1983: 46–51; Séguy 1993: 117–26; Hoare 1975; Hoare 1994: 164–5.

1967: 54–63, and Mitchell 1983, who briefly covers the Tokugawa period as well. Christiane Séguy 1993 focuses on the press, while Jay Rubin, *Injurious to public morals: writers and the Meiji state* (Seattle: University of Washington Press, 1984) deals in chapter 3 with some early cases of censorship.

CHAPTER NINE

LIBRARIES AND COLLECTORS

1   Libraries and book collecting before 1600
    1   Nara and Heian periods
    2   Kamakura and Muromachi periods
2   Libraries and book collecting after 1600
    1   Ieyasu, Yoshimune and the Bakufu library
    2   Institutional libraries
    3   Other libraries and collections
    4   Commercial lending libraries
3   Ownership
4   The Meiji transition and modern collections

This chapter traces the fate of books in their plurality, that is, the accumulation of books in the hands of individual owners, in institutional libraries and in commercial lending libraries. Systems for the ordering of books, and the preparation and significance of catalogues, are covered in the next chapter. It can be supposed that books as a plurality became a problem early in the history of the importation of texts from China and the Korean kingdoms, and that for the literate few access to a multiplicity of texts was frustrated by the paucity of existing copies. In all likelihood, those who could read Chinese very early on began to 'collect' texts initially by compiling their own volumes of extracts, but we have no clear evidence until later times. At any rate, books as material objects consisting of complete texts were already being formed into collections even by the middle of the seventh century, and the private individual, whether scholar, monk, or official in retirement, assumed an importance in the collecting and preservation of books in Japan that only gave way to institutional collections in the late nineteenth century.

As perhaps in all societies, libraries in Japan exhibit in varying degrees the tension that Chartier has written of between the desire to be comprehensive and a preoccupation with trying to preserve the essentials.[1] However, there is a further tension between different conceptions of what constitute the 'essentials'. For much of Japanese history they were in fact the literary and philosophical classics of Chinese civilization. Buddhist texts provided an alternative definition, and much later other possibilities emerged, such as Japanese secular literature and in the eighteenth century the scientific literature of the West. Consequently, the quest for a 'comprehensive' library covering the sum of human knowledge is muted in Japan. Libraries of state proved far from comprehensive, for they were narrow rather than eclectic in their definitions of the essentials. Further, the collecting of books in Japan involved first an exercise of intellectual ordering, a choice between competing claims: particularly in the Tokugawa period, there was a plurality of intellectual systems and no consensus on what the 'essentials' might be. Collecting books in Japan, then, was in certain important respects very different from that in China: there, as mentioned in chapter one, the state took a much more central role in the collecting and preservation of books and in the determination and dissemination of the canon.

9.1   LIBRARIES AND BOOK COLLECTING BEFORE 1600

9.1.1   *Nara and Heian periods*

The first extant notice of a collection of books in Japan, naturally Chinese books, dates from the sixth century. According to an early Heian genealogical compilation, *Shinsen shōjiroku*, there was a Chinese Buddhist monk called Zhicong 智聡 living in the 'capital' in the reign of the emperor Kinmei (r. 539–71) who had brought with him from China 164 rolls of Buddhist and secular works, including pharmacological studies and medical books which showed the places on the body to be used for acupuncture or moxibustion. The date is not impossibly early, particularly since the owner was an immigrant, and the precision is striking, but the source is a late one and it is wise

---

[1] Chartier 1994: 69.

to be cautious. Ono Noriiaki dates book-collecting from the seventh century, citing the account in *Nihon shoki* of Soga no Iruka's insurrection in 645 which ended with the burning of his books. Ono also notes that the Hōryū Gakumonji 法隆学問寺, a temple eponymously devoted to learning, must also have had a library at this time, although nothing is known of it.[2]

It is in the eighth century that we have the first firm evidence of collections of books maintained by the state, by religious institutions, and by private individuals. The lawcodes promulgated in 702 established the first state library, the Zushoryō, which was supervised by a government ministry and was largely modelled on the Bi shu sheng 祕書省 of Tang China. It was responsible for collecting and conserving both Buddhist and Confucian books and, unlike the Bi shu sheng, was required to compile official histories. For these purposes it had a staff of 4 papermakers, 10 brushmakers, 4 inkmakers and 20 copyists, for collecting was partly dependent on the copying of texts held elsewhere. It consumed huge quantities of paper, drawn by the tenth century from 42 of the 66 provinces, and appears to have become increasingly absorbed in sūtra-copying. The statutes contained in the *Engishiki* include a number of regulations relating to the Zushoryō, such as a requirement that the books be aired regularly, which shows that it also functioned as a repository of books. Precisely what books is unclear, although a ruling in 728 refers to both secular and Buddhist works as well as screens and paintings, and by 757 the Zushoryō had its own catalogue. The same source stipulates that permission was needed if somebody wished to borrow more than one item at a time, but doubtless the right to borrow was restricted. In 833 some of the buildings were burnt down and in 1027 its treasures were destroyed by fire. It may have been revived, for there is a record of another fire in 1042, but it then disappears from the record until the Meiji government established a new Zushoryō in 1884.[3]

The Zushoryō was by no means the only state library or repository in the Heian period. Several of the organs of state had their own libraries or *fudono* 文殿 in which documents and books were deposited

---

[2] Saeki Arikiyo 佐伯有清, *Shinsen shōjiroku no kenkyū: kōshōhen* 新撰姓氏録の研究―考証編, 7 vols (Yoshikawa Kōbunkan, 1981–4), 5: 56–62; *NKBT* 68: 265; Ono Noriaki 1944: 33.

[3] *NST* 3: 162–3; *KT* 26: 387, etc., 25: 589, 11: 267; *DNK* 4: 244; Ono Noriaki 1944: 42–64.

and copies were made of items held elsewhere. The main such repository was burnt down with its contents in 1226, while the others disappear from the historical record earlier. The palace had its own libraries too in the Heian period, similarly for the purpose both of preservation and of taking copies of other books. In 905 the poet Ki no Tsurayuki was in charge of the Goshodokoro 御書所 and in 1187 orders were given for a catalogue of the collection to be made, but in 1225 robbers made off with some of the collection and by 1235 it was in ruins. There are numerous brief references to other palace collections of books in the Heian period, but none of them seem to have survived into the Kamakura period.[4]

The law code of 702 also established a University (*Daigakuryō* 大学寮). Since its purpose was initially to train men for the bureaucracy by giving them a Confucian education, it follows that it must have had some books from the outset. The syllabus survives in a slightly later version, so we have some idea of which Chinese texts might have been available, and we know that there was a library. Regulations in the *Engishiki* refer to two kinds of books, 'official books' (*kansho* 官書), which were perhaps the textbooks, and 'other books' (*zassho* 雑書), which may have been extra-curricular books. The provincial academies (*kokugaku* 国学), which were also established in the Nara period, followed the same curriculum as the University and doubtless had their own modest libraries as well, but after the tenth century there is no further mention of any of these institutions or of their books, and most must have succumbed to fire.[5]

During this same period Buddhist texts were also being collected in Japan. Buddhism reached Japan as a textual religion in the form of sūtras translated from Sanskrit and Prākrit into Chinese, and texts were one of the three central 'treasures' of Buddhism. Although it must be concluded from this that the earliest Buddhist institutions in Japan were equipped with some form of library facilities, there are no pertinent records. There are a number of references in the earliest historical chronicles to the distribution of copies of sūtras supposed to be particularly effective for the purpose of protecting of the state, and even to a requirement that all houses contain a sūtra. But there is not mention of the sūtra repositories (*kyōzō* 経蔵) which later became

---

[4] *KD* 1: 690, 2: 120, 5: 788; *GY* 3: 333; Ono Noriaki 1944: 91–7.
[5] *NST* 3: 262–8; *KT* 26: 525; Ono Noriaki 1944: 108–23.

a standard feature of many temples, particularly in the Shingon sect. This is even the case with the *kokubunji* 国分寺 and *kokubunniji* 国分尼寺, the network of monasteries and nunneries initiated in 741 by emperor Shōmu. Protective sūtras were a part of their equipment but, as Ono has argued, they may well have been akin to the statuary that was also distributed to them, and thus have been given for symbolic rather than practical purposes.[6]

Very little is known of temple libraries in the Nara period, for most records relate rather to the various sūtra-copying projects which greatly enhanced access to the full range of available texts and commentaries in Chinese (§3.3). These consumed prodigious amounts of paper and required constant institutional borrowing of sūtras for the purpose of copying, but the sūtra libraries that resulted have left little documentary trace.[7]

For the Heian period, on the other hand, we have much more to go on, though it is often in the form of notices of collections lost in fires. As described earlier (§7.1.1), Saichō and Kūkai in the early ninth century, and six other monks later in the century, travelled to China on official missions to seek Buddhist texts not yet transmitted to Japan. The collections they brought back remained in their possession, or perhaps in the possession of the temples to which they belonged, as we know from the fact that after their return to Japan Kūkai and Saichō frequently lent each other books from their collections. In 811 Saichō deposited in a temple on Mt Hiei the books and Buddhist implements he had acquired in China and drew up a catalogue of the collection, part of which survives in his own hand. This became the foundation of the collection in one of the three comprehensive Buddhist libraries on Mt Hiei in the early Heian period, which later became known as the Konpon Kyōzō 根本経蔵. Of the other two, the Shingonzō 真言蔵 was established in 864 when the books brought back from China by Ennin were transferrred there on his death. The third was the Sannōzō 山王蔵, which contained the books acquired in China by Enchin. He resided there after his return in 859 and gave his books to the court in Kyoto, but some

---

[6] Ono Noriaki 1944: 140–56.
[7] For the scholarship of monks in the Nara period, see Inoue Mitsusada 井上光貞, 'Tōiki dentō mokuroku yori mitaru Nara jidai sōryo no gakumon' 東域伝灯目録より観たる奈良時代僧侶の学問, *Shigaku zasshi* 57.3 (1948): 27–48, 57.4: 23–45.

were transferred to the Miidera, a temple at the foot of Mt Hiei, and some he evidently took with him up the mountain. A catalogue of the collection, drawn up by a disciple of his in 891, is partly extant in a copy made in 925: the half that survives lists 1,090 titles, and notes that some were copied from texts preserved either in the Konpon Kyōzō or the Shingonzō. There were several monk-librarians attached to the Sannōzō and it is known that they impressed in the books a seal indicating Sannōzō ownership, but the ultimate fate of the collection is unknown.[8]

Similarly, the Tōji in Kyoto had its own sūtra repository by 823 at the latest and Kūkai deposited there the Sanskrit manuscripts he brought back from China. He too appointed a follower to look after the contents after his death, a move which, as Ono has pointed out, was particularly important in view of the closely guarded transmission of texts in Shingon Buddhism. However, the repository building burnt down with Kūkai's manuscripts in 1000. On Mt Kōya a repository had been built at the Kongōbuji by 877, which survived until 1401, when it too was destroyed by fire. In northern Japan the Chūsonji, part of the Fujiwara cultural outpost at Hiraizumi, had a repository from the time of its foundation in 1105 which left a substantial documentary record, although it lost most of its sūtras when Toyotomi Hidetsugu gave them to the monasteries of Mt Kōya in the late sixteenth century. It is evident from these examples that by the end of the Heian period at the very latest, a sūtra repository had become an indispensible part of a monastic complex.[9]

In addition to these institutional libraries of official or monastic complexion, there were also some significant private libraries of which record has survived. The earliest is the Unteiin 芸亭院, described by some as 'Japan's first open-access library'. It was founded, probably in 771, by Isonokami no Yakatsugu 石上宅嗣 (729–81), a poet and government official. On his retirement from public life he turned his home into a temple and in the precincts constructed a store for his secular books, which could be freely consulted by any who wished. In 794 it was still in existence, but by 828 it was defunct. This is the only private library in the Nara period amply supported by

---

[8] On the libraries on Mt Hiei see Satō Tetsuei 1937.
[9] See *Dengyō daishi shōsoku* in *ZGR* 28上: 394–5, etc.; *DNBZ Jishi sōsho* 3265–311; Ono Noriaki 1944: 233–306.

contemporary sources, but it was certainly not the only one. Kibi no Makibi's library of books acquired in China must have been considerable, and a catalogue of it survived at least until the late ninth century. It is reported in an early ninth-century source that Tachibana no Naramaro 橘奈良麻呂 had a library of 480 volumes which were confiscated when the rebellion he had led was crushed in 757.[10]

The picture becomes much clearer in the Heian period. It is beyond doubt that many of the scholar aristocrats whose names and writings have survived possessed substantial collections of books. Sugawara no Michizane's books were kept in the Kōbaiden 紅梅殿, a part of the family school which he used as a study: they were reportedly accessible to scholars but Michizane did complain that some readers lacked seriousness of purpose. Evidence of other libraries and collections abounds. Fujiwara no Michinaga owned a large collection of more than 2,000 volumes and had shelves built for them. Ōe no Masafusa had a library built for his books, Gōke Bunko 江家文庫, which contained 10,000 volumes and burnt down in 1153. Hino Sukenari 日野資叢 (988–1070) retired to Uji in 1051 and established a library, Hōkaiji Bunko 法界寺文庫, of which part of one book survives. The collection of Fujiwara no Michinori (=Shinzei; 1106–59) partially survives in the form of an incomplete catalogue, which gives a valuable insight into the nature of a Heian poet's private library and which is discussed elsewhere (§10.1.1), but the books themselves were torched by warriors and his retainers slain. And Fujiwara no Yorinaga, whose reading and acquisitions of Chinese books have been discussed elsewhere (§6.2.1), was an avid collector who particularly appreciated the convenience and technology of the printed and bound Song-dynasty books that were reaching Japan in his time; in 1151 sent off an order for more than 120 Song editions.[11]

Although it seems to have become customary to prepare for the doleful inevitability of fire by keeping books in special wheeled

---

[10] *Shoku nihongi* Ten'ō 1 [781].6; Shinmura Izuru, *Tenseki sōdan* 典籍叢談 (Oka Shoin, 1925), 436–63; Kuwabara Ryōken 桑原寥軒, *(Nihon saisho no kōkai toshokan) Unteiin* (日本最初の公開図書館) 芸亭院 (Risōsha, 1962); Ono Noriaki 1944: 310–17; *KT 3 Shoku nihon kōki* 30.

[11] Ono Noriaki 1944: 318–68; *DNKK Midō kanpakuki*, 3 vols (Iwanami Shoten, 1953), 2: 74–75; *ST* 15: 187; *Taiki* 台記, 3 vols (Kyōto: Rinsen Shoten, 1966): 1: 149; *GY* 1: 251.

chests (*fuguruma* 文車), fire in the end consumed almost all. Fujiwara no Sanesada 実貞 had a collection of Japanese and Chinese books in more than 10,000 volumes but all were burnt in the great Kyoto fire of 1177, which reduced many such collections to ashes just when the cultural and political significance of Kyoto was facing the challenge of the warriors.[12]

Since barely a fragment of these collections has survived, it is not possible to reconstruct them, except by relying, somewhat uncertainly, on the titles referred to in their owners' writings. A few catalogues have survived, and they are discussed below (§10.1), but there is no way of knowing how representative they might be. All that can be said about the collections referred to above is that the bulk of them was formed by Chinese texts, either brought from China or copied from originals in Japan; that temple collections often included secular Chinese books, including Confucian works, as well as Buddhist texts and commentaries; and that scholarly collections were dominated by Chinese secular writing. To what extent Japanese texts, whether in Chinese or, as the Heian period progressed, in Japanese, formed a part of these collections is entirely unclear. What is incontrovertible is that many Japanese texts, obviously those that are extant but also some that are not, survived into the thirteenth century, for some are listed in a catalogue compiled then, but the conditions of their transmission are unknown.[13] It is possible that the loss of these texts is due to the fact that Japanese writings did not customarily form a part of scholars' libraries until it was too late. At any rate, two of the finest collections of Japanese literary material from the Heian period, the Reizei and Konoe collections, which are discussed below (§9.4), were taking shape at this time and do not feature in the documentary record of book collecting in the Heian period.

BIBLIOGRAPHY

Ono Noriaki 1944 is a magisterial study of pre-Tokugawa libraries that is unlikely to be bettered. Wada Mankichi 1983: 36–100 is also valuable, and Satō Tetsuei 1937 is excellent on the libraries on Mt Hiei. On libraries in China during this period see Drège 1991b.

---

[12] *GY* 1: 251.
[13] Wada Hidematsu 1936: 638–9.

9.1.2 *Kamakura and Muromachi periods*

The Kyoto fire of 1177 and the wanton destruction by Taira warriors in 1180 of monasteries supportive of their opponents, such as the Tōdaiji and Kōfukuji in Nara, incinerated much of the cultural production of the Nara and Heian periods. On the other hand, in the Kamakura period the supply of books from China was maintained by monks and the domestic production of books grew as more temples began to turn to printing.

One of the most important repositories of books in the Kamakura period was the treasure house of the Rengeōin, the temple now known as the Sanjūsangendō in the southern part of Kyoto. It was founded in 1174 by the retired emperor Go-Shirakawa and the focus of the collection, as recorded by his librarian, Yoshida Tsunefusa, was Japanese books and documentary records. It survived numerous fires and earthquakes, and since it provided the originals from which many surviving manuscripts were copied, as the colophons testify, its contribution to the preservation and transmission of texts was a considerable one: for example, the extant manuscripts of the *Tosa nikki* all owe their origins to copies made of the Rengeōin copy in Ki no Tsurayuki's own hand. By the fourteenth century, however, it had ceased to exist: there are records of thefts, of depredations by warriors, and of the failure of emperor Go-Daigo to return books he had borrowed.[14]

Some of the monastery collections mentioned in the previous sections survived into the Kamakura period and beyond, although often in new premises and with new collections to replace ones that had been burnt. They were joined by the collections established by new temples, particularly the Zen monastic complexes of Kyoto and Kamakura known as the Gozan, which were supplied not only with Japanese printed books but also with books printed in China and Korea, such the various editions of the Buddhist canon (§7.1.1–2). In Zen temples the libraries of individual monks often retained their integrity as collections. At the Tōfukuji, for example, there were at least two separate libraries: Enji 円爾 brought back from China a collection of Buddhist, Confucian and Daoist books, including some Song neo-Confucian texts, which were catalogued in 1280 and stored

---

[14] Ono Noriaki 1944: 469–77.

in one library, while another held the collection of Kokan Shiren. Although it is true that the textuality of Buddhism was on the decline in the new sects that emerged in Japan in the Kamakura and Muromachi periods, it is by no means true that texts were no longer sought or produced, and so by this stage it is hard to conceive of a temple without some sort of a scriptural collection.[15]

Similarly, there may well have been, as Ono points out, a decline in the levels of literacy and intellectual commitment found among the Kyoto aristocracy, but some also maintained significant libraries. Most were lost in the maelstrom of fire and violence that overwhelmed Kyoto during the Ōnin war of 1467–77, but a large part of the Kanmu Bunko 官務文庫 has survived up to the present day. This was privately established at the end of the twelfth century by the Mibu Kanmu family, but it contained copies of state documents which came into their own later when the originals were lost in a fire. Its importance was politically recognised in the Muromachi period, when it received state support, and particularly during the Ōnin war, when both sides banned their soldiery from its precincts. On the other hand, the scholar and collector Ichijō Kanera, who had a separate building devoted to his books, was, along with many others, less fortunate in the Ōnin war. In the preface to his *Fude no susabi* he lamented the fate of his books as his home became part of the battleground and was burnt to the ground while his library was ransacked: 'of my Japanese and Chinese books, handed down over more than ten generations, not one volume is left: I am no different from an aged crane that has left its nest, a blind man who has lost his stick.'[16]

The most significant new library founded in the Kamakura period was in the east, close to the headquarters of the Kamakura shōgunate. The Kanazawa Bunko 金沢文庫 was established some time in the late thirteenth century by the Hōjō family, who exercised political power in place of a succession of figurehead shōguns. Whether or not it was founded by Hōjō Sanetoki 北条実時, as some hold, surviving copies of some of the library's books carry colophons which attest to his involvement in procuring of copies of important texts in the years 1243–76. The management of the library was entrusted to the abbots

---

[15] Ono Noriaki 1944: 676–93.
[16] Ijichi Tetsuo 伊地知鉄男, ed., *Rengaronshū* 連歌論集, 2 vols, Iwanami Bunko (1953–6), 1: 283.

of the nearby Shōmyōji 称名寺, which had its own collection of predominantly Buddhist works, and which took over the library after the fall of the Hōjō from power in 1333.[17]

The Kanazawa Bunko librarians were in the habit of impressing a seal of ownership at least in the books that were lent out. This makes it possible to reconstruct the collection from books that have survived in the library itself, which still exists, and in numerous other institutions. There are difficulties because of the known existence of forged seals, presumably manufactured to improve the supposed provenance of a book, and because it is not clear when the books in question became part of the library. Nevertheless, Seki has managed to assemble a photographic record of 215 survivors, and these throw light on the nature of the collection. The Chinese works include manuscript copies made in the Kamakura period and Song printed editions, which were probably part of the collection from early on, together with some Korean printed editions: these must have been acquired in the Muromachi period, which corresponds with the period when they were printed in Korea. The Buddhist books comprise Song editions and Japanese manuscript copies of the Kamakura period, but also a Japanese manuscript copy of the *Lotus sūtra* made in 758 and a number of texts printed at temples in the Kamakura period. And the collection of Japanese books consists mostly of manuscripts made in the Kamakura period. It is probable that these survivors are not unrepresentative of the shape of the collection as a whole, which was unusually eclectic in embracing the literary culture of the whole of East Asia.[18]

The library has preserved a number of interesting letters dating from the Kamakura period which show that it was open and widely used. These include an undated one from a woman who had borrowed and then lost a copy of the *Pillow book* of Sei Shōnagon. She observes that there are no copies as good to be had in Kyoto and undertakes to send to the Bakufu in Kamakura to have a copy made to replace the one she had lost. It is evident from this that both men and women could borrow from the library and that it contained books in Japanese as well as Chinese. The lack of good copies in Kyoto may have been the result of the destruction of Kyoto collections at the end of the

---

[17] Ono Noriaki 1944: 586–91.
[18] Ono Noriaki 1944: 596–613.

Heian period, but what is particularly significant is the suggestion that good books had migrated to Kamakura, the new locus of political power.[19]

In the early Muromachi period it was reported by some visitors that the books were not being well cared for, that some were being removed from the collections, and that access was being denied even to scholars. Although it was never burnt and was actually protected during the warfare at the end of the sixteenth century, it is clear that it lost many books at that time. Toyotomi Hidetsugu took some books, and others ended up in Tokugawa Ieyasu's collection, although it is not clear whether they were taken by him or by some other person and then given to him.

The most important library founded during the Muromachi period was that attached to the Ashikaga Gakkō, the school established in the village of Ashikaga in the province of Shimotsuke. The details of its foundation are unclear, for the records were lost in a fire in 1754. The conventional view has long been that the school was revived in 1439 by Uesugi Norizane 上杉憲実 (1411–66), but, as Kawase Kazuma has argued, it may well be that there was in fact no school in Ashikaga before this date.

Norizane had school buildings constructed, installed the first rector, donated four Song printed editions as a foundation for a library, and established rules for readers and the use of books. The instructions he laid down for the school in 1439, and rearticulated in 1446, emphasized the secular character of the education to be offered. Some of the teachers were Zen monks, for there were few other sinologists at this time who could match their abilities, and as a result some of the students too were Zen monks, but Uesugi banned the study of Zen texts and other non-canonical literature. His son and grandson maintained the tradition of looking after the library and adding to it, and up to the end of the sixteenth century it continued to grow through donations, recorded in inscriptions in the surviving books. The school and its library were, like the Kanazawa Bunko, respected and protected during the warfare at the end of the sixteenth century.[20]

By the early Tokugawa period the school had ceased to function

---

[19] Seki Yasushi, 'Kanazawa Bunko no saiginmi (7)' 金沢文庫の再吟味, *Rekishi chiri* 62.5 (1933): 23–26.

[20] Kawase 1974: 22–3, 29, 35; Ono Noriaki 1944: 628–46; some of the books are illustrated in *KD* 1, plates between pp. 168–9, and in Kawase 1974.

as an educational institution, although the library was intact. Ieyasu returned some of the books removed by Hidetsugu and through San'yō, a former rector, donated ten books, including four that had recently been printed in Japan with movable type. Throughout the Tokugawa period it continued to enjoy the financial support of the Bakufu and the patronage of daimyō, and the collection became increasingly well known and used. In the 1720s Yamanoi Konron spent three years there working on texts used in his *Shichikei mōshi kōbun* (§7.2.1), and later Dazai Shundai and other scholars prepared reprint editions of rare texts preserved in the library. In 1725, Bakufu officials wrote to the library on behalf of the shōgun Yoshimune asking for a catalogue of the collection to be forwarded for the shōgun's perusal. Three years later Yoshimune sent some scholars to examine the books and then ordered 28 items to be sent to Edo for his personal use. The library was not large, for just 271 titles were recorded in the catalogue prepared in 1725, but they were of outstanding quality and accessible to scholars. The bulk of the library consisted of Confucian texts and exegetical works, but there were also some Buddhist texts and some Japanese works, mostly written in Chinese.[21]

In the Muromachi period several daimyō are known to have accumulated substantial collections, and it is probable that the more scholarly shōguns, such as Ashikaga Yoshimitsu and Yoshimasa, had libraries at their disposal. Of the daimyō, Ōta Dōkan 太田道灌 established a library in his castle at Edo in 1477 consisting of several thousand book-boxes. The most avid collectors were probably the Ōuchi, who acquired 13 printed copies of the Buddhist canon from China and Korea, exchanged books with members of the Kyoto nobility for the purpose of making copies, and themselves engaged in printing.[22]

By 1600 book collecting had spread from temples and the court aristocracy to the samurai and their educational institutions. There was all the same no Bakufu or palace collection of any significance at this time, and the dispersal of books in different institutions throughout Japan reflects the decentralization of power in this period. This trend was dramatically reversed in the Tokugawa period in which power and book-collecting came together again.

---

[21] *KT* 38: 341; Kawase 1974: 223–5, 250–5, 258; Ono Noriaki 1944: 628–46;
[22] Ono Noriaki 1944: 652–70.

BIBLIOGRAPHY

Ono Noriaki 1944 is still the most thorough study of libraries in this period. Seki Yasushi 関靖, *Kanazawa Bunkobon zuroku* 金沢文庫本図録, 2 vols (Yūgakusha, 1935–6). Kawase Kazume 1974.

9.2 LIBRARIES AND BOOK COLLECTING AFTER 1600

9.2.1 *Ieyasu, Yoshimune and the Bakufu library*

Ieyasu's interest in books unsurprisingly shows itself mostly in his later life when campaigning demanded less of his attention. It is, however, recorded that in 1592–3 he had Fujiwara Seika 藤原惺窩, a Buddhist priest who had a major rôle to play later in the development of Tokugawa neo-Confucianism, lecture to him at Edo on the *Zhen guan zhen gyao* 貞観政要. This book concerns the principles of government: it had long been used in China as a manual for officials, it had been the subject of lectures given to previous shōguns in the Muromachi period, and it was subsequently printed at Fushimi in 1600 on Ieyasu's orders. This seems to have been one of a number of Chinese works, including the Confucian *Analects*, which, along with *Engishiki* and *Azuma kagami*, constituted Ieyasu's favourite books. His interest in learning was not simply part of the hagiographic tradition perpetuated in the Tokugawa period.[23]

The scholarly side of Ieyasu undoubtedly stimulated his sponsorship of printing, which is discussed elsewhere (§4.2.3), but it also guided his interests as a collector and his concern for the preservation of books. According to the *Tokugawa jikki*, in seeking to acquire books he was motivated by the concern that the 'books of Japan' (*tenka no shoseki* 天下の書籍) had been scattered and put into disorder during the decades of turbulence and civil strife since the Ōnin war broke out in 1467. How exactly he acquired all his books is not clear, but thanks partly to the labours of Kondō Seisai, the most learned of the shōgunal librarians, we do know the identity of many of the books he owned and most have survived intact. His collection included some

---

[23] *NST* 28: 189; see also Herman Ooms, *Tokugawa ideology: early constructs, 1570–1680* (Princeton: Princeton University Press, 1985), 112 and n.3; Mori Junzaburō 1933: 9.

Song, Yuan and Ming editions of Chinese texts and his concentration on Chinese books indicates that the 'books of Japan' was a concept that had less to do with authorship or provenance than with ownership. He did not neglect Japanese books, but to him the Japanese patrimony in terms of books did not exclude some of the large numbers of books that had been brought to Japan from Korea and China over the previous millenium and had been preserved in Japan.[24]

There cannot be much doubt that Ieyasu acquired at least some of his books through the exercise of secular power even while he was still subordinate to Toyotomi Hideyoshi. He may or may not have been the first ruler of Japan to build a collection of books in this way, but he did so far more systematically than any predecessor or any successor until the Meiji state intervened in the late nineteenth century. The Kanazawa Bunko was one of the victims in the late sixteenth century. Toyotomi Hidetsugu, Hideyoshi's son, took some Japanese books and Ieyasu some Chinese books, including some Song editions. Korea was another victim, for among his books were a large number of editions of Chinese texts printed with movable type in Korea. These must have come from the invasions of Korea led by Toyotomi Hideyoshi in 1592–8, which resulted in the transmission to Japan of many looted books (§7.1.2). Since Ieyasu himself declined to take part in the invasion, it must be supposed that they were donated to him by others who did participate.[25]

In 1602 Ieyasu established a repository at Fujimi no tei 富士見亭 in Edo castle, to which his books and his treasured paintings and scrolls were transferred later that year. In 1607, on his retirement to Sunpu (=Shizuoka), he established another library there taking some of his books from Edo with him, and it is from this time that he devoted himself to book collecting, with the assistance of Hayashi Razan and Konchiin Sūden, who acted as librarians. To the substantial collection of Korean imprints he already had he now added freshly imported Ming editions. Also, he was continuing to receive tributary gifts of books, such as the thirteenth-century copy of *Ise monogatari* in the hand of Fujiwara no Teika, which was given to him in 1614 by his son and successor as shōgun, Hidetada.[26]

---

[24] *KT* 38: 341.
[25] Kawase 1934: 1–8.
[26] Kawase 1934: 9–10.

In 1614 he sought information about the rare books and manuscripts in the collections of religious institutions and members of the nobility in Kyoto. Armed with that information he then put pressure upon the owners to make their hidden family treasures available for the purpose of having copies made. Ten monks with good calligraphic hands were recruited from each of the five Gozan temples in Kyoto, and they were set to work in the Nanzenji for a year, making one copy each for the court in Kyoto, for the Edo castle library and for his own collection at Sunpu. On 1615.4.2 a set was sent to Ieyasu at Sunpu, and in the same year or in 1616 it appears that some books he had kept in Nijō castle in Kyoto were also moved to Sunpu. In spite of his concern to build up his library at Sunpu, however, he did not neglect the Edo collection, for he sent Hidetada some books which were not available in Edo, most notably 28 Korean editions and 2 Ming editions of Chinese works, which he sent in 1614. In 1616 Ieyasu died, and Hidetada ordered Razan to deal with the collection at Sunpu. Certain early Japanese books and manuscripts were to be sent to Edo, while the remainder were divided up between the three collateral Tokugawa houses of Owari, Kii and Mito.[27]

In 1633 the Edo collection began its transformation from the shōgun's personal library into the Bakufu Library when the first four commissioners of books (*shomotsu bugyō* 書物奉行) were appointed to care for it and it thus became a part of the Bakufu's administrative apparatus. One of them was on duty each day in rotation, and since the work in time became too much for one, four assistants (*dōshin* 同心) were added to the establishment in 1693. Later there were further increases in the numbers of men in both positions, until in 1866 the office of commissioner of books was abolished and the assistants took over, under the supervision of the Bakufu Academy. The reasons for this change are unclear, but must be connected to the crisis facing the Bakufu, which was shortly to collapse.[28]

On 1639.8.11 a fire destroyed all the buildings in the main part of Edo castle, including the library. All the books, however, were moved out of danger and, as the diarist put it, 'the old books of our country for which Ieyasu and his successors had with divine favour searched the land since the Keichō and Genna eras [1596–1624]' were saved.

---

[27] Kawase 1934: 10–11, 13–22; *KSZ* 2: 228–38; Fukui 1980: 34–6.
[28] *KT* 39: 615, 52: 76–7; Fukui 1980: 18–28; Mori Junzaburō 1933: 28.

The decision had already been made to construct new library buildings at Momijiyama 紅葉山 in the grounds of the castle, and later in the year the Edo collection was transferred to its new and permanent home. This collection rapidly developed, and it is now known as the Momijiyama Bunko, although prior to 1868 it was referred to simply as Gobunko 御文庫, 'the exalted library [of the shōgun]'. Over the course of the Tokugawa period more buildings were added for storage as the collection grew, and the Library survived all the fires that afflicted Edo.[29]

The main responsibility of the library was providing books for the use of the shōgun. Other members of the Bakufu's administrative apparatus, daimyō and the commissioners of books themselves were also allowed to borrow books, but the shōgun's needs and wants had priority. Thus on 1708.9.14 Hayashi Hōkō 林鳳岡, the head of the Bakufu Academy, borrowed a copy of *Tōbu jitsuroku* 東部実録, a manuscript account of the reign of Tokugawa Hidetada, but on 1709.2.26 the shōgun himself requested to see it so it was hurriedly recovered and two days later delivered to him; he did not return it for nearly four years.[30]

Early in 1716 the direct line of shōgunal descent came to an end with the death of the child shōgun Ietsugu, and in the fifth month Yoshimune, head of the Kii branch of the family and the daimyō of the Kii domain, became shōgun. This caused an immediate acceleration in the pace of work at the library. In the modern printed edition of the Library's records, the first five months of that year occupy just 15 pages, while the rest of the year fills 123, with the sixth month alone filling 35. Yoshimune's personal and determined engagement with the library began on 1716.6.3, when he asked if there was a catalogue of the contents. The book commissioners informed him that there was a catalogue compiled by Hayashi Hōkō, and later the same day he asked to see it. It had actually been compiled in 1680 on Bakufu orders, and since it took the form of a book it was embarrassingly out of date and full of slips of paper that had been stuck in giving the titles of new acquisitions in order to keep it up to date. Nevertheless, it was of course presented to the shōgun. On the following day he ordered 15 books, including a book on the battle of

---

[29] *KT* 40: 144, 148; Fukui 1980: 10–18.
[30] *DNKS Bakufu shomotsukata nikki* 1: 5–6, 42.

Sekigahara at which Ieyasu had vanquished his rivals, a collection of the rules and regulations drawn up since Ieyasu's time (*Keichō irai shohatto* 慶長以来諸法度), and a number of books on shōgunal ceremonial.[31]

It was also under Yoshimune that many of the policies that determined the running of the library were put in place, and in terms of new acquisitions he seems to have been the most active of the 14 shōguns after Ieyasu. Books were acquired by having manuscript copies made of books in other libraries, by confiscation, by donation, and by purchase. An instance of the first occurred in 1735 when the commissioners were ordered to make good the defective copy of Fujiwara no Teika's *Meigetsuki* by copying the missing parts from the copy held by the Mito domain, which was brought to Edo for this purpose. Confiscations only occurred incidentally, as when an Osaka merchant had all his possessions confiscated in 1740 on account of some transgression, or when Takahashi Kageyasu 高橋景保, who was himself a commissioner of books and Bakufu Astronomer (Tenmongata), was imprisoned in 1828 for his part in the von Siebold affair. In each case their collections were investigated and a few choice specimens taken into the Library. The most significant of the many donations was that of Mōri Takanaka 毛利高翰, who in 1828 presented 20,000 volumes from the personal collection of his grandfather, Mōri Takasue, the daimyō of Saiki domain in Kyūshū: they were all Chinese books and included 4,150 volumes of the Daoist canon.[32]

Purchase was, however, the main mechanism by which books entered the Library. From 1639, if not earlier, this was conducted at Nagasaki by the Bakufu censors who monitored incoming cargoes of books from China to prevent books concerning Christianity from entering Japan (§§7.1.3 & 8.1.1). The Library took large numbers of books from these cargoes up to 1662, after which orders were much reduced. However, Yoshimune's accession brought with it a dramatic increase in the numbers of books taken. After relaxing the strict censorship rules for imported Chinese books in 1720, orders began to rise in 1723, reaching a peak of 307 in 1726. He personally examined

---

[31] *DNKS Bakufu shomotsukata nikki* 2: 17–20.
[32] *DNKS Bakufu shomotsukata nikki* 11: 27, 16: 69; Fukui 1980: 54; Mori Junzaburō 1933: 54, 153–4 and 253 n. 56.

the catalogues of Chinese books on offer and selected many of practical use, such as copies of the Qing statutes and books on medicine, astronomy and administration. He did not, the Bakufu diarist tells us, choose literary works but only books that had a bearing on governance.[33]

Three commercial booksellers had access to the Library and were known as *goshomotsushi* 御書物師. They were Izumoji Bungorō 出雲寺文五郎, Yamagataya Iemon 山形屋伊右衛門 and Tōhon'ya Seibee 唐本屋清兵衛, who was, as his name suggests, a specialist in books from China. When their special status was made formal is unknown, but in 1714 all three were officially informed of the appointment of a new commissioner of books and they evidently enjoyed privileged access to the Library by then. In time Tōhon'ya and Yamagataya went out of business and were not replaced, and only the Izumoji establishment survived to the end. In addition to fulfilling the commissioners' orders for books to be purchased in Japan, they also assisted with the regular airings of books, undertook the preparations of bindings, and disposed of duplicates, defective books and other books no longer wanted.[34]

It is thought to have been Yoshimune who insisted that only 'good copies' were acceptable for the Library, although there is no good evidence to support this and it is unclear what it meant and what changes in practice might have occurred later. It certainly seems to have been true that in general Chinese books printed in Japan were not sought by the Library, except in the case of editions published by the Bakufu itself or by the domains. In 1816 when the commissioner of books placed an order with the official booksellers for four Chinese books, he made it clear that copies with Japanese seals of ownership or inscriptions were unacceptable, although there would be no problem if they contained inscriptions written by Chinese owners. This indicates that the Library had become so purist as to disdain Chinese books that had passed through the hands of Japanese collectors.[35]

---

[33] *KT* 46: 243; Ōba 1984: 187–200, 227–95; Henderson 1970–71. The figures given for books imported in given years depends upon Ōba's hypothesis that the quantities of books mentioned in Gobunko mokuroku 御文庫目録 relate to books despatched each year from Nagasaki to the Library.
[34] Fukui 1980: 23–4; Mori Junzaburō 1933: 70–71, 76–7. On Tōhon'ya Seibee, see also Ōba 1984: 184–6.
[35] Fukui: 30–31.

The fundamental character of the collection was sinological. Mori's examination of the last catalogue, compiled by the commissioners of books and the head of the Bakufu Academy in 1864–6, reveals that there were over 107,000 bound volumes and about 6,000 items in other formats. Of these over 65% were sinological, mostly imports from China, and the percentage rises to 85% if the documentary items related to the Tokugawa house itself are excluded. This is not to say that no current Japanese books at all were acquired, for the records of borrowing by the shōguns and of purchases made show that some commercially published Japanese books were indeed purchased, and not on sinological subjects. Yoshimune himself, the official diarist recorded, read not only sinology and early Japanese literature but even the populist works of Kaibara Ekken and the classic farming manual *Nōgyō zensho* (1697). Nevertheless, it is a fact that Japanese books were heavily outnumbered by the sinological collections.[36]

In spite of the overwhelming sinological orientation of the Library, however, the growing significance of Western books was also represented. Dutch books and maps found their way into the shōgun's library as early as the seventeenth century, and by 1836 the collection included Engelbert Kaempfer's *Geschichte und Beschreibung von Japan* (1777–9), a number of Russian books and maps, a few English dictionaries and a number of Dutch works. The Institute for the Investigation of Foreign Books (Bansho shirabesho), established by the Bakufu in 1855, and its successor institutions possessed by 1868 more than 3,600 books in Western languages, mostly in Dutch but some in French and English. The bulk of these are nineteenth-century works and were presumably acquired either via the Dutch factory on Deshima or, after 1854, from Westerners in Japan and returning members of overseas missions.[37]

The Library survived intact and *in situ* until 1884, although the government agencies responsible for it went through numerous changes. Fukui has traced the administrative history in detail and it

---

[36] Fukui 1980: 32–3; e.g., *KT* 46: 235; *DNKS Bakufu shomotsukata nikki* 1: 39–40, 74, etc.

[37] Fukui Tamotsu 福井保, *Naikaku Bunko shoshi no kenkyū* 内閣文庫書誌の研究, *NSGT* 12 (1980), 91–128; Nichiran Gakkai 日蘭学会 ed., *Edo bakufu kyūzō ransho sōmokuroku* 江戸幕府旧蔵蘭書目録, Edo jidai nichiran bunka kōryū shiryōshū 2 (Yoshikawa Kōbunkan, 1980).

need not be rehearsed here. It is significant, however, that whereas the Bakufu librarians had impressed no seal of ownership in the Library's books, the various Meiji institutions in charge of them began impressing seals identifying them as former Momijiyama books. Their identity and the integrity of the collection were respected in spite of the collapse of the régime that had nurtured them. After Edo castle had become the new palace and its precincts full of government offices, a disastrous fire in 1873 destroyed almost everything, including more than 5,000 Library books which had been on loan to various government departments, but the Library escaped damage. In 1884 a new government library was established, which the following year took the name it still has, the Cabinet Library (Naikaku Bunko), and the Momijiyama books became part of the foundation collection.[38]

Fukui has argued that the Momijiyama Bunko had all the functions of a modern reference library. In terms of staffing, cataloguing, custodianship and conservation this is true. It is also impressive that books could be borrowed, although it is a little alarming that the commissioners were allowed to take home for further study even priceless Song editions. However, in two respects the Library fails the test and reveals the character of the state it served.

Firstly, access was highly restricted. All loans were recorded in the Library diary, and from these it is clear that the principal users were the shōguns, the members of the Senior Council and of Bakufu institutions such as the Finance Office, the Academy, the Observatory and the Medical Academy, and the commissioners of books themselves. There are few cases of loans to daimyō, and when asked in 1791 who had been borrowing books recently outside the Bakufu, the commissioners replied that loans had only been made lately to the Observatory and the daimyō of the three collateral Tokugawa houses. Ogyū Sorai was probably not the only one to be resentful of the inaccessibility of the collections and to express the view that all sinologists should be able to have access to them. Books and knowledge may have been preserved, but while Ieyasu had made texts available by printing them, his successors in effect hoarded the texts and treated them with the same concern for status and hierarchy that permeated official Tokugawa society.[39]

---

[38] Fukui 1980: 130–8.
[39] Mori Junzaburō 1933: 75–6; Fukui 1980: 118–29; *NST* 36: 438.

Secondly, for all the magnificence of its rare book collections, the Library became increasingly eccentric and unrepresentative. At the time of its foundation there were few printed secular Japanese texts, but by the nineteenth century the commercial press in Japan had published a large body of scholarly editions, commentaries and studies on Chinese texts, not to mention early Japanese texts. Few of these had a place in the Library, let alone the popular literature and other works issuing from the publishers of Edo. Eccentric though it was in rejecting even Japanese sinology, the sinophile orientation of course mirrored the educational philosophy of the Bakufu, and so the nearest approximation to a national repository of books in the Tokugawa period came to be dominated by imports.

BIBLIOGRAPHY

The official records of the shogunal library are extant for the years 1706–1857, though the years 1828–30, 1832–40, 1844–6, 1848–9 and 1854–5 are missing: the library records are being printed in *DNKS Bakufu shomotsukata nikki*, 18 vols to date (up to 1745); it will be many years before this series is completed, but selected extracts from the whole are contained in Mori Junzaburō 1933; on the library see also Fukui 1980. On Ieyasu's collecting, see Ono Noriaki 1978: 151–94, Kawase 1934: 1–5. Kondō Seisai's writings are contained in *KSZ*.

9.2.2 *Institutional libraries*

After the Bakufu Library the most important collection in Edo was that of the Bakufu Academy. The Academy had been founded in 1630 as the private school of Ieyasu adviser, Hayashi Razan, with a grant of land and money from the Bakufu, and it was closely connected with the Seidō 聖堂, or 'Sages' Hall', the shrine to Confucius. It gradually evolved into an institution intimately associated with the Bakufu, and in 1797 it came directly under the control of the Bakufu under the new name of Shōheizaka Gakumonjo 昌平坂学問所. Similarly, what eventually became the Academy Library started life as the private library of Hayashi Razan, who had already amassed a considerably personal collection by 1604 and who was appointed Ieyasu's librarian at Suruga in 1608.

The greater part of Razan's collection was destroyed in the fire that devastated Edo in 1657, and he died just days later. In a move that bespoke the semi-official nature of the library by this stage, in the following year the shōgun Ietsuna ordered the librarians of the Bakufu Library to give Razan's son and heir, Gahō, 60 duplicates from the Momijiyama Bunko and the substantial sum of 500 *ryō* with which to purchase replacements. The power of the state also helped the Hayashi library in another way. In 1662 Gahō was ordered to undertake a scholarly history of Japan, which was eventually completed in 1670 and presented to the shōgun as *Honchō tsugan* 本朝通鑑. Since the project was being undertaken at the Bakufu's behest, shōgunal retainers and daimyō in Edo were required to submit lists of the Japanese books they owned and temples and shrines were required to submit their diaries. Two copies of relevant items submitted were taken, with no apology to the owners, one of which remained in the Hayashi library while the other went to the Bakufu Library.[40]

In 1797, the library, together with the school, came under the direct control and financial support of the Bakufu. It received duplicate or unwanted books from the Bakufu Library, and a substantial sum for the purchase of Chinese books from Nagasaki. Its association with the state went considerably further in 1842 when the Academy was, under the Tenpō reforms, made responsible for secular censorship: the library benefited incidentally from this onerous new duty, for the new legislation stipulated for the first time that one copy of each work approved for publication had to be deposited with the Academy (§8.1.2).[41]

In 1800 the library established a set of rules to regulate the use of books, and as these evolved it became systematized in ways that are barely distinguishable from Meiji libraries. Thus staff were appointed to handle loans, and borrowers were required to affix their personal seal to borrowing slips recording the title of the book, the number of volumes and the date it was to be returned on. However, it remained the case that the library was open only to the Academy staff and students.[42]

While the Academy in Edo was closely associated with the

---

[40] Ono Noriaki 1978: 195–212; *KSZ* 3: 196.
[41] *DNKS Shichū torishimari ruishū* 18: 124–32, 135–7; *NKSS* 7: 496.
[42] Ono Noriaki 1978: 195–252. For various versions of the regulations see *NKSS* 7: 212, 502–4.

Bakufu and its educational policy for samurai, the domains established their own academies (*hankō* 藩校), in some cases not until the final years of the Tokugawa period, and they responded to their own perceptions of need. Sinology was of course dominant, and some schools opted for Zhu Xi orthodoxy from the time of their foundation, such as the Meirindō 明倫堂 in Kanazawa, which was founded in 1792. Other schools included studies in Japanese history or even, in the nineteenth century, Western studies, usually medical or military science. Since all of them valued book learning, they had need of libraries and detailed record has survived of many of them. At the Meirindō, for example, students were expected to provide their own copies of the basic texts studied in class, such as the *Five Classics* and the *Four Books* of Confucianism, or, in the case of Japanese texts in Chinese, *Kojiki* and *Nihon shoki*. They were allowed to borrow from the library, and teachers were allowed to take books home. At the Sakura 佐倉 domain school even students were allowed to take books home, provided that they entered the details in a borrowing register, and it was doubtless because they tended to allow borrowing that most domain academies impressed heavy and imposing seals of ownership in their books. Although it is probable that sinological texts formed the bulk of all domain school libraries, many were eclectic as well. The Tatebayashi 館林 domain academy, which was only founded in 1846, possessed 220 Chinese books, plus an indeterminate number of Japanese texts and books concerning Western studies and military science. And even the Mito 水戸 domain school, founded by Tokugawa Nariaki in 1841, had Western books in its collection in spite of the nationalistic stance of its founder.[43]

Shintō shrines also began to maintain libraries during this period. Perhaps because of the weak textual traditions of Shintō, prior to the Tokugawa period there are few signs of shrine libraries. This is not to say that there were none, for we know that the Ise Jingū had one by the mid eighth century, and in 766 recorded some losses. However, established libraries like those of temples date mostly from the eighteenth century. Some of them acquired collections of rarities by donation, such as the Kashima shrine library, which was consulted

---

[43] Kasai 1960: 274–91 provides a useful table of all domain schools with their dates of foundation and intellectual orientation. On the Meirindō and other schools mentioned, see Ono Noriaki 1978: 409–25, 376–92, etc.

by the compilers of the great history of Japan, *Dainihonshi*, and in 1815 by Hanawa Hokiichi for the compilation of his huge collectanea, *Gunsho ruijū*.[44]

In Kyoto and Osaka shrines were used as libraries of deposit by the booksellers' guilds, which undertook to maintain the library buildings and assist with maintenance and conservation work. From the early eighteenth century publishers in Osaka and Kyoto donated a copy of each of their publications to the Kitano Tenmangū in Kyoto or, in Osaka, to either the Sumiyoshi shrine or the Tenmangū. The motive for this, piety aside, was the need to preserve a copy of every publication so that, if the blocks were burnt in a fire, at least one copy would be preserved which could be cannibalized to form the basis of a reprint using the *kabusebori* process (§5.2.1–2). In the case of the Sumiyoshi shrine the publishers explicitly reserved the right to retrieve books needed in such circumstances.[45]

The primary significance of the domain libraries lay in their geographical dispersion, for they maintained access to good collections of books even in regions far removed from the centres of book production. However, access was far from unrestricted and the collections were predominantly sinological, so the perception of 'books' that underlay these libraries was one that was exclusive and narrow in its focus. The shrine libraries were equally well dispersed, and often more diverse in their range of books, but the collections had no obvious constituency and as a result the shrine libraries functioned largely to preserve donated texts rather than to make them accessible.

BIBLIOGRAPHY

On the Academy library and the domain libraries, see the essays collected in Ono Noriaki 1978. Ono Noriaki 1952 does not always indicate his sources but covers the full range of libraries in the Tokugawa period. On shrine libraries see Ono Noriaki 1978: 502–44.

---

[44] Ono Noriaki 1952: 202–22. On the Ise Jingū in 766 Ono cites *Jingū zōjiki* 神宮雑事記, a manuscript that is inaccessible to me.
[45] Ono Noriaki 1952: 201–22.

9.2.3 *Other libraries and collections*

It is obvious from the large number of seals of ownership that can be identified that there were numerous private libraries in the Tokugawa period. These testify to the holdings of scholars, doctors, popular writers and many unknown others. Very few of these collectors have left any hints about the acquisition or organization of their collections, and for the most part all that is left are the books, scattered often all over the world. A handful kept catalogues, but for the rest we have to wait until attempts have been made to reconstruct these libraries by taking note of seals of ownership.

In Ono's view private book-collecting, and especially the establishment of private libraries, only became widespread from the end of the seventeenth century. However, the output of the commercial publishing industry was already considerable by that time and it is likely that collecting established itself much earlier in the century. Ono treats as exceptions the cases of Suminokura Soan, who had an important part to play in the printing of the Saga editions in Kyoto (§4.2.3), and the Confucian scholar Matsushita Kenrin (1637–1703), but they are more likely to be simply cases that we happen to know of. Soan built up a substantial library on the foundations of a collection of Ming medical texts brought back from China by his grandfather, while Kenrin amassed 100,000 volumes, sending a man to Nagasaki every year to buy imports from China, and ungrudgingly lent them to other scholars.[46]

It is also Ono's view that the commoner residents of the towns only began to establish personal libraries from the end of the eighteenth century onwards, but again this is probably a matter of the paucity of records. We have no record, for example, of the collection of the Osaka merchant Kizuya Kichibei, but when in 1740 he suffered the confiscation of his worldly goods a catalogue of his books came to light and on the basis of this several rare items were chosen for the Bakufu library. And even before that it is difficult to suppose that a writer such as Ihara Saikaku did not have a library: he certainly used

---

[46] Ono Noriaki 1952: 143–66. It should be mentioned here that the common practice in the Tokugawa period of publishing books in multi-volume sets means that the number of volumes must be divided by 5 to arrive at an approximate number of titles.

an ownership seal, but no attempt has yet been made to reconstruct his library.[47]

By the end of the Tokugawa period there were certainly a number of very substantial collections in private hands. Ajiro Hironori 足代弘訓 (1784–?), who lived in Edo and moved in the circles of the eminent bibliographers Kariya Ekisai and Hanawa Hokiichi 塙保己一, attempted a ranking list of the biggest collections in Edo. The largest, he concluded, was that of the Bakufu Academy, but second was that of Morimura Jirōbei 守村次郎兵衛, one of the wealthy rice brokers catering to the needs of daimyō: he dabbled in haiku under the penname Hōgi 抱義 and, according to Ajiro, had 100,000 volumes of works in Japanese and Chinese. Third came Hachisuka Haruaki 蜂須賀治昭, daimyō of Awa domain, with 60–70,000; and fourth Hanawa Hokiichi himself with 60,000 and, according to Ajiro, nothing but books of quality. Another large collection was that of Oyamada Tomokiyo 小山田与清 (1783–1847), who used the commercial wealth of his adoptive family and an extensive network of contacts to build up a collection of some 50,000 volumes. It should be noted that Ajiro confined his ranking list to Edo, thus excluding the huge collection of the Maeda daimyō of Kanazawa, and that, presumably for reasons of tact, he did not include the Bakufu Library itself.[48]

The lending and borrowing of books by scholars and collectors in the absence of any public collections was an integral part of scholarly life, as was the need to copy out rare books by hand if printed copies could not be obtained. Oyamada Tomokiyo was unusually reflexive about his collecting, for he kept a diary recording the growth of his library and the exchanges that facilitated its growth, but he was also hard-headed enough to compile a set of rules for those borrowing from his library. Another working library engaged in the constant exchange of books was that of Yashiro Hirokata 屋代弘賢 (1758–1841), who worked in the Secretariat (Okuyūhitsu) in the shōgun's castle compiling the genealogical works *Hankanfu zokuhen* and *Kansei chōshū shokafu* and who also put his editorial skills to work assisting Hanawa Hokiichi with his *Gunsho ruijū*.[49]

---

[47] Ono Noriaki 1952: 150; Mori Junzaburō 1933: 58; for Saikaku's seals, see Shimabara 1985.
[48] Okamura 1996: 10; see *Ise no iezuto* in *Nihon geirin sōsho* 日本芸林叢書, 12 vols (Rikugōkan, 1927–9), 5: 2 (separately paginated).
[49] Okamura 1996: 11–20, 34–40. Oyamada's diary, *Yōshorō nikki* 擁書楼日記,

There were even in the Tokugawa period a few libraries explicitly accessible to the public at large. In Takayama in 1784 a local literary society constructed a library and stocked it with more than 1,000 volumes for the use of the neighbourhood. In 1818 officials of Fukuoka domain arranged for the construction of a library in the grounds of a shrine which was to be open to townsmen: it appears to have been closed because it was too popular and readers were neglecting their occupations to spend time in the library. And in Sendai domain a public library open to all and sundry was opened on private initiative in 1831 and subsequently supported by the domain.[50]

While many did make their books available to others, there were some who did not, and under this head must come not only the Bakufu Library itself but also those with charge of the 'secret traditions' (*hiden*), that is, manuscripts on medicine, the Nō, flower arrangement and other pursuits which were reserved for initiates. Inevitably, such collections were shrouded in secrecy and little is known about them as collections, even though the manuscripts may have survived. There were protests about the inaccessibility of books. Murata Harumi 村田春海, for example, railed against the practice of treating books as private possessions and hoarding them. He advocated a longer historical view of the past and the future of books, and he deplored the habit of keeping rare books secret and not showing them to others, which he claimed had led to the loss of some texts that could otherwise have been copied and could possibly have survived.[51]

BIBLIOGRAPHY

Ono Noriaki 1952 does not always indicate his sources but covers the full range of libraries in the Tokugawa period. Okamura 1996 is the first book to examine private collections and their functions, but he too does not adequately identify his sources.

---

is contained in *Kinsei bungei sōsho* 近世文芸叢書, 12 vols (Kokusho Kankōkai, 1910–12), 12: 208–391.

[50] Ono Noriaki 1952: 178–91.
[51] *NZT*, 1st series, 3: 274; Ono Noriaki 1954: 5–7.

9.2.4 *Commercial lending libraries*

In the second half of the Tokugawa period the most widespread means of access to books, especially but not exclusively popular and current works of fiction, was the network of *kashihon'ya*, commercial lending libraries, which spread to most parts of Japan. Readers were certainly accustomed by the end of the seventeenth century to renting books as an alternative to buying them, but at this stage this was just one of the facets of a bookseller's business, which might also include dealing in second-hand books and publishing. Pedlars dealing in books were in existence well before 1650, and they appear in a number of book illustrations in the second half of the century with packs of books on their back, the familiar trademark of *kashihon'ya* until the late nineteenth century (§5.1.1). In the course of the eighteenth century it became common for specialized *kashihon'ya* to be at work in the large towns, and in the nineteenth century these became widespread. They were observed by Western visitors, such as Edward Morse, who was professor of zoology at Tokyo Imperial University: 'One sees often on the streets a man with a huge pack on his back; this pack covered by a blue cloth reminding one of a hand organ. The bundle is a large stack of books; in truth, a circulating library. The books are carried everywhere, and as there is no illiteracy in Japan these books go to every house, new books being left and old ones taken away.'[52]

The earliest explicit reference to the commercial lending of books comes in a poem included in a collection published in 1703: 'The end of the year – when the bill comes in for books borrowed' (*karihon no kakidashi ga kuru toshizakai* 借り本の書出しか来ル年境イ). Apart from demonstrating that the practice of renting books was familiar enough to be the subject of comic verse, this indicates that a credit system was operated, and consequently that the proprietors had to be not just 'scholars of titles alone', as another verse put it, but also sufficiently literate and numerate to be able to keep accounting records.[53]

---

[52] Nagatomo 1982: 20-1, 26-32, 247-8; Morse: 1936: 120.
[53] The 1703 poem is contained in the collection *Sugatanazo*: *MZS* 14.2: 56b; *Haifū yanagidaru* 俳風柳多留, 5 vols, Iwanami Bunko (1950–56), 3: 39

Fig. 18 A label affixed to books by a haberdashery shop that also functioned as a *kashihon'ya*: the location is not specified, but the text requests customers to look after the book and not to sublend it.

Although *kashihon'ya* operated on a credit system they took the precaution of identifying their books with ownership seals. Since very few inventories of *kashihon'ya* collections, let alone complete collections themselves, have survived, the seals now provide valuable evidence of precisely what books circulated via this means and of how far they circulated in Japan. In addition to the seals of ownership, there are other unmistakable attributes of former *kashihon'ya* books which have reduced their value in the eyes of modern collectors but help to identify them. Given that they earned their keep by being circulated to as many customers as possible before being sold to another establishment, it is not surprising that the books themselves are often grubby and sometimes disfigured by graffiti. The graffiti may be lewd or take the form of uncomplimentary comments on the text, but in any case they reduced the contemporary resale value of the books and so, as a poem put it, '*kashihon'ya* are bothered by customers who are ready with the brush'. Many of them therefore attached printed labels to their books, often with a sketch of the owner in a supplicating position on his knees, requesting customers neither to sublend nor to scribble in the books they had borrowed.[54]

If it is not difficult to identify books from *kashihon'ya* collections, what sorts of books, then, did they deal with? There is no gainsaying that current or recent fiction formed an indispensible part of the stock, whatever other books might also be on offer. The earliest fictional works which can now be identified as having regularly been a part of *kashihon'ya* collections are the works of Ihara Saikaku. For the most part dating individual *kashihon'ya* is difficult, but given that Saikaku's literary reputation did not last long and he was rediscovered in the early Meiji period, it is probable that the seals impressed in his books are those of contemporary establishments, dating from the first decades of the eighteenth century or earlier. For example, a copy of his *Shoen ōkagami* carries the seals of two *kashihon'ya* in Nagasaki, having evidently passed from one to the other once no further customers could be found for it, and two of his other works carry the seals of Wakayama establishments, one a dealer in second-hand books and the other a haberdasher, both evidently renting books out as a sideline.

---

[54] *Haifū yanagidaru* (see previous note), 5: 156; for some examples of the labels see Nagatomo 1982: 244–5, Nogami 1975, and Kornicki, 'Some former *kashihonya* books in the Library of the School of Oriental and African Studies', *BSOAS* 43 (1980): 544–7.

It appears from these examples that Saikaku's works may have travelled far in his time.[55]

The combination of trades is made unequivocally clear in a seal from a Nagasaki establishment indicating that in addition to books for rent they also stocked a proprietary brand of toothpaste. Fiction not only continued to dominate the book rental market, but in the early nineteenth century came to depend on the existence of *kashihon'ya* for the sales and circulation of the long historical novels now known as *yomihon*. Bakin, the leading writer of *yomihon*, refers constantly in his diaries to the essential role of *kashihon'ya*, and his contemporary, Santō Kyōden, likening books to brides, wrote that, 'the publisher is the bride's parents, the readers are the bridegroom, and the *kashihon'ya* is the go-between.' Serialised forms of fiction, such as the multi-part *ninjōbon* and *gōkan*, were in the 1830s and 1840s commonly handled by *kashihon'ya*, as numerous internal references indicate.[56]

Customers could also rent erotica, travel guides and various other printed books, and in making these works and fiction available *kashihon'ya* were already fulfilling a marginally subversive role in Tokugawa society, given the Bakufu's expressed views on popular commercial publications. What confirms this perception is the fact that *kashihon'ya* also handled unpublished manuscripts. These were not all illicit, but some provincial establishments carried in their stocks local histories which it would have been imprudent to publish since they contained references to Tokugawa Ieyasu (§8.1.2). Thus a copy of *Mitsubo kikigaki* 三壷聞書 was circulated by several *kashihon'ya* in Kanazawa, including one that supplied books to the local daimyō: this is a history of the Kaga domain, which was centred on Kanazawa, and could not avoid mention of Ieyasu.[57]

---

[55] Hayashi and Kornicki 1991: #626; for the other two works, copies of *Kōshoku seisuiki* and *Saikaku okimiyage* in Ōsaka Furitsu Nakanoshima Toshokan, see the respective volumes of *Kinko bungaku shiryō ruijū* 近古文学資料類従, Saikakuhen 12 and 15 (Benseisha, both 1975).

[56] For the toothpaste seal, see vol. 5 of the copy of *Yōkyoku hyakumanguruma* 謡曲百万車 in Tenri Library (91362.321). On Bakin see Hamada 1953, and the Kyōden quotation is from *Sōchōki* 双蝶記, in *Kyōden kessakushū* 京伝傑作集, Teikoku Bunko (Hakubunkan, 1893), 372–3; *NKBT* 64: 383; *NKBZ* 47: 430.

[57] For some examples, see Kornicki, 'Some former *kashihonya* books in the Library of the School of Oriental and African Studies', *BSOAS* 43 (1980): 544–7, and 'Some books from Japanese circulating libraries in the British Library', *British*

Fig. 19 Seal of a *kashihon'ya* called Kameya operating in Watauchi in the province of Shinano in central Japan. It is impressed frequently throughout a copy of *Shūyū kidan*, a work of fiction published in 1806.

Many of the manuscripts were, however, illicit and were named as such in the list of banned books printed by the booksellers' guild in Kyoto in 1781 (§8.1.2). They were banned, for the most part, because they concerned current or recent scandals, sometimes in a more or less fictionalized form. *Kashihon'ya* were implicated in number of these cases. The practice of lending out illicit manuscripts was clearly widespread by 1790, for included in the Kansei Reforms was an edict expressly stating that it was forbidden to rent out manuscripts dealing with 'baseless rumours'. In 1805 a number were caught making available copies of a manuscript account of a sensational sex scandal involving ladies of the shōgun's castle and the abbot of a fashionable temple, and 15 were sentenced to spells in handcuffs (§3.3). Surviving manuscripts of this sort often carry the seals of *kashihon'ya*, in spite of the apparent risks involved. A few examples will suffice: the famous *kashihon'ya* Daisō of Nagoya (see below) owned a number of these manuscripts, including *Kinshi kaseiroku* 金氏苛政録 which deals with a scandal involving the Kanamori daimyō. And Ōshio Heihachirō's rebellion in Osaka in 1837 was the subject of several manuscript works, including one that circulated in Odawara. It is clear, then, that *kashihon'ya* played a subversive role in the Tokugawa period in circulating illicit books that undermined the Bakufu's attempt to restrict the flow of information relating to the Bakufu itself or to the domains (§3.3).[58]

The largest *kashihon'ya* of all in the Tokugawa period was the Daisō 大惣 establishment in Nagoya founded by Ōnoya Sōhachi in 1767, which uniquely maintained stationary premises to which

---

Library journal 6 (1980): 188–98. The copy of *Mitsubo kikigaki* mentioned is in Kanazawa Shiritsu Toshokan.

[58] Miyatake 1926: 59–60; Kornicki 1982; *Kinshi kaseiroku* in Kyōto University Library (4–41 シ 7); for the many other such manuscripts owned by Daisō, see Shibata 1983 1: 806–11; Hayashi and Kornicki 1991: #1301.

customers had to come. It was visited by numerous writers, including Kyokutei Bakin, and patronised by famous Nagoya scholars and writers such as Hosono Yōsai and Tsubouchi Shōyō. The catalogue of its holdings prepared in 1898 lists some 20,000 titles with a further 7,000 duplicates for items in heavy demand. The range of books was extensive, covering medicine, Buddhism and classical Japanese literature, but sinology was not represented and more than a quarter were works of fiction from the Tokugawa period, the mainstay of any *kashihon'ya* business. The distribution of the duplicates was even more revealing: there were a remarkable 17 copies of *Tsurezuregusa*, and ten of *Ehon taikōki* (1797), the fictionalized and illustrated biography of Hideyoshi mentioned elsewhere (§8.1.2), six of Ikku's *Hizakurige*, five each of *Hakkenden* and two other of Bakin's novels, and five each of *Umegoyomi* and another of Shunsui's *ninjōbon*. So although Daisō was exceptional in size and range, it is abundantly clear that the weight of the demand rested with current fiction, just as was the case with all *kashihon'ya*. Similarly, Daisō also stocked erotica and numerous manuscripts on forbidden topics, such as foreign travel by castaways and domestic political scandals.[59]

The impact of *kashihon'ya* on Tokugawa society was profound. By the nineteenth century at least they had spread to all castle towns and even to what is now called Hokkaidō, as the surviving seals of ownership demonstrate. The social range of their customers stretched from daimyō residences to the entertainment quarters and the residential districts of the urban commoners, and the delivery system made books more readily available to women readers. The fees they charged, between 35% and 15% of the purchase price of a given book, and the density of the trade, with several hundred operating in both Edo and Osaka alone by the 1830s, expanded the range of reading possibilities for all readers, and enabled those of modest means to keep abreast of literary trends, although higher fees were usually charged for the latest works of fiction. They also made knowledge of scandals easily available, and, by circulating the literature of Edo in the second half of the period, they helped unify literary

---

[59] Nagatomo Chiyoji, 'Ōnoya Sōhei no kashihon ni tsuite' 大野屋惣兵衛の貸本について, *Aichi Kenritsu Daigaku jūshūnen kinen ronbunshū* 愛知県立大学十周年記念論文集 (Nagoya, 1975), 75–84; Nagatomo 1982: 153–8. For Hosono Yōsai's record of borrowing an account of the revenge of the 47 rōnin, see *NS* 19: 326.

culture and make the tastes of Edo increasingly the tastes of all Japan.[60]

Daisō and some of the larger establishments survived until well into the Meiji period, but by that time the heyday of *kashihon'ya* was long past. The numbers had gone into a decline, owing to the publication of newspapers containing serialized fiction and the availability of cheap movable-type reprints, but *kashihon'ya* continued to peddle the light fictional genres of the Tokugawa period for some time, and numerous distinguished writers, politicians and others became extensively familiar with such literature in the 1860s and 1870s. It was precisely for this reason that in 1876 a journalist proposed that the lending of fiction by *kashihon'ya* be banned, on the grounds that *ninjōbon* and other fictional genres of the late Tokugawa period corrupted the young and distracted them from the more useful studies of geography and mathematics they ought to be applying themselves to. In the 1880s it became more common for *kashihon'ya* to stock translations of Western literature and the works of contemporary writers, and a handful established themselves as businesses catering to the new student market and offering scholarly or instructive books, or even books in English. Public libraries were still few in the 1880s and *kashihon'ya* were often the only alternative to purchase; and even in the few places where libraries were functioning it was unusual for them to lend books, so there was a commercial space in which *kashihon'ya* could operate. But as the century drew to a close they found it increasingly difficult to compete with public institutions offering access to books free of charge.[61]

---

[60] Nagatomo 1982: 4160–62, 186, etc.; Hironiwa 1967: 194–6. There is good evidence to indicate that there were 656 *kashihon'ya* in Edo in 1808: *Saikaku: kenkyū to shiryō* 西鶴研究と資料, Kokubungaku ronsō 1 (Shibundō, 1957), 176–7.

[61] *Tōkyō nichinichi shinbun*, 4 March 1876, 211–2; for the identity of the writer of this piece, see *Chihōbetsu Nihon shinbunshi* 地方別日本新聞史 (Nihon Shinbun Kyōkai, 1956), 293–4. Kornicki 1980: 336–7, 339–42; Kutsukake 1982: 200–24.

BIBLIOGRAPHY

Nagatomo 1982 is the first substantial study of *kashihon'ya*, but see also Nogami 1975 and Hironiwa Motosuke 1967; on Daisō, see A. L. Markus, 'The Daisō lending library of Nagoya, 1767-1899' *GLJ* 3 (1989): 5-34, and Shibata 1983. On *kashihon'ya* in the Meiji period, see Kutsukake 1982: 200-24 and Kornicki 1980.

9.3 OWNERSHIP

A characteristic of East Asian books is that they frequently carry signs left by previous owners, not only in the form of handwritten inscriptions and annotations, which are universal, but especially in the impressions of seals of ownership, or *zōshoin* 蔵書印. Personal and institutional seals were in use in the Han dynasty in China, albeit not for the purpose of indicating ownership of books, and the practice spread to Japan and Korea and other countries on the periphery of Chinese civilization. Many Nara-period documents contained in the Shōsōin, for example, carry impressions of government seals, not of course to indicate ownership but to confirm their authenticity and status as official papers.

The practice of using seals in books began in the Nara period in Japan, and it eventually became much more widespread than in either China or Korea. They were used to assert ownership of the books and thus to prevent loss through inadvertent or deliberate misappropriation. For this they were an effective means, since they cannot easily be removed: in some books there are obvious signs that the impression of a seal has been removed by erasure, but this is less common than resorting to scissors to excise a seal or to the brush to obliterate it. This was not done necessarily for dishonest reasons, for the circulating libraries known as *kashihon'ya*, which customarily passed books from one to another, sometimes found it convenient to avoid confusion about the current owner in this way.

The oldest impression of a seal used as a *zōshoin* seems to be that of emperor Shōmu's consort, Kōmyō, which is found in a copy of a Chinese work allegedly in her hand. But this is a rare and isolated instance. Better attested is the case of Hino Sukenari 日野資業 (988–1070), who in 1051 retired to Uji and put his books in order, impressing in them a vermilion seal reading 日野法界寺文庫, 'Hino's

Hōkaiji library', of which one example survives. In the Muromachi period there are a few instances of daimyō using seals, but individual *zōshoin*, which are usually limited to the lifetime of the owner, were still a rarity.[62]

It was primarily in the Tokugawa and Meiji periods that Japanese book-owners, institutional and individual alike, enthusiastically imposed their presence on the books they owned. They did so more visibly than collectors in the West, who attach their ex-libris to the inside front cover of their books, by making that presence felt at the start of the text itself. This is partly a matter of security and the assertion of ownership, but there is more to it than that, for, as with paintings, seal impressions become a text in themselves, telling the story of the transmission of that copy of that particular book and often interacting with the text by giving it a context. A difficult sinological text sporting an imposing domain library seal immediately betrays its ideological and cultural associations with the mostly sinological curricula in use in such schools; and the manuscript of a banned book carrying a lending library seal is a token of the literary underground which relied on such means for books to be circulated, or indeed 'published'. Seal impressions have for the most part been neglected in published catalogues, while guides to seals usually do not mention the books they are to be found in, let alone the location of the copy in question. In this respect *Shoryōbu zōshoinfu*, an illustrated guide to the seal impressions found in books preserved in the Shoryōbu, breaks new ground, and it will over the coming years become increasingly possible to reassemble the libraries of the Tokugawa and Meiji periods, and to some extent those of earlier periods too.

Since seals of ownership came into widespread use in the Tokugawa period, books that frequently contain several of them, enabling its movements to be traced.[63] Usage of ownership seals dates from the very beginning of the period: the shōgunal adviser Hayashi Razan used his in a Ming herbal published in 1523, and the shōgunal library itself used one from the time of its foundation in 1639. Most daimyō tended to use large and imposing seals as a visual symbol of their

---

[62] Ono Noriaki 1954: 11–20; *Yōshū fushi* in 雍州府志 *ZZGR* 8: 144; Seki Yasushi 1951: 448–577.

[63] Ono Noriaki 1954: 92 traces the movements of the Tenmon edition of the Confucian *Analects* through five owners represented by their seals.

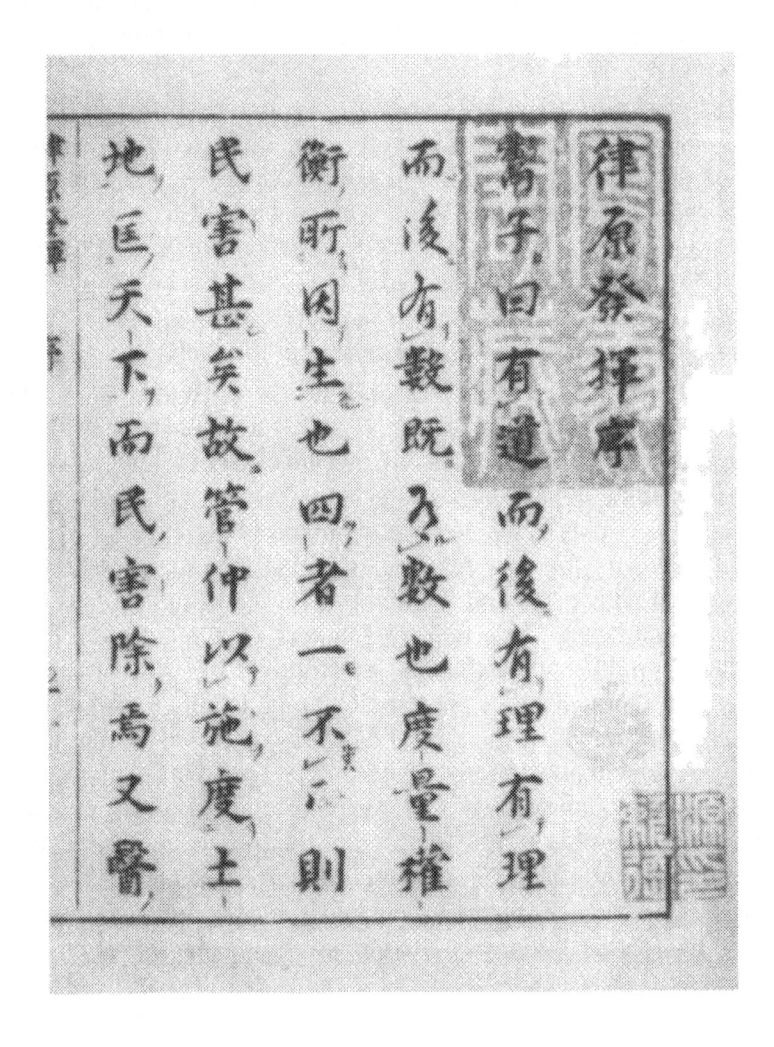

Fig. 20 The seal of Naitō Masaaki 内藤政陽 (1737–1781), daimyō of the Nobeoka domain in south-western Kyushu. The seal, in which the text appears in white on a vermillion ground, reads 'Hōshōkaku zō' 鳳翔閣蔵, Hōshō being one of his pennames. It is impressed in a copy of *Ritsugen hakki* 律原発揮, a study of measurements published in 1692: Hayashi and Kornicki 1991: #1910.

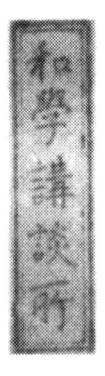

Fig. 21   The seal of the Wagaku Kōdansho, the institution for the study of Japanese texts established by Hanawa Hokiichi. It is impressed in a manuscript which he had intended to include in his collectanea *Gunsho ruijū* but which was evidently not returned to him or to his heirs and so was never included. Hayashi and Kornicki 1991: #1385.

status. By the end of the Tokugawa period seals were in widespread use by the various Bakufu academies, the domain schools, intellectuals and writers, and a variety of commercial enterprises engaged in lending books, from bookshops and circulating libraries to dry goods stores, tobacconists and pharmacists. In the late Tokugawa and Meiji periods a number of foreign bibliophiles began collecting Japanese books and a few of them had their own seals made. Léon de Rosny, who became the first professor of Japanese in Paris in 1868, identified himself with 「羅尼印」, and Ernest Satow with 「英国薩道蔵書」. Unfortunately, the seals used by foreign collectors are omitted from most guides to this subject.

How were the seals used? It was most common to impress them on the first page of the preface or of the text, where it would stand out more and not be lost if the book were rebound. Some commercial lenders of books, in the desire to assert their ownership as unmistakably as possible, marred the visual presentation of the text by impressing their seal in every conceivable place. The majority were impressed in vermilion, because the contrast with the colour of the text made them easily visible, although black was often used as well, especially by commercial enterprises, and in very rare instances other colours were also used. Almost all have a border, and a rectangular shape is most common; round or oval ones are also found, while some, especially writers, used the shape of a gourd or elephant. The inscribed texts are subject to great variation: most simply give the name of the individual or private library or institution followed by 蔵, 蔵書 or something similar to indicate ownership. Temple libraries often used seals containing the legend 'shutsumon o yurusazu' 不許出門,

indicating that the book was not to leave the temple. Some commercial seals, used by enterprises which also engaged in booklending, carry advertisments; some carry texts expressing the owner's delight in the possession of rare books, or desire that a descendant inherit the collection, or anxiety about the eventual dispersal of the collection; some Kokugaku scholars, such as Kamo Mabuchi, Kishimoto Yuzuru and Motoori Ōhira, made cultural statements on their seals by including some *waka* poetry, or a text in faked or authentic early scripts (*jindaimoji* and *man'yōgana*); and some seals, both private ones and ones used by lending libraries, request borrowers not to pass the book on to a third person, not to lick the finger when turning the pages, or not to fold the corners of pages.[64]

Ex-libris (*zōshohyō* 蔵書票) were not unknown in Japan in the Tokugawa period. A number of temples used them, particular those assocated with the Zōjōji in Edo and the Kenninji and Daigoji in the vicinity of Kyoto. They were usually attached to the front cover in a prominent manner and came with an injunction not to remove the book from the temple precincts. Personal book-plates with artistic pretensions only came into use in the late nineteenth century on the inspiration of Western examples.[65]

Many owners also imposed their presence on their books in another way, by adding punctuation in the case of Chinese texts, and by adding marginal comments, annotations or other inscriptions. These are collectively known as *shikigo* 識語. In some cases they replace the use of seals, and provide additional information: for example, Shikitei Sanba, a popular writer of comic fiction in the early nineteenth century, wrote in his copy of a *sharebon* published in 1751, 'I acquired this in the Kansei era [1789–1801] at a secondhand bookshop; owned by Shikitei'. Ryūtei Tanehiko, another popular writer, who came to grief in 1842 following the Tenpō reforms, was also a pioneer bibliographer and his inscriptions, which are gradually being gathered, are of particular importance because he had access to books and other documents that are now lost. *Shikigo* can add considerably to our understanding of the owner's intellectual development, and they

---

[64] Ono Noriaki 1954: 21–39, 40–50.
[65] Ono Noriaki 1954: 8; Hotta Ashio 堀田葦男, 'Wayō zōshohyō no koto' 和洋蔵書票の事, *Shomotsu tenbō* 5.3 (1935): 43–6 and accompanying illustrations.

LIBRARIES AND COLLECTORS 403

Fig. 22   Label attached to the front cover of a copy of *Hyakunin isshu Saga no yamafumi* 百人一首嵯峨の山ふみ, a commentary on Fujiwara no Teika's anthology *Hyakunin isshu*; it was published in 1816. The label identifies the book as the property of one of the subtemples of the Zōjōji 増上寺 in Edo and the legend at the top forbids its removal from the temple precincts. Hayashi and Kornicki 1991: #972.

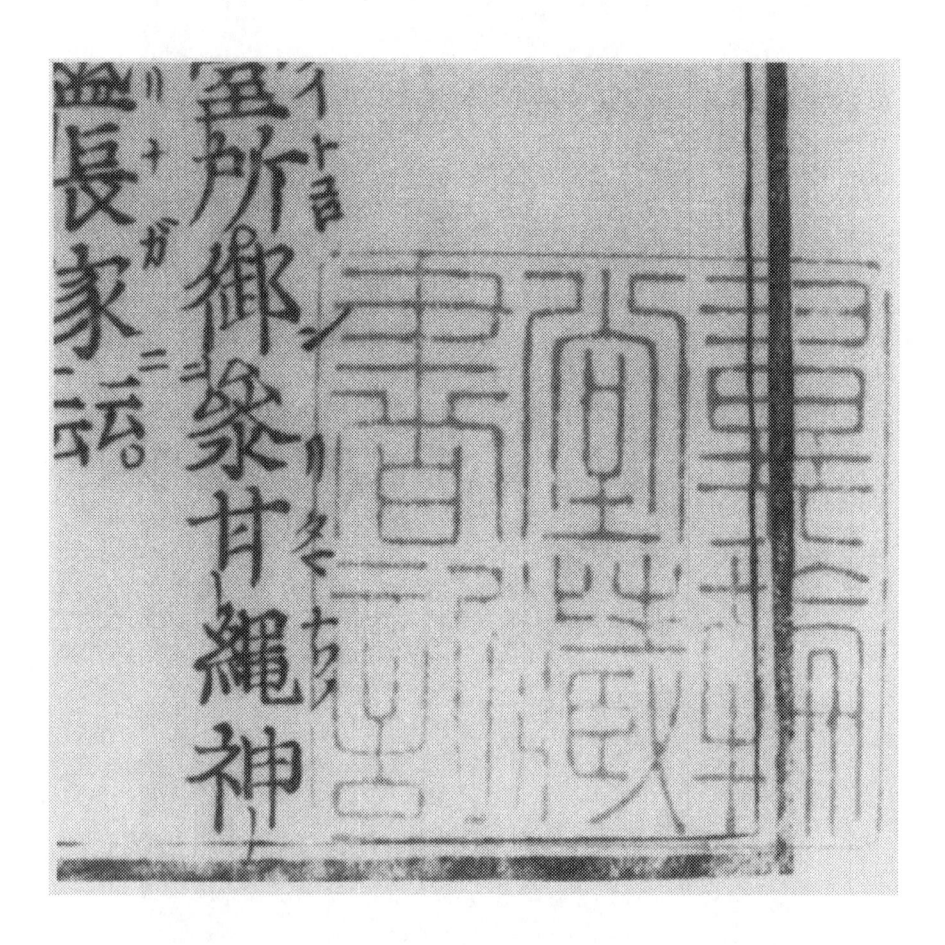

Fig. 23 The legend on this seal reads 'Yokurindō zōshoki' 翼輪堂蔵書記. The Yokurindō was the domain school of the Minakuchi 水口 domain in Ōmi province, to the east of Kyoto. The school was founded in 1855. It is impressed in a copy of *Shinkan Azuma kagami* published in 1626. Hayashi and Kornicki 1991: #1174.

have of course been used in some cases for just such purposes. Hitherto few efforts have been made to collect and reprint them, but the recently-published collected works of Ōta Nanpo 大田南畝 (1749–1823), who was both a Bakufu official and a popular writer, have included all those that could be found.[66]

Ōta Nanpo also illustrates another way in which collectors and scholars treated their books. In the absence of public libraries, and for those without access to the closed libraries of the Bakufu and the domain schools, it was common practice to borrow, lend and exchange books. In a letter he wrote in 1822 to Yamazaki Yoshishige, a pharmacist and scholar, he noted that he was returning some books that he had borrowed and expressed his willingness to exchange books. This practice has a long history, and we know that by the late seventeenth century there were networks of readers lending each other books in villages in the vicinity of Osaka (§6.2.2). Although widespread, the practice was not without its dangers. Motoori Norinaga bemoaned the bad habits of borrowers who often mistreated his books, and, as mentioned above, a number of seals requested borrowers to be careful with the books and not to sublend them. A collector who identified himself only as Fujii had a label printed for his books requesting borrowers to read carefully, to keep away from fire when reading, to use bookmarks rather than bending over the corners of pages and under no circumstances to sublend to third parties.[67]

BIBLIOGRAPHY

Ono Noriaki 1954 is the best study of *zōshoin*. *Shoryōbu zōshoinfu* 書陵部蔵書印譜, 2 vols, Zushoryō sōkan (Kunaichō Shoryōbu, 1996-) is the most sophisticated treatment yet of seal impressions, reproducing impressions of seals and identifying the books they are to be found in; it is a pity that foreigners' seals are excluded. Shimabara 1985 is an invaluable index to the texts of seal impressions. Bunkenka 1979–81 shows some of the deliberately imposing institutional *zōshoin* of the Meiji period. Nearly 400 are illustrated and identified in *KD* 8 (plates following p. 540). For help with reading the

---

[66] The *sharebon* owned by Sanba and some of the books owned by Tanehiko are in Cambridge University Library: see Hayashi and Kornicki 1991: #685, 771, 1012, 1057, 1080 & 1083. *ONZ* 19: 687–731. On Tanehiko's library see Satō Satoru 佐藤悟 1989, 'Ryūtei Tanehiko to sono zōsho' 柳亭種彦とその蔵書, in *KSS*, 337–49.

[67] *ONZ* 19: 302; Ono Noriaki 1954: 31–2; Fujii's label is found in the copy of *Edo suzume* in the Seikadō Bunko in Tōkyō.

texts of seals written in seal script, see Oka Shōji 丘襄二, *Tenkai jiten* 篆楷字典 (Kokusho Kankōkai, 1976).

9.4 THE MEIJI TRANSITION AND MODERN COLLECTIONS

The number of libraries and collections that have survived intact over the centuries is negligible. The years of internecine war in the Kamakura and Muromachi periods, the institutional upheavals of the Meiji period, the devastating Tokyo earthquake of 1921 and the bombing of the Second World War have all taken their toll, not to mention the attention of insects with a taste for paper. From the Nara period, the Shōsōin, which contains a few books as well as many documents, is the most famous survivor. From the Kamakura period the Kanazawa Bunko has survived, although without many of its finest books. And a few temple libraries have survived all this as well as the campaign against Buddhism of the 1870s. But the most significant literary collections to have weathered the centuries are undoubtedly the libraries of the Konoe 近衛 and Reizei 冷泉 aristocratic families of Kyoto, both of which date back to the Heian period. The Konoe family is descended from the Northern Branch (Hokke 北家) of the Fujiwara and the library, now known as the Yōmei Bunko 陽明文庫, contains the holograph of *Midō kanpakuki* 御堂関白記, the diary kept by one of the most distinguished members of the family, Fujiwara no Michinaga, during the years 995–1021. It also contains many other Japanese rarities from his time, and Chinese printed books of the Song, Yuan and Ming dynasties, though it is not clear when these were acquired.[68]

The Reizei family library probably owes its survival to the decision not to move to Tokyo after the Meiji Restoration. The family is descended from Fujiwara no Michinaga's sixth son, Nagaie 長家 (1005–1064), who was himself an accomplished poet, and it counts among its ancestors two of the most famous poets of the late Heian and early Kamakura periods, Fujiwara no Shunzei (1114–1204) and

---

[68] *KD* 14: 352 and supplement following p. 364; Kanda Kiichirō, 'Yōmei Bunko no kanseki ni tsuite' 陽明文庫の漢籍について, *Yōmei sōsho kokusho hen geppō* 陽明叢書国書篇月報 14 (1978): 1–2. Facsimiles of texts in the library are being published in the *Yōmei sōsho* series.

Fujiwara no Teika (1162–1241). The family archive became known in the Tokugawa period for the rich collection of books and documents dating from the time of Teika, including his important diary, *Meigetsuki*, and a copy of the first anthology of court poetry, *Kokin wakashū*, in his hand. As early as 1614 Ieyasu had requested permission to take a copy of *Meigetsuki*, which was accomplished at the Nanzenji using a team of copyists (§9.2.1). Later in the seventeenth century emperor Reigen placed a ban on use of the archive without permission from the throne in order to prevent losses, and although this ban was removed in the Meiji period, the collection remained virtually inaccessible until in 1981 the heirs named it the Shiguretei Bunko 時雨亭文庫, altered its legal status to preserve the collections, and began the process of making the contents, some 20,000 items, accessible to the public.[69]

These two aristocratic libraries, with their integrity as collections unscathed, survived not only through centuries of warfare and innumerable fires in Kyoto, but also through the upheavals surrounding the collapse of the Bakufu and the establishment of the early Meiji state. Those upheavals were undoubtedly the most serious interruption to the stability of book collections since the foundation of the Tokugawa Bakufu. The most obvious consequence of the shifting intellectual values and the impoverishment of large swathes of former samurai in the mid nineteenth century was the appearance on the antiquarian book market of huge collections of rarities. As yet this is a matter of hypothesis rather than demonstrable fact, for the only evidence we have is that of surviving books which were purchased on the open market at the time and which bear the ownership seals of samurai, domain schools and other institutions. It was in those years too that the market was distorted by the sudden and pressing demand for Western books, which pushed down the prices of older Japanese books. This was the very time when foreign visitors were just getting interested in Japanese books, or at least in Japanese book illustration. The shrewd book collecting of Adolf Nordenskiöld, Ernest Mason Satow, William George Aston, Basil Hall Chamberlain, Feliks Jasień-

---

[69] Tsunoda Bun'ei 角田文衞, 'Reizeike to Shiguretei Bunko' 冷泉家と時雨亭文庫, *Gakushikai kaihō* 学士会会報, 750 (1981): 57–62; some of the treasures are listed in Fukui Keiichi 福井恵一, 'Reizeike Shiguretei Bunko', *Kokubungaku* 26.16 (1981): 40–3; *KD* 14.698 and supplement following p. 700.

ski, Sergei Kitaev and Heinrich von Siebold, to name just a few of those who endowed European collections, would not have been possible were it not for these circumstances.

For the most part books have undergone a massive internal migration since the early Meiji period. The Bakufu academies and the domain schools were closed in or around 1868, and the institutions that succeeded them could not achieve stability in the administratively unsettled early years of the Meiji period. The contents of a few of the domain school libraries survived more or less intact in local prefectural libraries, while those of the Meirindō in Kanazawa were absorbed into the Sonkeikaku 尊経閣 library, the collection of Maeda Tsunanori (1643–1724) and his successors as daimyō of the Kaga domain, and are still intact in the Sonkeikaku in Tokyo. More often than not, however, the domain school libraries were broken up and divided amongst several institutions. And it is obvious from items in European libraries that some of their books were sold on the open market: for example, in 1879 Nordenskiöld purchased for 2 yen a copy of the 1724 Japanese edition of the Tang law code, *Da tang liu dian* 大唐六典, which bore an impression of the seal of the Zeze domain school near Kyoto.[70]

It was not only foreigners, of course, who took advantage of the topsy-turvy antiquarian book market. The artist Tomioka Tessai (1836–1924) was able to buy a Tang manuscript of the *Lotus sūtra*, a manuscript from the Nara period originally in the collection of the Hōryūji, and various other items with seals showing that they came from the libraries of religious institutions. Much the same is true of the collecting possibilities that the journalist Tokutomi Sohō and the Iwasaki family of industrialists found when building up their collections, which now constitute the Seikidō Bunko 成簣堂文庫 and the Seikadō Bunko 成嘉堂 respectively. It is evident from these as well as from other collections that many books from temple libraries came onto the market in the Meiji period. This is yet to be satisfactorily explained, but it is undoubtedly connected with the campaign against Buddhism in the early Meiji period which deprived many temples of their lands, their income and their property.[71]

---

[70] Edgren 1980: 326, #1010.
[71] Ōsaka Furitsu Toshokan, ed., *Tomioka Bunko zenpon shoei* 富岡文庫善本書影 (Kyōto: Kobayashi Shashin Seihansho shuppanbu, 1936), 1, 24, 49, 50–1, etc.

It is still difficult to grasp the extent of the internal migration of books over the last hundred years, or of the totality of institutions possessing rare pre-1868 books. The national catalogue of pre-modern books, *Kokusho sōmokuroku* (1963–76), covered only a limited range of institutions; this has been made good by *Kotenseki sōgō mokuroku* (1990), which covered a number of small and less well known institutions and discovered many works not recorded at all in its predecessor. But this is by no means the end of the story, for there are many local libraries, in small towns or cities or undistinguished temples, which contain books that would otherwise be lost. One example will suffice: in Tanabe the modest City Library and a small local temple both possess small collections of books published during the Tokugawa period, including some not otherwise recorded, and there are parallel cases in other towns and cities as well.

As a result of the collecting activities of many foreigners who visited Japan in the late nineteenth century, there was also a considerable migration of Japanese books overseas. The full scale of this is still unknown: most, but by no means all, of these books ended up in institutional collections, in national libraries, museums, galleries and university libraries. In the last twenty years most of the larger and more important such collections, with the exception of the Bibliothèque Nationale in Paris, have been fully described in print. From time to time some of the private collections have come onto the market, like the superb Donald and Mary Hyde Collection which was put together in the 1960s. Some of these books are reported to have been purchased by Japanese collectors and institutions and to have returned to Japan, while the equally fine collection of illustrated books assembled by Jack Hillier went into the British Museum before his death.[72]

The early years of the Meiji period literally left their mark on many collections as public institutions were dissolved, reorganised, amalgamated with others and went through innumerable changes of name, all necessitating, in the case of libraries, new ownership seals, and in the Meiji period these tended to be large and imposing. One example will suffice: the Gakushūin, an educational establishment for children of the nobility, was founded in 1847 in Kyoto; on 1868.1.15

---

[72] See the well-illustrated auction catalogue, Christies 1988: such catalogues are often the only record of particularly fine books.

it was renamed Daigakuryōdai and on 1868.9.18 renamed again Kangakusho, but on 1869.12.10 it joined with the Kōgakusho, founded the previous year, to form the Daigakkōdai. Of the books owned by the original Gakushūin some went to the new Gakushūin founded in Tokyo in 1877, and some followed its various transformations eventually to become in 1899 part of the foundation collection of Kyoto Prefectural Library (Kyoto Furitsu Toshokan, now called Kyoto Furitsu Sōgō Shiryōkan). The migrations of these books can now be traced using some of the old catalogues that survive from the original Gakushūin, but the seal impressions in the Kyoto Furitsu Sōgō Shiryōkan books today tell the story more eloquently.[73]

The emergence of public libraries in the Meiji period was a long-drawn out affair. It goes without saying that the initial inspiration for libraries offering unrestricted access to all came from the West. The perception that Meiji libraries were fundamentally different from their predecessors led to the emergence of a new word, *toshokan* 図書館, to distinguish them. As with many other aspects of life in the West, it was Fukuzawa Yukichi who was the first to disseminate knowledge of Western libraries. He had visited Europe as a member of a Bakufu diplomatic mission in 1862 and his experiences formed the basis of his *Conditions in the West* (*Seiyō jijō* 西洋事情; 1866). He describes libraries as *bunko* 文庫 (hitherto a term for a private library) or bibliothèques and emphasizes that they contain both rare books and quite ordinary books, and that anybody can come and read them, but not take them away. It appears that he was thinking of the British Museum, the Bibliothèque Nationale and the Imperial Library in St Petersburg, for he gives the large number of volumes held at the library in each city, and notes that foreign books were purchased while those published in the country in question were deposited on publication.[74]

As emphasized by Fukuzawa and other early Meiji writers, the cardinal features of the modern public library were that it was open to all irrespective of status and that no fees were charged. As I have shown in previous sections, circulating libraries were open to all but charged fees, while some altruistic collectors did make their books available to others, but not as a public facility. For the state to become

---

[73] Bunkenka 1979–81: 1–29.
[74] *Fukuzawa Yukichi zenshū*, 22 vols (Iwanami Shoten, 1958–71), 1: 305.

involved in an undertaking of this sort was indeed novel, and the pioneer was the Shojakkan 書籍館 established by the Ministry of Education in 1872 in the newly-established Museum (Monbushō Hakubutsukan 文部省博物館), which was the forerunner of the modern National Museum in Tokyo. The association with the Museum betrays the example of the British Museum and its library, but the conception and the collections were modest, and as an institution it was extremely unstable. It was the responsibility of several different bodies in succession, and in 1885 it introduced a fee for access to the books, thus differing from circulating libraries only in that provision came from the state. In the course of the 1870s the British model became less influential and the links between the Shojakkan and the Museum were severed. What replaced it was a new linkage with educational institutions. This was espoused by a senior member of the Ministry of Education, Tanaka Fujimaro 田中不二麻呂, who had visited the United States with the Iwakura Mission in 1872 and again in order to attend the Centennial Exposition in Philadelphia in 1876 and who had been impressed by the network of school district libraries.[75]

At the same time the new organs of local government and some entrepreneurs were beginning to see the advantages of enhancing access to print in the interests of the new rhetoric of 'civilization and enlightenment.' In Kyoto in 1872 a library called Shūshoin was founded by a local *kashihon'ya*, a local publisher and two others with the support of prefectural officials: in their publicity statement they allied themselves with the 'civilization and enlightenment' policies of the Kyoto prefectural government, and undertook to provide foreign and Japanese books and newspapers for people to borrow; readers had to pay a fee for their enlightenment, however.[76]

It was in the same year, 1872, that newspaper reading rooms (*shinbun jūransho* 新聞縦覧所) began to spread to all parts of Japan, some established by prefectural authorities and some by commercial enterprises. They offered newspapers from all over Japan, and occasionally from overseas as well. Customers came to the premises

---

[75] Nagasue 1984: 18–28, 30–2; on the Shojakkan, see Ono Noriaki 1978: 610–14.

[76] Takemori Kumahiko 竹森熊彦, 'Shūshoin ni tsuite no shiteki kōsatsu' 集書院についての史的考察, *Kyōto Furitsu Sōgō Shiryōkan kiyō* 2 (1973): 3–63; *Kyōto shomin seikatsu shi* 京都庶民生活史 (Kyōto Shin'yō Kinko, 1973), 434.

to read and paid a fee for the privilege, although some were free in the interests of 'progress' or of the interests represented by the Popular Rights Movement in the 1870s. In the 1880s they went into decline, partly because some popular newspapers became cheaper but also because reading newspapers, other than those issued by the government, was increasingly seen as subversive: in various regions policemen, local officials and school pupils were forbidden to read anything other than government newspapers.[77]

What is striking about libraries in the early part of the Meiji period is their instability. The lack of institutions that could take over the roles of the domain libraries or the Bakufu's academic libraries brought many books onto the open market, which was good for collectors, foreign and domestic alike, but less good for the integrity of the collections. Further, the educational needs perceived by the new government were of a utilitarian cast, and for the purposes of acquiring a knowledge of world geography, international law, or mechanics, translations from Western works or newly written books in Japanese had the edge. It was not until the end of the century that the notion of modern libraries with a mission to conserve the past as well as to provide for the present began to gain widespread acceptance.

BIBLIOGRAPHY

Ono Noriaki 1952; Nagasue Toshio 1984, ch. 1; Takebayashi Kumahiko 竹林熊彦, *Kinsei Nihon bunkoshi* 近世日本文庫史 (Taigadō Shuppan, 1943). Theodore F. Welch, *Toshokan: libraries in Japanese society* (London: Clive Bingley/ Chicago: American Library Association, 1976). On newspaper reading facilities, Hironiwa Motosuke 1973–74 is excellent. There is no study of the dispersal of Japanese books throughout the world since the 1850s, but all collections in Europe are being covered in the *Union catalogue of early Japanese books in Europe* project, which is based in Cambridge University Library.

---

[77] Hironiwa 1973: 143–5 and *passim*.

CHAPTER TEN

CATALOGUES AND BIBLIOGRAPHY

1   Catalogues and categories
      1   Pre-Tokugawa
      2   Tokugawa period
2   Bibliography in the Tokugawa period

Whereas the previous chapter dealt with the formation and typology of collections of books in Japan, here the focus is on the systems of intellectual ordering applied to those collections and on the significance of the categories used and the hierarchies they formed. In all these respects the impact of China was considerable, for even before Chinese books had reached Japan Chinese bibliographical scholarship had evolved systems for the ordering of the growing corpus of texts. Furthermore, the very large number of texts in Chinese which had reached Japan by the end of the eighth century, especially Buddhist texts, necessitated systems for the physical control of books in Japan too as well as for their intellectual ordering. On the other hand, the expanding corpus of Japanese texts from the Heian period onwards fell outside the normative sinological systems of textual categories and posed a challenge to them that was not adequately met until the nineteenth century, so here too, as in many other of the fields of cultural production covered in this book, there was a continuing tension between sinological texts and Japanese texts.

Catalogues were another response to the plurality of texts, and were certainly being compiled in the eighth century, either as bureaucratic records or as lists of books brought back from China. Some from later centuries that survive to this day in multiple copies, or were even printed, are evidence of the circulation of catalogues, and it is evident that they were beginning to transform what Chartier has called a 'closed world of individual libraries' into a 'universe of books'.[1] However, in Japan the divides between Buddhist books, secular Chinese books and Japanese books remained normative and the sense of a single universe of books is elusive. Much the same was true of the development of bibliographical knowledge and the encounter with books as material objects. It is in the nineteenth century that those divides began to be broken down, and it is not clear that they have been completely broken down yet, even though the history of books in Japan cannot be written without a balanced appreciation of the complementary functions those three textual strands have fulfilled in the cloth of Japanese literate culture.

Bibliography as the study of texts or of the sociology of texts becomes clearly identifiable in the Tokugawa period, but undoubtedly had been practised much earlier. Like the bibliographic traditions of Europe, it was primarily concerned with the 'recovery of the past' and it functioned to shape perceptions of the canon.[2] Although there are some signs of nationalist bibliography, for the most part bibliography is a field divided between the sinologists and the Kokugaku scholars. Towards the end of the period independent scholars begin to ignore that divide and treat of both old Chinese and Japanese texts, and in the Meiji period, with the advent of Kokubungaku, that is 'studies of national [ie, Japanese] literature', as a discipline, more nationalistic perceptions of the literary past begin to dominate, and indeed their influence is still to be detected.

10.1 CATALOGUES AND CATEGORIES

In China, and later by extension in Japan, systems for ordering books developed from simple classification procedures and evolved into complex structures that have less to do with classification than with the intellectual typologies and genealogies of books. This process has its roots in the Han dynasty: in the preceding Qin dynasty books had been burnt and suppressed because of the perceived dangers of the diversification of scholarly opinion, and in the Han efforts were made to reassemble and order the corpus of available literature from copies scattered far and wide under the censorship of the old régime.

---

[1] Chartier 1994: 70, 88.
[2] Balsamo 1990: 5, 19, etc.

The classification system devised by the bibliographers responsible for this project is not extant but it is thought to have generated that used in the *Yi wen zhi* 芸文志, the bibliographical section of the dynastic history of the Later Han. This used six basic categories: the first three, consisting of the classics, literature and the various schools of thought, constituted the textual traditions which the educated had to be familiar with, while the second three, military studies, mathematics, and medicine and divination, were for specialists alone. With the addition of a seventh category for maps and geographical texts, and the reservation of Buddhist and Daoist books in their own categories, this system for classifying the textual legacy of the past was satisfactory in its time but was unable to cope with literary production in the subsequent centuries and was therefore abandoned in favour of other formulations.[3]

By the time of the Sui dynasty a classification system based on a division into four areas of literary production had become standard, and in *Sui shu jing ji zhi* 随書経籍志, the bibliographic section of the Sui dynastic history, it took the form of a new typology which became the standard until modern times not only in China but in Japan and Korea as well. This consisted of the following four categories: *jing* 経 (classics), *shi* 史 (history), *zi* 子 (masters), *ji* 集 (anthologies) with two additional categories for Daoist books and Buddhist books. So great was the corpus and variety of texts by this time that it was necessary to subdivide all of these categories, and by ordering these sub-categories it proved possible to represent the genealogy and hierarchy of schools of thought and of textual traditions in addition.[4]

The *Sui shu jing ji zhi* had definitely reached Japan by the late ninth century, for it informs the ordering of material in the *Nihonkoku genzaisho mokuroku*, which is discussed below (§10.1.1). It is unsurprising that Chinese perceptions of the hierarchies of Chinese texts were adopted in Japan, but there were on the other hand no corresponding attempts made to encompass the totality of texts produced or available in Japan. On the contrary, efforts in Japan were directed in three different and quite separate directions, secular Chinese books, Buddhist books, and Japanese books, and the tensions

---

[3] Kuraishi 1973: 10–28, 43.
[4] Kuraishi 1973: 57–61.

between these three textual traditions are evident both in catalogue production and in bibliographic practice.

BIBLIOGRAPHY

The most thorough study of classifications and typologies of books in China is Kuraishi Takeshirō 1973. See also Drège 1991b.

10.1.1 *Pre-Tokugawa*

Cataloguing activity was an inevitable accompaniment of the vast manuscript copying enterprises of the Nara period, and some of the lists and catalogues produced for control purposes have survived in the collections of the Shōsōin. The earliest is *Sha daishōjōkyō mokuroku* 写大小乗経目録, a list made in 733 of Mahāyāna and Hīnayāna scriptures which had been copied that year. There also survive several inventory catalogues listing the contents of the book chests at the Tōdaiji sūtra scriptorium and a list of missing parts of multi-volume works, missing either because of the transmission of faulty copies or as a result of loss in Japan. The list of missing parts was compiled in 742 by Takaya no Akamaro, an employee of the Tōdaiji who also did an inventory of the chests containing the Buddhist canon in the previous year.[5]

All of the works appearing in these catalogues are of course of Chinese origin; the one exception is to be found in *Shashōsho mokuroku* 写章疏目録, a list of non-canonical works copied at the Tōdaiji which includes 43 non-Buddhist works and an item described as follows: *Teiki nikan nihonsho* 帝記二巻日本書 [chronicle of sovereigns, 2 volumes, Japanese book]. This is almost certainly the lost mid-sixth-century record of the Japanese monarchs and their reigns which is referred to in the *Nihon shoki*, the *Kojiki* and other eighth-century works.[6]

Most of these records, however, are more akin to bureaucratic documents than to catalogues, as is clearly the case with records surviving from 781 of borrowings and returns of books from the Shōsōin repository. Nevertheless, they bespeak a concern for imposing

---

[5] *DNK* 24: 17–22, 185–6, 197; 8: 131–2; 7: 5–32, 495, 500.
[6] *DNK* 3: 84–91.

order and control over books that is a direct result of the quantity of texts available by the early eighth century and at the same time they reveal a tangible desire for intellectual order, at least in the case of Buddhist texts. *Shashōsho mokuroku* (748) goes further than this, listing 128 Buddhist texts, 42 secular Chinese texts and in addition other Chinese texts divided into literary, political, military and medical categories. This is, it must however be remembered, primarily a list of books copied at a particular time, not a catalogue of a collection. Also, it remains a fact, as Wada Mankichi has emphasized, that there is at this stage little interest in Japan in compiling bibliographical catalogues as there had been in China since the Han dynasty, and that such interests only come fully into their own in the Tokugawa period.[7]

Catalogues of other kinds were also compiled in the Nara period, but they do not survive. A catalogue of the Chinese books, probably mostly secular works, brought back from China by Kibi no Makibi in 734 survived for at least 150 years to be referred to in a later catalogue, but it is no longer extant. We know too that by 757 the Zushoryō (Palace Library) had its own catalogue, but this too is not extant.[8]

In the Heian period the quantities of Buddhist texts reaching Japan made catalogues an ever more pressing necessity, although here political and bureaucratic exigencies also had a part to play. The eight monks who travelled to China in the ninth century with the sponsorship of the court submitted catalogues of the works they brought back with them (*shōrai mokuroku* 請来目録), and these have been preserved. The court's motives for sponsoring the collection of sūtras were multi-layered: the desire for improved translations, for better texts, and for the texts of newly-translated works was there, but so was the desire to keep abreast of sectarian developments in China, to use Buddhism as a means of ritually protecting the state, and to assert Japan's claim to be 'civilized' by Tang standards. As the persecution of Buddhism became fiercer and the Tang sank into chaos, Japanese missions to China were brought to an end in the ninth century and with them court sponsorship of monks seeking to gather texts in China, for they had already served their purpose.[9]

---

[7] *ZZGR* 16: 1–9; Wada Mankichi 1983: 5, 23–31.
[8] Yajima 1984: 86; *DNK* 4: 244.
[9] The eight *shōrai mokuroku* are in *T*, vol. 55, #2159–68, 2173–4.

By the Tang dynasty there were already in existence in China a number of specialist sūtra catalogues. The oldest one extant, *Chu san cang ji ji* 出三蔵記集, was compiled around the end of the fifth century A.D. but the compiler states that he had examined other catalogues to discover what texts he should include in his library. More important than that, however, was the imperially commissioned catalogue produced in 594, *Zhong jing mu lu* 衆経目録, because what prompted its compilation was the need to identify and determine a scriptural and exegetical canon for the purpose of producing state-sponsored manuscript copies of the Buddhist canon for distribution to the temples of state in the capital and the provinces.[10]

Saichō and Kūkai, the founders respectively of Japanese Tendai and Shingon Buddhism, were not the first to bring back quantities of Buddhist texts from China, for Genbō had in 735 brought back many more than they did. They were, however, the first to prepare catalogues for presentation to the throne, in 805 and 806 respectively. These catalogues were valuable simply as lists of what had been acquired and was now available in Japan, although it is not clear just how accessible the texts they brought back were. Kūkai's catalogue survives in a copy made by Saichō and we know from Saichō's letters that he asked Kūkai to lend him certain texts that he had not acquired himself; other copies of Kūkai's catalogue survive, such as that preserved in the Hōganji on Chikubujima, which was formerly thought to be Kūkai's holograph and probably dates from the ninth century, and their existence lends credence to the idea that the catalogues were valuable for the information they contained and therefore circulated in manuscript copies. But these catalogues had more significance than that, for they also served to determine the textual canons of different schools of Buddhism.[11]

Of the two, Kūkai's has often been described as the more important collection, and his catalogue is certainly the more interesting. Moriyama Seishin has suggested that he may have investigated temple holdings in Japan beforehand and endeavoured to bring back texts that were not available in Japan, pointing out that certain important

---

[10] *T*, vol. 55, #2145; *BKD* 5: 227–31.

[11] Ishida Hisatoyo 1982; Moriyama Seishin 守山聖真, *Bunkashijō yori mitaru Kōbō Daishi den* 文化史上よりみたる弘法大師伝 (Kokusho Kankōkai, 1973; facsimile of 1933 edition), 229–54.

texts which are known to have reached Japan by Kūkai's time are not included in his catalogue, possibly because he already knew that those texts were available in Japan. At any rate, the catalogue breaks down Kūkai's collection into a number of categories that seem to privilege political rather than sectarian considerations. After the preface, written in 806 in China, and a list of Buddhist ritual implements, he gives a list of 142 'newly translated sūtras' (*shin'yakkyō* 新訳経), of which he was perhaps rightly proud: some of these had only been completed the year before and some again were copies given to him by the translators themselves. Ishida has pointed out that the list of sūtras translated by Amoghavajra (Bukong 不空) in this section corresponds closely with *Zhen yuan xin ding shi jiao mu lu* 貞元新定釈教目録, which was compiled in China in 800: even the order is the same, and the only difference is that six items are missing from Kūkai's catalogue, possibly because he was unable to obtain copies. This raises the possibility that Kūkai may have used Chinese catalogues as a shopping list while he was in China. After the 'newly translated sūtras' he lists a small number of 'old translations', followed by 42 hymns in Sanskrit, which he is reputed to have been able to read, then lists of statues and mandalas, and finally 32 commentaries and exegetical works written by Chinese monks. The categories he utilised are not so much doctrinal or sectarian as concerned with externals, and possibly also with a perceived need to justify the whole exercise as a success.[12]

Kūkai's catalogue and the other seven were the product of hazardous voyages made by their authors in the ninth century and were much valued by their contemporaries, but in a sense they only added to the textual confusion. There was consequently a felt need, by the end of the century if not before, for more comprehensive catalogues. The first sign of this is a catalogue of Shingon sūtras and texts compiled in 823 on imperial orders, which explicitly addresses the problem of determining which Shingon scriptures and texts were to be found in Japan, or at least in the vicinity of Kyoto. A much more sophisticated classification was adopted by Annen at the end of the century when he combed through all eight of the *shōrai mokuroku* for Shingon texts, listing them with an indication of their contents and of which

---

[12] Ishida Hisatoyo 1982; Moriyama Seishin 1973: 229–54 (see previous note); *T*, vol. 55, #2157.

monks had brought them to Japan. Control of the expanding corpus of Shingon and esoteric texts in general was a continuing problem, if we can judge from the succession of works of a similar nature, which stretches well into the Tokugawa period (see next section).[13]

Shingon was not, however, the only problem, and sectarian divisions are increasingly reflected in the preparation of catalogues. This started in 914, when the emperor Daigo asked each of the six Nara sects to make catalogues of their books to prevent loss and dispersal. Later, Hōnen (1133–1212) made the sectarian associations of particular texts much more explicit in his *Shoshū kyōsho mokuroku* 諸宗経疏目録, in which he gave a brief account of the tenets of each of 11 sects and appended a list of the principal sūtras and exegetical works associated with them. This is not, of course, a catalogue of a specific collection or collections, rather a catalogue constructed as a bibliographic guide. It is only in the Tokugawa period that the compilation of explicitly sectarian catalogues for such purposes becomes widespread, and in earlier periods it is more common for individual monastic institutions to draw up catalogues of their actual holdings.[14]

One of the earliest temple catalogues known is that of the Sannōin on Mt Hiei, which survives in part in a manuscript copied in 925. Enchin resided there after his return from China in 859, and the catalogue was compiled by one of his followers in 891, just after his death. As mentioned in the previous chapter (§9.1.1), only some of the books he brought from China were kept in the Sannōin, but the collection was a large one, and the two surviving parts of the catalogue list respectively tantric Buddhist texts and texts associated with the Tendai school of Buddhism, without, however, attempting any more detailed classification. How widespread the compilation of temple catalogues was in the Heian period is unclear, although they must have had a compelling practical purpose for temples possessing large quantities of texts: when Kujō Kanezane visited the Byōdōin at Uji in 1187 he found there a catalogue which covered both the contents of its copy of the Buddhist canon and its material treasures. When Eichō compiled in 1094 his *Tōiki dentō mokuroku* 東域伝灯目録, a catalogue of extant Buddhist books in Japan, he made explicit use of

---

[13] Annen's catalogue has alternative titles: the version in *T*, vol. 55, #2176, is titled *Sho ajari shingon mikkyō burui mokuroku* while that in *DNBZ, Bukkyō shoseki mokuroku* 2, is titled *Nittō hakke shōrai mokuroku*; see *BKD* 5:252–3.

[14] *DNBZ, Bukkyō shoseki mokuroku* 1: 85–90.

a number of temple catalogues that have not survived. It is reasonable to conclude that temples with scholarly collections or a large number of scriptural texts were forced by the need for order to keep stock of their books, and that these catalogues functioned also as guides to available texts for monks attached to other temples.[15]

By the middle of the thirteenth century the Kōzanji in Kyoto had a very substantial collection of books stored in two repositories. In 1250 a catalogue of this collection was prepared at the request of the retired emperor Go-Saga. A duplicate of the original presentation copy is preserved in the Kōzanji and this reveals a concern for locating the items desired. Thus the first sections list the contents of two copies of the Buddhist canon and several other large texts, which were presumably stored separately and in order, and the remainder lists the contents of 101 boxes, consisting almost entirely of Buddhist texts with just a few boxes of secular Chinese and Japanese works at the end. However, it is also clear that the assignment of books to boxes was based on their categories, and books belonging to the same category were stored together. The categories used for classification include both sectarian affiliation and subject matter, so there is some overlap in their potential scope and the scheme is not intellectually rigorous. Nevertheless, the catalogue reveals a concern both for intellectual order and for accessibility, and as such it has no earlier parallel in Japan that is extant.[16]

It is clear that in the Heian period the very substantial collections of books and documents held by some temples were making catalogues a growing necessity for the sake of order and preservation, and this was true of secular collections as well. According to a source cited by Ichijō Kanera, in 917 emperor Daigo ordered that a detailed catalogue be compiled of the contents of a palace storehouse which kept 197 volumes of the writings of previous emperors, so that in the future it would be easier to use the collection. Similarly, in 1187 emperor Go-Toba ordered that catalogues be made of the contents of

---

[15] Satō 1937: 1–13; *GY* 3: 392; *T*, vol. 55, #2183; Inoue Mitsusada, 'Tōiki dentō mokuroku yori mitaru Nara jidai sōryo no gakumon' 東域伝灯目録より見たる奈良時代僧侶の学問, *Shigaku zasshi* 53.3 (1948): 32.

[16] Okuda Tsutomu 奥田勲, 'Kōzanji kyōzō komokuroku ni tsuite' 高山寺経蔵古目録について, *Utsunomiya Daigaku kyōiku gakubu kiyō* 26 (1976): 1–9; *Kōzanji kyōzō komokuroku*, Kōzanji shiryō sōsho 14 (Tōkyō Daigaku Shuppankai, 1985), 6–48, 278–91.

two other palace buildings that had been given over to the storage of books. Neither the catalogues nor the collections survive in either of these cases.[17]

The most important secular catalogue produced in the Heian period is undoubtedly *Nihonkoku genzaisho mokuroku*, which was compiled at imperial command by Fujiwara no Sukeyo in the closing years of the ninth century. It is the oldest extant catalogue of Chinese books in Japan, and it provides valuable evidence for the transmission of Chinese texts, as well as for the existence in Japan of texts not included in the official bibliographies attached to the Chinese dynastic histories. However, in the absence of a preface or other indications, the reasons for its compilation are a mystery. It has long been assumed that what occasioned this catalogue was the destruction by fire of the Reizen'in 冷然院 and its collection of books in 875. A number of entries indicate that the items are from the Reizen'in, and the understanding has been that they survived the fire and prompted a survey of the Chinese books left extant in Japan. However, as Ōta Masujirō has argued, this is no more than a hypothesis and does not give any sure indication of the motives or of the date of compilation. Further, with regard to the meaning of the title, Ōta suggests that the emphasis in the title is not a temporal 'what is available/extant now', as has been the common understanding, but a spatial 'what is here in Japan'.[18]

The problems posed by *Nihonkoku genzaisho mokuroku* are exacerbated by the fact that the only surviving manuscript, which dates from the late Heian period, appears to be in some sense an abbreviated version. How representative this may be of the original version is impossible, of course, to say. A further oddity is the inclusion of a small number of Japanese books in Chinese, although it is possible that they were not recognised as such and mistakenly assumed to be works of Chinese authorship. Also, the absence of a number of Chinese works which are known to have reached Japan by this time is puzzling. Some may have been lost in the Reizen'in fire, but others are known to have survived, and this raises questions about just how comprehensive *Nihonkoku genzaisho mokuroku* might be, and how

---

[17] *Kachō yosei* 花鳥余情, in *KCZ* 3: 246 (separately paginated).
[18] Kawaguchi 1964: 148; Ōta Masujirō 太田晶二郎, 'Nihon kansekishi sakki' 日本漢籍史札記, *Shoshigaku geppō* 6 (1980): 1–16; Onagaya 1976: 5–9.

extensive Sukeyo's searches were.[19]

Sukeyo undoubtedly had access to the catalogue of books attached to the official history of the Sui dynasty, *Sui shu jing ji zhi*, for Kano Naoki has demonstrated that some entries in *Nihonkoku genzaisho mokuroku* are identical to those in *Sui shu jing ji zhi*. He was also dependent on it for his scheme of classification. The *Sui shu jing ji zhi* assigns books to one of the four familiar categories of Chinese bibliographic practice, classics, history, masters, and anthologies, or to one of two additional categories, Daoist books and Buddhist books. Sukeyo omits both Buddhist and Daoist works, and does not adopt the four main categories, although he does take over, almost in their entirety, the 40 sub-categories into which they are divided. This represents, then, the first known adoption in Japan of the intellectual typology underlying the 'traditional' classification system used in China.[20]

Nevertheless, it is clear that Sukeyo was not wholly dependent on *Sui shu jing ji zhi*. He is more comfortable with the categorization of books by authors rather than with analytical categorization based on the contents, for the sub-categories are described in terms of authors not subjects, thus 'poets' rather than 'poetry'. In another departure from Chinese practice he appears to have invented a number of bibliographical terms for the description of the texts at his disposal.[21] Further, the exclusion, not only and inevitably of Japanese works but also of Buddhist and Daoist works, bespeaks the strict compartmentalization of books in Japan that is not resolved until commercial interests override intellectual loyalties in the seventeenth-century booksellers' catalogues. Finally, it should be noted that *Nihonkoku genzaisho mokuroku* appears to reflect, in the balance of texts cited, a preference for poetry and other literary works rather than the canonical Confucian texts and this probably owes much to the tastes of Tang China that Japanese were familiar with.

Another important catalogue that reveals much of Japanese tastes in the Heian period is *Tsūken nyūdō zōsho mokuroku*. This is purportedly the catalogue of the collection of Fujiwara no Michinori

---

[19] Onagaya 1976: 18–26, 38–56.

[20] Ono Noriaki 1970: 92; Kano Naoki 1973: 87–92; Onagaya 1976: 16–7; see also Kōzen Hiroshi 興膳宏 & Kawai Kōzō 川合康三, *Zuisho keikishi shōkō* 随書経籍志詳攷 (Kyūko Shoin, 1995); Kawaguchi 1964: 148.

[21] Wang Zhen-pin 1991: 63, n. 54.

and is certainly the oldest extant guide to the contents of a private library in the Heian period. Michinori was indeed a collector of books, but there is no evidence to support the supposition that the books listed, almost all in Chinese by Japanese and Chinese authors, actually came from his collection. Further, as Ono has noted, the catalogue does not include any music books although he was a musician, and does not mention any of the books he is known to have possessed. Either parts of it are missing, or there must be some doubts about the ownership of the collection. And if the books did come from Michinori's collection, then the catalogue must have been compiled after his death: rather than being a classified catalogue it is a list of the contents of 84 book-chests, and the fact that a further 86 chests are listed as missing at the time of compilation suggests strongly that the owner was already dead. Nevertheless, the contents of the chests available to the compiler provide, as Smits has demonstrated, a unique guide to the library of a leading exponent of Chinese poetry in Japan.[22]

While some Japanese books in Chinese were, as indicated above, occasionally included in catalogues of what were mainly sinological collections, there is no firm evidence to indicate that Japanese books were even listed in inventories or simple catalogues, let along subjected to a system of intellectual ordering, until around the twelfth century. In 1174, as he notes in his diary, Yoshida Tsunefusa went to the treasure house of the Rengeōin, which is known today as Sanjūsangendō and was the most important repository of books in the Kamakura period, in order to make a catalogue of the Japanese books and documents there on the orders of the retired emperor Go-Shirakawa. This catalogue does not survive and nothing more is known of it, but several Heian-period catalogues of limited scope are extant: *Honchō kokushi mokuroku* 本朝国史目録 is of uncertain date and is little more than a guide to the six national histories of Japan starting with *Nihon shoki*; *Honchō hōke bunsho* 本朝法家文書 deals with legal books and documents, and it must date from before the end of the twelfth century for it is mentioned in *Tsūken nyūdō zōsho mokuroku*; and *Waka genzaisho mokuroku* 和歌現在書目録, a list of extant books of *waka* poetry, has a preface dated 1166. These are all

---

[22] Yoshimura 1928; Smits 1995: 40–44; *(Shinkō) Gunsho ruiju* 新校群書類従 21: 545–54; Ono Noriaki 1944: 359–61.

little more than lists and there is no evidence at this stage of the development of any system of classification or hierarchy; indeed the lack of movement in that direction is indicated by the fact that each of these catalogues covers a separate category of books.[23]

Much more comprehensive and ambitious than these is *Honchō shojaku mokuroku*, although the date and circumstances of its compilation are uncertain. The current view is that it was compiled some time in the Kamakura period, probably in the thirteenth century, but there are more than 70 manuscript versions extant, which testify to its perceived value but at the same time in their variety pose difficult questions relating to its genesis and transmission. In its original form it probably consisted of little more than a list of titles with numbers of volumes, although many manuscripts include some annotation. The oldest extant manuscript dates only from the early seventeenth century and it is not clear how much has been added and when. A further difficulty is this: what exactly is it a catalogue of? It is not a catalogue of a particular collection, and in some sense seems to be a representation of the cultural production of Japan. It is certainly underpinned by the notion that there is a corpus of Japanese books which deserve to be kept distinct from Chinese books and valued in their own right. In some cases the compiler, unidentified but presumably a man, refers to the text of a handwritten colophon in the book he is describing and clearly has in mind a specific copy which he has seen. In other cases, however, he states that he has not seen a copy of the work. It has also been suggested that some entries may have been transferred from other catalogues and that the books in question may even no longer have been extant by the time *Honchō shojaku mokuroku* was compiled.[24]

In spite of these difficulties it has compelling interest. In the first place, it describes 493 Japanese books but as many as 299 of them are no longer extant. A few are mentioned in other sources but the greater part are otherwise unknown, which in part is due to the fact that although printing was currently being used for Buddhist texts it was not applied to Japanese texts, so they escaped being 'fixed' in print and failed to gain a better chance of survival. There are many

---

[23] *ST* 22: 54; *ZZGR* 16: 148–56; *ZGR* 17 上: 232–6; Ono Noriaki 1944: 464–77; Wada Hidematsu 1936: 2–6.

[24] Wada Hidematsu 1936: 13–6.

losses to regret, such as the biography of Kibi no Makibi and several lost tales of the Heian period, such as *Matsudono monogatari*, and others not mentioned even in the Tamakazura chapter of the *Tale of Genji*, where a number of other lost tales are mentioned. Of greater significance here is the division into 20 categories, which represents the first attempt to apply analytical categories to Japanese books based on an assessment of their subject matter. The first category is *shinji* 神事, which may be loosely described as books relating to Shintō and which is unmistakably intended to have pride of place; it is followed by *teiki* 帝記, which denotes the records of the historical emperors, and then by books concerning governance. This pattern of precedence has enjoyed remarkable longevity, for it has long served as the standard and is used even now in the catalogues of the Japanese books in the Naikaku Bunko. The only significant departure came in the system for ordering the Japanese books in the Bakufu Library, which will be mentioned below.[25]

There are few important catalogues from the Muromachi period, but mention must be made of *Sentō gobunsho mokuroku* 仙洞御文書目録, which reveals in brief outline the library collections of the Northern Line of emperors during the period in the fourteenth century when two rival lines of emperors were in conflict. The catalogue was compiled in 1354–5 in two parts, of which the second lists various documents and holographs in two libraries associated with the throne. The first part covers the contents of the imperial library in Kyoto, and lists the contents of the storage boxes without any careful classification, but in doing so it brings together Chinese, Japanese and Buddhist books under one head, thus disregarding the intellectual divisions that had been so influential. It does so because those three orders of books happened to be represented in the library, rather than because of any intellectual commitment to catholicity, but it is nonetheless a signficant harbinger of the abandonment of those divisions in the Tokugawa period.[26]

---

[25] Wada Hidematsu 1936: 512, 638–9; Ono Noriaki 1970: 93.
[26] *NSMT* 1: 113–5.

BIBLIOGRAPHY

The eight *shōrai mokuroku* are in *T*, vol. 55, #2159–68, 2173–4; the subsequent Buddhist catalogues mentioned are either in the same volume of *T* or in *DNBZ, Bukkyō shoseki mokuroku* 1 & 2; Wada Mankichi 1983. On Kūkai's *shōrai mokuroku*, see Ishida Hisatoyo 1982 and Moriyama Seishin, *Bunkashijō yori mitaru Kōbō daishi den* (Kokusho Kankōkai, 1973; facsimile of 1933 edition). On *Nihonkoku genzaisho mokuroku*, see Yajima 1984 and Onagaya 1976. On *Tsūken nyūdō zōsho mokuroku*, see Smits 1995: 41–4, and Yoshimura Shigeki 1928. Wada Hidematsu 1936, introduction and 512, 638–9, etc. See also the catalogues in *NSMT*. Ono Noriaki 1970 provides an introduction to the history of classification.

10.1.2 Tokugawa period

It is in the Tokugawa period that the compilation of catalogues and the construction of categories and hierarchies assumes an importance that reaches both into the commercial world of the book trade and into the scholarly world of bibliographers and historians. The booksellers' catalogues, which first make their appearance in the seventeenth century, were indisputably driven by the rapidly increasing volume of new publications and books in print. At the same time catalogues from the Heian period were printed and published for the first time in answer to scholarly and sectarian needs. Meanwhile, individuals were compiling catalogues of their own collections and making them available for copying as a source of information about books that were difficult to locate, and the Bakufu library was wrestling with the question of how to deal with Japanese books in what was predominantly a sinological library. Of all these new developments the booksellers' catalogues are the most innovative, largely because they are tied to the needs of the commercial nexus in publishing and bookselling, while the catalogues of the Bakufu institutions of learning remain closely tied to Chinese perceptions of the world of books.

At the Momijiyama Bunko, the Bakufu Library, the work of cataloguing the growing collections was taken so seriously that constant efforts were made to keep the catalogues up to date, although this was difficult, for the catalogues were in the form of books, as were all premodern library catalogues. All the books in the Library were kept in wooden boxes containing books of related content. The boxes were ranged in a classified order so that the intellectual and physical arrangements of the books fully coincided, perhaps for the first time in a Japanese library. The basic divisions were Chinese books, Japanese books and books closely connected with the Tokugawa house, and as these collections expanded it became necessary from time to time to undertake a complete revision of the catalogue. The catalogues did not exist, however, for the purpose of making the collections better known and access to them was restricted. Thus when a new version was made in 1733 only three copies were made, one for presentation to the shōgun, one for the head of the Bakufu Academy and one to be retained for the use of the librarians.[27]

Since each revision made its predecessor redundant, the nine earlier catalogues prepared at intervals from 1602 onwards have not survived. The 1836 catalogue, which was similarly restricted to the shōgun, the head of the Bakufu Academy and the Library itself, was intellectually the most thorough. The compilers were fully aware of the choices they were making, for they noted the profusion of catalogues of various sorts being prepared for various purposes in Japan, and they based it on the classification scheme used for the *Siku quanshu*, the huge but carefully controlled collection of texts initiated by the Qianlong emperor in 1772. The *Siku quanshu* scheme was not followed slavishly, for some alterations were made to accommodate Korean and Manchu books, and the compilers distinguished imported books from the movable-type editions produced in Japan in the early seventeenth century and from the editions sponsored by the Bakufu itself. Nevertheless, Japanese books could not fit into the *Siku quanshu* straitjacket, and were therefore consigned to an 'extra' (*bangai* 番外) section.[28]

The final version, prepared in the years 1864–6, has survived in full and again reveals the consistent sinological priorities of the Library. The Chinese books come first, ranged in the usual quadripartite classification scheme but with an additional section containing popular drama and fiction of the Ming dynasty, some Western books, Korean books and Manchu books. The Japanese books follow, in a classification scheme based closely on that used in *Honchō shojaku*

---

[27] Mori 1933: 48–9; Fukui 1980, ch 5.
[28] Mori 1933: 155–63.

mokuroku, with Shintō books coming at the head, followed by records of the emperors.[29]

The Bakufu Academy had a similar sinological preoccupation, as reflected in a catalogue compiled in 1857. This simply follows the quadripartite classication scheme, and if the Academy possessed any Japanese books then they must have been excluded from the catalogue altogether.[30]

Both the Academy and the Library derived some of their books from the China book trade, as described elsewhere (§§7.1.3, 9.2.1). Most of these books were, at least in their Chinese editions, rare and hard to come by in Japan; consequently information about them was scarce and potentially of value to sinologists with access to the Bakufu collections. A number of manuscript catalogues were compiled in the second half of the Tokugawa period to furnish bibliographic guides to the range of books that had been imported, and the most thorough of these is *Bunrui hakusai shomoku tsūran* 分類舶載書目通覧. This was originally compiled at the end of the eighteenth century and covers all books imported in the first half of that century, arranging them in accordance with Chinese bibliographic practice. But there were many other manuscript catalogues of these imported rarities, compiled by booksellers, by officials at Nagasaki or the Bakufu Library, or by others with access to imports, such as the Confucianist and botanist Matsuoka Gentatsu. These showed contemporaries what was available, but the only such catalogues that were published were guides to the contents of imported Chinese collectanea, enabling sinologists to locate texts of works that were not otherwise easily available.[31]

Although the importation of Chinese books enabled Japanese sinologists to maintain an intellectual dialogue with China, the commercial publishing industry in Japan was, even in the seventeenth century, a much more significant and voluminous source of books, including reprints of Chinese texts and the work of Japanese sinologists, to say nothing of domestic literature and scholarship. By the middle of the seventeenth century, as we have already seen (§5.1.2), the

---

[29] Fukui 1980: 80–6, 88–94; *Tokugawa bakufu zōshomoku* 徳川幕府蔵書目, 10 vols, *SSS* 16 (1985), vols 1–7 (for the Japanese books see 7: 81–286).

[30] The Academy catalogue is contained in *Tokugawa bakufu zōshomoku* (see previous note), vol. 10.

[31] Ōba 1984: 152–8, 205–8, etc.

output of the commercial publishers of Osaka and Kyoto was already so large and varied that catalogues of books in print became necessary for commercial bookselling purposes if nothing else. The oldest one extant survives only in a manuscript copy made in 1659, but it must have been produced at around that time for it includes two works published in that year.

The arrangement in this manuscript catalogue is crude, and was superseded by that in the printed catalogue produced c1666, which established the order that became the standard in booksellers' catalogues: first come Buddhist books, then secular Chinese books, dictionaries, Shintō books, and other categories of Japanese book. The relatively low priority accorded to Shintō books is striking, but much more so is the fact that this was the first catalogue to embrace the three orders of Chinese books, Buddhist books and Japanese books in the one schematic representation and to bring an end to the compartmentalization that had characterized the representation of books and collections for a millenium. Further, in the medical and dictionary sections Chinese and Japanese books appear together without any discrimination, and in the Japanese sections ephemeral works are listed as well as classics. Commercial bookselling had no need of the divisions that had ordered intellectual life, and the consequence was a catholic comprehension of the output of the press, although it is evident that Japanese books still came a poor third in esteem at this stage.[32]

Given the reasons for their compilation, it is not surprising that all the books listed in the booksellers' catalogues were commercially published books that were currently available or forthcoming, and that in consequence no manuscripts, private publications or official publications were included. This was a limitation, especially in view of the continuing importance of manuscript production throughout the Tokugawa period, but on the other hand there was a commercial drive to keep the catalogues up to date and to make them more useful. In 1670 an augmented edition of the 1666 catalogue was published in recognition of the frenetic growth of the publishing industry in Osaka and Kyoto, and the significance of the newly emergent publishing industry in Edo is apparent from the fact that one of the two publishers of this catalogue was based in Edo.

[32] *YMC* 2: 142–4.

To cope with the tide of publications the compilers in 1670 were forced to add more categories for such items as women's books, Nō texts and mathematics texts. In a subsequent catalogue published in 1685 cookbooks, travelogues and books on flower arrangement had to be treated in separate categories of their own as various niche markets grew in strength. These categories were, however, simply a mechanical response to the growth of certain areas of the publishing industry and do not appear to reflect any concern to establish an intellectual order of books. Between 1675 and 1696 there was also a series of catalogues published in Edo in which the detailed classification was replaced by a listing in *iroha* syllabic order according to the initial syllable of the title. The books listed under each syllabic symbol were crudely subdivided into Confucian books, medical books, Buddhist books and *kana* books (i.e., other books in Japanese).

Some of the seventeenth-century catalogues gave retail prices and even short guides to the contents of some works, but in the eighteenth century the pressure on space dictated a sparer format and the exclusion of most seventeenth-century publications, even though some of them were still in print and available. The last of the booksellers' catalogues was published in 1801, but it was a composite catalogue covering publications from the early seventeenth century up to 1801: it consisted of sections of various earlier catalogues, with additions and alterations but with no attempt to impose any chronological or logical order on the sections taken from different sources. It was reprinted without change several times in the nineteenth century, but was never brought up to date or superseded. This must have been partly due to the sheer volume of books being published or remaining in print in the nineteenth century, which would have made the task of compiling a new catalogue with some pretensions to comprehensive coverage a more daunting one than it had been in the seventeenth century. To some extent also the need was no longer so great, for publishers had got into the habit of attaching catalogues of their own publications (*zōhan mokuroku*) to their books, often stretching to as many as a dozen pages, and there were more and more specialized catalogues being published as well (§5.1.4).

The booksellers' catalogues were largely compiled by members of the book trade and in the first instance for the convenience of the trade. It is likely that they were also used as reference tools, for the earlier booksellers' catalogues were themselves included as entries in later editions. Ōta Nanpo is known to have owned several of them along with a catalogue of the Bakufu Academy, which must have been earlier than the 1857 version mentioned above, and various other bibliographic tools.[33]

In addition to the booksellers' catalogues there were also more specialized published catalogues available that were clearly aimed at the customers or, to put it less narrowly, at particular interest groups. One such group was the world of amateur *haikai* poets, and several catalogues of *haikai* books were published in the Tokugawa period, the earliest being *Haikai waratibōkō* (c1676), which consists of a chronological list of published *haikai* books followed by a list of unpublished ones and then by a collection of *hokku* verses. A few years later came *Haikai shojaku mokuroku* (c1692), which incorporates and expands on *Haikai waratibōkō*. In 1707 the first of several even more specialized *haikai* catalogues appeared, focussing solely on books connected with the *haikai* school of Matsuo Bashō.[34]

Popular literature and drama also achieved the respectability of bibliographic attention at this time. *Gedai nenkan* 外題年鑑 is a guide to *jōruri* plays originally published in Osaka in 1757 which was reissued in updated versions in 1768, 1779 and 1793 and also published in a pirate edition in 1763. Similarly, *Gesaku gedai kagami* 戯作外題鑑 is a retrospective listing of light fiction published in the years 1775–1806, while Kyokutei Bakin's *Kinsei mono no hon Edo sakusha burui* is a more careful study of writers and their works up to the early nineteenth century.[35]

Buddhism remained of course a subject of bibliographic attention, and a number of catalogues were published in the Tokugawa period which were devoted to books pertaining to specific sects of Buddhism.

---

[33] See *Shokusanjin zōsho mokuroku* 蜀山人蔵書目録, *SSS* 13 (1984), 370–71.

[34] *KSS* 9–148; Ishikawa Iwao 石川巌, *(Ashinken henshū) Haikai shojaku mokuroku* (阿誰軒編集)誹諧書籍目録 (Inoue Shoten, 1924); *Haisho sōkan* 俳書叢刊, 1st series, vol. 7 (Tenri: Tenri Daigaku Toshokan, 1950); there is a useful index to these catalogues of *haikai* books: Inui Hiroyuki 乾裕幸, ed., *Kohaisho mokuroku sakuin* 古俳書目録索引 (Kyoto: Akao Shōbundō, 1974).

[35] Nihon engeki bunken kenkyūkai, ed., *Jōruri kenkyū bunken shūsei* 浄瑠璃研究文献集成 (Hokkō Shobō, 1944), 402–573, 662–4; *Enseki jisshu* 燕石十種, 10 vols (Kokusho Kankōkai, 1908), 3: 209–255; Kimura Miyogo 木村三四吾, ed., *Kinsei mono no hon Edo sakusha burui* 近世物之本江戸作者部類 (Yagi Shoten, 1988).

For the Zen sect there was *Zensekishi* 禅籍志 (1716), a classified list of Zen books from China and Japan, and *Nihon zenrin senjutsu shomoku* 日本禅林撰述書目, which covers the works of Japanese Zen monks from the Kamakura period up to the seventeenth century. *Jōdo shinshū shōgyō mokuroku* 浄土真宗聖教目録 (1752) and *Hokke shūmon chojutsu mokuroku* 法華宗門著述目録 (1847) focus on the intellectual genealogy of the Jōdo shinshū and Nichiren sects respectively, subordinating the texts to their authors and, in the latter case, appending short biographical sketches. In some cases these catalogues were explicitly designed as study aids, such as *Shinshū kyōtenshi* 真宗教典志 (1780), which includes biographical information about the authors and brief explanations of the contents. The connection between these catalogues and the publishing industry is brought out clearly in *Misshū shojaku mokuroku* 密宗書籍目録 (1734), which lists books pertaining to the Shingon sect and promises to reappear in updated editions, of which one was published in 1757.[36]

To give one final example of a specialized catalogue, by the last years of the Tokugawa period there were already so many translations of Western books available that there was room for a catalogue aimed at the growing numbers seeking to work their way into the new field of 'Western studies' (*yōgaku* 洋学). To meet that need *Seiyō gakka yakujutsu mokuroku* 西洋学家訳術目録 was published in 1854 and furnished a list of some 400 translations already available.[37]

In the course of the Tokugawa period it became commonplace for institutions and individual collectors alike to compile catalogues of their holdings, and there is evidence to suggest that some of these circulated and were valued as guides to the contents of collections and the location of rare books. The Bakufu official and litterateur Ōta Nanpo had a catalogue of his library prepared towards the end of his life by Yamazaki Yoshishige, a well known scholar and bibliographer with whom he was in the habit of exchanging books. The original survives together with several copies taken from it, presumably with Nanpo's permission and presumably in order to get acquainted with the contents of his library. A similar case is *Isshūdō zōsho mokuroku* 聿修堂蔵書目録, the catalogue of the medical

---

[36] *DNBZ*, Bukkyō shoseki mokuroku 1: 271–320, 325–36, 427–530, 541–62, 2: 404–17; *BKD* 6: 96, 98–9, 205, 399, 8: 339, 10: 72, 338; Hayashi & Kornicki 1991: #2.

[37] Nakamura Kiyozō 1972:146-7.

collection belonging to the Bakufu doctor Taki Mototane (1789–1827), which survives in at least 16 copies.[38]

By the nineteenth century some writers of popular fiction were becoming serious collectors of books and keeping records of their collections. Kyokutei Bakin's catalogue, in his own hand, lists a number of banned manuscript books and thus indicates in passing that even a writer as nervous of the authorities as Bakin felt safe owning such works. There was clearly no danger in the private possession of banned books in manuscript. Bakin also compiled other catalogues of his *haikai* books and so on, but a more discriminating collector was Ryūtei Tanehiko. Tanehiko may have used his collection partly as a source of ideas for his more ephemeral works, but it is also clear that his approach to collecting was more scholarly, for he used some of the seventeenth-century booksellers' catalogues to familiarize himself with earlier publications. He compiled catalogues of his old *jōruri* books, his early erotica (*kōshokubon*), his *haikai* books and his collection of books relating to the Yoshiwara pleasure quarter.[39]

The catalogue of Ōta Nanpo's collection is of interest because of the ordering of the categories he established for his library. Since he was a Bakufu official, it is perhaps not surprising that he placed at the head books associated with the Bakufu and the shōgunal household, but it is surprising that the next category is books about vendettas, including the case of the 47 rōnin, and that he consigned the few Shintō books he owned and some Buddhist books to the very end. It is difficult to read this as anything other than a deliberate rejection of the established hierarchy that placed Shintō books before all others.[40]

Only a few of the many extant institutional catalogues can be mentioned here. The 1683 catalogue of the collection of the Sō daimyō of the Tsushima domain reveals the extent of their connections with Korea, and the principal divisions relate to the country of origin, Japan, Korea or China. The collection is uniquely rich in seventeenth-century Korean printed books, which had probably been received as gifts, for the Sō had a monopoly of diplomatic dealings with Korea

---

[38] *ONZ* 19: 302, 347–42. In additon to the copies of *Isshūdō zōsho mokuroku* listed in *KSM* 1:254.1, there is also a copy in Berlin: Kraft 1982–94: 1 #309.

[39] See the essays by Satō and Suzuki, and the various catalogues contained in *KSS*; *Shin gunsho ruijū* 7: 145–71, 173–84; *Mikan zuihitsu hyakushu* 18: 405–37.

[40] *Shokusanjin zōsho mokuroku*, *SSS* 13 (1984).

in the Tokugawa period. The only category relating to content is medical books, which in other catalogues too are treated as belonging to a single tradition irrespective of country of production.[41]

Two catalogues of the Ashikaga Gakkō collections were compiled in the Tokugawa period, the first in 1725 giving pride of place to the books associated with Ieyasu. The second, compiled in 1797, uses a scheme embracing Confucian, Buddhist, Japanese and medical books, in that order. The Japanese books were mostly in Chinese but did also include *Taiheiki* and some other items in Japanese, which by this time were considered worthy of standing alongside Chinese and Buddhist books. This catalogue is important because it awakened the interest of two leading bibliographers, Kariya Ekisai and Kondō Seisai, in the collection and encouraged them to visit it.[42]

A number of manuscript catalogues survive at the Manjuin, a temple on the northern outskirts of Kyoto, the oldest dating from the early eighteenth century. They are carefully classified, but, unlike temple catalogues of earlier centuries, they include large numbers of non-Buddhist works, including many of the popular works of seventeenth-century fiction known as *kanazōshi*. It is probable that temples had always had collections of secular books, at least in Chinese, but they were rarely included in catalogues of temple holdings. The Manjuin catalogues demonstrate the disintegration of the boundary between sacred and secular books, but it is of course impossible to extrapolate from this one example and the extent to which that disintegration characterized other temple libraries in the Tokugawa period remains uncertain.[43]

Yayoshi Mitsunaga has argued that the rise of Kokugaku fostered a new hierarchy of books, and certainly by the end of the Tokugawa period it is safe to agree with him. Both the Bakufu Academy and the Library followed Chinese classification practice and treated books lacking an appropriate sinological category as 'miscellaneous'. This was the fate of all Japanese books, which therefore enjoyed a second-class existence. And the seventeenth-century booksellers' catalogues placed Japanese books last after Buddhist and Chinese books. But

---

[41] Fujimoto 1981.
[42] Kawase 1974: 250–78.
[43] Satake Akihiro 佐竹昭広 et al., eds, *Manjuin zōsho mokuroku* 曼殊院蔵書目録, Kyōto Daigaku kokugo kokubun shiryō sōsho 50 (Kyoto: Rinsen Shoten, 1984).

there was resistance to this cavalier treatment of Japanese books, and the growing impact of Kokugaku ideas can be seen at work in the Kokugaku scholar Fujii Sadamoto's *Kokuchō shomoku* 国朝書目 (1791), a bibliographical guide to Japanese books. Fujii's arrangement is unusual, for he demotes Shintō books from their usual place at the head to a place alongside Buddhist books in the middle, and gives priority to historical works. The title and the very subject matter, however, bespeak a concern to draw attention to Japanese books and, by implication, away from Chinese books.[44]

There are other signs of this change too, such as Toda Ujinori's *Bangai zassho kaidai* (1826), which is a guide to the contents of the non-sinological books in the Bakufu Library. This deals first with Shintō books and then other Japanese books, and relegates sinological books by Japanese, listed in the usual Chinese categories, to the end in a deliberate inversion of the customary hierarchy. It can also be detected in the *Gunsho ruijū* project (§10.2) and in *Gunsho ichiran* 群書一覧 (1802, and reprinted in 1814, 1821 and 1824). The latter is an encyclopaedic guide by Ozaki Masayoshi to around 2,500 Japanese books: he places the initial focus on Japanese history and Shintō and disregards books associated with sinological traditions such as medicine and Buddhism. Ozaki elaborated a detailed classification scheme for Japanese books, not because, as was the case with the booksellers' catalogues, there just happened to be lots of books published which needed ordering in a catalogue, but because he considered Japanese books worthy of the same degree of bibliographical attention as Chinese books. Further, he provided at the outset an explanation of the 34 categories he used and an indication of the scope of each.[45]

By the end of the Tokugawa period these and other works were reasserting the worth of Japanese books vis-à-vis Chinese books and creating a new hierarchy which privileged what was Japanese. Within that hierarchy there was another which, with but few exceptions, placed Shintō at the apex of Japanese literary production and looked forward to the aggrandizement of Shintō in the early Meiji period.

---

[44] *NSMT* 3: 173–233.
[45] *YMC* 2: 151ff; *NSMT* 1: 119–468. *Bangai zassho kaidai* is reprinted in *Zoku shiseki shūran* 続史籍集覧, 10 vols (Kondō Shuppanbu, 1930), 10: 3–556.

BIBLIOGRAPHY

On classification, Ono Noriaki 1970 and Okamura 1995. The booksellers' catalogues are reprinted and extensively discussed in Shidō Bunko 1962-4. The texts of a number of catalogues and bibliographic studies ddating from the Tokugawa period are contained and briefly discussed in *NSMT*. Many others, some no longer extant, are discussed in one of the catalogues of the Unsen Bunko, Sugiura Saburōbei 杉浦三郎兵衛, *Edo jidai no shomoku* 江戸時代之書目 (Kyoto: Sugiura Kyūen, 1929). On private collections see the essays contained at the end of *KSS*.

10.2 BIBLIOGRAPHY IN THE TOKUGAWA PERIOD

When did the engagement of scholars with the Japanese or Chinese textual tradition become 'bibliography'? As we have seen above, book catalogues fulfilled many and various roles well before the Tokugawa period and their compilation required the exercise of discrimination and the imposition of order, but there is no sign that the history or transmission of a particular text was a concern of the compilers or that they were interested in books as material objects. As Kurita Mototsugu argued in 1939, it is probable if not certain that in the late Heian period literary scholars such as Fujiwara no Teika were forced by the complexity of the manuscript traditions confronting them to face up to the materiality of texts and the need to determine their relative reliability. Teika's diary makes it clear that in certain senses he was undoubtedly an 'editor' of the *Tale of Genji*. And the printing of Buddhist texts similarly required the exercise of editorial concern for the best texts. Little, however, has survived from the centuries before the Tokugawa period to cast light on the actual editorial processes involved, except for annotations correcting faulty manuscript readings (§3.2).[46]

It is not until the Tokugawa period, then, that we first encounter clear signs of scholarly engagement with the materiality of texts. This is first apparent in the editorial aspects of the project for the compilation of a great history of Japan, the *Dainihonshi*, which was initiated in 1657 by Tokugawa Mitsukuni, the daimyō of Mito. During the last 30 years of the seventeenth century the search for books and

---

[46] Kurita 1979: 12.

documents to be used in this project was put on an organized footing: researchers were sent to Kyoto and elsewhere, and gradually the search was extended to cover 'the old books and records of [all] sixty-six provinces'. The Mito scholars also took the close examination of texts seriously enough to publish reference works on early Japanese war-tales such as *Taiheiki*.[47]

In the late seventeenth century, when the *Dainihonshi* project was getting under way, the scholars of the Kogaku school, such as Itō Jinsai, and others like Ogyū Sorai were also beginning to pay close attention to texts and their contingency. Their textual scholarship was originally a product of their commitment to a branch of the Confucian tradition, known in Japan as *kōshōgaku* 考証学. This came to the fore in China in the late seventeenth century and manifested itself in the search for better texts, in studies of the transmission of texts and in a concern for correct interpretation. It was originally and predominantly concerned with the texts of the Confucian canon, but it stimulated the development of similar concerns with textual traditions and questions of interpretation in the Kokugaku studies of Motoori Norinaga and his intellectual successors, in Taki Keizan's studies of medical texts, and in the Sanskrit studies of Jiun (1718–1804). In the sinological tradition this textual empiricism was taken much further in the early eighteenth century by Yamanoi Konron, whose sophisticated textual criticism made some impact in China, as has already been mentioned (§7.2.1).[48]

The Bakufu was also becoming increasingly interested in gathering old documents and texts. The first clear sign of this is the anthology *Butoku taisei* 武徳大成 (1686), which was an edited collection of documents that had been requisitioned from the daimyō. In 1722 the shōgun Yoshimune, whose interventions leading to the growth of imports from China have been described elsewhere (§7.1.3), issued an edict listing a number of early Japanese works he wished to consult which were either unavailable in the Bakufu Library or were available only in incomplete copies. The implied recipients of the edict were daimyō and they were required to submit to the Bakufu items in their possession which were on Yoshimune's list. Similarly, if any of the items were in the possession of their retainers or of temples, shrines,

---

[47] Aida 1939: 1157–70.
[48] *KD* 5: 386–7.

farmers or merchants within their domains, they were to arrange for these to be submitted also.[49]

In the 1730s and 1740s the Bakufu, still under Yoshimune's direction, took more active steps to locate and appropriate books and documents in the provinces. Firstly, in 1736 temples, shrines and farmers in the province of Suruga were ordered to submit copies of documents in their possession. Later, in the years 1740–42 Aoki Kon'yō was commissioned by the Bakufu to travel around the provinces of Kai, Shinano, Musashi, Sagami, Izu, Tōtōmi and Mikawa in search of old books and documents. His visits were reinforced by local officials, who issued edicts requiring all to cooperate fully, to produce rarities from their collections, and to permit Aoki to copy them or to take temporary possession of them if he thought it necessary. The books and documents he removed were sent to Edo where they were meticulously copied, down to and including any impressions of seals of ownership, and were finally returned to their owners with instructions that they were to take good care of their possessions.[50]

At the end of the eighteenth century the scholar and statesman Matsudaira Sadanobu took the collection and study of historical documents to a level of sophistication that was not bettered until well after the end of the Tokugawa period. He published a lavish series of facsimiles under the title *Shūko jisshu* in 1800, but he also developed a scientific appreciation of the importance of recognising and identifying the status of documents, and invented a classification system to represent these different statuses. In this he differed from his contemporaries, who for the most part gave precedence to the extrinsic character of documents over the intrinsic and divided them up according to their owners not their contents. Such a tendency is discernible, for example, in the report compiled in 1792 by Shibano Ritsuzan and others following their official inspection of various temples and shrines in Yamashiro and Yamato provinces. They listed the manuscripts that they found not simply as texts but in terms of the calligrapher or the owner, fthus identifying one item as a 'sūtra in

---

[49] Aida 1939: 1150–51; *OKS* 991–3 #2017.

[50] Aida 1939: 1151–7; *OKS* 995–6 #2028–9; Aida Jirō, 'Genbun Kanpō nenkan ni okeru Bakufu no komonjo saihō' 元文寛保年間に於ける幕府の古文書採訪, *Rekishi chiri* 53.6 (1929): 72–88, 54.1 (1929): 66–9; *idem*, 'Aoki Kon'yō no komonjo saihō' 青木昆陽の古文書採訪, *Rekishi chiri* 51.2 (1928): 61–71.

the hand of Shōtoku Taishi'.[51]

Undoubtedly the most ambitious attempt to gather in and preserve lost texts in an editorially rigorous process in the Tokugawa period was the *Gunsho ruijū* project initiated by the blind bibliographer Hanawa Hokiichi (1746–1821). This had its origins in his fear that valuable Japanese texts, surviving perhaps in only one manuscript, might be irretrievably lost. This fear was justified, for a number of texts now survive only in their *Gunsho ruijū* versions. Hanawa and his editorial staff established the texts for *Gunsho ruijū* on the basis of manuscripts from a variety of sources. Some came from the Bakufu Library itself, and were made available to him by being deposited in the house of the Hayashi, hereditary heads of the Bakufu Academy. Further support came from the Bakufu in 1815 when it issued an edict instructing two shrines not only to show Hanawa and his researchers all the old documents they had in their libraries, but also to allow them to copy any documents they wished.[52]

Although it was purely private in its conception, the project benefited considerably from the Bakufu's growing interest and support. In 1793 Hanawa obtained permission from the Bakufu to establish an institution for the prosecution of 'Japanese studies', and this marked the start of his Wagaku Kōdansho 和学講談所, where the scholarly editorial work was carried out. In 1795 he received a grant of money from the Bakufu and presented a set of the 43 volumes that had so far been published, and the financial basis of the project was by that time secure. However, by 1797 he was already having problems with the storage of the printing blocks for the sections that had already been printed and published, and he was forced to request from the Bakufu the loan of some land so that he could construct some additional storage facilities. When the project was complete in 1819 there were 33,719 printing blocks in storage. Over the years 1795–1813 he published a further 556 volumes, but he remained dependent on the Bakufu's support, for he was forced to seek a substantial loan in 1814. Although gigantic in its conception, this was not the only such project Hanawa originated, for in 1798 he initiated a parallel one

---

[51] Aida 1939: 1176–81, 1184; *ZZGR* 16: 158–216.
[52] Sakamoto Tarō 坂本太郎, 'Wagaku Kōdansho ni okeru henshū shuppan jigyō' 和学講談所における編集出版事業, in *Koten to rekishi* 古典と歴史 (Yoshikawa Kōbunkan, 1972), 376; *OTS* 2: 811–12 #6424.

which would concern itself with the preparation of scholarly editions of, and the publication of, early Japanese historical texts. This was never completed, but it formed the basis of the *Kokushi taikei* series, which was first published in 1897–1901 and is still the standard edition of many of the texts contained in it.[53]

It is significant that Hanawa concerned himself with Japanese texts rather than Chinese. There can be no doubt that in the course of the Tokugawa period a fundamental shift took place in favour of Japanese books and texts, but it is yet to be given anything more than cursory treatment. The first clear sign of movement known to me is Hayashi Gahō's explanatory guide to Japanese books and texts, *Nihon shojaku kō* 日本書籍考 (1665; see below). It is in the eighteenth century, however, that political tension between Chinese and Japanese learning comes into the open, for example in the writings of Motoori Norinaga, who rejected the common interpretation of 'learning' (*gakumon*) to mean sinology and insisted that the primary meaning should be japanology. Miyazaki Rikken drew attention to the quantity and variety of Japanese books, implying that in neither respect had Japan anything to be ashamed of. And, as mentioned above, in his *Bangai zassho kaidai* Toda Ujinori placed sinological books after Japanese books, reversing the usual hierarchy.[54]

Let us now turn back to consider the growth of interest in books as material objects and to the emergence of a tradition of bibliographic enquiry. The earliest published books about books were Hayashi Razan's *Keiten daisetsu* 経典題説 (1667) and his son Gahō's *Nihon shojaku kō* (1665), which gave brief summaries of a selection of Chinese and Japanese texts respectively. Although not explicitly stated, Razan and Gahō had these works published as educational aids to guide inexperienced readers, perhaps particularly those without teachers who were trying to find their way through the bewildering variety of printed works currently available. The publication of *Bengisho mokuroku* in 1710 went considerably further. The author was Nakamura Magobee, a Kyoto publisher and bookseller, and it was written for fellow members of the book trade. He considered

---

[53] Sakamoto (see previous footnote), 367–85.
[54] *Motoori Norinaga zenshū* 本居宣長全集, 20 vols (Chikuma Shobō, 1968–75), 1: 47; *YMC* 2: 146–51; *Zoku shiseki shūran* 続史籍集覧, 10 vols (Kondō Shuppanbu, 1930), 10: 1.

books printed with movable type as a separate category and was the first to draw up a catalogue of them. He directed some attention to the formal qualities of books, but mostly with a view to the book trade, which also explains his attention to the titles of books not yet published and to books with homophonic titles that could easily be confused. At the same time, the compilation of catalogues for commercial and for private purposes was becoming commonplace, and bespeaks a growing concern with the identification of books by their distinguishing characteristics.[55]

At the end of the eighteenth century we encounter the first scholars whose work is not only recognisable as bibliography in a modern sense but which is in some cases still cited, both for their judgments and for their access to archives that are now lost. It was to this period too that the talented bibliographic circles active at the very end of the Tokugawa period traced their ancestry, and above all to the work of Kariya Ekisai (1775–1835). Ekisai was the precocious son of a bookseller and publisher operating in Edo. Before the age of 11 he had purchased a copy of the second of the eighth-century Japanese chronicles in Chinese, *Shoku nihongi*. He later built up a remarkable personal library of Song and Yuan printed editions and of movable-type books printed in Japan, which was dispersed in the early Meiji period. In 1790, about the same time as he took over his father's business, he travelled to Kyoto and managed, in spite of his youth, to examine several manuscripts of great antiquity and rarity, and either on this trip or on a subsequent one he made in 1797, he purchased one of the Hyakumantō Darani (§4.1.1), which were on sale at the Chikuhōrō 竹苞楼 bookshop in Kyoto. In 1798 he published a sheet on the Hyakumantō Darani as a contribution to the history of printing in Japan. It is evident from this, from the study he wrote on the movable type used for some of the editions printed by Ieyasu, and from his interest as a publisher in producing facsimiles of rarities he had found that he had from an early age an interest in the history of the book in China and Japan.[56]

Ekisai is particularly known now for his editorial work and his

---

[55] *NSMT* 3:75–152.
[56] Kurita 1979: 17; Umetani 1994: 11, 17–26, and *passim*; Kawase 1935. On his collection of books, Nagasawa Kikuya, 'Ekisai kyūzō sōgen kanpon ni tsuite', *Shoshigaku* 4.6 (1935): 44–6, and Kawase Kazuma, 'Kyūkorō shomoku' 求古楼書目, *Shoshigaku* 4.6 (1935): 54–68.

textual criticism. He took care to compare copies in his possession with others he had access to and corrected errors in the work of others. Although the inscriptions in the books and manuscripts he left at his death reveal a high order of bibliographic expertise, he was reluctant to publish even the concordances and indexes he compiled, and it has fallen to modern scholars to establish his reputation. However, it was at his initiative that a small group of fellow intellectuals with bibliographic interests began in 1815 to meet occasionally at his house to exhibit and discuss early Chinese printed books and manuscripts; the group included Izawa Ranken, Taki, Yashiro Hirokata and several others. Records of at least 11 meetings were kept in 1815–6, and these show that the focus of discussion was not texts but books as bibliographical objects. Thus at the first meeting Ekisai himself produced the pagoda and printed dhāraṇī from his Hyakumantō Darani, and the Northern Song printed edition of *Yü zhu xiao jing* 御注孝経, which is the oldest extant printed version of any of the works in the Chinese canon and which Ekisai himself published in facsimile in 1826. When the meetings came to an end is not known, but he did run a similar group in his declining years, and his example was followed by several of those who had been associated with him.[57]

One of these successor groups was the Tankikai 耽奇会, a circle led by Yamazaki Yoshishige for the discussion of books and other aspects of material culture. These meetings were attended by Kyokutei Bakin, Tani Bunchō and Yashiro Hirokata, amongst others. Yashiro also features in Ōta Nanpo's miscellany *Ichiwa ichigon*, in a section giving Nanpo's questions and Yashiro's answers on various bibliographical questions including, for example, the origins of blockprinting and of movable type. A further link between these men is their possession of the sole surviving manuscript of *Nihonkoku genzaisho mokuroku*: Ekisai acquired it some time before 1826 from a Kyoto bookseller and was the first to make a close study of this important guide to Chinese books extant in Japan in the early Heian period. He passed it on to Yashiro, who in turn gave it to Mori Shien, a participant in another bibliographical circle mentioned below.[58]

---

[57] Kawase 1935; Umetani 1994: 105–24.
[58] Okamura 1996: 51, 54; *Ichiwa ichigon*, *NZT bekkan*, 2: 603; Onagaya 1976: 56ff.

The most significant such venture, however, was the circle formed in 1852 by Taki Motokata with Shibue Chūsai, Mori Shien, and others connected with Ekisai, in order to work on a set of bibliographic studies of rare books. The books in question belonged to private collectors such as Ekisai himself, who was already dead, and Izawa Ranken, or to the Bakufu Library, the Academy library, the Ashikaga Gakkō and other institutional collections. They consisted of Song and Yuan printed editions from China, Korean printed books, and Japanese printed books and manuscripts. The members met 12 times a month at Taki's home for discussion of their findings and then subsequently wrote up the fruits of their studies in the form of contributions to a volume entitled *Keiseki hōkoshi* 経籍訪古志. These underwent a further process of revision and were finally ordered in the familiar four-part classification system of Chinese catalogues. The whole, although incomplete as originally conceived, was first published in 1885 in China.[59]

It cannot be gainsaid that there was a definite scholarly shift in favour of books as cultural artifacts, of editorial projects and of bibliographic questions in the first half of the nineteenth century. This shift has yet to be closely examined, and indeed much of the work which exemplifies it best is still only available in manuscript. Here there is room merely to cite a few further examples. Kondō Seisai, who served in the office of the Nagasaki city commissioner and was one of the shōgunal librarians from 1808 to 1819, had as a result of these positions privileged access to books and documents. His studies of the banning of imported Chinese books concerning Christianity and of Tokugawa Ieyasu's collection of books have already been referred to in earlier chapters and need not be discussed again here (§8.2.1).

Several booksellers had a scholarly interest in books and had the means to pursue that interest. In Kyoto the best known example is that of the owner of the Chikuhōrō bookshop, while in Edo Matsuzawa Rōsen (1769–1822) stands alone. Rōsen was a publisher who traded under the name Izumiya Shōjirō 和泉屋庄次郎 and who rose from obscurity in the course of just one generation to become one of the leading establishments with the right to reprint publications of the Kan'eiji in Edo and the Bakufu Academy. His diary records his

---

[59] *NKC* 2: 211; *Kaidai sōsho* 171.

acquaintance with Kariya Ekisai and gives details of his editorial work in 1818 with Ekisai, Shibue Chūsai and others on the text of *Qun shu zhi yao* 群書治要, for which they consulted copies from the Bakufu Library, the Kanazawa Bunko and the collection of the daimyō of Owari. He also published in 1821 a volume of corrections to a Qing catalogue, *Hui ke shu mu* 彙刻書目, and his various other bibliographical works include a lists of banned secular books and of Korean sinological books reprinted in Japan.[60]

These remarkable scholars, working entirely within a tradition of East Asian bibliography which they had done a great deal to create, had no successors. As Kurita put it, come the Restoration in 1868 and the 'turn to the West', the books they had treasured counted for little and the intellectual tradition they had nurtured went into stagnation, with the result that many of the books went abroad and that foreign bibliographers, especially Ernest Satow with his studies of early printing and the Jesuit editions, took the lead. It was not until the late Meiji period that the value of bibliography was recognised once more, but then that was largely as an ancillary tool for historical research and it owed much to the traditions of the German historical profession.

BIBLIOGRAPHY

For the texts of some of the bibliographic works mentioned here see *Kaidai sōsho* 1916. The only history of bibliography is Kurita 1979: 11–58, which covers the period up to 1932. Aida 1939 covers the development of editorial work with particular reference to documentary materials. Wada Mankichi 1983: 221–51 covers the compilation of catalogues by bibliographers. On Kariya Ekisai see Umetani Fumio 1994, and Kawase Kazuma 1935; on Yashiro Hirokata see *Mori Senzō chosakushū* 森銑三著作集, 12 vols (Chūō Kōronsha, 1988-9), 7: 115–91; Kondō Seisai's bibliographic works are contained in *KSZ*; on Ryūtei Tanehiko's bibliographic work see Andrew Lawrence Markus, *The willow in autumn: Ryūtei Tanehiko, 1783–1842* (Cambridge, Mass.: Harvard University Press, 1992), 102–9.

---

[60] *Matsuzawa Rōsen shiryōshū* 1982: 136, 215–6, 454–5, etc. See also Morikawa Akira 森川彰, 'Keigendō ni tsuite' 慶元堂について, in *Toshokangaku to sono shūhen (Amano Keitarō sensei koki kinen ronbunshū)* 図書館学とその周辺（天野敬太郎先生古希記念論文集）(Gannandō, 1971), 384–400.

AFTERWORD

Having reached the end of this book, readers may well feel, as does the author, that it has raised many more questions than it has answered, and that its coverage is patchy. One of the most obvious omissions is the economics of publishing. What were the break-even points for publishers? What determined the prices of books? What were the costs incurred in publishing, and how did they fluctuate? These important issues will, alas, have to await further research. I append here, therefore, merely a few final thoughts relating to the Tokugawa period that touch on questions only tangentially covered elsewhere, if at all.

In a recent and stimulating essay comparing the history of the book in Edo and Paris, Henry Smith has observed that 'the general absence of seditious publications in Japan, in all but the most indirect and parodic forms, is in striking contrast to the situation in France.' It is certainly true that attacks on, or criticisms of, the Tokugawa régime in print were almost non-existent and that print did not constitute a 'public political sphere' before the Meiji period. But this is not the whole story, for, as I have attempted to show in §3.3, print had to share cultural space with manuscripts and other forms of textual production, both written and oral, and here the picture is rather different. In oral performance and published manuscripts there was much that was seditious, and in addition there was a world of leaflets, graffiti and other forms of transient writing that were sometimes overtly critical of the Bakufu, particularly in the times of the shōgun Tsunayoshi and in the closing decades of the period, when inflation, famine and the threatening presence of foreign ships undermined the Bakufu's authority. Furthermore, the Bakufu made little attempt to restrain the publication of works expounding alternative ideologies: both Kokugaku and Rangaku writings, which undermined the sinocentrism of the Bakufu, encountered no difficulties. Defiance of the law and of the official ideology of the state was therefore not wanting, but the self-censorship of the guild system ensured that what was seditious remained outside the world of officially-approved print. Publishers benefiting from the monopolistic advantages the guild system conferred stood to lose more than they could possibly gain by turning to 'seditious publications.' That did not apply to the non-commercial publishers of books printed with movable type in the first half of the nineteenth century, who, as explained in §4.4.1, also challenged the limits of the permissible until they too became subject to state control in the 1840s.[1]

It is important, then, to acknowledge here that the focus on printed books, and the neglect of other forms of textual communication, which this book is guilty of, are likely to lead to mistaken conclusions about the extent of subversive, and indeed all forms of, cultural production in the Tokugawa period. The prevalence and ubiquity of print in Japan in that period makes it tempting to conclude that, as in England, 'print ... had become by the early eighteenth century ... the basic, inescapable technological fact of letters, the medium in which writing must exist and communicate in the world', but I hesitate to do so. Even in the case of prose literature this was not so, as the manuscript genre of *jitsuroku* clearly demonstrates (§3.3). In short, although print and its languages achieved a level of penetration of social and cultural life in urban Japan that at the time can only find parallels in Europe and north America, there were other ways in which writing could 'exist and communicate in the world'. Even in the late eighteenth century there were in existence establishments devoted to the production and marketing of manuscript books, and in the 1850s a catalogue of such scribal publications was printed in Edo.[2]

In his valuable study of the commercialization of literature in the Tokugawa period, May has drawn attention to the dominance of the market mechanisms of supply and demand in the production of prose literature, all of which was subject to market forces and published commercially not privately. He signals the need for study of the

---

[1] Smith 1994: 345, 352; Yoshihara Ken'ichirō 吉原健一郎, *Edo no jōhōya: Bakumatsu shominshi no sokumen* 江戸の情報屋－幕末庶民史の側面 (Nihon Hōsō Shuppan Kyōkai, 1978); Yajima Takanori 矢島隆教, *Edo jidai rakusho ruijū* 江戸時代落書類聚, 3 vols (Tōkyōdō, 1984–5); Konta 1978; Hirai Ryūtarō 平井龍太郎, 'Edo jidai ni okeru nyūsu rufu no ichiyōsō - nyūsu monjo no tensha ni tsuite' 江戸時代におけるニュース流布の一様相－ニュース文書の転写について, *Tōkyō Daigaku Shinbun Kenkyūsho kiyō* 2 (1953): 77–90. On the printing of Ōshio Heihachirō's critique of Bakufu policy in 1837, see Kōda Shigetomo 幸田成友, *Ōshio Heihachirō* 大塩平八郎 (Sōgensha, 1942), 261–7.

[2] Kernan 1987: 9; Nakamura Kiyozō 1972: 40–44.

effects of commercialization on the form and structure of narrative, and suggests, for example, that the marketing of illustrated fiction, in which the quality of the illustrations and the name of the illustrator counted for a great deal, may have impeded the textual development of fiction. His exploration of publishers' strategies in prolonging the life and profitability of successful works by resorting to sequels and continuations is valuable, too, but there is a sense in which he, and other writers, have reified Japanese literature and detached it from the thick matrix of print, scribal and oral culture in which it subsisted. On the one hand, since almost all publication was commercial, the inference must be that in other fields, too, such as maps, directories, conduct books and travel guides, commercialization had its impact, but what impact? And important though May has shown the effects of commercialization to have been on prose literature, there are other forces at work, too: it was not commercialization that created the enormous and costly *yomihon* of Bakin, which could only be published if the lending libraries would buy them, or the demand for *setsuyōshū* or conduct books for women. In short, the world of print that prose literature inhabited, and the print language in which it was expressed, can only be understood with reference to its non-literary components as well.[3]

We still know far too little about the experiences of readers, their social and gender composition, and it is time to discard assumptions that are widespread. A project such as the 'Reading experience database', which takes as its motto the words of Martial, 'Laudant illa sed ista legunt', 'They praise those but read these', and which is being run jointly by the Open University and the Centre for the Book at the British Library, would be invaluable in the case of Japan too. We must ask the question, when did Japan learn to read? The answer will lie in the Tokugawa period, but the complexities are yet to be understood. As in Qing China, we know that the élite definitions of reading and literacy in Tokugawa Japan are inadequate, but we know little about the public and private dimensions of reading. We do not know how Japanese men and women read the Chinese and Japanese texts they encountered and how they reacted to them, nor do we know about the differences between rural and urban readers. And what about the impact of the 'unified national market' for goods that

---

[3] May 1983: xi–xiv, 140, 150–81.

emerged in the late seventeenth century: what effect did this have on the reading habits of Japanese readers?[4]

As Jeffrey Brooks has shown for Russia, secular texts can sometimes be read in unexpected ways by unsophisticated readers, and recovering the reading experiences of Japanese readers will not be easy.[5] But some attempt must be made, for our assumptions about what Japanese read and how they read are at present inadequate. This is perhaps the most urgent challenge. For if we are to come to grips with the mentalities and mental constructs of literate Japanese of the past, then we need to learn more about their uses of books, how they fitted books into their conceptual worlds, and ultimately how they read.

---

[4] Smith 1994: 352; Evelyn Sakakida Rawski, *Education and popular literacy in Ch'ing China* (Ann Arbor: University of Michigan Press, 1979); Gilbert Rozman, *Urban networks in Ch'ing China and Tokugawa Japan* (Princeton: Princeton University Press, 1973), 111, 135.

[5] Jeffrey Brooks, *When Russia learned to read: literacy and popular literature, 1861–1917* (Princeton: Princeton University Press, 1985), 32.

APPENDIX

THE BIBLIOGRAPHY OF BLOCK-PRINTED BOOKS

There is, unfortunately, no universally accepted set of bibliographical conventions for the description, and the determination of the status, of books produced in Japan before the twentieth century. There is not even a universally accepted set of terms, for some use terms derived from Chinese bibliography and the nomenclature of the Chinese book, while others eschew these terms in favour of a Japanese vocabulary.

Since only a small proportion of the output of the commercial and private presses of the Tokugawa and Meiji periods has so far been reprinted in easily accessible modern editions, dealing with pre-modern editions remains unavoidable for historians, literary scholars, intellectual historians and others. But here the terminological confusion and lack of bibliographical clarity make the task not only palaeographically taxing but often one that is in addition bewildering in terms of textual history and reliability. For the benefit of those who are forced to refer to editions printed in the Tokugawa period or who need to trace the textual history and ecology of a given work in the Tokugawa period, I append here an outline of the problems. This will serve to draw attention to the fluidity of texts in the Tokugawa period, a fluidity that situates them somewhere between manuscript culture and the solid state of the modern printed book.

The principal point at issue here concerns the nature of the blockprinting process in the Tokugawa period and the practices of the commercial publishing industry, and it focusses on the question of what an 'edition' is. The word commonly used in contemporary Japanese catalogues and works of reference in a sense approximating to that of the English 'edition' is *han* 版, but this word as customarily used is fundamentally flawed when applied to the blockprinted books of the Tokugawa period, as will now be demonstrated.

Although, as Elizabeth Eisenstein has argued, the replication of a text in print fixed that text in the standardized form of identical copies, it is in fact rare that any two copies of the same text printed in the Tokugawa period are today found to be actually identical. There is an almost infinite range of variation possible between two copies of what is purportedly the same book (§2.3). At one end of the range would be two books that were physically identical in all respects but for different seals of ownership. Although the reading history of those two books would be demonstrably different just as would presumptively be the case with any two other identical copies, their textual status would be identical. At the other end would be two copies bearing the same title and apparently containing the same text but actually printed from different printing blocks. Visually they would be quite distinct, since they would be the product of different calligraphic hands, to make no mention of other possible difference of illustration, binding, and so on. It would be appropriate to describe these latter two as belonging to two different editions, and it would be necessary to establish whether or not they were textually identical.

Between these two extremes lie a number of other possibilities, and it is these that create the problems. Let us take the example of an edition of the *Heike monogatari* published in the fifth year of Enpō 延宝 (1677), and by 'published' I mean that the blocks were prepared and first used for the production of printed copies in that year, as ascertained by examining the date given in the colophon. The term used for published in that narrow sense in certain catalogues, such as those of the Naikaku Bunko in Tokyo, and by certain bibliographers such as Nagasawa Kikuya, is *kan* 刊, and that is what will be used here because it explicitly identifies the status of a book. This particular edition of the *Heike monogatari* published in 1677 is therefore described as 延宝5刊, and this would unequivocally distinguish it from other editions printed from different printing blocks in other years.

The set of blocks used to print that 1677 edition of the *Heike* would be used to print a certain number of copies in that year, as many as the publisher thought the market could take, perhaps, and then the blocks might be put in storage. Some time later, and it could be months, years, or decades later, the publisher gets them out again to print more copies; alternatively, he might wish to realise the capital investment and so sell the blocks to another publisher, who thought it worthwhile to print some more copies. The results of either of these renewed printing operations could take one of a number of

different forms, of which three possibilities are given here:
1   The new copies are visually identical to the earlier ones and virtually indistinguishable from them except for slightly greater wear on the blocks.
2   The new copies have a quite distinct cover, but are otherwise identical to the earlier ones, except for the wear on the blocks.
3   The new copies have a new colophon giving the current year either in addition to or instead of the old date, 1677; they could appear with a new cover design or with the old one.

Textually they would all necessarily be identical, given that they were printed from the one unchanged set of blocks. Why, then, should they be distinguished, and how can they be distinguished bibliographically? The value of distinguishing them lies in the fact that they testify to a continuing market demand for copies of that text in that edition, but the task of doing so requires more detailed bibliographical knowledge than is at present easy to acquire, concerning for example the covers of the first printed copies, and demands a laborious comparison of the texts to determine if there is appreciable wear on the blocks. Where evidence of worn blocks indicates a later printing of types 1 or 2 above, this can be shown in the form 延宝5刊・後印. In the case of type 3, where the date of printing is indicated, there is a need to distinguish between the date of the blocks and the date of printing, and this is done in the form 延宝5刊・元禄5印. Of course, in some cases the date of the blocks given in the colophon may have been removed and replaced by the date of printing: these cases require laborious comparisons to determine which edition has been reprinted, and sometimes this is not possible if no early dated copies have survived. If one is fortunate enough to be able to determine the original date of the blocks, then that is best indicated in square brackers, [延宝5]刊・元禄5印.

Although the complexity is already testing, no mention has yet been made of changes to the blocks, which set the printed copies visually and textually apart from other copies printed from the same blocks before they were altered, and which require some bibliographic notation to indicate this important difference in status. What sorts of changes might be made to the blocks and why? The following list is by no means exhaustive but will serve to reveal the covert world of textual manipulation in the Tokugawa period.

1 An old work might be given a fresh lease of commercial life by reissuing it under a different title. The original blocks are used, of course, and the extent of the changes depends on the publisher's ingenuity and estimation of the gullibility of the reading public. He might merely change the title on the covers or he might resort to *umeki*, the practice of substituting a plug of wood for undesired text and carving on it a new text, to change the internal titles as well.
2 Mistakes and orthographical errors might be corrected using *umeki*.
3 Changes or additions to the text or to the illustrations might be made by *umeki* or even by the replacement of a whole block or blocks. In many cases the changes are of importance in the evolution of the text or the aesthetic presentation of the illustrations.
4 Some or many of the blocks of a popular work might have become so worn down that they need to be replaced. The easiest ways to do this was to cannibalize a printed copy by pasting the pages onto new blocks and carving new printing blocks; they will of course not be identical to the old ones, but they will be calligraphically consistent.

It will be obvious that none of these changes are easy to discern, obviously important though they are. It is again a laborious matter of comparisons of extant copies and of careful attention to the appearance of each page, for the experienced eye can learn to recognise the signs of *umeki* in most cases. Copies printed from altered blocks in one or more of these ways are represented bibliographically by the notation 延宝5刊・元禄5修, where *shū* 修 indicates the date of alteration of the blocks.

It will be clear from the above brief discussion that the bibliographical unit must be the blocks, and that the task, often well nigh impossible, of the bibliographer must be to determine the hierarchy and genealogy of texts generated by a given set of blocks in their often long and varied life. The very gradual elucidation of these hierarchies and genealogies is making it possible in some cases to discern the interventions of the commercial publishers, the repackaging and remaking of texts, and the longevity of the market for specific texts.

BIBLIOGRAPHY

Nagasawa Kikuya 長沢規矩也, *Zukai kosho mokuroku hō* 図解古書目録法 (Kyūko Shoin, 1974) and his *(Zukai) Shoshigaku nyūmon* （図解）書誌学入門 (Kyūko Shoin, 1976) are excellent illustrated introductions to Japanese bibliography, and Fujii Takashi 藤井隆, *Nihon koten shoshigaku sōsetsu* 日本古典書誌学総説 (Osaka: Izumi Shoin, 1991) covers bibliographic terminology. Nagasawa has also discussed the significance of colophons when determining the status of printed books with numerous examples in 'Shoinbon to kōinbon' 初印本と後印本, *NKC* 4: 205-28. For a superb guide to bibliography of the printed books of the Tokugawa period see Nakano 1995, and for a detailed discussion in English of the bibliographic terminology and a system for the representation of bibliographic difference see Hayashi & Kornicki 1991: 13-37.

GLOSSARY

Bakufu the name given to the successive samurai governments of the Kamakura, Muromachi and Tokugawa periods.
chokusenshū the anthologies of Japanese poetry commissioned by the court
ehon a book consisting wholly or mostly of illustrations
Five Classics the earliest set of 'classics' in the Chinese tradition, consisting of the *Book of songs*, the *Book of Documents*, the *Book of changes*, the *Spring and autumn annals* and the *Book of rituals*
Four Books the Confucian classics, consisting of the Confucian *Analects*, the *Great learning*, the *Doctrine of the mean*, and *Mencius*
furigana glosses in one of the *kana* syllabaries placed on the right of characters printed vertically, and above characters printed horizontally
ireki see *umeki*
gozanban one of the editions printed by the Gozan Zen monasteries in the Kamakura and Muromachi periods
hanshita the written form of the text which is pasted onto the wooden blocks prior to carving
hiragana the cursive *kana* syllabary
jūhan a copyright infringement which involves copying an entire work
kabusebori the carving of a new block using a printed page as the *hanshita*
kana the Japanese syllabaries
katakana the angular *kana* syllbary
kokatsujiban books printed in Japan with movable type in the seventeenth century
Kokugaku the so-called Nativist tradition of the eighteenth and nineteenth centuries, which rejected the sinophilic aspects of Japanese culture

kunten reading marks inserted into Chinese texts to enable Japanese readers to read those texts as if they were Japanese

ninjōbon a genre of romantic fiction that arose in Edo in the early nineteenth century

Rangaku 'Dutch studies', the school of learning that depended on Dutch books brought into Japan via Deshima and that was largely scientific in focus

renga chains of linked verse

rōnin a samurai who has no master

ruihan a copyright infringement which involves copying part of, or imitating, another work

Sagabon books printed with movable type at Saga, to the west of Kyoto, in the early years of the seventeenth century

santo the so-called 'three capitals'; a term used in the Tokugawa period to refer to Kyoto, Osaka and Edo

umeki the insertion of pieces of wood into existing printing blocks to alter the colophon or part of the text

yomihon a genre of mostly historical novels that developed in the late eighteenth century and was popular until the end of the nineteenth

zōhan 'ownership of the blocks', a term used mostly by private publishers

ABBREVIATIONS

AA	*Acta Asiatica*
ARI	*Abe Ryūichi ikōshū* 阿部隆一遺稿集, 4 vols (Kyūko Shoin, 1985–93)
BKD	*Bussho kaisetsu daijiten* 仏書解説大辞典, ed. Ono Genmyō 小野玄妙, 11 vols (Daitō Shuppansha, 1933–35)
BKK	*Bukkyō kōkogaku kōza* 仏教考古学講座, 4 vols (Yūsankaku Shuppan, 1970–71)
BN	*Bakin nikki* 馬琴日記, 4 vols (Chūō Kōronsha, 1973)
BOS	*Bakumatsu ofuregaki shūsei* 幕末御触書集成, ed. Ishii Ryōsuke 石井良助 & Harafuji Hiroshi 腹藤弘司, 7 vols (Iwanami Shoten, 1992–95)
BSOAS	*Bulletin of the School of Oriental and Afrcian Studies*
DBZ	*Dainihon bukkyō zensho* 大日本仏教全書, 151 vols (Dainihon bukkyō zensho Hakkōsho, 1912–22
DNK	*Dainihon komonjo* 大日本古文書, 46 vols to date (Tōkyō Daigaku, 1910–)
DNKK	*Dainihon kokiroku* 大日本古記録, 57 vols to date (Iwanami Shoten, 1952–)
DNKS	*Dainihon kinsei shiryō* 大日本近世史料, 214 vols to date (Tōkyō Daigaku Shuppankai, 1953–)
EHSK	*Edo hon'ya shuppan kiroku* 江戸本屋出版記録, 3 vols, *SSS* 10 (1980–2)
EZ	*Ekken zenshū* 益軒全集, 8 vols (Ekken Zenshū Kankōkai, 1910–11),
GBZ	*Gozan bungaku zenshū* 五山文学全集, ed. Kamimura Kankō 上村観光, 5 vols (Gozan Bungaku Zenshū Kankōkai, 1936)
GLJ	*Gest Library journal*
GUDJ	*Genshoku ukiyoe daihyakka jiten* 原色浮世絵大百科事典, 11 vols (Taishūkan Shoten, 1980–82)
GY	*Gyokuyō* 玉葉, 3 vols (Kokusho Kankōkai, 1906–7)
HJAS	*Harvard Journal of Asiatic Studies*
JAOS	*Journal of the American Oriental Society*
JAS	*Journal of Asian Studies*

KCZ	*Kokubun chūshaku zensho* 国文注釈全書, 20 vols (Teikoku Shoin, 1907–10)
KD	*Kokushi daijiten* 国史大辞典, 15 vols (Yoshikawa Kōbunkan, 1979–97)
KSM	*Kokusho sōmokuroku* 国書総目録, 8 vols (Iwanami Shoten, 1963–72)
KSS	*Kinsei shomokushū* 近世書目集, ed. Suzuki Jūzō 鈴木重三 & Satō Satoru 佐藤悟, Nihon koten bungaku eiin sōkan 32 (Nihon Koten Bungakkai, 1989)
KSZ	*Kondō Seisai zenshū* 近藤正斎全集, 3 vols (Kokusho Kankōkai, 1905–6)
KT	*Kokushi taikei* （増補改正）国史大系, 60 vols (Yoshikawa Kōbunkan, 1929–58)
MFC	*Mizutani Futō chosakushū* 水谷不倒著作集, 8 vols (Chūō Kōronsha, 1973–77)
MN	*Monumenta Nipponica*
MZS	*Mikan zappai shiryō* 未刊雑俳資料, 49 sections (*ki* 期), (Suzuki Katsutada, 1958–; referred to in the form 4.3: 56b, meaning 4th *ki*, section 3, page 56 verso)
NKBT	*Nihon koten bungaku taikei* 日本古典文学大系, 102 vols (Iwanami Shoten, 1957–68)
NKBZ	*Nihon koten bungaku zenshū* 日本古典文学全集, 51 vols (Shōgakkan, 1973)
NKC	*Nagasawa Kikuya chosakushū* 長沢規矩也著作集, 11 vols (Kyūko Shoin, 1982–7)
NKSS	*Nihon kyōikushi shiryō* 日本教育史資料, 9 vols (Monbushō, 1890–92)
NS	*Nagoya sōsho* 名古屋叢書, 25 vols (Nagoya: Nagoya-shi Kyōiku Iinkai, 1959–65)
NSGT	*Nihon shoshigaku taikei* 日本書誌学体系, 120 vols in 74 parts to date (Musashi-Murayama, 1978–; references are made to part numbers)
NSMT	*Nihon shomoku taikei* 日本書目大系, ed. Nagasawa Kikuya 長沢規矩也 and Abe Ryūichi 阿部隆一, 4 vols (Kyūko Shoin, 1979)
NST	*Nihon shisō taikei* 日本思想大系, 67 vols (Iwanami Shoten, 1970–82)
NYK	*Nihon yōgakushi no kenkyū* 日本洋学史の研究, ed. Arisaka Takamichi 有坂隆道, 10 vols (Osaka:

ABBREVIATIONS

	Sōgensha, 1968–91)
NZT	*Nihon zuihitsu taisei* 日本随筆大成, 41 vols in three series (Nihon Zuihitsu Taisei Kankōkai, 1927–31)
OATD	*Ōsaka Aoyama Tanki Daigaku Shozōhin zuroku* 大阪青山短期大学所蔵品図録 (Minō: Ōsaka Aoyama Tanki Daigaku, 1992)
OHNK	*Ōsaka honya nakama kiroku* 大坂本屋仲間記録, 18 vols (Osaka: Osaka Furitsu Nakanoshima Toshokan, 1975–93)
OHS	*Ofuregaki hōreki shūsei* 御触書宝暦集成, ed. Takayanagi Shinzō 高柳真三 and Ishii Ryōsuke 石井良助 (Iwanami Shoten, 1935)
OKS	*Ofuregaki kanpō shūsei* 御触書寛保集成, ed. Takayanagi Shinzō 高柳真三 and Ishii Ryōsuke 石井良助 (Iwanami Shoten, 1934)
ONZ	*Ōta Nanpo zenshū* 大田南畝全集, 20 vols (Iwanami Shoten, 1985–90)
OSSM	*(Kyōhō igo) Ōsaka shuppan shoseki mokuroku* 享保以後大阪出版書籍目録 (Osaka: Ōsaka Tosho Shuppangyō Kumiai, 1936)
OTS	*Ofuregaki Tenpō shūsei* 御触書天保集成, ed. Takayanagi Shinzō 高柳真三 & Ishii Ryōsuke 石井良助, 2 vols (Iwanami Shoten, 1937–41)
SNKBT	*Shin nihon koten bungaku taikei* 新日本古典文学大系, 81 vols to date (Iwanami Shoten, 1989–)
SR	*Sen'yō ruishū* 撰要類集, ed. Tsuji Tatsuya 辻達也, 3 vols (Zoku Gunsho ruiju Kanseikai, 1967–79)
SSS	*Shoshi shomoku shiriizu* 書誌書目シリーズ, 290 vols to date (Yumani Shobō, 1986–)
ST	*Shiryō taisei* 史料大成, 43 vols (Naigai Shoseki, 1934–44)
T	*Taishō shinshū Daizōkyō* 大正新修大蔵経, 100 vols (Daizō Shuppan/ Taishō Issaikō Kankōkai, 1924–34)
TASJ	*Transactions of the Asiatic Society of Japan*
TKKZ	*Tokugawa kinreikō, zenshū* 徳川禁令考　前集, ed. Ishii Ryōsuke 石井良助, 5 vols (Sōbunsha, 1959)
YMC	*Yayoshi Mitsunaga chosakushū* 弥吉光長著作集, 6 vols (Nichigai Asoshiētsu, 1981–3)

ZEJ	*Zoku enseki jisshu* 続燕石十種, 2 vols (Kokusho Kankōkai, 1908–9)
ZGR	*Zoku gunsho ruijū* 続群書類従, 67 vols (Zoku Gungsho Ruijū Kankōkai, 1902–28)
ZZGR	*Zokuzoku gunsho ruiju* 続続群書類聚, 16 vols (Kokusho Kankōkai, 1906–9)

BIBLIOGRAPHY

Listed here are only those books and articles which have been referred to twice or more often in the footnotes. Items referred to only once in the footnotes or in the short bibliographies following each section are not included here.

Abe Yoshio 阿部吉雄 1965, *Nihon Shushigaku to Chōsen* 日本朱子学と朝鮮 (Tōkyō Daigaku Shuppankai)
Aeba Kōson 饗庭篁村 1910, 'Mukashi no sakusha no sakuryō oyobi shuppan busū' 昔の作者の作料および出版部数, *Aoi* あふひ 4: 1–3 (facsimile in *SSS* 2)
Aida Jirō 相田二郎 1939, 'Edo jidai ni okeru komonjo no saihō to hensan' 江戸時代に於ける古文書の採訪と編纂, in Shigakkai, ed., *Honpō shigakushi ronsō* 本邦史学史論叢, 2 vols (Fuzanbō 1939), 2: 1147–84
Alford, William P. 1995, *To steal a book is an elegant offence: intellectual property law in Chinese civilization* (Stanford: Stanford University Press)
Altman, Albert A. 1975, 'Shinbunshi: the early Meiji adaptation of the Western-style newspaper', in W. G. Beasley, ed., *Modern Japan: aspects of history, literature and society* (London: George, Allen and Unwin), 52–66
Anderson, Benedict 1991, *Imagined communities: reflections on the origin and spread of nationalism*, revised edition (London: Verso)
Ariga Yōen 有賀要延 1984, *Shakyō ganmon taisei* 写経願文大成 (Kokusho Kankōkai)
Asakura Haruhiko 朝倉治彦 1983, *Kinsei shuppan kōkoku shūsei*, 近世出版広告集成 6 vols, *SSS* 11
Asakura Haruhiko 1990, 'The origins of newspapers and magazines in the Bakumatsu and Meiji periods', in Yu-Ying Brown 1990: 179–87
Asakura Haruhiko 朝倉治彦 and Ōwa Hiroyuki 大和博幸 (eds) 1993, *Kinsei chihō shuppan no kenkyū* 近世地方出版の研究 (Tōkyōdō Shuppan)
Asakura Haruhiko & Sakuma Nobuko 佐久間信子 1971, *(Meiji shoki)*

Santo shinkoku shomoku 明治初期三都新刻書目 (Nihon Kosho Tsūshinsha)

Asano, Shūgō & Timothy Clark (eds) 1995, *The passionate art of Kitagawa Utamaro*, 2 vols (London: British Museum Press)

Ashikaga Enjutsu 足利衍述 & Ashikaga Chiburi 足利知夫 1932, *Kamakura Muromachi no jukyō* 鎌倉室町時代之儒教 (Nihon Koten Zenshū Kankōkai)

Atiyeh, George N. (ed.) 1995, *The book in the Islamic world: the written word and communication in the Middle East* (Albany: SUNY Press)

Balsamo, Luigi 1990, *Bibliography: history of a tradition*, trans. William A. Pettas (Berkeley, Ca.: Bernard M. Rosenthal)

Barthes, Roland 1977, 'The death of the author', in Stephen Heath, ed., *Image music text* (London: Fontana), 142–9

Bowring, Richard 1982, *Murasaki Shikibu: her diary and poetic memoirs* (Princeton: Princeton University Press)

Brown, Louise Norton 1924, *Block-printing and book-illustration in Japan from the earliest period to the twentieth century* (London: George Routledge & Sons Ltd)

Brown, Yu-Ying (ed.) 1990, *Japanese studies*, British Library occasional papers 11 (London: The British Library)

Bunkenka 文献課, ed., 1979–81, 'Meiji shoki no zōsho' 明治初期の蔵書, *Kyōto furitsu sōgō shiryōkan kiyō* 京都府立総合資料館紀要 7.51–70 & 9.1–29

Chartier, Roger (ed.) 1989, *The culture of print: power and the uses of print in early modern Europe*, trans. Lydia G. Cochrane (Cambridge: Polity Press)

Chartier, Roger 1994, *The order of books: readers, authors, and libraries in Europe between the fourteenth and eighteenth centuries*, trans. Lydia G. Cochrane (Cambridge: Polity Press)

Chen Guoqing 陳国慶 1984, *Kanseki hanpon nyūmon* 漢籍版本入門, trans. Sawaya Harutsugu 沢谷昭次 (Kenbun Shuppan)

Chibbett, David 1977, *The history of Japanese printing and book illustration* (Tokyo: Kodansha International)

Ch'ŏn Hyebong 千恵鳳 (ed.) 1976, *Hanguk koinswaesa* 韓国古印刷史 (Seoul: Hanguk Tosogwanhak Yŏnguhoe)

Christie's 1988, *The Donald and Mary Hyde collection of Japanese books and manuscripts* (New York: Christie's)

Drège, Jean-Pierre 1986, 'Le livre manuscrit et les débuts de la

xylographie,' in Drège, Ishigami-Iagolnitzer and Cohen 1986: 19–39
Drège, Jean-Pierre 1991a, 'La lecture et l'écriture en Chine et la xylographie', *Études chinoises* 10: 77–111
Drège, Jean-Pierre 1991b, *Les bibliothèques en Chine au temps des manuscrits (jusqu'au Xe siècle)*, Publications de l'École française d'extrême-orient 161 (Paris)
Drège, Jean-Pierre, Mitchiko Ishigami-Iagolnitzer and Monique Cohen (eds) 1986, *Le livre et l'imprimerie en extrême Orient et en Asie de sud* (Bordeaux: Société des Bibliophiles de Guyenne)
Ebihara Hachirō 蛯原八郎 1980, *Nihon ōji shinbun zasshi shi* 日本欧字新聞雑誌史 (facsimile of 1934 edition; Meicho Fukyūkai)
Egami Yasushi 江上綏 1989, *Sōshokukyō* 装飾経, Nihon no bijutsu 278 (Shibundō)
Eisenstein, Elizabeth 1979, *The printing press as an agent of change: communications and cultural transformations in early-modern Europe* (Cambridge: Cambridge University Press)
Farrington, Anthony 1991, *The English factory in Japan, 1613–1623* (London: The British Library)
Formanek, Susanne & Sepp Linhart (eds) 1995, *Buch und Bild als gesellschaftliche Kommunikationsmittel in Japan einst und jetzt* ([Vienna], Literas)
Matthi Forrer 1979, *Egoyomi and surimono: their history and development* (Uithoorn: J. C. Gieben)
Forrer, Matthi 1985, *Eirakuya Tōshirō, publisher at Nagoya*, Japonica Neerlandica 1 (Amsterdam: J. C. Gieben)
Fujimoto Yukio 藤本幸夫 1981, 'Sōke bunkozō chōsenbon ni tsuite' 宋家文庫蔵朝鮮本について, *Chōsen gakuhō* 99/100: 195–224
Fujiyoshi Masumi 藤善真澄 1981, 'Jōjin no motarashita higa no tenseki' 成尋の齎した彼我の典籍, *Bukkyō shigaku kenkyū* 仏教史学研究 23.1: 33–70
Fukui Tamotsu 福井保 1980, *Momijiyama Bunko: Edo Bakufu no sankō toshokan* 紅葉山文庫－江戸幕府の参考図書館 (Kyōgakusha)
Fukui Tamotsu 1985, *Edo bakufu kankōbutsu* 江戸幕府刊行物 (Yūshōdō Shuppan)
Fukuzawa Yukichi 1966, *The autobiography of Fukuzawa Yukichi*, trans. Eiichi Kiyooka (New York: Columbia University Press)
Gardner, Kenneth B. 1990, 'Centres of printing in medieval Japan:

late Heian to early Edo period', in Yu-Ying Brown 1990: 157–69.
Gardner, Kenneth B. 1993, *Descriptive Catalogue of Japanese Books in the British Library printed before 1700* (London: The British Library; Tenri: Tenri Central Library)
Goodman, Grant K. 1986, *Japan: the Dutch experience* (London: Athlone Press)
Groemer, G. 1994, 'Singing the news: *yomiuri* in Japan during the Edo and Meiji periods', *HJAS* 54: 233–261
Haga Kōshirō 芳賀幸四郎 1981, *Higashiyama bunka no kenkyū* 東山文化の研究, 2 vols, Haga Kōshirō rekishi ronshū 1-2 (Kyoto: Shibunkaku)
Hagitani Boku 萩谷朴 1971–3, *Murasaki Shikibu nikki zenchūshaku* 紫式部日記全注釈, 2 vols (Kadokawa Shoten)
Hamada Keisuke 浜田啓介 1953, 'Bakin ni okeru shoshi sakusha dokusha no mondai' 馬琴に於ける書肆、作者、読者の問題, *Kokugo kokubun* 国語国文 22.4: 21–38
Hamada Keisuke 1956, 'Kinsei kōki ni okeru Ōsaka shorin no sūkō - shorin Kawachiya o megutte' 近世後期における大阪書林の趨向ー書林河内屋をめぐって, *Kinsei bungei* 3: 15–28
Hanpon 版本 1990 (Tabako to Shio no Hakubutsukan)
Hashimoto Fumio 橋本不美男, *Genten o mezashite - koten bungaku no tame no shoshi* 原典をめざしてー古典文学のための書誌 (Kasama Shoin, 1974)
Hawks, Francis L. 1857, *Narrative of the expedition of an American Squadron to the China seas and Japan ...* (New York: D. Appleton & Co.)
Hayashi, Nozomu & Peter Kornicki 1991, *Early Japanese books in Cambridge University Library: a catalogue of the Aston, Satow and von Siebold collections*, University of Cambridge Oriental Publications 40 (Cambridge: Cambridge University Press)
Hayashi Yoshikazu 林美一 (ed.) 1987, *Sakusha tainai totsuki no zu* 作者胎内十月図, Edo gesaku bunko 10 (Kawade Shobō Shinsha)
Henderson, Dan Fenno 1970–71, 'Chinese legal studies in early eighteenth century Japan: scholars and sources', *JAS* 30: 21–56
Higuchi Hideo 樋口秀雄 1963, 'Kinsei ni okeru shuppan to ken'etsu' 近世における出版と検閲, *Kokubungaku* 8.4: 174–81
Higuchi Hideo & Asakura Haruhiko 朝倉治彦 1962, *(Kyōhō igo) Edo shuppan shomoku* 享保以後江戸出版書目, Mikan kokubun shiryō bekkan 1 (Toyohashi: Mikan Kokubun Shiryō Kankōkai)

Hillier, Jack 1988, *The art of the Japanese book* (London: Philip Wilson, for Sotheby's Publications)
Hirako Takurei 平子鐸嶺 1908, *Hyakumantō shikō* 百万塔肆攷 (n.p.: Hirako Nao)
Hironiwa Motosuke 広庭基介 1967, 'Edo jidai kashihon'ya ryakushi' 江戸時代貸本屋略史, *Toshokan kai* 図書館界 18.5: 158–66 & 178; 18.6: 188–203
Hironiwa Motosuke 1973–74, 'Shinbun jūransho shōron' 新聞縦覧所小論, *Toshokan kai* 25.3: 84–100; 25.4: 133–52; 26.2: 67–8
Hoare, J. E. 1975 'The "Bankoku Shinbun" Affair: foreigners, the Japanese press and extraterritoriality in early Meiji Japan', *Modern Asian studies* 9: 289–302
Hoare, J. E. 1994, *Japan's treaty ports and foreign settlements: the uninvited guests, 1858–1899* (Folkestone: Japan Library)
Ikeda Kikan 池田亀鑑 1941, *Koten no hihanteki shochi ni kansuru kenkyū* 古典の批判的処置に関する研究, 3 vols (Iwanami Shoten)
Inoue Masamichi 井上順理 1972, *(Honpō chūsei made ni okeru) Mōshi juyōshi no kenkyū* 本邦中世までにおける孟子受容史の研究 (Kazama Shobō)
Inoue Takaaki 井上隆明 1981, *Kinsei shorin hanmoto sōran* 近世書林板元総覧, *NSGT* 14
Ishida Hisatoyo 石田尚豊 1982, 'Kūkai shōrai mokuroku o megutte' 空海請来目録をめぐって, *Aoyama shigaku* 青山史学 7: 1–35
Ishida Mosaku 石田茂作 1930, *(Shakyō yori mitaru) Narachō bukkyō no kenkyū* 写経より見たる奈良朝仏教の研究, Tōyō Bunko ronsō 11 (Tōyō Bunko)
Ishida Mosaku 1952, *Yasuda Bunko kokyō seikan* 安田文庫古経清鑑 (Nihon Kaigai Shōji)
Ishida Mosaku 1977–78, *Bukkyō kōkogaku ronkō* 仏教考古学論攷, 6 vols (Kyoto: Shibunkaku)
Ishizaki Matazō 石崎又造 1967, *(Kinsei nihon ni okeru) Shina zokugo bungakushi* (近世日本に於ける) 支那俗語文学史 (Shimizu Kōbundō Shobō)
Itazawa Takeo 板沢武雄 1959, *Nichiran bunka kōshōshi no kenkyū* 日蘭文化交渉史の研究 (Yoshikawa Kōbunkan)
Itō Tasaburō 伊東多三郎, 'Kinsho no kenkyū' 禁書の研究, *Rekishi chiri* 歴史地理 68.4 (1936): 35–48
Itō Tasaburō 1972, 'The book banning policy of the Tokugawa

shogunate', *AA* 22: 36–61

Iwata Toyoki 岩田豊樹 1980, *Edozu sōmokuroku* 江戸図総目録, *NSGT* 11

Kabutogi Shōkō 兜木正亨 1983, *Hoke shakyō no kenkyū* 法華写経の研究 (Daitō Shuppansha)

Kaidai sōsho 解題叢書 1916 (Kokusho kankōkai)

Kanno Ginpachi 菅野銀八 n.d., 'Kōraiban daizōkyō ni tsuite' 高麗板大蔵経に就いて, in *Chōsenshi kōza tokubetsu kōgi* 朝鮮史講座特別講義 ([Keijō=Seoul], Chōsenshi Gakkai, n.d.)

Kanmuri Ken'ichi 冠賢一 1983, *Kinsei Nichirenshū shuppanshi kenkyū* 近世日蓮宗出版史研究 (Kyoto: Heirakuji Shoten)

Kano Naoki 狩野直喜 1973, *Shinagaku bunsō* 支那学文藪 (Misuzu Shobō)

Kasai Sukeharu 笠井助治 1962, *Kinsei hankō ni okeru shuppansho no kenkyū* 近世藩校に於ける出版書の研究 (Yoshikawa Kōbunkan)

Katagiri Kazuo 片桐一男 1985, *Oranda tsūji no kenkyū* 阿蘭陀通司の研究 (Yoshikawa Kōbunkan)

Kawada Hisanaga 川田久長 1981, *Kappan insatsushi* 活版印刷史 (Insatsu Gakkai Shuppanbu)

Kawaguchi Hisao 川口久雄 1964, *Heianchō Nihon kanbungakushi no kenkyū* 平安朝日本漢文学史の研究, 2nd edition (Meiji Shoin)

Kawase Kazuma 川瀬一馬 1934, 'Suruga oyuzuribon no kenkyū' 駿河御譲本の研究, *Shoshigaku* 3.4: 1–5

Kawase Kazuma 1934, 'Jōdai ni okeru kanseki no denrai' 上代に於ける漢籍の伝来, *Shoshigaku* 書誌学 2.5: 11–17

Kawase Kazuma 1935, 'Kariya Ekisai no gakuseki', *Shoshigaku* 4.6: 1–22

Kawase Kazuma 1945, *Nihon shoshigaku no kenkyū* 日本書誌学之研究 (Dainihon Yūbenkai Kōdansha)

Kawase Kazuma 1967, *(Zōho) Kokatsujiban no kenkyū* 増補古活字版之研究, 3 vols. (The Antiquarian Booksellers Association of Japan)

Kawase Kazuma 1970, *Gozanban no kenkyū* 五山版の研究 (The Antiquarian Booksellers Association of Japan)

Kawase Kazume 1974, *Ashikaga Gakkō no kenkyū* 足利学校の研究 (Kōdansha)

Kawada Hisanaga 川田久長 1981, *Kappan insatsu shi* 活版印刷史

(Insatsu Gakkai Shuppanbu)
Kernan, Alvin 1987, *Printing technology, letters and Samuel Johnson* (Princeton: Princeton University Press)
Kimiya Yasuhiko 木宮康彦 1932, *Nihon koinsatsu bunkashi* 日本古印刷文化史 (Fuzanbō)
Kimiya Yasuhiko 1955, *Nikka bunka kōryūshi* 日華文化交流史 (Fuzanbō)
Kimoto Yoshinobu 木本好信 1989, *Narachō tenseki shosai bussho kaisetsu sakuin* 奈良朝典籍所載物仏書解説索引 (Kokusho Kankōkai)
Kishi Masahiro 岸雅裕 1981, *Kyōto shorin nakama shiryō* 京都書林仲間資料 (Iwakura: privately published)
Kishimoto Masane 岸本真実 1986, 'Kinsei mokkatsujiban gaikan' 近世木活字版概観, *Biburia* ビブリア 87: 72-94
Kobayashi Zenpachi 小林善八 1978, *Nihon shuppan bunkashi* 日本出版文化史, *NSGT* 1
Koda, S. 1939, 'Notes sur la presse jesuite au Japon', *MN* 2: 374-85
Koike Masatane 小池正胤 1980, 'Kinsei dokusha ron' 近世読者論, *Kokubungaku kaishaku to kanshō* 45.10: 44-7
Kokugakuin Daigaku Nihon Bunka kenkyūsho (ed.) 国学院大学日本文化研究所編 1990, *Wagakusha sōran* 和学者総覧 (Kyūko Shoin)
Kokuritsu Kokkai Toshokan 1971-6, *(Kokuritsu Kokkai Toshokan shozō) Meijiki kankō tosho mokuroku* 国立国会図書館所蔵明治期刊行図書目録, 7 vols (Kokkai Toshokan)
Kokuritsu Kokkai Toshokan 1989, *(Kokuritsu Kokkai Toshokan shozō) Kokatsujiban zuroku* 国立国会図書館所蔵古活字版図録 (Kyūko Shoin)
Komatsu Shigemi 小松茂美 1976, *Heike nōkyō no kenkyū* 平家納経の研究, 3 vols (Kōdansha)
Konta Yōzō 今田洋三 1974, 'Edo no shuppan shihon' 江戸の出版資本, in Nishiyama Matsunosuke 西山松之助, ed., *Edo chōnin no kenkyū* 江戸町人の研究 (Yoshikawa kōbunkan), 3: 109-95
Konta Yōzō 1977, *Edo no hon'yasan* 江戸の本屋さん (Nihon Hōsō Shuppan Kyōkai)
Konta Yōzō 1978, 'Edo no saigai jōhō' 江戸の災害情報, in Nishiyama Matsunosuke, ed., *Edo chōnin no kenkyū*(Yoshikawa kōbunkan), 5: 171-282
Konta Yōzō 1981, *Edo no kinsho* 江戸の禁書, Edo sensho 6

(Yoshikawa kōbunkan)

Konta Yōzō et al. 1981, 'Kinsei no shuppan' 近世の出版, *Bungaku* 9.11: 1–31

Kornicki, P. F. 1977, '*Nishiki no Ura*: an instance of censorship and the structure of a *Sharebon*', *MN* 32: 153–88

Kornicki, P. F. 1980, 'The publisher's go-between: *kashihonya* in the Meiji period', *Modern Asian studies* 14: 331–44.

Kornicki, P. F. 1982, 'The Enmeiin affair of 1803: the spread of information in the Tokugawa period', *HJAS* 42: 503–33

Kornicki, P. F. 1985, 'Chihō shuppan ni tsuite' 地方出版について, in Yoshida Mitsukuni 吉田光邦, ed., *Jūkyū seiki nihon no jōhō to shakai hendō* 十九世紀日本の情報と社会変動, (Kyoto: Shibunkaku), 449–466

Kornicki, P. F. 1990, 'Provincial publishing in the Tokugawa period', in Yu-Ying Brown (ed.) 1990: 188–197

Kornicki, P. F. 1993a, 'The Japanese collection in the Bibliotheca Lindesiana', *Bulletin of the John Rylands University Library of Manchester* 75: 209–300

Kornicki, P. F. 1993b, 'European japanology at the end of the seventeenth century', *BSOAS* 56: 505–506

Kornicki, P. F. 1997, 'Japanese medical and other books at the Wellcome Institute', *BSOAS* 60: 489–510

Kotenseki sōgō mokuroku 古典籍総合目録, 3 vols (Iwanami Shoten, 1990)

Kōzato Haruo 上里春生 1970, *Edo shosekishō shi* 江戸書籍商史, facsimile of 1932 edition (Meicho Kankōkai)

Kraft, Eva 1982–94, *Japanische Handschriften und traditionelle Drucke aus der Zeit vor 1868*, 5 vols (Wiesbaden: Franz Steiner Verlag)

Kuraishi Takeshirō 倉石武四郎 1973, *Mokurokugaku* 目録学, Tōyōgaku Bunken Sentā sōkan 20 (Tōyōgaku Bunken Sentā)

Kurita Mototsugu 栗田元次 1979, *Shoshigaku no hattatsu* 書誌学の発達, *NSGT* 8

Kutsukake Isakichi 沓掛伊佐吉 1983, *Kutsukake Isakichi chosakushū: shomotsu bunka shikō* 沓掛伊佐吉著作集－書物文化史考 (Yashio Shoten)

Laures, Johannes 1940, *Kirishitan bunko: a manual of books and documents on the early Christian missions in Japan* (Tokyo: Sophia University; supplements in 1941 and 1951)

Lawson, Simon D. 1982, 'A catalogue of Indian Buddhist sealings in British Museums', unpublished D.Phil. thesis (University of Oxford)

Lewis, Mark (forthcoming), *Writing and authority in early China* (New York: SUNY Press)

Maeda Ai 前田愛 1973, *Kindai dokusha no seiritsu* 近代読者の成立 (Yūseidō)

Makita Inashiro 蒔田稲城 1968, *Keihan shosekishō shi* 京阪書籍商史, facsimile of 1926 edition (Osaka: Takao Hikoshirō shoten) [this work is divided into three sections, each paginated separately; '2.87' indicates p. 87 of part 2]

Matsudaira Susumu 松平進 1988, *Moronobu Sukenobu ehon shoshi* 師宣祐信絵本書誌, *NSGT* 57

Matsuki Hiroshi 松木寛 1988, *Tsutaya Jūzaburō* 蔦屋重三郎 (Nihon Keizai Shinbunsha)

Matsuzawa Rōsen shiryōshū 松沢老泉資料集, *NSGT* 25 (1982)

May, Ekkehard 1983, *Die Kommerzialisierung der japanischen Literatur in der späten Edo-Zeit (1750-1868): Rahmenbedingungen und Entwicklungstendenzen der erzählenden Prosa im Zeitalter ihrer ersten Vermarktung* (Wiesbaden: Otto Harrassowitz)

Miller, Roy Andrew 1952, 'Some Japanese influences on classical scholarship of the Ch'ing Period', *JAOS* 72: 56–67

Minami Kazuo 南和男 1975, 'Bakumatsu bukan no nedan' 幕末武鑑の値段, *Nihon rekishi* 324 : 34–7

Minami Kazuo 1976, 'Tenpō kaikaku to shuppan tōsei' 天保改革と出版統制, *Kokugakuin zasshi* 国学院雑誌 77.6: 1–18

Mitchell, Richard H. 1983, *Censorship in imperial Japan* (Princeton: Princeton University Press)

Miyako no Nishiki 都の錦 1937, *Genroku taiheiki* 元禄大平記, in *Hyōshaku Edo bungaku sōsho* 評釈江戸文学叢書, Ukiyozōshi meisakushū 浮世草子名作集, ed. Fujii Otoo 藤井乙男 (Dainihon Yūbenkai Kōdansha)

Miyatake Tobone 宮武外骨 1974, *Hikkashi* 筆禍史 (Yamanosama Shobō; reprint of 1926 edition published by Asakaya Shoten)

Mizuhara Gyōei 水原堯栄 1932, *Kōyaban no kenkyū* 高野板之研究 (Morie Shoten)

Mori Junzaburō 森潤三郎 1933, *Momijiyama Bunko to shomotsu bugyō* 紅葉山文庫と書物奉行 (Shōwa Shobō)

Mori Junzaburō 1979, *Kōshōgaku ronkō - Edo no kosho to zōshoka no chōsa* 考証学論攷－江戸の古書と蔵書家の調査, *NSGT* 9

Mori Katsumi 森克巳 1975, *(Zōho) Nissō bunka kōryū no shomondai* 増補日宋文化交流の諸問題, Mori Katsumi chosaku senshū 4 (Kokusho kankōkai, 1975), 204–242

Morris, Ivan (trans.) 1971, *As I crossed a bridge of dreams: recollections of a woman in eleventh-century Japan* (London: Oxford University Press)

Morse, Edward S. 1936, *Japan day by day: 1877, 1878–9, 1882–3* (Kobunsha Publishing Co.; reprint of 1917 edition)

Mote, Frederick W. & Hung-Lam Chu 1988, *Calligraphy and the East Asian Book* (Boston, Mass.: Shambhala Publications)

Mukai Shinobu 向井信夫 1995, *Edo bungei sōwa* 江戸文芸叢話 (Yagi Shoten)

Munemasa Isoo 宗政五十緒 1979, 'Gakkai jihyō - kinsei' 学界時評－近世, *Kokubungaku* 24.3: 186–7

Munemasa Isoo 1982, *Kinsei Kyōto shuppan bunkashi no kenkyū* 近世京都出版文化史の研究 (Kyoto: Dōhōsha)

Munemasa Isoo & Wakabayashi Seiji 若林正治 (eds) 1965, *Kinsei Kyōto shuppan shiryō* 近世京都出版資料 (Nihon Kosho Tsūshinsha)

Murase, Miyeko 1986, *Tales of Japan: scrolls and prints from the New York Public Library* (New York: Oxford University Press)

Nagasawa Kikuya 長沢規矩也 1976, *Zukai wakan insatsushi* 図解和漢印刷史 (Kyūko Shoin)

Nagasawa Kikuya 1976–80, *Wakokubon kanseki bunrui mokuroku* 和刻本漢籍分類目録, 2 vols (Kyūko Shoin)

Nagasawa Kikuya & Nagasawa Kōzō 長沢孝三 1979, *Kanbungakusha sōran* 漢文学者総覧 (Kyūko Shoin)

Nagasue Toshio 永末十四雄 1984, *Nihon kōkyō toshokan no keisei* 日本公共図書館の形成 (Nihon Toshokan Kyōkai)

Nagatomo Chiyoji 長友千代治 1982, *Kinsei kashihon'ya no kenkyū* 近世貸本屋の研究 (Tōkyōdō Shuppan)

Nagatomo Chiyoji 1987, *Kinsei no dokusho* 近世の読書, *NSGT* 52

Nagatomo Chiyoji 1994, *(Kinsei Kamigata) Sakka shoshi kenkyū* 近世上方作家書肆研究 (Tōkyōdō Shuppan)

Nakada Katsunosuke 仲田勝之助 1950, *Ehon no kenkyū* 絵本の研究 (Bijutsu Shuppansha)

Nakamura Kiyozō 中村喜代三 1972, *Kinsei shuppanhō no kenkyū*

近世出版法の研究 (Nihon Gakujutsu Shinkōkai)
Nakamura Yukihiko 中村幸彦 1961, *Kinsei shōsetsushi no kenkyū* 近世小説史の研究 (Ōfūsha)
Nakamura Yukihiko 1966, *Gesakuron* 戯作論 (Kadokawa Shoten)
Nakamura Yukihiko 1973, 'Kinsei no dokusha' 近世の読者, *Ōsaka furitsu toshokan kiyō* 大阪府立図書館紀要 9: 80–98
Nakane Katsu 中根勝 1987, *Hyakumantō darani no kenkyū* 百万塔陀羅尼の研究 (Osaka: Hyakumantō darani no kenkyū kankō iinkai)
Nakano Mitsutoshi 中野三敏 1995, *Shoshigaku dangi: Edo no hanpon* 書誌学談義－江戸の板本 (Iwanami Shoten)
Nakayama Einosuke 中山栄之輔 1974, *(Edo Meiji) Kawaraban senshū* 江戸明治かわらばん選集 (Kashiwa Shobō)
Nara Kokuritsu Hakubutsukan 奈良国立博物館 1983, *Narachō shakyō* 奈良朝写経 (Daitō Shuppansha)
Nishimura Keishō 西村冏紹 1987, '*Ōjō yōshū* shoshakanpon no kenkyū', in Ōjō yōshū kenkyūkai, ed., *Ōjō yōshū kenkyū* 往生要集研究 (Kyoto: Nagata Bunshōdō)
Nishimura Tei 西村貞 1941, *Nihon dōban shoshi* 日本銅版書志 (Shomotsu Tenbōsha)
Nogami Mamoru 埜上衛 1975, 'Wakabayashi Seiji shi shozō kashihon'ya shuppan tosho tō kōkoku harimazechō (honkoku)' 若林正治氏所蔵貸本屋・出版図書等広告貼交ぜ帳（翻刻）, *Kinki Daigaku tandai ronshū* 近畿大学短大論集 8.1: 41–104
Noma Kōshin 野間光辰 1958, 'Ukiyozōshi no dokushasō' 浮世草紙の読者層, *Bungaku* 26.5: 63–73
Notehelfer, F. G., ed. 1992, *Japan through American eyes: the journal of Francis Hall, Kanagawa and Yokohama, 1859–1866* (Princeton: Princeton University Press)
Nunn, G. Raymond 1969, 'On the number of books published in Japan from 1600 to 1868', in *East Asian occasional papers* 1, Asian studies at Hawaii 3 (Honolulu: University of Hawaii), 110–19
Ōba Osamu 大庭脩 1967, *(Edo jidai ni okeru) Tōsen mochiwatashisho no kenkyū* 江戸時代における唐船持渡書の研究 ([Suita], Kansai Daigaku Tōzai Gakujutsu Kenkyūsho) [apart from the material reprinted in the second half, this is superceded by Ōba 1984]
Ōba Osamu 1984, *(Edo jidai ni okeru) Chūgoku bunka juyō no kenkyū*

江戸時代における中国文化受容の研究 (Kyōto: Dōhōsha)
Ōba, Osamu 1991a, 'Imported Chinese books in late Edo period and their influences on Japan', *International Association of Orientalist Librarians Bulletin* 38: 55-60
Ōba Osamu 1996a, *Kodai chūsei ni okeru nitchū kankeishi no kenkyū* 古代中世における日中関係史の研究 (Kyōto: Dōhōsha)
Ōba Osamu 1997, *Kanseki yunyū no bunkashi - Shōtoku taishi kara Yoshimune e* 漢籍輸入の文化史－聖徳太子から吉宗へ (Kenbun Shuppan)
Ōba Osamu and Wang Yong 王勇 1996, *Tenseki* 典籍, Nitchū bunka kōryūshi sōsho 9 (Taishūkan Shoten)
Ōe Fumiki 大江文城 1935, *Honpō shisho kunten narabi ni chūkai no shiteki kenkyū* 本邦四書訓点並に注解の史的研究 (Seki Shoin)
Oka Masahiko 岡雅彦 & Wada Yasuyuki 和田恭幸 1996, 'Kinsei shoki hanpon kanki shūei', *Chōsa kenkyū hōkoku* 調査研究報告 17: 293-327
Okada, H. Richard 1991, *Figures of resistance: language poetry, and narrating in The tale of Genji and other mid-Heian texts* (Durham: Duke University Press)
Okada Tetsu 岡田哲 1987, *Baba Bunkō shū* 馬場文耕集, Sōsho Edo bunko 12 (Kokusho Kankōkai)
Okamoto Katsu 岡本勝 1980, 'Kinsei shuppan no issokumen - Motoorike kankei monjo o chūshin ni' 近世出版の一側面－本居家関係文書を中心に, *Kinsei bungei* 近世文芸 31: 43-52
Okamura Keiji 岡村敬二 1995, 'Wakete wakaru - Edo jidai no shojaku mokuroku to sono bunrui' 分けて分かる－江戸時代の書籍目録とその分類, *Ōsaka furitsu toshokan kiyō* 31: 19-32
Okamura Keiji 1996, *Edo no zōshokatachi* 江戸の蔵書家達 (Kōdansha)
Okuno Hikoroku 奥野彦六 1982, *Edo jidai no kohanpon* 江戸時代の古版本, revised edition (Kyoto: Rinsen Shoten)
Olson, D. R., and N. Torrance (eds) 1991, *Literacy and orality* (Cambridge: Cambridge University Press)
Onagaya Keikichi 小長谷恵吉 1976, *Nihonkoku genzaisho mokuroku kaisetsukō* 日本国見在書目録解説稿 (Komiyama Shuppan; facsimile of 1956 edition)
Ono Hideo 小野秀雄 1960, *Kawaraban monogatari* かわら版物語 (Yūsankaku Shuppan)
Ono Noriaki 小野則秋 1944, *Nihon bunkoshi kenkyū (jōkan)* 日本文

庫史研究 上巻 (Kyoto: Taigadō) [no further volumes published]

Ono Noriaki 1952, *Nihon toshokan shi* 日本図書館史 (Kyōto: Ranshobō)

Ono Noriaki 1954, *Nihon no zōshoin* 日本の蔵書印 (Kyoto: Geibunsha)

Ono Noriaki 1970, 'Wagakuni ni okeru tosho bunruihō no rekishiteki kōsatsu - toku ni kokusho bunruihō wo chūshin to shite' わが国に於ける図書分類法の歴史的考察－特に国書分類法を中心として, in Senda Masao kyōju koki kinenkai 仙田正雄教授古希記念会, ed., *Toshokan shiryō ronshū* 図書館資料論集 (Tenri: Tenri Daigaku Shuppanbu), 87–108

Ono Noriaki 1978, *(Koki kinen) Ono Noriaki toshokangaku ronbunshū* 古希記念小野則秋図書館学論文集 (Kyōto: Ono Noriaki sensei ronbunshū kankōkai)

Ōta Masahiro 太田正弘 1995, *Owari shuppan bunkashi* 尾張出版文化史 (Kōbe: Rokkō Shuppan)

Ōta Shōjirō 太田晶二郎 1959, 'Kibi no Makibi no kanseki shōrai' 吉備真備の漢籍将来, *Kagami* かがみ 1: 55–8

Ōuchida Sadao 大内田貞郎 1981, 'Kinsei mokkatsuji ni yoru insatsu to shuppan' 近世木活字による印刷と出版, *Bungaku* 49.12: 59–69

Ōwa Hiroyuki 大和博幸 1991, 'Edo jidai chihō shoshi no kisoteki kōsatsu' 江戸時代地方書肆の基礎的考察, *Kokugakuin zasshi* 92.3: 86–114

Ōya Tokujō 大屋徳城 1923, *Nara kangyō shi* 寧楽刊経史 (Kyoto: Naigai Shuppan)

Ōya Tokujō 1926, *Nara kokyō sen*, 3 vols 寧楽古経選 (Kyoto: Benridō)

Rose, Jonathan 1992, 'Rereading the *English common reader*: a preface to the history of audiences', *Journal of the history of ideas* 53: 47–70

Rose, Mark 1993, *Authors and owners: the invention of copyright* (Cambridge, Mass.: Harvard University Press, 1993)

Rosenfield, John M., Fumiko E. Cranston & Edwin A. Cranston 1973, *The courtly tradition in Japanese art and literature: selections from the Hofer and Hyde collections* (Boston, Mass.: Fogg Art Museum, Harvard University)

Rubinger, R. 1988, 'Problems in research on literacy in 19th-century Japan', in *Nihon kyōikushi ronsō* 日本教育史論叢 (Kyoto:

Shibunkaku), 1–24
Sakamoto Muneko 坂本宗子 1982, *(Kyōhō igo) Hanmotobetsu shoseki mokuroku* 享保以後板元別書籍目録 (Osaka: Seibundō)
Sakanishi, Shio 1937, 'Prohibition of import of certain Chinese books and the policy of the Edo government', *JOSA* 57: 290–303
Satō Tetsuei 佐藤哲英 1937, 'Sannōin zōsho mokuroku ni tsuite' 山王院蔵書目録に就いて, *Eizan gakuhō* 叡山学報 13: 1–21
Screech, Timon 1996, *The Western scientific gaze and popular imagery in later Edo Japan: the lens within the heart* (Cambridge: Cambridge University Press)
Seeley, Christopher 1991, *A history of writing in Japan* (Leiden: E. J. Brill)
Séguy, Christiane 1993, *Histoire de la press japonaise: la développement de la presse à l'époque Meiji et son rôle dans la modernisation du Japon* (Paris: Publications Orientalistes de France)
Seki Yasushi 関靖 1951, *Kanazawa Bunko no kenkyū* 金沢文庫の研究 (Kōdansha)
Sekine Masanao 関根正直 1903–04, 'Tokugawa seifu no shuppan hōki' 徳川政府の出版法規, in Kokugakuin 国学院, ed., *Hōsei ronsan* 法政論纂 (Dainihon tosho)
Shibata Mitsuhiko 柴田光彦 1983, *Daisō zōshomokuroku to kenkyū* 大惣蔵書目録と研究, 2 vols, *NSGT* 27
Shidō Bunko 斯道文庫 (ed.) 1962–4, *(Edo jidai) Shorin shuppan shojaku mokuroku shūsei* 江戸時代書林出版書籍目録集成, 4 vols
Shimabara Yasuo 島原泰雄 1985, *Zōshoin teiyō* 蔵書印提要, *NSGT* 44
Smith, Henry D. II 1994, 'The history of the book in Edo and Paris', in James L. McClain, John M. Merriman & Ugawa Kaoru, eds, *Edo and Paris: urban life and the state in the early modern era* (Ithaca: Cornell University Press), 332–52
Smits, Ivo 1995, *The pursuit of loneliness: Chinese and Japanese nature poetry in medieval Japan, ca. 1050–1150*, Münchener ostasiatische Studien 73 (Stuttgart: Franz Steiner Verlag)
Son Pogi [Sohn Pow-key] 孫宝基 1971, *Hanguk e kohwalja* (Seoul: Hanguk Tosogwanhak Yŏnguhoe)
Son Pogi 1987, *Hanguk e kohwalja*, new edition (Seoul: Pojinjae)
Sorimachi Yūichi 反町雄一 1997, *(Sorimachi Shigeo tsuizen) Kōbunsō zenpon zuroku* 反町茂雄追善弘文荘善本図録, 2 vols (Kōbunsō)

Sugano Yō 菅野陽 1974, *Nihon dōbanga no kenkyū* 日本銅版画の研究 (Bijutsu Shuppansha)

Suwa Haruo 諏訪春雄 1978, 'Kinsei bungei to chosakken' 近世文芸と著作権, *Bungaku* 46.12: 50–62

Suzuki Jūzō 鈴木重三 1979, *Ehon to ukiyoe: Edo shuppan bunka no kōsatsu* 絵本と浮世絵 - 江戸出版文化の考察 (Bijutsu Shuppansha)

Suzuki Toshio 鈴木敏夫 1980, *Edo no hon'ya* 江戸の本屋, 2 vols, Chūkō shinsho 568 & 571 (Chūō Kōronsha)

Takagi Gen 高木元 1995, *Edo yomihon no kenkyū - jūkyū seiki shōsetsu yōshiki kō* 江戸読本の研究―十九世紀小説様式攷 (Perikansha)

Tanaka Kaidō 田中塊堂 1973, *Nihon koshakyō genzon mokuroku* 日本古写経現存目録 (Kyoto: Shibunkaku)

Tanaka Kaidō 1974, *Nihon shakyō sōkan* 日本写経綜鑑 (Kyoto: Shibunkaku)

Tenri Toshokan 天理図書館 1961, *Kokatsujibon mokuroku* 古活字本目録 (Tenri: Tenri Daigaku Shuppanbu)

Tenri Toshokan 1973, *Kirishitanban no kenkyū* きりしたん版の研究 (Tenri: Tenri Daigaku Shuppanbu)

Thomas, Rosalind 1990, *Literacy and oriality in ancient Greece* (Cambridge: Cambridge University Press)

Sarah E. Thompson 1991, 'The politics of Japanese prints', in Thompson and H. D. Harootunian, *Undercurrents in the floating world: censorship and Japanese prints* (New York: The Asia Society Galleries,), 29–91

Tōdō Sukenori 藤堂祐範 1976, *Jōdokyōban no kenkyū* 浄土教版の研究, revised edition (Sankibō Busshorin)

Tokushi Yūshō 禿氏祐祥 1951, *Tōyō insatsushi josetsu* 東洋印刷史序説 (Kyoto: Heirakuji Shoten)

Tokushi Yūshō 1991, *Tōyō insatsushi kenkyū* 東洋印刷史研究, *NSGT* 17

Tōno Haruyuki 東野治之 1977, *Shōsōin monjo to mokkan no kenkyū* 正倉院文書と木簡の研究 (Hanawa Shobō)

Tsien Tsuen-hsuin 1985, *Paper and printing*, Part 1 of Volume 5, 'Chemistry and Chemical Technology,' of Joseph Needham's *Science and Civilization in China* (Cambridge: Cambridge University Press)

Tsukahara Jūshien 塚原渋柿園 1910, 'Edo jidai no nanbungaku' 江

戸時代の軟文学, *Aoi* あふひ 3: 7–9

Twitchett, Denis 1983, *Printing and Publishing in Medieval China* (London: The Wynkyn de Worde Society)

Ueda Yutaka 上田穰 1982, 'Yōfū bunka no juyō to denpa' 洋風文化の受容と伝播, in *NYK* 6: 21–66

Umetani Fumio 梅谷文夫 1994, *Kariya Ekisai* 狩谷掖斎 (Yoshikawa Kōbunkan)

Unno Kazutaka 1994, 'Cartography in Japan', in J. B. Harley & David Woodward, eds, *The history of cartography*, vol. 2, book 2, *Cartography in the traditional east and southeast Asian societies* (Chicago: The University of Chicago Press), 346–477

Verschuer, Charlotte von, 1991, 'Le voyage de Jōjin au Mont Tiantai', *T'oung Pao* 77.1-3: 1–48

Wada Hidematsu 和田英松 1936, *Honchō shojaku mokuroku kōshō* 本朝書籍目録考証 (Meiji Shoin)

Wada Hidematsu 1940, *Kokusho itsubun* 国書逸文 (edited and privately published by Mori Katsumi)

Wada Mankichi 和田万吉 1983, *Nihon bunkenshi josetsu* 日本文献史序説, *NSGT* 32

Wada Tsunashirō 和田維四郎 1918, *Hōsho yoroku* 訪書余録 (privately published)

Walthall, Anne 1991 *Peasant uprisings in Japan: a critical anthology of peasant histories* (Chicago: Chicago University Press)

Wang Zhen-ping 1991, 'Manuscript copies of Chinese books in ancient Japan', *GLJ* 4.2: 35-67

Wang Zhenping 1994a, 'The use of Japanese records in Sung Official Histories', *East Asian library journal* 7: 43–71

Wang Zhenping 1994b, 'Chōnen's pilgrimage to China, 983–986', *Asia Major*, 3rd series 7.2: 63–97

Watanabe Toshio 渡辺敏夫 1984, *Nihon no koyomi* 日本の暦, 2nd edition (Yūsankaku, 1984

Yajima Genryō 矢島玄亮 1976, *Tokugawa jidai shuppansha shuppanbutsu shūran* 徳川時代出版者出版物集覧, 2 vols (Sendai: Man'yōdō Shoten)

Yajima Genryō 1984, *Nihonkoku genzaisho mokuroku - shūshō to kenkyū* 日本国見在書目録一集証と研究 (Kyūko Shoin)

Yayoshi Mitsunaga 弥吉光長 1988-93, *Mikan shiryō ni yoru Nihon shuppan bunka* 未刊資料による日本出版文化, 8 vols, *SSS* 26

Yan Shaodang 厳紹璗/玉 1992, *Han ji zai ri ben di liu bu yan jiu*

漢籍在日本的流布研究 (Jiang su gu ji chu ban she)
Yi Chun'gil 李峻杰 1986, *Chosŏn sidae ilbon kwa sŏjŏk kyoryuyŏngu* 朝鮮時代日本과書籍交流硏究 (Seoul: Hŭng'ikjae)
Yi Honjik 李弘稙 1954, *Hanguk komunhwasa nongo* 韓国古文化史論攷 (Seoul: Ŭlyu Munhwasa)
Yokota Fuyuhiko 横田冬彦 1995, 'Ekkenbon no dokusha' 益軒本の読者, in Yokoyama Toshio 横山俊夫, ed., *Kaibara Ekken: tenchi waraku no bunmeigaku* 貝原益軒－天地和楽の文明学 (Heibonsha), 315–53
Yoshihara Ken'ichirō 吉原健一郎 1980, 'Kansei kaikaku to Edo hangiya nakama' 寛政改革と江戸板木屋仲間, in *(Haga Kōshirō sensei koki kinen) Nihon bunkashi kenkyū* 芳賀幸四郎先生古希記念日本文化史研究 (Kasama Shoin), 245–61
Yoshimura Shigeki 吉村茂樹 1928, '*Tsūken nyūdō zōsho mokuroku ni tsuite no gimon*' 通憲入道蔵書目録についての疑問, *Shigaku zasshi* 39.10: 96–107

INDEX

Abe Yoshio 157
actor critiques 177
Adachi Ginkō 322 n.4
advertising 187–92
Aeba Kōson 142, 239, 241
Aesop's *Fables* 126, 134, 301
Aguranabe 57
aiaiban 179
Ajiro Hironori 389
akahon 57, 234
Akamatsu Kozaburō 149
Akisato Ritō 217
Aleni, Julius 326, 330
Amakusa 125
Amano Shinkei 260
Amoghavajra 419
An Chŏngbok 312
Analects, Confucian 123, 155, 279, 280, 376, 399 n.63
Anderson, Benedict 16, 33
Annen 419
Aobyōshi 345
Aōdō Denzen 167
Aoki Kon'yō 439
Aoki Michio 274
Arabic 22, 27
Arai Hakuseki 302, 312, 330
Araki, James 301
aratamein 340, 343
Aseishū 197
Ashikaga Gakkō 130, 374, 435, 444
Ashikaga shōgunate 294
Ashikaga Takauji 91, 100
Ashikaga Yoshimasa 93, 288, 375
Ashikaga Yoshimitsu 375
Ashikaga Yoshimochi 294
Aston, William George 316–7, 407
Astronomical Bureau 346, 353–4
Astronomie 354
Atan yume monogatari 108
authorship 189, 201, 223
Azuma kagami 130, 135, 143, 309, 311, 313, 376

Baba Bunkō 108–9
Bacon, Francis 20
Bakufu Academy (Shōheizaka Gakumonjo) 75, 130, 145–6, 339, 342–3, 378–9, 382, 384, 389, 428–9, 432, 435, 440, 444
Bakufu Library 15, 75–6, 304, 378–9, 383, 385, 426, 427, 436, 438, 440, 444
Bakufu Medical Academy 342
bakuryō 74
bakusho 74–5
Bangai zassho kaidai 436, 441
Bankoku shinbunshi 66
Banreki ryōmen kagami 248
Bansho shirabesho (see Institute for the Investigation of Foreign Books)
banzuke 72
baren 48
Barthes, Roland 223
Batavia 301
Ben cao gang mu 130

Ben'en 288
Bendō 230, 310
Bengisho mokuroku 176, 232, 441
Benmei 310
Bi shu sheng 祕書省 365
Bible 21, 23
Bibliotheca universalis 14
binding 47
Binjin taiheiki 350 n.54
block-carvers guild 202
Blomhoff, Jan Cock 314
Bo Juyi 282-3, 292
Bohai 277
Book of Changes 255
book trade, pre-Tokugawa 170
bookburning 12
books, Dutch 301-3, 382
Books, Dutch 303
Books, Dutch 303
books, English 304
books, European 304
books, Russian 382
booksellers' guild 196, 179-84
Borgen, Robert 271
Brownlee, John 321
Buddhist canon 84, 418
bukan (see directories, samurai)
Buke Shohatto 333
bunjin 36
Bunrui hakusai shomoku tsūran 429
Bunshō kanazukai 189 n.29
Bureau of Astronomy and Calendrical Science (Tenmon rekidōkyoku) 357

Butoku taisei 438
Byōdōin 420

calendars 43, 67-8, 353-8
calligraphy 27, 29, 86
Camphuijs, Johannes 302
censorship 11-13, 320-62
ch'ŏnggyŏngsa 請経使 294
Ch'ŏnmyŏng tosŏl 157
Chamberlain, Basil Hall 142, 407
Chartier, Roger 9, 35-6
Chikamatsu Monzaemon 352
Chikuhōrō 442, 444
Chinsetsu yumiharizuki 188, 240
Chishakyō 308
chitsu 46
cho 著 227
chōai 48
Chōjiya Heibee 344-5
chokuhan 130
chokusenshū 91, 95
Chōnen 286-7, 308
Chōrakuji 124
Chosakken hō 251
Chōsen seibatsuki 332, 334
Chou hai tu bian 289
Christian books 297, 302
Christianity 325-31, 337, 380
chroniques scandaleuses 14
Chu san cang ji ji 418
Chŏng Yagyong 312
Chūgan Engetsu 323
Chūjō 101
Chūshin suikoden 299
Chūshingura 310

Chūsonji 368
Cicero 126
Clanchy, M. 24
Classic of filial piety 155
Cocks, Richard 313
colophon 45, 54, 338
Conditions in the West (Seiyō jijō) 410
conservation 74–7
Contemptus mundi 125
Copperplate printing 166–8
copyright 242–51
Council of State (Dajōkan) 146
courtesan critiques 71
covers 56, 57, 60
Curtius, Jan Hendrik Donker 314

Da pu ning si 287, 293
Da tang liu dian 408
Da xue 124
Da xue zhang ju 124
Daianji 119
Daigakkōdai 410
Daigaku wakumon 162, 333
Daigakuryō 270
Daigakuryōdai 410
Daigo, emperor 420–1
Daigoji 402
Daihannya kyō 81, 83, 252
daikan 327
Daikokuya Kōdayū 316
Daikyōshi 353
Dainihonshi 147, 387, 437, 438
daisen 46
daishi 81
Daisō 395

Daitokuji 100
Dajōkan nisshi 66, 209, 358
Daoism 290
Daoist books 290–91, 415
Daoist canon 290, 380
Darnton, Robert 9, 37
Dazai Shundai 155, 312, 375
Dazaifu 280–82
Deshima 167, 301, 302, 303, 328, 354
dhāraṇī 114–6
Diamond sūtra 89, 118
dictionaries 52
Diderot 21
directories 52, 54, 69, 185, 187, 188, 211
directories, samurai 69, 186, 211, 315–6
Dodoens, Rembert 302
Dodonaeus 167 n.76
Dokusho hajime 253
Dokusho no gi 253
Dokusho shidai 263
Dōkyō 83, 117
domain academies 146, 386
Dong chan si 287
Doryōkō 186
Douglas, Ann 31
Dourado, Constantino 125
Drège, Jean-Pierre 254
Du Fu 49
Dunciad 37
Dunhuang 254, 280, 283
Dushu fa 259–60
Dutch East India Company 157, 164, 314

E ingakyō 96–7
East India Company 313

edaisen 46, 136
Edo hanjōki 345, 317
Edo meibutsu shi 211 n.66
egoyomi 355
ehon 36, 58, 59, 139, 214, 219
Ehon hitorigeiko 189 n.29
Ehon imayō sugata 54 n.14
Ehon mushierami 58
Ehon ōshukubai 315
Ehon taikōki 193, 341, 396
Ehon toyotomi kunkōki 193
Eiga monogatari 89
Eirakuya Tōshirō 191, 205, 213-4
Eiri genji monogatari 232
Eisenstein, Elizabeth 24-5
Ejima Kiseki 188, 231-2
emaki 96-7
emakimono 42, 96
Emi no Oshikatsu 116
Enchin 285, 367, 420
Engishiki 75, 365-6, 376
Engyō 285
Enji 371
Enmeiin 109
Ennin 252, 285, 307, 367
enpon 351
Enryaku sōroku 307
Enseiji 15
Eun 285
ezōshiya 175
ezu 61

Feather, John 9, 242
Fisscher, Johan Frederik Overmeer 314
Five Classics 148
Forrer, Matthi 207, 355

Forty-seven (actually 46) *rōnin* 106, 109, 171-172, 227-228, 299, 310, 311, 336, 348
Foucault, Michel 224
Four Books 123, 148, 260
Franklin, Simon 25
Fude no susabi 372
fudono 文殿 365
fuguruma 文車 370
Fujii Sadamoto 436
Fujiwara no Kōzei 93
Fujiwara no Michinaga 88, 95, 118, 286, 369, 406
Fujiwara no Michinori 283, 369, 423
Fujiwara no Nakamaro 116
Fujiwara no Sanesada 370
Fujiwara no Shunzei 406
Fujiwara no Sukeyo 282, 422
Fujiwara no Takemori 282
Fujiwara no Tameie 94
Fujiwara no Teika 15, 75, 87, 93-6, 377, 380, 403, 407, 437
Fujiwara no Yorinaga 254-5, 287, 369, 376
Fujiwara Seika 157, 295
Fukui Tamotsu 382
Fukunaga Mitsuji 290
fukuro-toji 44, 56
Fukuzawa Yukichi 250, 267, 305, 410
Fuller, Margaret 31
Fushimi 130, 376
Fūgetsu Shōzaemon 182
Fūgetsudō Magosuke 214
Fūryū fumi hyōban 350
Fūzoku haijin katagi 266

Gakkōkan 359
Gakumon no susume 250, 267
Galton, Francis 227
Gamble, William 165
Ganjin 83, 114, 117, 284
ganmon 82
gedai 46
Gedai gakumon 264
Gedai nenkan 432
Genbō 83–4, 284–5, 418
Gendō hōgen 229
Gengendō 168
Genji monogatari emaki 97
Genkō shakusho 252, 290, 311
Genroku taiheiki 233, 240
Gensei 327
Genshin 121, 308
gesaku 227
Gesaku gedai kagami 432
Gesaku hana no akahon sekai 234
Gesner, Konrad 14
Gion monogatari 184 n.21
go 353
Go-Daigo, emperor 91, 371
Go-Mizunoo, emperor 100, 130, 134
Go-Momozono, emperor 100
Go-Reizei, emperor 309
Go-Saga, emperor 421
Go-Shirakawa, emperor 371, 424
Go-Toba, emperor 421
Go-Yōzei, emperor 129, 130, 143, 155
Gobunko 379
gōkan 57, 343

Gōke Bunko 369
Gokokkin yaso shomoku 330
Gokurakuji 121
Golovnin 274
Gomō jigi 230
Goodman, Grant 304
Goody, Jack 30
goroku 122
Gōrui shojaku mokuroku taizen 177
Goseikin gomen shoseki yakusho 326, 327
Goshodokoro 366
goshomotsukata 297
goshomotsushi 381
Gozan editions 3, 44, 56, 121–2, 289
Gu jin tu shu ji cheng 329
Gu yi cong shu 311
gunsho 334
Gunsho chiyō 148
Gunsho ichiran 436
Gunsho ruijū 16, 101, 387, 389, 401, 440, 436
Guy, Kent 11
gyobi 55
gyōji 181–2, 195, 219
gyokuhen 52

Hachimonjiya Jishō 183, 231
Hachisuka Haruaki 389
Haeinsa 294
Hai guo tu zhi 329
Hai wai qi tan 海外奇談 310
haikai 141, 152, 174, 175, 207, 215, 216, 219, 220, 236, 432, 434

Haikai shojaku mokuroku 432
haikai shorin 175
Haikai wataribōkō 432
Hakkenden 185, 267, 396
Hall, David 9
Hall, Francis 76, 171, 305
Hamada Hikozō 66
Hamada Keisuke 197, 240
Han shu 253, 282
Hanabigusa taizen 174
Hanaoka Seishū 101, 304
Hanawa Hokiichi 16, 101, 387, 389, 401, 440–1
hanchin 板賃 247
Hangiya-nakama 201
hankabu 182–3, 209, 211, 243, 247
Hankanfu zokuhen 389
Hanken jōrei 250
hankō (domain academies) 146, 272, 386
hanmoto 201
Hannya haramitta rishushaku 317
hansatsu 147
Hanshan shi 122
hanshin 55, 150
hanshita 47, 49, 52, 178
hanshitagaki 47
Hasegawa Takejirō 142
hashira 150
Hattori Hitoshi 240
Hawks, Francis 315
Hayabiki setsuyōshū 248
Hayashi Gahō 385, 441
Hayashi Hōkō 379
Hayashi Jussai 339
Hayashi Razan 130, 157, 230, 295, 377, 384, 399, 441
Hayashi School 297
Hayashi Shihei 104, 341
He Yan 123
Heco, Joseph 66
Heike monogatari 58 n.20, 126, 132, 265
Heike nōkyō 90
Hepburn, James Curtis 142
Hesse, Carla 224
hidarihan 136
hiden 101
Hiei, Mt 131, 160
Hifuryaku 282
hikkō 47
Hillier, Jack 56, 409
Hino Sukenari 369, 398
Hiraga Gennai 241
hiragana 270
Hiragana mori no shizuku 109
Hirata Atsutane 152, 190, 244, 330
Hishikawa Moronobu 350
Hizakurige 396
Hobson, Benjamin 156
Hoffmann, Johann Joseph 318
Hōganji 418
Hōjō family 372
Hōjō Sanetoki 372
Hōjō Tokiyori 322
Hōjōji 286
Hōkaiji Bunko 369
Hokekyō (see *Lotus sūtra*)
Hokekyō gisho 79, 306
Hokke shūmon chojutsu mokuroku 433
Hokke shūmon shodō 208
hokokuchō 52

Hokusai (see Katsushika Hokusai)
Hokusai manga 59, 206, 214
hōmen 45, 150
Hon'ami Kōetsu 132
hon'an 299
hon'ya 175
hon'ya nakama 180, 245
Hon'ya Shinshichi 174
hon-okugaki 45
Honchō hōke bunsho 424
Honchō kokushi mokuroku 424
Honchō shojaku mokuroku 77, 91, 425
Honchō suikoden 299
Honchō tsugan 385
Hōnen 121, 310, 322, 420
honkadori 243
Honkokuji 131
Honnōji 131
Honzō kōmoku 130
Hōrei burui 345-346
Hōryū Gakumonji 365
Hōryūji 92
Hōseidō Kisanji 241
Hosono Yōsai 263, 396
Hua Shou 156
Hui ke shu mu 彙刻書目 329, 445, 442-3
Hyakunin isshu 403
Hyakunin isshu Saga no yamafumi 403
Hyakushō seisuiki 350 n.54
Hyeja 慧慈 306
hyōshiya 48

Ibukinoya 190
Ichijō Kanera 257, 372, 421

Ichion 106
Ichiwa ichigon 443
Igakkan 342
Ihara Saikaku 32, 38, 63, 88, 233, 235, 240, 243, 265-266, 350, 388, 393
Imagawa Ryōshun 294
Imperial Printing Office Manual for Movable Type 159
inbutsu 117-9
Indijck, Hendrick 302
ingō 淫号 233
inkokubon 136
Inoue Masamichi 291
Inoue Takaaki 205
Institute for the investigation of foreign books (Bansho shirabesho) 146, 164, 346, 382
Institute for the investigation of Western books (Yōsho shirabesho) 66, 146
Institute of Divination 353
Iphak tosŏl 57
Ippen 97
Iro denju 337
Ise monogatari (see *Tales of Ise*)
Ise Shrine 357-8
Iseya Han'emon 192
Ishibashi Ken 332
Ishibashi Seian 173
Ishida Mosaku 84
Ishinpō 101, 102, 145
Isho taizen 123
Isoho monogatari 134, 301
Isonokami no Yakatsugu 307, 368

Isshūdō zōsho mokuroku 433
Itazawa Takeo
   272, 302–3
Itō Jinsai 230, 312, 438
Itō Tasaburō
   324, 326, 330
Itō Tōgai 180
Iwademo no ki 241
Iwakura Mission 305
Iwasaki family 408
Izawa Banryū 189
Izawa castle 85
Izawa Ranken 443
Izumiya Ichibee 172
Izumiya Shōjirō 444
Izumoji Bungorō 145, 381
Izumoji Izumi-no-jō 69, 200
Izumoji Manjirō 186

Jager, Herbert de 313
Jasienski, Feliks 317, 407–408
Jesuit Mission Press 129
Jesuit missions 166
Jia li yi jie 229
Jian Hongchu 308
Jianzhen (see Ganjin)
jihon 地本 202, 219
Jihon toiya nakama 202
Jin Jian 159
Jinbō Kazuya 337
jindai-moji 269
Jippensha Ikku 240
Jishū sect 97
jitsuroku 14, 108, 110
jittetsu 十哲 195
Jiun 438
Jōdo sect 44
Jōdo shinshū 433
Jōdo shinshū shōgyō
   mokuroku 433
Jōgyō 285
Jōjin 286, 309
Jōkyū war 322
Jonston, Jan 302
jōruri 177, 200, 202, 211, 261
Jōyuishikiron 119
Junshi 228
Juntoku, emperor 322
jūhan 181, 182, 245, 247
Jūtei eikoku hohei renpō 148

kabusebori 49, 52, 121–4,
   130, 135, 138, 145, 153,
   195, 229, 246, 288, 387
Kachū Myōhō rengekyō shō
   160
Kadomaruya Jinsuke 214
Kaempfer, Engelbert 314,m
   382
Kagoshima 124
Kai yuan si 287
Kaibao canon 286–7
Kaibara Ekken 76, 189, 261,
   261–4, 382
Kaifūsō 75, 279
Kaigai shinbun 66
Kaihan shishin 250 n.34
Kaihō chōreki benran 356
Kaikoku heidan 104, 341
Kaiseisho 146
Kaiyuan canon 284
Kako genzai ingakyō 96
Kamo no Mabuchi 402
Kan'ei gyōkōki 42, 134–5
Kan'eiji 152, 444
Kanagaki Robun 57
Kanamori Yorikane 109
Kanazawa 206

Kanazawa Bunko 257, 372, 377, 406, 445
kangakujuku 262
kango 188
kanki 45
kankyo 359
Kanmu Bunko 372
Kano Naoki 423
kanpan 14–6
Kanpan Batabiya shinbun 65-66
Kansei chōshū shokafu 389
Kansei reform 15, 219
kansubon 42
Kanzan shi 122
Kanzanji 15
Karasumaru Mitsuhiro 41, 100
Karei gisetsu 229
Kariganeya Seikichi 176
Kariya Ekisa 389, 435, 442–3, 445
Kasedaya Heiemon 215–6
kashihon'ya 103, 105, 203, 259, 265, 267, 340, 350, 391, 393, 411
Kashiwaraya Seiemon 189
Kashōki 184
Kasuga-ban 119
katagi 188
Katsukawa Shunshō 219
Katsushika Hokusai 214, 240
Kawachiya Kihee 191
Kawachiya Mohee 183, 221–2
Kawachiya Wasuke 183
kawaraban 63, 65, 335, 337
Kawaradera 80
Kawase Kazuma 279, 374

Kazunomiya, princess 65
Keian taiheiki 107
Keichō irai shohatto 380
Keikokushū 271
keisei 188
Keisei Shima-bara kaeru gassen 352
Keiseki hōkoshi 444
Keishishi yōran 264
Keiten daisetsu 441
Keizaiben 162
Kenchōji 121
Kenninji 402
Kernan, Alvin 38
Keyes, Roger 349
Ki no Haseo 93
Ki no Tsurayuki 93–4, 366, 371
Kibi no Makibi 281, 284, 369, 417, 426
kibyōshi 57, 219, 240, 340, 347
Kichimonjiya Ichiemon 221
Kii no kuni meisho zue 217
Kikō Daishuku 256
Kimura Kahei 164
Kinbusen, Mt 88
Kinmei, emperor 364
Kinmō kyūri taizen 191
kinsei mokkatsujiban 159
Kinsei mono no hon Edo sakusha burui 235, 432
Kinshi kaseiroku 395
kinsho 禁書 324
Kinsho mokuroku 105–6, 110, 348
kiriezu 62
Kirishitan taiji monogatari 332

kirishitanban 127
Kishimoto Yuzuru 402
Kishin shinron 190
Kitaev, Sergei 317, 408
Kitagawa Utamaro 58, 218, 220, 342, 179 n.13
Kitamura Kigin 209
Kitamura Shirōbee 216
Kitano Tenjin engi 97
Kitano Tenmangū 387
Kiyomizu monogatari 137, 184, 258
Kizuya Kichibei 388
Klaproth, Heinrich 317-8
kō 講 195
Kōbaiden 369
kochōsō 43
Kodera Gyokuchō 109
Kōdōkan 147
kōdoku 256-7
Kōfukuji 119, 307, 371
Kogaku school 438
Kōgakusho 410
Koguryŏ 40, 306
Koikawa Harumachi 241
Koike Masatane 265
Kojiki 213, 278, 386, 416
Kojiki den 206, 213-4
Kojima Noriyuki 283
Kojōzoroe 332
Kōkaku, emperor 100
Kokan Shiren 290, 310, 372
kokatsujiban 130
Kōkeisai kyūhō 152
Kōken, empress 83
Kokin wakashū (*Kokinshū*) 96, 407
Kōko shinbun 359
Kōkoku sanbutsu ōrai 191

kokubungaku 235, 414
kokubunji 84, 367
kokubunniji 367
Kokubyaku mizukagami 341
Kokuchō shomoku 436
Kokugaku 2, 16, 29, 33, 146, 152, 212, 282, 321, 402
Kokushi taikei 441
kokusho 1-2
Kokusho sōmokuroku 1, 2, 5, 140, 205, 409
Kōkyō 155
Kōmyō, empress 81, 83, 398
Konchiin Sūden 377
Kondō Seisai 324, 326, 376, 435, 444
Kongōbuji 368
Kongōjō daranikyō 80
Konoe family 406
Konoe Iehiro 100
Konpon Kyōzō 367
Konta Yōzō 332
Korean edition of the Buddhist canon 294
Korean movable type 128
Koreki benran 356
Koryŏ 287, 294
kōsatsu 272, 335, 346
kōshōgaku 438
kōshoku 188
Kōshoku fumi denju 350
Kōshoku gonin onna 350
kōshokubon 194, 335, 337, 344, 348, 350, 434
Kotenseki sōgō mokuroku 1, 409
Kotoba no kayoiji 185
kouta 261
Kōya, Mt 119, 131, 152, 170

Kōya-ban 119
Kōzanji 421
kuge-kagami 71
Kujō Kanezane 75, 420
Kumano sensei nanzan kikō 215
Kumazawa Banzan 162, 333
Kunaichō Shoryōbu 298
kunten 88, 123, 135, 153, 261
Kurita Mototsugu 437
Kurodani shōnin gotōroku 121
Kwŏn Kŭn 157, 295
Kyō suzume 170
kyōka 216, 218–20
Kyōka kaiawase 216
Kyokutei Bakin 37, 48, 76, 137, 178, 184, 188, 203, 214,, 218, 227, 235, 238–41, 267, 344, 394, 396, 432, 434, 443
kyōzō 366
kyūhan 183
Kūkai 15, 119, 285, 310, 367–8, 418, 419

Lalande, Joseph de 354
lei shu 42, 283
Lewis, Mark 11, 32
Li ji 280
Li Madou 326
lithography 22
Liu yu yan yi 144
Lotus sūtra 79, 82–3, 87–90, 100, 118, 160, 209–10
Lun yu (see Analects)

machi-bugyō 324
machibure 324, 337

machidoshiyori 324
Maeda Ai 266–7
Maeda daimyō 389
Maeda Tsunanori 408
Mainichi shinbun 66
Majima Seigan 101
Majimaryū 101
Makita Inashiro 196, 246
Makura no sōshi 132
Man'yōshū 93, 132, 191, 260, 269, 279–80
Man'yōshū ryakuge 191
Manase Shōrin 295
manga 59
Manjuin 435
Mantei Ōga 317
mappō 88
maps 54, 60–2
Martial 42
Matsudaira Sadanobu 339, 439
Matsudaira Shigeyoshi 108
Matsudono monogatari 426
Matsumoto Yasuoki 167
Matsuo Bashō 243, 432
Matsuoka Gentatsu 429
Matsushita Kenrin 388
Matsuzawa Rōsen 444
Matteo Ricci 324, 326
McCormack, Gavan 4
Medical Academy (Igakkan) 102, 145, 152, 245, 383
Meerdervoort, J. L. C. Pompe van 164
Meibutsu rikujō 180
Meigetsuki 380, 407
Meijikan 356
Meirindō 263, 386
meisho zue 217, 231

Mencius 257, 290–1
Mibu Kanmu family 372
Midō kanpakuki 406
mikaeshi 45, 150
Mikusazashi 216
Military Academy (Rikugunsho) 146, 165
military science 146, 148
Miller, Roy Andrew 311
Minabuchi no Jōan 280
Minamoto no Tametomo 240
minchōtai 165
Ming fiction 299
Mingkong 306
Ministry of Education (Monbushō) 146
Misa ji yi 326
Misshū shojaku mokuroku 433
Mito 206
Mitraśanta 115
Mitsubo kikigaki 394
Mitsukuri Genpo 342
Miura Chikke 264
Miyako meisho zue 217
Miyako no Nishiki 195, 209, 233, 240
Miyatake Tobone 322–3, 325, 332, 349
Miyazaki Antei 273
Miyazaki Rikken 441
Miyazaki Yasusada 52
Mizuno Tadakuni 302, 343, 346
Mizutani Futō 178, 186, 317
mokkan 85, 270, 280
mokuroku-daisen 46

Momijiyama Bunko (see Bakufu Library)
Momotaro; or, Little Peachling 142
mononohon 244
Monzen jibiki 248
Mori family 273
Mori Katsumi 282
Mori Shien 443–4
Mōri Takanaka 380
Mōri Takasue 291, 380
Morimura Jirōbei 389
Morioka mitsugi monogatari 108
Moriyama Seishin 418
Moroshigure momiji no aigasa 138
Morse, Edward 26, 391
Moscow 21
mosho 摸書 94
Mote, Frederick 27
Motoki Shōzō 164–5
Motoori Norinaga 152, 185, 189, 206, 212–3, 217, 236, 241, 244, 249, 405, 438, 441
Motoori Ōhira 217, 402
Mujaku Dōchū 252
Mukai family 297
Mukai Genshō 327
Muku jōkō dai daranikyō 115–6
Müller, Andreas 314
Munemasa Isoo 244
Murakami Kanbee 208–9
Murasaki Shikibu 95, 253, 271
Murasaki Shikibu nikki emaki 97
Murata Harumi 390

Muro Kyūso 144
musha-ehon 59
mushibarai 75
mushiboshi 75
Myōhō rengekyō 82

Nabeshima daimyō 303
Nagaidō Kiyū 266
Nagasaki 125, 325
Nagasaki city commissioner (Nagasaki bugyōsho) 146, 164
Nagasaki shipping list and advertiser 65, 165
Nagatomo Chiyoji 262
Nagoya 213
naidai 46
Naikaku Bunko 295, 298, 383, 426
Naitō Masaaki 400
Nakahara Yasutomi 257
Nakamura Chōbee-no-jō 174
Nakamura Kiyozō 337
Nakamura Magobee 176, 441
Nakamura Yukihiko 239, 258
Nakane Genkei 328
Nakano Kōichi 256
Namaei katagi 266
names 238
nanushi 324
Nanzenji 287, 293, 378, 407
Nara ehon 98
Negoroji 124
newspaper reading rooms 411
Nichiren 152, 322, 433
Nichiren sect 208, 210
Nihon fūkeiron 227
Nihon gaishi 262

Nihon shojaku kō 441
Nihon shoki 92, 130, 193, 252, 257, 260, 278–9, 290, 293, 365, 386, 416, 424
Nihon zenrin senjutsu shomoku 433
Nihonkoku genzaisho mokuroku 281–2, 290, 291, 415, 422–3, 443
Nihonsho 323
ninjōbon 35, 44, 103, 139, 188, 265–6, 341, 344, 396
Nise murasaki inaka Genji 138, 345
Nishikawa Joken 262
Nishiki no ura 352
Nishimura Denbee 332
Nishimura Shigeki 263
Nishizawa Tahee 197
Nisshin shinjishi 361
Nō 44
Nōgyō zensho 52, 73, 382
Nordenskiöld, Adolf 3, 317–8, 407–8
Noro Genjō 302
Nunn, G. Raymond 140
nyūgin 150

Ōba Osamu 256, 290, 296, 326
Ōbaku sect 152, 165
Obiya Ihee 206, 215–7
Odyssey 301
Ōe no Masafusa 75, 369
Ofuregaki shūran 346
Ogyū Sorai 33, 104, 144, 189, 230, 264, 309–10, 312, 329–30, 383, 438
oie-sōdō 108

Ōishi Matora 193 n.35
Ōjin, emperor 278
Ōjō yōshū 121, 124, 308
Okada Gyokusan 341
Okada, Richard 255
Okadaya Kashichi 189
Okamoto Katsu 244
Okuyūhitsu 389
okuzuke 4–6
Ōmi no Mifune 307
Ōmiya Jirōemon 197
Ōnendaiki 308
Onmyōryō 353
Onna suikoden 299
onna-de 270
Ono Hideo 63
Ōno Hiroki 345
Ono no Takamura 92-93
Ono Noriaki 365
Ōnoya Sōhachi 395
ōraimono 140
oranda tsūji 302
orihon 43
Ōshio Heihachirō 275, 395
Ōshū meisho zue 347
Ōta Dōkan 375
Ōta Masujirō 422
Ōta Nanpo 176, 405, 432, 433–4, 443
otogizōshi 98
otoko-de 270
Ōtori Keisuke 165
Ōuchi daimyō 294, 375
Ōuchi Yoshitaka 294–5
Ōuchida Sadao 163
Ōwa Hiroyuki 219
Oyamada Tomokiyo 389
Ozaki Masayoshi 436
Oze Hoan 131, 341

Paekche 254, 278, 290
Paekchegi 293
papermaking 40–1
Parhae 277, 279–80, 293, 295, 353
Parkes, Sir Harry 41
pen-names 238
Perry, Commodore M. C. 65, 304, 315
Peter the Great 21
Popular Rights Movement 412
prefaces 45
Printing Office (書籍院 sŏjŏkwŏn 128
proofreading 52
publishing procedures 182
Pulguksa 114
Pure Land sect 121, 159

Qian zi wen 279
Qianlong emperor 11, 15, 428
Qing merchants 296
Qiu Jun 230
Qun shu zhi yao 148, 445

Rai San'yō 262
Rakkun 261
Rakuyōshū 126
Raleigh, Sir Walter 301
Rangaku 16, 34, 167, 272, 304, 321, 330, 342
Ranwa tsūben 164
Razan sensei bunshū 230
Reigen, emperor 407
Reizei family 406
Reizeike Bunko 93
Reizen'in 422

Rengeōin 93–4, 371, 424
Ricci, Matteo 104, 329–30
Rikuyu engi 144
Risshō ankokuron 322
Ritsugen hakki 400
Rōben 83
Robinson, Francis 22
Rodrigues 127
Rongochō 310
Rose, Jonathan 31, 36
Rose, Mark 242
Rosny, Léon de 67, 317–8, 401
rufubon 92
ruihan 181–2, 246–7
Ryō no shūge 283
Ryūtei Tanehiko 138, 235, 345, 402, 434
Sagabon 41, 56, 57, 132, 134
Saichō 285, 307, 310, 367, 418
Saidaiji 119
sairai mokuroku 齋来目録 296, 298
Saitō Shōzō 358
Sakaiya Magobee 174
Sakanishi Shio 324
Sakugen Shūryō 288
Samukawa Masachika 262
San cai tu hui 77
San guo zhi 281–2
Sanda family 274
Sangeya Gorōbee 206
Sangō shiiki 119, 290
Sangoku tsūran zusetsu 104, 341
Sanjōnishi Sanetaka 94, 98, 257
Sanjūsangendō 371

Sannōin 420
Sannōzō 367
Santō Kyōden 176, 184, 205, 218–9, 239, 241, 340–1, 347, 352, 394
Sarashina nikki 93, 95, 256
Saris, John 313
Satō Shin'en 330
Satow, Ernest 69, 76, 316–8, 401, 407
Satsuma 356
Schliemann, Heinrich 274
Screech, Timonq59
Seeley, Christopher 269
Sei Shōnagon 256–7, 271, 373
Seijukan 152
Seikadō Bunko 408
Seikidō Bunko 408
Seikyō yōroku 333
Seiwa emperor, 88
Seiyō gakka yakujutsu mokuroku 433
Seiyō jijō 250, 410
Sekine Masanao 332
Sen'yūji 119
Senmyōreki 353
senryū 139
Senshu sengankyō 84
Sentō gobunsho mokuroku 426
setsuyōshū 52, 72, 139, 209, 248
Setto 摂都 193 n.35
Sha daishōjōkyō mokuroku 416
Shaken nichiroku 256
Shakyōjo 81, 92, 284
Shang shu 308

Sharaku 220
sharebon 219, 239-1, 347, 402
shasho 写書 94
Shashōsho mokuroku 416-7
Shenzong, emperor 286
Shi ji 253, 282
Shi xue da cheng 123
Shiba Kōkan 167
Shibano Ritsuzan 439
Shibue Chūsa 444-5
Shibukawa Harumi 353
Shichikei mōshi kōbun 309, 375
shichū torishimarigakari 249, 344
Shiga Shigetaka 227
Shigaku taisei 123
Shigeno no Sadanushi 282
Shiguretei Bunko 407
shikigo 402
Shikitei Kosanba 234
Shikitei Sanba 28, 238, 266, 402
Shimabara pleasure quarter 331
Shimabara uprising 352
Shin usuyuki monogatari 179 n.13
shinbun jūransho 411
shinbun-yomi 268
shinbunshi 66, 359
Shinbunshi hakkō jōmoku 360
Shinbunshi inkō jōrei 360
Shinchokusenshū 322
Shingaku 237
Shingaku michi no hanashi 237
Shingon sect 118-9, 420, 433

Shingonzō 367
shinjū 335
Shinkan Azuma kagami 404
Shinsaku jūniban no uchi 141
Shinsen shōjiroku 364
Shinshū kyōtenshi 433
Shintei sanraizu 216
Shintō books 434, 436
Shinzō 317
Shiraishi Chōkō 76
Shirōto kyōgen monkirigata 28
Shisi jing fa hui 155
shobō 175
Shoen ōkagami 393
Shogaku dokushohan 260
Shōhaku 257
Shōheizaka Gakumonjo (see Bakufu Academy)
shōhonya 175
Shojakkan 411
shojaku mokuroku 177
Shojaku mokuroku taizen 185
Shōkai Ichirōbee 200
Shōkōkan 147
Shoku nihongi 114, 116, 252, 442
Shokuinryō 308
Shōmangyō gisho 306, 311
shōmenzuri 137
shomotsu bugyō 378
shomotsu-aratameyaku 297, 327
shomotsuya 175
Shomotsuya nakama 202, 211, 219
Shōmu, emperor 81, 83, 84, 97, 367, 398
Shōmyōji 373

shōrai mokuroku 請来目録 285, 417, 419
shorin 175
Shoryōbu 399
shosha-okugaki 45
shoshi 175
shoshidai 61
Shoshū kyōsho mokuroku 420
Shōsōin 40, 75, 81–3, 92, 406, 416
shōsokukyō 消息経 88
Shōtei Kinsui 229
Shōtoku Taishi 80, 279, 284, 306, 311, 440
Shōtoku, empress 14, 83, 117, 271
shugendō 290
Shui hu chuan 299
Shun'oku Myōha 122
shunga 340, 350–1, 358
Shunjō 119, 288
Shunjō awase kagami 233 n.12
Shunshō yumiharizuki 188
Shuppan jōrei 250, 360
Shushi dokusho no yō 260
Shushi gorui 49
shūchinban 159
Shūko jisshu 439
shūsha-kuyō 118
Shūshoin 411
Shūzenji 15
Sidotti 302
Siebold, Heinrich von 408
Siebold, Philipp Franz von 164, 304, 314, 380
Siku quanshu 11, 12, 14, 310, 428
Silla 114, 280

sirhak 実学 311
Smits, Ivo 283, 424
Sō daimyō 294, 300, 434
Società dei Classici Italiani 14
sodoku 148, 267
Sōei 285
Soga hyakubutsu 193 n.35
Soga no Iruka 365
Sōgi 257
Son'en 41
Song shi 308
Sonkai 294
Sonkeikaku 408
sōrōbun 272
sōshiya 175
Spencer, Herbert 263
Spufford, Margaret 34
Stone, Lawrence 274
Suetonius 301
Sugawara no Michizane 93, 308, 369
Sui shu jing ji zhi 415, 423
Sumidagawa ryōgan ichiran 42
Suminokura Soan 132, 150, 388
Summers, James 67
surimono 355
surishi (printer) 48
Suruga 130
Suwa Haruo 243
Suwaraya Ichibee 341
Suwaraya Ihachi 211
Suwaraya Mohee 61, 69, 145 n.48, 186, 203, 210, 211, 212, 213, 220, 241
Suwaraya Shinhee 155, 191, 247
Suwaraya Yasujirō 206

Suzuki Jūzō 56
Suzuki Shōsan 156
Suzunoya 152
Sŏng Hyŏn 128
sūtra mounds (*kyōzuka*) 88
sūtra-copying 40, 80, 82

T'ai-tsung, emperor 308
Tachibana Morikuni 315
Tachibana no Naramaro 369
Tachikawa school 323
Taga castle 85
Tai ping yu lan 287
Tai xi shui fa 326, 329
Taihei gishinden 336
Taiheiki 98, 132, 257, 265, 274, 435, 438
taiisho 297–8, 327
Taiki 254
Taikōki 341
Taira no Kiyomori 90, 287
Taisei meii ikō 342
Taisei shinbun 67
Takahashi Kageyasu 380
Takaya no Akamaro 416
Takechi Shiyū 215, 217
Takemura Ichibee 209
Taki family 152
Taki Keizan 438
Taki Motokata 443–4
Taki Mototane 434
Tale of Genji 24, 95, 98,, 132, 187, 209, 232, 257, 262, 270, 426, 437
Tales of Ise 98, 132, 257, 262, 377
Tamagami Takuya 255–6

Tamenaga Shunsui 139, 188, 229, 233, 265, 266, 344, 396
Tanaka Fujimaro 411
Tanaka Kaidō 81, 84
Tanba Yasuyori 101
Tang lü 283
Tang shu 281
Tani Bunchō 443
Tankikai 443
tanrokubon 57
Tanuma Okitsugu 341
Tasmania 17
techōsō 44
Tendai sect 118, 131, 208
Tendai shikyōgi shūge 131
tendoku 252–3, 258
Tenmangū gobunko kō 198
Tenmangū shrine 198
Tenmongata (see Astronomical Bureau)
Tenpō reforms 196, 249, 343–6
Tenpōreki 354
Tenryūji 122
Terakado Seiken 345
terakoya 272, 275
Tetsugan 153 n.58
Thomas, Rosalind 30
Thunberg, Karl Pieter 314
Tian zhu shi yi 326
Tiantai si jiao yi ji jie 131
Tiantai, Mt 286, 307
Titsingh, Isaac 314
Tōbu jitsuroku 379
Toda Ujinori 436, 441
Tōdaiji 83, 116, 119, 371, 416
Tōfukuji 288, 371
Tōfukumon'in 100

Tōhon'ya Kichizaemon 180
Tōhon'ya Seibee 180, 381
tōhonya 175
Tōiki dentō mokuroku 420
Tōji 368
Tōkaidō meisho zue 172
Tokiwa village 275
Tokugawa Hidetada 377, 379
Tokugawa Ieyasu
  15, 106, 130, 135, 143, 153, 174, 295, 332, 374, 376–7, 407, 442, 444
Tokugawa jikki 328, 376
Tokugawa Keiki 164
Tokugawa Mitsukuni 437
Tokugawa Nariaki 386
Tokugawa Tsunayoshi 144
Tokugawa Yoshimune 15, 144, 186, 298, 302, 309, 328, 337, 375, 379, 380, 438
Tokushi Yūshō 118
Tokutomi Sohō 408
Tōkyō nichinichi shinbun 66
Tokyo Observatory (Tenmondai) 358
tomehan 180
Tomioka Tessai 408
Tonoibukuro 345
Tosa nikki 93–4, 371
Tōsei onna katagi 350
Tōshisen 191, 247
Tōyō Bunko 295
Toyotomi Hidetsugu 368, 374–5, 377
Toyotomi Hideyori 106, 332
Toyotomi Hideyoshi 106, 129, 295, 332, 341, 377
Tsubouchi Shōyō 396

Tsuchimikado family 354, 357
Tsuda Mamichi 358
Tsukahara Jūshien 259
Tsurezuregusa 10, 396
Tsuruguya Kyūhee 248
Tsuruya Kiemon 232, 241
Tsutaya Jūzaburō 71, 139, 173, 205, 212, 216, 218, 239, 241, 340
Tsūken nyūdō zōsho mokuroku 283, 423, 424

Uchida Roan 103
Uchiko, princess 271
Ueda Akinari 243
Uemura Fujiemon 189
Uesugi Norizane 374
Ukai Sekisai 49
Ukibotan zenden 184
Ukita Hideie 295
ukiyoe 219
ukiyozōshi 231
Umegoyomi 396
Umehara Tōru 272
umeki 52, 185
University (Daigaku Nankō) 146
University (Daigakuryō) 282, 366
Unjō meikan 71
Unjō meiran 71
Unteiin 368
Urami no suke 134
uridashi 201
Urokogataya Magobee 200, 219
Ursis, Sabbatinus de 326, 329

urushigami 85
Utagawa Toyokuni 342
Utsunomiya Ton'an 332

Valignano, Alessandro 125
Virgil 126

Wada Mankichi 417
Wada Tokutarō 141
Wagaku Kōdansho 401, 440
Wagenaer, Zacharias 302
waka 91-2, 95-6, 141, 207, 217, 226, 236, 243, 261, 335
Waka genzaisho mokuroku 424
Wakamatsu Sadatsugu 257
Wakan 倭館 300
Wakayama 148, 173, 206, 215, 216
Wang Bo 280
Wang Bo ji 王勃集 280
Wang Zhenping 281, 308
Wani 278-9
Wazoku dōjikun 261
Wen xuan 248, 280
Weng Guangping 309
Western studies 146, 148, 303, 433
Witsen, Nicholas 313
Woodmansee, Martha 224
Wu za zu 291, 329
Wu, empress 116-7
Wutaishan 286
Wuyue 308

Xavier, Francis 125
Xiao jing 85, 129, 155, 253
Xuan ming li 295

yagō 141
yakusha hyōbanki (see actor critiques)
Yakusho dokuhō 263
Yamaga Sokō 333
Yamagataya Iemon 381
Yamaguchi 157
Yamamoto Gentan 148
Yamamoto Shunshō 232
Yamanoe no Okura 280
Yamanoi Konron 275, 309, 311, 438
yamato-toji 43-44
Yamazaki Ansai 157, 260, 312
Yamazaki Yoshinari 329
Yamazaki Yoshishige 405, 433, 443
Yang Liang 228
Yang Shoujing 311
Yano Fumio 263
Yashiro Hirokata 389, 443
Yayoshi Mitsunaga 435
Yi dynasty 294, 312
Yi Ik 311
Yi shu da quan 123
Yi T'oegye 157, 295
Yijing 85
Yin jing yuan 印経院 286
Yo-no ouvasa 67
yōgaku (see Western studies)
Yōhōji 131
Yokohama 19

Yōmei Bunko 406
yomeiribon 44, 101
yomihon 44, 103, 139, 184–5, 203, 221, 226, 240, 299, 352, 394
yomikudashi 254
yomiuri 63
yonaoshi 275
Yorozuya Heishirō 66
Yosano Akiko 32
Yoshida Kenkō 10
Yoshida Tsunefusa 371, 424
Yoshiwara 139, 171, 173, 200, 219, 220
Yoshiwara saiken 71, 218–9
Yōsho shirabesho (see Institute for the investigation of Western books)
Yu Liangfu 122
yu lu 語録 288
Yu Yue 12, 310
Yü zhu xiao jing 443
Yuan Zhen 282
Yuanqing 308
Yugyō shōnin engi e 97
Yui Shōsetsu 106–7
Yuriwaka Daijin 301
yūjo hyōbanki (see courtesan critiques)

Zen 121–2, 433
Zeng ding guang yu ji 328
Zenrin shōkisen 252
Zensekishi 433
Zenshōji 293
Zhen guan zhen gyao 376
Zhen yuan xin ding shi jiao mu lu 419
Zheng Ruoceng 289, 292
Zhicong 364
Zhong jing mu lu 418
Zhouyi 255
Zhu Xi 15, 49, 98, 124, 157, 230, 255, 259, 260, 263, 264, 289, 333, 339, 357, 386
Zhu zi yu lei 49, 260
Zōeki shojaku mokuroku 185
zōhan 149, 150, 244
zōhan mokuroku 431
(Zōho) Shojaku mokuroku 225-226
Zōjōji 15, 402, 403
zōshoin 398
zuihitsu 63
Zushoryō 40, 75, 85, 91, 365, 417

CPSIA information can be obtained
at www.ICGtesting.com
Printed in the USA
BVHW04s1738210618
519379BV00009B/15/P